JOHN CAMPBELL

The Iron Lady

Margaret Thatcher:
From Grocer's Daughter
to Iron Lady

ABRID

Davi

VINTAGE BOOKS
London

Published by Vintage 2012

6 8 10 9 7

Vintage
Random House, 20 Vauxhall Bridge Road,
London SW1V 2SA

www.vintage-books.co.uk

Addresses for companies within The Random House Group Limited
can be found at: www.randomhouse.co.uk/offices.htm

The Random House Group Limited Reg. No. 954009

A CIP catalogue record for this book
is available from the British Library

ISBN 9780099575160

Typeset in Bembo by Palimpsest Book Production Limited,
Falkirk, Stirlingshire
Printed and bound by CPI Group (UK) Ltd, Croydon CR0 4YY

For Robin and Paddy – two of Thatcher's children

Contents

Illustrations

CREDITS

The author and publishers are grateful to the following sources for permission to reproduce illustrations: Camera Press, images 2, 3, 4,

5, 14, 15; Topham Picturepoint, image 6; PA News, images 7, 9; Hulton Getty, image 8; Rex Features, images 10, 13, 16; PA Photos, images 11, 12. They would also like to thank the Local Studies Collection, Grantham Library, Lincolnshire County Council Education and Cultural Services Directorate for image 1.

Acknowledgements

THIS book was originally published in two volumes totalling
more than 1,200 pages. The present volume is drastically reduced
to make it more accessible to the general reader. Inevitably much of
the detail and some of the colour of the original have been sacrificed. But I hope that the integrity of the book has been preserved.
I am immensely grateful to David Freeman of the University of
California for carrying out the work of abridgement so skilfully.
I could not have done it myself, but I think he has done a superb
job. If there is now a somewhat greater emphasis on foreign relations and the major enduring themes of Lady Thatcher's life and
rather less on her early life and the small change of party politics,
I think that is appropriate as her career moves into a longer historical perspective. It is now 30 years since she came to power and
19 since she fell. In that time the world has continued to evolve:
some of the hopes raised by the ending of the Cold War have not
been realised, while Islamist terrorism, climate change and now a
global financial crisis pose new problems scarcely imagined in her
day. Beyond a very brief contemporary conclusion to the last
chapter, however, I have not attempted to rewrite the original
book. Remarkably little new information has emerged which
requires substantial reinterpretation or revision. Most of the assumptions and judgments I made in 2000 and 2003, I believe, still stand.
They are themselves part of the record of the time. For two decades
after her fall Margaret Thatcher continued to exercise a powerful
grip on the imagination of the country and of her successors. But
already a new generation is growing up who scarcely remember
her. I hope that this book, in its shortened form, may serve as a
useful introduction to them, as well as a reminder to those who
lived through the high drama of what will always be the Thatcher

years. Those whose appetite is whetted may wish to go back to the original volumes for more detail.

I incurred an immense number of debts during the nine years it took me to write this book: scores of interviews, dozens of more casual conversations, many valuable pointers from friends and colleagues, much help from librarians and archivists. But I made due acknowledgement for all this help in the original volumes, and I hope it will be understood if I do not repeat my thanks in detail here: most of the interviewees are credited in the notes. I do, however, need to thank again HarperCollins, for allowing me to use substantial quotation from Lady Thatcher's memoirs and also from Carol Thatcher's biography of her father; Macmillan for allowing me to quote from Woodrow Wyatt's diaries; David Higham Associates for permission to quote from Barbara Castle's diaries; and Brook Associates for allowing me to quote from interviews for their television series *The Seventies* and *The Thatcher Factor*. I confess that I have not sought specific permission for every quotation I have made from the many other memoirs and diaries of the period but I am grateful to all those authors who put their memories into the public realm. I am also grateful to the United States Government for allowing access to and quotation from the papers of Presidents Carter, Reagan and Bush under the Freedom of Information Act, and to the staff of the three presidential libraries who guided me to what I needed to see on a necessarily short visit to the States in 2001. Finally I should like to thank again my publishers – Dan Franklin at Jonathan Cape for the original volumes and now Alison Hennessey at Vintage for handling the abridgement; my agent Bruce Hunter; my children Robin and Paddy; and finally, for her love, faith and companionship over the past five years, Kirsty Hogarth. To all of them my debt is incalculable.

John Campbell
December 2008

I

Dutiful Daughter

Grantham born

A FORMER town clerk once described Grantham as 'a narrow
town, built on a narrow street and inhabited by narrow people'.[1]
It is a plain, no-frills sort of place, brick-built and low-lying: at first
sight a typical East Midlands town, once dubbed by the *Sun* 'the
most boring town in Britain'.[2] Yet Grantham was once more than
this. Look closer and it is a palimpsest of English history. Incorp-
orated in 1463, it was a medieval market town. Kings stopped there
on their journeys north: Richard III signed Buckingham's death
warrant in the Angel Hotel. St Wulfram's church boasts one of the
tallest spires in England. England's greatest scientist, Isaac Newton,
was born seven miles south of the town in 1642 and educated at
the grammar school.

Beatrice Stephenson – Margaret Thatcher's mother – was
Grantham born and bred. She was born on 24 August 1888. Her
father, Daniel Stephenson, is euphemistically described as a railway-
man: he was actually for thirty-five years a cloakroom attendant.[3]
He married, in 1876, Phoebe Crust, described as a farmer's daughter
(which might mean anything) from the village of Fishtoft Fen, near
Boston, who had found work in Grantham as a factory machinist.
Beatrice, one of several children, lived at home in South Parade
until she was twenty-eight, working as a seamstress. Her daughter
says she had her own business; but whether she worked alone or
employed other girls there is no record. In December 1916 Daniel
died. Five months later, on 28 May 1917, Beatrice married an ambitious young shop assistant – four years younger than herself – whom
she had met at chapel: Alfred Roberts.

He was not a Grantham man, but was born at Ringstead, near

Oundle in Northamptonshire, on 18 April 1892, the eldest of seven children of Benjamin Roberts and Ellen Smith. The Roberts side of his family came originally from Wales – but had been settled in Northamptonshire as boot and shoe manufacturers for four generations. Alfred broke away from shoemaking. A bookish boy, he would have liked to train to be a teacher, but was forced to leave school at twelve to supplement the family income He spent the rest of his life reading determinedly to make up for the education he had missed. He went into the grocery trade and after a number of odd jobs over the next ten years came to Grantham in 1913 to take up a position as an assistant manager with Clifford's on London Road. It was while working for Alderman Clifford that he met Beatrice Stephenson. They are said to have met in chapel; but she may well have been a customer as well. However they met, Alfred soon began a lengthy courtship.

As a young man born in 1892 Alf was lucky to survive the Great War. He was tall, upright and good looking, but seriously short sighted. All his life he wore thick pebble glasses. He tried to enlist, but was rejected on the grounds of defective eyesight. Spared the fate of so many of his contemporaries, he was free to pursue his chosen trade. He worked hard and saved hard, and by 1917 he and Beatrice – he called her Beatie – had saved enough to marry. At first Alf moved in with Beatie and her mother, but within two years they were able, with a mortgage, to buy their own small shop at the other end of town in North Parade. Phoebe came to live with them over the shop. Their first child, christened Muriel, was born in May 1921. Their second, another daughter, did not come for another four years, by which time Beatrice was thirty-seven. Margaret Hilda Roberts – the choice of names has never been explained – was born over the shop on 13 October 1925.

The shop was a general store and also a post office. This is something which the iconography of Thatcherism tends to overlook; yet it subtly changes the picture of Alfred as the archetypal small businessman and champion of private enterprise. He was that; but as a sub-postmaster he was also an agent of central government, a sort of minor civil servant. The post office franchise was an important part of his business. The Post Office Savings Bank was the only bank most people knew; and old-age pensions had been paid through the post office since their introduction in 1908. The elderly of north Grantham collected their weekly ten shillings from North Parade. To this extent Alfred – even in the 1920s and much more so after 1945 – was an agent of the nascent welfare state; and Margaret was brought up with first-hand knowledge of its delivery system.

The post office was open from 8.00 a.m. to 7.00 p.m., Monday to Saturday, with Thursday early closing. During these hours either Alfred or Beatie was always in the shop – Alfred normally at his corner by the bacon slicer – but they also employed two or three assistants, plus another permanently in the post office. In the early years Grandmother Stephenson served in the shop too; and later, as they grew up, the girls helped out when they were not at school – not only serving, but weighing out the sugar, tea, biscuits and lentils in the back. From an early age young Margaret gained a close awareness of the market in its purest form.

Alfred's move into politics was a natural extension of his business. In a place like Grantham most members of the town council were tradesmen of one sort or another, effectively representing the Chamber of Trade. It happened that in April 1927 the council was expanded from twelve members to eighteen. Alfred was one of six candidates put up by the Chamber of Trade to fill the additional vacancies. He represented St Wulfram's for sixteen years until he was elected an alderman in 1943.

His overriding purpose in local politics was keeping the rates down. He very quickly became chairman of the Finance and Rating Committee, and retained that position for more than twenty years. He established a formidable reputation for guarding the ratepayers' pennies as carefully as his own. One need seek no further for the origin of Mrs Thatcher's visceral hostility to public spending. In 1936 he successfully opposed a proposal that the council should employ its own direct labour force to maintain the town's newly built stock of public housing. 'I do not believe', he argued, 'that there is an instance where jobs done by direct labour save money over jobs done by contract.'[4] He faced his greatest embarrassment in 1937 when he was obliged to ask for a seven pence rate increase to fourteen shillings in the pound. Characteristically he blamed his colleagues for having approved excessive commitments; his job, he protested, was merely to find the money. 'It is just brought to your notice now', he told them, 'what exactly you have been approving.'[5]

On top of his seat on the council and chairmanship of the Finance Committee, Alfred was active in many other areas of Grantham life. In 1943 he was elected the town's youngest alderman and in 1945–6 served as mayor. He was a good mayor in a particularly testing year, presiding not only over victory celebrations and Remembrance Day parades but also the rebuilding necessitated by Grantham's extensive bomb damage.

The most celebrated episode in Alfred's political career was its ending. By 1950 Labour had won a majority on Grantham council for the first time; they naturally installed one of their own councillors as chairman of the Finance Committee. Two years later they used their majority, quite legitimately, to elect their own aldermen, thereby displacing Roberts from the council after twenty-seven years. His removal was widely deplored as an act of petty ingratitude to an outstanding servant of the local community. Thirty-three years later his daughter famously shed tears when she recalled his deposition in a television interview.

At the heart of all Alfred's community activity was his religion. As a devout Methodist, he made no distinction between commercial, political and religious values. Simultaneously shopkeeper, local politician and lay preacher, he conducted his business on ethical principles and preached business principles in politics. In all three spheres he prided himself on hard work, high standards and integrity. He was indeed a proud man, with a powerful sense of his own worth – tempered by proper Christian humility.

Alfred Roberts' Methodism was a religion of personal salvation. His preaching was fundamentalist, Bible-based, concerned with the individual's responsibility to God for his own behaviour. Unlike the nonconformist tradition which played such a large part in the foundation of the British labour movement, it was not a social gospel, but an uncompromisingly individualistic moral code which underpinned an individualist approach to politics and commerce. A man's duty was to keep his own soul clean, mind his own business, and care for his own family. At best it was a philosophy which instilled a further obligation to look after neighbours in need and thence, by extension, to wider community service and private charity. At the same time, however, it carried a strong undercurrent of self-righteousness and moral superiority.

Relative Values

Margaret's childhood was dominated by her parents' faith. Sundays – the only day in the week the shop was closed – were almost wholly taken up with church attendance. Sunday school at ten was followed by morning service at eleven. There was just time to get home for lunch before afternoon Sunday School at 2.30 at which Margaret, from the age of about twelve, played the piano for the younger ones; then it was back again for evening service at six. During the week, too, the family's social life was almost entirely church-based. Beatie attended a sewing circle on Tuesdays, often taking Margaret with her; Muriel and Margaret attended the

Methodist Guild on Fridays. Life at home was austere, teetotal, governed by strict rules, particularly while Beatie's mother was still alive. Grandmother Stephenson, Margaret told one of her first biographers, was 'very, very Victorian and very, very strict'.[6] The greatest sin of all was wasting time. Every minute of the day was to be filled with useful occupation. Never was a childhood lesson more thoroughly taken to heart.

Alf Roberts was not poor. As a successful shopkeeper he belonged by the 1930s to the middle middle class; he could scarcely have devoted so much of his time to politics had his business not been securely profitable. At a time when quite ordinary middle-class families up and down the country were discovering the liberation of vacuum cleaners, washing machines and even cars, he could certainly have afforded his family the luxury of a few modern conveniences; at the very least hot water. They did in fact have a maid before the war, and later a cleaning lady two days a week. It was for religious and temperamental reasons – puritanism and parsimony – not economic necessity, that Alfred kept his family in such austerity. The flashes of rebellion that illuminate Mrs Thatcher's recollections fifty years later betray a sense that she felt the parsimony, like the churchgoing, was taken too far. Ironically Alf and Beatie did move to a larger house with more home comforts soon after Margaret left to go to Oxford.

The family did get a wireless set after Grandmother Stephenson died in 1935 (when Margaret was ten). This was such an event that she remembers running all the way back from school that day. The wireless was the one form of popular entertainment that was allowed. Margaret unquestionably longed for a bit more glamour than her parents' principles allowed. The highlight of her whole childhood was a visit to London, without her parents, when she was twelve. She was sent to stay with friends – a Wesleyan minister and his wife – in Hampstead. 'I stayed for a whole week', she recalled, 'and was given a life of enjoyment and entertainment that I had never seen.' As well as all the usual sights – the Tower of London, the Changing of the Guard, the Houses of Parliament and the zoo – 'we were actually taken to the theatre'. The show was the musical *The Desert Song* at the Catford Theatre. 'We saw the crowds and the bright lights and I was so excited and thrilled by it that I've never forgotten that week.'[7]

What she did do during her childhood was to read precociously. This was undoubtedly the medium of her father's most direct and lasting influence. Alfred was a voracious autodidact, reputed to be 'the best-read man in Grantham' (though one has to wonder when he found the time).[8] 'Each week my father would take two books out of the library – a "serious" book for himself (and me) and a novel for my mother.'[9] From an early age Margaret shared her father's – rather than her mother's – taste. Reading was a means of self-improvement and advancement in the world; perhaps because he had no son, Alfred encouraged his younger daughter to read influential books of the moment, like John Strachey's *The Coming Struggle for Power*, and discussed them with her. He was a member of the library committee, so he got first pick of these topical books. Of course she read some classic fiction too; but she confessed that her favourite Dickens novel was *A Tale of Two Cities*, because it was about politics.[10]

This utilitarian attitude to literature was reinforced by her education. At school she specialised in science, went on to read chemistry at Oxford, and then took up law. From Oxford onwards she devoted most of her spare time to politics. As a result she never had much time to enlarge on her youthful reading. What she read and learned in her first eighteen years, under her father's influence, remained the bedrock of her literary education. In this sense it is literally true that she learned 'almost everything' from her father. She always insisted that the most important lesson he taught her was to follow her own convictions. 'Never do things just because other people do them,' he told her when she wanted to go dancing.[11] 'Make up your own mind what you are going to do and persuade people to go *your* way.'[12] 'Never go with the crowd,' she paraphrased his advice in 1982. 'Never, never, never.'[13] The paradox, of course, is that she went on, with no sense of contradiction, to pride herself on taking all her ideas from him. 'He brought me up to believe all the things I do believe and they are the values on which I fought the election.'[14]

It is a curious thing for a strong-minded woman to proclaim in this way her debt to her father, as if she was no more than his echo. In fact she exaggerated the extent of her fidelity to Alfred's teaching – presumably to divert attention from the important respects in which she had abandoned it. Once she had got away from Grantham and embarked upon her own career she quickly adopted a style of life and political values a world away from his spartan ethic. Symbolically, she abandoned her parents' church and gravitated to the Church of England. She gave her own children an upbringing as different as possible from the puritanical austerity she always claimed had been so good for her. Mark and Carol were not made to go to church, she told Patricia Murray, 'because I'd had so much insistence myself'.[15] 'There was not a lot of fun and sparkle in my life,' she told an audience of children in 1980. 'I tried to give my children a little bit more.'[16] An alternative interpretation is that Mark and Carol were smothered in material comforts in guilty compensation for their mother's absence, for most of their childhood, in pursuit of her political career.

Yet clearly much that Alfred taught his daughter did go into the forging of her creed. The political personality that Margaret Thatcher became was moulded by her upbringing. Essentially she took three things from her father's example. First, it was Alfred who instilled in her the habit of hard work, as something both virtuous in itself and the route to self-advancement. Second, it was the example of Alfred's tireless community activity which bred in his daughter a powerful impulse towards public service. The third, and perhaps most important, legacy which Alfred gave his daughter was an exceptionally powerful moral sense. More than anything else in her political make-up, it was her fierce confidence that she knew right from wrong – even if what was right was not always immediately attainable – which marked Margaret Thatcher out from contemporary politicians. She believed absolutely in her own integrity and habitually disparaged the motives of those who disagreed with her. This rare moral certainty and unreflective self-righteousness was her greatest political strength in the muddy world of political expediency and compromise; it was also in the end her greatest weakness.

The most extraordinary thing about Mrs Thatcher's mythologisation of her father is that it was entirely retrospective. Having once escaped from Alfred at the age of eighteen she saw very little of him for the remainder of his life. In 1951 she took her fiancé to meet his prospective in-laws. Alfred Roberts and Denis Thatcher had nothing in common. Once they were married, Margaret and Denis went back to Grantham very rarely. When Beatie died in 1960, Alf remarried – a local farmer's widow called Cissie Hubbard, with grown-up children. 'I suppose that's a good thing,' Margaret witheringly confided. 'She's a nice homely little woman.'[17] He lived until February 1970. He was proud of his daughter being a Member of Parliament, and was said to have been listening to her on a radio discussion programme just before he died. But he did not live quite long enough to see her in the Cabinet – though, curiously, she believed he did.[18] Perhaps she was thinking of the Shadow Cabinet; but her mistake suggests that he did not share very closely in her triumphs. He had only a graduation photograph of her in his house: nothing more recent, and no pictures of his grandchildren.[19] Mark and Carol were sixteen when Alfred died, yet appear to have little memory of him. The impression is inescapable that Margaret was very much less devoted to her wonderful father while he was alive than she became to his sanctified image after he was dead.

Educating Margaret

The key to Margaret Roberts' escape from Grantham was education. Her formal schooling began a few weeks before her fifth birthday, on 3 September 1930, at Huntingtower Road County Elementary School, reputed to be the best council school in Grantham. According to her own account she could already read by the time she went there, and she quickly moved up a year. She was already formidably diligent and competitive. At the age of nine she won a poetry recital competition at the local music festival When the head congratulated her, saying she was lucky, she denied it indignantly: 'I wasn't lucky. I deserved it.'[20] She would always believe that if she worked hard she would deserve to win. The following year, when still only ten, she won a scholarship to the fee-paying girls' grammar school, Kesteven and Grantham Girls' School (known as KGGS), where her sister Muriel had already gone before her.

In fact Alfred paid Margaret's fees too, since the scholarship was means-tested; it was nevertheless a useful insurance, and a considerable achievement.

Her reports give a clear picture of her character. At Christmas 1936 she was said to have 'worked steadily and well throughout the term. She has definite ability, and her cheeriness makes her a very pleasant member of her form. Her behaviour is excellent.' The following July she won praise for 'neat and careful work'. The next year she was 'a very helpful member of her form' and 'achieved a high standard in every subject'. In her fifth year (the summer of 1941) she sat her School Certificate: she passed well in all subjects, but her methodical approach naturally directed her towards specialising in the sciences.

An interest in chemistry was not something she derived from her father, nor was it the most obvious subject for a girl precociously consumed by current affairs; later, when she had set her sights on a political career, she regretted having been sidetracked into science. At the age of sixteen, however, chemistry was her best subject. It suited the practical bent of her mind, and – most important at that age – she liked her teacher. It was a sensible subject, leading to good employment prospects.

Margaret was not quite fourteen when the war began, nearly twenty when it ended; it overshadowed her entire adolescence and was overwhelmingly the formative influence on her political development and specifically her approach to international relations. She came to political awareness in the mid-1930s at just the moment when international crises – in Abyssinia, the Rhineland, Spain and Czechoslovakia – began to dominate the news. Her first political memory was the so-called 'Peace Ballot' organised by the League of Nations Union in 1934. At a time when most Methodists inclined towards pacifism, Alfred appears to have been exceptionally aware of the threatening European situation, convinced of the need for rearmament to resist Nazism, and also – more unusually – concerned about the plight of the Jews. In 1938 the Roberts family briefly gave sanctuary to a seventeen-year-old Austrian girl – the penfriend of Margaret's sister Muriel – sent to England by her parents to escape the *Anschluss*. She did not stay long – Alfred persuaded other Rotary families to take her in turn – but she brought the reality of what was happening in Central Europe home to North Parade.

The war itself was a formative influence for Margaret Thatcher's whole generation, yet it affected her in a crucially different way from her male contemporaries. She was not only just too young to fight: she was the wrong sex. She could have joined one of the women's services when she left school, which would have got her into uniform and closer to the action; but still she could never have gained that first-hand experience of combat which left such a deep and lasting impression on practically all the young men who became her rivals and colleagues in the years ahead. Mrs Thatcher's experience on the home front – listening to Churchill in the blackout, following the campaigns with little flags on maps – taught her different lessons.

Unlike those who served during or after the war in France, Germany, the Mediterranean or the Far East, Mrs Thatcher never set foot out of England before her honeymoon in 1952, when she was twenty-six. Seen from Grantham, the peoples of the Continent were either odious enemies to be defeated, or useless allies who had to be saved from the consequences of their own feebleness by the British and Americans. By contrast the Americans were cousins, partners, friends: powerful and generous, the saviours of democracy, champions of freedom, prosperity and progress. Nor was this a merely abstract admiration: from 1942 onwards there was a large presence of American airmen stationed at bases around Grantham. Though they excited considerable interest among the local girls, there is no record that any of them tried to take up with Margaret

Roberts. She never had much time for that sort of thing. But she saw the Americans around the town, noted the spending power they brought to the local economy, and could hear them flying out each day to bomb Germany.

We are dealing with simplistic stereotypes here. But there can be no doubt that Mrs Thatcher's instinctive and lifelong belief in the Atlantic alliance as the first principle of British foreign policy, and her equally instinctive contempt for the continental Europeans, both derived from her particular experience of the Second World War – an experience unique among British politicians of the post-war era. It is impossible to overemphasise the significance of this gulf of perception. It was not just her sex which made Mrs Thatcher different: the most important consequence of her sex was her lack of military experience.

Though she did not sit her Higher School Certificate until 1943, she had already received offers from both Nottingham ('our local university') and Bedford College, London, before the end of 1942. However, she was determined, with Alfred's support, to try for Oxford. ('I regarded it as being quite simply the best, and if I was serious about getting on in life that is what I should always strive for . . . I was never tempted to opt for Nottingham.')[21] So she sat a scholarship exam in December 1942. She narrowly missed the prize (she was, as she points out in her memoirs, only seventeen); but she was offered a place at Somerville College, Oxford, for October 1944. The lost year was important since, under wartime regulations, unless she went up in 1943 she would only be allowed to take a two-year degree before being called up for National Service. Still, it was a considerable achievement to have won a place.

With a university place secured, but a year to fill before she could expect to take it up, the natural thing for a patriotic eighteen-year-old in the middle of the war might have been to do as many of her contemporaries had already done and join one of the women's services; or, if that would have committed her for too long a period, at least find some other form of war work while she waited to go to Oxford. It is a little odd that she chose instead to go back to school for another year.

The autumn term began in August, three weeks early to allow an October break for potato picking. Just three weeks into the term, however, there came a telephone call from Somerville: a vacancy had arisen – another girl had presumably decided that she had more compelling priorities – so Miss Roberts was offered the chance to take up her place immediately. She therefore left KGGS in the middle of the term, left home and Grantham and went up to Oxford in October 1943, with the opportunity, after all, to enjoy a full three years.

Oxford

Going to Oxford was the great opportunity which changed Margaret Roberts' life, opened doors to her and set her on the way to a political career. Yet Oxford was not for her, as it was for so many others, a golden period of youthful experiment and self-discovery. In the four years she eventually spent there she made no lasting friendships, underwent no intellectual awakening. She did not light up the university in any way: none of her contemporaries saw her as anything remarkable, still less picked her as a future Prime Minister. Yet she was already more than half-determined to go into politics and used her time at Oxford quite deliberately to make connections which would be useful to her in years to come. The fact that no one noticed her was largely a function of her sex: Oxford in the 1940s was still a predominantly male society. The Union, in particular, was barred to women, who were obliged to confine their political activity to the less glamorous back rooms of the Conservative Association and the Labour Club. But even within the Conservative Association Margaret Roberts seemed no more than diligent. The most remarkable thing about her Oxford career, in fact, was how little the experience seemed to change her.

Admittedly, Oxford in wartime was a shadow of its normal self. There were more women than usual and fewer young men; rather than giving the women more opportunity to shine, however, the men's absence seemed to drain the place of much of its energy. Margaret was given rooms in college, but was slow to make friends. 'Yes, I was homesick,' she admitted to Patricia Murray. 'I think there would be something very wrong with your home life if you weren't just a little.'[22] She gradually filled her rooms with familiar pictures and bits of furniture brought from home.

Her principal antidote to loneliness was work; but in some ways this only increased it. Chemistry is an unsociable course of study, involving long hours alone in the laboratory: years later she recalled that science was 'impersonal', compared with arts subjects which gave more opportunity for discussion and debate.[23] She was probably already beginning to regret having chosen chemistry; but she stuck at it conscientiously and she was more than competent at it, combining as she did a clear mind with an infinite capacity for taking pains. In her third year she devoted more of her time to politics and less to work. Had she dedicated herself single-mindedly to getting a first she might – by sheer application – have succeeded. As it was she won a university essay prize, shared with another Somerville girl. But she was not so single-minded. Moreover she was ill during her final exams. In the circumstances she did well to take a solid second. It was good enough to allow her to come back for a fourth year to do a B.Sc.

Outside her work, her most active commitment in her first two years was the John Wesley Society. This was a natural refuge for a shy provincial girl of Methodist upbringing, an opportunity to meet people like herself with similar habits and assumptions. She attended the Wesley Memorial Church on Sundays, and her social life revolved around the Methodist Study Group and tea parties run by the Students' Fellowship. It would be easy to conclude that the re-assuring familiarity of Methodism was simply a comfort blanket while she found her feet: 'a sober but cheerful social life', as she put it, 'which I found the more valuable in my initially somewhat strange surroundings'.[24] But she took it more seriously than that. The Wesley Society used to send its members out in pairs to preach in the surrounding villages – exactly as Alfred preached in the villages around Grantham. Margaret readily joined in this activity. Fifty years later, a Somerville contemporary and fellow Methodist clearly remembered a sermon she preached on the text 'Seek ye first the Kingdom of God; and all these things shall be added unto you', which was regarded by all who heard it as 'outstanding'.[25] No doubt it owed a lot to Alfred; but it should not be forgotten that when, much later, she was invited to expound her faith from a number of famous pulpits, she had done it before. She was a preacher before she was a politician.

By far the most important thing she did in her first term was to join the Oxford Union Conservative Association (OUCA). There was no question of her joining any other party, or all the political clubs, as some new undergraduates did. She had no doubt of her allegiance; Winston Churchill was her hero and she already took her political commitment very seriously.

To Janet Vaughan, Principal of Somerville and proud of the college's left-wing reputation, Miss Roberts was an embarrassment, a cuckoo in her progressive nest.

> She fascinated me. I used to talk to her a great deal; she was an oddity. Why? She was a Conservative. She stood out. Somerville had always been a radical establishment and there weren't many Conservatives about then. We used to argue about politics; she

was so set in steel as a Conservative. She just had this one line . . . We used to entertain a good deal at weekends, but she didn't get invited. She had nothing to contribute, you see.[26]

It would be hard to overestimate the effect of this sort of snobbish condescension on the formation of Margaret Thatcher's character. The discovery that all the trendy people were against her only confirmed her certainty that they were all wrong and reinforced her righteous sense of persecution. She encountered the same patronising attitude when she first became Leader of the Opposition in 1975. She had probably met it already at school, where she was used to being a loner who was not allowed to go to dances: it was precisely the attitude Alfred had tried to arm her against by urging her to follow her own – or his – convictions and ignore the crowd. But nowhere can it have been more brutal than at Oxford, where she went up naively expecting to find rational inquiry but met only arrogant superiority. This was her first encounter with the liberal establishment and she did not like it. It hardened her heart: one day she would get even.

Miss Roberts made her first recorded political speech during the 1945 General Election. As soon as the term ended she went back to Grantham to work for the Conservative who was trying to regain the seat from Denis Kendall – an Independent who had won it at a by-election during the war. The new candidate was Squadron Leader Worth. The twin themes of his campaign were encapsulated in an advertisement in the *Grantham Journal*: 'Worth stands for Agriculture and Churchill.'[27] Margaret Roberts, still only nineteen, acted as warm-up speaker at meetings before the Squadron Leader arrived. At one such meeting on 25 June, the *Sleaford Gazette* reported, 'the very youthful Miss M. H. Roberts, daughter of Alderman A. Roberts of Grantham', did not talk about agriculture, but spoke with precocious confidence about the need to punish Germany, to cooperate with both the Soviet Union and the United States, and to 'stand by the Empire' – as well as the importance of confirming Churchill in power. Having lost Roosevelt, she urged, the world could not afford to lose Churchill too.[28]

If she expected Kendall to lose and Churchill to be returned, however, she was wrong on both counts. Kendall held Grantham by a huge majority while the Conservative Government was swept from office by a totally unanticipated Labour landslide. Miss Roberts was shocked by the result. 'I simply could not understand how the electorate could do this to Churchill,' she wrote.[29] She was still more shocked to find that others whom she had assumed to be right-thinking Conservatives were not equally dismayed but elated by the election of a Labour Government. She always had difficulty believing that otherwise decent people could genuinely hold opposite opinions to her own. Looking back over half a century she portrayed the 1945 election as the start of the rot which did not begin to be set right until she herself was elected in 1979.

Returning to Oxford for her third year she found a university transformed by returning servicemen, older than normal peacetime undergraduates, keen both to build a new world and to celebrate their own survival. Lady Thatcher claims to have enjoyed the seriousness of the new influx; but she also allowed herself to unbend slightly and enjoy a little of the new hedonism. 'It was at this time', she wrote in *The Path to Power*, 'that I first went out to dances and even on occasion drank a little wine.'[30] She tried smoking, did not like it and decided to spend her money buying *The Times* every day instead. She went to the theatre. But she was not, so far as we know, tempted to act: nor did she develop any lasting interest in the theatre. What she did discover was a love of ballroom dancing, a taste which stayed with her, though rarely indulged, all her life.

But who did she dance with? There is no record that she had any serious male friends at Oxford, let alone a boyfriend. The fact is that her social life was wholly subordinated to politics. By her third year, despite competition from the returning servicemen, she was senior enough to stand for office within OUCA. She was first elected to be Secretary, in which capacity she attended a Conservative student conference in London; then Treasurer in the summer term; and finally President in Michaelmas 1946, when she went back to Oxford for a fourth year to take her B.Sc.

In her memoirs Lady Thatcher described her time at Oxford as an important period of intellectual foundation-building. Yet the only books she specifically mentions having read are Friedrich Hayek's *The Road to Serfdom*, which was first published in 1944, and *Who are 'The People'?* by the anti-socialist journalist Colm Brogan, published in 1943. Reading chemistry for her degree, rather than history or PPE (politics, philosophy and economics) like most aspiring politicians, she was not exposed to the discipline of sampling the whole spectrum of political thought; she was free to read only what she was likely to agree with. But if she did read *The Road to Serfdom* at this time, she also read Keynes' seminal White Paper on Full Employment, published the same year. Many years later she produced a heavily annotated copy from her handbag to berate the young Tony Blair in the House of Commons.[31] She made very little acknowledgement of Hayek's influence over the next thirty years.

But this is not surprising: she was always a gut politician, to whom intellectual arguments were no more than useful reinforcement. It is only retrospectively that she would like to claim an intellectual pedigree that was no part of her essential motivation.

Then, in early October 1946, she attended her first party conference, at Blackpool. She loved it. One of the sources of Mrs Thatcher's strength in the 1980s was that – almost uniquely among Tory leaders – she was in tune with ordinary party members. That love affair began at Blackpool. Now she met for the first time the Tory rank and file en masse already reacting defiantly to the outrageous impositions of socialism. She was impressed by the sheer number of the representatives, disproving any idea that Conservatism was an extinct creed, and she felt that she was one of them.

From now on she was on the inside track. No one she met at Oxford directly helped her or advanced her career; but having been President of OUCA gave her a standing at Central Office which helped her on to the candidates' list. What Oxford did not give her was a liberal education. She did not mix very widely or open herself to new views or experiences. She arrived in Oxford with her political views already settled and spent four years diligently confirming them. Undoubtedly her scientific training gave her a clarity and practicality of thought very different from the wishful woolliness of much arts and social science thinking. At the same time she read little or no history at university; and neither then nor later did she read much literature.

This amounted to more than a gap in cultural knowledge. More important, she did not receive the sort of education that delights in the diversity of different perspectives or might have exposed her to the wisdom of philosophic doubt. Her mind dealt in facts and moral certainties. She left Oxford, as she went up, devoid of a sense of either irony or humour, intolerant of ambiguity and equivocation. Her study of science at school and university chimed with her strict moral and religious upbringing and reinforced it, where a more liberal education in the arts or humanities might have encouraged her to question or qualify it. This rigid cast of mind was a source of unusual strength in Mrs Thatcher's political career. But it was also a severe limitation, exacerbating a lack of imaginative sympathy with other views and life-experiences which ultimately restricted her ability to command support.

She left Oxford in the summer of 1947, a qualified research chemist. For the past year she had been working under Dorothy Hodgkin, trying to discover the protein structure of an antibiotic called Gramicidin B, using the same technique of passing X-rays through crystals that Professor Hodgkin had successfully applied to penicillin. As it happened Gramicidin B was more complicated than penicillin, and she failed to crack it. There was no discredit in this: success was not finally achieved until 1980. She was still awarded her degree, but it was not the degree she wanted. In the short run it was the only qualification she possessed: it was as a chemist that she must start her working life. But she had already set her mind on going into politics.

2

Young Conservative

Standing for Dartford

ONLY twenty-one and fresh down from university, Margaret Roberts at least had a marketable qualification. In her final term at Oxford she had signed on with the University Appointments Board. She attended a number of interviews with prospective employers before being taken on by a firm called BX Plastics, based at Manningtree in Essex.

BX Plastics was a well-established company which developed new materials for such products as spectacle frames, raincoats and electrical insulation. During the war it had been taken over by Distillers; later, it was swallowed by the American Union Carbide Corporation, and finally by BP. In 1947 the company employed about seventy researchers. Margaret Roberts was one of ten graduates taken on that summer − three of them women, who were paid £50 a year less than the men. (The men got £400, the women £350.) She had understood that she was going to be Personal Assistant to the Research and Development Director, but was disappointed to find herself just another laboratory researcher, working on surface tensions to develop an adhesive for sticking polyvinyl chloride (PVC) to wood or metal.

During the eighteen months she worked at BX Plastics she lived in digs ten miles away in Colchester. She lodged with a young widow, Enid Macaulay, at 168 Maldon Road. Another lodger, probably not by coincidence, was the secretary of the local Young Conservatives. The likelihood must be that the first thing Margaret did on coming to Colchester was to approach the YCs for help with finding accommodation. Mrs Macaulay, interviewed in the early 1980s, remembered two things about Miss Roberts: first that she was always very smartly turned out – 'nice suits, nice blouses, nice gloves'; and second, her determination to be a politician. She was always busy with political activity of one kind or another, either with the YCs in Colchester or away at weekend conferences.[1]

When she was not away on Sundays, however, she kept up her religious observance. She attended the Culver Street Methodist Church and, as she had done at Oxford, joined other young people on missions to the surrounding villages. She may have preached: she is certainly remembered reading the lesson, with her too-perfect elocution. To her fellow Methodists in Colchester she appeared very grown up and sophisticated, more at ease with older people than she was with her contemporaries.

So far as we know she took no active steps to advance her political career. Though she attended weekend conferences, cultivated her contacts and practised her speaking, it was too soon to start looking for a constituency. She did not even apply to go on the Central Office list of prospective candidates. One would like to know what her imagined timetable was, how long she intended staying with BX Plastics before starting to read for the Bar, her next objective. As it was she had a lucky break. She attended the 1948 party conference at Llandudno – not as a representative from Colchester, but representing the Oxford University Graduates Association. An Oxford acquaintance introduced her to the chairman of the Dartford Conservative Association, John Miller, who happened to be looking for a candidate. This introduction changed her life.

Dartford had already been seeking a new candidate for a year. For twelve months Conservative Central Office had been sending lists of possible contenders, but Miller and his committee did not think much of any of them. Dartford, admittedly, was not an enticing prospect – though it was a good place for a first-time candidate to cut his teeth. It was a rock-solid Labour seat with a majority in 1945 of more than 20,000, and one of the largest electorates in the country, covering the three north Kent estuary towns of Dartford, Erith and Crayford. The local Association was run down, following 'a succession of mediocre agents'.[2] Miller, an energetic local builder, was determined to pull it round. He was initially doubtful about the idea of a woman candidate, taking the conventional view that a tough industrial constituency was no place for a woman. But he introduced Miss Roberts to other members of his delegation over lunch on Llandudno pier, and they were impressed. Miller could see that the novelty of a forceful young woman might be the shot in the arm his Association needed. She was invited to put her name forward. Meanwhile, Miller wrote again to Central Office mentioning her, but also requesting more names for consideration. They sent him another eleven, but agreed to see Miss Roberts if she would like to come into the office. She did, and 'created an excellent impression'.[3]

Miller still tried to persuade a number of local businessmen to stand – among them a paint manufacturer named Denis Thatcher who had recently stood as a Ratepayers' candidate for Kent County Council. 'He came to my office in Erith and asked me to think about it,' Denis recalled. 'I said no without hesitating.' Instead a slate of Central Office-approved hopefuls was interviewed in London in late December, from whom five were shortlisted for a run-off in Dartford at the end of January 1949. On 14 January the deputy area agent wrote to the deputy party chairman:

> Although Dartford is not a good constituency for a woman candidate there is a possibility that Miss Margaret Roberts will be selected; her political knowledge and her speaking ability are far above those of the other candidates.[4]

The Dartford Executive agreed with the area agent. Miss Roberts was selected over four male rivals and recommended for adoption by the full Association four weeks later.

The same area agent attended the formal adoption meeting on 28 February and reported enthusiastically to Central Office that Miss Roberts had made a 'brilliant' speech attacking the Labour Government, and the decision to adopt her was unanimous.[5] The meeting was also notable for Alfred's presence on the platform – the first time that father and daughter had ever spoken from the same platform.

There is a piquant symbolism in Alfred's presence at this meeting; also present that evening was Denis Thatcher. He was there as an ordinary member of the Association, but he was invited to supper afterwards to meet the candidate. Denis was then aged thirty-three, general manager of Atlas Preservatives, the family paint and chemicals business founded by his grandfather. During the war he had married a girl named Margaret (known as Margot) Kempson; but she was unfaithful while he was away fighting in Italy, and the marriage did not survive. He was now divorced, and openly looking to remarry. It seems that he was immediately struck by Margaret Roberts, who bore a startling resemblance to Margot. After supper he drove her back to London to catch the last train home to Colchester. This was the start of the relationship that became the anchor of her life. It developed gradually over the next two years;

but it began that evening of her adoption meeting, which therefore marks the critical watershed of her career. She arrived, as it were, on her father's arm: she left with her future husband. Her adoption for Dartford was thus the moment when she turned her back on Grantham. Oxford was an escape route; Colchester no more than an interlude. But though she did not go on to win Dartford she did put down roots, both political and personal, in suburban Kent. By marrying Denis Thatcher she embraced a Home Counties lifestyle. Of course Grantham remained in her blood, but for the next twenty-five years she steadily suppressed it.

Once adopted, Margaret threw herself into the constituency with total commitment. Though she could not seriously hope to win, she had been given an unexpected chance to make her name. She had at most fifteen months before the election to make an impact. First of all, though, she had to move nearer the constituency. So long as she was living and working in Essex she had a very awkward journey into London and out again to get to Dartford. But she could not afford to give up her job with BX Plastics until she had found a more convenient replacement; and this was not easy. She had several interviews, but found employers understandably reluctant to take on someone who made no secret of her political ambitions. Eventually she was taken on by the food manufacturers J. Lyons as a research chemist, working in Hammersmith. The job has usually been described as testing ice cream and pie-fillings, but Lady Thatcher writes in her memoirs that 'there was a stronger theoretical side to my work there, which made it more satisfying than my position at BX had been'.[6] Be that as it may – she was never very interested in theory – she stayed in pie-fillings scarcely longer than she had in plastics: less than two and a half years.

Three months after her adoption she was able to move to Dartford, where she stayed with a local Tory couple. For the next few months her routine was punishing. Commuting to London every day meant getting up before six to catch a bus to the station, a train to Charing Cross, then another bus to Hammersmith; the same in reverse when work finished, followed by an evening of canvassing or meetings, chauffeured around the large constituency by a rota of members; and, finally, speechwriting or other political homework late into the night. It was at this time in her life that she discovered, or developed, the ability to manage on only four hours' sleep.

But Margaret Roberts was having more fun than she had ever had in her life before. She was in her element. She was busy, she had a mountain to climb and she was the leader. She led from the front, by exhortation and tireless example, and she was the centre of attention: not only local attention, but the first stirrings of national attention, drawn by the still-novel spectacle of a young woman hurling herself into politics. By sheer energy and enthusiasm she pulled a moribund constituency party up by its bootstraps.

Attlee called the General Election, exceptionally, in the middle of winter. Polling day was 23 February; the campaign was fought in miserably cold, wet weather. Miss Roberts' energy, tackling a solid Labour stronghold in these conditions, won universal admiration. Whether or not she really believed it, she managed to persuade her supporters that she had a real chance of winning.

She fought on the slogan, unveiled at her formal adoption meeting on 3 February, 'Vote Right to Keep What's Left' – six words which brilliantly encapsulated her message, simultaneously identifying the Conservatives with morality and Labour with ruin and decline. Of course she sounded the same themes as other Tory candidates up and down the country, urging lower taxes, lower public spending and incentives to enterprise in place of rationing and controls. But she expressed these routine prescriptions with unusual fundamentalism. Hayek may have been in her mind as she painted the election as a choice between two ways of life – 'one which leads inevitably to slavery and the other to freedom'. While other Conservatives – particularly those who had been in the war – were anxious to blur such sharp distinctions, accepting that 1945 had shifted the political argument permanently to the left, Margaret Roberts made no such concession:

> In 1940 it was not the cry of nationalisation that made this country rise up and fight totalitarianism. It was the cry of freedom and liberty.[7]

Of course, she did not win, yet such was the enthusiasm of her campaign that her agent persuaded himself that she had an even chance. In reality the mountain was far too steep for her:

N. Dodds (Labour)	38,128
M. Roberts (Conservative)	24,490
A. Giles (Liberal)	5,011
Labour majority	13,638

But Miss Roberts had cut Dodds' majority by a third and won herself golden opinions. After such a successful blooding there could be little doubt that she would get a winnable constituency before long. Her problem was that nationally the Conservatives had almost, but not quite, overturned Labour's 1945 majority. Attlee survived with an overall majority of just five. This meant that there was likely to be another election very soon, making it difficult for candidates like Margaret Roberts to seek greener pastures.

Marriage to Denis

Margaret Roberts' first parliamentary campaign must have done wonders for her self-confidence. She knew now that she was on her way. With her course firmly set, she could begin to equip herself professionally for the career that lay within her grasp. Testing pie-fillings was no preparation for the House of Commons. As soon as the 1950 election was out of the way she applied to the Inns of Court to start reading for the Bar. She gave up her digs in Dartford and rented a flat in Pimlico. Instead of commuting daily to Hammersmith and returning to Dartford every evening to canvass, she could now devote her evenings to the law, visiting the constituency only when required. She did not really believe that one more push would win it. Yet she was still more visible than most candidates in hopeless seats.

Living in London also enabled her to see more of Denis Thatcher, who drove down to Atlas Preservatives each day from Chelsea. Since their first meeting on the night of her adoption, their relationship had developed slowly. Margaret had little time for social life in the eleven months up to the election; moreover, they were commuting every day in opposite directions. It was 'certainly not', she later insisted, love at first sight.[8]

Margaret and Denis were not an obviously well-matched couple: they had very few interests or enthusiasms in common. Yet at the time they met each was exactly what the other was looking for. Denis was thirty-three in February 1949. He had been deeply hurt by the failure of his first marriage. He wanted to marry again before he got too old, but was wary of making another mistake. What he liked about Margaret Roberts, on top of her looks, her energy and her youthful optimism, was her formidable practicality. She was not a girl who was going to make a mess of her life, or complicate his with feminine demands. Dedicated to her own career, she would leave him space to get on with his. She too was ready to get married, on her own terms. Hitherto she had never had much time for boyfriends. She had male friends – indeed, she preferred the company of men to women – but they were political associates with whom she talked and argued, rather than kissed. She always preferred men older than herself.

Though she had made a great impact in Dartford as a single woman, Alfred Bossom – leader of the Kent Conservatives and something of a mentor at this time – advised her that to advance her career she really should be married. Moreover, in sheer practical terms, marriage would enable her to give up her unrewarding job and concentrate fully on law and politics.

At the same time her practicality disguised a romantic side to her nature. At the height of her political power Mrs Thatcher was notoriously susceptible to a certain sort of raffish charm and displayed a surprising weakness for matinee-idol looks. Denis did not have these exactly, but he was tall (which she liked), upright and bespectacled (like her father, though Denis was more owlish). He had fought in the war and retained a military manner, at once slangy, blunt and self-deprecating. As managing director of his family firm he was comfortably off, drove a fast car and had his own flat in Chelsea. In the still grey and rationed world of 1950 he had, as she writes in her memoirs, 'a certain style and dash . . . and, being ten years older, he simply knew more of the world than I did'.[9] But she would not have fallen for a playboy. It was his work that took Denis round the world, and she admired that. She was a great believer in business, and export business in particular. Atlas Preservatives was just the sort of company on which British economic recovery depended. Beneath his bluff manner, Denis was a serious businessman of old-fashioned views and a moral code as rigorous as her own. He was much more relaxed about politics than she was, but he shared her principles and embodied them in practice. It was not an accident that politics brought them together.

Thus they complemented one another perfectly. While each answered the other's need for security and support, each also appreciated the other's self-sufficiency. Both were dedicated to their own careers, which neither ever curtailed for the other – not Margaret when their children were young, nor Denis when she became a Cabinet Minister.

Only once, around 1964, did Margaret's growing political prominence strain Denis's tolerance near to breaking point. For the most part he accepted, in a way remarkable for a man of conservative views born in 1915, the equality – and ultimately far more than equality – of his wife's career with his own. In this he was indeed 'an exceptional man'.[10] Needing a husband, Margaret chose shrewdly and exceedingly well. Marriage to Denis was the rock of her career.

He actually proposed in September 1951. He says he made up his mind while on holiday in France with a male friend. 'During the tour I suddenly thought to myself "That's the girl" . . . I think I was intelligent enough to see that this was a remarkable young woman.'[11] She claims that she 'thought long and hard about it. I had so much set my heart on politics that I hadn't figured marriage in my plans.'[12] Be that as it may, she accepted. But the 1951 General Election came first. Attlee went to the country again in October. Miss Roberts – for the last time under that name – threw herself back into electioneering. It can have done her no harm that Central Office leaked the news of her engagement the day before polling. But of course the seat was still impregnable. She took another thousand votes off Dodds' majority. More important, the Tories were narrowly returned to power (on a minority of the national poll). Just seven weeks later Miss Roberts became the second Mrs Thatcher.

The wedding, on 13 December, emphasised the bride's new life in the Home Counties rather than her Midland roots. She was married in London, in the Wesleyan Chapel, City Road – 'the Westminster Abbey of the Methodist Church'[13] – but this was mainly because Denis, as a divorced man, could not remarry in an Anglican church. Alfred thought the ceremony 'half-way to Rome',[14] and from now on Margaret increasingly identified herself with the Established Church. She did not even wear white, but a brilliant blue velvet dress with a matching hat decorated spectacularly with ostrich feathers, a replica of the dress worn by Georgiana, Duchess of Devonshire, in Gainsborough's painting.

Typically, the honeymoon combined holiday with work – a few days in Madeira sandwiched between business trips to Portugal and Paris. It was Margaret's first experience of foreign travel, but she never had much time for holidays; she was almost certainly impatient to get back to start homemaking, passing her Bar exams and looking for another seat. On their return she moved into Denis's flat in Swan Court, Flood Street, Chelsea, just off the King's Road, and began life as Margaret Thatcher. With marriage accomplished, she told Miriam Stoppard many years later, 'this was the biggest thing in one's life now sorted out'.[15]

Motherhood and law

After the precocious triumphs of her two Dartford candidacies, Margaret Thatcher's career was stalled for the next six years. Just when she had made such a spectacular beginning, marriage and then motherhood took her abruptly out of the political reckoning. In the long run, marriage set her up, both emotionally and financially: Denis's money gave her the security and independence to dedicate her life to politics. But in the short run it set her back five years.

Not that she became a housewife: far from it. But she was obliged to concentrate her energies on her secondary ambition – to become a lawyer – while putting her primary political goal temporarily on hold. She was forced – reluctantly – to sit out the 1955 General Election. Not until 1958 was she able to secure a winnable constituency from which to resume her march on Westminster. Frustrating though it was at the time, this enforced period of retrenchment did her no harm. In 1950 she was young, conspicuous and headstrong: had she got into Parliament at that age she would inevitably have attracted a lot of attention and probably identified herself irreparably as a naively vigorous right-winger. As it was, six years of marriage, motherhood and law both matured her and made her much less visible, enabling her to slip easily into a career path of rapid but inconspicuous promotion, without weakening her fundamental instincts and convictions. Those who make their move too soon in British politics seldom make it to the top.

For the first time in her life she had money. She could at last surround herself with all those enviable mod cons she did not have in Grantham or in any of her cheerless digs. In Swan Court she could afford to entertain and quickly turned herself into a formidable hostess. But of course she also worked. Along with the cooking and the housework, she now had time to pursue her legal studies. She attended courses at the Council for Legal Education, working towards her intermediate Bar exams in the summer of 1953. If she did not know it already, Denis discovered that he had married a workaholic who would stay up long after he had gone to bed, or get up early, to finish whatever she had to do.

Almost certainly Margaret Thatcher wanted to have children – she would have regarded it as part of her duty, one of those social expectations she was programmed to observe – even though she must have known it would make finding a seat more difficult. She was confident of her own ability to handle the competing demands on her time; but local Conservative Associations were a different matter. Whatever her calculations, they were knocked sideways in August 1953 when she surprised herself and her doctors by producing twins. This was a wonderful piece of Thatcherite efficiency – two babies for the price of one, a boy and a girl, in a single economy pack, an object lesson in productivity. She had been expecting a single child in late September, but her labour pains started six weeks early. She went into Queen Charlotte's Hospital on Thursday 13 August, was X-rayed next day and found to be carrying twins; they were delivered by Caesarean section on Saturday the 15th, weighing 4lbs each, and were christened Mark and Carol.

Giving birth to twins with the minimum disruption of her career became part of the Thatcher legend. She did not enjoy her pregnancy, which made her feel uncharacteristically unwell, so getting two children for the labour of one suited her admirably. 'As she now had one of each sex', Carol has written, 'that was the end of it as far as she was concerned – she needn't repeat the process.'[16] She could get on with what was more important to her. There and then, in her hospital bed, she committed herself to taking her final Bar exams in December. She had passed her intermediates in May and, twins or no twins, she was not going to postpone her finals. In fact their arrival six weeks early gave her more time.

On coming out of hospital she first hired an Australian nurse for six weeks while she found a permanent nanny, called Barbara, who stayed for five years. To give themselves more space, she and Denis rented the adjoining flat, knocking through a connecting door: this arrangement, with Denis and Margaret in one flat and Barbara and the twins next door, ensured undisturbed nights and maximum peace and quiet in the daytime for Margaret to work. She duly passed her final exams, was called to the Bar and joined her first chambers in January 1954.

While she was practising at the Bar, in Mark and Carol's pre-school years, she told Patricia Murray, 'I was never very far away – my chambers were only about twenty minutes from home, so I knew I could be back very quickly if I were needed.'[17] That was true – though perhaps optimistic – so long as the family was living in Chelsea. 'I was there with them quite a lot during the early stages,' she claimed in 1979.[18] But in 1957, when the twins were four, the hitherto very low rent on their two flats in Swan Court was steeply increased as a result of the Conservative Government's abolition of rent controls – an act which the Thatchers in principle approved. Rather than pay the new commercial rent they moved out of London to a large suburban house in Lock's Bottom, Farnborough, in Kent. This gave Denis a much shorter daily drive to Erith. But it meant Margaret commuting every day. She could not now be home in twenty minutes. Then, when she got into Parliament in 1959, she was not at home in the evenings either. The nannies had to cope – first Barbara, later another, much older, known as Abby. 'They kept the children in order and I always telephoned from the House shortly before six each evening to see that all was well.'[19]

Mark and Carol were not exactly spoiled, but they were certainly indulged. They did not lack for clothes or expensive toys: their childhood was very different from the constricted existence Margaret had endured in Grantham. They had family holidays – traditional English seaside holidays, first at Bognor, then on the Isle of Wight where they rented the same house for six years running from 1959. But Carol notes bleakly: 'Family holidays didn't appeal to Denis or Margaret.'[20] More adventurously they also went skiing as a family every Christmas from 1962 – quite an unusual thing to do in the early sixties. Carol describes her mother as 'a cautious skier' who worked hard on perfecting her technique but eschewed speed: 'she had no intention of returning with a leg in plaster'.[21]

'When I look back', Carol goes on, 'I have no doubt that my mother's political ambitions – and the single-mindedness with which she pursued them – eclipsed our family and social life.' She does not blame Margaret. 'No woman gets to the top by going on family picnics and cooking roast beef and Yorkshire pudding for Sunday lunch with friends.'[22] As a working woman bringing a second full-time income into an already prosperous home (and then spending a good deal of it on child care and private school fees) Mrs Thatcher was blazing a trail which became commonplace in her daughter's generation. Moreover she was not just working for her own fulfilment, or for money: she had a mission, and ultimately she achieved it. Plenty of prominent men – political leaders, businessmen and artists – have followed their calling at the expense of their families. History will not blame Margaret Thatcher for having done the same. But she deceived herself if she believed her family did not suffer for her single-mindedness.

Seeking a winnable constituency

Margaret Thatcher's legal career was brief and undistinguished, but nevertheless an important stage in her political apprenticeship. Less than six years elapsed between her being called to the Bar in January 1954 and her entering the House of Commons in October 1959. For those six years, however, her commitment to the law was characteristically thorough and purposeful, and it achieved its purpose. She had recognised even before she went to Oxford that law would be a much better profession than chemistry from which to launch into politics, first as a means of gaining practical experience of legislation in action, and second as a profession whose short terms and flexible hours would allow her both to nurse a constituency – supposing she could find one – and feel that she could always get home in an emergency if required. So it proved.

Women were still conspicuous by their rarity in the Inns of Court: the few exceptions tended to stick to 'feminine' specialisms like divorce and family law, rather than challenge hard masculine preserves like tax. Undoubtedly Mrs Thatcher did meet some prejudice at the Bar. Wherever she did encounter male chauvinism, her technique was simply to ignore it while giving it nothing to feed on. She worked at least as hard as any man. She arrived promptly in the morning, wasted no time on gossiping or long lunches, went home at 5.30 and usually took work with her. As a woman she was different because she did not mix socially with other barristers and pupils: she did not go to the pub at the end of the day. But she pulled her weight professionally: she relished showing the men that she expected no concessions. If anything, Patrick Jenkin remembers, her reputation with her peers was the more formidable because they knew that she had passed her exams while nursing twins, and that she went home every evening to look after her husband and children.[23]

She was not a brilliant lawyer. In the two years she practised under her own name she impressed everyone who worked with her as highly competent, thorough and meticulous; but as soon as she got into Parliament she was happy to give it up. 'You can do two things,' she explained to Miriam Stoppard in 1985. 'You cannot do three things.'[24] The law, like chemistry, was part of her apprenticeship: its discipline shaped her mental equipment, but she never joined the legal tribe. She retained an elevated, almost mystical, reverence for the rule of law as the foundation of English liberty. But she had seen enough of the profession from the inside not to be in awe of its pretensions As Prime Minister she treated lawyers as just another professional conspiracy to be brought to heel in the public interest; appeals to her professional solidarity fell on deaf ears. Her experience between 1953 and 1959 valuably inoculated her against the claims of legal protectionism.

In 1957, when the twins were three, Mrs Thatcher began again actively seeking a winnable constituency. Despite her record at Dartford and glowing references from Central Office, she did not find it easy. Conservative Associations, frequently dominated by women, are notoriously reluctant, even today, to select women candidates; that they were reluctant in the mid-1950s to adopt a young mother of twins is scarcely surprising. In truth it is more remarkable that she did, at only the fourth attempt, manage to persuade a safe London constituency that she could handle the double burden.

Before that she was shortlisted for two Kentish seats and one in Hertfordshire. The next safe seat where the sitting Member announced his intention to stand down was Finchley, a prosperous slice of north-west London which eventually turned out to be ideal for her. But here again she had a struggle initially against powerful prejudice. She was helped by the fact that the local Association was in bad shape. Despite a comfortable Conservative majority of nearly 13,000 in 1955, the Liberals had been making a big effort – specifically targeting the large Jewish vote – and had captured several council seats.

Sir John Crowder announced that he was stepping down in March 1958. By 15 May Central Office had sent the Association the names of some eighty hopefuls to consider. In June this long list was reduced to twenty, including Margaret Thatcher. Then the seventeen members of the selection committee voted for a short-list of three: Mrs Thatcher was on everyone's list, coming top with seventeen votes. 'It will be interesting', the deputy area agent minuted, 'to see whether the 100 per cent vote for Mrs Thatcher contained some people who were willing merely to include one woman in the list of four, but there is no doubt that she completely outshone everyone we interviewed.'[25]

The selection was a close-run thing, but on the second ballot Mrs Thatcher squeezed home by 46 votes to 43. She had won the vote, but she had still to win the acceptance of the whole Association. 'Woman Chosen as Conservative Prospective Candidate', the *Finchley Press* reported. 'Barrister, Housewife, Mother of Twins.'[26] The London *Evening Standard* featured the same angle. 'Tories Choose Beauty' ran its headline.[27] Her sex remained a contentious issue. Sir John Crowder made no secret of his disgust at being succeeded by a woman; and Central Office feared trouble at the formal adoption meeting on 31 July. In the event she had a triumph:

> We had anticipated that there might have been some volume of opposition to Mrs Thatcher as a clique in the constituency were known to be opposed to a woman candidate. In fact the Chairman handled the meeting extremely well and Mrs Thatcher gave a most excellent speech and altogether went down splendidly. When the resolution proposing her adoption was put, it was carried with about five descensions [*sic*] who looked extremely red-faced and stupid.[28]

Over the next fifteen months she threw herself into the task of getting to know the constituency with her usual thoroughness, holding meetings in each of the ward branches, leading canvassing parties and conducting 'an intensive campaign to meet as many of the electors as possible'.[29] Her pace was perhaps not quite so hectic as it had been in Dartford nine years earlier. There she had been a single woman with no obligations outside her work; now she was married with children and a home to run. Moreover, though she took nothing for granted, Finchley was in fact a safe seat. She had not the urgent sense of being a missionary in enemy territory; she was among friends – once she had overcome initial reservations – securing her base for a long parliamentary career. For that purpose Finchley suited her admirably. The only drawback was that she had just gone to live in Kent, and the constituency was the wrong side of London.

Affluent middle-class homeowners, relatively highly educated and concerned for the education of their children, with a strong Jewish element – this was to be Mrs Thatcher's personal electorate. These were 'her people', who embodied her cultural values and whose instincts and aspirations she in turn reflected and promoted for the next thirty years. One can only speculate how differently her career might have developed if she had become Member for Maidstone or Oxford or Grantham; as it was she became perfectly typecast as Mrs Finchley.

The Thatcher family was on holiday on the Isle of Wight in early September 1959 when Macmillan called the election. Margaret hurried back to throw herself into what the *Finchley Press* hyperbolically dubbed 'the political struggle of all time'.[30] Her election address spelled out in conventional terms how eight years of Conservative Government had made life better for the voters of Finchley. She fought an energetic but courteous campaign, sharing platforms with both her Labour and Liberal opponents. The result was never in doubt. The Liberals' effort was enough to gain them some 4,000 votes from Labour but not quite enough to put them into second place: they made almost no impact on the Tory vote. Mrs Thatcher thus increased the Tory majority from 12,825 to 16,260.

Margaret Thatcher (Conservative)	29,697
Eric Deakins (Labour)	13,437
Ivan Spence (Liberal)	12,260
Conservative majority	16,260

Though she held the seat without serious alarm through various boundary changes for the next thirty-two years, her majority was never so large again. The lowest it ever fell was in October 1974, when it dipped below 4,000; but even in her years of dominating the national stage her majority in Finchley never again hit five figures.

Finchley was a microcosm of the national result. Macmillan increased his overall majority to exactly 100. This was the high point of Tory fortunes in the post-war period, a zenith of confidence not to be touched again until Mrs Thatcher's own unprecedented run of three consecutive victories in the 1980s. The party she joined at Westminster in October 1959 was riding high; political analysts wondered if Labour would ever hold office again. But within a few years the pendulum had swung, and the first fifteen years of Margaret Thatcher's parliamentary career were served against a background of increasing uncertainty and loss of confidence within the party – from which it fell to her, eventually, to lead an astonishing recovery.

3

First Steps

Member for Finchley

WITH the Conservatives winning a three-figure majority, Margaret Thatcher was one of sixty-four new Tory Members elected in 1959. Among such a large new intake being a woman was simultaneously an advantage and a handicap. As one of only twelve women Members on the Conservative side of the House (Labour had thirteen) she was immediately conspicuous – the more so since she was younger, prettier and better dressed than any of the others – but for this very reason she was also patronised and disregarded. 'She appeared rather over-bright and shiny', one contemporary recalled. 'She rarely smiled and never laughed . . . We all smiled benignly as we looked into those blue eyes and the tilt of that golden head. We, and all the world, had no idea what we were in for.'[1]

She was always combative, another remembered, but in those early days she would generally back down gracefully when she had made her point. The alternative was to be written off as strident and bossy. She had to be careful to keep this side of her character out of sight for the next twenty years while she climbed the ladder: not until she was Prime Minister did Tory MPs come to enjoy being hectored by a strong-minded woman. To a remarkable extent she succeeded, while extracting the maximum advantage from her femininity.

Mrs Thatcher's parliamentary career received a fortunate boost within a few weeks of arriving at Westminster when she came third in the ballot for Private Members' Bills. This threw her in at the deep end, but also gave her the opportunity to make a conspicuous splash: instead of the usual uncontroversial debut delivered in the dinner hour to empty benches, she made her maiden speech introducing a controversial Bill. Inevitably she seized her chance and made certain of a triumph. She brought herself emphatically to the attention of the whips, demonstrated her competence and duly saw her Bill on to the Statute Book with the Government's blessing. Behind the scenes, however, neither the origin nor the passage of the Bill were as straightforward as they appeared. The newly elected thirty-four-year-old endured some bruising battles, both in the House of Commons and in Whitehall; and the measure that emerged was neither the one she originally intended nor the one she introduced. It was a tough baptism.

An MP who wins a high place in the Private Members' ballot is swamped with proposals for Bills which he or she might like to introduce. The issue Mrs Thatcher eventually chose was the right of the press to cover local government. This was thought to have been enshrined in an Act of 1908. Recently, however, some councils had been getting round the requirement of open meetings by barring the press from committees and going into a committee of the whole council when they wanted to exclude reporters. The 1959 Tory manifesto contained a pledge to 'make quite sure that the press have proper facilities for reporting the proceedings of local authorities'.[2] But the Government proposed to achieve this by a new code of conduct rather than by legislation. Mrs Thatcher considered this 'extremely feeble' and found enough support to risk defying the expressed preference of the Minister of Housing and Local Government, Henry Brooke, and his officials.

Her problem was that she needed the Department's help to draft her Bill; but the Department would only countenance a minimal Bill falling well short of her objective. Eventually she settled for half a loaf. Her Bill published on 24 January 1960 was judged by *The Times* 'to have kept nicely in line with Conservative thinking'.[3] In fact, it was a fairly toothless measure which increased the number of bodies – water boards and police committees as well as local authorities – whose meetings should normally be open to the press; required that agendas and relevant papers be made available to the press in advance; and defined more tightly the circumstances in which reporters might be excluded – but still left loopholes. It was still open to a majority to declare any meeting closed on grounds of confidentiality.

Maiden speech

The Second Reading was set down for 5 February. To ensure a good attendance on a Friday morning, Mrs Thatcher sent 250 handwritten letters to Tory backbenchers requesting their support. She was rewarded with a turnout of about a hundred. She immediately ignored the convention by which maiden speakers begin with some modest expression of humility, a tribute to their predecessor and a guidebook tour of their constituency. Margaret Thatcher wasted no time on such courtesies:

> This is a maiden speech, but I know that the constituency of Finchley which I have the honour to represent would not wish me to do other than come straight to the point and address myself to the matter before the House. I cannot do better than begin by stating the object of the Bill . . .

She spoke for twenty-seven minutes with fluency and perfect clarity, expounding the history of the issue and emphasising – significantly – not the freedom of the press but rather the need to limit local government expenditure. Only at the very end did she remember to thank the House for its traditional indulgence to a new Member.[4]

Her seconder, Frederick Corfield, immediately congratulated her on 'an outstanding maiden speech . . . delivered with very considerable clarity and charm'. She had introduced her Bill 'in a manner that would do credit to the Front Benches on either side of the Chamber'.[5] Later speakers reiterated the same compliments. It was practically compulsory in 1960 to praise a lady speaker's 'charm'; but the tributes to the Member for Finchley's front bench quality were more significant and probably more sincere.

In any case, the Bill passed its Second Reading – on a free vote, with many Labour Members supporting and some Tories opposing – by 152 votes to 39. Eventually it went into committee in mid-March. Over the next few weeks Mrs Thatcher had to battle hard for her Bill. She suffered a serious defeat when she failed to carry a clause giving public access to all committees exercising delegated functions; she had to settle for committees of the full council only. *The Times* regretted that this reduced the Bill to a 'half-measure'.[6]

Back on the floor of the House the emasculated Bill carried its Third Reading on 13 May, without a vote. For the Government Keith Joseph paid another compliment to Mrs Thatcher's 'most cogent, charming, lucid and composed manner', which had contributed to the passage of 'a delicate and contentious measure perhaps not ideally suited for a first venture into legislation'.[7] In the Lords the Bill earned another historical footnote when Baroness

Elliot of Harwood became the first peeress to move a Bill in the Upper House, before it finally received the Royal Assent in October. After exactly a year it was an achievement of sorts, but rather more of an education. As a piece of legislation it was ineffective. Nevertheless Mrs Thatcher had learned in a few months more about the ways of Whitehall – and specifically about the ability of officials and the Tory establishment together to stifle reform – than most backbenchers learn in a lifetime.

Mrs Thatcher's conduct of the Public Bodies (Admission to Meetings) Bill, as a novice backbencher taking on a senior Cabinet Minister of her own party, his Permanent Secretary and the parliamentary draftsmen, in the belief that they were all being either feeble or obstructive, displayed a degree of political aggression to which Whitehall was unaccustomed. Officials did not know how to handle a forceful woman who did not play by bureaucratic rules or accept their departmental wisdom. Their successors were to have the same problem twenty years later, multiplied tenfold by her authority as Prime Minister. No one in 1960 imagined that a woman could ever become Prime Minister. But her luck in winning a high place in the Private Members' ballot, and her plucky exploitation of the opportunity, had certainly put her in line for early promotion.

The Common Market

In the summer of 1961, after months of cautious soundings, the Macmillan Government finally announced Britain's application to join the European Economic Community – the Common Market, as it was then universally known. This was the biggest decision in post-war politics, which determined – even though it was another decade before Britain's third application was successful – the gradual redirection of British policy towards ever closer involvement with the Continent. In time, Mrs Thatcher as Prime Minister came to feel that this process had gone too far, and set herself to slow or even to reverse it. She felt no such doubts in 1961. In a characteristically thorough speech in her constituency on 14 August, she tackled the question of sovereignty head-on.

First she denied that Britain faced a choice between Europe and the Commonwealth, as many older Tories feared, arguing that the Commonwealth would only benefit from Britain being strong and prosperous. Besides, she frankly admitted, the Commonwealth was not the same as twenty or thirty years earlier: 'Many of us do not feel quite the same allegiance to Archbishop Makarios or Doctor Nkrumah or to people like Jomo Kenyatta as we do towards Mr Menzies of Australia.' Seldom has that point been more bluntly put.

Second, she warned that it was important to join the Community quickly in order to be able to help shape the Common Agricultural Policy. In fact it was already too late for that: the Six were pressing on deliberately to settle the CAP before Britain was admitted. But the principle she enunciated – that Britain needed to be in at the beginning of future developments – was an important one whose truth did not diminish.

Third, and most crucially, Mrs Thatcher faced up to fears of loss of sovereignty and national identity and dismissed them as groundless. Britain already belonged to alliances – principally NATO – which limited her independence. These were an *exercise* of national sovereignty, not a derogation of it.

> Sovereignty and independence are not ends in themselves. It is no good being independent in isolation if it involves running down our economy and watching other nations outstrip us both in trade and influence . . . France and Germany have attempted to sink their political differences and work for a united Europe. If France can do this so can we.[8]

What is remarkable about this statement, in retrospect, is its unblinking acceptance of the political dimension of a united Europe and Britain's proper place within it. Yet it only reflected the common assumption of British politicians in the early 1960s – and still in the early 1970s – that Britain would be joining the Community in order to lead Europe, or at least to share in the joint leadership. It was the confidence that Britain would still be a great power within Europe – indeed a greater power as part of Europe – which allowed them to contemplate with equanimity the loss, or pooling, of formal sovereignty. It is a striking illustration of this confidence that even so ardent a nationalist as Margaret Thatcher felt no qualms in 1961 on the subject which exercised her so furiously thirty years later.

Pensions minister

Less than two months later she was invited to join the Government as joint Parliamentary Secretary at the Ministry of Pensions and National Insurance (MPNI). The offer had come a little sooner than she would have liked, when the twins were only eight; but she knew that in politics, 'when you're offered a job you either accept it or you're out', so she accepted.[9] It was an exceptionally rapid promotion – equal first of the 1959 intake. Probably Macmillan and his Chief Whip simply wanted another woman to replace Patricia Hornsby-Smith in what was regarded as a woman's job. But their choice made Mrs Thatcher the youngest woman and the first mother of young children ever appointed to ministerial office.

She stayed in the Ministry of Pensions and National Insurance for three years, longer than she might have wished in one department; but it was a good department in which to serve her ministerial apprenticeship. The nature of the work suited her perfectly. Though she knew next to nothing about social security when she arrived, she quickly set herself to master both the principles of the system and the immensely complex detail. With her tidy mind – honed by both chemistry and law – and her inexhaustible appetite for paperwork, she rapidly achieved a rare command of both aspects which enabled her to handle individual cases confidently within a clear framework of policy. The MPNI was not a department where a minister – certainly not a junior minister – had large executive decisions to take, rather a mass of tiny decisions investigating grievances and correcting anomalies across the whole range of benefits and human circumstances. Three years of this gave Mrs Thatcher a close working knowledge of the intricacies of the welfare system which – since she never forgot anything once she had learned it – became a formidable part of her armoury twenty years later (though much of her detailed knowledge was by then out of date).

Her first minister was John Boyd-Carpenter, a pugnacious character who had been at the MPNI since 1955. 'He was a marvellous teacher,' she later recalled, 'fantastic man, total command of his department.'[10] He won her undying gratitude by coming down to meet her at the door the first morning she turned up bright and early at the department just off the Strand. This gallantry made such an impression on her that she made a point of extending the same courtesy to her own juniors at the Department of Education ten years later.

In her memoirs she conceded that generally 'the calibre of officials I met impressed me'.[11] Yet the enduring lesson she took from her time at the MPNI was that civil servants have their own agenda. She was shocked to catch them offering advice to Boyd-Carpenter's successors which they would not have dared to offer him because they knew he would not take it. 'I decided then and there that when I was in charge of a department I would insist on an absolutely frank assessment of all the options from any civil servants who would report to me.'[12] Whether this always happened in Downing Street in the 1980s is debatable, but Mrs Thatcher never had any doubt of the need to show her officials very quickly who was boss. Even as a junior minister she always wanted the fullest possible briefing. On one occasion she found herself unable to answer a series of deliberately arcane questions put by her Labour shadow, Douglas Houghton, to catch her out. She was furious and told her officials that it must never happen again. It never did.[13]

In July 1962, when Macmillan sacked a third of his Cabinet in an ill-judged effort to revive his faltering Government, Boyd-Carpenter was finally promoted. His successor at the MPNI was Niall Macpherson, who in turn was replaced the following year by Richard Wood. Both were much milder personalities than Boyd-Carpenter. The result was that Mrs Thatcher, though still only joint Parliamentary Secretary in charge of National Insurance and National Assistance, was allowed to assume a much more dominant role within the Department than is usual for a junior minister.

Her finest moment in the 1959 Parliament came on the day following Macmillan's culling of his Cabinet. The House met in a state of shock. By chance the first business was questions to the Minister of Pensions; but Boyd-Carpenter had been promoted to the Cabinet as Chief Secretary to the Treasury and his successor at the MPNI had not yet been named. Into the breach stepped the two joint Parliamentary Secretaries. Of fifteen questions tabled, Mrs Thatcher answered fourteen. It was not simply the fact that she answered, but the way she did it, that made an impact. 'Amid the gloom and depression of the Government benches', one observer wrote, 'she alone radiated confidence, cheerfulness and charm.'[14] It was a performance of exceptional composure under pressure.

In January 1963 General de Gaulle unilaterally vetoed Britain's application to join the Common Market. The collapse of his European policy holed Macmillan's Government very near the waterline: by the summer of 1963 it was listing badly and beginning to sink. The restructuring of the Cabinet had failed to rejuvenate the Government, which now faced a dynamic new Leader of the Opposition, Harold Wilson, twenty-two years younger than the Prime Minister. Macmillan was made to look even more out of touch by the titillating revelations of the Profumo scandal, which threatened to engulf the administration in a slurry of sexual rumour and suspected sleaze. There were stirrings in the party that it was time for the old conjuror to retire. Privately Margaret Thatcher made no secret of her support for this view.

Macmillan considered stepping down; but then, as Prime Ministers do, determined to soldier on – until, three months later, on the eve of the party conference, ill health suddenly compelled him to retire after all, leading to an undignified scramble for the succession. Mrs Thatcher's first preference was for 'Rab' Butler, but she was quite happy with the unexpected 'emergence' of Sir Alec Douglas Home. If she was pleased by the result, however, she was disappointed that the new Prime Minister did not undertake a wider reshuffle. When Richard Wood arrived at the MPNI to replace Niall Macpherson he found his Parliamentary Secretary in 'some turmoil', on tenterhooks to see what her own future might be.[15] She evidently felt that two years of Pensions and National Insurance was enough. She could hardly have expected promotion, but she had hoped for a sideways move to another department to widen her experience. It is not surprising that Wood found her a difficult subordinate over the last year of the Government's life.

Retaining Finchley

As the 1964 General Election, which seemed certain to end the Tories' thirteen-year rule, approached, Mrs Thatcher could not be absolutely confident of retaining Finchley. But she was an exceptionally visible Member who, in five years, had won herself a strong personal vote. Despite her family and ministerial commitments, the *Finchley Press* reckoned on 18 September, 'there can be few Members who have spent more time among their constituents than Mrs Thatcher'. She herself, unusually, predicted a majority of 10,000 and she was nearly right.[16]

Margaret Thatcher (Conservative)	24,591
John Pardoe (Liberal)	15,789
Albert Tomlinson (Labour)	12,408
Conservative majority	8,802

Her vote was down by 4,000, her majority nearly halved; the Liberals had succeeded in pushing Labour into third place. But Finchley was still a safe Tory seat. More significant was the impact of the Liberal advance on the national result. By nearly doubling their share of the vote largely at the Conservatives' expense, they helped Labour back into government with a wafer-thin majority of four. After thirteen years of Tory rule and the shambles of 1963,

Douglas-Home came astonishingly close to winning re-election. But he failed, narrowly, and his failure ended Mrs Thatcher's first experience of government.

More seriously, she also suffered a personal reaction. Her daughter Carol suggests that she was exhausted after a particularly strenuous campaign in Finchley on top of her ministerial work, and driving back to Farnborough late every night. In one respect her family life was eased, since both Mark and Carol were now at boarding school so neither was at home in mid-October; but she was having problems with Denis, who seems to have undergone some sort of mid-life crisis in 1964. This was first disclosed in Carol's biography of her father, published in 1996, and we only know what little she reveals. It appears that he was working too hard, partly because Atlas Preservatives was under-capitalised and struggling to survive, and he worried that not only his own family but the life savings of his mother, sister and two aunts depended on its continuing success. To someone as robust as Margaret, the idea of Denis having a nervous breakdown must have been alarming. She must have worried about the implications for herself and the twins if he were seriously ill. Not that he did not thoroughly support her ambition. On the contrary, the decision he took, after pondering the direction of his life on safari in southern Africa, to sell the family firm was not only intended to secure his family's future but represented a deliberate subordination of his career to hers. He was nearly fifty; she was not yet forty. He had done as much as he could with Atlas; he had been warned that he needed to slow down if he was not to kill himself. She was well launched on a trajectory which, win or lose in 1964, might reasonably be expected to lead to the Cabinet within ten years. So he made his decision. But he did not discuss it with Margaret until it was a *fait accompli*.[17]

In fact, the sale of Atlas to Castrol turned out very well for Denis. According to Carol it realised £530,000, of which his personal share was just £10,000. But other accounts suggest that it was worth very much more than that. In practice the sale of his family firm made Denis a millionaire. Secondly, instead of narrowing his responsibilities it widened them. Denis had expected to carry on running Atlas for Castrol, but now as an employee without the stress of ultimate responsibility. To his surprise Castrol offered him a place on the board, with salary and car to match. (The car was a Daimler with a personalised number plate, DT3.) When, just a few years later, Castrol in turn merged with Burmah Oil, Denis did very well in terms of share options and once again was invited on to the board. From being the overworked chairman of an insecure paint and fertiliser business, Denis spent the last decade of his working life as a highly paid executive in the oil industry, which in turn left him well placed to pick up lucrative non-executive directorships after his retirement.

4

Opposition

Shadow boxing

FOR the next six years Margaret Thatcher was the Conservative Opposition's maid of all work. Between 1964 and 1970 she held six different portfolios – three as a junior spokeswoman, successively on pensions, housing and economic policy, and three as a member of the Shadow Cabinet, shadowing Power, Transport and finally Education. When the Conservatives returned to power in 1970 she was confirmed in the last department. But in the meantime she had been given an unusually wide experience of shadow responsibilities which stood her in excellent stead as Prime Minister two decades later, going some way to compensate for her relatively narrow ministerial experience. Though her average tenure of each portfolio was less than a year she did nothing by halves, but always thoroughly mastered each one before moving on.

When in July 1965 Alec Douglas-Home announced his resignation of the Tory leadership, Mrs Thatcher was 'stunned and upset'. It is a measure of her isolation from Westminster gossip that she claims to have had no inkling that Sir Alec was coming under pressure to step down, allegedly orchestrated by supporters of Ted Heath. 'I never ventured into the Smoking Room so I was unaware of these mysterious cabals until it was too late.'[1] Her exclusion was partly a function of her sex, but also reflected her compartmentalised life and her nose-to-the-grindstone view of politics. Harder to explain is why she was so upset. Much as she admired Sir Alec, he was clearly not cut out to be Leader of the Opposition; the party needed a more aggressive and modern style of leadership to wrest the political initiative back from Labour and rethink its policies. She had known Heath since their time as candidates in adjacent Kentish seats in 1949–51. They had spoken on one another's platforms, but they had not become close and their acquaintance, as she later put it, 'had never risked developing into friendship'.[2] They were in truth very similar people – from similar social backgrounds, both humourless, single-minded and ambitious. But Mrs Thatcher disguised her ambition with a cloak of femininity: her manners were impeccable and she responded to a certain style of masculine gallantry. Heath had a curt manner and made no pretence at gallantry; long before he had any special cause to dislike Margaret Thatcher he was uncomfortable with her type of Tory lady, with her immaculate clothes, pearls, hats and gushing manner. So until she forced herself on his attention he barely noticed her. What attracted her to his standard – and kept her loyal for nine years, despite a personal relationship that never became warm – was respect for his seriousness of purpose, which matched her own. She evidently did not consider backing Enoch Powell, the leading advocate of free-market economics, who was then regarded as a fringe eccentric, but voted for Heath, who beat Maudling by 150 votes to 133, with Powell taking just 15.

Though elected as a new broom, Heath initially felt obliged, with an election possible at any moment, to retain all his predecessor's Shadow Cabinet. But in October he did reshuffle his front bench. Margaret Thatcher was delighted to be switched at last from Pensions and National Insurance (which she had been doing in and out of office for four years) to shadow Housing and Land.

Wilson was only biding his time before calling a second election in March 1966 which the Tories, even with a new leader, had no hope of winning. In Finchley, Mrs Thatcher did her best to project enthusiasm. But privately she was critical of Heath's prosaic manifesto. Her own address led on the fundamental theme that every action of the Labour Government increased the power of the state over the citizen. Conservative philosophy was the opposite: 'The State was made for Man, not Man for the State.'[3]

The result was never in doubt. Though her vote actually fell slightly, Mrs Thatcher was one of only three Tories to increase her majority, with Labour pushing the Liberals back into third place:

Mrs M. Thatcher (Conservative)	23,968
Mrs Y. Sieve (Labour)	14,504
F. Davis (Liberal)	13,070
Conservative majority	9,464

Nationally Labour won a landslide, with a majority of nearly a hundred. The Tories were condemned to another five years of opposition. With the certainty of a long haul ahead, Heath reshuffled his team, taking the chance to drop several of the older hands. There was some discussion of putting Mrs Thatcher in the Shadow Cabinet. Jim Prior, then Heath's PPS, remembers suggesting her as the statutory woman. There was a long silence. 'Yes,' he said. 'Willie [Whitelaw, the Chief Whip] agrees she's much the most able, but he says once she's there we'll never be able to get rid of her. So we both think it's got to be Mervyn Pike.'[4]

Actually, the idea of a statutory woman was a new one. There had not been a woman in a Tory Cabinet since Florence Horsburgh in 1954, nor in the Shadow Cabinet since the party went into opposition. But Wilson had included Barbara Castle in his first Cabinet in 1964 and promoted her the following year. If the Tories had to be seen to follow suit, Margaret Thatcher was a more obvious counterpart to Mrs Castle than the much gentler Mervyn Pike. Whitelaw's preference for keeping Mrs Thatcher down for a little longer suggests that she was already seen as an uncomfortable colleague. Iain Macleod, however, had spotted her potential and specifically asked for her in his shadow Treasury team. Heath agreed. She became Treasury and Economic Affairs spokeswoman, outside the Shadow Cabinet but in some respects better placed to make a mark than she would have been inside it.

This was one of the very few periods in Mrs Thatcher's career when she operated as a team player, contributing her own particular expertise as a tax lawyer to a delegated effort, opposing the Labour Government's Selective Employment Tax. She clearly found it a liberating experience. When her own time came to lead she was not so good at delegating, yet she copied much of Macleod's method of working.

At the party conference in Blackpool in October Mrs Thatcher had the opportunity of replying to a debate on taxation. She spent nine hours preparing her speech, and was rewarded with her 'first real conference success'.[5] 'Thoroughly relaxed,' the *Daily Telegraph* enthused, 'she banged out sentences with the elusive rhythm some of her peers find it so hard to achieve.'[6] The still pre-Murdoch *Sun* hailed a new star under the headline, 'A Fiery Blonde Warns of the Road to Ruin': 'Mrs Margaret Thatcher, the pretty blonde MP for Finchley, got a standing ovation for one of those magnificent fire-in-the-belly speeches which are heard too seldom.'[7]

In 1967 she paid her first visit to the United States. It was a revelation to her. In her forty-two years she had scarcely been out of Britain before, apart from her honeymoon and, since 1962, her annual skiing holiday. Ever since the war she had been well disposed towards America as the arsenal of democracy and Britain's great English-speaking ally in the cause of Freedom. But the potential love affair had not been consummated until now. In the spring of 1967 she went on an American government 'leadership programme' designed to show rising young British politicians the American way of life; for six weeks she was whisked all round the country. 'The excitement which I felt', she wrote in her memoirs, 'has never really subsided. At each stopover I was met and accommodated by friendly, open, generous people who took me into their homes and lives and showed me their cities and townships with evident pride.' Her theoretical awareness of the 'brain drain' was brought into focus by meeting a former constituent from Finchley who had fled 'overregulated, high-taxed Britain' to become a space scientist with NASA.[8] Two years later she went back for a four-week speaking tour under the auspices of the English Speaking Union. Henceforth America became for her the model of an enterprise economy and a free society: not only American business practice, but American private health care, American penal policy and American business sponsorship of the arts were the examples she encouraged her ministers to study in the eighties.

Shadow Cabinet

After eighteen months working with Macleod she got her reward in October 1967. By her performances in the House, Mrs Thatcher had certainly earned promotion to the Shadow Cabinet; but still she only gained it when she did because Mervyn Pike stepped down on grounds of health. She now had no rival as the statutory woman. Significantly, however, Heath did not simply give her Miss Pike's social services portfolio – which would have been a traditionally feminine responsibility. Instead he set her to shadow the Ministry of Power, an unmistakably masculine brief comprising coal, nuclear energy, electricity and North Sea gas. More important than the portfolio, however, admission to the Shadow Cabinet marked Mrs Thatcher's arrival at the top table, just eight years after entering Parliament. As Whitelaw had foreseen, she would not easily be got rid of now. In less than another eight years, in fact, she had toppled Heath and leapfrogged over Whitelaw to seize the leadership.

In her memoirs Lady Thatcher wrote that she felt marginalised as a member of Heath's Shadow Cabinet. 'For Ted and perhaps others I was principally there as the "statutory woman" whose main task was to explain what "women" . . . were likely to think and want on troublesome issues.'[9] It is clear that she no longer felt – as she had done as Treasury spokesman – part of a team. If initially she talked too much she soon learned to keep quiet and bide her time.

Meanwhile, shadowing Power gave her the chance to master another important area of policy. Interviewed by the *Sunday Telegraph* just after her appointment she said it was 'a great surprise'; she was now 'busy genning up on the subject for all she was worth'.[10] It was still the era of cheap imported oil. North Sea gas had recently been discovered, but not yet oil. The Labour Government was running down the coal industry, a policy the Conservatives broadly supported against a good deal of traditional Labour anguish. Altogether Power was another excellent portfolio for her, using her scientific training in handling technical questions of nuclear energy and mineral deposits, but also facing her directly for the first time with the political problem of the nationalised industries.

Shadowing Power, in fact, was all about the nationalised industries. Every speech that Mrs Thatcher made during the year that she held this portfolio – and the following year when she was switched to Transport – shows her developing ever more clearly the conviction that public ownership was economically, politically and morally wrong. Though she never cited him, all the signs are that she had been reading – or rereading – Hayek, whose two-volume elaboration of *The Road to Serfdom*, *The Constitution of Liberty*, was published in 1960. She was certainly beginning to come under the influence of the independent free-market think-tank, the Institute of Economic Affairs (IEA), run by Arthur Seldon and Ralph Harris. But already she had the gift of putting their arguments into clear unacademic language of her own. On one hand she delighted in demonstrating that public ownership was inefficient, on the other that it was destructive of individual freedom.

In 1968 she was invited to give the annual Conservative Political Centre (CPC) lecture at the party conference in Blackpool. This was a considerable honour: previous lecturers had been recognised party thinkers. Mrs Thatcher, the *Times* diarist noted, was being offered 'an opportunity much coveted by the party's intellectuals through the years – and certainly the best chance a high-flying Tory politician ever gets to influence party thinking on a major theme'.[11]

The Tory party was in a considerable ferment in the summer of 1968, as grass-roots loathing of the Government combined with mounting criticism of Heath's leadership to fuel demand for a sharper, more distinctive Conservatism. Mrs Thatcher's lecture did dimly reflect this rising tide. Instead of nailing her colours boldly to the mast, however, she offered an uncharacteristically woolly, largely conventional Tory critique of the growth of government. Concern about the size, complexity and facelessness of modern government was a commonplace right across the political spectrum in the sixties. The New Left warned of 'alienation' and demanded more 'participation'. The right blamed socialism and talked vaguely of 'getting government off people's backs' and 'rolling back' the state. Mrs Thatcher's CPC lecture was just another Shadow Cabinet expression of this line – padded with some oddly naive banalities and altogether much less strikingly expressed than many of her Commons speeches. Such press coverage as the lecture received was typified by the *Guardian's* headline: 'Time to reassert right to privacy'.[12]

The fact is that it would have been imprudent for an ambitious young frontbencher, only recently appointed to the Shadow Cabinet, to have come out openly as a Powellite in October 1968. Only six months earlier Enoch Powell had been sacked from the Shadow Cabinet for making his notorious 'River Tiber' speech calling for a halt to coloured immigration and the assisted repatriation of immigrants. This speech transformed him overnight from a cranky economic theorist into a national figure with a huge popular following, a hate figure to the left and a looming challenge to Heath's leadership. Mrs Thatcher was never close to Powell in the few months they sat together in the Shadow Cabinet: Powell was an explicitly masculine politician who frankly deplored the intrusion of women into politics. But she was becoming increasingly interested in his economic ideas; she also 'strongly sympathised' with his argument about immigration. She regretted that Powell's new notoriety henceforth overshadowed his economic agenda, allowing opponents to tar free-market thinking with the same brush as either right-wing extremism or crackpot nostalgia, or both at once.[13]

That autumn, in the run-up to the party conference – just when she was writing her lecture – Heath had made a speech in Scotland firmly repudiating those Tories who were attracted by the seductive Powellite prescription of rolling back the state. 'That', he declared, 'though a century out of date, would certainly be a distinctive, different policy.'

But it would not be a Conservative policy and it would not provide a Conservative alternative. For better or worse the central Government is already responsible, in some way or another, for nearly half the activities of Britain. It is by far the biggest spender and the biggest employer.[14]

That was precisely what Powell, the IEA and, in her heart, Mrs Thatcher, wanted to reverse. Most practical Conservatives, however, though they might pay lip service to the idea of some marginal denationalisation, took it for granted that a large public sector was a fact of life.

It was in the context of this overwhelming orthodoxy that Mrs Thatcher spoke at Blackpool. The most significant section of her lecture was its ending, an unfashionable defence of party politics, rejecting the widespread hankering for 'consensus'. 'We have not yet appreciated or used fully', she suggested, 'the virtues of our party political system.' The essential characteristic of the British system was the concept of the Opposition, which ensured not just an alternative leader but 'an alternative policy and a whole alternative government ready to take office'. Consensus she dismissed as merely 'an attempt to satisfy people holding no particular views about anything'. It was more important to have 'a philosophy and policy which because they are good appeal to sufficient people to secure a majority' – in other words, what she later called 'conviction politics'. She concluded:

No great party can survive except on the basis of firm beliefs about what it wants to do. It is not enough to have reluctant support. We want people's enthusiasm as well.[15]

More than anything else it was this crusading spirit which was Mrs Thatcher's unique contribution to the anti-collectivist counter-revolution which ultimately bore her name. Others developed the ideas which she seized on and determinedly enacted. The force which transformed British politics over the next twenty years was Mrs Thatcher's belief that politics was an arena of conflict between fundamentally opposed philosophies, her contempt for faint hearts and her ruthless view that a party with a clear philosophy needed only a 'sufficient' majority – not an inclusive 'consensus' – to drive through its programme. Few who heard the shadow Minister of Power set out this credo in Blackpool in October 1968 paid much attention at the time. Even when she grasped the party leadership seven years later few colleagues or commentators really believed she meant what she said. In fact the essence of Thatcherism was there in her words that day: not so much in the unremarkable policies as in her fierce belief in them.

That autumn she was switched again, to Transport. Interestingly, she did not see her job as simply championing the road lobby. Though famous later for her enthusiasm for 'the great car economy' and a corresponding detestation of the railways, she was at this time strikingly positive – in her first Commons speech on the subject – that the most urgent need was for more capital investment in British Railways. 'If we build bigger and better roads', she warned – thirty years before the argument was widely accepted – 'they would soon be saturated with more vehicles and we would be no nearer solving the problem.'[16]

In the summer of 1969 she paid her first visit to the Soviet Union, the counterpart of her visit to the United States two years before. She was invited as Opposition Transport spokeswoman, principally to admire the Moscow metro and other Soviet achievements in the transport field, but she also found time to take in nuclear power stations as well as the usual tourist sights. Of course she had no illusions about the moral and material bankruptcy of the Soviet system: her instinctive hostility had been sharpened by her experience of campaigning for the past four years for the release of a British lecturer, one of her constituents, whom the Russians had charged with spying in the hope of swapping him for two of their own spies. (A swap was finally agreed just before her visit.) Her own self-congratulatory account of the trip tells of embarrassing her guides by asking awkward questions and correcting their propaganda; but while the drab streets and empty shops confirmed her preconceptions she also saw enough of the long-suffering victims of the system to convince her that they must sooner or later reject it. Believing passionately that Communism was contrary to human nature she was confident that it could not endure. She always thought that the Cold War was there to be won.[17]

That October she celebrated ten years in Parliament, marking the anniversary with a ball at the Royal Lancaster Hotel. In her speech she noted how the world had changed in those ten years: in 1959 South Africa had still been a member of the Commonwealth, Eisenhower was President of the United States, Britain had not yet applied to join the Common Market and the first man had not yet gone into space. There were no Beatles, no David Frost, no hippies and no 'permissive society'. But some things, she asserted, did not change: 'Right is still right and wrong is wrong.'[18]

In years to come Mrs Thatcher regularly blamed the decline in the moral standards of society on the liberalisation of the legal framework promoted by the Labour Government in the sixties – what she called in her memoirs the 'almost complete separation between traditional Christian values and the authority of the State'.[19] Yet at the time she supported much of this agenda. It is true that she opposed the 1968 liberalisation of divorce law. She also remained firm in her support for capital punishment. But she voted for the legalisation of homosexuality between consenting adults, and also for David Steel's Abortion Bill. In both cases she was influenced by the individual suffering she had witnessed in her work at the Bar.

Shadow Education Secretary

With hindsight the appointment of Margaret Thatcher to replace Sir Edward Boyle as shadow Education Secretary is a symbolic moment in the transformation of the Tory party. A gentle, liberal, high-minded Old Etonian baronet who had already been Education Secretary in 1962–4, Boyle personified the educational consensus which had promoted comprehensive schools and 'progressive' teaching methods: as a result he was the principal target for the right-wing backlash. Angry Conservatives in the shires and suburbs fighting to preserve their grammar schools regarded Boyle as a traitor – a socialist in all but name. Mrs Thatcher – grammar school-educated, defiantly middle class and strenuously anti-socialist – was in every way his opposite. Yet Heath intended no change of policy by appointing her.

On the contrary the appointment was widely applauded as a shrewd piece of party management – for example by the *Financial Times*.

> The choice of Mrs Thatcher shows that Mr Heath has resisted the pressure from the Right to appoint a dedicated opponent of the comprehensive system. Instead he has picked an uncommitted member of the 'shadow' Cabinet who has won a high reputation for her grasp of complex issues in the fields of finance, social security, power and transport.[20]

In fact, of course, she did have strong views on education. As Nora Beloff in the *Observer* was almost alone in pointing out, she 'has made no secret of her desire to see the party campaign more aggressively in favour of freedom of choice and against regimentation'.[21] She had sent her own children to the most expensive private schools – Mark was now at Harrow, Carol at St Paul's Girls' School; but no one in 1969 considered this a disqualification for running the state system. Since 1965 the Labour Government had required Local Education Authorities to draw up schemes to convert their grammar and secondary modern schools to comprehensives. In Finchley at the 1966 election she promised that a Tory government would withdraw Labour's circular requiring the preparation of plans; she always insisted that the party was not against comprehensivisation where appropriate but she deplored the disappearance of good grammar schools.[22]

Nationally, however, comprehensivisation was proceeding rapidly. Progressive opinion took it for granted that the momentum was unstoppable. There were still 'pockets of resistance', Boyle admitted just before he resigned. It was 'a difficult subject for our Party', and the next Conservative Government would have to take 'a number of most uncomfortable decisions when we are returned to power'; but he was sure there were 'absolutely no political dividends to be gained from any attempt to reverse the present trend in secondary education'.[23] Even with Boyle gone, this remained the general view of the Shadow Cabinet. Whatever her own preference might have been, Mrs Thatcher inherited an agreed line which left her very little room for manoeuvre.

Looking back in her memoirs, Lady Thatcher wished she could have argued for preserving grammar schools on principle, not just case by case.[24] In fact she did, from the first weeks of her responsibility for education, clearly assert the principle of diversity. She lost no time in lending her support to the nine LEAs which were refusing to go comprehensive. But at the same time she accepted that she could save only 'a small top layer' of the most famous grammar schools.[25] She was not proposing to stake her career on fighting the march of comprehensivisation.

Mrs Thatcher may have hoped that such a pragmatic compromise would prevent her tenure of Education being dominated by the issue of comprehensivisation. But in practice her hand was forced by Labour's Education Secretary, Edward Short – a former headmaster and a doctrinaire proponent of comprehensives – who blew her compromise apart by introducing a Bill in February 1970 to compel the handful of recalcitrant LEAs to comply. Even Boyle called this 'highly dictatorial';[26] it was in fact unnecessary and counterproductive, since all it did was to provoke resistance to a process which was already proceeding very rapidly. Mrs Thatcher was bound to fight it, and in doing so she could not help revealing her gut instincts. But still Conservative policy did not materially change.

Short's Bill fell when Wilson called an early election. All it achieved was to expose Mrs Thatcher's lack of sympathy with the policy she very soon found herself having to pursue in office.

Meanwhile, she was coming to terms with the rest of her new brief. The policy she had inherited was confidently expansionist. At a time when the Tories were promising to cut public expenditure overall, they were committed to higher spending on education. They were pledged to implement the raising of the school-leaving age to sixteen (which Labour had postponed in 1968), to maintain spending on secondary education while giving a higher priority to primary schools, and to double the number of students in higher education over ten years. Mrs Thatcher's consistent theme as shadow Education Secretary was the need for more money and the promise that the Tories would find it. She was even sympathetic to the teachers' claim for higher salaries.

For the first three or four months of 1970 the Conservatives were still confident of winning the next election, whenever it was held. Although Heath personally never established much rapport with the electorate, the party had enjoyed huge leads in the opinion polls for the past three years. Then, in the spring, the polls went suddenly into reverse. Wilson could not resist seizing the moment. With the polls temptingly favourable and the Tories commensurately rattled he called the election for 18 June.

Once Heath's victory had made nonsense of the polls, many Conservatives claimed to have been confident all along that they would win. More honest, Lady Thatcher admits that she expected to lose.[27] Not personally, of course: she was secure in Finchley, where the local Labour party did not even have a candidate in place when Wilson went to the Palace. But this was the first election in which she featured as a national figure, albeit in the second rank. Central Office arranged for her to speak in a number of constituencies beyond her own patch, all over the south and east of England; she did not detect the enthusiasm which others claimed to have felt.

She was also chosen to appear in one of the Tories' election broadcasts. Despite a television training course she had taken in the 1950s and regular appearances on the radio, she was not a success; her planned contribution had to be cut. Characteristically, however, she realised that television was a skill that had to be mastered. 'She was clever enough to ask for help,' one media adviser acknowledged. 'Margaret wanted to learn while most of the rest of the senior Tories wished television would just go away.'[28] The man she turned to for coaching, who would eventually get the credit for transforming her image, was Gordon Reece.

In her memoirs Lady Thatcher described attending her own count in Hendon Town Hall, then going on to an election night party at the Savoy where it became clear that the Conservatives had won.[29] In fact, Finchley did not count until the Friday morning. Carol's memory is more accurate:

We were on our way to Lamberhurst* when the news of the early exit polls came over the car radio. 'If that result is right, we've won,' exclaimed Margaret, obviously surprised. Denis turned the car round and we went to the *Daily Telegraph* party at the Savoy.[30]

That first exit poll, from Gravesend, was announced by the BBC at 10.30; the first results were declared soon after eleven. For both Labour, who had thought themselves to be cruising towards re-election, and for the Tories, resigned to defeat and just waiting to turn on their leader, the reversal of expectations was hard to grasp. For Mrs Thatcher the result meant the likelihood of Cabinet office. She returned to Finchley after an hour and a half's sleep to learn that she had increased her own majority by nearly two thousand:

Mrs M. Thatcher (Conservative)	25,480
M. Freeman (Labour)	14,295
G. Mitchell (Liberal)	7,614
Conservative majority	11,185

She was not in the first batch of Cabinet ministers named that day, but was summoned to Downing Street on Saturday morning to be offered, as expected, the Department of Education and Science. She was immediately asked if she would like to be the first woman Prime Minister. Her reply was categoric – but also barbed: '"No," she answered emphatically, "there will never be a woman Prime Minister in my lifetime – the male population is too prejudiced."'[31] She preferred to get on with the job in hand. She went home to read her first boxes, before turning up at the Department bright and early on Monday morning.

---

*The Thatchers had moved from Farnborough to Lamberhurst, near Tunbridge Wells, in 1965.

5

Education Secretary

The minister and her department

MARGARET Thatcher was Secretary of State for Education and Science for three years and eight months. Her time at the DES formed a crucial period of her political development, if only because it constituted her only experience of heading a government department before she became Prime Minister, responsible for running the entire Whitehall machine, just five years later. Unfortunately it was an unhappy experience; or at least that was how she came to remember it. Yet there was an element of hindsight in her recollection. In truth, her time at the DES was a good deal less embattled – and a good deal more successful – than she later suggested.

Heath sent her to Education mainly because he had to send her somewhere, and after all her switches of the previous six years that was the portfolio she happened to be shadowing when the music stopped in June 1970. Education was not high on the Government's agenda; no major policy initiatives were planned. When Iain Macleod died suddenly just four weeks after the Government took office, Mrs Thatcher's name was canvassed in some quarters as a possible replacement Chancellor. Though inexperienced she had proven expertise. But it is most unlikely that Heath ever considered her before choosing the more amenable Tony Barber. In his view Education was about her ceiling. Yet it was in some ways the worst possible department for her.

It was a department with an entrenched culture and a settled agenda of its own which it pursued with little reference to ministers or the rest of Whitehall. The convention was that education was above politics: government's job was to provide the money but otherwise leave the running of the education system to the professionals. Political control, such as it was, was exercised not by the DES but by the local educational authorities up and down the country; the real power lay with the professional community of teachers, administrators and educational academics, all of whom expected to be consulted – and listened to – before any change in the organisation or delivery of education was contemplated. Political interference in the content of education was taboo. The Secretary of State, in fact, had very few executive powers at all. One of Mrs Thatcher's Labour successors complained that his only power seemed to be to order the demolition of an air raid shelter in a school playground. It was not a department for an ambitious minister keen to make her mark.

Politically as well as temperamentally, Mrs Thatcher was antipathetic to the DES. She instinctively disliked its central project, the spread of comprehensive schools, and the whole self-consciously 'progressive' ideology that lay behind it. She disliked the shared egalitarian and collectivist philosophy of the educational establishment, and resented the fact that they all knew each other extremely well. Attending her first teachers' union dinner soon after coming into office she was disturbed to discover that her senior officials were 'on the closest of terms' with the NUT leaders.[1] She particularly disliked the assumption that her views were immaterial and her only function, as the elected minister, was to get the money to carry out the predetermined policy. In addition she correctly sensed that the educational mafia frankly disliked her.

The DES traditionally looked for two qualities in its Secretary of State. On the one hand, the Department's self-esteem required a leader of high intellectual calibre and broad liberal culture. Senior officials were sniffy about Mrs Thatcher's science degree and her lack of cultural interests. At the same time, however, the DES wanted a minister who would fight its corner in competition with Cabinet colleagues and against the Treasury; and in that respect Mrs Thatcher quickly proved her mettle. She was not a heavyweight but she was a fighter. The stubbornness which exasperated her officials within the Department delighted them when it was deployed against the rest of Whitehall. She could be 'brutal' and 'a bully'; but the obverse was that she was 'strong, determined and bloody-minded enough to wear down the Treasury'. She was 'absolutely maddening', one of her most senior mandarins recalled. 'We liked that.'[2] Despite her intellectual limitations – perhaps because of them – she turned out to be highly effective at winning the resources to carry out the Department's policies; so that in the end they came reluctantly to regard her as one of the best of recent Secretaries of State. In fact, once they had explained to her the constraints of her office, Mrs Thatcher was in some ways the civil servant's ideal minister: hard-working and demanding, but a good advocate for the Department, with no educational agenda of her own.

That is not to say that she did not have strong views, only that she had no power to impose them. Her attitude to education was simple, prescriptive and defiantly old-fashioned: she saw it not as a process of awakening or intellectual stimulation but as a body of knowledge, skills and values to be imparted by the teacher to the taught. ('Mrs Gradgrind Thatcher', one profile not unfairly called her.)[3] She deplored the new child-centred teaching which held that everything was relative and value-free.

As Secretary of State she took great pride in her own (very slight) experience of teaching. In her first Oxford summer vacation she had taught maths and science for six weeks at a Grantham boys' school. She used to recall this brief exposure to the chalkface to establish her credentials. At the same time she recognised that teaching was 'a vocation which most people just do not have'.[4] Teachers, of course, regarded such pieties as simply an excuse for underpaying them. In principle she did value good teachers – it was the teaching unions she blamed for protecting bad teachers while imposing a left-wing political orthodoxy of underachievement. But in 1970 the Secretary of State had very little power to affect either the quality or the content of education.

Ironically, it was her very success as a departmental minister, winning resources for policies she did not in her heart approve, which retrospectively poisoned her memory of the DES. From the perspective of the 1980s her record as a high-spending minister with the reputation of having 'gone native', who had tamely followed the departmental line and failed to halt the spread of comprehensivisation, was an embarrassment to her which never ceased to rankle. Stuart Sexton, a special adviser to successive Education Secretaries in the 1980s, felt that the Prime Minister 'hated the Department of Education, because I think she realised they had taken her for a ride'.[5] The fact is, however, that she did not hate them all at the time; nor did all of them hate her.

She certainly had her difficulties, beginning with the Permanent Secretary, Sir William Pile. Newly appointed in June 1970, Pile was an old DES hand who had spent most of his career in the Department, now coming back as its head after a spell in the Home Office as Director of Prisons. Described by the Whitehall historian Peter Hennessy as 'a genial, quiet, pipe-smoking official who . . . liked to look on the bright side',[6] he was at the same time 'a doughty defender' of the DES line who 'liked to stick to his guns'.[7] So did Mrs Thatcher. Generally, however, Mrs Thatcher and Pile got along. Other senior officials in the Department saw nothing wrong with their relationship, and feel that reports of their hostility were greatly overdone.

Mrs Thatcher arrived at the DES on Monday morning 22 June determined to show that she was the boss. She marched in, with no conversational preliminaries, and presented Pile with a list of points for immediate action written on a page torn out of an exercise book. Number one was the immediate withdrawal of Short's circular requiring local authorities to prepare schemes for comprehensivisation. But she had no positive agenda. She was committed by the Tory manifesto to a number of broad objectives all of which, apart from the slowing down of comprehensivisation and more Government support for direct grant schools, were uncontroversial, even consensual. Her main priority was switching more resources into primary education, with an ambitious new school building programme. 'This', she told the party conference revealingly in October, 'is the thing the Government controls.'[8] The Government was committed to raising the school-leaving age to sixteen – a long-planned change postponed by Labour in 1966 – and to continuing the expansion of higher education. The manifesto also promised an inquiry into teacher training. All this she carried out.

In practice – to her subsequent chagrin – comprehensivisation proceeded faster than ever during Mrs Thatcher's time at the DES. Under Section 13 of the 1944 Education Act final approval of every local scheme still lay with the Secretary of State; and Mrs Thatcher took this responsibility very seriously. She was meticulous in examining every scheme personally, burdening herself with a 'massive workload'[9] and giving rise to allegations of deliberate delay; in November 1971 she told the Commons that she currently had 350 schemes under consideration.[10] Where she could discover valid grounds for refusing approval she did so; but in practice she found few schemes that she could reasonably stop. In many cases schools had to merge, on purely practical grounds, to create Sixth Forms to cope with the raised school-leaving age. The result was that over the four years of Mrs Thatcher's tenure of the DES she rejected only 326 out of 3,612 schemes which were submitted to her; that is about 9 per cent. But it was this small minority which made the headlines. Wherever she withheld approval from a scheme she laid herself open to the charge that she was making nonsense of the Government's professed policy of leaving local decisions to local option.

Defending her budget

Her first serious challenge on coming into office in June 1970 was to defend the education budget. Just like her own Government nine years later, the Heath Government took office promising immediate economies in public spending to pay for tax cuts. Macleod's first act as Chancellor – virtually his only one before his sudden death – was to demand a series of savings from the departments. Having established in opposition that the Tories were committed to increasing education spending, Mrs Thatcher was in a better position than most of her colleagues to resist. Even so, she was required to find some short-term economies. She did so by raising the price of school meals and stopping the supply of free milk to children over the age of seven. These were from her point of view unimportant cuts, falling only on the welfare benefits which had got loaded on to education while protecting the essential business of education itself – in particular the expensive commitment to proceed with the raising of the school-leaving age, and her promise to improve the standard of primary school buildings. In 1971 she was able to announce 'a huge building drive' to replace old primary schools, spending £132 million over three years from the savings on school meals and milk.[11] She also reprieved the Open University, which Macleod had earmarked for the axe before it had enrolled its first students. 'With all our difficulties', she boasted, 'the cuts have not fallen on education.'[12]

When Tony Barber announced his package in October, she was generally thought to have done well: the row over school milk did not blow up until the following year. As Prime Minister a decade later she insisted that her ministers owed their first duty to the Government's collective strategy, not to their departments; but in 1970, like every other departmental minister, her priority was to fight her own corner. She made a point of telling journalists that she had taken on the Treasury and won.

Her most remarkable feat was saving the Open University. The Tories in opposition had sneered at the projected 'university of the air' as a typical Wilson gimmick. But Mrs Thatcher took a different view. She was persuaded that it was a worthwhile enterprise which would genuinely extend opportunity. It was also good value for money, an economical way to produce more graduates. So even though the Department itself was not strongly committed to it, she had already determined to defy the Treasury death sentence and allow it to go ahead. She indicated her intention at a press conference two days after taking office. Contrary to the impression he gives in his memoirs, Heath was furious at this exercise of 'instant government': she had unilaterally reversed the party's policy before he had even appointed the junior minister who would be responsible for the universities. Within days of appointing her he was already talking 'quite openly' of getting rid of his Education Secretary 'if he could'.[13] Thirty-nine years later, when the Open University is established as a great success, the credit for its conception is usually given to Harold Wilson and Jennie Lee; but Margaret Thatcher deserves equal credit for single-handedly allowing it to be born when her senior colleagues were intent on aborting it. It is one of her more surprising and unsung achievements.

'Milk snatcher'

She blamed her officials for failing to foresee the hornets' nest she would stir up by cutting free school milk. To the Department it seemed an obviously sensible and uncontentious economy. The Government was currently spending more on providing free milk than on books for schools; much of the milk was never drunk – partly because the crates of little bottles were not refrigerated, partly because children's taste had simply moved on since Attlee's day. Labour had already stopped the supply to secondary schools, with no public outcry and no ill effect on children. By ending the provision to children aged seven to eleven, Mrs Thatcher was merely continuing a process which Labour had begun: as she pointed out, milk would still be provided free to those children who were prescribed it on medical grounds, and schools could still sell milk.[14] Insofar as she was withdrawing a previously universal benefit in accordance with the Tory belief that those who could afford to pay should do so, it could be presented as an ideological measure; but in truth it was a minor administrative rationalisation, ending a wasteful anachronism.

She was unprepared for the furore it aroused. It was the personal nature of the attacks which shook her. The *Sun* asked 'Is Mrs Thatcher human?'[15] and dubbed her 'The Most Unpopular Woman in Britain'.[16] For the first time in her political career her sex was being used against her. The fact of a woman, a mother, taking milk from children was portrayed as far more shocking – unnatural even – than a man doing the same thing; and the cruel nickname 'Thatcher – Milk Snatcher' (coined by a speaker at the 1971 Labour Party Conference) struck a deep and lasting chord in the public mind. For better or worse it made her name: image recognition was never a problem for her again.

At the beginning of 1972 there was speculation that Heath might sack his Education Secretary. In fact, he stood by her in her darkest hour. At the end of the month he invited her, with Pile and other of her officials, to Chequers to discuss her future plans. This was a clear signal that she was not about to be removed. She 'emerged radiant', the *Daily Mail* reported. 'The comeback has begun.'[17]

From this low point her fortunes sharply improved: the second half of her time at the DES was, at least in terms of public perception, dramatically more successful than the first. This was partly due to the fact that from late 1971 she had a new press officer with whom she got on exceptionally well. Terry Perks had a lot to do with Mrs Thatcher's more professional presentation of herself from 1972 onwards. The first sign that she had turned the corner actually came before the end of January when she won an unexpectedly good reception from an NUT dinner. She was able to reap the credit for having finally given the go-ahead to raising the school-leaving age. She made 'a splendid speech', *The Times* reported, 'full of warmth, wit and friendly reproach to her critics. Seasoned Thatcher-watchers reckoned it her best public appearance yet.'[18]

Mrs Thatcher sealed her rehabilitation in the eyes of the educational establishment with the publication, towards the end of 1972, of her White Paper, *A Framework for Expansion*. This represented the culmination of a whole raft of policies the DES had been working on for twenty years. In truth she had remarkably little to do with its conception: she was merely the midwife. It projected a 50 per cent rise in education spending (in real terms) over the next ten years, pushing education's share from 13 to 14 per cent of total government expenditure (overtaking defence for the first time). Within this overall growth there was to be a vast expansion of nursery education, designed to provide free part-time nursery places for 50 per cent of three-year-olds and 90 per cent of four-year-olds by 1981 (concentrated at first in areas of greatest need); a 40 per cent increase in the number of teachers – from 360,000 in 1971 to a projected 510,000 in 1981, which would cut the average teacher–pupil ratio from one to 22.6 to one to 18.5; and the continued expansion of higher education, evenly divided between the universities and polytechnics, to a target of 750,000 students by 1981 (an increase from 15 to 22 per cent of eighteen-year-olds).[19]

This was a hugely ambitious plan, and a triumph for the DES. Pile was afraid that Mrs Thatcher would not swallow it: in fact she took it all on board without demur. At a time when Government spending was expanding on all fronts she was determined to get her share of it. Having had to fight the Treasury hard over her first two years to get the money she wanted for school building and improving teachers' pay, she was taken aback by the ease with which the Cabinet accepted her proposed White Paper. She had expected another battle. Very soon she came to repudiate her own enthusiasm for it. Looking back, she wrote in her memoirs, it was 'all too typical of those over-ambitious, high-spending years . . . In retrospect the White Paper marks the high point of the attempts by Government to overcome the problems inherent in Britain's education system by throwing money at them.'[20] At the time, however, she basked in the almost universal praise her plans attracted. Every minister likes to put his or her name to something big; and she was happy to be seen as less of a reactionary than had been thought.

Alas, her optimism was blown away within a year by the quadrupling of oil prices following the Yom Kippur war and the consequent recession which forced cutbacks in Government spending for the next decade. Mrs Thatcher's bold plans were under threat before she had even left office. They were not pursued by her Labour successors after February 1974; and by the time she returned to Downing Street as Prime Minister in 1979 her interest in using the state to extend educational opportunity had passed. Not until 1995 did the aspiration to offer nursery places to all pre-school children creep back on to the political agenda. A generous vision which might have been the most far-reaching legacy from Mrs Thatcher's time as Education Secretary was sadly destined to go down as one of the great might-have-beens of recent history.

In the end, however, even she could not protect her department from the heavy cuts Barber was forced to impose at the end of 1973. Excluding Scotland, science and the arts, the DES share of the cuts amounted to £157 million out of a total departmental budget of £3.5 billion. This she described as 'serious but not disastrous': she gave the impression that the cuts would only slow the projected building programme and procurement by LEAs, insisting that the department's priorities – including the nursery programme – had been substantially preserved.[21] But this was her last speech as Education Secretary. Just over a week later the miners – whose overtime ban had already reduced the country to a three-day week – voted for a full-scale strike. Confronted with this challenge, Heath finally gave in to the hawks in his Cabinet and called the General Election which removed him from office.

U-turns

Mrs Thatcher's wider role as a member of the Heath Government subsequently came to embarrass her. Not only did she pursue policies in her own department which she later repudiated, and fail to promote others which in retrospect she wished she had embraced more vigorously; she also conspicuously failed to dissent from economic policies which she soon came to regard as disastrously flawed and which, she now implied, she had instinctively known to be wrong all along. For someone who would later make so much of being a 'conviction politician' this was a singularly unheroic performance, which she and her biographers had to expend much effort trying to explain or deny.

The Government notoriously made two major U-turns in economic policy, both in 1972. First, in response to rising unemployment – which in January 1972 passed the symbolic and at that time politically intolerable figure of one million – Heath reversed the policy of not bailing out 'lame ducks' on which he had fought the 1970 election and started to throw money indiscriminately at industry in a successful (but inflationary) effort to stimulate the economy into rapid growth. Second, when inflation rocketed – as a result partly of sharp increases in the price of imported commodities (copper, rubber, zinc and other raw materials) even before the 1973 oil price shock, but also, it was almost universally believed, of excessive domestic wage increases – the Government abandoned its apparently principled rejection of incomes policy and introduced, from November 1972, an increasingly complex system of statutory wage and price control. Both policies commanded wide support on the Conservative benches and in the press. A handful of eccentric monetarists warned that the Government was itself fuelling the very inflation it was attempting to cure; while a rather larger number of more traditional right-wingers were disturbed by the socialistic overtones of the Government's increasing interference in the economy. But in the short term both policies appeared to be working: the economy boomed, unemployment fell and inflation was contained. Until the double blow of the oil crisis and the miners' strike at the end of 1973 the Government seemed to be surmounting its problems with a good chance of re-election in the autumn of 1974 or spring of 1975.

There is little evidence that Mrs Thatcher offered any serious objection to either U-turn. Indeed, she positively supported what many regarded as the forerunner of the later reversals, the nationalisation of the aircraft division of Rolls-Royce in 1971. It is true that a report in *The Times* in 1972 named her as one of a number of Cabinet Ministers who 'frankly confess their uneasiness about the socialist implications' of the Government's new industrial strategy; but that was all.[22] She stoutly defended prices and income control as 'absolutely necessary'.[23] Cabinets did not leak so freely in those days, nor did ministers brief the press with their private views. Mrs Thatcher uttered no public indication of dissent, unless there was a coded message in her speech to the party conference in October, when she declared pointedly that 'I believe it is right for any Government to honour the terms of its manifesto. That is precisely what we are doing in education.'[24]

The third major issue of the Heath Government on which Mrs Thatcher expressed no contrary view at the time was Britain's entry into the European Community. Heath's achievement in persuading President Pompidou to lift de Gaulle's veto, negotiating acceptable terms, winning a substantial bipartisan majority in the House of Commons and forcing the enabling legislation through against the determined opposition of a section of his own party, finally joining the Community on 1 January 1973, was the one unquestioned success of his ill-fated Government. Despite her later change of heart, Mrs Thatcher was firmly and conventionally supportive of the European project throughout, as she had been since Macmillan first launched it in 1961.

She had no reservations, either, about supporting the Government in its stand against the miners. While she condemned the miners' leaders and attacked Communist influence in the NUM, she insisted that the Government's offer to the miners – in the range of 13–16 per cent – was 'generous' and argued that the Government had 'kept faith with the miners' when it could have switched to other energy sources. She appealed to the miners in turn to vote against a strike. At the same time she pointed out that North Sea gas and oil would soon give the Government alternatives to both coal and imported oil. 'The prospects are enormous.'[25] In the prevailing mood of almost apocalyptic gloom, this was an unusually optimistic message.

On 4 February 1974, however, the miners voted overwhelmingly to step up their action, and Heath finally bowed to the clamour for an election, though still seeking a settlement of the dispute by referring the miners' claim to the Pay Board while the election was in progress. He was honourably determined not to fight a confrontational campaign against the miners, even though that would almost certainly have given him his best chance of winning. Mrs Thatcher in all her published and reported statements loyally followed her leader's line.

Boundary changes meant that she could no longer take her seat for granted. Moreover, she had a potential problem with the Jewish vote as a result of Heath's even-handed policy of refusing to supply Israel with military parts, or even allow American planes to supply Israel from British airfields, during the Yom Kippur war. This issue allied Mrs Thatcher with Keith Joseph, the only Jewish member of the Cabinet. Together they protested, but Heath and Alec Douglas-Home were determined to avert an Arab oil embargo by maintaining strict neutrality. She met the Finchley branch of the Anglo-Israel Friendship League to assure them that she opposed the Government's policy.[26] This was the most difficult period in her long and close relationship with her Jewish constituents; but her position was not seriously threatened.

This was an election the Tories confidently expected to win. Indeed, one reason Heath fought such a poor campaign was that he was afraid of winning too heavily. In the event he failed to polarise the country sufficiently. By referring the miners' dispute to the Pay Board the Government seemed to call into question the point of having an election at all. Labour was still in disarray over Europe and beginning to be torn apart by the new hard left: Wilson did not expect to win any more than Heath expected to lose. In these circumstances the electorate called a plague on both their houses and turned in unprecedented numbers to the Liberals.

Out of office

Mrs Thatcher was still perfectly safe in Finchley. As usual the Liberal hype could achieve only so much. On a reduced poll (and revised boundaries) her vote was 7,000 down, the Liberals nearly 4,000 votes up, but Labour still held on to second place. Her majority was nearly halved but the two opposition parties cancelled each other out.

Margaret Thatcher (Conservative)	18,180
Martin O'Connor (Labour)	12,202
Laurence Brass (Liberal)	11,221
Conservative majority	5,978

Nationally it was a different story. The Liberals won an unprecedented six million votes, nearly 20 per cent of the poll. They were rewarded with just fourteen seats, but their advance fatally damaged the Tories, helping Labour to scrape a narrow majority – 301 seats to 297 – despite winning a slightly lower share of the poll – 37.1 per cent against 37.9 per cent. Heath held a last Cabinet before being driven to the Palace to resign. It was by all accounts a bleak occasion: he was determined that it was not the end of his Government, merely a temporary interruption, so there were no thanks, tributes or recriminations. Only one minister felt she could not let the moment pass without a word of valediction. It was Margaret Thatcher who insisted on speaking 'in emotional terms of the wonderful experience of team loyalty that she felt she had shared since 1970'.[27]

From her time at the DES, however, she had learned a number of lessons which she would carry back with her into government in 1979. First, as she reflected on her experience, she became convinced of the malign power of officials to block, frustrate and manipulate all but the most determined ministers. Secondly, she learned from the failure of the Government as a whole to maintain its sense of direction and purpose in the face of mounting political pressure. At its simplest this expressed itself as a determination not to duplicate Heath's notorious U-turns. But this was not so much an ideological point as a political one.

Heath lost the ability to control events, paradoxically, because he tried to control too much: all the complex machinery of prices and incomes control – the Pay Board, the Price Commission and the rest – left the Government still helpless in the face of soaring imported food and commodity prices on the one hand, and the industrial muscle of the miners on the other. The lesson Mrs Thatcher took from the Heath Government was not so much monetarism, which she grasped later as a useful technical explanation, but rather a compelling affirmation of an old Tory article of faith – the self-defeating folly of overambitious government. Government – she instinctively believed – must be strong, clear, decisive; but the experience of the Heath Government taught that it could only appear strong by holding itself above the economic fray, not taking responsibility upon itself for every rise in unemployment or inflation. It was that lesson, more than any other, which enabled her Government to rise above the economic devastation of the early 1980s.

6

The Peasants' Revolt

The roulette wheel

LESS than a year after losing office in March 1974 Margaret Thatcher was elected leader of the Conservative party. This was a stunning transformation which no one would have predicted twelve months earlier: one of those totally unexpected events – which in retrospect appear predestined – that constitute the fascination of politics. One of the most extraordinary things about Mrs Thatcher's seizure of the Tory leadership is that scarcely anyone – colleague or commentator – saw her coming. Even after the event her victory was widely disparaged as a freak of fortune of which she was merely the lucky beneficiary. As Enoch Powell put it, with a mixture of envy and grudging admiration: 'She didn't rise to power. She was opposite the spot on the roulette wheel at the right time, and she didn't funk it.'[1]

But the fact that she did not funk it was crucial, and not at all an accident. It should have been foreseen by anyone who had worked closely with her over the previous twenty-five years, for she had been quietly preparing for the opportunity all her life. When it came she was ready. It takes extraordinary single-mindedness and stamina to reach the topmost rung of British politics, an obsessive dedication to the job to the exclusion of other concerns like money, family, friendship and the pursuit of leisure. Like Harold Wilson, like Ted Heath, but more than any of her Conservative contemporaries, Margaret Thatcher possessed that quality of single-minded dedication to her career. She never made any secret of her ambition: it was only because she was a woman that the possibility that she might go right to the top was not taken seriously. No one who had known her at Oxford, at Colchester or

Dartford should have been surprised that when the chance offered she left her male rivals at the post.

Yet it was still an unpredictable combination of other factors which created her opportunity. First, she benefited from an intellectual revolution – or counter-revolution – in Tory thinking which had been building over the previous ten years but which was suddenly brought to a head by the shock of electoral defeat, creating the opening for a radical change of direction. This was a development in which she played very little part, yet one which reflected her most deeply held convictions, so that she had no difficulty taking advantage of it. At the same time a fortuitous pattern of personal circumstances ruled out of contention virtually all the other candidates who might, a year earlier, have hoped to harness this opportunity to their own careers.

The revolution in Tory thinking had two strands – economic and political. On the one hand there was a sudden revival of interest in the free-market economic ideas quietly propagated for years on the margins of serious politics by the Institute of Economic Affairs but largely derided by the conventional wisdom in both Whitehall and the universities. Throughout the 1960s the fact that the only prominent politician to preach the beauty of the unfettered market was Enoch Powell was enough to tar the message with the taint of crazed fanaticism.

From the middle of 1972 onwards, however, the Government's U-turns in economic policy had begun to make converts for the Powellite critique. Treasury mandarins attached little importance to the money supply. But in Fleet Street an influential group of economic journalists led by Samuel Brittan on the *Financial Times* and Peter Jay and William Rees-Mogg on *The Times* took up the cause and began to expound it in their columns. When the Heath Government fell, therefore, there was quite suddenly a fully-fledged monetarist explanation of its failure available for disillusioned Tories – including ex-ministers – to draw upon.

At the same time there was among ordinary Tories in the country a more generalised mood of mounting frustration at the failure of successive Conservative Governments to halt or reverse what seemed a relentless one-way slide to socialism. Not only in the management of the economy but in almost every sphere of domestic and foreign policy – immigration, comprehensive schools, trade unions, Northern Ireland, Rhodesia – Heath had appeared almost deliberately to affront the party's traditional supporters while appeasing their tribal enemies. Strikes, crime, revolting students, pornography, terrorism, inflation eating away at their savings – all stoked a rising anger that the country was going to the dogs while the Tory Government was not resisting but rather speeding the process. By the time Heath lost the February 1974 election an ugly mood had built up in the Tory party which lacked only heavyweight leadership to weld together the two elements – the political backlash and the economic analysis – to form a potent combination which ultimately became known as Thatcherism.

The unlikely catalyst was Keith Joseph – hitherto no one's idea of a rebel or a populist, but a former Cabinet Minister of long experience and unimpeachable integrity who was almost uniquely qualified to lend intellectual rigour to political revolt. He subsequently described how he had thought he had been a Conservative for the past thirty years, but now realised that he had been a 'statist' all along, bewitched by the delusive power of government.[2] Having seen the light, he set out with a religious fervour rare in high-level politics to atone for his past sins by bringing the Tory party – and ultimately the country – to a realisation of the true faith.

Mrs Thatcher by contrast never pretended to be a thinker. She was a politician, and – unlike Joseph – an intensely practical and ambitious one. It is not the job of politicians to have original ideas, or even necessarily to understand them. Professional economists like Peter Jay used to sneer that Mrs Thatcher never really understood monetarism. But she did not need to. It was enough that she saw its importance; she possessed – as Joseph did not – the much more important and rare ability to simplify complex ideas and mobilise support for them. No intellectual herself, she was nevertheless unusual among politicians in acknowledging the importance of ideas. She had always believed that politics should be a battle between fundamentally opposed philosophies; it was a characteristic of her leadership that she systematically used intellectuals and academics – those whom she thought were on her side – to underpin her policies and furnish her with arguments and intellectual ammunition. As Prime Minister she developed an informal think-tank of her favourite academics to advise her.

The result of the February election had left the Tory party in a sort of limbo. With another election certain within a few months – as soon as Wilson saw an opportunity to increase his precarious majority – there was no early possibility of challenging Heath's leadership, even if there had been an obvious challenger in waiting. The lesson he drew from the debacle of confrontation with the miners was that the Conservatives must try harder than ever to show themselves moderate and consensual in order to unite the country and win back the votes lost to the Liberals. This was the opposite of what his party critics wanted.

The one area in which Heath saw a need for new policies was housing. He told the Shadow Cabinet that the voters he met wanted 'some radical and drastic changes in policy aimed particularly at the problems of ordinary people' – specifically the cost of mortgages and the burden of the rates – 'which should take priority over rather more abstract principles'.[3] The key job of developing and selling these shiny new policies which would form the centrepiece of the party's appeal at the next election he entrusted to Margaret Thatcher: an indication that he still saw her as an efficient and amenable agent of his will, not as a potential troublemaker.

Shadow Environment Secretary

In fact, up to October 1974 he was not wrong. The job of shadow Environment Secretary was a high-profile opportunity in an area of policy she had always been interested in but had not previously covered. It took her all her time to get on top of it. An Oxford contemporary who had known her in the Department of Education ran into her soon after she had taken it over and found her uncharacteristically harassed, complaining that the wide-ranging DoE empire – taking in transport as well as housing and local government – was too big to master in her usual detail.[4] Parliamentary opposition, however, was just a matter of going through the motions – more than ever this summer when the Conservatives had to hold back for fear of precipitating another election before they were ready for it. Mrs Thatcher's real brief was to come up with the bright new housing policies which Heath wanted to put in the forefront of the party's next manifesto to win back the middle-class voters who had cost the Tories the February election by defecting to the Liberals. Frankly, what he was seeking was a short-term electoral bribe, but one which could be presented as consistent with the long-standing Conservative philosophy of encouraging home-ownership.

Suppressing her doubts, Mrs Thatcher loyally complied. The package she eventually announced at the end of August comprised three different forms of housing subsidy. First she promised to hold mortgages to a maximum interest rate of 9.5 per cent, to be achieved by varying the tax rate on building societies. Second, council tenants were to be helped to buy their houses at a 33 per cent discount. Third, first-time buyers would be encouraged to save by a direct

Government bribe of £1 for every £2 saved. Most significant for the long term, however, was her fourth commitment: a promise to abolish domestic rates.

Here too she was pressured to go further than she wanted. A meeting of party heavyweights – Heath flanked by most of his senior colleagues – 'bludgeoned' her into promising abolition of the rates before they had decided what to put in their place. Her August package eventually spoke of replacing the rates with 'taxes more broadly-based and related to people's ability to pay', meanwhile transferring to the Treasury the cost not only of teachers' pay but of parts of the police and fire services. 'I felt bruised and resentful', she wrote in her memoirs, 'to be bounced again into policies which had not been properly thought out.' Yet she was still too loyal, or too junior, to refuse. Heath was still the leader, backed by almost the whole of his former Cabinet. In the last resort she was still willing to conform to protect her career. 'I thought that if I combined caution on the details with as much presentational bravura as I could muster I could make our rates and housing policies into vote-winners for the Party.'[5]

Mrs Thatcher's performance over the summer and autumn of 1974 – arguing in private against policies which she would then defend equally passionately in public – demonstrated the maturing of a formidable political skill. By her championing of subsidised mortgages she showed that she possessed not only the good lawyer's ability to argue a weak case; any self-respecting politician can do that. She also had a preacher's ability to invest even a poor case with moralistic force: this more than anything else was the secret of her success over the next fifteen years. In the years of her success she boasted of being a 'conviction politician', but it should not be forgotten that both words carried equal weight. She had powerful convictions, certainly; but she could be brilliantly insincere too, when the situation required it, and such was her reputation for burning integrity that few could spot the difference. At a number of critical points in her later career it was only this which enabled her to skate on some very thin ice and get away with it.

She was the Tories' star performer in the October 1974 campaign. She still made only two trips out of London; but largely because her policies were their only new ones, she appeared more than ever before on television and radio, featuring in three of the party's election broadcasts and three of the morning press conferences, including the final one with Heath. She was coached for her television appearances by Gordon Reece, who began for the first time to get her to relax in front of the camera. With Reece's help she was judged to have done so well in the Tories' first broadcast that she was promoted to introduce the second.

Labour was seriously alarmed, but could not make up its mind how to respond. In the event polls soon showed that the public did not believe the Tories' promises.[6] Despite this, however, the high-profile exposure did Mrs Thatcher much more good than harm. It temporarily damaged her credentials with the right, who were dismayed to see her once again betraying her professed beliefs, using public money to distort the market in pursuit of votes. But the sheer feistiness of her performance, and indeed her pragmatism, stood her in good stead when she came to appeal to the whole body of middle-of-the-road MPs just three months later. She had valuably shown herself not as a naive right-winger but as a vigorous vote-getter and a seasoned pro.

In the event, with just 39.2 per cent of the vote (against 35.8 per cent), Labour gained only eighteen seats for an overall majority of four. Mrs Thatcher's personal majority was cut by another 2,000 (on a lower turnout), but it was still sufficient:

Margaret Thatcher (Conservative)	15,498
Martin O'Connor (Labour)	12,587
Laurence Brass (Liberal)	7,384
Janet Godfrey (National Front)	993
Conservative majority	2,911

In fact, as events turned out, the national result was probably the best possible for her. An unexpectedly successful rearguard action was creditable enough to enable Heath to dismiss calls that it was time for him to stand down; yet at the same time it was still a defeat, the party's third in four elections under his leadership, so it only fuelled the gathering consensus that he could not survive much longer. Meanwhile, such a tiny majority was unlikely to sustain Labour in office for a full term – thus offering an unusually fruitful prospect of opposition for whoever succeeded in replacing him.

'Someone had to stand'

As soon as the October election was out of the way, the struggle for the Tory leadership was unofficially on. Quite apart from the simmering revolt on the right, too many Tory MPs with no quarrel with Heath's policies came back to Westminster convinced that the party could never win under his leadership. Several of his friends urged him to step down immediately, or at least submit himself for re-election. By refusing, however, he not only threw away his own best chance of survival, but he also made it practically impossible for Willie Whitelaw or any other candidate from the left of the Tory party to succeed him. By clinging on, he allowed time for a dark horse to emerge who would eventually consolidate all the various strands of party discontent against him.

Joseph was the obvious standard-bearer of the right – not because he possessed any of the qualities of political leadership but because by his speeches over the summer he alone had staked out a clear alternative to Heath's discredited centrism. Mrs Thatcher quickly cast herself as his loyal supporter, explicitly discouraging speculation about her own chances. 'You can cross my name off the list,' she told the London *Evening News* the day after the General Election. 'I just don't think I am right for it.'[7] But then, just two weeks after the election, Joseph made a speech in Birmingham which spectacularly confirmed the doubts of those who thought he lacked the judgement or the nerve for leadership. Exactly four weeks after this speech, he concluded that he was not the stuff of which leaders are made and decided that he would not be a candidate.

The first person he told – on 21 November – was Mrs Thatcher. We have only her account of the conversation, but if that can be believed she did not hesitate. 'I heard myself saying: "Look, Keith, if you're not going to stand, I will, because someone who represents our viewpoint *has* to stand."'[8] The telling is disingenuous: in practice she was a good deal more cautious than this suggests. Yet there is no reason to doubt that it accurately represents her instinctive reaction. In all her carefully phrased denials of the idea that she could ever aspire to the highest offices, there was always a qualification which suggests that she did not, in her heart, quite rule them out.

On 25 November Mrs Thatcher thought it right to tell Heath of her purpose in person, though it had already been heavily trailed in the weekend papers. She saw him in the Leader's room at the House of Commons. It was reported at the time – and the story can only have come from her – that he neither stood up nor invited her to sit down, but merely grunted, 'You'll lose.'[9] Lady Thatcher's published version is that 'He looked at me coldly, turned his back, shrugged his shoulders and said, "If you must."'[10] Either way the interview was evidently brief and chilly. But there is no suggestion that Heath was greatly worried by her candidature or thought it uniquely treacherous of her to stand. Having reluctantly agreed that new rules should be drawn up to allow a challenge to a sitting leader, he probably imagined that she would be the first of several hopefuls who might now throw their hats into the ring. This, she wrote in her memoirs, was her expectation, too. She thought it 'most unlikely' that she would win.[11]

Heath had inadvertently given his challenger another opportunity which she grasped with both hands. In reshuffling his front bench team at the beginning of November he moved Mrs Thatcher from Environment – which she had only shadowed for nine months – to become deputy Treasury spokesman under Robert Carr. It is not clear whether Heath intended this as a promotion or a snub. 'There is an awful tendency in Britain', she had once complained, 'to think of women as making excellent Number Twos, but not to give them the top job.'[12]

Nevertheless, making her deputy to so bland a performer as Carr simply invited her to outshine her nominal superior. Unwittingly, Heath had given her the perfect opportunity to show her paces by taking on Labour's powerful Treasury team, giving demoralised Tory MPs something to cheer for the first time in months. By her usual combination of hard work and calculated aggression Mrs Thatcher quickly assumed the leadership of the Tories' opposition to Labour's Finance Bill, leading a team of junior spokesmen almost all of whom became members of her own Cabinet a decade later.

It is often said that Tory MPs did not know what they were doing when they elected Mrs Thatcher leader. This is true only in that she did not set out a detailed agenda of specific policies – monetarism, tax cuts or privatisation. But it cannot be said that she disguised her beliefs to win the leadership. On the contrary, she declared her philosophy very clearly: if some who voted for her did so without fully realising where her ideas would lead, the fault was theirs for failing to believe that she meant what she said. In fact what the party responded to was not so much her beliefs themselves as the burning self-belief with which she expounded them: it was not her convictions that they voted for, but her conviction.

As important as her message, however, was the need to humanise her image, neutralise the gender question and persuade both the public and Tory MPs that she was a credible leader. Paradoxically she no longer needed to prove that she was tough enough for the job: it was becoming a cliché, as David Wood noted in *The Times*, to say that she was 'the best man among them'.[13] But that raised the alarming spectre of a feminist harridan – the worst sort of woman. What she now had to do was to make a virtue of her femininity. With Gordon Reece's help, therefore, she presented herself to the press and television as an ordinary housewife, old-fashioned, home-loving and non-feminist, thus allaying both male fears and female disapproval. 'What people don't realise about me', she told the *Daily Mirror*, 'is that I am a very ordinary person who leads a very normal life. I enjoy it – seeing that the family have a good breakfast. And shopping keeps me in touch.'[14] She played along with the pretence that she was 'just' a housewife and milked it for all it was worth. For the benefit of the *Daily Mail* she went shopping with her sister. On the morning of the ballot she was filmed cooking Denis's breakfast and photographed putting out the milk bottles.

Heath's supporters never really believed it possible for the former Prime Minister to be beaten by an inexperienced woman. He had the support of the whole Shadow Cabinet, except Keith Joseph. Elder statesmen like Alec Douglas-Home and Reggie Maudling were wheeled out to consolidate support for the status quo. The constituency chairmen came out overwhelmingly for Heath: a poll in the *Daily Express* found that 70 per cent of Tory voters still thought him the best leader.[15] As a result, while Mrs Thatcher's team were assiduously combing the lists of Tory MPs – as systematically and professionally as Peter Walker had done for Heath in 1965, finding the right colleague to influence each individual – Heath this time had no proper campaign at all. The Heath camp simply believed what they read in the newspapers and repeated to one another, that all sensible people were still for Ted and only a small fringe of right-wingers and diehard anti-Marketeers would vote for 'that dreadful woman'.

They underestimated the extent of disillusion with Heath among a significant body of MPs who were neither particularly on the right nor anti-Europe. By his remoteness, insensitivity and sheer bad manners, Heath had exhausted the loyalty of a large number of backbenchers who had no reason to be grateful to him: this group simply wanted a change of leader. Most of them did not want Mrs Thatcher to become leader; they certainly did not want a lurch to right-wing policies; but they were persuaded to vote for Mrs Thatcher on the first ballot in the hope that they would then be able to vote for Whitelaw or some other more experienced candidate in the second round.

The result of all this second-guessing was that the unfancied filly not only gained enough votes to open up a second ballot, but actually topped the poll. Heath mustered only 119 supporters: Mrs Thatcher – for whatever mixture of motives – attracted 130, while sixteen voted for Hugh Fraser and another eleven abstained. 'The word sensational', the *Daily Mail* reported, 'was barely adequate to describe the shock wave that hit Westminster' when the figures were declared.[16] From the Establishment's point of view the figures were not only bad enough to oblige Heath to step down immediately. ('We got it all wrong,' he told his stunned team.)[17] They also made it very difficult for anyone to pick up his banner with any prospect of success.

By the normal British understanding of elections, Mrs Thatcher had won already. She had defeated the incumbent and therefore asserted an unanswerable moral claim on the prize. Willie Whitelaw was bound to announce that he would now come forward as the unity candidate who could bind the party's wounds; but it was too late – Mrs Thatcher's stature was hugely increased by her unexpected victory. The fact that three more contenders threw their hats into the ring as well merely underlined that none of them had any chance of catching her. They were simply putting down markers: had they been serious about trying to stop her they should all have backed Whitelaw. Saluting her achievement, the *Daily Telegraph* suggested that it was almost bad form to force a second ballot at all after she had done the dirty work of getting rid of Heath.[18]

In the week between the two ballots the novelty and kudos of being the first major political party in the Western world to elect a woman leader overcame the previous doubts of many who had intended to switch their votes, and of a good many more who had voted for Heath. 'Electing Margaret Thatcher would be the most imaginative thing the party has done for years', one supporter told the *Daily Mail*; 'The time has come for a change', said another, 'and it would be absolutely right for the Tories to come up with a woman leader, who may even be a woman Prime Minister.'[19]

Though she gained only another sixteen votes overall – just seven more than the simple majority required to win on the second ballot – Whitelaw's poor showing and the fragmentation of the vote among the rest made her margin of victory look more decisive than it really was. The figures were:

Margaret Thatcher	146
William Whitelaw	79
Geoffrey Howe	19
James Prior	19
John Peyton	11
Abstentions	2
Majority	276

The new leader's first engagement on receiving the result was a press conference in the Grand Committee Room, off Westminster Hall. She began by being suitably gushing and humble, carefully paying tribute to all her predecessors:

To me it is like a dream that the next name in the lists after Harold Macmillan, Sir Alec Douglas-Home, Edward Heath is Margaret Thatcher. Each has brought his own style of leadership and stamp of greatness to the task. I shall take on the work with humility and dedication.

The only surprise was that she did not go back as far as Churchill – the Tory leader she was really proud to be succeeding – but she made good the omission with a tearful tribute to 'the great Winston' on television that evening.[20] Having got the pieties out of the way, she 'took complete charge' of the press conference in a manner that would become very familiar.

The new Tory leader stunned her audience into silence with her rapid, almost brusque replies to questions. She kept calling 'Next question, next question', as she outpaced the flustered press gang. At one time she called out confidently: 'You chaps don't like short, direct answers. Men like long, rambling, waffling answers.'

Asked if she had won because she was a woman, she replied crisply: 'I like to think I won on merit.' She even had the confidence to risk a joke. Asked about foreign affairs, she replied: 'I am all for them.' She then acknowledged, with 'disarming feminine charm', 'I am the first to understand that I am not expert in every subject.'[21] Swivelling this way and that to give all the photographers a good picture, she announced pointedly, 'I am now going to take a turn to the right, which is very appropriate.'[22] It was an astonishing performance: already she had the press eating out of her hand.

7

Leader of the Opposition

On trial

MARGARET Thatcher said that it was 'like a dream' to follow in the footsteps of Macmillan, Home and Heath. But none of these predecessors had faced such a daunting prospect on becoming leader. She was the first Conservative leader since 1921 to lack the prestige of having already been Prime Minister. She had seized the leadership as a result of a backbench revolt against the party establishment, opposed by practically the whole of her predecessor's Shadow Cabinet. Even those who had campaigned for her were not sure what they had persuaded the party to elect, and the party in the country did not know her at all. For all these reasons, in addition to the startlingly novel factor of her femininity, she was even more on trial than most new leaders, facing a mixture of scepticism, curiosity and snobbish condescension, shading into latent or outright hostility.

Nevertheless, not everything was against her. First, she was protected by the Tory party's traditional instinct to rally round a new leader – reinforced in her case by an old-fashioned sense of chivalry. Second, party elders such as Alec Home, Quintin Hailsham and Peter Carrington – all loyal friends of Heath who could easily have made her life impossible had they so wished – determined that the new leader must be supported and set a strong example to that effect. Above all Willie Whitelaw, the principal rival whom she had defeated in the leadership contest, determined to be both a good loser and a loyal deputy. This was by no means easy for him, since he and Mrs Thatcher had little in common, either personally or politically. Though she immediately named him deputy leader and consulted him about other appointments, Mrs Thatcher was not at first quite sure that she could trust him. Having stood against her and lost, however, Whitelaw felt an almost military sense of duty to subordinate his views to hers. With his deep knowledge of the party he would sometimes warn her what the backbenchers or the constituencies would not wear; but he would not oppose her. In opposition and later in government, Whitelaw steadfastly refused to lend himself to any appearance of factionalism. His un-wavering support over the next thirteen years was indispensable to her survival and her success.

Yet her position remained insecure for the whole period 1975–9. Though Whitelaw and Carrington made sure there was no overt move against her, a powerful section of the party, including most of Heath's senior colleagues whom she was obliged to retain in the Shadow Cabinet, remained conspicuously uncommitted to her. They were not greatly worried by her tendency to embrace simplistic panaceas like monetarism since they took it for granted, as experienced politicians, that no one could take such nonsense seriously for long. If she did become Prime Minister, the combination of Civil Service advice and the realities of office would quickly educate her. All parties, they assured themselves, tend to play to their extremes in opposition, but they return to the centre ground when back in government.

Mrs Thatcher was formally elected Leader of the Conservative party at a meeting of MPs, candidates, peers and party officials on 20 February, her nomination proposed by Lord Carrington and seconded by Lord Hailsham. Before that she had already been raptur-ously acclaimed by the 1922 Committee and presided rather awkwardly over a meeting of the existing Shadow Cabinet, minus only Heath himself. Owing to the circumstances of her election, however, her room for reshuffling the personnel she had inherited from Heath was very limited; just because they had almost all voted against her, paradoxically she was bound to keep most of his colleagues in post.

It was the backbenchers, not her front bench colleagues, who had made Mrs Thatcher leader; and for the first ten years of her leadership at least she never forgot it. She was determined not to repeat Heath's mistake. Ironically in view of her ultimate fate, she welcomed the new rules requiring the leader to be re-elected every year, believing that the regular renewal of her mandate made her position stronger.[2] Her official channel for communicating with her backbenchers was the 1922 Committee, via its chairman Edward du Cann who had guaranteed access to her. In these early years du Cann found her very approachable and anxious to listen.

Awkward baptism

Moving out from Westminster to the country at large, Mrs Thatcher had next to sell herself to the party in the constituencies. She began well, with a tumultuous visit to Scotland ten days after her election. She was mobbed by a crowd of 3,000 in a shopping centre in Edinburgh and had to abandon a planned walkabout on police advice. That evening she spoke at a packed rally in Glasgow with overflow meetings in two additional halls near by. Yet somehow she never created the same excitement again. A similar walkabout in Cardiff drew only minimal crowds. John Moore, who accompanied her on a number of constituency visits, remembers the first two years as 'an uphill struggle', with a lot of 'ghastly trips' north of Watford, where the party was still demoralised and doubtful; there was no supportive network, poor response to her efforts to arouse enthusiasm, and little belief that she would be leader very long. In the first few weeks and months she addressed every sort of sectional and regional conference within the Tory party: Scottish Conservatives, Welsh Conservatives, Conservative women, Conservative trade unionists, the Federation of Conservative Students and the Conservative Central Council. She gave them all ringing patriotic statements of her determination to halt Britain's decline by reawakening the virtues of freedom, enterprise, individual opportunity and self-reliance. For all her rousing rhetoric, however, she was careful to present her policies as simple common sense: moderation contrasted with Labour's extremism. Wealth must be created before it could be distributed; the country could not consume more than it produced; taxes should be cut to increase incentives. These were the familiar axioms of Tory leaders, not the blueprint for a counter-revolution. As a result she was politely rather than rapturously received.

Mrs Thatcher faced a peculiarly awkward baptism just weeks after her election in the form of the imminent referendum on Britain's continued membership of the Common Market. Suspected of being a good deal less keen on Europe than her predecessor, she nevertheless had no choice but to campaign for a vote to confirm the one unquestioned achievement of Heath's Government – even though a 'yes' vote would also help to get Wilson off the hook on which the Labour party had been impaled for the past four years. It was a no-win situation for a new leader anxious to set her own agenda. Her difficulty was somewhat relieved by Heath declining her invitation to lead the Conservative campaign, preferring to conduct his own under the umbrella of the all-party organisation,

Britain in Europe, chaired by Roy Jenkins. Then Wilson elected to take a back seat, placing the Government's authority officially behind the 'Yes' campaign while playing little active part himself, which lent a sort of symmetry to Mrs Thatcher doing the same. Nevertheless, her low profile drew a good deal of criticism.

In her memoirs Lady Thatcher blamed herself for going along too tamely with the Establishment consensus in favour of continued membership, ducking the hard questions about Britain's constitutional integrity and national identity which would come back to haunt her a decade and a half later.[3] At the time, however, she was under pressure to dispel the persistent impression that she was privately cool about Europe. She did so emphatically on 8 April in the Commons debate approving the referendum with a characteristically practical but wholly positive case for staying in the Community. 'Mrs Thatcher stills anti-Europe clamour', *The Times* reported.[4] She based her case on four arguments: security; guaranteed food supplies; access to the expanded European market; and the prospect of a wider world role. 'The Community opens windows on the world for us which since the war have been closing.'[5]

All in all she did just enough. She was able to hail the decisive result as a 'really thrilling' vindication of the Tory party's long-standing vision, compared with Labour's record of unprincipled somersaults, while feeling privately relieved that the divisive issue was shelved for the foreseeable future.[6] Right up to 1979 she continued to take a positive line on Europe, repeatedly berating the Government for failing to make the most of Britain's membership by being too negative and adversarial.

Cold Warrior

But Europe was never a subject on which Mrs Thatcher was going to be able to speak with conviction. By contrast the Cold War, and the need for strong defence in the face of the ever-present threat of Soviet expansionism, was a cause close to her heart, and one she determined very early on to make her own. There was no inconsistency with her primary domestic mission, since she regarded the core problem of the British economy as too much socialism, which was merely a weaker local variant of Communism. Her immediate purpose might be freeing the British economy, but her ultimate ambition was to eradicate not just the symptoms of socialism, but the virus itself, whose source and breeding ground was the Soviet

Union. Thus the struggle for the British economy was part of the global struggle against Communism. Moreover, it was a good deal easier for an opposition leader to define the battleground rhetorically in terms of the grand abstractions of Freedom against Tyranny than by getting bogged down in petty arguments about incomes policy and trade union law.

In particular she saw the forthcoming Helsinki conference, at which Western leaders were preparing to offer Russia all sorts of aid and recognition in exchange for promises of improved human rights, as a second Munich in the making; and could see a role for herself as the clear-sighted Churchill figure whose mission was to warn the West of impending disaster before it was too late.

Just before the Helsinki conference convened, therefore, she resolved to make a speech. The only Tory elder she consulted was Lord Home, whose unblinking view of Soviet intentions she had long respected. Replying to his congratulations on her election, she asked him for a meeting; and after Easter they began a series of informal conversations whenever he was in London. In June she specifically asked his help with her proposed speech: 'It is time I made a comprehensive speech about "Britain's Place in the World",' she wrote. 'I wonder if you would give me some advice about it.'[7] Afterwards she thanked him 'first for providing the framework . . . and then for going through it so carefully. It gave me all the confidence I should otherwise have lacked.'[8] Home in turn congratulated her. 'One always hopes that the communists will change their spots but they have not done so yet, and until there is firm evidence of change people must be warned.'[9]

A second expert to whom she turned for help was the British historian Robert Conquest, whose book *The Great Terror* is still the most comprehensive exposé of Stalin's purges. Her third inspiration was Alexander Solzhenitsyn, then at the height of his prestige in the West following his expulsion from the Soviet Union the previous year. It was Solzhenitsyn's dramatic assertion the year before that the West had been losing the Third World War ever since 1945, and had now 'irrevocably lost it', that gripped her imagination. Mrs Thatcher did not swallow the whole of this nightmare vision; but she was already repeating the essence of his warning before the end of 1975, and the Russian prophet quickly joined her gallery of heroes. She finally met him in 1983.

She delivered her speech to a hastily arranged meeting of the Chelsea Conservative Association on 26 July, two days before Wilson left for Helsinki. It was quite short but stunningly direct. She started from the premise that 'Freedom has taken a major battering in the last few months'. The background to Helsinki, she asserted, was that the Soviet Union was spending 20 per cent more than the United States each year on military research and development; 25 per cent more on weapons and equipment; 60 per cent more on strategic nuclear forces; while the Soviet navy possessed more nuclear submarines than the rest of the world's navies put together. 'Can anyone truly describe this as a defensive weapon?'

> *Détente* sounds a fine word. And to the extent that there really has been a relaxation in international tension, it is a fine thing. But the fact remains throughout this decade of *détente*, the armed forces of the Soviet Union have increased, are increasing and show no signs of diminishing.

She recalled the crushing of the Czechoslovak spring just seven years before, and the Soviet writers and scientists – Solzhenitsyn among them – jailed for voicing their belief in freedom. The Soviet leaders, she declared uncompromisingly, were 'in principle arrayed against everything for which we stand'. The power of NATO was 'already at its lowest safe limit', she concluded. 'Let us accept no proposals which would tip the balance of power still further against the West.'[10]

This was a speech of extraordinary simplicity and power. It expressed Mrs Thatcher's own uncompromising but essentially optimistic view of the Cold War. She had no time for the static view that the best outcome to be hoped for was a managed stand-off between two equally balanced superpowers; still less did she accept any moral equivalence between the two sides. She always believed, instinctively and passionately, that the Cold War should and could be won by the unwavering assertion of Western values backed by military strength. She boldly declared her position as a newly elected opposition leader more than five years before Ronald Reagan was elected President of the United States. She held to it unflinchingly as Prime Minister, in alliance with Reagan, throughout the 1980s, and saw it triumphantly vindicated just before she left office. She made other, more celebrated speeches over the next few years; but she never essentially departed from the position she took up at Chelsea in July 1975.

By contrast the new Leader of the Opposition failed to shine in the House of Commons, either at Prime Minister's Questions or in debate. The fact was that the sort of simple certainties that went down well with party audiences cut no ice at Westminster. As a result she spoke less and less frequently in the House. Apart from certain fixed occasions in the parliamentary calendar which she could not avoid, she made no more than seven major speeches in the next two years and only one in 1977–8. She spoke slightly more over the winter of 1978–9 as the Labour Government began to crumble, but still much less than Heath had done when he was Leader of the Opposition. Her neglect of Parliament continued even after she became Prime Minister, when she had all the information and authority needed to command the House but still spoke as rarely as she could and never memorably.

'Quite a dame'

If her voice was carrying little weight at home, however, Mrs Thatcher was nevertheless determined that it should be heard in the wider world. Against the advice of the experienced heads around her, she insisted on going to America at the earliest opportunity to announce herself as a robust new partner in the Western alliance. British opposition leaders have often been humiliated by the lack of attention paid to them in Washington. Not so Margaret Thatcher. Her public relations wizard, Gordon Reece, went ahead of her to stir up media interest. By the time Mrs Thatcher flew into New York in the middle of September – she made a point of flying by Freddie Laker's free enterprise airline – the novelty of her sex and the unusual clarity of her message did the rest.

Her first speech, for the most part a perfectly standard lecture to the Institute of Socio-Economic Studies in New York on the evils of excessive taxation, was beefed up at the last minute by Adam Ridley in breach of the convention that opposition leaders do not criticise their own country when speaking abroad. Mrs Thatcher did not scruple to paint a grim picture of the British economy groaning under socialism, graphically endorsing the common American perception that Britain was going down the tube. Rebuked by James Callaghan for running Britain down, she retorted that she was 'not knocking Britain: I'm knocking socialism'.[11]

By the time she moved on to Washington, she had captured the media's attention. She met President Ford, had breakfast with Secretary of State Henry Kissinger and had talks with both Treasury and Defense Secretaries. Her next speech, to the National Press Club, was broadcast live on CBS television. She seized the opportunity with both hands. First she put her own gloss on Solzhenitsyn's warning that the West was losing the ideological struggle by default.

No, we did not lose the Cold War. But we are losing the Thaw in a subtle and disturbing way. We are losing confidence in ourselves and in our case. We are losing the Thaw politically.

Then she answered the critics of her earlier speech by emphasising her faith in Britain's potential to surmount its problems, stressing the huge windfall of North Sea oil and her favourite measure of British genius, the proud tally of seventy-two scientific Nobel Prize winners. She claimed to see a new willingness to reject the easy options. 'We may suffer from a British sickness now, but our consti-tution is sound and we have the heart and will to win through.'[12]

This combination of Churchill and Mrs Miniver went down a storm. Hard-nosed bankers were heard to declare that Britain's alter-native Prime Minister was 'quite a dame'.[13] This first American trip marked the beginning of a love affair between Margaret Thatcher and the American press and public which lasted with ever-increasing enthusiasm for the next twenty years. It also greatly boosted her self-confidence. To journalists on the flight home she boasted: 'The very thing I was said to be weak in – international affairs – I've succeeded in.'[14] She felt she had now proved herself on the inter-national stage.

The one domestic forum where Mrs Thatcher could unfailingly project her faith and rouse a large audience to enthusiasm was the Tory party's annual conference in October. Unlike any other Tory leader, Mrs Thatcher had always loved the Tories' annual seaside jamboree, ever since she first attended it in 1946. The annual confer-ence speech henceforth became the high point of her year, a shame-less festival of orchestrated leader-worship for which she prepared with meticulous care. The latent actress in her responded instinc-tively to the cameras and the razzmatazz, the flagwaving and Elgar, and her speech was almost always intensely patriotic, associating Labour relentlessly with national decline and looking forward to the recovery of 'greatness' under the Conservatives.

'Ronnified'

Her first conference speech as leader was a critical test. Over the summer she had made two poorly received economic speeches in the House of Commons, and one controversial outburst on defence. Blackpool in October was her first major opportunity to tell the party and, via television, the whole country what she was about.

She was determined that she did not want to make 'just an economic speech. So I sat down at home over the weekend and wrote out sixty pages of my large handwriting. I found no difficulty: it just flowed and flowed.'[15] Then, on the Wednesday of conference, week she summoned Ronald Millar to Blackpool for the final rewrite.

Millar was a popular West End playwright who had written occasional material for Ted Heath. He responded reluctantly, but he was instantly captivated. He read her some material which he had hastily prepared, ending with some lines of Abraham Lincoln:

> You cannot strengthen the weak by weakening the strong. You cannot bring about prosperity by discouraging thrift. You cannot help the wage-earner by pulling down the wage-payer . . .

When he had finished Mrs Thatcher said nothing, but produced from her handbag a piece of yellowing newsprint containing the same lines. 'It goes wherever I go,' she told him.[16] In that moment they clicked. For the next fifteen years no major speech of hers was complete until it had been 'Ronnified'.

With his experience of the theatre, Millar also coached her in how to deliver her lines, writing in the pauses and emphases she should observe. 'I'm not a performer, dear,' she told him once;[17] but she was, and much of his success with her was due to the fact that he handled her like a highly-strung actress. As she delivered this first conference speech, Millar stood in the wings, feeling like Henry Higgins watching Eliza Doolittle at Ascot. But the speech was a triumph.

She began with nicely judged humility, recalling her first conference in the same hall in 1946, when Churchill was leader and she never dreamed that she might one day speak from the same platform, paying tribute in turn to Eden, Macmillan, Home and Heath ('who successfully led the party to victory in 1970 and brilliantly led the nation into Europe in 1973'). Getting into her stride, however, she repeated her defence of her speeches in America. She damned the Labour Government not just for high unemployment, high taxation, low productivity and record borrowing but, more fundamentally, for threatening the British way of life itself. 'Let me give you my vision', she went on – with characteristic disregard for feminism:

> A man's right to work as he will, to spend what he earns, to own property, to have the State as servant and not as master –

these are the British inheritance. They are the essence of a free country and on that freedom all our other freedoms depend.

'We want a free economy,' she conceded, 'not only because it guarantees our liberties but also because it is the best way of creating wealth.' There followed a fairly standard recital of the need to stimulate private enterprise, cut the share of the economy taken by public spending and rebuild profits and incentives. The purpose of increasing prosperity, she proclaimed, was 'not merely to give people more of their own money to spend as they choose but to have more money to help the old and the sick and the handicapped'. Yet she ended with another explicit endorsement of inequality: 'We are all unequal,' she declared boldly.

No one, thank heavens, is quite like anyone else, however much the Socialists may like to pretend otherwise. We believe that everyone has the right to be unequal. But to us, every human being is equally important ... Everyone must be allowed to develop the abilities he knows he has within him – and she knows she has within her – in the way he chooses.

Finally, after a strong assertion of the primacy of law and order, and a pledge to uphold the Union with Northern Ireland, she returned to her intensely patriotic personal faith.

I believe we are coming to yet another turning point in our long history. We can go on as we have been going and continue down, or we can stop and with a decisive act of will say 'Enough'.[18]

The representatives in the hall loved it. The press loved it. 'Now I *am* Leader,' she told her entourage, accepting that she had been on probation up to that moment.[19]

Back at Westminster for the autumn session, however, Wilson continued effortlessly to dominate her at Prime Minister's Questions every Tuesday and Thursday, alternately taunting her with her shared responsibility for 1970–74 and chiding her if she disowned it. He patronised her inexperience: 'It is a pity she never served on the Public Accounts Committee or she would have known these things.'[20] He mocked her reluctance to intervene more often, and once caught her out quoting newspaper reports of a White Paper instead of the paper itself.[21]

Emergence of the 'Iron Lady'

Mrs Thatcher maintained her attack on the Helsinki process with several more speeches during 1976. It was the first, delivered at Kensington Town Hall in January, which succeeded in striking a most satisfactory response from the Soviets. Russia, she bluntly asserted, was 'ruled by a dictatorship of patient, far-sighted men who are rapidly making their country the foremost naval and military power in the world'. They were not doing this for self-defence: 'A huge, largely landlocked country like Russia does not need to build the most powerful navy in the world just to guard its own frontiers.'

> No. The Russians are bent on world dominance, and they are rapidly acquiring the means to become the most powerful imperial nation the world has seen. The men in the Soviet Politburo do not have to worry about the ebb and flow of public opinion. They put guns before butter, while we put just about everything before guns. They know that they are a superpower in only one sense – the military sense. They are a failure in human and economic terms.[22]

This was breathtakingly undiplomatic. She was immediately attacked for warmongering. Such bluntness was simply not the language of serious statesmanship. Old hands like Callaghan and Wilson prided themselves on their ability to do business with the enduring Soviet Foreign Minister, Andrei Gromyko, and his hard-faced colleagues. Calling the Soviet leaders dictators bent on world domination was in this view merely childish and counterproductive. It certainly annoyed them. A few days after the Kensington speech the Soviet army newspaper *Red Star* denounced the Conservative leader, calling her – in what was meant to be an insult – 'the Iron Lady'. As she later noted, 'They never did me a greater favour.'[23] She immediately seized on the sobriquet and made sure it stuck. If ever there was a doubt that a woman could be Prime Minister, this Soviet epithet did more than anything else to dispel it.

The next month her personal rating shot up by seven points. Realising that she was on to a winner, she kept up the attack. She undertook an extensive programme of globetrotting over the next three years – partly to spread her message and polish her credentials as a world leader in waiting, partly to educate herself and meet the other leaders with whom she hoped to deal once she had attained office. In all she visited twenty-three countries, including all Britain's major European partners at least once, and one or two outside the EC like Switzerland and Finland. She visited the two Iron Curtain countries least controlled by the Soviet Union – Ceauşescu's Romania and Tito's Yugoslavia; but was – unsurprisingly – not invited to Moscow. Her strong anti-Soviet stance did, however, earn her an invitation to China in April 1977. She visited Egypt, Syria and Israel in early 1976, and later the same year made an extended tour of India, Pakistan and Singapore, going on to Australia and New Zealand. She did not set foot, however, in sub-Saharan Africa, South America or the Gulf. For the most part she did not lecture her hosts about free markets – where she tried it, in Australia, it went down badly. But she did project herself successfully as a staunch defender of Freedom with a capital F, capitalising skilfully on the curiosity which attended a forceful woman politician. In Israel she visited a kibbutz and predictably did not like it. She then infuriated the Israelis by inspecting a Palestinian refugee camp in Syria; but she was even-handed in her condemnation of terrorism and refused to recognise the PLO.

On her main battleground of Helsinki and the Cold War, however, she made an undoubted impact, at least while the Republican administration of Ford and Kissinger was still in the White House. Jimmy Carter, elected in November 1976, was a different kind of President, genuinely but naively determined to work for disarmament and human rights. Mrs Thatcher met him on her second visit to the States in September 1977 – a mark of some respect in itself, since Carter did not normally receive opposition leaders. She could not help liking him and was impressed by a mastery of detail equal to her own; but she was dismayed by his determination to pursue a nuclear test ban treaty and did not let him get a word in for forty-five minutes while she told him so. Even Carter, however, was constrained by the evidence that the Soviets were flouting the assurances they had given at Helsinki. Several prominent dissidents, including the founder of the Helsinki monitoring group, Yuri Orlov, were sentenced to long spells in labour camps. Despite her enthusiastic reception in 1975, Mrs Thatcher's influence in Washington should not be exaggerated. She was only a British opposition leader, and Carter had very good relations with Jim Callaghan. Yet by pointing out loudly and repeatedly the nature of the Soviet regime she certainly contributed to a general stiffening of Western resolve, evidenced in NATO's decision to increase defence spending by 3 per cent a year from 1977 and the agreement of West Germany and other European countries to accept American nuclear missiles on their soil to counter the Soviet deployment of SS-20s. These were both decisions which Mrs Thatcher strongly supported in opposition and implemented when she came to power.

Another sign of hardening American opinion was the emergence of Ronald Reagan as a presidential challenger. Mrs Thatcher first met Reagan soon after her election as leader, when he happened to be visiting London and called on her at the House of Commons. Their meeting was scheduled to last forty-five minutes, but actually lasted twice as long. 'We found', Reagan told Geoffrey Smith, 'that we were really akin with regard to our views of government and economics and government's place in people's lives and all that sort of thing.'[24] In fact, Mrs Thatcher already knew of Reagan's reputation as a successful Governor of California who had got rid of a lot of controls and cut expenditure: Denis had heard him speak to the Institute of Directors back in 1969. 'In a way', she recalled, 'he had the advantage of me because he was able to say: "This is what I believe! This is what I have done!"'[25] Yet in 1975 few took the former film star seriously as a potential President. They met a second time when Reagan next came to London three years later, and again got on exceptionally well. This time their conversation ranged across international as well as domestic politics, defence as well as economics: on both their views instinctively tallied. It was not until five years later that Reagan, two years into his Presidency, called the Soviet Union 'the evil empire'. But those two words precisely encapsulated what Mrs Thatcher had been saying in her speeches ever since Chelsea.

In March 1976 the nature of Mrs Thatcher's domestic task suddenly changed when Harold Wilson unexpectedly resigned. When told the news, Mrs Thatcher thought for a moment that the whole Government had resigned. Instead she had to pay gracious tribute to Wilson and adjust to the challenge of a new antagonist in Number Ten.

She immediately tipped Jim Callaghan to win the succession and predicted that he would be the hardest of the contenders to beat.[26] She was right on both counts. Four years older than Wilson and thirteen years older than Mrs Thatcher, Callaghan was the first Prime Minister ever to have held all three of the senior offices of state before finally reaching the premiership. Mrs Thatcher found him just as patronising as Wilson and even harder to come to grips with. As Barbara Castle – no admirer of Callaghan – wrote in her memoirs: he 'ran rings round an uncertain Margaret Thatcher, metaphorically patting her on the head like a kindly uncle'.[27]

When she lectured him on what he ought to know, he thanked her ironically for the information but told her that it was not possessing information which mattered, but what one did with it.[28] By now she was much less shy of intervening, since Callaghan was not so skilful as Wilson at turning her questions against her. On the contrary, Labour MPs increasingly complained that she was monopolising Question Time by always taking her permitted three bites at the cherry. She scored one palpable hit when Callaghan called her a 'one-man band'. 'Is that not one more man than the Government have got?' she retorted.[29] But she rarely succeeded in disturbing Callaghan's masterly impersonation of a wise old statesman calmly in control of events, while she fussed about details like a terrier yapping at an elephant.

The 1976 sterling crisis gave Labour a bad nine months, as further rounds of spending cuts and raising the minimum lending rate to 15 per cent failed to stop the pound sliding to a low point of $1.56 in late October. After rapidly exhausting two previous standby credits from the IMF, the Chancellor of the Exchequer, Denis Healey, could only secure a third on stringent conditions. In the short term this apparent humiliation – as Mrs Thatcher strenuously portrayed it – actually served Callaghan well, enabling him to make a stand against the left and taking much of the wind out of Mrs Thatcher's sails. In her speech at the Tory conference she was inhibited from making her usual slashing condemnation of the Government by the need not to appear to be talking down the pound. By contrast Callaghan had boldly told his conference the previous week that Keynesianism was dead: the Government could no longer spend its way out of recession.

For the next two years, under IMF tutelage Healey enforced a regime of strict financial discipline which Mrs Thatcher could only – through gritted teeth – applaud. She was obliged to welcome the Chancellor's conversion to the importance of controlling the money supply – 'the only final way in which inflation can be held and reduced. He knows it and we know it.'[30] The one benefit of the Government's conversion to monetary virtue, she wrote in her memoirs, was that 'it outflanked on the right those of my own Shadow Cabinet who were still clinging to outdated nostrums of Keynesian demand management'.[31]

In March 1977 Callaghan lost his Commons majority, but managed to secure the Government's survival for another two years by means of a pact with the Liberals. This frustrated Mrs Thatcher at the time, but in fact this twilight period worked to her advantage in the long run. Had she come to power in 1977 she personally would have been less experienced, less confident and less prepared for office than she was in 1979, while the tide of intellectual and public opinion which eventually carried her into Downing Street and made possible – just – the uncompromising economic policies which she and Geoffrey Howe pursued in 1980–81, would not have been so strong. When the Tories did return to power, it was immensely helpful that Healey and Callaghan had already been keeping a tight grip on monetary policy for the past two years. It is a recurring pattern in politics that when one party reluctantly adopts the other's policies, the electorate tends to go for the party which actually believes in them. 'If you want a Conservative government', she told listeners to Jimmy Young's morning radio programme in 1978, 'you'd better have a Conservative government and not a half-hearted Labour government practising Conservative policies.'[32] By May 1979 Callaghan and Healey had made much of her case for her.

8

Thatcherism under Wraps

Cautious crusader

THE years of opposition were a peculiarly difficult and ambiguous time for Margaret Thatcher. She was a woman of strong convictions and a powerful sense of mission whose instinct, once she unexpectedly found herself leader, was to lead from the front. Yet at the same time, she was very conscious of the weakness of her political position, a little frightened of her own inexperience and the heavy responsibility which had suddenly been thrown upon her, and well aware of the formidable combination of habit, convention and vested interest that was ranged against her. She did not have the authority to impose a thoroughgoing free-market agenda on the Tory party, let alone project it unambiguously to the country. Moreover, even if she had been in a position to proclaim her long-term vision, there was a huge gap between knowing what was right in theory and translating that knowledge into practical policies that could be compressed into a manifesto.

Even after she achieved power, and a political dominance she could never have imagined in 1975, it still took her the best part of two terms, with the full resources of the Civil Service at her command, to begin to frame an explicitly 'Thatcherite' programme. So long as she was in opposition her overriding priority was to make sure she did not lose the General Election, whenever it came. She could not risk getting too far ahead of her party, so had to disclaim objectives which might alarm the voters or allow her opponents to label her 'extreme'. She had to be prepared to fight on a vague prospectus that gave only the broadest hint of her true ambition. As a result, for the whole of this period in opposition, she was obliged to speak with two voices – one clear, didactic and evangelical, the other cautious, moderate and conventional – displaying a confusing mixture of confidence and caution. Right up to May 1979 no colleague or commentator could be sure which was the real Margaret Thatcher.

It is not even certain that she knew herself. Looking back from the perspective of the 1990s, Lady Thatcher in her memoirs naturally subscribed to the heroic legend of a leader who knew clearly from the outset what she wanted to achieve and was only constrained to dissemble her intentions by her dependence on colleagues less clear-sighted and resolute than herself. And, of course, there is plenty of evidence to support this view. '*This* is what we believe,' she famously told a seminar at the Centre for Policy Studies, producing from her handbag a well-worn copy of Hayek's *The Constitution of Liberty* and banging it down on the table.[1] More than once she announced that her purpose was nothing less than to eliminate what she called socialism permanently from British public life. 'Our aim is not just to remove a uniquely incompetent Government from office,' she declared in May 1976. 'It is to destroy the whole fallacy of socialism that the Labour party exists to spread.'[2]

Yet rarely if ever did Mrs Thatcher speak in public of abolishing exchange controls or serious denationalisation, still less of curbing local authorities or renewing the Tories' battle with the miners. In an ideal world all this may have been among her long-term aspirations, but it is doubtful if she ever imagined that any of them would become practical politics. In the short term she thought more in terms of stopping things than of pursuing a radical agenda of her own. Her repeated refrain to colleagues and advisers from the think-tanks who told her what she should do in office was 'Don't tell me *what*. I know what. Tell me *how*.'[3] It was by no means certain that the necessary public support would ever be attainable, even if she won the election. Even as Prime Minister, it is clear from the memoirs of Nigel Lawson, Geoffrey Howe and others that Mrs Thatcher was often the last to be persuaded that key 'Thatcherite' policies, from the scrapping of exchange controls to the reform of the National Health Service – however desirable in principle – were in fact practicable or politically prudent. She was still more hesitant in opposition.

The truth is that caution was just as integral a component of Margaret Thatcher's character as faith. She was pretty sure she would only get one chance, and as an ambitious politician she did not intend to blow it. Nor was it simply that she dare not risk commitments that might split the party. She always had a superstitious fear of giving hostages to fortune or crossing bridges before she came to them. She hated the detailed pledges Heath had forced her to make on rates and mortgages in October 1974. Back in 1968 she had argued in her lecture to the Conservative Political Centre that elections should not be turned into competitive auctions. Now she seized on an essay by the political scientist S. E. Finer which lent academic authority to her distrust of the modern doctrine of the mandate, and quoted it triumphantly to her aides.[4] She believed that politics should be a contest between opposed philosophies, not catchpenny bribes. Her purpose was to win the battle of ideas.

The battle of ideas

Thus it was because she had faith that she could afford to be cautious. She was confident that the correct policies would become clear in time so long as she got the direction right. In the meantime she could compromise, bide her time and go along with policies in which, in her heart, she fundamentally disbelieved – as she had been doing, after all, for most of her career – with no fear that she would thereby lose sight of her objective or be blown off course. She felt no contradiction, for example, in telling David Butler and Dennis Kavanagh that she was utterly opposed in principle to the trade union closed shop, but recognised that for the moment she had to live with it. She explained that politics was all about timing. You could kill a good idea by floating it five years ahead of its time, she told them; but two years ahead it could take off. Judging the right moment was the test of 'real political leadership'.[5]

To win the battle of ideas Mrs Thatcher recognised that she had first to educate herself. Having come to the leadership so unexpectedly she knew she had an immense amount to learn, not merely to master the whole field of politics and government – where previously she had only had to cover one department at a time – but to equip herself intellectually to seize the opportunity which confronted her. With characteristic application, but remarkable humility, she set about learning what she needed to understand about the theory and practice of the free market and its place in Tory philosophy. She read the books that Keith Joseph and Alfred Sherman told her to read, attended seminars at the Centre for Policy Studies and the IEA, and was not ashamed to sit humbly at the feet of Milton Friedman and Friedrich Hayek when they came to London, absorbing their ideas but transmuting them skilfully into her own practical philosophy.

The main theme of all her speeches in these years was simple. One day very soon – 'and it will be a day just like any other Thursday' – the British electorate would face a simple choice between opposed governing philosophies: on the one hand what she loosely labelled socialism, and others would call social democracy, corporatism, Keynesianism or the mixed economy; on the other 'what socialists call capitalism and I prefer to call the free economy'.[6] When a Labour MP interrupted her in the Commons to ask her what she meant by socialism she was at a loss to reply.[7] What in fact she meant was Government support for inefficient industries, punitive taxation, regulation of the labour market, price controls – everything that interfered with the functioning of the free economy. She accepted that many of these evils were in practice unavoidable. Even so, there were in principle, as she put it in a speech to the West German Christian Democrats, 'only two political philosophies, only two ways of governing a country', however many party labels might be invented to obscure the fact: the Marxist-socialist way, which put the interest of the state first, and the way of freedom, which put people first.[8]

Moderate Western forms of democratic socialism as practised by the German Social Democrats or the British Labour party she regarded contemptuously as merely watered down versions of Marxism without the courage of Moscow's convictions. It fitted her political model perfectly that the Labour Party – under the influence of its increasingly dominant left wing – was becoming ever more openly Marxist. True to Hayek, she believed that socialism was a slippery slope – literally the road to serfdom – which would lead inexorably to Communism if the slide was not halted and reversed. Hence she did not, like other Tory leaders in the past, attribute the failures of the Labour Government merely to incompetence or inefficiency, but to fundamental error, which in her more generous moments she could recognise as well-intentioned. Labour Governments, she believed – and Tory ones when they fell into socialist fallacies – inevitably caused inflation, unemployment and stagnation because socialism was by its very nature simply wrong. It was wrong in practice, since self-evidently it did not work: and the reason it did not work was because it was morally wrong. It was essentially immoral and contrary to everything that she believed was best in human nature.

The Right Approach

Meanwhile, despite her determination not to saddle herself with specific commitments, the opposition had to have some policies. In keeping with the strategy of presenting a moderate face to the electorate, and the necessity of keeping the party outwardly united, Mrs Thatcher was content to leave the official process of policy-making in the hands of the Conservative Research Department fed by a network of backbench committees. Some were more active than others, and the process was nothing like so thorough as Heath's comprehensive policy exercise in 1965–70; but Mrs Thatcher was happy to encourage it as a harmless way of keeping her MPs out of mischief.

Meanwhile, the important policy work was being done on a freelance basis by shadow ministers, particularly Geoffrey Howe and his shadow Treasury team. Some of this Mrs Thatcher followed closely; other ideas appear to have been worked up without her direct knowledge. In between there was a lot of thinking, planning and discussion which she was more or less aware of; but very little of this work found its way into her public pronouncements. Though she was evidently persuaded, for instance, that exchange controls should be abolished as soon as possible after winning office, the proposal never appeared in any policy document. Howe, with Nigel Lawson and others, was working on the practicalities of abolition long before the election, but Mrs Thatcher made no commitment, in public or in private. The battle for her approval had to be undertaken from square one the day after she entered Number Ten.

Likewise Howe and Lawson were working on the theory and practice of measuring and controlling the money supply, laying the foundations of what became the Medium Term Financial Strategy, introduced in 1980; and Lord Cockfield, the Tory party's long-standing taxation expert, was working with Howe on possible tax reforms, above all the proposed switch of emphasis from direct to indirect taxation. In retrospect the biggest dog that scarcely barked before 1979 was privatisation – or, as it was then known, 'denationalisation'. In his memoirs Lawson insists that he and others all saw privatisation as 'an essential plank of our policy right from the start'; but he admits that 'little detailed work [was] done on the subject in Opposition', on account of 'Margaret's understandable fear of frightening the floating voter'.[9]

Mrs Thatcher's nervousness of the subject was demonstrated in March 1978 when Howe floated the suggestion that a Tory Government might sell some of the Government holding in British Petroleum. She firmly denied any such intention.[10] Soon afterwards, ironically, the Labour Government started selling BP shares as a way of raising money for the Treasury. In 1979 the Tory manifesto promised to 'offer to sell back to private ownership the recently nationalised aerospace and shipbuilding concerns, giving their employees the opportunity to purchase shares'; to try to sell shares in the National Freight Corporation; and to open up bus services to private operators. Beyond that it promised only that a Tory Government would 'interfere less' with the management of the nationalised industries and set them 'a clearer financial discipline in which to work'.[11] For all Mrs Thatcher's brave talk of reversing socialism, the thrust of Howe and Lawson's preparatory work in opposition – as it remained for the first three years in government – was on ways of controlling the cost of the public sector, not on fantasies of eliminating it.

Mrs Thatcher actually allowed only one general statement of Conservative policy to be officially published by the party between February 1975 and the 1979 manifesto. This was *The Right Approach*, a studiously bland document whose sole purpose was to paper over the evident differences in approach between the two wings of the party before the 1976 conference. Launching *The Right Approach* at Brighton, Mrs Thatcher stated that the party's first task would be to 'put our finances in order. We must live within our means.'[12] But she was at pains not to make this prescription sound too draconian or harsh. Moreover with memories of the three-day week still vivid, it was imperative that the Tories should be seen to be able to 'get on' with the unions.

There was no subject on which Mrs Thatcher's public words were at greater variance with her real views. 'Let me make it absolutely clear', she promised in 1976, 'that the next Conservative Government will look forward to discussion and consultation with the trade union movement about the policies that are needed to save our country.'[13] In private conversation and off-the-record interviews, by contrast, she made no secret that she regarded the trade-union leaders as full-time Labour politicians who would never have any interest in cooperating with a Tory Government. She left no doubt of her wish to see the overmighty unions confronted; and if she could not in the short term confront them herself, she gave covert support to a variety of ginger groups on the fringe of the Tory party which were not so inhibited. She took a close interest, for instance, in the work of the Institute for the Study of Conflict, founded in 1970 to expose Trotskyist subversion in industry and the Communist links of left-wing Labour MPs; she also gave private encouragement to the National Association for Freedom (later renamed the Freedom Association) founded by Norris McWhirter in 1975.

Yet she remained reluctant to commit herself to the strategy urged on her by John Hoskyns and Norman Strauss in a secret paper entitled *Stepping Stones*, which argued that everything an incoming Tory Government hoped to do would depend on facing down trade-union opposition. Right up to the end of 1978 the only piece of new legislation she was prepared to sanction was the introduction of postal ballots for union elections. She ruled out legislation on the closed shop, strike ballots or intimidatory picketing, let alone the unions' legal immunities or the political levy. Had Callaghan gone to the country in October 1978 no trace of *Stepping Stones* would have found its way into the Tory manifesto. It was only the industrial anarchy of the Labour Government's last winter which shifted the debate in favour of the Tory hawks and persuaded Mrs Thatcher that it was safe to come off the fence.

Pocket Britannia

In no respect did Mrs Thatcher conduct herself more like a conventional Leader of the Opposition than in her ritual condemnation of Labour's responsibility for unemployment. From the moment she became leader, the ever-rising rate of unemployment offered the easiest stick with which to beat first Wilson and then Callaghan at Prime Minister's Questions. From 600,000 in February 1974 the numbers had more than doubled to 1.5 million by 1978. Perhaps no Leader of the Opposition could be expected to resist a sitting target; but there was the most blatant opportunism in the way Mrs Thatcher repeatedly tried to tag Labour 'the natural party of unemployment'[14] and Callaghan 'the Prime Minister of unemployment'.[15] 'Our policies did not produce unemployment', she had the nerve to tell the House of Commons in January 1978, 'whereas his policies have.'[16] She contrasted Callaghan's denial of blame with Heath's acceptance of responsibility when unemployment touched a million in 1972 – the intolerable figure which more than anything else impelled him to his notorious U-turn.[17] When Callaghan and Healey retorted that her monetarist prescription would increase unemployment – as Joseph on occasion candidly admitted – she vehemently denied it. 'No,' she insisted on television in October 1976. 'This is nonsense and we must recognise it as nonsense . . . A very, very small increase would be incurred, nothing like what this government has and is planning to have on present policies.'[18] 'We would have been drummed out of office if we had had this level of unemployment,' she asserted in a party broadcast the following year.[19]

As the General Election approached the Tory campaign focused more sharply on jobs than on any other issue, starting with Saatchi & Saatchi's famous poster in the summer of 1978 featuring a winding dole queue with the caption 'Labour Isn't Working'. If not quite a promise, the poster unmistakably suggested that Tory policies would quickly bring the figure down. After two or three years of Conservative Government, however, when the numbers out of work had doubled again to a hitherto unimaginable figure of more than three million, Mrs Thatcher's glib exploitation of the problem in opposition had begun to look more than a little cynical. The best excuse that can be offered is that she, Joseph and Howe genuinely did not anticipate that their monetarist experiment would coincide with the onset of a world recession. Arguably the pain of an economic shake-out had to be gone through: eventually – after seven years – the figure did begin to fall. But given that the starting point of Joseph's analysis had been that cutting the dole queues should cease to be the central priority of economic management, a scrupulous Leader of the Opposition would not have made quite so much political capital of unemployment.

Ever since the furore stirred up by Enoch Powell's 'River Tiber' speech in 1968 immigration had been a taboo subject, carefully avoided by the respectable politicians of all parties. Mrs Thatcher had hitherto observed this polite convention; but as an ardent nationalist with a scarcely less mystical view of British identity than Powell himself she shared his concern about the impact of the growing immigrant population. In private she used to sound off about the 'two Granthams' worth' of coloured immigrants she believed were still arriving in Britain each year.[20] She believed that continued immigration was something ordinary voters worried about, and that politicians therefore had the right, even a duty, to articulate their worry. But she also had a baser motivation. With the economy picking up in the latter part of 1977, the Tories' private polls indicated that their most profitable issues were rising crime and other social problems. So it was not a gaffe, but quite deliberate, that when Mrs Thatcher was interviewed on Granada's *World in Action* two days after a racial incident in Wolverhampton she chose to speak sympathetically of people's fear of being 'swamped by people of a different culture'. Some of her staff tried to dissuade her; but she had determined what she was going to say – without consulting her shadow Home Secretary, Willie Whitelaw – and refused to moderate the emotive word 'swamped'. 'We are not in politics to ignore people's worries,' she declared, 'we are in politics to deal with them . . . If you want good race relations, you have got to allay people's fears on numbers', by holding out 'the prospect of a clear end to immigration'.[21]

Her words sparked an immediate outcry. In the Commons Labour MPs accused her of stirring up racial prejudice. Callaghan hoped she was not trying to appeal to 'certain elements in the electorate', and asked her to explain how she proposed to end immigration, given that all but 750 of the 28,000 admitted in 1977 – actually about one Grantham's worth – were dependants of those already here.[22] Six months later he charged that by speaking as she did she had 'knowingly aroused the fears of thousands of coloured people living in this country and it will take them a long time to recover their composure'.[23] But she hit her intended target. Like Powell in 1968, she received a huge postbag, some 10,000 letters thanking her for speaking out. The Tories gained an immediate boost in the polls, taking them from neck and neck with Labour at 43–43 into a clear lead of 48–39; and four weeks later they won a by-election at Ilford North, where polls showed that immigration was the key issue in swinging votes.

Yet Tory policy did not change. Whitelaw was furious, and briefly considered resignation. But short of assisted repatriation there was no way the policy could change. The party was already committed to a register of dependants; Mrs Thatcher could hardly reverse Whitelaw's promise not to break up families. Powell was disappointed that she never referred to the subject again, claiming that 'a chloroformed gag was immediately clapped over the leader's mouth'.[24] But as he reflected in a later interview: 'If you're trying to convey what you feel to the electorate, perhaps you only have to do it once.'[25] In one respect Powell was wrong. She did return to the subject, quite unapologetically, in an *Observer* interview just before the election, when she denied that she had modified her original statement and defiantly repeated it.[26]

But in another sense Powell was right. Her words did not have to change Tory policy in order to achieve their purpose of signalling her real views to supporters in the country who wanted to believe that she was on their side. It was a trick she often used, even as Prime Minister, to suggest that she was not responsible for the lamentable timidity of her colleagues. She did the same thing over capital punishment, losing no opportunity in the run-up to the election to remind radio and television audiences of her long-standing support for hanging murderers. Most of the time she was obliged to keep her true feelings to herself. Her immigration broadcast was one of those vivid moments that helped bring Mrs Thatcher's carefully blurred appeal into sharp focus, revealing, both to those who shared her views and those who loathed her, exactly what her fundamental instincts were.

This episode is a good example of the way Mrs Thatcher learned to project herself to the public independently of the party she led, not through specific policies or even in big ideas expressed in major speeches, but by constructing an image of the type of person she was, with attitudes, sympathies and instincts which could be guessed at when they could not prudently be spelled out. She realised the importance of projecting her message through her personality, selling the public a wide repertoire of carefully contrived images. It is ironic that Mrs Thatcher, who actually had an unusually clear ideological programme to put across, was the first leader to be packaged to this extent, beginning a process which, taken ever further by her successors, has practically drained politics of ideological content altogether. It was another measure of her political weakness, however, that she was obliged to hint at attitudes whose implications she could not fully expound; and a measure of her political skill that she was able to do so successfully.

The result of this emphasis on promoting her personality rather than her policies was to enable Mrs Thatcher to overcome the perceived handicaps of her class and her sex. In place of the Home Counties Tory lady in a stripy hat, married to a rich husband, whose children had attended the most expensive private schools, she forced the media to redefine her as a battling meritocrat who had raised herself by hard work from a humble provincial background – an inspiration to others, whatever their start in life, who had the ambition, ability and guts to do the same. The transformation did not convince everyone. But long before 1979 she had shown that she could appeal much more widely than her critics had thought possible in 1974. She was not popular, but she was no longer patronised. On the contrary, she had immensely widened the range of available stereotypes for a woman politician, and in doing so transformed her gender from a liability into an asset. First of all she did not try to escape the traditional female stereotype of the housewife, but positively embraced it and turned it to her advantage. Her willingness to act up to the role of ordinary wife and home-maker infuriated feminists, who thought she thereby devalued the whole project of a woman storming the seats of male power. But Mrs Thatcher knew what she was doing. By boasting that she still cooked Denis's breakfast for him every morning, still did her own shopping and even used to 'pop up to the launderette' regularly, she encouraged millions of women to identify with her as they had never been able to identify with any previous politician, male or female. Rich though she was, she sounded as if she understood the problems of daily living in a way that Heath and Callaghan never could. 'They will turn to me', she told John Cole, 'because they believe a woman *knows* about prices.'[27] Mrs Thatcher's homely lectures on 'housewife economics', expressed in the language of domestic budgeting, made monetarism sound like common sense.

But Mrs Thatcher was also able to tap into another range of female types: established role models of women in positions of authority whom men were used to obeying. Thus she was the Teacher, patiently but with absolute certainty explaining the answers to the nation's problems: and the Headmistress exhorting the electorate to pull its socks up. She was Doctor Thatcher, or sometimes Nurse Thatcher, prescribing nasty medicine or a strict diet which the voters knew in their hearts would be good for them.

Finally she was Britannia, the feminine embodiment of patriotism, wrapping herself unselfconsciously in the Union Jack. No politician since Churchill had appealed so emotionally to British nationalism. Unquestionably it was her sex that enabled Mrs Thatcher to get away with it. She was not yet the full-blown Warrior Queen, the combination of Britannia, Boadicea and Elizabeth I that she became after the Falklands war. But already, thanks to the Russians, she was 'the Iron Lady' – recognised as a strong leader ready to stand up to foreign dictators, calling on the nation to look to its defences. While visiting British forces in Germany she was even able to be photographed in a tank without looking silly. No previous woman politician could have done that. As a result, when *The Economist* announced at the beginning of the 1979 election campaign that 'The issue is Thatcher' it meant her personality and her politics, not her sex.[28] That was already a huge achievement.

9

Into Downing Street

'Labour Isn't Working'

THE summer of 1978 was the lowest point of Mrs Thatcher's leadership, when it suddenly began to look possible that she might lose the coming election. Though unemployment was still around 1.5 million, inflation was down to single figures and the pound was riding high. The economic outlook was unquestionably improving, and in his April budget Denis Healey was able to make some modest tax cuts. The Tories' leap in the polls following Mrs Thatcher's immigration broadcast in January proved to be short-lived. By May the parties were neck and neck again, and in August Labour took a four-point lead. Callaghan's personal approval rating was consistently above 50 per cent, Mrs Thatcher's often below 40 per cent. Her efforts to portray Labour as wildly left wing were becoming increasingly implausible; on the contrary, Callaghan was widely recognised as 'the best Conservative Prime Minister we have',[1] while it was she who came over as scarily extreme.

It was specifically to try to forestall an early election that Saatchi & Saatchi came up with 'Labour Isn't Working'. The dole queue design broke the conventions of political advertising, first because it mentioned the other party by name, and second because unemployment was traditionally a 'Labour' issue on which the Tories could never hope to win. In fact only twenty posters ever went up, but their effect was hugely amplified by Labour howls of protest, which meant that the image was reproduced – often several times – in every newspaper and on television. The revelation that the queue was actually made up of Young Conservatives made no difference to the message. The public was reminded that unemployment was still intolerably high. The impact of 'Labour Isn't Working' had exactly the desired effect of making Callaghan draw back from an early election. Instead he committed himself to trying to get through the winter, with a tough limit on pay increases of just 5 per cent. It was a fateful mistake.

At the beginning of December 1978 Callaghan came back from a European Council meeting in Brussels and announced that Britain, in common with Ireland and Italy, would not be joining the European Monetary System (EMS) – the latest venture in European integration originally foreshadowed by Heath, Georges Pompidou and Willy Brandt in 1972 and now brought to fruition by Valéry Giscard d'Estaing, Helmut Schmidt and the first British President of the Commission, Roy Jenkins. Mrs Thatcher immediately condemned the Government's decision. 'This is a sad day for Europe,' she declared in the Commons.[2]

In the light of her own adamant determination to stay out of the EMS over the next ten years her enthusiasm for joining in 1978 is remarkable. Yet her own attitude to Europe was always firmly Gaullist. She wanted Britain to *lead* in Europe, not because she had a vision of European integration but because her vision of Britain demanded nothing less. In this at least she was at one with Heath. 'If we always go to the Community as a supplicant,' she told Callaghan in December 1976, 'either for subsidies or for loans, that prevents us carrying out the wider creative role which was very much expected of us when we joined the Community.'[3] She hated seeing Britain stay out of the EMS, not because she believed in the system for itself but because exclusion cast Britain 'in the second division economically of European countries, and since Britain was the victor in Europe, this comes very hard to the British people'.[4] Her view of Britain's proper relationship to the Continent continued to be shaped by the memory of the war. Thus she never really grasped the idea of a European *community* as understood by the other members, but always saw it primarily as a defence organisation, an arm of NATO.

Winter of discontent

The winter of industrial action against the Government's 5 per cent pay limit began in the private sector with a short but successful strike at the Ford Motor Company, which was doing well and preferred to pay increases of 15–17 per cent rather than suffer a long strike. On 3 January the road haulage drivers went on strike, demanding 25 per cent, followed by the oil tanker drivers, stopping deliveries to industry, power stations, hospitals and schools. Action quickly spread to local authority and National Health Service manual workers – porters, cleaners, janitors, refuse collectors and the like – demanding a £60 minimum wage. There followed two or three weeks of near anarchy, displaying the ugliest face of militant trade unionism. The transport of goods by road practically dried up. Employees were laid off as businesses were crippled by lack of deliveries, enforced by intimidatory and often violent picketing of docks and factories. Piles of rubbish lay uncollected in the streets. Roads were not gritted (in very cold weather), schools were closed and hospitals admitted only emergency cases, while shop stewards took it on themselves to determine what was an emergency. Most famously, in Liverpool, the dead went unburied. On 22 January 1.5 million workers joined in a national Day of Action, the biggest stoppage since the General Strike in 1926. All this left the Government looking helpless and irrelevant – an impression damagingly reinforced by Callaghan's ill-judged attempt to play down the seriousness of the crisis on his return from a sunny G7 summit in Guadeloupe. He never actually used the words 'Crisis? What crisis?' but the *Sun*'s headline accurately paraphrased the impression he conveyed.[5] The whole shambles could not have been better scripted to turn Labour's hitherto biggest asset, the party's close relations with the unions, into its greatest liability and deliver the Conservatives an irresistible mandate for tougher action against the unions than Mrs Thatcher had previously dared contemplate.

Yet she was initially hesitant in gathering this electoral windfall. Public opinion was the key. Mrs Thatcher was still determined not to commit herself to any confrontation with the unions without first making sure that the public would be on her side. She was convinced that the great majority of decent trade unionists wanted only to be allowed to work for a fair wage without being bullied by politically motivated militants. But to win their support she must not seem to be spoiling for a fight. The critical test was the speech she was due to make when Parliament reassembled on 16 January, followed by a party political broadcast on television the next day.

In the Commons she therefore offered the Government Tory support for three specific measures: a ban on secondary picketing, funding of strike ballots and no-strike agreements in essential services. There was never any likelihood that Callaghan would accept – he brushed her off with his usual weary assurance that it was all much more difficult than she imagined – but the offer gained her the patriotic high ground, particularly when she repeated it on television. The Government's refusal left Mrs Thatcher free to assert that it was now up to the Tories to shoulder alone the responsibility of bringing the unions 'back within the law'. 'That's the task which this government will not do, it'll run away from it,' she mocked. 'I don't shirk any of it. I shall do it.'[6]

For the first time Mrs Thatcher had a clearly understood cause to which the long-suffering public now emphatically responded. The polls which at the beginning of the year had still shown the Tories neck and neck with Labour, or even a few points behind, now gave them a twenty point lead, while Mrs Thatcher's personal rating had leapt to 48 per cent. The various disputes were eventually settled, on terms mostly around 9 per cent, and life returned to something like normal. But the legacy of bitterness remained. It seemed that nothing could now stop the Tories winning the election, whenever it was held.

Callaghan could still have tried to hang on until the autumn in the hope that the memory of the winter's humiliation would gradually fade, but his heart was not in it. The issue which finally precipitated the Government's demise was devolution. On 1 March the Welsh and Scottish people were finally given the chance to vote on Labour's proposals for assemblies in Cardiff and Edinburgh. On turnouts which suggested a profound lack of interest, the Welsh overwhelmingly rejected their proposed talking-shop (by a margin of 8–1), while the Scots voted in favour of an Edinburgh parliament by a margin too small to meet the condition written into the Bill by dissident Labour backbenchers. The Scottish result left the Scottish National Party with no reason to continue to support the Government (except that, had they considered the alternative, they were even less likely to get a Scottish parliament from Mrs Thatcher). For the first time the parliamentary arithmetic gave the Tories a real chance of bringing the Government down. On 28 March, therefore, Mrs Thatcher tabled yet another vote of confidence.

There was still no certainty that it would succeed, even when the SNP, the Liberals and most of the Ulster Unionists declared their intention to vote against the Government. There were in that Parliament an exceptionally large number of small parties and maverick individuals: Labour still held a majority of 24 over the Conservatives, but the two main parties together accounted for only 592 MPs out of the total of 635. In the days before the vote the corridors and tearooms of the Palace of Westminster saw a frenzy of arm-twisting and bribery, bluff and double bluff. But by this time Callaghan saw no point in bartering his soul for a few more precarious weeks in office. He had already pencilled in 3 May for an election, whether he lost or won the crucial vote.[7]

For her part Mrs Thatcher made it clear that she would do no deals with anyone. 'In my heart of hearts', she confessed in her memoirs, she thought the Government would probably survive.[8] On the day of the confidence debate she made – as usual on these big occasions – a pedestrian speech indicting the Government on four charges: high taxation, centralisation of power, the abuse of union power and the substitution of 'the rule of the mob for the rule of law'. 'The only way to renew the authority of parliamentary government', she concluded, 'is to seek a fresh mandate from the people and to seek it quickly. We challenge the Government to do so before this day is through.'[9]

It reads well enough, but it was heard 'in complete silence'. Callaghan made a good debating speech twitting Mrs Thatcher for putting down her confidence motion only when she knew the Liberals and Scottish Nationalists were going to vote against the Government. 'She had the courage of their convictions.'[10] At the end of the debate Michael Foot wound up with a brilliant barnstorming performance; and then came the vote. Kenneth Baker best describes the scene:

> We returned to the Chamber looking rather crestfallen while the Labour benches looked very cheerful. Margaret was looking very dejected when suddenly Tony Berry, who had been counting in the Labour Lobby, appeared from behind the Speaker's chair and held up his thumb. We couldn't believe it. Spencer le Marchant holding the teller's slip stepped up to the table and read out 'Ayes 311 – Noes 310' . . .[11]

Callaghan immediately announced that he would ask the Queen for a dissolution. The next day he announced that the General Election would be held on the same day as the local government elections on 3 May.

Into battle

Generally speaking, Mrs Thatcher was pretty confident, though she never liked to count her chickens: she had a superstitious nightmare that she might win the national election but lose her own seat in Finchley.[12] Unlike many politicians, however, she thoroughly enjoyed electioneering, and after four years of frustration she threw herself into the contest – her ninth – with relish, knowing that it would either make or break her.

The Tories' electoral strategy had three strands – neutral, negative and positive. The first priority was to protect the Tory lead by keeping the campaign as dull as possible and allowing Mrs Thatcher to say nothing that might frighten the voters. The negative strand was to keep the heat on Labour, reminding the electors in simple language of the Government's record since 1974: inflation ('prices'), unemployment ('jobs'), cuts in public services (schools, homes and hospitals) and above all the strikes and picket line violence of the winter. For a party wishing to present itself as the wind of change without being specific about the precise nature of that change, Mrs Thatcher's gender was a godsend. The possibility of electing the first woman Prime Minister gave the Tory campaign a radical *frisson*, independent of anything she might say. If the country needed a new broom, who better to wield it than a brisk, no-nonsense woman? 'Maggie' – as she was now universally known – symbolised a fresh start before she even opened her mouth.

Above all she shamelessly played up to her conviction that 'they will turn to me because they believe a woman knows about prices'.[13] She visited a supermarket in Halifax, bought four jars of instant coffee and a lump of cheese and discoursed knowledgeably about the prices of butter and tea, holding up two shopping bags, red and blue, to illustrate how much prices had risen under Labour. She repeatedly insisted that managing public expenditure was no different from running a household budget: the country, like every ordinary household, must live within its means. In Bristol she was presented with an outsize broom with which to sweep the country clean of socialism.

Mrs Thatcher dominated the Conservative campaign. Ironically the next most prominent figure was Ted Heath, who threw himself into the election with a belated display of loyalty transparently intended to make it impossible for her to exclude him from her Government. He kept off the sensitive subject of incomes policy but spoke mainly about foreign affairs – practically the only candidate in the election to do so – and clearly had his eye on the Foreign Office. Pressed in every interview to say if she would include him, however, Mrs Thatcher firmly declined to name her Cabinet in advance.

After the morning press conference she made flying sorties into the country, sometimes by air from Gatwick, sometimes in a specially equipped campaign 'battlebus', but almost always returning to London the same evening. The usual pattern was a factory visit or a walkabout in two or three key constituencies, an interview for regional television or local radio, followed by a big speech to a ticket-only rally of local Conservatives in the evening. Security was necessarily tight, following the murder of Airey Neave, blown up by an Irish car bomb two days after the election was declared, but the ticket-only rule – copied by Reece from his experience of Republican campaigning in the United States – reflected the Tories' strategy of shielding Mrs Thatcher from the possibility of encountering hostile audiences or demonstrations: as far as possible she was shown only in controlled situations, speaking to rapturous congregations of the faithful.

In fact she was warmly received wherever she went and enjoyed meeting real people when she could get to them through the mass of journalists and film crews. In Ipswich – against the advice of her handlers – she 'braved a frightening crush of supporters to walk among the enthusiastic crowds' and made 'a short, confident, impromptu electioneering speech to a crowd of shoppers and passers-by . . . from the steps of the Town Hall'. '"It was like being on the hustings thirty years ago," enthused one of her entourage.'[14]

But of course it was all for the benefit of the cameras. Mrs Thatcher, normally with Denis in tow, lent herself patiently to every sort of charade in order to get a good picture in the local paper or clip on the television news. In a Leicester clothing factory she took over a sewing machine and stitched the pocket on a blue overall. In Cadbury's factory at Bourneville she operated a machine wrapping and packing chocolates. In Milton Keynes she and Denis had their heartbeats and blood pressure tested. '"Steady as a rock," she declared triumphantly as the figures . . . flashed on the screen. "They can't find anything wrong with me. They never can."' When someone said that her heart and lungs would last till polling day, she shot back confidently, 'Yes, and for the next twenty years in Downing Street.' She took the chance to remind the press that she would be not only the first woman Prime Minister, but the first with a science degree, and 'proceeded to deliver a brisk lecture on the system to monitor the temperature in containers at Tilbury', talking about computers 'with the same ease with which she had been discussing prices with shoppers'. Then she suddenly flashed a winning smile and said, 'There – didn't I learn my briefing well?'[15]

Most famously, visiting a farm in Norfolk, she cradled a newborn calf in her arms. She held it for thirteen minutes, while the cameramen covered all the angles, until Denis warned that if she held it much longer they would have a dead calf on their hands. 'It's not for me – it's for the photographers,' she announced. 'They are the really important people in this election.'[16] 'Would you like another take?' she would ask them until they were happy.[17] Callaghan was contemptuous of these vacuous photo-opportunities. 'The voters don't want to see you cuddling a calf,' he told her. 'They want to be sure you're not selling them a pig in a poke.'[18] Some journalists began to realise that they were being manipulated. Adam Raphael wrote an article in the *Observer*, 'The Selling of Maggie', criticising the way the Tory leader was being packaged in a series of cosy images, devoid of political content.[19] But Gordon Reece knew exactly what he was doing. The press were offered seats on the Thatcher battlebus for £600 per head, and took them gratefully. In future elections they would grow more cynical. In 1979 they were still happy to print what they were fed.

The only serious interrogation she faced was on television and radio. Even Reece could not deny the heavyweight media their chance entirely. But Mrs Thatcher accepted only one major television interview and two audience question-and-answer sessions during the campaign, plus two radio interviews and a phone-in. Contrary to Labour hopes that she would crack under the strain of a long campaign she made no serious blunders.

As the three-week campaign progressed the Tory lead in the polls was steadily cut back, from an average of around 11 per cent down to around 3 per cent, while Callaghan's personal lead over Mrs Thatcher widened. The Liberals, as usual during elections, picked up support, leading to renewed speculation about a hung Parliament. Mrs Thatcher naturally insisted that she wanted and expected to win an overall Conservative majority, and vowed that she would do no deals with the Liberals or anyone else if she fell short. But from about the middle of the second week she began to sound more defensive, and sometimes a bit rattled. Her adviser Angus Maude asked speechwriter Ronald Millar to try to calm her down. 'It's urgent,' Maude told him. 'If she blows up at this stage it could blow the election.' Ever resourceful, Millar came up with the slogan 'Cool, calm – and elected' and persuaded Mrs Thatcher to adopt it, telling her that of course she was perfectly calm, but it was important that she help to keep those around her calm. She fell for it.[20]

'Hello, Maggie'

After a quiet Saturday on home ground in Finchley and Enfield, publicly shrugging off the narrowing polls, her campaign moved into top gear over the last three days. First Harvey Thomas staged a spectacular rally of Conservative trade unionists at the Wembley Conference Centre on Sunday afternoon. This was her highlight of the whole campaign – 'an inspiring sight', she told Patricia Murray, 'and one which I will never forget'.[21] Mrs Thatcher entered the hall to the strains of *Hello, Dolly*, rewritten by Millar and recorded by Vince Hill:

> Hello, Maggie,
> Well, hello, Maggie,
> Now you're really on the road to Number Ten . . .

With this event, wrote the *Daily Mail*, 'the barn-storming, star-studded traditions of American politics arrived in Britain'.[22]

She spent the rest of that day working on her final TV broadcast which went out on Monday evening. She spoke solemnly for ten minutes direct to camera, stressing the need for a change of direction and her own deep sense of responsibility, promising – in a phrase she had already tried out several times during the campaign – that 'Somewhere ahead lies greatness for our country again'.[23]

On Sunday night, after recording her final broadcast, she shyly asked Ronnie Millar if he had by any chance thought of a few words that she might say on the steps of Downing Street if it should turn out that she needed them. At that stage he would not tell her what he had in mind.[24] Three days later, at her last press conference, a journalist asked her about the G7 summit conference coming up in June. 'I have got it in my diary,' she replied crisply.[25] There is no doubt that she was genuinely confident. 'She looks more powerful', Jean Rook noted in the *Daily Express*, 'and her soaring ambition and huge mental span are beginning to show.'[26] The final opinion polls all showed the Tories clearly ahead – the margins ranging from 2 per cent (Gallup) to 8 per cent (London *Evening Standard*).

The polling day headlines hailed her expected victory. 'The Woman Who Can Save Britain', trumpeted the *Daily Mail*; 'Give The Girl A Chance', urged the *Daily Express*; while the *Sun*, urging Labour supporters to 'Vote Tory This Time – It's The Only Way To Stop The Rot', looked forward to 'The First Day of the Rest of Our Lives'.[27] Yet up to the last minute she was still nervous that it might all be snatched away. She talked anxiously during the day of Thomas Dewey, the American presidential candidate who had appeared to have the 1948 election for the White House sewn up before Harry Truman unexpectedly pipped him at the last.[28] Jim Callaghan – a solid incumbent who had never expected to become Prime Minister but had turned out surprisingly popular – was not unlike Harry Truman.

By the time Mrs Thatcher and Denis arrived at Barnet Town Hall for her own count just before midnight it was clear that she would be Prime Minister, with an adequate if not overwhelming majority, though she still made a point of not claiming victory until she had 318 seats. In the end the Conservatives won 339 seats to Labour's 269, with the Liberals holding 11, the Scottish and Welsh Nationalists reduced to 2 each and the various Ulster parties 12, giving an overall majority of 43. Yet at just under 44 per cent her share of the total vote was the lowest winning share – apart from the two inconclusive elections of 1974 – since the war. (Heath in 1970 had won 46.4 per cent.)[29] Her fear that she might lose her own constituency was, of course, groundless. When her result was declared at 2.25 a.m. she had doubled her majority to nearly 8,000:

Margaret Thatcher (Conservative)	20,918
Richard May (Labour)	13,040
Anthony Paterson (Liberal)	5,254
William Verity (National Front)	534
Elizabeth Lloyd (Independent Democrat)	86
Conservative majority	7,878

She arrived in triumph at Central Office around 4.00 a.m. still only admitting that she had moved from 'cautiously optimistic' to 'optimistic'. She was punctilious in thanking all the party workers who had helped in the campaign. Eventually she beckoned Millar into a corridor. 'I think it's going to be all right,' she said cautiously. Now would he tell her what she should say on the steps of Number Ten? Millar offered her the supposed prayer of St Francis of Assisi – it was actually a nineteenth-century invention – beginning 'Where there is discord, may we bring harmony . . .'

The lady rarely showed deep feelings but this . . . proved too much. Her eyes swam. She blew her nose. 'I'll need to learn it,' she said at length. 'Let's find Alison and get her to type it.'[30]

She returned home around 5.15 a.m. for a few hours' sleep but was back at Central Office by 11.30 a.m. to hear the final results and await the call to the Palace. When the telephone rang it was not Buckingham Palace but Ted Heath, ringing to offer his congratulations. Mrs Thatcher did not go to the phone, but quietly asked an aide to thank him. Eventually, soon after three o'clock, the call came. After an audience with the Queen lasting forty-five minutes she arrived in Downing Street around four o'clock as Prime Minister.

The words that Millar gave her to intone on the steps of Number Ten sounded uncharacteristically humble, consensual and conciliatory:

> Where there is discord, may we bring harmony;
> Where there is error, may we bring truth;
> Where there is doubt, may we bring faith;
> And where there is despair, may we bring hope.

Actually the second and third lines bear a more didactic interpretation than anyone noticed at the time. Mrs Thatcher had no time for doubt or error: she was in the business of faith and truth. But for a woman with a reputation for plain speaking she had a remarkable gift for clothing harsh ideas in deceptively honeyed words.

St Francis's apocryphal prayer was not the only piety she uttered on the steps of Downing Street. She also seized the chance to pay tribute to Alfred Roberts.

> Well, of course, I just owe almost everything to my own father. I really do. He brought me up to believe all the things I do believe and they're just the values on which I've fought the Election. And it's passionately interesting to me that the things that I learned in a small town, in a very modest home, are just the things that I believe have won the Election. Gentlemen, you're very kind. May I just go . . . [31]

And so the grocer's daughter entered Number Ten.

10

The Blessed Margaret

'Where there is discord . . .'

M ARGARET Thatcher entered Downing Street on 4 May 1979 carrying an extraordinary weight of public expectation, curiosity, hope and apprehension. Her achievement in becoming the first female leader of a major Western democracy lent her an unprecedented novelty value. Even when she led in the polls there had remained a lingering doubt whether the British electorate, when it came to the point in the privacy of the voting booth, would really bring itself to vote for a woman Prime Minister. Conceding defeat, the outgoing James Callaghan made a point of acknowledging that 'for a woman to occupy that office is a tremendous moment in this country's history'.[1] It represented, as a writer in the *Guardian* put it, 'one small step for Margaret Thatcher, one giant stride for womankind'.[2]

Yet Mrs Thatcher determinedly played down the feminist aspect of her victory. She always insisted that she did not think of herself as a woman, but simply as a politician with a job to do, the standard-bearer of certain principles, who happened to be female. Though in her thirty-year progress from Grantham via Oxford to Westminster and now Downing Street she had skilfully exploited her femininity for whatever advantages it could bring her, she had rarely presented herself as a pathfinder for her sex and did not intend to start now. It was symptomatic of her uniqueness that the 1979 election saw fewer women returned than at any election since 1951 – just nineteen compared with twenty-seven in the previous Parliament. 'It never occurred to me that I was a woman Prime Minister,' she claimed in her televised memoirs.[3] She preferred to boast of being the first scientist to reach the office.

More important than the novelty of her gender was the widespread sense that she represented a political new dawn and a decisive break with the recent past. Of course no one in 1979 imagined that she would remain Prime Minister for eleven years, stamping her personality and even her name indelibly on the whole of the next decade. But she was unquestionably different. Her admirers – who included, crucially, many former Labour voters – saw her election as the last chance for a failing country to pull itself out of the spiral of terminal decline. Others – including many in her own party – feared that on the contrary she was a narrow-minded dogmatist whose simple-minded remedies would prove disastrous if she was not restrained by wiser counsel. In between, of course, there were plenty of cynics who were confident that she would in practice turn out no different from any of her recent predecessors whose lofty rhetoric had quickly turned to dust. With all her brave talk of restoring Britain's 'greatness' – whatever that meant – by reviving the spirit of enterprise, Mrs Thatcher had been remarkably unspecific in opposition about how she was going to do it. Why then should she be expected to succeed where they had failed?

Mrs Thatcher herself was fiercely determined that her government would indeed be different. She was driven by a burning sense of patriotic mission and historic destiny. 'I can't bear Britain in decline. I just can't,' she insisted during the election.[4] 'I know that I can save this country and that no one else can', the Earl of Chatham is supposed to have declared on taking office in the middle of the Seven Years War in 1757. 'It would have been presumptuous of me to have compared myself with Chatham,' Lady Thatcher wrote in her memoirs. 'But if I am honest I must admit that my exhilaration came from a similar inner conviction.'[5]

Of course this was written many years later. But from the moment she walked through the door of Number Ten her officials felt the force of this passionate self-belief. Kenneth Stowe, her first principal private secretary, recalls that from the first moment she was 'absolutely focused, absolutely committed' and 'very hands-on': she wanted to be briefed about everything and to take charge of everything immediately, even before she sat down to pick her Cabinet. The contrast with the relaxed style of her predecessor could not have been more marked.[6] Mrs Thatcher appeared to need no sleep, nor did she expect anyone else to need it. All her life, and specifically for the past four years, she had been training herself for this moment. 'I have always had an onerous timetable, but I like it,' she told an interviewer on the first anniversary of her taking office.

'I have a tremendous amount of energy and for the first time in my life it is fully used.'[7]

Yet her missionary impatience was, as always, overlaid with caution. She knew in broad terms what she wanted to achieve. She knew there was a tide to seize, a powerful movement of economic thinking in favour of the New Right free-market agenda that she and Keith Joseph had been preaching for the past four years. But at the same time she knew that the opposition of established interests and entrenched assumptions – in Whitehall, in the country and not least in the Tory party – was still very strong, so that she would have to proceed carefully in order to carry the party and the country with her. The election had delivered her an adequate parliamentary majority of forty-three. But the outstanding feature of the result, emphasised by all the press, was the imbalance between the prosperous Tory south of England and the struggling old industrial areas of the north of England, Wales and Scotland, which had still predominantly voted Labour.

She frequently remarked that she would be given only one chance to get it right and she did not intend to blow it. In making her first pronouncements, therefore, in choosing her Cabinet, in taking over the machinery of government and in setting out her initial agenda, she was a great deal more cautious than her rhetoric in opposition had suggested, disappointing her keenest supporters while reassuring those who had feared she might be dangerously head-strong. The heroic picture painted in her memoirs of a radical reformer determined to shake the country from its socialistic torpor is not untrue; but her radicalism was in practice tempered by a shrewd awareness of political reality and a streak of genuine humility. She had no illusions about the scale of the task before her.

Her long-term ambition, as set out in opposition, was nothing less than the elimination of what she called 'socialism' from British politics, the reversal of the whole collectivising trend of the post-war era and thereby, she believed, the moral reinvigoration of the nation. 'Economics is the method', she declared in 1981. 'The object is to change the soul.'[8] In the short term, however, she was determined to keep her attention firmly on the method. She would not be distracted by foreign affairs; she had no interest in flashy constitutional reform; nor did she have any immediate plans for tackling the welfare state. Even the reform of trade-union law – for which she had an undoubted popular mandate – was not to be rushed. Hence for the leader of a determinedly radical government she had a remarkably thin agenda of specific reforms in May 1979. In opposition since 1975 she had deliberately stuck to general principles and avoided precise commitments. Her fundamental philosophy of anti-socialist economics prescribed a number of broad objectives: the Government should cut public spending, cut taxes, keep tight control of the money supply, refrain from detailed intervention in the economy and generally trust the operation of the free market. But very little of this required legislation. Most of it simply involved not doing things which previous governments of both parties had believed it their function to do.

She had three important factors working in her favour. First, she gained a huge advantage from the timing of the election which had brought her to power. Had the Labour Government fallen at any time in the previous four years, Mrs Thatcher would have been obliged to launch her free-market experiment in far less propitious conditions. But the trade-union-orchestrated chaos of the previous winter had played into her hands. In the ten years since 1969, the unions had destroyed the Wilson, Heath and now the Callaghan Governments. Public tolerance of the assumption that the country could only be governed with the consent of the unions – the conventional wisdom of the past four decades – had finally snapped. There was a powerful mood that it was time for someone to make a stand and face them down; and that someone was Margaret Thatcher.

At an official level, too, a significant shift had already occurred. Though monetarism – the theory that there was a direct causal relationship between the amount of money in the economy and rising inflation – was still deeply controversial, disputed by many economists and used by politicians as sloppy shorthand for all manner of right-wing extremism, it had in practice been largely accepted and quietly applied by the Labour Government, under the instruction of the International Monetary Fund, for the past two years. Callaghan and his Chancellor, Denis Healey, had kept a tight squeeze on monetary growth on pragmatic, not dogmatic, grounds; the new Conservative Government – or at least the inner group of ministers who would direct its economic policy – believed in controlling the money supply as a matter of principle, even of faith. But the soil had already been prepared for them, and the change of policy within the Treasury was more cosmetic – a matter of presentation – than real. The incoming Government was actually a good deal less innovative in this respect than either the Tories pretended or Labour ex-ministers liked to acknowledge.

The third enormous benefit the new Government enjoyed, which cushioned to some extent the impact of the policies it intended to pursue, was the coming on flow of North Sea oil. It was in June

1980 that Britain became for the first time a net oil exporter. The effect of this fortunate windfall was disguised by the fact that the Government's coming to power coincided with the onset of a major world recession, so that for the first two or three years the economic news appeared to be all bad as unemployment and inflation soared. But the impact of the recession would have been a great deal worse, and maybe politically unsustainable, had it not been for the fortu-itous subsidy that Britain's independent oil supply gave to both government revenue and the balance of payments.

Unlike all her recent predecessors, Mrs Thatcher's purpose was not to run the economy from Whitehall, but to teach British industry to survive by its own competitiveness instead of looking to the Government for its salvation. Her immediate priority, therefore, was to take three or four big, bold decisions and then have the courage to stick to them. As it happened, this turned out to be more diffi-cult than anticipated as the recession bit, provoking a concerted demand from every shade of the political spectrum that the Govern-ment must set aside its ideological preconceptions and act in the national interest in exactly the ways Mrs Thatcher was determined to eschew. It took a strong nerve to resist this chorus of advice, but Mrs Thatcher was morally armoured by her certainty that what she was trying to do was right. Indeed, her combative nature positively relished the adversity. The more the apologists of the old consensus insisted that she must change course, the more determined she became not to be deflected, until the importance of being seen not to be deflected became an end in itself, irrespective of the economic arguments. Thus the style of the Thatcher premiership was forged in these first two testing years.

A traditional Tory Cabinet

The formation of the Cabinet reflected this mixture of long-term determination and short-term realism. For all her brave talk in opposition of having a 'conviction Cabinet' with 'no time for internal arguments',[9] Mrs Thatcher had in practice no choice but to confirm in office most of those who had comprised the Shadow Cabinet before the election. Having maintained a broad front of party unity in opposition, she could not suddenly appoint an aggressively Thatcherite Cabinet in the moment of victory. As it was, when she sat down that first evening in Downing Street with Willie Whitelaw and the outgoing Chief Whip, Humphrey Atkins, to settle the allo-cation of departments to be announced next day, she let herself be guided to a great extent by Whitelaw. With one major exception, no figure of importance was left out and no new faces were brought in, while several old ones were brought back. It did not look like a Cabinet to launch a social revolution. Yet at the same time Mrs Thatcher made sure that the key economic jobs were reserved for those she called 'true believers'.

So far as most commentators were concerned, her trickiest dilemma was whether to include Ted Heath. In fact she never seriously considered it. As she frankly explained to one of her first biographers: 'He wouldn't have wanted to sit there as a member of the team. All the time he would be trying to take over.'[10] She sent him by motorcycle a brief handwritten letter informing him that, after thinking 'long and deeply about the post of Foreign Secretary', she had 'decided to offer it to Peter Carrington who – as I am sure you will agree – will do the job superbly'.[11] She later added public insult to this perceived injury by offering Heath the Washington Embassy – a transparent way of trying to get him out of domestic politics – even though he had made clear his determination not to leave the Commons. For the next eleven years the former Prime Minister's glowering resentment on the front bench below the gangway served as the most effective deterrent to Tory malcontents tempted to criticise the Government.

The price of excluding Heath was that Mrs Thatcher was bound to fill her Cabinet with his former colleagues. Thus Whitelaw became Home Secretary, Francis Pym had to settle for Defence and Carrington asked for and was granted Ian Gilmour as his deputy in the Commons, with a seat in the Cabinet as Lord Privy Seal. James Prior was confirmed as Employment Secretary. Most significantly, Peter Walker was brought back as Agriculture Secretary. It was widely assumed that she considered Walker (unlike Heath) too dangerous a potential critic to leave on the back benches. In fact, she had always regarded him as an effective minister, as she proved by keeping him in a succession of departments for the next ten years.

She had much less regard for Michael Heseltine, whom she already distrusted as dangerously ambitious as well as ideologically unsound, but she could not afford to leave him out. In opposition Heseltine had accepted the shadow Environment portfolio only on condition that he would not have to take the same job in government; but after turning down the Department of Energy he reluctantly accepted Environment after all, and then found that it suited him admirably.

Other former Heathites filled most of the spending departments. The engine room of the new Cabinet, however, lay in the economic departments. The relationship between the Prime Minister and Chancellor is central to the success of any Government. Four years earlier Mrs Thatcher had chosen the dogged Geoffrey Howe, rather than her intellectual mentor Keith Joseph, to be her shadow Chancellor and now, slightly reluctantly, she kept faith with him. Howe had worked hard in opposition to lay the groundwork of monetarist policies and was said to be 'the only man who can work with Margaret at his shoulder';[12] but she always found his mild manner exasperating and was already inclined to bully him.

Howe was joined in the Treasury by John Biffen as Chief Secretary (in the Cabinet) and the most brilliant of the younger monetarists, Nigel Lawson, as Financial Secretary (outside the Cabinet). Keith Joseph went to the Department of Industry – amid accurate predictions that he would prove too compassionate in practice to implement the sort of ruthless withdrawal of subsidies which he advocated in theory;[13] while John Nott got the Department of Trade. These five – Howe, Joseph, Biffen, Nott and Lawson – with Mrs Thatcher herself, formed the central group in charge of the Government's economic strategy. The only non-monetarist allowed near an economic job was Jim Prior, whose appointment to the Department of Employment was welcomed as a signal that the new Government did not want an early confrontation with the unions. Mrs Thatcher accepted this analysis. 'There was no doubt in my mind', she wrote in her memoirs, 'that we needed Jim Prior . . . Jim was the badge of our reasonableness'.[14]

Most press comment found the moderate composition of the Cabinet reassuring and failed to anticipate the way Mrs Thatcher would get around it. In fact, with an instinct for the reality of government which belied her relative inexperience, Mrs Thatcher had calculated better than either her supporters or her opponents that neither the individuals nor the numbers around the Cabinet table mattered. So long as those she came to call the 'wets' had no departmental base from which to develop an alternative economic policy, she and her handful of likeminded colleagues (who naturally became the 'dries') would be able to pursue their strategy without serious hindrance. Short of resigning – which none of them was keen to do – the 'wets' could only stay and acquiesce in policies they disliked, in the belief that political reality must force a change of direction sooner or later.

From the start, the full Cabinet never discussed economic policy at all. Yet in her early days as Prime Minister Mrs Thatcher operated for the most part quite conventionally through the Cabinet committee structure: economic policy was determined by the 'E'

Committee, chaired by herself. She held weekly breakfast meetings with the monetarist inner circle, Howe, Joseph, Biffen and Nott, with just one or two of her own staff in attendance. These Thursday breakfasts remained secret until they were revealed by Hugo Young in the *Sunday Times* in November 1980 – by which time they had achieved most of their purpose and the group was anyway beginning to unravel. On wider matters Mrs Thatcher allowed much freer discussion in the Cabinet than Ted Heath had ever done; partly because she lacked his personal authority among her colleagues (nearly half of whom were older than her and several much more experienced), partly because she always enjoyed a good argument. In the early years she quite often lost the argument; but she never lost control, not only because she had her key allies in the posts that mattered, but also because in a crunch Willie Whitelaw and Peter Carrington would not let her be seriously embarrassed. She never held a vote, so she could not be outvoted. At the same time it was undoubtedly good for her to have powerful opposition within the Cabinet, composed of colleagues of her own age and independent standing who would argue with her, even though she could usually prevail in the end. In later years, when her colleagues were all much younger and owed their positions entirely to her, she lacked that sort of opposition. For this reason her first Cabinet was in some respects her best.

The linchpin of her authority was Whitelaw. It was many years later that she made the immortal remark that 'Every Prime Minister should have a Willie',[15] but it was in her first term that she needed him most. As the acknowledged leader of the paternalistic old Tories, he could easily have rallied a majority of the Cabinet against her had he chosen to do so. Instead, having stood against her in 1975 and been defeated, he made it a point of honour to serve her with an almost military sense of subordination to his commanding officer. He had strong views of his own on certain matters which he did not hesitate to argue, normally in private. He would warn her when he thought she was getting ahead of the party or public opinion. But he saw his job as defusing tension and ensuring that she got her way. In the last resort he would never set his judgement against hers or countenance any sort of faction against her. Some of his colleagues felt that he thereby abdicated his proper responsibility to act as a traditional Tory counterweight to her more radical instincts; but so long as Willie stood rocklike beside her it was impossible for any other group in the Cabinet successfully to oppose her.

In effect she used him to chair the Cabinet. In business terms Mrs Thatcher acted more like a chief executive than a chairman, concerned not with seeking agreement but with driving decisions forward. She would normally speak first, setting out her own view and challenging anyone with a good enough case to dissent. 'When I was a pupil at the Bar,' she once told the House of Commons, 'my first master-at-law gave me a very sound piece of advice, which I tried to follow. He said: "Always express your conclusion first, so that people do not have to wait for it."' As Prime Minister she made this her regular practice.[16] After a brisk exchange of views, often head-to-head with a single colleague, she would then leave Whitelaw to sum up, which he would do with skilful bonhomie, blandly smoothing away the disagreements while making sure the Prime Minister got her way, or at least was not visibly defeated.

'She certainly was aggressive,' one member of that Cabinet confirms, but 'I never felt that she was dominant . . . On all sorts of issues there was a pretty good ding-dong discussion . . .' Yet more often than not she did dominate, not only because she was always thoroughly prepared, but because she had no hesitation in berating ministers in front of their colleagues if she thought they did not know their stuff. Moreover, as Jim Prior wrote, colleagues were given no time to develop an argument at length. 'If a minister tended to be in the slightest bit longwinded, or if she did not agree with his views, Margaret would interrupt.'[17] She was the same in smaller meetings, with both ministers and officials.

She was in fact a very good listener when she respected the expertise of the person she was talking to, and really wanted to hear what he had to tell her. To hold her attention, however, it was essential to make your point quickly and then stick to it. 'Waffle was death,' a senior mandarin recalled.[18] Much of her irritation with Geoffrey Howe stemmed from the fact that he never learned to make his point quickly. She relished argument for its own sake, and would often take a contrary line just to provoke one. It was through argument that she clarified her own mind. 'She would argue vigorously,' the head of her policy unit, John Hoskyns, recalled, 'to satisfy herself that the thinking she was being given was good.'[19] Though she read all the papers, her staff quickly learned that she was never persuaded of anything on paper alone: she had to test the case in argument before she would accept it.[20]

At the same time she was extraordinarily difficult to argue with, because she would never admit to losing an argument, but would become 'unbelievably discursive' and illogical if the point was going against her, abruptly changing the subject in order to retain the upper hand.[21] Alan Clark, recording a bout with the Prime Minister some years later, characteristically saw her illogicality as quintessentially feminine: 'no rational sequence, associative lateral thinking, jumping rails the whole time'. Yet he concluded: 'Her sheer energy and the speed with which she moves around the ring makes her a very difficult opponent.'[22] She argued not merely to clear her mind, but to *win*.

It was possible to change her mind, but she would never admit to having been wrong. She would furiously resist an argument by every device at her disposal one day, only to produce it unblushingly the next day as her own, with no acknowledgement that she had shifted her ground or that her interlocutor might have had a point.[23]

Some colleagues reckoned that this aggressive manner was both necessary, at least in the beginning, and effective. Lord Carrington suggests that it was the only way that Mrs Thatcher, as a woman, could have asserted her authority in the circumstances of 1979–81.[24] John Hoskyns likewise believes that she had to be 'impossible, difficult, emotional, in order to try to bulldoze . . . radical thinking through' against those he termed 'the defeatists' in the Cabinet.[25] Even Geoffrey Howe, the butt of so much of her worst bullying, told Patricia Murray in 1980 of the exhilaration of working with Mrs Thatcher in these early days:

> Oh, yes she is *dramatically* exciting! She has an openness, a frankness, an enthusiasm and an unwillingness to be cowed . . . which makes her enormous fun to work with. You can never be quite sure on issues you have never discussed with her what her instinctive reaction will be, but it's bound to be interesting . . . Even on the days when it isn't fun, she thinks it is well worth having a try.[26]

Others, however – particularly those colleagues less resilient than Howe and less robust than Prior – thought her method of government by combat counterproductive and inimical to sensible decision making. David Howell, a thoughtful politician who had naively imagined that the Cabinet would function as the forum for an exchange of ideas, was disillusioned to discover that, on the contrary, 'certain slogans were . . . written in tablets of stone and used as the put-down at the end of every argument'. 'In my experience,' Howell concluded, 'there is too much argument and not enough discussion.'[27] Another member of the 1979 Cabinet thought it 'an absurd way to run a Government'.[28] To these critics, Mrs Thatcher's inability to delegate and her insistence on interrogating her ministers about the smallest detail of their own departments reflected a deep-seated insecurity, not so much political as psychological: she had to be on top all the time, and keep demonstrating that she was on top. The schoolgirl had not only done her homework, but had to prove that she had done it. On this analysis her aggression was essentially defensive.

The negative results of this method were that she exhausted herself and did not get the best out of others. Though she liked to boast that she was never tired so long as there was work to be done – 'it's when you stop that you realise you might be rather tired'[29] – and wrote in her memoirs that there was 'an intensity about the job of Prime Minister which made sleep a luxury', many of those who worked most closely with her insist that this was not true. Undoubtedly her stamina was remarkable. She could go for several days with four hours' sleep a night, and rarely allowed herself more than five or six. But her staff could see that she was exhausted more often than she ever admitted: one sign was that she would talk more unstoppably than ever.[30] Her refusal to acknowledge physical weakness was another way of asserting her dominance. Any minister unwise enough to admit that he needed sleep would find himself derided as a feeble male. Alternatively, she would express motherly concern; but this, George Walden noted, was another stratagem:

> What she was saying when she commented on how terrible you looked was that you were a man and she was a woman, you were a junior and she was Prime Minister, and yet unlike you she was *never* tired.[31]

In the same way she would insist that other people must have their holidays while refusing to admit that she might need one herself. 'I must govern,' she told a member of her staff in the summer of 1979.[32] Holidays, she frequently implied, were for wimps.[33] But her inability to relax also conveyed the message that she did not trust anyone to deputise for her. She believed that if she stopped for a moment, or let slip her vigilance, the Civil Service would quickly resume its paralysing inertia, her feeble colleagues would backslide and her enemies would combine against her. By not trusting her ministers to run their own departments, however, Mrs Thatcher ultimately diminished them.

Thus from the very beginning Mrs Thatcher's restless interference centralised the business of government, while by concentrating everything on herself she underused the talents of others. As she grew more dominant, colleagues and officials became increasingly reluctant to tell her things she did not want to hear. The free circulation of information and advice within Whitehall was constrained by the requirement to refer everything upwards to Number Ten; while by battering and badgering, second-guessing and overruling her colleagues she strained their loyalty – ultimately to breaking point.[34] As early as March 1980 her devoted PPS, Ian Gow, was worried that 'Margaret did treat colleagues badly and it would boomerang'.[35]

Unlike Ted Heath's exceptionally harmonious Cabinet half a dozen years before, which had kept its own counsel even when pursuing sensitive and controversial policies, Mrs Thatcher's Cabinet was prone to leaks from the very beginning. The fact that more than half the Cabinet had serious doubts about the economic strategy to which they were committed was well known and widely reported. Mrs Thatcher blamed the so-called 'wets' for trying to subvert by hints and whispers policies they were unable to defeat in Cabinet. The truth was that both sides leaked; this was an inevitable consequence of a fundamentally divided Cabinet. The 'wets' confided their misgivings to journalists because they were denied any opportunity to influence policy from within; while for her part Mrs Thatcher, having been obliged to appoint a Cabinet most of whom she knew were out of sympathy with her objectives, felt justified in bypassing them and appealing, via the press, directly to the public, which she believed understood what she was trying to do. She was never a good team player, still less a good captain, because she never trusted her team. Even when she had replaced most of her original opponents with younger colleagues more loyal to her – whether from conviction or ambition – the habit of undermining them was too established to be abandoned. She was not loyal to them, she drove an unprecedented number of them to resign, and ultimately in November 1990 the collective loyalty of the survivors cracked.

Inside Number Ten

The wider field over which the new Prime Minister had quickly to assert her authority was Whitehall. From the moment she took office she became responsible for the entire government machine. Yet the British Prime Minister has no department of his or her own through which to coordinate this extensive bureaucracy, merely a small private office, based in Number Ten, Downing Street, composed of an anomalous mixture of career officials inherited from the outgoing government, whose job is to provide continuity;

a handful of personal staff carried over from the very different world of opposition, more often than not with no experience of government; and a scrum of more or less informal political advisers. Nowhere else in the democratic world does the changeover of power from one government to the next take place so quickly. Some discreet preparations are made at official level for a possible transition; but Mrs Thatcher was always wary of taking anything for granted, so this critical central structure had to be put together over a single weekend, ready to start running the country on Monday morning.

The two key permanent officials who met her when she walked through the door were her principal private secretary, Kenneth Stowe, and the Cabinet Secretary, Sir John Hunt. Both were due to be replaced before the end of the year, but both played important roles in introducing Mrs Thatcher to her new responsibilities. Emollient and self-effacing, Stowe managed the transition from Callaghan to Mrs Thatcher with exemplary smoothness, but stayed in Number Ten for only six weeks – 'six very intensive weeks' as he recalled.[36] His replacement, Clive Whitmore, came from the Ministry of Defence. Though 'very much the machine man', in the view of one internal critic,[37] Whitmore was instinctively in sympathy with her political objectives and they quickly formed a close working relationship, which lasted for the next three years, after which she sent him back to the MoD as Permanent Secretary at the unusually young age of forty-seven.

Sir John Hunt had been Cabinet Secretary – in effect the Prime Minister's Permanent Secretary – since 1973: Mrs Thatcher was thus his fourth Prime Minister in seven years. He remembered her as Education Secretary under Heath, when it had never occurred to him that she might one day be Prime Minister.[38] Hunt's style was brisk and businesslike: as a newcomer feeling her way, Mrs Thatcher found him a bit managing. When he retired at the end of 1979 she was happy to choose as his successor the more obliging, indeed positively Jeeves-like, Robert Armstrong, a classic Eton and Christ Church–educated mandarin who had long been tipped for the top job. His only handicap was that he had been Heath's principal private secretary and was still close to his old chief. But he was the model of Civil Service impartiality and selfless professionalism; and the conservative side of Mrs Thatcher's character respected those traditional qualities so long as they were employed to serve and not obstruct her. Though far from Thatcherite by inclination, Armstrong served her, rather like Willie Whitelaw, with absolute loyalty and discretion for the next seven years.

The private office was headed by her political secretary, Richard Ryder, and the somewhat shadowy figure of David Wolfson. But Mrs Thatcher's personal support team also had a strong female component, particularly in the early years, largely because she made so little distinction between work and home. When she titled the first chapter of her memoirs 'Over the Shop' and wrote that living in Number Ten was like going back to her girlhood in Grantham, it was not just a literary flourish, but described exactly how she lived. During her working day she was always popping upstairs to the flat at the top of the building to eat or change or work on a speech before coming down again for a Cabinet committee or to meet a foreign leader: smaller meetings with colleagues and advisers were often held in the flat. Denis, if he was around, sometimes sat in on these informal meetings: late at night it was frequently he who ended them by telling Margaret firmly that it was time for bed. Because she was 'always on the job' – as she once told a delighted television audience[39] – she made no effort to protect her private space from the intrusion of work. Far more than with a male Prime Minister – who might wear the same suit all day and have his hair cut once a month – her clothes, her hair, her make-up were all essential props of her public performance, needing frequent, but very rapid, attention throughout the day. Thus her personal staff was much more mingled with her professional staff than was the case with Jim Callaghan or Ted Heath; secretaries might be pressed into cooking scratch meals at any hour of the day or night.* Though Mrs Thatcher made no secret that she enjoyed being surrounded by subservient men, and in eleven years appointed only one other woman – briefly – to her Cabinet, there was always a distinctly feminine flavour in her immediate entourage.

Lady Thatcher was justifiably proud of having created a happy family atmosphere inside Number Ten. However roughly she may have treated her colleagues and advisers, she was always immensely considerate towards her personal staff and towards all those – drivers, telephonists and the like – who kept the wheels of government turning. When her driver died suddenly in March 1980, she insisted, at the end of a very busy week, on attending the funeral in south London and comforting his widow.[41] Likewise, when Bernard

---

*Mrs Thatcher herself frequently cooked late-night meals too, often insisting on running up a quick supper (lasagne or chicken Kiev from the freezer) for aides or MPs helping with a speech. 'Don't stop her cooking,' Denis would tell them. 'It's her form of therapy.'[40]

Ingham's wife was involved in an accident in the middle of the Falklands war, she insisted that he must go and look after her: she told him firmly that she did not expect to see him back at work for several days.[42]

Finally, there is the joyfully repeated story of a lunch at Chequers when one of the service personnel waiting at table spilled a plate of hot soup in Geoffrey Howe's lap. The Prime Minister immediately leapt up, full of concern, not for her Foreign Secretary but for the girl. 'There, there,' she comforted her. 'It's the sort of thing that could happen to anyone.' The contrast between the way Mrs Thatcher fussed over her staff and the cavalier way she treated her colleagues – particularly Howe – was perfectly emblematic. With the benefit of hindsight, Ronnie Millar wondered whether she was 'altogether wise to treat Sir Geoffrey any old how'.[43]

Bernard Ingham became the Prime Minister's chief press secretary towards the end of 1979. A pugnacious former Labour supporter, he quickly transferred his loyalty to his new mistress and became one of her most devoted servants. His robust and highly personalised briefings strained Civil Service neutrality to the limit, but Mrs Thatcher trusted him absolutely and he remained at the heart of her entourage until the end.

Another key figure in her first administration was her Parliamentary Private Secretary, Ian Gow. MP for Eastbourne since February 1974, Gow was a balding, tweedy solicitor who cultivated a self-consciously old fogeyish manner, though only in his early forties. He had scarcely met Mrs Thatcher before May 1979, and was astonished to be invited to become her PPS; but he too immediately fell under her spell. 'Ian loved her,' Alan Clark wrote after Gow's murder in 1990, 'actually loved, I mean, in every sense but the physical.'[44] He escorted her everywhere, protected her in public and helped her unwind in private with late night whisky and gossip. At the same time he was the most sensitive link with the back benches that any Prime Minister ever had. 'Known affectionately as "Supergrass",' according to Ronald Millar, 'he had a knack of reporting back to the lady everything she needed to know about the gossip of the bazaars without ever betraying a confidence, a rare feat in the political world.'[45] He was also an old friend of Geoffrey Howe, which helped lubricate the key relationship at the heart of the Government, one that later turned disastrously sour. Gow played a crucial part in Mrs Thatcher's political survival in the dark days of 1981–2 when her premiership hung in the balance. She felt bound to reward him with a ministerial job in 1983; but thereafter she never found a successor with the same qualities. As a result her relationship with her backbenchers steadily deteriorated. Gow was unique and irreplaceable.

Finally there was Denis. It was the presence of the Prime Minister's husband, coming and going as he liked amid the press of government business, frantic speechwriting and impromptu meals, that gave Mrs Thatcher's Downing Street much of its special flavour. Denis had officially retired from Burmah Oil in 1975, but he still had a string of non-executive directorships as well as his drinking chums and his golfing companions. He lived his own life, as he and Margaret had always done; but he was continually in and out, and when he was there he often sat in on meetings contributing his views without restraint. On business matters where he had real expertise – for instance on British Leyland – Margaret listened seriously to what he had to say. (She once said that she did not need briefing on the oil industry because 'I sleep with the oil industry every night.')[46] On other subjects he served to keep her, and her staff, in touch with what the man in the golf-club bar was thinking.

Normally Denis would go to bed long before Margaret, leaving her working. But he was also very protective and she deferred to him. There are numerous stories of Denis breaking up late night speechwriting sessions by insisting in his inimitable way that it was time she went to bed ('Woman, bed'); or reminding her, 'Honestly, love, we're not trying to write the Old Testament.'[47] At least at a superficial level he never lost the masculine authority which a husband of his class and generation expected to assert over his wife.* His interventions often came as a relief to her hard-pressed staff. Willie Whitelaw was another who frequently found that a quiet word with Denis was the way to get through to her when all else failed.

In fact, living and working above the shop, with neither of them commuting any more, the Thatchers were closer in Downing Street than at any previous time in their marriage. They were both excellent hosts, and Denis was infinitely skilful at supporting and protecting Margaret, talking to those she could not or did not want to speak to and deflecting people who tried to monopolise her. He accompanied her on the most important of her overseas trips, and developed his role as the Prime Minister's consort with extraordinary

---

*It could work the other way, however. Ronnie Millar recalls one time when she dragged Denis away from a party, telling him, 'If you want me to poach your egg, come *now*.'[48] Right to the end, she made a point of getting back to Downing Street if she possibly could to cook his breakfast in the morning – even though she herself had only an apple and a vitamin pill.

tact and skill. He stuck firmly to his policy of never giving interviews and the press – particularly the travelling press accompanying the Prime Minister to international summits, who had ample opportunity to witness him sounding off over several stiff drinks on long flights home – respected his privacy by never quoting him. 'He was off limits, out of bounds,' Bernard Ingham wrote. 'Everybody loves him because he is straight and decent and loyal.'[49]

Lady Thatcher has always paid extravagant tribute to Denis's part in her career. In the early days his contribution was frankly more material than emotional: his money gave her the financial security to pursue her legal and political career. They lived very separate lives, which suited her admirably. But theirs was a rare marriage, which grew deeper the longer it went on: being the Prime Minister's husband gave him the best retirement job imaginable. He had no defined functions, but he played an important humanising role and was always on hand when required, helping to calm her when she was upset or buck her up when she was depressed. At the end of the day, she told the 1980 party conference, 'there is just Denis and me, and I could not do without him'.[50] Many of her closest advisers felt that the one thing that might have induced her to resign before 1990 would have been Denis becoming seriously ill.

The Prime Minister and Whitehall

Mrs Thatcher hit Whitehall, in Peter Hennessy's words, 'with the force of a tornado'.[51] While many officials had welcomed the prospect of a dynamic government which knew its own mind, and enjoyed a secure parliamentary majority, after years of drift and hand-to-mouth expediency under Labour, they were not prepared for the degree of positive hostility which the new Prime Minister exuded, and encouraged her ministers to express, towards the Civil Service as an institution. Both from her personal experience of the Department of Education and the Ministry of Pensions, and as a matter of political principle, she came into office convinced that the Civil Service bore much of the blame for Britain's decline over the past thirty-five years: that civil servants as a breed, with some individual exceptions, were not the solution to the nation's ills but a large part of the problem. She considered the public service essentially parasitic, a drag upon national enterprise and wealth creation: too large, too bureaucratic, self-serving, self-satisfied and self-protective, corporatist by instinct, simultaneously complacent and defeatist. She was determined to cut the bureaucracy down to size, both metaphorically and literally. Word quickly spread through Whitehall that Mrs Thatcher's purpose was to 'deprivilege' the Civil Service.

First, the Civil Service was the softest target for the new government's promised economies in public spending. An immediate freeze was placed on new recruitment and pay levels were held down. The resentment that resulted led to an unprecedented strike which in 1981 closed down regional offices, delayed the collection of tax revenues and altogether cost the Government around £500 million before it was settled. All those directly involved would have liked to compromise earlier; but Mrs Thatcher was determined to make a demonstration of the Government's resolve to control public spending and believed that cutting its own pay bill was the best possible place to start.

Second, she set up an Efficiency Unit in Number Ten, headed by Sir Derek Rayner, to scrutinise the working of every department, looking for economies. By the end of 1982 'Rayner's Raiders', as they were known, had carried out 130 of these departmental scrutinies, saving £170 million a year and 'losing' 16,000 jobs. In the first four years of the Thatcher Government Civil Service numbers were cut by 14 per cent; over the following six years, as the privatisation of nationalised industries removed whole areas of economic activity and administration from the public sector, that figure climbed to 23 per cent, while salaries relative to the private sector fell still further.[52] At the same time the core function of the service was shifted inexorably from policy advice to management: the efficient implementation of policy and the delivery of services. Senior officials who preferred writing elegantly argued memos increasingly found their time taken up by targets, performance indicators and all the other paraphernalia of modern business methods.

The new Prime Minister imposed her will not by structural reform or sacking people but by sheer force of personality: by showing the Whitehall village who was boss. One way of doing this was by constant requests for figures or information at short notice: even quite junior officials felt the presence of the Prime Minister continually prodding and pressing their minister for results, never letting an issue go but demanding 'follow-through'.[53] Another way was by personally visiting every department in turn, something no previous Prime Minister had ever done, confronting civil servants on their own territory, questioning their attitudes and challenging their assumptions. This alarming innovation dramatically signalled Mrs Thatcher's determination to make her presence felt; at the same time it reflected her awareness of her inexperience of departments other than the Department of Education and Science (DES) and her genuine desire to learn. In fact these visits had two distinct aspects. On the one hand she was marvellous – as she had been at the DES – at going round talking to the junior staff, taking an interest in their work, thanking and encouraging them: something which most ministers do far too little beyond the immediate circle of their private office. Her encounters with their superiors, on the other hand, were often bruising: she lectured more than she listened, and the exercise tended to confirm rather than modify her preconceptions.

Over the next decade it was often alleged that she 'politicised' Whitehall by appointing only committed Thatcherites to senior positions. But she was not so crude as that. Mrs Thatcher certainly took a close interest in appointments and intervened more directly than previous Prime Ministers in filling vacancies, not just at Permanent Secretary level but further down the official ladder. She undoubtedly advanced the careers of her favourites, sometimes those who had caught her eye with a single well-judged briefing; conversely she sidetracked or held back those who failed to impress her. Thus the longer she stayed in office, the more she was able to mould the Civil Service to her liking. By 1986 the entire upper echelons of Whitehall were filled by her appointees.

There was nothing wrong in principle with this approach: quite the contrary. It was natural for a radical Prime Minister to want activist officials who would help, not hinder or obstruct. Most of the more unconventional choices Mrs Thatcher made were excellent appointments, fully merited. But questions did arise about her judgement, particularly lower down the scale: her instant estimates of people were not always accurate or fair. Officials often felt that she made up her mind about individuals on first impression and then never changed it. She did not always appreciate that it was sometimes the civil servant's job to raise objections. In her memoirs Lady Thatcher boasted: 'I was never accused of thinking like a civil servant. They had to think like me.'[54] But equally it was not the official's job to think like a politician. It was only in this sense, however, that she could be accused of 'politicising' the service. Even after ten years, Peter Hennessy wrote, 'the Prime Minister . . . would . . . find it hard to muster a true believer from the top three grades of the Civil Service'.[55] Really what she did over the next eleven years was to personalise it. Nevertheless there is no doubt that the effect was seriously to demoralise it.

11

Signals of Intent

The economy

THE new Parliament met on Wednesday 9 May to re-elect the Speaker. But the House did not meet again for serious business until the State Opening the following Tuesday, with the formal unveiling of the Government's legislative programme in the Queen's Speech. It comprised a curiously modest assortment of Bills, since the radical thrust of the Government's agenda was not primarily legislative. There was – there had to be, after the events of the previous winter – a measure of trade-union reform. There was legislation to oblige local authorities to sell council houses and slow the advance of comprehensive schools. In addition the Government announced tighter immigration controls, the deregulation of inter-city coach services and the establishment of a second commercial television channel.

As usual, however, Mrs Thatcher's language implied a good deal more than the Gracious Speech promised. Contradicting Callaghan, who complacently predicted that the period of Tory rule would be 'a brief interruption' before Labour resumed its forward march, and the Liberal leader David Steel, who reminded her that she had won the lowest share of the poll of any post-war Conservative Government, Mrs Thatcher hailed her victory as 'a watershed election' which marked a decisive rejection of 'the all-powerful corporatist state'. In its place she promised to restore incentives and individual choice, particularly in housing, health and education. Where once she had been sceptical about selling council houses, she now saw the right to buy as one of those things 'so fundamental that they must apply to all citizens regardless of the local authority area in which they live'. The Government was taking power to force reluctant Labour authorities to sell their housing stock because 'we believe that the right to buy council houses should belong to everyone'. She also warned that 'there is no such thing as a free service in the Health Service'.

Significantly, she dealt with the trade-union question under the heading of law and order. Yet she was careful – as she had been during the election – not to be provocative. She still went out of her way to stress that 'a strong and responsible trade union movement must play a large part in our economic recovery.'[1] Perhaps fearing that she had been too conciliatory, however, she emphasised her personal commitment to action on union reform. 'I am not known for my purposes or policies being unclear,' she assured a backbench questioner. 'I believe that my policies on this are known.' She believed that they were 'overwhelmingly supported by the vast majority of people in this country, who believe that a law must be introduced to deal with certain aspects of the closed shop, picketing and the postal ballot'.[2] To the disappointment of the Tory right, however, Jim Prior's Employment Bill, when it was eventually published at the end of the year, turned out to be a very cautious measure. While she hinted at her sympathy for the hardliners behind Prior's back, Mrs Thatcher had no wish to plunge into battle with the unions before she was ready. All the Government's initial energy was concentrated on setting a new course for the economy. Howe's first budget was fixed for the earliest possible date, 12 June, just five weeks after the election.

The first objective was quite clear. The Prime Minister and her inner group of economic ministers were determined to mount an immediate assault on public spending. But this was a goal easier to proclaim in opposition than to realise in government. On taking office, ministers found their room for major economies seriously constrained – partly by inescapable external factors, but also by their own political choices. On the one hand the value of sterling, already high due to the recent tripling of the price of oil (since sterling was now a petrocurrency), was boosted further by the weakness of the dollar and the markets' satisfaction at the Government's election. The high pound sharply increased the cost of British exports, creating unemployment, which swelled the social security budget while reducing revenue. But at the same time ministers had tied their own hands by commitments they had made during the election.

In opposition the Iron Lady had lived up to her reputation by supporting NATO's request for an extra 3 per cent annual spending on defence. Once in office, Howe tried to row back from this pledge, but Mrs Thatcher was immovable: in her book, strong defence took precedence over everything else, even cutting public spending. Likewise she had promised substantial pay rises to the armed forces and the police; and the Tory manifesto also committed the new Government to increase old-age pensions. Finally Patrick Jenkin as Shadow Health Secretary had bounced Howe into promising that spending on the NHS would be protected for at least three years. All these undertakings left very little scope for the sort of big savings the Prime Minister and Chancellor were looking for. As Mrs Thatcher wrote in her memoirs: 'We seemed to be boxed in.'[3]

In fact, Howe squeezed £1.5 billion from a variety of soft targets. Civil Service recruitment was frozen and tough limits imposed on local government spending. Prescription charges were raised for the first time in eight years, foreshadowing virtually annual increases for the next decade. Cuts were announced in the provision of school meals and rural school transport. Most significantly, though the basic old-age pension was increased in the short term, the long-term link between pensions and average earnings was broken – a major saving in the future. Another projected £1 billion was saved by imposing cash limits on departmental budgets; and a further billion by selling shares in public-sector assets, following the lead already set by Labour and condemned by the Conservatives in opposition. This saving of £3.5 billion announced in the June budget was quickly followed by a further £680 million package in October, made up of more Civil Service cuts and steep rises in gas and electricity prices.

These economies were designed to make room for dramatic tax cuts. In the end Howe was able to cut the standard rate of income tax by three pence in the pound, from 33 to 30 per cent, and reduce the top rate from Labour's penal 83 per cent to a more moderate 60 per cent. This was a bold early signal of the new Government's intentions. But it was made possible only by virtually doubling Value Added Tax (VAT). It had always been part of the Tories' strategy to switch a greater proportion of the burden from direct to indirect taxation. But during the election Howe specifically denied that he planned to double VAT. In the event he could not finance the income-tax cuts he was determined on in any other way. Mrs Thatcher was very worried by the drastic impact that such a steep hike would have on prices. With inflation already rising, she had reason to be worried: however long planned, it was the worst possible moment for such a switch. In his memoirs Howe wryly noted 'the ambivalence which Margaret often showed when the time came to move from the level of high principle and evangelism to practical politics'.[4] Nigel Lawson wrote more bluntly that she was 'fearful' of the political fallout, 'but Geoffrey persuaded her that if we did not grasp this nettle in the first budget it would never be grasped at all'.[5] For her part Lady Thatcher acknowledged that 'Geoffrey stuck to his guns' and overcame her doubts.[6] But this – the first really unpopular decision the Government had to take, within three weeks of taking office – was not the last time that a cautious Prime Minister had to be hauled over the hurdle by her more resolute colleagues.

Another instance was the abolition of exchange controls. This was arguably the single most important step the Thatcher Government took to give practical effect to its belief in free markets: by doing away with the restrictions on the movement of capital which had been in place since 1939, the Government dared to expose the British economy to the judgement of the global market. It was an act of faith which might have resulted in a catastrophic run on sterling. In the event it had the opposite effect: the markets were impressed by the new Government's show of confidence and the pound, already strong, dipped only momentarily and then went on rising. Howe later wrote that the abolition of controls was 'the only economic decision of my life that ever caused me to lose a night's sleep. But it was right.'[7]

In the long run it undoubtedly was; and it was brave to take the decision in the first few months in office. But in the short run it played havoc with the Government's monetary policy. Controlling the money supply was supposed to be the linchpin of the Government's new monetarist approach. The trouble was that Labour had already been controlling it very effectively before the election. Denis Healey and the Permanent Secretary of the Treasury, Douglas Wass, were not ideological monetarists like Joseph, Howe and Lawson, who had embraced monetarism with quasi-religious certainty: they were 'reluctant monetarists' who had pragmatically concluded – at the prompting of the International Monetary Fund (IMF) – that tight monetary targets were a necessary part of economic policy. But in practice monetary policy did not change in May 1979 so dramatically as either Labour or the Government liked to pretend. When Healey denounced Tory policies it sometimes suited Mrs Thatcher to remind the House that 'the previous Labour Chancellor was more of a monetarist than he now cares to admit'.[8]

Howe's first budget was a bold statement of intent, taking a huge gamble on early tax cuts at the risk of inflation. It was taken for granted that, though the Chancellor held up the dispatch box outside Number Eleven, the political will had come from Number Ten. 'Either she succeeds,' the *Daily Mirror* commented, 'or we go bust.'[9]

Mrs Thatcher was widely reported to have insisted on a bigger tax cut than the expenditure savings warranted and on a steeper rise in VAT than her Chancellor had wanted. The reality was in fact quite the opposite.

The impact of Howe's June budget was as damaging as its critics predicted. The virtual doubling of VAT and the cutting of subsidy to the nationalised industries, along with the ending of pay and dividend controls and John Nott's swift abolition of the Price Commission, added 6 per cent to the Retail Price Index almost overnight, leading inevitably to large compensating pay claims, while the income-tax cuts boosted consumption and further fuelled inflation that way. For a Government that had come into office proclaiming the conquest of inflation as its first priority, this was a perverse beginning. Inflation actually doubled from 10.3 to 21.9 per cent in the first year. As industry laid off workers under the impact of the high pound, benefit payments had to keep pace with inflation, while Government revenue fell.

Set against these rising commitments, Howe's two packages of spending cuts were insufficient to dent the inexorable rise in Government borrowing. The Government's only other means of curbing the growth of money was raising interest rates. Howe had already raised the minimum lending rate (MLR) from 12 to 14 per cent in June. He warned that it would not fall until the money supply and public-sector borrowing were under control; but this only caused more money to flow into London. Instead of falling, £M3 – which measures the amount of money in circulation, including bank deposits – actually rose by 14 per cent in four months between June and October. In November Howe was obliged to hike the lending rate another three points to 17 per cent – an unprecedented rise to an unprecedented level. Thinking more of the effect on mortgages than of the cost to industry, Mrs Thatcher hated having to do this. 'It bothered me enormously,' she told Patricia Murray. 'It really was devastating.'[10] But monetarism prescribed no other remedy, so she bit the bullet. 'We would not print money,' she insisted at Prime Minister's Questions; therefore 'it was necessary to raise interest rates to conquer inflation'.[11] Thus the Government got the worst of both worlds: its first actions were simultaneously too much and too little, painful enough to raise howls of fury from industry, unions, home-owners, educationists and others, yet ineffective in cutting spending and positively counterproductive with regard to inflation. Mrs Thatcher and her economic team had come into office with a doctrinaire prescription which they proceeded to apply, undeterred by the most unfavourable economic circumstances. After a few months of rising unemployment, rising inflation and record interest rates, the Government's monetarist experiment was already widely dismissed as a dogmatic folly.

This, however, was where the composition of the Cabinet prevented any loss of purpose. The central quintet of Mrs Thatcher, Howe, Joseph, Nott and Biffen was firmly in control of economic policy. Sceptics like Prior, Ian Gilmour, Peter Walker and Michael Heseltine first learned of the abolition of exchange controls when they read it in the newspapers.[12] While individual ministers fought more or less successfully to defend their own budgets, it was too soon for any concerted rebellion. The most unflinching doctrinaire was Geoffrey Howe. It is clear from the memoirs of both Howe and Lawson, and the recollections of Nott and Biffen, that if any one of the central directorate faltered in the early days it was the Prime Minister herself. Not that her sense of purpose faltered. Relentlessly every Tuesday and Thursday in the House of Commons and in radio and television interviews she reiterated the simple message that the country must learn to live within its means, that public expenditure must be cut to a level the wealth-producing taxpayer could support, that the Government must tax and spend less of the national income.[13] Publicly she never weakened; but she was always vividly conscious of the political risks. It was the Chancellor, intellectually stiffened by Lawson, who stubbornly put his head down and got on with what he was determined must be done. The Prime Minister's function, quite properly, was to be the last to be persuaded that each course of action – doubling VAT, abolishing exchange controls, scrapping the Price Commission or raising interest rates – was both necessary and politically practicable. In her memoirs, despite their later differences, she paid due tribute to Howe's tenacity: 'In my view these were his best political years.'[14] In truth she could not have done without him. Though their relationship deteriorated later, for these first two or three years of the Thatcher Government they made a formidable combination, perhaps the most successful Prime Minister–Chancellor partnership of the twentieth century.

First steps in foreign policy

It was really after Howe moved to the Foreign Office in June 1983 that their relationship deteriorated. By that time – after the Falklands war and with the assurance of a second term in front of her – Mrs Thatcher's self-confidence in foreign affairs had grown and she was ready to be her own Foreign Secretary. In 1979, by contrast, she was conscious of her relative lack of experience and was content to leave foreign policy largely to Lord Carrington. This was a surprising abdication, since one of her prime ambitions was to restore Britain's 'greatness' in the eyes of the world. Like Churchill she had a clear view of Britain's place as America's foremost ally in the global battle against Communism, and she regarded the Foreign Office as a nest of appeasers. For her first sixteen years after entering Parliament in 1959 her energies had been almost exclusively diverted to domestic responsibilities: pensions, energy, transport and education. On becoming Leader of the Opposition in 1975, however, she had quickly made up this deficit, marking her arrival on the world stage by launching a series of uncompromising verbal assaults on the Soviet Union. For four years she had avoided appointing a shadow Foreign Secretary with the authority to make the portfolio his own, but travelled tirelessly in parliamentary recesses to educate herself and meet the leaders she hoped to have to deal with in office.

Once elected, however, she recognised that she could not do everything. Her priority was the economy. Moreover, she believed that restoring British influence abroad depended essentially on restoring the economy at home. 'A nation in debt,' she told the House soon after becoming party leader, 'has no self-respect and precious little influence.'[15] For all these reasons she told her aides that she did not intend to waste her time on 'all this international stuff'.[16] In appointing Peter Carrington as her first Foreign Secretary, with Ian Gilmour his deputy in the Commons, she made a tacit concordat to leave the detail of foreign policy to them, while Carrington in return suppressed his doubts about her economic policy.

In fact, she soon found that there was a crowded calendar of international meetings which she was bound to attend: European councils, G7 summits (attended by the leaders of the seven leading industrial nations) and Commonwealth conferences. That first summer there was one of each, respectively in Strasbourg, Tokyo and Lusaka. She confessed to Patricia Murray in 1980 that she had been 'surprised at the amount of time we actually have to spend on foreign affairs. The amount of summitry we have now is terrific.'[17] At first she was nervous – though she was careful not to show it. Conscious of her inexperience, she felt patronised by senior European leaders like the West German Chancellor Helmut Schmidt and the French President Valéry Giscard d'Estaing, who treated her with patrician disdain which stopped barely short of outright rudeness. She did her homework more anxiously than ever, only to find that they were much less well briefed than she was. Her self-confidence visibly increased as she discovered that with the Rolls-Royce machine of the despised Foreign Office behind her, she was more than a match for any of them.[18]

By chance one of her first meetings was with the Soviet leadership. The Soviet Union was one major country she had not visited in opposition, preferring to denounce the Communist menace from the safety of Kensington Town Hall. But on her way to the Tokyo summit at the end of June her plane made a refuelling stop in Moscow. To her surprise Prime Minister Kosygin, with half the Politburo, came out for an unscheduled dinner in the airport lounge. They were reported to be 'very curious' to meet the famous 'Iron Lady' who wore their intended insult as a badge of pride. 'They were absolutely mesmerised by her,' Lord Carrington recalled, 'because . . . she was very direct with them.'[19] She questioned them specifically on the plight of the Vietnamese 'boat people' – refugees from Communist persecution who had taken to the sea in a perilous effort to reach Hong Kong – and was unimpressed by their answers. This brief stopover confirmed her contempt for the moral and intellectual bankruptcy of the Soviet system, without in the least diminishing her perception of the challenge it posed to the West.

Nevertheless, as Carrington recalled, 'distrust of the FO . . . was never far from the surface, and could erupt in impatient hostility unless ably countered'.[20] Ably countered it usually was: this was Carrington's great skill. Certainly they had their rows. But better than anyone else in her first Cabinet he knew how to handle the Prime Minister. For all her belief in meritocracy, Mrs Thatcher had a curious weakness for a genuine toff; and the sixth Baron Carrington was the real thing. Though a close colleague of Ted Heath who personified many of the attitudes of the Establishment she most despised, Carrington's hereditary peerage gave him a special immunity: unlike the other Heathites in the Cabinet he posed no threat to her leadership. At the nadir of her popularity in 1981 there was actually a flurry of speculation that he might renounce his peerage to challenge her; but Carrington firmly quashed the idea.[21] He was delighted to get the Foreign Office and had no greater ambition. Moreover, he was effortlessly charming, undeferential and irreverent: he made her laugh. Sometimes when she was inclined to lecture visiting foreign leaders without drawing breath, he would pass her a note saying, 'He's come 500 miles, let him say something.' Once, with the Chinese leader, Chairman Hua, the situation was reversed: it was Mrs Thatcher who could not get a word in as Hua talked non-stop for fifty minutes. So Carrington passed her a note saying, 'You are speaking too much, as usual.' 'Luckily,' he recalled, 'she had a handkerchief – she held it in front of her face and didn't laugh too much.'[22] The episode became part of Foreign Office mythology; but none of her subsequent Foreign Secretaries would have dared to tease her in this way.

Whatever her general intentions, there was one central area of foreign policy where Mrs Thatcher was always going to take the lead. She came into office determined to restore Britain's credentials as America's most reliable ally in the war against Soviet expansionism. That central ideological struggle was the global reflection of her mission to turn back socialism at home. Although in practice she was quickly drawn into two major foreign-policy questions in other spheres – the acrimonious quarrel over Britain's contribution to the European Community budget and the long-running saga of Rhodesia – these were to her mind subordinate sideshows to the over-arching imperative of the Cold War. Accordingly she was keen to visit Washington as soon as possible to forge a special relationship with President Jimmy Carter.

Mrs Thatcher's premiership overlapped so closely with the presidency of her Republican soulmate Ronald Reagan that it is easily forgotten that Reagan was not elected President until November 1980. For her first twenty months in Downing Street Mrs Thatcher had to deal with his very different Democratic predecessor. She had first met Jimmy Carter when visiting Washington in 1977 and again at the G7 summit in Tokyo in June, when Carter was not altogether impressed. 'A tough lady', he wrote in his diary, 'highly opinionated, strong willed, cannot admit that she doesn't know something.'[23] After this encounter the State Department put Mrs Thatcher off until December. Before she left Carrington privately 'doubted whether Mrs Thatcher would become great buddies with President Carter'.[24] In fact, they got on better than he expected. As she later wrote, 'it was impossible not to like Jimmy Carter'. He was a more serious man than his rather folksy manner suggested – 'a deeply committed Christian and a man of obvious sincerity', with a scientific background like her own. Though in retrospect she was scathing about his 'poor handle on economics' and what she saw as weakness in the face of Soviet expansionism, he was the leader of the free world and she was determined to get on with him.[25]

She arrived in Washington six weeks after the seizure of fifty American diplomats in Teheran. It was a measure of her early uncertainty that she initially intended to say nothing about the prolonged hostage crisis, feeling that to do so would be to intrude on a private

American agony. Carrington and Frank Cooper (Permanent Secretary at the Ministry of Defence) had to tell her that the Americans were interested in nothing else at that moment: she must give them unequivocal support. She agreed only reluctantly ('Margaret, you have got to say yes. You have got to,' Carrington urged her). But then, once persuaded, she came out with a 'clarion call' on the White House lawn which instantly confirmed the impact she had made on her first visit to Washington as leader in 1975:

> At times like these you are entitled to look to your friends for support. We are your friends, we do support you. And we shall support you. Let there be no doubt about that.[26]

'The effect was like a trumpet blast of cheer to a government and people badly in need of reassurance from their allies,' the British Ambassador, Sir Nicholas Henderson, recorded.[27] The rest of her visit was a triumph. On Henderson's advice she was carefully non-polemical in her conversations with Carter; but then, addressing Congress, she threw off all restraint and wowed her audience with a ten-minute 'harangue' on the virtues of the free market and the evil of Communism, followed by questions which she handled with an informality and relish the like of which Washington had never seen before from a visiting leader. More than one Congressman invited her to accept the Republican nomination for President. She went on the next day to address an audience of 2,000 at the Foreign Policy Association in New York, where the directness of her message again made a tremendous hit. The Russians, she boasted, had called her the Iron Lady: 'They're quite right – I am.'[28] In that moment – a year before Reagan entered the White House – Margaret Thatcher became a heroine to the American right.

Ten days later the Soviet Union invaded Afghanistan. In her memoirs Lady Thatcher described this action as 'one of those genuine watersheds which are so often predicted, which so rarely occur'. She immediately saw the invasion as bearing out her warnings of worldwide Soviet expansionism, part of a pattern with Cuban and East German intervention in Angola and Namibia, all taking advantage of the West's gullible belief in *détente*. She was determined that the Russians must be 'punished for their aggression and taught, albeit belatedly, that the West would not only talk about freedom but was prepared to make sacrifices to defend it'.[29] On this occasion Carter needed no prompting. When he rang her at Chequers three days after Christmas he likened the Soviet action to their invasion of Czechoslovakia in 1968. 'In effect Moscow had changed a buffer nation into a puppet nation under Soviet direction,' he told her. 'This would have profound strategic consequences for the stability of the entire region . . . He did not think we could let the Soviets get away with this intervention with impunity.' Mrs Thatcher agreed, 'and observed that when something like this occurred it was important to act right at the beginning'.[30] She quickly pledged British support for economic and cultural sanctions to punish the invader. In particular they agreed that the best way to hurt the Russians would be a Western boycott of the forthcoming Moscow Olympics. To her fury, however, she found that this was something she could not deliver. While the United States Olympic Committee did stay away from Moscow the following summer, most British athletes declined to give up their medal hopes at the behest of the Prime Minister.

More seriously she discovered that her call for a resolute response to the Soviet action was not supported by the rest of Europe. The invasion of Afghanistan sharply highlighted the gulf between American and European perceptions of the Cold War. The Europeans, particularly the Germans, had always gained more tangible benefits from *détente*, in the form of trade and cross-border cooperation, than the Americans and British, and were anxious not to jeopardise them. They were disinclined to view the Soviet action as part of a strategy of world domination, but rather as an understandable response to Iranian-type Islamic fundamentalism on their southern border. Mrs Thatcher's instincts were strongly with the Americans; but to Washington's disappointment she proved unable to deliver concerted European backing for significant sanctions.

'The Bloody British Question'

If Mrs Thatcher could not bring her European partners with her on Afghanistan, this was partly because she had already antagonised them over Britain's contribution to the Community budget. This was a matter she could not possibly leave to the Foreign Office, combining as it did her two favourite themes of patriotism and good housekeeping. It was exactly the sort of issue on which she thought the Foreign Office liable to give up vital British interests for the sake of being good Europeans. It offered a wonderful early opportunity to be seen battling for Britain on the international stage, cheered on by the tabloid press, on a simple issue that every voter could understand. At a time when the economy was already proving intractable, Europe offered a much more popular cause in which to display her determination not to compromise, and she seized it with relish. It took five years before she finally achieved a satisfactory settlement. The long battle helped set the style of her premiership. It also got her relationship with the European Community off to a bad start from which it never recovered.

There is no dispute that there was a genuine problem, left over from the original terms of Britain's entry to the Community negotiated by Ted Heath in 1971 and not resolved by Callaghan's essentially cosmetic renegotiation in 1974–5. The fundamental imbalance derived from the fact that Britain continued to import more than other members from outside the Community, so paying more in import levies, while having a much smaller farming sector, and consequently gaining much less benefit from the Common Agricultural Policy (CAP). Over the past decade Britain's growth had fallen behind that of other countries, so the budget contribution fixed in 1971 had become disproportionately high. By 1980 Britain was paying about £1,000 million a year more into the Community than she was getting out.

The existence of an imbalance was recognised in Brussels. Callaghan and his Foreign Secretary, David Owen, had been making efforts to correct it; but Labour was handicapped by its history of hostility to the Community. The election of a Conservative Government with a more positive attitude to Europe was expected to make agreement easier. Callaghan exaggerated when he told the House of Commons: 'We took the shine off the ball, and it is now for her to hit the runs.'[31] But with goodwill it should not have been difficult, by the normal processes of Community bargaining, to achieve an equitable adjustment without a bruising confrontation. The Foreign Office would have considered a rebate of about two-thirds both satisfactory and achievable.[32] It was the heads of government on both sides of the Channel – Mrs Thatcher on one side, but equally Schmidt and Giscard on the other – who played to their domestic galleries and elevated the issue into a trial of political strength.

By chance the first overseas leader to visit London the week after the British election was Helmut Schmidt. Their talks in Downing Street actually went quite well. Though he was supposed to be a socialist, Mrs Thatcher approved of his sound economic views, while Schmidt in turn told the Bundestag (a touch patronisingly) that he was impressed by her 'knowledge, authority and responsibility'.[33] But she left the German Chancellor in no doubt that she regarded Britain's present budget contribution as unacceptable and intended to seek a rebate. That was quite right and proper;

but she soon struck a discordant note by talking truculently about getting 'our' money back, as though the Community had stolen it, and declaring that she was not going to be 'a soft touch', as though her European partners were a bunch of con men.[34] This sort of talk went down badly in Paris, Bonn and Brussels, because it showed a fundamental failure to understand how the Community worked.

First of all, the Community did not recognise the concept of 'her' money; funds contributed by each member country belonged to the Community, to be expended by the Commission for the benefit of the Community as a whole. The idea of each member keeping a profit-and-loss account was strictly *non-communautaire*. Within this broad principle there was certainly a case that Britain was paying more than her fair share; but if Mrs Thatcher was going to be legalistic about it, her partners could argue that Britain had signed up in 1972 and could not now rewrite the contract because it had turned out to be disadvantageous. They were particularly unsympathetic since Britain's economic position had now been transformed by North Sea oil, a benefit which no other member enjoyed. Moreover, in the wider context of European trade, the sums involved were really very small.

Second, Mrs Thatcher exasperated her partners – and not least the President of the Commission, Roy Jenkins, whose job it was to broker a deal – by insisting that Britain's demand for a budget rebate should be treated as an issue entirely on its own, not settled as part of a wider package, as was the Community's normal way. Schmidt and several of the other leaders were willing to help Britain, but they expected Mrs Thatcher in turn to be flexible and constructive in other difficult areas like lamb, fish, oil and the European Monetary System. This she adamantly refused. 'We simply cannot do so,' she told the Commons in March 1980.[35] In opposition just twelve months earlier she had repeatedly condemned Labour's counterproductive obstructiveness towards Europe.[36] But now she wanted Britain's grievance settled before she would allow progress on anything else.

The other leaders first realised what they were up against at the European Council at Strasbourg on 21–2 June, where Mrs Thatcher began by trying to get the budget issue placed first on the agenda, which naturally irritated Giscard. When they eventually reached it, Jenkins wrote in his diary, she 'immediately became shrill' and picked an unnecessary quarrel with Schmidt, 'which was silly because he was absolutely crucial to her getting the result that she wanted'.[37] She herself was well pleased with her performance. 'I felt that I had made an impression as someone who meant business.' She was delighted to overhear 'a foreign government official' comment that 'Britain is back' – 'a stray remark that pleased me as much as anything I can remember'.[38]

She deliberately set out to be difficult. But Giscard and Schmidt, the experienced European statesmen, both in office since 1974, should have handled her better. After five years of Wilson and Callaghan, they had every reason to welcome the return of a British Government unambiguously committed to Europe. Giscard particularly welcomed British support for the French nuclear *force de frappe*. They should have set out to disarm her. Instead, at the purely personal level, Giscard as the host at Strasbourg went out of his way to snub her, first by failing to seat her next to himself at either lunch or dinner, and then by insisting on being served first – asserting his precedence as head of state over the normal courtesy due to her sex.[39] French gallantry alone might have dictated an effort to make a fuss of her. She was susceptible to Gallic charm, as François Mitterrand later proved. Instead she thought Giscard's behaviour, with reason, 'petulant, vain and rather ill-mannered'.[40] When the French President came back to dinner in Downing Street later that year she got her own back by deliberately seating him opposite full-length portraits of Nelson and Wellington.[41] More seriously, the two European leaders (and Giscard in particular) seem to have decided that the way to deal with the British Prime Minister was to put her down.

They misjudged their woman. Once she had defined the issue as a trial of her strength, she would not – could not – back down. Carrington, caught uncomfortably in the crossfire, thought the Europeans' handling of her was 'pretty stupid . . . enormously shortsighted and selfish'.[42] They would have done much better to have taken her aside right at the outset, before Strasbourg, and offered her a generous out-of-court settlement before the political stakes were raised too high. As it was, Mrs Thatcher spent the interval between Strasbourg and the next European Council at Dublin in November working herself into a position of determined intransigence. In Luxembourg in October to deliver a Winston Churchill memorial lecture, she declared truculently: 'I cannot play Sister Bountiful to the Community while my own electorate are being asked to forgo improvements in the field of health, education, welfare and the rest.'[43] In the House of Commons, pressed both by Labour and by anti-Market Tories, she talked up what she hoped to achieve at Dublin. What she wanted was 'a broad balance between what we put in and what we get out'.[44]

In fact she was offered a refund of just £350 million for the current year. Instead of taking it as a starting point for bargaining, she rejected it with contempt as 'a third of a loaf'. Roy Jenkins had a ringside view of what followed. 'She kept us all round the dinner table for four interminable hours,' he wrote in his diary,[45] 'for the greater part of which,' he later recalled, she talked without pause, but not without repetition.[46] 'It was obvious to everyone except her that she wasn't making progress and was alienating people.'

What infuriated her was that no one bothered to argue with her. Giscard ostentatiously read a newspaper, while Schmidt pretended to go to sleep. This was perhaps inexcusable, though they for their part felt provoked by her aggressive insensitivity. But it was not only the big players that she antagonised. For good measure she gratuitously 'upbraided . . . the little countries for their pusillanimous attitude' to nuclear weapons.[47] There was only one flash of light relief. In the middle of a tirade about 'my oil' and 'my fish', she exclaimed 'My God', at which someone audibly interjected, 'Oh, not that too!'[48]

The next morning she continued 'banging away' at the same points, still getting nowhere, before Jenkins and Carrington took her aside and persuaded her to agree to a postponement on the basis – 'the words coming out of her with almost physical difficulty' – 'that she would approach the next meeting at Luxembourg in April in a spirit of genuine compromise'.[49]

Back in the Commons she was constantly under pressure from both Labour and Tory anti-Europeans to leave the Community altogether. But that was an option she refused to countenance. She certainly felt no emotional or visionary commitment to the idea of Europe; and the more she saw of its institutions in practice, the less respect she felt for them. She regarded it as an organisation founded upon compromise and horse-trading, which she despised. Nevertheless she still accepted without question, as she had done since Macmillan's first application in 1961, that Britain's place was in the Community. When pressed, however, she always tended to justify membership in the context of her overriding preoccupation with defence. In his first conversation with her after the election Roy Jenkins was disconcerted to find her 'thinking always a little too much in terms of the EEC and NATO as two bodies which ought to be amalgamated'.[50] Nine months later she was happy to agree with a friendly questioner in the Commons that 'Europe needs to be united, and to stay united as a free Europe against the unfree part of Europe which is bound by bonds of steel around the Soviet Union'.[51] The Cold War set the framework of her thinking.

On this basis she started out moderately pro-European. In her speech to the Tory Party Conference just before Dublin she promised to fight Britain's corner as a committed member of the Community, asserting that it was 'no good joining anything half-heartedly'.[52] She was happy to acknowledge that there were lessons Britain could profitably learn from Europe: 'If we want a German and French standard of living we must have a German and French standard of work.'[53] Or again: 'There are many Continental practices that one would like to assume in this country, including the Continentals' tendency not to spend money that they have not got.'[54] But the budget dispute quickly brought out her instinctive underlying hostility to Europe and an unpleasant streak of contempt for the Europeans. 'They are all a rotten lot,' she told Roy Jenkins just before Dublin, couching her scorn as usual in terms of defence. 'Schmidt and the Americans and we are the only ones who would do any standing up and fighting if necessary.'[55] Her belief in the essential superiority of the British was founded on two ideas. First, her memory of the war, when most of continental Europe had been overrun and occupied and had to be liberated by Britain (and the Americans). 'We,' she once exclaimed, 'who either defeated or rescued half Europe, who kept half Europe free when otherwise it would have been in chains . . .'[56] The idea that the Europeans were not permanently grateful to Britain – as she was to the Americans – never ceased to offend her. Second, she contrived to believe that the sense of justice was an essentially British (or, more specifically, English) characteristic which foreigners did not understand. 'There's not a strand of equity or fairness in Europe,' she declared in her television memoirs. 'They're out to get as much as they can, that's one of those enormous differences.'[57]

The next European Council met in Luxembourg in April 1980. This time Britain was offered a rebate of £700 million a year, roughly two-thirds of the disputed loaf, which Jenkins regarded as 'a very favourable offer'. 'To almost universal amazement', however, Mrs Thatcher again rejected it.[58] She was 'much quieter, less strident, less abrasive than at Dublin', but still adamant. When Jenkins told her she was making a great mistake, 'she good-humouredly but firmly said "Don't try persuading me, you know I find persuasion very counterproductive."'[59] The French Commissioner, Claude Cheysson, sensed that Mrs Thatcher positively relished her isolation. 'Not only didn't she mind about it,' he recalled, 'but she was pleased with that. She was very anxious that Britain would be Britain, and Britain needed no ally. Britain could stand on its own.'[60] Long before the Falklands she was already striking Churchillian poses.

Faced with another impasse at heads of government level, the Commission now dressed up 'approximately the same deal in somewhat different form' – still only a two-thirds refund but extended for the next three years – to present to the council of foreign ministers the next month in Brussels. On their own responsibility Carrington and Gilmour accepted this, and thought they had done well. Carrington, in Jenkins' view, 'showed himself a more skilful and sensible negotiator than his head of government. He knew when to settle. She did not.'[61] The Foreign Secretary and his deputy then flew back to Britain and drove straight to Chequers, feeling pleased with themselves. But if they expected congratulation they were swiftly disillusioned. 'My immediate reaction,' Lady Thatcher wrote in her memoirs, 'was far from favourable.'[62] 'Had we been bailiffs arriving to take possession of the furniture,' Gilmour wrote, 'we would probably have been more cordially received. The Prime Minister was like a firework whose fuse had already been lit; we could almost hear the sizzling.' Without even offering them the drink they were dying for, she bombarded them with 'an interminable barrage of irrelevance', accusing them of selling the country down the river, vowing to resign rather than accept it.[63] Eventually they escaped back to London, where Gilmour ignored the Prime Minister's reaction and briefed journalists that they had secured a diplomatic triumph. The next day's papers duly hailed a great victory for her tough tactics. Temporarily outmanoeuvred, Mrs Thatcher was forced to swallow her objections and accept the deal, consoling herself that if not the end of the matter, it represented 'huge progress from the position the Government had inherited'.[64]

'Her objection,' Gilmour believed, 'was to the fact of the agreement, not its terms. That was not because we had succeeded where she had failed. It was because, to her, the grievance was more valuable than its solution.'[65] There is no doubt that the dispute was a godsend to her in her first year, providing what she always needed, an external enemy against whom to vent her aggression and prove her mettle. Greedy foreigners trying to get their hands on Britain's money offered the perfect outlet for patriotic indignation, a priceless distraction as inflation continued to rise and unemployment began to mount alarmingly. The EC budget battle set the style of her premiership and fixed the tabloid image of battling Maggie swinging her handbag and standing up for Britain against the wiles of Brussels. For the moment she was obliged to make the best of the interim settlement Carrington had secured, while still holding out for a permanent solution, which was not finally achieved until the Fontainebleau council of June 1984. Until then the 'Bloody British Question', as it was known in Brussels, continued to paralyse all other progress in the Community and poison Britain's relationship with Europe.

She won in the end when two new leaders, François Mitterrand in France and Helmut Kohl in Germany, realised that they would get no peace till Mrs Thatcher got what she demanded. But her victory was achieved at a considerable cost. First, however much she claimed to be a full and equal member, her exclusive preoccupation with the budget prevented Britain playing a full role in the development of the Community, thus confirming the dismal pattern of critical semi-detachment already set by Labour. Second, Mrs Thatcher's jingoistic rhetoric, gleefully amplified by the *Sun* and the *Daily Mail*, set a tone of popular prejudice, hostile to the Community and all its works, which endured long after the budget problem was resolved. Third, the ultimate success of her uncompromising campaign encouraged Mrs Thatcher's conviction that intransigence was the only language foreigners understood. 'The outcome,' Nigel Lawson observed, 'persuaded her that it always paid to be bloody-minded in dealings with the Community. This was to prove increasingly counterproductive in practice.'[66]

In this way she began to undermine the Tory commitment to Europe which she had inherited from Macmillan and Heath, leading within ten years to a deep split in the party which would eventually destroy her and bedevil the life of her successors. As Roy Jenkins wrote, 'It was a heavy price to pay for 400 million ecus.'[67]

Rhodesia into Zimbabwe

The long-running problem of ending colonial rule in Rhodesia, by contrast, was a subject on which Mrs Thatcher, very soon after taking office, dramatically changed her mind and modified her initial instinct, leading to a settlement which reflected her flexibility and pragmatism. Unlike Europe or the Cold War, Rhodesia was not an issue with which she felt any visceral involvement. Her sympathies were instinctively with the white settlers – 'our kith and kin', as the British press liked to call them. Denis had business connections with Rhodesia, and she could not forget that Ian Smith, the rebel Prime Minister, had served in the RAF during the war. The African leaders, by contrast, she regarded as Communist-sponsored terrorists. Nevertheless Rhodesia was marginal to her central concerns, a tiresome responsibility which she simply wanted to dispose of honourably.

Ten years after Smith's illegal declaration of independence from Britain, it was the collapse of the Portuguese empire in Angola and Mozambique in 1975 which spelled the end of the line for rebel Rhodesia. As the two rival African guerrilla groups, ZIPRA and ZANU, led by Joshua Nkomo and Robert Mugabe, stepped up their military incursions from neighbouring Zambia and Mozambique, South Africa decided it could no longer go on shoring up its northern satellite and began to put pressure on Smith to bow to the inevitable and accept majority rule. In 1977 Smith rejected an Anglo-American peace plan put forward by David Owen and the US Secretary of State, Cyrus Vance, and negotiated his own internal settlement – heavily favourable to the whites – with the more accommodating Bishop Abel Muzorewa. Callaghan and Owen – and Carter – immediately declared it unacceptable and refused to recognise it.

Mrs Thatcher's instinct was to support the Smith/Muzorewa settlement, and this remained her position up to the General Election. In April she sent the former Colonial Secretary Lord Boyd to observe the Rhodesian elections for the Tory party. Bishop Muzorewa won and duly became the country's first black Prime Minister at the head of a power-sharing government. But with Nkomo and Mugabe (now allied as the Patriotic Front) boycotting the elections, most international opinion declared them meaningless. Boyd, however, declared them fair and valid, and Mrs Thatcher accepted his report. In her first speech in the Commons as Prime Minister she warmly welcomed the elections as marking a 'major change' and promised to build on them.[68] Six weeks later, stopping off in Canberra on her way back from the Tokyo summit at the end of June, she again hinted that Britain would recognise Muzorewa, provoking a storm of protest led by the Australian Prime Minister Malcolm Fraser, who warned her that she was isolating herself from the rest of the Commonwealth, and indeed the world. President Carter had already rejected the result of the elections and announced – in defiance of Congress, which voted to lift them – that American sanctions against Rhodesia would be maintained.

On her return to Britain, Carrington persuaded her to change her mind. Recognition of Muzorewa, he argued, would not only split both the Commonwealth and the Atlantic alliance, boost Soviet influence in Africa and damage Britain economically; it was also futile, since the internal settlement would not end the war in Rhodesia, but only widen it, with the Soviet Union backing Nkomo and China backing Mugabe. Britain would be left holding nominal responsibility before the United Nations for an escalating conflict.

As Lady Thatcher subsequently wrote in her memoirs: 'Unpleasant realities had to be faced . . . He turned out to be right.'[69]

She also found other grounds to change her mind. She was persuaded that there were legal flaws in Smith's gerrymandered constitution, which was unlike any other that Britain had bequeathed her former colonies. Strict regard for legality was something Mrs Thatcher always took very seriously. In addition, following the failure of the Vance–Owen initiative, she liked the idea of Britain going it alone to achieve a settlement without American help. 'How do we decolonise a colony when there is no problem at all?' she asked her advisers. 'We get all the parties round a table at Lancaster House,' they replied. 'They work out a constitution that suits them all; then they have an election on that constitution and that's goodbye.' Very well, she concluded, 'Let's go down that road and see what happens.'[70]

For all these reasons – though not without a last-minute wobble when she appeared to go cold on the whole idea – Mrs Thatcher had made up her mind before she flew to Lusaka for the Commonwealth Conference in August that the only solution lay in a comprehensive settlement involving all the parties. She actually signalled her shift of view in the House of Commons on 25 July, when the Foreign Office succeeded in writing into her speech a carefully phrased statement that any settlement must be internationally recognised. But scarcely anyone noticed the significance of her words: it is not certain that she fully recognised it herself.[71] Carrington insists that she had determined what she wanted to achieve before she went to Lusaka. But it was still generally assumed that she would be walking into a lions' den, setting herself against the united view of the rest of the Commonwealth. She was certainly prepared for a hostile reception.

Though Denis had travelled extensively in Africa, Mrs Thatcher had no connection with either the old or the new Commonwealth; nor – unlike Callaghan or Wilson – did she feel any political sympathy with Africa's liberation struggle. On the contrary, like Ted Heath, she found the hypocrisy of the African leaders preaching democracy for others while operating one-party states themselves, reviling Britain one moment while demanding increased aid the next, very hard to swallow. Yet she did not want to see the club break up; and in practice, once exposed to them privately in the relaxed atmosphere of a Commonwealth Conference, she discovered most of the African leaders to be much more agreeable and a good deal less 'Marxist' than she had expected.[72] In particular, as Carrington noted, she 'blossomed in the warmth of Kenneth Kaunda's friendly personality'.[73] At Lusaka she even scored a memorable diplomatic coup by dancing with him: since her Oxford days she had been an excellent dancer, and the resulting photographs did more than any diplomatic communiqué to dissolve tensions.

Much of the credit for the success of Lusaka has been given to the Queen for helping to create the family atmosphere in which Mrs Thatcher and President Kaunda were able to overcome their mutual suspicion.[74] But at least as much is due to Mrs Thatcher herself, first for allowing Carrington to change her mind on the central issue and then, having changed it, for her determination to hammer out – with Malcolm Fraser, Michael Manley (of Jamaica) and the Commonwealth Secretary-General Sonny Ramphal – the lines of an agreement which could bring Mugabe and Nkomo to Lancaster House. Carrington paid tribute to the skill with which she exploited the element of surprise at her unexpected reversal. Always concerned to get the legal framework right, she insisted that Rhodesia must first return to its constitutional status as a colony, with the appointment of a new Governor and all the flummery of British rule. In return she agreed that Britain would send troops to enforce and monitor the ceasefire. This was a risk which Callaghan had not been prepared to take. But Mrs Thatcher accepted that Britain had a responsibility to discharge; she was determined not to have the United Nations involved.[75] More than anything else it was this guarantee of British military commitment which persuaded the Patriotic Front to lay down its arms. By the concerted pressure of South Africa, the neighbouring 'Front Line' states, the rest of the Commonwealth and the United States, all parties to the conflict were cajoled into agreeing to attend peace talks in London in September.

Carrington still had no great hopes of a settlement. But for fifteen weeks he put the whole weight of the Foreign Office into the effort to achieve one, believing that his tenure would not last long if he failed.[76] Having played her part at Lusaka, Mrs Thatcher left her Foreign Secretary to chair the talks with minimum interference. While Kaunda flew to London to impress on Nkomo that he must settle, and Samora Machel of Mozambique similarly leaned on Mugabe, Mrs Thatcher's role behind the scenes was to make plain to the whites that they could not look to Britain to bail them out. The negotiations were tense and protracted – a walkout by one or other party was never far away; but an agreement was eventually signed just before Christmas, providing for elections in the New Year, a ten-year embargo on the transfer of land and British help in forging a united army out of the previously warring forces. Christopher Soames was appointed Governor to oversee the elections and bring the new state of Zimbabwe to independence.

Mrs Thatcher would frankly have preferred that the Marxist Mugabe had not won the elections. Right up to the last moment, diehard whites still hoped that she would declare the result invalid. But she refused to do so, and firmly quashed any thought that she might recognise a military coup. She was their last hope, and when she spelled out the reality they knew the game was up. Mugabe's victory was in fact the best possible outcome, since winning power through the ballot box served – at least in the short term – to de-radicalise the Patriotic Front. Once in power, Mugabe quickly declared Zimbabwe a one-party state; but for the best part of twenty years it seemed a relatively successful one. Only at the end of the century did the issue of the unequal ownership of land – shelved at Lancaster House – erupt in Government-sponsored violence against white farmers as the ageing dictator clung to office, wrecking the country's once-prosperous economy and throwing its multi-racial future into doubt.[77]

The contrary pulls of patriotic sentiment and geopolitical realism recurred in relation to other remnants of Britain's imperial past: the Falklands, Grenada and Hong Kong. In the case of Rhodesia, as in Hong Kong, realism prevailed. For fourteen years since 1965 the colony had been a running sore in British politics, the annual vote on the maintenance of sanctions a source of division and embarrassment to the Tory party in particular. All Mrs Thatcher wanted in 1979 was to be honourably rid of it. She was lucky that the circumstances came together to make a solution possible just as she came into office. But she deserves credit for seizing the opportunity, against her initial instinct, and for exerting her influence to secure a tolerable settlement. The outcome gained her a good deal of international credit, not only with black Africa but also in Washington, at a time when the Government's domestic economic record was already looking bleak. After seven difficult months, the Zimbabwe settlement was her Government's first unquestionable success.

The end of the beginning

By the time the Zimbabwe settlement was signed at the end of 1979 the Government's honeymoon, such as it was, was over. The Lancaster House agreement was the one bright spot in an otherwise darkening picture. The novelty of a woman Prime Minister had quickly worn off. Her style was established: brisk, didactic, combative, with a touch of syrup. There was no lingering doubt about her capacity to do the job. She had established her domination of the Cabinet and Government machine, despite the barely concealed scepticism of many of her senior colleagues. By her mastery of detail and clarity of purpose she had asserted her command of the House of Commons despite having to shout over a perpetual hubbub of heckling and interruption.

She had achieved a notable coup in November by her unprecedentedly full disclosure of the facts surrounding the unmasking of the distinguished art historian Sir Anthony Blunt – the Keeper of the Queen's Pictures – as a one-time Soviet spy, the 'fourth man' who had tipped off his friends Guy Burgess and Donald Maclean, enabling them to escape to the Soviet Union in 1951, and then done the same for Kim Philby in 1963. It was a tricky task for a new Prime Minister to reveal that Blunt's treachery had been suspected since 1951 and known to the security services since 1964, but covered up by successive Home Secretaries and Attorneys-General in return for a full confession. But she carried it off with considerable aplomb, raising hopes – not to be fulfilled – that she would inaugurate a more open regime where MI5 and MI6 were concerned. Willie Whitelaw was actually working on a new Protection of Information Bill to replace the catch-all provisions of the 1911 Official Secrets Act; but this was abandoned when Andrew Boyle, the journalist who had exposed Blunt, asserted that he could not have done so under the new provisions. It was another ten years before her government returned to the reform of the Official Secrets Act, and then it was to tighten, not loosen, its provisions.

Mrs Thatcher also won considerable admiration for her response to further Irish atrocities. At the end of August the former Viceroy of India, Lord Mountbatten, and two members of his family were blown up while on holiday in the Irish Republic; and the same day eighteen British soldiers were killed at Warrenpoint in County Down. Mrs Thatcher not only condemned the attacks but paid an unannounced visit to Northern Ireland two days later to demonstrate her defiance of the terrorists and her support for the troops. She visited some of the victims of previous IRA bombs in hospital, went on a courageous walkabout in the centre of Belfast protected by just a handful of flak-jacketed policemen, had lunch with army commanders at Portadown and then flew by helicopter to the republican stronghold of Crossmaglen, where she 'enthusiastically donned a combat jacket and a beret of the Ulster Defence Regiment'.[78] This 'nation-rallying trip,' *The Times* wrote at the end of the year, 'was a stroke of genius'.[79] She repeated it just before Christmas and made a point of going at least once a year over the next decade.

She enjoyed a rapturous victory conference at Blackpool in

October, at which she thanked her party for keeping faith during the years of opposition and boldly looked forward to 'the far longer years of Conservative government that are to come'.[80] In this and other speeches Mrs Thatcher repeated the Government's determination to tackle the four linked problems of inflation, public spending, taxation and industrial relations. But by the end of 1979, as the commentators looked back on the Government's first six months, it seemed that in every one of those areas its first actions had only made a bad situation worse. On the credit side, opinion polls still showed overwhelming public support for action to curb the unions, and the Government was further heartened by votes against strike action by the miners and the British Leyland car workers. Yet despite lurching hard to the left since losing office, Labour was once again ahead in the polls. Even those who wished the Government well were holding their breath. Fred Emery, political editor of *The Times*, wrote that the dominant reaction to the Prime Minister's first six months was one of awe for the 'marvellous flair' of 'this unflinching woman' who had swept her doubtful party into 'a high-risk policy gamble'. 'The awe reflects Mrs Thatcher's private and public dominance, making our system more presidential than ever.' But many wondered 'whether Mrs Thatcher has quite grasped yet how bad the economy could be'.[81]

The Government was sailing into stormy waters.

12

Heading for the Rocks

The failure of monetarism

THE two years 1980 and 1981 were the critical period for the Thatcher Government, when the Prime Minister and her Chancellor, with dwindling support even from former true believers in the Cabinet, confronted by appalling economic indicators and widespread predictions of disaster, set their faces against the storm and stubbornly held – more or less – their predetermined course. Economically, in truth, things did not go according to plan. Some targets were quietly abandoned, others were hit only at huge cost: economists still dispute whether more lasting good or harm was done to the economy by the monetarist experiment. Politically, however, Mrs Thatcher won through without being seen to change course. There was no overt U-turn, such as her critics had confidently predicted. Instead, by the end of 1981 she had purged her Cabinet of the most persistent doubters and laid the basis of the reputation for unwavering resolution which would keep her in Downing Street for another nine years.

By all the normal measures of economic management the Government's performance was dismal during 1980. Inflation went on climbing for several months, reaching 22 per cent in May before finally starting to fall. By the end of the year it had fallen to 13 per cent, but that was still higher than it had been when the Conservatives came in. Meanwhile unemployment continued to soar, reaching 2.8 million by the end of 1980: the sort of level no one had ever expected to see again. The Tories' 1978 poster showing a winding dole queue with the caption 'Labour Isn't Working' was revealed as a cynical mockery.

The worst problem was the pound, which reached $2.40 in

September 1980 (compared with $2.08 in May 1979). The rise was partly due to the rising oil price, partly to the falling dollar and partly – some economists would say mainly – to the Government's determination to keep interest rates high, which impressed the markets. Whatever the cause, the effect on British manufacturing industry was devastating. Hundreds of small companies went out of business, while even the giants struggled. Industrial leaders queued up to blame the Government. In November the chairman of the CBI (Confederation of British Industry), Sir Terence Beckett, called dramatically for 'a bare-knuckle fight' with the Government.[1] Sir Michael Edwardes of British Leyland said it would be better to leave North Sea oil in the seabed than let it do such damage.[2] In principle, however, she was inclined to believe that the high pound was a good thing: first because she always had a simple patriotic belief that the currency was a barometer of national prosperity, and second because she thought it would administer a healthy shock to industry, forcing it to become more competitive to survive. Industrialists faced with closure were not so sanguine. 'I am aware that the exchange rate is causing some difficulty for some exporters,' Mrs Thatcher conceded, 'but it is also keeping down the rate of increase in inflation in this country.'[3] The monetarists' real problem, one sceptic told the *Observer*'s William Keegan, 'was that they could not make up their mind whether the squeals from British industry were a good thing or not'.[4]

The critics' case is that by sticking to their predetermined strategy, despite the oil-price increase and deepening world recession, Mrs Thatcher and her Treasury team wilfully exacerbated an already threatening situation. 'Undeterred by the prospect of a world recession ahead,' Ian Gilmour later wrote, 'they proceeded to create their own far worse recession at home', permanently destroying in the process much of Britain's manufacturing base.[5] The Thatcherites, by contrast, argued at the time – and still argue – that British industry was overmanned and featherbedded and needed shaking out. A shift from old manufacturing to new service industries – what Mrs Thatcher called 'tomorrow's jobs'[6] – was both inevitable and necessary: the recession of 1980–81 merely accelerated this process which was the precondition for subsequent recovery. To which the Keynesians reply that there was bound to be some recovery eventually from such a deep trough, but that it was only partial, and more delayed than it need have been, while much of manufacturing industry never recovered at all.

Geoffrey Howe's second budget, introduced in March 1980, unveiled what Lady Thatcher later called the 'cornerstone' of her

Government's success – the so-called Medium Term Financial Strategy (MTFS).[7] Its purpose was to bring down public spending and monetary growth by announcing fixed targets for several years ahead, instead of just one year at a time. The strategy was the brainchild of Nigel Lawson, Financial Secretary to the Treasury, who successfully sold the idea to Howe with the slogan 'Rules rule, OK'.[8] Howe pragmatically agreed: he always insisted that the MTFS was 'commonsense rather than revolutionary'.[9] As so often with ideas she subsequently adopted as her own, however, Mrs Thatcher was initially hostile. Though in theory all in favour of squeezing the money supply, 'she reacted instinctively against what she called "graph-paper economics"', which smacked of socialist planning. In the end she was persuaded that fixed targets would both put a ceiling on high-spending ministers and make it possible to reduce interest rates.[10] In fact the targets were not fixed at all. The MTFS was no more than a statement of desirable objectives. Its effect – as Mrs Thatcher came to realise – was essentially declaratory. 'Its credibility depended . . . on the quality of my own commitment, about which I would leave no one in doubt. I would not bow to demands to reflate.'[11] On that basis she was converted, elevating the MTFS into a symbol of her personal resolution.

The fact is that monetarism in the strict sense did not work. Paradoxically, the importance of controlling the money supply was now almost universally accepted. Although it suited both parties to gloss over the fact after 1979, Healey had run a pretty successful monetary regime from 1976. The difficulty Howe and Lawson had was in measuring the growth of money – particularly after they had scrapped exchange controls. As Biffen anticipated, by elevating the control of money into the central totem of policy the Government made a rod for its own back. At one level it was perfectly correct for the Prime Minister and Chancellor to maintain that monetarism was not some 'minority doctrinal obsession, pursued blindly for its own sake',[12] but 'simple common sense', long accepted in Switzerland and Germany.[13] 'Monetarism,' she insisted in the House of Commons, 'means honest money. It means that money is backed properly by the production of goods and services.'[14] The trouble lay not in the principle but in the practice. Of the various available yardsticks they took as their measure of money in circulation £M3, which included not only notes and coins but bank deposits. They were then made to look ridiculous when £M3 rose during 1980, despite the Government's best efforts to curb it, by 18 per cent – that is, nearly twice as fast as before 1979.

This embarrassing inability to control the very indicator on which the Government had publicly staked its reputation caused serious friction between Downing Street and the Bank of England. Mrs Thatcher took a closer personal interest in the minutiae of monetary control than any previous Prime Minister. Yet she lacked a trained economist's sense of the subject's intrinsic fallibility. Rather, she had a scientist's literal belief in money as a finite substance which must be able to be measured. The result, as Jock Bruce-Gardyne observed, was 'a conflict of personalities between an exceptionally determined Prime Minister and an exceptionally formidable Governor'.[15] Appointed by Ted Heath in 1973, and now serving his fourth Prime Minister, Gordon Richardson was the most dominant Governor of the Bank of England since Montagu Norman in the 1930s. He objected to being treated like an errant schoolboy who had got his sums wrong. The crunch came in the summer of 1980, when Mrs Thatcher was taking a rare, brief holiday in Switzerland. £M3 rose 5 per cent in July alone and another 5 per cent in August. She furiously consulted various Swiss bankers, then came storming home to charge the Deputy Governor, Eddie George – Richardson was on holiday – with rank incompetence. While Downing Street insisted that the Prime Minister was 'not rattled, they admit that she needs some sturdy reassurance'.[16] It was provided by the return from the United States of her favourite monetarist guru Alan Walters, who told her to forget about £M3. 'Bugger £M3!' he is supposed to have said. 'Sterling is obviously far too high. That can only mean that sterling is scarce.'[17] He proposed commissioning an independent report from another monetarist academic, Professor Jurg Niehans of Berne University, who duly supported Walters' diagnosis, giving Howe impeccable authority to loosen the monetary squeeze. 'The appreciation of sterling in the last two years,' he reported, 'is largely a monetary phenomenon' – in other words, it was not due to oil.[18]

The theory was right, but the implementation was wrong, he told John Hoskyns. 'If the Government goes on with its present monetary squeeze, you won't just have a recession, you'll have a slump.'[19] To the CBI's relief, Minimum Lending Rate was cut by 2 per cent in November, and previous monetary targets were discreetly modified in the 1981 budget. At the beginning of 1981 Walters formally moved into Downing Street as the Prime Minister's personal economic adviser.

Thereafter what finally got inflation back to single figures by the spring of 1982 was not the control of money but heavy pressure on public spending, higher indirect taxation and lower borrowing, resulting in nearly three million unemployed.[20] In other words the MTFS was a blind – just a fancy smokescreen for old-fashioned deflation. 'If Keynesianism stood accused of buying employment at the price of inflation,' Peter Clarke has written, 'Thatcherism could plausibly be accused of simply inverting the process.' The Government came in preaching the painless alchemy of Milton Friedman but ended up delivering the harsher medicine of Friedrich Hayek.[21]

Howe's 1980 budget took another £900 million out of planned public spending for 1980–81, mainly from social services. Sickness and unemployment benefit were made liable to income tax, child benefit was raised by less than the rate of inflation, prescription charges were doubled again – to £1 per item, five times the level of a year before. Higher education took the heaviest cuts; university funding was severely (but unequally) reduced, and overseas students were required to pay the full cost of their tuition. All these measures evoked a furious outcry from those affected. The *Guardian* accused the Government of waging 'war against the poor'.[22] In July the Cabinet agreed a further package, though several of the biggest spenders – Patrick Jenkin at the DHSS and, above all, Francis Pym at Defence – fought successfully to limit the impact on their departments. Pym threatened resignation and deployed the Chiefs of Staff to exercise their right of access to the Prime Minister to defend his budget. The more the Government tried to cut, however, the more the cost of social security kept on rising. In her memoirs Lady Thatcher recalled that cutting public expenditure at this time felt like 'running up the "Down" escalator'.[23] Obliged to make a virtue of failure, she pointed out that spending in 1979–80 was actually slightly up on the year before, 'which should give the lie to those who accuse us of savage cuts'.[24] In October 1980 she admitted that the Government's revised objective was merely to hold spending to its current level; but insisted that since some expenditure was expanding, this inevitably necessitated economies elsewhere.[25]

At least half the Cabinet, however, believed it was wrong to be trying to cut spending at all when unemployment was rising. Not only the established 'wets' but even some of those previously counted 'dry' were beginning to shrink from the social consequences – notably John Biffen, who as Chief Secretary was responsible for wielding the Treasury axe, but quickly concluded that no really major cuts were practicable. Conventional wisdom took it for granted that no Government could survive unemployment at two or three million. Less than a decade earlier the Heath Government had been forced to reverse its strategy when unemployment hit one million. It was not as if the Conservatives had given warning that unemployment would have to rise. On the contrary, they had denounced Labour's employment record as opportunistically as any opposition. Ever since 1975 Labour (and, privately, many Tories) had warned that monetarism, strictly applied, would inevitably cost jobs: Keith Joseph had on occasion admitted it. Yet it seems that Mrs Thatcher and her economic team had genuinely not expected unemployment to take off as it did as soon as they got into office. They were alarmed by the mounting figures and protested that they were doing everything possible by means of tax cuts and other incentives to encourage the new industries and businesses which would create new jobs. But Mrs Thatcher had staked her political reputation on not repeating Heath's U-turn. Whatever the economic arguments which came from every part of the political spectrum, her credibility would have been destroyed if she were seen to reverse her insistence that squeezing inflation must remain the top priority. From political necessity, then, but also with extraordinary nerve (and a good deal of luck), Mrs Thatcher contrived to stand conventional wisdom on its head by making a virtue of her refusal to change tack – almost indeed making a virtue of unemployment itself.

In the House of Commons she faced uproar every month when the latest figure was published: Labour MPs accused her of creating 'an industrial desert' and using unemployment deliberately to cow the unions. She responded with a mixture of angry retaliation, recalling that unemployment had doubled under Labour too, and patient lectures on the facts of economic life.

She insisted that there was no painless remedy. Only by becoming competitive would new jobs in the new industries eventually be created. Cutting public expenditure, far from exacerbating unemployment, was actually the way to reduce it by releasing resources for the private sector, which was the productive sector. 'It is the sector from which the jobs will come.'[26] As the recession endured and deepened, she increasingly accepted an obligation on the Government to 'cushion the harsher effects of change' by promoting enterprise zones, training schemes and new technology.[27] But finding that she could not prevent the numbers of the jobless rising remorselessly, Mrs Thatcher found a way of turning the pain of unemployment to her advantage. Skilfully seizing on one of the most positive role models peculiarly available to a woman Prime Minister, she portrayed herself as a nurse – or sometimes a doctor – administering nasty medicine to cure the country's self-inflicted illness. 'Which is the better nurse?' she asked:

The one who smothers the patient with sympathy and says 'Never mind, dear, there, there, you just lie back and I'll bring you all your meals . . . I'll look after you.' Or the nurse who says 'Now, come on, shake out of it . . . It's time you put your feet on the ground and took a few steps . . .' Which do you think is the better nurse? . . . The one who says come on, you can do it. That's me.[28]

This was clever presentation, and it worked. After the dismal spiral of inflation, strikes and steadily mounting unemployment through the 1970s, the public was at least half ready to believe that any effective cure for the nation's sickness was bound to be painful, and was masochistically ready to endure it. The figure of the strict Nurse Thatcher struck a chord in the British psyche. Though the Conservatives had not campaigned on any such prospectus, and opinion polls showed the Government's popularity sinking ever lower, Labour was increasingly distracted and marginalised by its bitter internal power struggle, which the left was clearly winning. In November 1980, when Callaghan retired, the party abdicated any claim to be a serious opposition by electing the sentimental old left-winger Michael Foot in preference to the robust and realistic Denis Healey. At a level deeper than opinion polls the electorate seemed to accept that there was indeed, as Geoffrey Howe asserted, 'no alternative'.[29] The phrase was originally the Chancellor's, but the nickname TINA – 'There Is No Alternative' – quickly attached itself to the Prime Minister. She declared in a confidence debate just before the House rose in July 1980: 'We are doing what the country elected us to do. The Government will have the guts to see it through.'[30]

Three months later, at the party conference in Brighton, she made her most famous retort to the fainthearts who were calling for a U-turn, supplied as usual by Ronnie Millar. 'You turn if you want to,' she told the delighted representatives, then paused while they laughed, thinking that was the punchline. 'The Lady's not for turning.'[31]* Privately she had already given the same assurance to her staff. 'She made it absolutely clear,' John Hoskyns recalled, 'she would really rather be chucked out than do a U-turn.'[32] Whether the policy was economically right or wrong, whether or not it was true that there was no alternative, her resolution conveyed itself to

---

*The line derived from the title of Christopher Fry's 1948 verse play, *The Lady's Not for Burning*, which Mrs Thatcher may well have seen during her courtship with Denis.

the country and won its grudging admiration. After the Wilson–Heath–Callaghan years of drift and compromise, Mrs Thatcher's sheer defiance was a bravura performance which deflected – or at least suspended – criticism.

Softly, softly

But the heart of Thatcherism was not in monetarism anyway. Monetarism was merely an economic theory which few ministers, let alone commentators or the public, fully understood. To Mrs Thatcher monetarism was essentially a tool, not a dogma, to be discarded if it did not work. Her real purpose was much more political: purging what she called socialism from the economy by encouraging enterprise in place of subsidy and regulation, cutting overmanning and restrictive practices, particularly in the public sector, and above all curbing the power of the overmighty unions.

Union power was the great symbolic dragon which she had been elected to slay. It was the unions which had humiliated and ultimately destroyed the last Conservative Government in 1972–4, and union-fostered anarchy which had done more than anything else to bring the Conservatives back to power in 1979, with a clear mandate to bring the bully-boys to heel.

Nevertheless this was another area in which Mrs Thatcher proceeded cautiously. Her treatment of trade-union reform, indeed, offers a casebook example of prudence overruling instinct, her head ruling her heart. For one thing she needed Prior in her first Cabinet. He had invested heavily in his consensual approach to industrial relations and enjoyed the support of other old Heathites like Willie Whitelaw and Peter Carrington. Mrs Thatcher had little choice but to confirm him as Employment Secretary in May 1979, and having once appointed him she could not afford to lose him, so she had to go along with his approach, frustrating though it was to her backbench zealots.

At the same time she recognised that Heath had courted disaster in 1971 by trying to reform the whole of industrial relations law in one comprehensive Bill. The political climate was much more propitious now than then. But still there was a shrewd argument for tackling the problem one step at a time, carrying public opinion with the Government and denying the unions a single emotive cause to rally round. Her strategy, therefore, was not to confront the unions but to outflank them by appealing over the heads of the unrepresentative and timewarped leaders to the rank-and-file members who had voted Conservative in unprecedented numbers in May and who – polls showed – overwhelmingly supported reform. Her constant theme was that it was not only the public but ordinary trade unionists who suffered from the abuse of union power. These ordinary members had voted Tory, she believed, because they recognised that 'our policy represents their ambition for their own future and for their families, for a better standard of living and better jobs'.[33] The purpose of the Government's reform was to encourage those ordinary Tory-voting trade unionists to reclaim their unions from the control of the militants.

She further marginalised the union barons by ignoring them. The TUC Secretary-General, Len Murray, complained that Mrs Thatcher 'rejected the idea of trade unions as valid institutions within society . . . which, even if you didn't like them, you were stuck with and had to come to some sort of agreement'.[34] For her part she firmly denied them the role they had come to see as their right by eschewing any form of pay policy, refusing to intervene in industrial disputes and letting economic realities and the rising toll of unemployment educate the workforce and emasculate the militants.

Legislation played only a supporting role in this process. Following a consultation document in July, Prior published his Employment Bill in December 1979. Its scope was modest, proposing only what had been promised in the Tory manifesto. Secondary picketing – that is, picketing workplaces not directly involved in a dispute – was outlawed, but not secondary strike action. Employees who refused to join unions were given increased rights of appeal and compensation against the operation of closed shops; but the closed shop itself was not banned (despite Mrs Thatcher repeating that she was 'absolutely against the closed shop in principle').[35] Thirdly, Government money was made available to encourage unions to hold secret ballots. There was no mention in the Bill of any of the more draconian measures demanded by the Tory right: cutting strikers' entitlement to benefits, making union funds liable to action for civil damages, or making members who wished to support the Labour party 'opt in' to paying the political levy, instead of requiring those who did not to opt out. All these were more or less explicitly left to further Employment Acts further down the road.

The skill of this approach was demonstrated by the unions' predictably exaggerated response. By vowing 'total opposition' to what Murray called 'a fundamental attack' on workers' rights, the TUC only confirmed its reputation as an unthinking dinosaur.[36] Prior's strategy was perfectly designed to demonstrate that the union leaders were out of touch with their members. When the TUC tried to revive the memory of its successful campaign against Heath's Industrial Relations Bill by calling a 'Day of Action' in May 1980, it failed dismally when no more than a few thousand activists stayed off work. 'People will have no truck with political strikes,' Mrs Thatcher asserted in the House of Commons. 'They would rather get on with the job.'[37]

Up to the end of January 1980, Mrs Thatcher stoutly defended Prior's 'modest and sensible' Bill as 'a very good start'. Even after the steel unions began a bitter strike against the British Steel Corporation's plans to rationalise the industry, she specifically ruled out – 'for the moment' – action on secondary strikes and strikers' benefits.[38] In February, however, the situation was transformed. First, the steel dispute spread, with secondary picketing of private steelmakers leading to violent scenes reminiscent of the previous winter. At the same moment the House of Lords' judgement in an important test case, *Express Newspapers v. McShane*, confirmed the trade unions' legal immunity from liability for the consequences of their members' actions. These events increased the pressure on the Government to widen the scope of Prior's Bill. The papers built up the issue as the critical first test of the Government's mettle. 'If you don't act now,' the *Daily Express* warned, 'the writing will be on the tombstone of the Tory Government.'[39]

Mrs Thatcher was bound to respond. She accordingly pressed Prior to add a new clause outlawing secondary action. Since that would not have immediate effect on the steel strike, she also wanted to rush forward a single-clause Bill to ban secondary picketing immediately, without waiting for the Employment Bill to go through all its stages. But Prior resisted both proposals, and was supported in Cabinet by a powerful combination of senior ministers. Defeated in Cabinet in the morning, however, Mrs Thatcher got her own back the same afternoon by simply announcing at Prime Minister's Questions that plans to cut strikers' benefits were going ahead after all, and provision for cutting strikers' benefits was duly included in Howe's budget six weeks later.

Meanwhile – before his Bill was even on the Statute Book – Prior was pressured to publish a Green Paper foreshadowing further curbs on the closed shop and other measures. But he still firmly resisted ending the unions' legal immunity. Mrs Thatcher missed no opportunity to repeat that she intended to go further: 'The Bill is a first step,' she said in July. 'It is not a last step.'[40] But it was clear that the next step would have to await a new Employment Secretary; and she was not yet strong enough to be rid of Prior.

In this way she got the best of both worlds. On the one hand she saw a significant first measure of reform enacted without provoking serious union opposition, and opened the way for another, while gaining credit for moderation and keeping her Cabinet intact. On the other she contrived to preserve her reputation with her core supporters as a radical who would have liked to do more, were she not constrained by her colleagues. Her blatant undermining of Prior was an early instance of what became a familiar tactic whereby she distanced herself from her own Government, running with the hare while hunting with the hounds. It was clever politics, but it was essentially two-faced and disloyal to colleagues who never felt they could rely on her support. In the short run this skilful ambiguity helped establish her authority over colleagues, many of whom were not naturally her supporters. But over time it strained the loyalty even of her handful of 'true believers', undermined the cohesion of her Government and ultimately wrought her downfall.

Over the whole decade 1979–90, curbing the power of the unions was perhaps the Thatcher Government's most unarguable achievement, ending a culture of institutionalised abuse which had hobbled enterprise and broken three previous Governments – Labour and Conservative – in the previous ten years. The Government's legislation was successful partly because it was introduced against a background of high unemployment which weakened the unions' industrial muscle and shrank their membership from thirteen million to ten million over ten years, but also because it was implemented in cumulative instalments which offered the unions no popular cause on which to make a stand. The result vindicated Prior's gradualism – but also Mrs Thatcher's caution in backing him.

Joseph on the rack

The second great dragon waiting to be tackled was the nationalised sector of the economy. Here again the Government's first steps disappointed its keenest supporters. The fact that privatisation on the scale that occurred after 1983 was not foreshadowed in the 1979 manifesto subsequently gave rise to a belief that it was not on the Government's agenda when Mrs Thatcher first came to power, but was merely a sort of opportunist afterthought. There is enough truth in this to give the story an ironic piquancy, but it is not the whole truth.

It was always a central part of the vision of an enterprise economy that the nationalised sector, if it could not be wholly eliminated, should at least be substantially reduced. Mrs Thatcher was instinctively much keener on privatisation than Heath had ever been. She believed that the public sector was inherently inefficient and a drag on the wealth-creating enterprise of the private sector, and talked freely in private about the need to reduce it. But up to 1979 her overriding concern was not to alarm the voters by striking attitudes that could be labelled 'extreme'.

There is no question that privatisation did take off unexpectedly after 1983. That is not to say, however, that finding ways of cutting the public sector was not a high priority from the beginning. In her very first speech as Prime Minister, Mrs Thatcher spoke of making a start 'in extending the role of private enterprise by reducing the size of the public sector' – adding emphatically: 'It needs reducing';[41] and a few weeks later she promised proposals for 'attempting to have less public sector ownership and more private sector ownership'.[42] Her language constantly suggests that she did not think it would be easy. What she mainly meant in these early days was selling shares in profitable state-owned companies like BP – where Labour had already shown the way – and dismantling the ragbag portfolio of odd companies taken into public ownership by Labour's National Enterprise Board (NEB). She was particularly keen to give priority to the workers employed in these firms, so that 'those who work in industry ... should make great strides towards being real capital owners'.[43] Neither she nor anyone else at this stage envisaged selling whole industries, mainly because their concern was less with ownership than with promoting competition. The Government's early effort was concentrated on selling off profitable ancillary parts of the nationalised industries, like gas and electricity showrooms, British Rail hotels and the cross-Channel hovercraft. They did not see how the core utilities themselves could be sold. 'In those industries,' Mrs Thatcher told the Commons in November 1981, 'we must ensure that the absence of market forces is replaced by other pressures to induce greater efficiency.'[44] While clear about the desirability of the objective, she remained persistently cautious, always talking of 'trying' to denationalise 'wherever possible' and stressing the practical difficulties.[45]

Nevertheless a very substantial start was made in 1979–82. Only by comparison with what came later can it be represented as small beer. Norman Fowler, as Transport Secretary, duly sold the National Freight Corporation, but also deregulated long-distance coach travel, creating new private competition with the state-owned railways. Keith Joseph began the process of selling British Aerospace. Several large NEB holdings were successfully sold. As Energy Secretary,

David Howell began the process of turning the British National Oil Corporation (BNOC), the North Sea oil exploitation company, into Britoil as a first step to privatising it. The sale of British Airways was also planned, under the dynamic leadership of John King, one of Mrs Thatcher's favourite businessmen, but had to be delayed for commercial reasons. Most significantly, Joseph split up the Post Office, creating a separate telecommunications company (British Telecom), initially as a way of attracting private money to pay for new technology; he also licensed a private telephone company, Mercury, to inject some competition into the telecommunications business.

By any standard except that of the bonanza years 1983–90, this was a remarkable record. Moreover, in November 1981 Lawson announced the principle that 'No industry should remain under State ownership unless there is a positive and overwhelming case for it so doing.'[46] The momentum of privatisation was well under way before the 1983 election. The Tory manifesto for that election targeted British Telecom, British Airways and the profitable parts of British Steel, British Shipbuilders and British Leyland. Yet ministers themselves did not realise the scale of the revolution that was around the corner.

In a sense, however, all this activity was marginal because it did not touch the core of the Government's problem – the great loss-making dinosaurs of the nationalised sector: British Rail, British Steel, the National Coal Board (NCB) and the permanently struggling car maker British Leyland. Much as they would have loved to have been rid of them, Mrs Thatcher and Keith Joseph were stuck with these monsters. Their ambition in 1979–81 was limited to trying to cut their costs, to reduce the drain on the Exchequer of their annual losses as part of the drive to cut public borrowing. To this end Joseph imposed tight cash limits on each industry, within which financial discipline they were expected to operate as far as possible like commercial companies – shedding surplus labour, raising productivity, selling off ancillary businesses and resisting unearned pay demands in order to meet their financial targets within a fixed timescale; meanwhile, the Government ostentatiously stood back and proclaimed its refusal to print money to buy off strikes or underwrite further losses. In 1981 the CPRS proposed a scheme for groups of outside industrialists to monitor the nationalised industries; and a search was set in hand for a new breed of tough, commercially minded managers from the private sector to replace the old style of corporatist bosses.

Joseph, however, found the practice of non-intervention much harder than the theory. As a humane man, and as a practical politician, he could not wash his hands while whole industries went to the wall. He could not simply close down British Steel, British Leyland or Belfast shipbuilders, however chronic their losses. So he agonised and, against his principles, ended up – to his subsequent shame – spending more taxpayers' millions: in two years his budget actually increased by 50 per cent, from £2.2 billion to £3.3 billion per annum.

Mrs Thatcher despaired of him. He was both her economic mentor and the man who, more than anyone else, had opened the way for her to become Prime Minister. She still listened to his advice in private; but he was a hopelessly indecisive minister. 'In the end', Jim Prior wrote, 'it all became impossible and Keith was moved to Education.'[47]

Joseph's first big test was a major steel strike at the beginning of 1980. The ostensible issue was pay; but behind that lay the British Steel Corporation's plans for drastically restructuring – that is, shrinking – the industry. In the first half of 1979 British Steel lost £145 million; by the end of the year it was losing £7 million a week. Clearly this could not continue. Joseph set the BSC a target to cut its deficit by the end of 1980. At the end of November 1979 the corporation announced the closure of plants with the loss of 50,000 jobs – one-third of the workforce. At the same time it offered the remainder a pay rise of just 2 per cent. The two main steel unions called a strike from 2 January; both unions and management then sat back and waited for the Government to come up with more money. But Joseph refused to intervene. The effect of a long steel strike on the rest of industry was potentially devastating. Mrs Thatcher was worried – she personally chaired a special group of ministers and officials to keep close watch on the situation – but she was adamant that the Government would not weaken. She was determined to teach the lesson that steel must stand on its own feet.

Finally, the two sides agreed to an old-fashioned inquiry, headed by the former Labour Cabinet Minister Harold Lever. Mrs Thatcher was deeply suspicious; her doubts were confirmed when Lever predictably split the difference between the BSC's final offer and the union's demand and recommended a settlement around 16 per cent, including productivity deals. (Inflation was then around 20 per cent.) Both sides accepted it and the strike was called off at the beginning of April.

On the face of it this was not much of a victory for the Government. Yet Joseph and Mrs Thatcher had made their point by not intervening, despite great pressure from the rest of industry (and much of the Cabinet), leaving management and unions to make their own deal. The real victory for the Government was that, under cover of the pay rise, BSC's plant closures were accepted. On this basis Joseph agreed to carry on subsidising the corporation for another year. Then, after a long search, the sixty-eight-year-old Scottish-born but Americanised Ian MacGregor – a tough manager with a reputation for defeating strikes – was recruited from Lazard Frères at a huge salary.

MacGregor earned his salary. In two years he transformed British Steel from the least efficient to one of the best steelmakers in Europe, bringing it almost into profit – at the cost of losing nearly half the workforce. Five years later the slimmed-down corporation was successfully privatised. This was Thatcherite industrial policy as it was meant to work – the long-term reward for the Government standing firm in the early months of 1980. The casualties – apart from the workers who lost their jobs – were, ironically the private steelmakers who were forced out of business while BSC was subsidised into profitability.

Less happy in the short term – indeed a major embarrassment to a government pledged not to support lame ducks – was the necessity to go on funding British Leyland. BL symbolised everything that was wrong with British industry: it was overmanned, underproductive, racked by unofficial strikes, a once-major car manufacturer increasingly unable to compete with European and Japanese rivals. Here was a prime candidate for the new Government's free-market philosophy: if Joseph was true to his convictions, he would refuse to subsidise BL any further but simply close it down. Nothing the Government could have done in its first year would have sent a clearer message to the rest of industry. But two considerations pulled the other way. First, BL was a big employer in the politically marginal West Midlands. The effect of closure would have been devastating. Second, BL had a dynamic new chairman, the South African-born Michael Edwardes, who was making a real effort to solve the company's labour problems. This was a factor that made a special appeal to Mrs Thatcher. 'I knew that whatever we decided to do about BL would have an impact on the psychology and morale of British managers as a whole', she wrote in her memoirs, 'and I was determined to send the right signals . . . We had to back Michael Edwardes.'[48]

In December 1979 BL was given an additional £300 million, with a warning that if the latest Corporate Plan was derailed by the militants there would be no more. Yet the company lost another

£93 million in the first half of 1980. By the end of the year Edwardes was asking for another £900 million to carry forward his restructuring during 1981–2. The same arguments applied. In Cabinet Committee before Christmas Joseph still favoured paying up. Mrs Thatcher was pragmatically clear that, for political not economic reasons, 'BL had to be supported.'[49]

On television she graphically presented the decision to keep on funding BL as a matter of timing. With productivity improving and a new model – the Metro – soon to be launched, she explained in one of those surprising phrases which occasionally came to her that this was not the moment to say, 'No, I'm going to chop you off at the stocking tops.'[50] This was a bravura defence of what might easily have been seen as a U-turn. In fact this rescue too was vindicated in the long run. After a couple of hiccups, BL – its name by then changed to Rover – was finally sold to the already privatised British Aerospace in 1987. By that time Mrs Thatcher was just glad to be rid of it.

Two hard-nosed managers like Michael Edwardes and Ian MacGregor provided cover for the Government continuing to fund British Leyland and British Steel through their difficulties. No such fig leaf was available to explain a third reversal, which really did seem to suggest that the Government's resolution was weaker than its rhetoric when it came to implementing its industrial strategy. This third challenge came from the miners – still the vanguard of the union movement, whose two strikes in 1972 and 1974 had humiliated and then destroyed the previous Conservative Government. Of all the beasts in the industrial jungle, the National Union of Mineworkers (NUM) was the one Mrs Thatcher knew she would have to take on and defeat at some point. Detailed planning to withstand a coal strike had begun the moment the Government came into office. Yet when the opportunity for a showdown with the NUM arose in February 1981 it was Mrs Thatcher who backed down. It was her decision, overriding her Energy Secretary who was preparing to stand firm. (The Cabinet was not consulted.) Three years later, of course, it was very different. That epic confrontation in 1984–5 sealed her rout of the unions. From the perspective of 1985 the earlier retreat could be understood as merely tactical. But at the time it appeared to show that Mrs Thatcher had learned from Ted Heath's experience that it was wiser not to tangle with the miners.

The issue, as in 1984, was the closure of uneconomic pits. The NCB's announcement of plans to close twenty-three pits with the loss of 13,000 jobs raised fundamental fears for the future of the industry. Faced with the threat of a strike, Mrs Thatcher was initially robust. Asked by Michael Foot in the Commons if she would reconsider the closures before she was forced to, she replied defiantly: 'No, Sir . . . I am not forced to do many things.'[51] Pit closures were a matter for the NCB. 'I am not directing that industry.'[52] But she was appalled to discover that the NCB had made no contingency plans to withstand a strike: surplus coal was piling up at the pithead, but there were only minimal stocks at the power stations where it was needed. With her instinct for the realities of power she swiftly concluded that this was a dispute the Government could not win.

'All we could do', she wrote in her memoirs, 'was cut our losses and live to fight another day.'[53] But the NUM's crowing, and her own supporters' undisguised dismay, must have been hard to bear. The *Observer* gleefully reported that the Government 'did not even wait to see the whites of their eyes before climbing down'. The NUM was unwise to gloat, however. In the long war between the miners and the Tories, 1981 was a Pyrrhic victory. Her ignominious retreat only hardened Mrs Thatcher's determination to exact a decisive revenge when the time was ripe.

One group of workers she had no compunction about taking on, however, was the Civil Service. Any Government intent on cutting public spending was bound to start with its own servants. But more than that, it was Mrs Thatcher's positive intention to 'deprivilege' the Civil Service. Though she admired individual officials, she regarded the bureaucracy as a whole as an obstacle to the culture she was trying to create. One of Geoffrey Howe's first actions in 1979 was to set a target to cut the Civil Service by 100,000 jobs over the next five years. At the beginning of 1981 he announced that the 6 per cent cash limit already set for local authorities would also apply to central government. The nine Civil Service unions promptly rejected an offer of 7 per cent and started a highly effective campaign of selective strikes directed at Inland Revenue collection, customs and excise, vehicle licences and other Government agencies – including the secret intelligence monitoring centre at Cheltenham (GCHQ).

This last enraged Mrs Thatcher more than all the others; but after three months the loss of revenue to the Government was becoming serious. The Cabinet Office minister responsible for the Civil Service, Christopher Soames – fresh from his proconsular triumph in Zimbabwe – applied his heavyweight experience to trying to negotiate a settlement. He succeeded, with a very modestly increased offer of 7.5 per cent; but Mrs Thatcher would not have it. She wanted to make a demonstration of the Government's determination to stick to its cash limit, whatever the cost. In fact a few weeks later – at the end of July – she was persuaded to settle at the same figure that she had earlier rejected, plus an inquiry to be chaired by a High Court judge. It was an expensive display of Prime Ministerial stubbornness which was estimated to have cost the Government anything between £350 million and £500 million. Nigel Lawson, still at the Treasury, thought it was worth it; but Geoffrey Howe felt that 'the line on which we were obliged to stand was not well chosen'.[54] As usual she took her revenge. In her Cabinet reshuffle that September Soames was sacked. More than that, the Civil Service Department itself was abolished, its Permanent Secretary prematurely retired and the management of the Civil Service split between the Treasury and the Cabinet Office. This was not only a matter of public spending, but a critical assertion of Mrs Thatcher's subordination of Whitehall.

The 1981 budget and the routing of the wets

The key turning point in the critical first two and a half years was Geoffrey Howe's third budget in March 1981. This was the make-or-break moment when the increasingly embattled Prime Minister and her dogged Chancellor defied the whole weight of conventional economic wisdom and political punditry to demonstrate beyond doubt their determination to stick to their fundamental strategy. The timing was important. It was just coming up to two years since the Government had taken office – exactly the point at which so many previous Governments which had started out with high ambitions had run into a brick wall of economic reality. Despite her defiant declaration at the party conference, there was widespread scepticism that Mrs Thatcher's experience would be any different.

Mrs Thatcher was acutely sensitive to such criticism. She believed that the Government's radicalism was being continually undermined by leaked whispers of the wets' unhappiness. In fact the dissenting ministers did not only voice their reservations off the record. Several of them, including Gilmour, Pym and Walker, did not shrink from making their barely coded criticism public. Over Christmas 1980, therefore, Mrs Thatcher determined on her first reshuffle.

The single victim, however, was the Leader of the House, Norman St John Stevas – the softest target among the wets. She wanted to move Francis Pym, who had fought too successfully against cuts in his defence budget, embarrassing her by turning her own arguments against her. Pym was too senior to be easily sacked, but the Leadership of the House offered a suitably dignified sideways move, appropriate for a former Chief Whip. So Stevas – an amusing lightweight who had tested her tolerance by inventing satirical nicknames for her – was the scapegoat. He was devastated.

With just this one dismissal Mrs Thatcher simultaneously achieved a significant rebalancing of the Cabinet. As well as Pym from Defence, she also moved John Biffen from the Treasury, where he had proved a disappointingly soft touch as Chief Secretary. Biffen was switched to Trade, while John Nott was sent to sort out the Ministry of Defence. Overall the effect of the changes represented a slight tilt to the right.

But something more dramatic was required. The first weeks of 1981 saw the British Leyland rescue, and the Government's retreat from confrontation with the NUM. At the end of February Ian Gow warned Mrs Thatcher of 'a serious deterioration in the morale of our backbenchers.'[55] In this atmosphere Howe's forthcoming budget took on huge importance. Though there were differences of emphasis, the Prime Minister with her private advisers essentially agreed with Howe and his Treasury team that the first priority must still be to maintain the pressure on inflation by redoubling the attack on public borrowing. Their argument among themselves was about how, and by how much, the borrowing requirement could be cut. The alternative strategy – the orthodox Keynesian approach, followed by every previous British Government since the war – prescribed on the contrary that at a time of increasing unemployment, public spending must be allowed to rise. This would have been the policy of three-quarters of the Cabinet, had they been consulted. But they were not.

Mrs Thatcher had staked her reputation on the need to keep on cutting borrowing, yet so far it had only kept on rising. What she wanted from the budget was above all an emphatic demonstration that the Lady was not for turning. Having cut income tax in 1979 she and Howe were determined not to have to raise it again. The solution was eventually provided by Lord Cockfield – the Tory party's long-standing tax specialist. By freezing personal allowances, withholding the usual increases in tax thresholds, he suggested, the Chancellor could achieve the same effect without the political odium.

The 1981 budget actually marked the abandonment of strict monetarism in favour of what has been termed 'fiscalism'.[56] But it delivered a massive deflationary squeeze to an already depressed economy. This was what horrified the wets when the budget was revealed to the Cabinet a few hours before Howe was due to present it in the House of Commons. It was also the objection of the 364 university economists – including five former Chief Economic Advisers to successive governments – who famously wrote to *The Times* to denounce it.[57] The budget's authors, on the contrary, argued that it was not deflationary at all, merely an unavoidable response to the Government's inability to control public expenditure. If anything it was actually reflationary.

Ian Gilmour, the most cerebral of the wets, rejected this – as he rejected the whole philosophy of Thatcherism – maintaining that the homely analogy of 'housewife' economics is false, since when Government cuts its spending it also cuts its income: it merely balances the books at a lower level of economic activity. This is what happened in 1981. In the short term the budget did further depress the economy – or would have done if the Government had stuck to its monetarist guns. Instead, the loosening of personal credit controls in the summer fuelled an expansion of demand which led to the beginnings of a recovery.[58] The fact is, once again, that the budget was less an act of economic management than of political will. Its strictly economic effect is still disputed. Howe and Lawson insist that it laid the foundations of the recovery, which took off spectacularly after 1983; Gilmour counters that recovery from the Government-exacerbated recession of 1979–81 would have come anyway, and was actually delayed by the budget. This is an argument that can never be settled. What is indisputable is that the budget marked a decisive stage in Mrs Thatcher's routing of the wets.

The real weakness of the wets' position was that – as Mrs Thatcher contemptuously jeered – they had no practical or principled alternative. They knew that they did not like the policy of deflation and high unemployment, and feared the social consequences; they congratulated themselves when the money supply turned out not to be the philosopher's stone the monetarists had pretended. But their criticism amounted to warning that the Government's measures were too harsh in current circumstances. As Conservatives they accepted in principle that public spending took too large a share of GDP and should be reduced: they were simply afraid of the consequences of trying to cut it during a recession. Right or wrong, the Prime Minister and her Chancellor were following a positive strategy which attracted admiration for its sheer conviction; by contrast the wets' anguished mutterings were easily portrayed as feeble. The universal adoption of the term 'wet' damned them to irrelevance.

Much of the press comment on the budget was fiercely critical. Even before the 364 economists published their anathema, words like 'disastrous', 'perverse' and 'economically illiterate' were common currency. The majority of Tory MPs were said to be 'bewildered and uneasy'.[59] The smack of unpopular measures, however, was just what those who feared that the Government had lost its way were looking for. The *Daily Telegraph* hailed the budget as 'bold, harsh and courageous'; *The Times*, rather more hesitantly, agreed.[60] 'Her enemies in the Cabinet and elsewhere began to realise that if she and Geoffrey could do what they had done, then they were far tougher and stronger than people had thought.'[61] Speaking to the Conservative Central Council in Cardiff at the end of the month, Mrs Thatcher dramatically reaffirmed, in characteristically personal terms, her determination to hold the moral high ground. 'I do not greatly care what people say about me . . . This is the road I am resolved to follow. This is the path I must go.'[62] She won a standing ovation. Boldness was its own reward.

She had flattened the wets and she could always trounce Michael Foot in the House of Commons, puncturing his windy outrage with reminders of his own record laced with helpful quotations from Callaghan and Healey. Within weeks of the budget, however, two new developments occurred which were harder to deal with. First, at the end of March the Labour party finally split. The pro-European right led by Roy Jenkins (recently returned from Brussels) and three former Cabinet Ministers (Shirley Williams, David Owen and Bill Rodgers) sealed their disillusion with the leftward direction of the party and resigned to form a new Social Democratic Party (SDP), which immediately linked up with the Liberals and began to register high levels of support in the opinion polls. In July, at the new party's first electoral test, Jenkins came within 2,000 votes of capturing the safe Labour seat of Warrington. The SDP's direct challenge was to Labour; but the huge appeal of the new Alliance sent a warning to worried Tories of the danger of abandoning the middle ground. One Conservative MP crossed the floor to join the SDP, and all summer there were rumours that others might follow.

Second, beginning in April in Brixton, then spreading in July to other rundown areas of Liverpool, Birmingham and other cities, there was a frightening explosion of riots and looting on a scale not seen in Britain since Victorian times. This was precisely the sort of civil disorder that Prior and Gilmour had predicted if the Government was not seen to show more concern about unemployment. The riots seemed to confirm the conventional analysis that a level of 2.5 million unemployed was not politically sustainable, and increased the pressure from worried backbenchers for a change of policy.

Mrs Thatcher reacted characteristically to both challenges. She despised the SDP defectors for running away instead of fighting their corner in the Labour party. There was no room in her conviction politics for centre parties. In her memoirs she called them 'retread socialists who . . . only developed second thoughts about socialism when their ministerial salaries stopped in 1979'.[63] There was enough truth in this to make it an effective argument. Though the Alliance undoubtedly represented an unpredictable electoral danger to the Government, tapping a deep well of public distaste for both the 'extremes' of militant Labour and Thatcherite Conservatism, it lacked a clear political identity; while clarity was Mrs Thatcher's principal asset. The SDP was just another gang of wets.

She was shaken by the riots, on two levels. First, she was genuinely shocked at the violence and destruction of property. Her famous exclamation, on seeing the extent of the damage, 'Oh, those poor shopkeepers!', was a heartfelt cry of identification with the victims.[64] She felt no sympathy whatever with the rioters, or interest in what might drive a normally quiescent population to rebel. She was determined to treat the episode as a purely law-and-order matter, though she did allow Whitelaw, as Home Secretary, to appoint a liberal judge to inquire into strained relations between the local black population and the police.

The second wave of disturbances, which started in Liverpool on 3 July and spread over the next three weeks to Manchester, Birmingham, Blackburn, Bradford, Leeds, Derby, Leicester and Wolverhampton, involving young whites as well as blacks, was much more serious, since it could be interpreted not simply as an outbreak of local tension but as a political challenge to the Government. Now she was alarmed at a different level. One colleague observed that 'the Prime Minister's nerve seemed momentarily to falter'.[65] On television she appeared unusually nervous and succeeded only in displaying the limitations of her law-and-order response. Two days later she visited Brixton police station and spent the night in the operations room at Scotland Yard to demonstrate her support for the police. She returned to Downing Street to impress on Willie Whitelaw the urgency of arming them with the latest American anti-riot equipment.

Back in the Commons she blamed the permissive society – and its godfather, Roy Jenkins. 'A large part of the problem we are having now has come from a weakening of authority in many

aspects of life over many, many years. This has to be corrected.'[66]
Prompted by a friendly backbencher, she condemned Jenkins' dictum
that 'a permissive society is a civilised society' as 'something that
most of us would totally reject. Society must have rules if it is to
continue to be civilised.'[67]

In truth, Mrs Thatcher was very lucky. The riots that summer
died down as suddenly as they had erupted, dissolved in a warm
glow of patriotic sentiment surrounding the 'fairytale' wedding of
the Prince of Wales to Lady Diana Spencer on 29 July. There was
a further outbreak in September 1985. But there was no political
violence directed against the Government until the anti-poll-tax
demonstrations of 1990, which did help to destroy her. In 1981 she
contrived to transform a potentially devastating crisis for her Government into a vindication of her own analysis of society. At the same
time police forces were supplied with the most modern anti-riot
technology: shields, truncheons, vehicles, rubber bullets and water
cannon. This armoury was to prove as critical as the building up
of coal stocks in the Government's confrontation with the miners
in 1984–5.

Mrs Thatcher *was* worried that summer. One of her staff was
concerned at her 'physical and mental exhaustion';[68] and David
Wood in *The Times* suggested that the Iron Lady was 'showing signs
of metal fatigue'. Nicholas Henderson, visiting London from Washington at the beginning of July, found the Prime Minister 'characteristically resilient, though worried by events in Ireland and the
falling pound'. Even American Republicans, Henderson reflected,
who once looked to Mrs Thatcher as 'a beacon of the true faith'
now saw her as an awful warning, 'a spectre that haunts them'. Yet
he was still 'impressed by her vitality and will'. Things might yet
come right, he concluded. It was bound to take time. 'It is not,
therefore, the moment to lose faith in her.'[69]

Some who had hitherto supported her, however, were losing
faith, or patience. Several senior Conservatives, including the party
chairman Peter Thorneycroft, were beginning to call for a change
of direction; and in July the revolt reached the Cabinet. The one
concession the wets had managed to wring from their defeat in
March was a promise that the Cabinet should never again have the
budget sprung on them without advance warning, but should be
allowed to discuss broad economic strategy in advance. Mrs Thatcher
agreed reluctantly as a sop to Geoffrey Howe, who felt that Prior
and Gilmour had 'some justification' for feeling excluded from 'a
secretive monetarist clique'; he believed that, given a more colle-
giate style, he could persuade them that there was no alternative

to his policy.[70] Howe's faith in his power of advocacy did him credit; but Mrs Thatcher's political sense was more acute. The first test of the new openness demonstrated exactly why she had been right to fear it.

Howe and Leon Brittan produced a paper proposing a further package of spending cuts for 1982–3. They were supported by Keith Joseph but by virtually no one else. Practically the whole of the rest of the Cabinet rebelled. Most seriously, from Mrs Thatcher's point of view, two of her original handful of 'true believers', John Biffen and John Nott, defected. But Biffen, though a monetarist by long conviction, was always sceptical by temperament and had been making damp noises for some time. It was Nott's desertion which most upset the Prime Minister. Hitherto she had seen him as her next Chancellor. Now she felt that he had been infected by 'the big-spending culture' of the Ministry of Defence.[71] The defection of Nott and Biffen left the Prime Minister and Chancellor danger-ously isolated.

At this potential crisis of her premiership Willie Whitelaw's posi-tion was crucial. As Home Secretary he had borne the full impact of the summer riots; he did not believe they had nothing to do with Government policies. Now, if ever, was the moment when he might have exerted his influence, without disloyalty, on the side of an easing of policy. In fact he stayed true, vainly urging loyalty on the rest of the Cabinet. With his protection, Mrs Thatcher was able to close the meeting without conceding any ground, promising that the discussion would be resumed in the autumn.

But that Cabinet never met again. The July revolt convinced her that she must assert herself or lose control of the Government. After two years she could legitimately drop some of those she had felt obliged to include in 1979. So in September – after the summer holidays but before the party conference – she struck. Yet once again she showed caution in her choice of victims, picking off only those of the wets – Gilmour, Soames and Education Minister Mark Carlisle – who had least following in the party. Gilmour went with the most style, marching out of Downing Street to announce that throwing a few men overboard would not help when the ship was steering 'full steam ahead for the rocks'.[72] Soames' outrage could be heard across Horse Guards' Parade. Carlisle was probably less surprised to be sacked than he had been to be appointed in the first place. But Mrs Thatcher wanted his job for Keith Joseph, who specifically requested Education when he earned his release from the Department of Industry.

Paradoxically, the biggest casualty of the reshuffle was Jim Prior, who remained in the Cabinet. He was clearly earmarked for a move, since Mrs Thatcher was determined on another measure of trade-union reform. Over the summer Downing Street let it be known that he was going to be offered Northern Ireland. Prior in turn told the press he would refuse. But Mrs Thatcher called his bluff. When it came to the point he could not refuse the poisoned chalice of Northern Ireland without appearing cowardly. In his memoirs he confessed ruefully that he had been outmanoeuvred. 'That is probably why she was Prime Minister and I was certainly never likely to be.'[73] More than the sacking of Gilmour and Soames, it was her trumping of Prior that showed the surviving wets who was boss.

Meanwhile, she used the vacancies she had created to shift the balance of the Cabinet to the right. In a wide-ranging reshuffle, three new entries were particularly significant. Nigel Lawson went to the Department of Energy, to give new impetus to the privat-isation of gas and ensure that the Government was ready the next time the miners threatened to strike; Norman Tebbit took over at Employment; and Cecil Parkinson, to general amazement, was plucked from a junior post in the Department of Trade to replace Thorneycroft as party chairman, with the additional job of Paymaster-General. In addition Patrick Jenkin moved to Industry and Norman Fowler began what turned out to be a six-year stint at the DHSS. David Howell moved from Energy to replace Fowler at Transport, while Mrs Thatcher picked Janet Young, the only other woman she ever appointed to the Cabinet, to take Soames' place as Leader of the Lords.

For the first time she had a Cabinet of whom perhaps nine or ten – out of twenty-two – were 'true believers'. Yet the autumn brought very little respite. The party conference gathered in Black-pool in an atmosphere of crisis, fuelled by the worst opinion-poll ratings of any Government since the war, a stock market crash, another rise in interest rates (back to 16 per cent) and a powerful intervention by Ted Heath, lending his voice to the chorus calling for a national recovery package to tackle unemployment. Heath was coolly received and was effectively answered by Howe, who quoted back Heath's own 1970 pledge to put the conquest of inflation first, 'for only then can our broader strategy succeed'. 'If it was true then,' Howe argued, 'when inflation was half as high, it is twice as true today.'[74] Howe won a standing ovation.

Two days later Mrs Thatcher's own speech was unusually concil-iatory. Yet she gave no ground where it mattered. She repeated that she would not print money to buy illusory jobs at the cost of further inflation. 'That is not obstinacy,' she insisted. 'It is sheer common sense. The tough measures that this Government have had to introduce are the very minimum needed for us to win through. I will not change just to court popularity.'[75] If her delivery was gentler than the previous year, she made it plain that the Lady was still not for turning. She too got her usual rapturous reception. Not for the first or last time, the party faithful at conference backed her against the parliamentary doubters.

The same slight softening of tone was detectable when the Commons returned at the end of October. Labour immediately tabled a confidence motion. Mrs Thatcher had no difficulty demolishing Foot's emotional demands for a full-scale Keynesian reflation. 'His recipe is to spend more, borrow more, tax less and turn a blind eye to the consequences. He wants all that,' she mocked, 'and he wants a reduction in interest rates!' But she also met her Tory critics by taking credit, for the first time, for the fact that public spending had not fallen, but was actually some £3 billion higher than the Government's initial plans. 'To accuse us of being inflexible is absolute poppycock,' she declared. 'We have increased public spending, but not to profligate levels.' As a result, she concluded, 'I believe that underneath the surface and beginning to break through is a spirit of enterprise which has lain dormant in this country for too long.'[76]

Still the Government's position in the country remained precarious, as the Alliance bandwagon gathered a heady momentum. First the Liberals won North-West Croydon, the Government's first by-election loss. Then, a month later, Shirley Williams swept aside a Tory majority of 18,000 to win the well-heeled Lancashire seat of Crosby for the SDP. This was a landslide of a wholly different order, suggesting that no Tory seat was safe. December's Gallup poll gave the Alliance 50 per cent, with Labour and the Conservatives equal on 23 per cent. The Government's approval rating was down to 18 per cent and Mrs Thatcher's to 25 per cent: she was now the most unpopular Prime Minister since polling began. Admittedly Michael Foot was even more unpopular; but with a credible third force for the first time offering a serious alternative to the Labour/ Conservative duopoly, it would take more than just a normal swing back to the Government to secure Mrs Thatcher's re-election.

In fact the end of 1981 was the nadir of her popularity. Despite unemployment hitting three million in January, there were some shoots of economic recovery – output was rising, inflation continued to fall and interest rates fell back again – and the polls responded. 'We are through the worst,' she claimed in an end-of-year message.[77]

By the spring the Alliance had slipped back and the three parties were roughly level-pegging at 30–33 per cent each. This is the basis for the claim that the Government was already on the way back before the Falklands war changed everything. Clearly it is true up to a point. Alliance support had hit a peak in December which it could never have sustained; but it gained a fresh boost with Roy Jenkins' stunning victory at Glasgow, Hillhead, in March 1982 – just a week before the Argentine invasion of the Falklands. There is no reason to think that the Alliance was about to fade away. Three-party politics introduced an unpredictability into election forecasting which makes it impossible to say that the Tories, without the Falklands, could not have won a second term. But it is most likely that no party would have won a majority in 1983 or 1984. Mrs Thatcher's popularity may indeed have touched bottom at the end of 1981. The economy may have been beginning to recover. But her Government was still desperately beleaguered when events in the South Atlantic turned the whole landscape of British politics upside down.

13

Salvation in the South Atlantic

Falklands or *Malvinas*?

THE Argentine invasion of the Falkland Islands on 2 April 1982 was by far the greatest crisis Mrs Thatcher ever faced. After nearly three years of mounting unemployment, a record level of bankruptcies and unprecedented public disorder, she was already the most unpopular Prime Minister in living memory, with a huge mountain to climb if she was to have any hope of being re-elected. If nothing else, however, she had taught the public to see her as the Iron Lady: she presented herself above all as a champion of strong defence, a resolute defender of British interests and British pride. Failure to prevent the seizure of British territory by a tinpot South American junta could easily have been the end of her. Instead, over the following ten weeks, she turned potential national humiliation to her advantage and emerged with an improbable military triumph which defined her premiership and set her on a pedestal of electoral invincibility from which she was not toppled for another eight years.

Yet it was a deeply ironic triumph, since it should not have been necessary at all but for serious errors by her own Government in the previous two years. Mrs Thatcher snatched victory out of a disaster caused by her own failure, for which she might easily have been arraigned before Parliament for culpable negligence. Not only that, but the result of her military recovery was to land Britain indefinitely with precisely the expensive and burdensome commitment which successive Governments had quite properly been trying to offload. By any rational calculation of political results the Falklands war was a counterproductive folly. Yet it was a heroic folly, the sort of folly of which myths are made, and, instead of finishing her, it was the making of her.

The legal title to the Falkland Islands – *las Malvinas* in Spanish – has been disputed between Spain, France, Britain and Argentina for centuries and still remains debatable. Mrs Thatcher took her stand on the defence of British sovereignty: she was on stronger ground asserting the islanders' right of self-determination. Situated just 300 miles off the coast of Argentina, but 8,000 miles from Britain, the islands were an anomalous legacy of imperial adventurism; it was natural that Argentina should claim them. But the awkward reality was that they had been colonised since 1833 by British emigrants who had built up a British way of life and developed a fierce loyalty to the British flag – as well as total dependence on the British taxpayer.

Successive British Governments had been discreetly trying to give away the sovereignty of the islands since at least 1965, so long as they could guarantee certain safeguards for the population. Since they were militarily indefensible if the Argentines chose to take them by force, the Foreign Office had concluded that the islanders' practical interests would be better served by reaching an accommodation with Argentina than by living in a permanent state of siege. But the islanders stubbornly refused to be persuaded. There were only 1,800 of them, yet they enjoyed an effective veto on any proposals to transfer sovereignty between London and Buenos Aires.

By the time Mrs Thatcher came into office, the Foreign Office's favoured solution was a 'leaseback' scheme by which Britain would have ceded sovereignty to Argentina in return for a ninety-nine-year lease which should protect the islands' British way of life. Mrs Thatcher instinctively disliked the idea of handing over British subjects to foreign rule. Nevertheless she was persuaded to go along with the scheme if the islanders could be brought to agree. Unfortunately the Minister of State given the task of persuading the islanders was the chronically undiplomatic Nicholas Ridley. In July 1980 the islanders sent Ridley home with a flea in his ear; they then mobilised their substantial lobby in the House of Commons to savage the scheme when Ridley tried to sell it there. Mrs Thatcher needed no more prompting to scotch the idea; and Peter Carrington saw no need to press it.

In truth some form of 'leaseback' offered the only sensible solution unless Britain was willing to defend the islands by military force. But John Nott, sent to the Ministry of Defence specifically to make the sort of economies Pym had resisted, judged that naval warfare was the least likely form of conflict the country could expect to face in the last decades of the twentieth century. He therefore proposed, with Mrs Thatcher's approval, to scrap one aircraft carrier, *Hermes*, and sell a second, *Invincible*, to Australia (leaving only one, the ageing *Illustrious*). As it happened these two ships provided the core of the task force which retook the Falklands in 1982; had the Argentines waited a few months longer before invading, they would no longer have been available.

After the war was over Mrs Thatcher proclaimed the victory as a triumph of her strong defence policy. 'By not cutting our defences,' she asserted in a speech in her constituency, 'we were ready.'[1] This was simply not true. The cuts she had made had not yet taken effect. But the announcement of these cuts sent a clear signal to Buenos Aires that Britain had no long-term will to defend the islands. To make the message clearer still, Nott also announced the withdrawal of the ice-patrol ship *Endurance* from the South Atlantic. Her removal – as Carrington strenuously argued – was practically an invitation to Argentina to invade. But Mrs Thatcher threw her weight behind Nott. At the same time the British Antarctic Survey announced the closure of its station on the uninhabited dependency of South Georgia; and, most bitter of all for the islanders, the new British Nationality Act which passed through Parliament in the summer of 1981 – a measure aimed principally at denying the Hong Kong Chinese the right to come to Britain – casually deprived them of their British citizenship. No one could have guessed that a few months later Mrs Thatcher would be declaring the Falkland islanders as British as the inhabitants of Margate or Manchester.

Negotiations with Argentina continued at the United Nations in New York. But with any discussion of sovereignty off the agenda, the Foreign Office had no cards to play. Reading the signals, the new Argentine junta headed by General Leopoldo Galtieri calculated that a swift seizure of the islands in the late summer of 1982 would present Britain and the world with a *fait accompli*. With a reduced navy, in the worst of the South Atlantic winter, there was no way Britain could have recaptured them even if she had wanted to. A few diplomatic protests and perhaps some half-hearted United Nations sanctions would have been the end of the matter. The humiliation might well have forced Mrs Thatcher's resignation, but no successor would have attempted to reverse the coup. The Argentines were actively planning the operation from January onwards. As so often happens, however, the intended timetable was upset by accident. At the beginning of March an Argentine scrap-metal merchant with a legitimate contract to dismantle a disused British whaling station on South Georgia landed without specific authorisation and raised the Argentine flag while his men went about their business. Carrington persuaded Mrs Thatcher that this was exactly the sort of thing *Endurance* existed to prevent; she agreed to send *Endurance* with twenty marines from Port Stanley to South Georgia to throw the intruders off. This in turn provoked the Argentines to accelerate their preparations.

The Saturday debate

Mrs Thatcher was genuinely outraged by the Argentine invasion of the Falklands. First, she had never believed that the Argentines, after all their blustering, would actually resort to anything so crude as military seizure. Second, she was outraged that anyone could seize British territory and think they could get away with it: it was a measure of the decline in Britain's standing in the world – the very decline she had come into office to reverse – that someone like Galtieri should imagine he could twist the lion's tail. Third, her human sympathies were immediately engaged by the thought of the islanders subjected to the daily indignity of foreign occupation. All these reactions expressed themselves over the following weeks in high-principled appeals to the great causes for which Britain was prepared to go to war. It was not just for the 1,800 Falklanders that she was prepared to fight, but for the principles of self-determination and democracy against dictatorship and naked aggression; the restoration not merely of Britain's national honour, but of the rule of international law.

All these emotions – of shock, anger, shame and sympathy – she undoubtedly felt deeply and instinctively. But she was also well aware, from the moment on 29 March when it suddenly became clear that the Argentines were seriously bent on invasion, that the unpreventable loss of the islands posed a desperate threat to her personal position and the survival of her Government. For two days she was seriously worried. Travelling to Brussels for an EC meeting, she and Carrington agreed to send three submarines south immediately; but these would take ten days to reach the islands. They sailed too late to deter; and in fact the news of their sailing only encouraged the Argentines to go ahead. In desperation Mrs Thatcher turned to the Americans. First, Carrington asked Secretary of State Alexander Haig; then she herself asked President Reagan to try to persuade the invader to stay his hand. On 1 April Reagan had a fifty-minute telephone conversation with General Galtieri, but failed to shift him. With ecstatic demonstrators already on the streets of Buenos Aires it was too late for the junta to back down. The Argentine flag flew over Port Stanley the next day.

But by then the decision to send a naval task force had already been taken. At a famous meeting in her room in the House of Commons on 31 March Mrs Thatcher was given the advice she wanted to hear – that, given the political will, the navy could recapture the islands. The man who gave this advice should not even have been at the meeting. The military advice was gloomy until the First Sea Lord, Sir Henry Leach, arrived with a very different story. Leach had bitterly opposed the shrinking of the navy. He had lost the battle within the MoD; but the Falklands crisis offered a heaven-sent opportunity to prove his case. He now gatecrashed the conclave at the Commons – in full dress uniform – telling the Prime Minister that, despite the difficulties, a naval task force could be assembled in a matter of days which could recapture the islands if they were indeed seized.

This was the advice Mrs Thatcher needed if she was to survive. There was, of course, no certainty that the navy could deliver what Leach promised. Sending a task force to retake the islands would be an enormous gamble: the problem, if it really came to fighting, would be assembling adequate air cover to permit an opposed landing. But the essential thing was that Mrs Thatcher had something positive to announce when the House of Commons met – for the first time on a Saturday since Suez in 1956 – on the morning after the invasion was confirmed.

The House met in a mood of high jingoistic outrage, but she was equal to it. When even Michael Foot – popularly seen as a sentimental old pacifist – was demanding a military response to wipe away the stain of national humiliation, Mrs Thatcher was not to be outdone.* The Argentine action, she declared bluntly, 'has not a shred of justification nor a scrap of legality'. Accordingly 'a large task force will sail as soon as preparations are complete'. HMS *Invincible* would be in the lead and would be ready to leave port on Monday.[2]

A task force ready to sail in forty-eight hours was more than the Government's most excited critics could have hoped to hear. The announcement regained Mrs Thatcher the initiative. Her mixture of moral indignation and uncompromising belligerence perfectly matched the mood of the House and of the country. There was still considerable anxiety and some muttering among dissident

---

* In fact, Foot was not a pacifist at all. As an ardent young journalist he had been one of the authors of *Guilty Men*, the famous indictment of the Chamberlain Government's unreadiness for war in 1939.

Tories who hoped that the crisis would destroy her. But from the moment the first ships of the task force – eventually comprising a hundred ships and 26,000 men and women – sailed from Portsmouth on 5 April amid scenes of Edwardian enthusiasm, Mrs Thatcher identified herself emotionally with 'our boys' and skilfully rode the wave of jingoism and national unity.

Yet if the announcement of the task force enabled her to recover the initiative, the House still craved a scapegoat to purge the sense of national disgrace. First, John Nott winding up the debate in the chamber, then Peter Carrington in a committee room upstairs, were savaged by furious backbenchers scenting blood. Carrington, unused to the rough manners of the Commons, determined to resign. Having warned repeatedly against the withdrawal of *Endurance*, his department bore less immediate culpability for the invasion than the MoD – or the Prime Minister. But a mixture of *noblesse oblige* and lordly disdain – the former prompting him that someone should carry the can and the latter that it might as well be him – made up his mind to go. Carrington's self-sacrifice was quixotic but it had exactly the desired effect, satisfying the need for someone to be seen to take responsibility so that the Government and the country could unite behind the task force.

Losing Carrington, whom she both liked and trusted – even if she did not always act on his advice – was nevertheless a blow, compounded by the fact that she was obliged to promote one of her least-favourite colleagues, Francis Pym, to take his place. Pym's elevation was ironic, not just because she disliked and thoroughly distrusted him, but because it was he who had fought for the defence budget in 1980 when she had been intent on cutting it. Yet she was now the Warrior Queen while he was cast as the voice of inglorious appeasement.

Britannia at war

On finding herself unexpectedly plunged into a possible war for which she had no training or preparation, Mrs Thatcher very sensibly sought advice. She invited Sir Frank Cooper to the upstairs flat at Number Ten for Sunday lunch. Cooper recalled: 'We had a gin and she asked me "How do you actually run a war?"'

> I said 'First you need a small War Cabinet; second it's got to have regular meetings come hell or high water; thirdly, you don't want a lot of bureaucrats hanging around.'[3]

She duly formed a small War Cabinet – officially the South Atlantic sub-committee of the Overseas and Defence Committee (ODSA) – to handle both the military and the diplomatic aspects of the crisis. It comprised Pym and Nott as Foreign and Defence Secretaries and Willie Whitelaw as deputy Prime Minister. The fifth member was Cecil Parkinson, chairman of the Tory party, chosen for his smooth presentational skills on television but also as a dependable supporter of the Prime Minister. Geoffrey Howe was excluded since the cost of the operation was not to be a factor. For the next ten weeks this group, plus Admiral Sir Terence Lewin (Chief of the Defence Staff), Frank Cooper and other officials, met at Number Ten every morning at 9.30, and at Chequers at the weekend.

As the conflict escalated, however, Mrs Thatcher was careful to cover her back by securing the endorsement of the full Cabinet for every major decision, starting with the sending of the task force. This was one of the very few occasions when she went round the table counting heads: only John Biffen openly dissented.[4] Throughout the crisis, indeed, Mrs Thatcher showed herself – as Peter Hennessy has written – 'almost Churchillian in the punctilio she showed to Cabinet and Commons'.[5] She even introduced a second weekly meeting, every Tuesday after the meeting of the War Cabinet, to keep the full Cabinet informed of developments.

The streamlined command structure worked extraordinarily smoothly, mainly because Mrs Thatcher got on well with the military top brass. Before March 1982 she had had very little to do with the armed forces – though the drama of the SAS's ending of the Iranian Embassy siege in May 1980 had given her a brief, exciting taste of what they could do.* But once she had stopped worrying about their cost, she greatly admired their dedication and professionalism. She trusted the military, and they in turn trusted her not to let them down halfway through the operation. They too remembered Suez.

---

* On 30 April 1980 six armed terrorists demanding autonomy for southern Iran seized the Iranian Embassy in Kensington, taking twenty hostages, including a police officer and two BBC journalists. Willie Whitelaw, as Home Secretary, was in charge of the six-day police operation to end the siege. But Mrs Thatcher took a close interest, making it clear that there should be no substantial negotiations and that the terrorists should not be allowed to get away with it. As soon as they started shooting hostages she approved Whitelaw's decision to send in the SAS to storm the building – live on television, at teatime on Bank Holiday Monday – killing five of the terrorists and capturing the sixth. Afterwards she and Denis went in person to congratulate the assault team at their HQ in Regent's Park.[6]

Nor was it only the top brass she admired. She established an even more remarkable rapport with the men who would actually do the fighting. Just as she identified with the aspirations of suburban home-owners whom she called 'our people', so a part of her reached out, adopted and idealised the tough young soldiers, sailors and airmen who became 'our boys'. She had first used the phrase in 1978, referring to the troops in Northern Ireland, but only took to doing so regularly and possessively during the Falklands campaign.[7] The forces recognised 'Maggie' as a politician with a difference, a fighter like themselves who actually understood them better than the would-be peacemakers, who sought a diplomatic settlement to prevent the loss of life which would be inevitable in retaking the islands by force. They had not been training all their lives to have their one chance of action denied them.[8] To the men in the South Atlantic 'Maggie' was not just a civilian Prime Minister playing politics with their lives. She was a leader they were proud to fight for 'with a passion and loyalty', the military historian John Keegan has written, 'that few male generals have ever inspired or commanded'.[9] Less intensely, the public at home recognised that she was no longer just another politician: the war transformed her from a bossy nanny into the breast-plated embodiment of Britannia.

From her teens Mrs Thatcher had idolised Churchill. She often invited ridicule – and infuriated the Churchill family – by suggesting a totally unwarranted familiarity with 'Winston'. Whether standing up to the Soviet Union or defying the wets in her Cabinet, she did not shrink from casting her struggle in Churchillian terms. At the time of the 1981 budget she stiffened her resolve by reading Churchill's wartime speeches and reciting them aloud to her staff.[10] She visited Churchill's underground war rooms beneath Whitehall before they were opened to the public. She could never have dreamed that she would have the chance to play Winston in reality. But the Falklands invasion gave her – on a minor scale – that opportunity. Eagerly, as if she had been in training for this moment all her life, she adopted a Churchillian rhetoric of Britain alone fighting for liberty, Britain standing up to the dictators, everything subordinated to the single aim of victory. 'Failure?' she declared grandly in one television interview, this time quoting Queen Victoria: 'The possibilities do not exist.'[11] She summoned the spirit of 1940 and, remarkably, by the power of her conviction and the heroism of her sailors and soldiers, she lived up to it.

In one way Mrs Thatcher's inexperience of war was a positive advantage. Practically every senior politician, soldier and diplomat involved in the Falklands was convinced that no male Prime Minister, except perhaps Churchill, would have done what she did – ordered the task force to sail and then backed it to reconquer the islands, accepting the certainty of casualties if it came to a shooting war. Most of the men around her had personal experience of war. Whitelaw and Pym both had the Military Cross; even the owlish Nott had served as a professional soldier with the Gurkhas in Malaya. A man, they all believed, would have been more vividly aware of what war involved. Admiral Lewin warned Mrs Thatcher that there would be casualties. She hated the idea, of course; but she accepted the inevitability so long as the navy and the army judged the risk proportionate to the goal. Fighting, after all, was what the forces were for.

When casualties occurred, however, she probably felt them more deeply than her male colleagues. Several of her closest confidants have described her 'acute distress' at the news of losses. Ronnie Millar was with her when she was told of the sinking of HMS *Sheffield*, just before she spoke to the Conservative Women's Conference on 29 May. She tensed, turned away, clenched her fists, struggled for control and quietly wept; then she composed herself and proceeded to make her speech, calmly and with dignity, but cut to twenty minutes.[12]

She made a point of writing personally to the families of all the men who died. She later claimed, without irony, that her own anxiety when Mark was lost in the Sahara earlier that year gave her an insight into what the Falkland mothers were going through. ('I was lucky,' she told Miriam Stoppard in 1985. 'They weren't.')[13] The old hands around her – not least Denis, who had served in Italy in 1943–5 – all had to console her at times with the reminder that casualties were inevitable. Once the casualties started, however, they only made her more determined to finish the job.

Her sex was really beside the point. What made Mrs Thatcher a successful war leader – apart from the quality of the forces under her command and a large slice of luck – was the clarity of her purpose. She had an unblinking single-mindedness about achieving her objective and an extraordinary simple faith that because her cause was right it would prevail. In war, as in economics, it was this moralistic certainty, not her gender, which set her apart from her male colleagues, enabling her to grasp risks they would have baulked at. In the messy trade-offs of domestic politics, her clear-cut sense of righteousness was a mixed attribute – a source of strength up to a point, but also a weakness which narrowed her capacity for human sympathy. In war it was pure strength. It was the job of her colleagues in the War Cabinet to weigh the risks, and specifically the job of Pym as Foreign Secretary to pursue every diplomatic possibility of averting war – if only to keep world opinion on Britain's side. As it happened, she was right to see from an early stage that there was no genuine compromise available. She recognised that General Galtieri could no more back down without winning the sovereignty of *las Malvinas* than she could accept their continued occupation. So she was vindicated in her determination that there was no alternative to war.

Yet the fact remains that even she, with all her determination, still could not have retaken the islands if the Chiefs of Staff had not advised her that it was militarily possible, or if they had judged the risk too great. Theirs was the real responsibility. Mrs Thatcher's role was to make and sustain the political judgement that if the military said it could be done, then it should be done. By the force of her own conviction she won and kept the backing of her Cabinet for her unswerving line. It is this judgement that colleagues doubted that any other modern Prime Minister, or potential alternative Prime Minister in 1982, would have made. In the event, she won her war and liberated the islands, with relatively little loss of life; and the victory was judged to have been worth the cost. Nevertheless the cost was high – 255 British lives; six ships sunk and others damaged; the huge cost of defending the islands for an indefinite future – and it could very easily have been much higher. The risk was never properly calculated in advance, and the Argentines should have inflicted much heavier damage than they did. It was in fact a very close-run thing. All the elements of the task force were operating at the extreme limits of their capacity, with virtually no margin for error; some units outside Stanley were down to their last six rounds of ammunition when the Argentine surrender came.[14] The peace-makers were right to explore every possibility of averting Mrs Thatcher's appalling gamble.

The diplomacy of war

As the task force steamed slowly south during April and early May, Mrs Thatcher's position was very delicate, since she had to be seen to be willing to accept a reasonable settlement, if one could be negotiated, even though she was personally determined to agree to nothing less than the full recovery of British sovereignty over the islands. She recognised that she must keep the diplomatic option open in order to retain world and above all American opinion on

Britain's side – though she had difficulty understanding how the Americans could fail to support their most faithful ally against what seemed to her a clear-cut case of unprovoked aggression. In fact, the first instinct of the Reagan administration, which had taken office in Washington at the beginning of 1981, was to remain neutral. There was a strong lobby, most powerfully represented by the outspoken Ambassador to the United Nations, Jeane Kirkpatrick, which considered the preservation of good relations with Latin America more important than pandering to British imperial nostalgia. President Reagan himself, bemused by the importance Mrs Thatcher attached to what he called 'that little ice-cold bunch of land down there', stated on 6 April that America was friends with both Britain and Argentina.[15] It was on this basis, to Mrs Thatcher's fury, that Secretary of State Alexander Haig set out to try to broker an even-handed settlement.

It was not, as is often assumed, Mrs Thatcher's special relation-ship with Ronald Reagan which swung American sentiment in Britain's favour over the next few weeks, but a brilliant exercise in old-fashioned diplomacy by two paladins of the despised Foreign Office – Sir Anthony Parsons, Britain's Ambassador to the United Nations in New York, and Sir Nicholas Henderson, the British Ambassador in Washington. In addition, and crucially, the US Defense Secretary, Caspar Weinberger, accorded Britain on his own initia-tive vital military cooperation – the use of the US base on Ascen-sion Island, with unlimited fuel and spares, accelerated purchase of Sidewinder missiles and access to American intelligence – long before the White House had officially come off the fence, and despite the fact that the US military viewed the attempt to retake the islands as 'a futile and impossible effort' which could not succeed.[16] For this help beyond the call of duty Weinberger was awarded an honorary knighthood after the war.

Anthony Parsons pulled off an extraordinary coup, just one day after the invasion, by persuading the UN Security Council to pass a resolution (Resolution 502) condemning the Argentine action and calling for the withdrawal of the occupying troops pending a diplo-matic solution. To obtain the necessary two-thirds majority – discounting the Communist and Latin nations – he had to twist the arms of Togo, Zaire, Uganda, Guyana and Jordan. He managed the first four, before calling in Mrs Thatcher to make a personal appeal by telephone to King Hussein. She succeeded. The Argen-tines had never imagined that Britain could mobilise the UN in support of an imperialist quarrel. As in Rhodesia, Mrs Thatcher would much rather have done without the involvement of the UN.

But in the eyes of the world, Resolution 502 gave priceless legitimacy to Britain's claim to be standing up for freedom, self-determination and international law. Over the next few days Nico Henderson toured the television studios of Washington projecting Britain's cause to the American public. Most crucially, the French froze the export of Exocet missiles and spare parts for those they already had. Mrs Thatcher was always grateful for President Mitterrand's prompt and unconditional support. Within a week of the invasion Galtieri and his junta – who had expected no more than token protests – found not only Britain in arms but most of the world arrayed against them.

This gratifying approval, however, was accorded on the assumption that Britain remained ready to negotiate. The six-week hiatus before the task force reached the South Atlantic allowed ample time for a peaceful settlement to be found as Al Haig shuttled back and forth between London and Buenos Aires. Even after hostilities had started, Reagan never ceased to beg her to accept a ceasefire. In fact Mrs Thatcher played an extraordinary lone hand against the entire foreign-policy establishment of both Britain and America to ensure that all their well-intentioned peace-mongering should not forestall the military victory which she was convinced was the only outcome Britain could accept. But she recognised that she would forfeit international support if she appeared inflexible.

Haig's initial proposals provided for Argentine withdrawal from the islands followed by an interim joint administration while a permanent settlement was negotiated. Over the next two months numerous variations were spun on these three central ideas. Through all the comings and goings, however, Mrs Thatcher remained adamant on two points: first, that the occupying force must withdraw before anything else could be considered and second, that the wishes of the islanders in any eventual settlement must be 'paramount'. But Galtieri and his colleagues were equally adamant that the islands were Argentine and they would not let go what they had seized without a guarantee of eventual sovereignty. Between these two sticking points there was no compromise. But thanks to Parsons' diplomatic coup Mrs Thatcher had UN authority for her position. Resolution 502 not only called for Argentine withdrawal and guaranteed the right of self-determination; Article 51 of the UN Charter asserted the right of self-defence against aggression. So long as she showed a willingness to compromise on hypothetical details the Charter endorsed her essential demands.

At first she did not have too much difficulty holding her line. On 23 April, to her disgust, Pym bowed to intense American pressure and was persuaded to recommend a package which she described as 'conditional surrender'.[17] 'I could not have stayed as Prime Minister had the War Cabinet accepted Francis Pym's proposals,' she wrote in her memoirs. 'I would have resigned.'[18] She averted that necessity, as she often did before crucial Cabinets, by squaring Willie Whitelaw in advance. As usual he did not let her down. Rather than send Pym back to Haig with a flat rejection, however, Nott proposed that they ask him to put his package to the Argentines first, in the expectation that they would reject it – as they duly did. 'It was the Argentine invasion which started this crisis,' she told the Commons, 'and it is Argentine withdrawal that must put an end to it.'[19] That was relatively easy. Next day came news of the recapture of South Georgia, and a few days later the US Government formally came out on Britain's side, promising material and intelligence support. 'We now have the total support of the United States,' Mrs Thatcher announced, 'which we would expect and which I think we always expected to have.'[20]

The next time round the track was much more difficult. On 2 May the British submarine *Conqueror* sank the Argentine cruiser *General Belgrano*, with the loss of 368 lives; next day, in retaliation, the Argentine air force sank the destroyer *Sheffield*, killing twenty-one of her crew. Suddenly war was a reality, and international pressure on Britain to refrain from escalating the conflict grew more urgent.

The question of why the War Cabinet agreed to sink the *Belgrano* has generated more controversy than any other aspect of the Falklands war. Britain had declared (on 12 April) a maritime exclusion zone of 200 miles around the islands, inside which it warned that any Argentine ship was liable to be sunk. But the *Belgrano* was outside the zone on 2 May and – it later transpired – steaming away from the islands. To attack her in these circumstances appeared to be an act of unprovoked escalation – even a war crime. In fact there were good military reasons for doing so. The Argentine fleet was at sea, with orders to attack British ships: the previous day it had launched, but aborted, an Exocet attack. The direction in which the *Belgrano*, with her two accompanying Exocet-armed destroyers, was temporarily headed was, in Lewin's view, 'entirely immaterial'.[21] The commander of the task force, Admiral 'Sandy' Woodward, suspected that she was engaged in 'a classic pincer movement' and requested permission to sink her.[22] Lewin backed his request, and the War Cabinet had little hesitation in agreeing. By 2 May the original exclusion zone had been superseded; the Argentines had been warned that from 26 April any ship operating in the area of the task force would be liable to attack. The *Belgrano*, Mrs Thatcher told the Commons next day, 'posed a very obvious threat to the men in our task force. Had we left it any later it would have been too late and I might have had to come to the House with the news that some of our ships had been sunk.'[23] She has always subsequently maintained that the decision was taken for strictly military reasons to counter 'a clear military threat which we could not responsibly ignore'.[24] Moreover even critics have had to admit that the action was justified by its result, since the Argentine navy never ventured out of port again for the duration of the conflict.[25]

The allegation that the *Belgrano* was sunk deliberately to scupper a peace plan proposed by the President of Peru does not stand up. On the contrary, the loss of the *Belgrano* and the *Sheffield* did more than anything else to get President Bellaunde's initiative off the ground. Now that both sides had shown the other what they could do, there was growing demand both at home and abroad for a ceasefire before further carnage was unleashed. On 5 May Mrs Thatcher felt obliged to seek the support of the full Cabinet. This time she did not get it. Bellaunde's scheme was essentially the same as Haig's – 'Haig in a poncho'; it was still clear that the Argentines were prepared to discuss interim administrations only on the understanding that sovereignty would eventually be theirs. But as the Prime Minister went round the table only Michael Heseltine and Quintin Hailsham held to the uncompromising line.[26] The next day Mrs Thatcher was obliged to announce that 'we have made a very constructive response' to the Peruvian proposals.

Once again she was relying on the Argentines rejecting half a cake; and once again Galtieri did not let her down. Nevertheless this was the first time since 2 April that Mrs Thatcher had let herself be committed to accept a compromise settlement, with some form of condominium or UN trusteeship replacing simple British sovereignty. The full Cabinet discussed a range of different options in exhaustive detail; she could no longer get her way by threatening resignation.[27] This was the moment when the junta could have achieved a share in the government of the islands, had they had the sense to grasp it. A word from Foreign Minister Costa Mendes to the UN Secretary-General in New York that evening, and Britain could not have defied American and world opinion by pressing on.

Instead the countdown now quickened. On 8 May the task force sailed south from Ascension Island. Nott and others had always felt that this was the critical point after which it would not be possible to recall it with the job half done.[28] The same day the War Cabinet approved Woodward's plan for an amphibious landing on the western side of East Falkland, at San Carlos Bay, to begin on 21 May. On 12 May the requisitioned passenger liner *Queen Elizabeth II* left Southampton carrying another 3,000 men of the 5th Infantry Brigade – Welsh Guards and Scots Guards – to reinforce the Marines and Parachute Regiment who would make the initial assault. In the Commons on 13 May Mrs Thatcher was visibly irritated by further talk of peace. 'May I make it perfectly clear,' she told a Tory questioner, 'that we are working for a peaceful solution, not a peaceful sell-out.'[29] Later she practically bit Reagan's head off when the President rang to urge further negotiations: 'He couldn't get a word in edgeways,' one of his aides recalled.[30]

The following day, Sunday 16 May, she held an all-day meeting of the extended War Cabinet at Chequers to agree the form of words of Britain's final negotiating stance – in effect an ultimatum. No one expected it to be accepted: Mrs Thatcher's mind was fixed on the trial ahead. But Parsons and Henderson were still concerned to frame as conciliatory a text as possible to demonstrate Britain's willingness to go to the limit of concessions to avert war. In response the Prime Minister harried them relentlessly with high-principled talk of democracy, aggression, self-determination and the Americans' moral obligation to take Britain's side, insisting on clarity where they favoured diplomatic fudge.

In the Commons three days later she explicitly cleared the decks for war. Blaming the Argentines' 'obduracy and delay, deception and bad faith' for thwarting every effort over the past six weeks to negotiate a peaceful settlement, she announced with ill-concealed relief that the effort was over. While Britain had offered reasonable proposals, including acceptance of interim UN administration of the islands, following an Argentine withdrawal and pending long-term negotiations 'without pre-judgement of the outcome', Argentina had 'sought merely to confuse and prolong the negotiations, while remaining in illegal possession of the islands. I believe that if we had a dozen more negotiations the tactics and results would be the same.' Therefore, she announced, the British proposals were now withdrawn. 'They are no longer on the table.'

> Difficult days lie ahead; but Britain will face them in the conviction that our cause is just and in the knowledge that we have been doing everything reasonable to secure a negotiated settlement . . . Britain has a responsibility towards the islanders to restore their democratic way of life. She has a duty towards the

whole world to show that aggression will not succeed, and to uphold the cause of freedom.[31]

Victory and after

Once the order was given, four days later, to launch the counter-invasion, Mrs Thatcher had little further role to play: like everyone else she could only wait for news and trust the forces to deliver what Leach and Lewin had rashly promised seven weeks before. The risk of failure was still very real. The landing at San Carlos Bay without adequate air cover (the navy had no airborne early-warning system, and only forty Harriers against 160 Argentine planes) broke all the canons of warfare. American admirals later admitted that they would not have attempted it.[32] Helped by bad weather, the assault force reached San Carlos Water undetected – the Argentines had expected a landing nearer to Port Stanley – beachheads were successfully secured and 4,000 men put ashore on 21 May. But in the crucial battle for air superiority over the next four days two frigates (*Ardent* and *Antelope*) and the destroyer *Coventry* were sunk, and several more ships damaged. The losses would have been worse if several Argentine bombs had not failed to explode; but they were bad enough to force Woodward to keep *Hermes* and *Invincible* at a greater distance than intended, which in turn reduced the combat capacity of the Harriers.

Militarily most serious was the sinking on 25 May of the transport ship *Atlantic Conveyor*, with the loss of three of the task force's four Chinook helicopters, with which it had been planned to lift the Marines and Paras across the island to Port Stanley. Now they had to 'yomp' the whole way on foot, carrying their heavy equipment. Fortunately – and inexplicably – the Argentines failed to bomb the beachheads before the troops were ready to move off. Fortunately the Harriers performed better than could have been predicted, inflicting heavier losses on the Argentine air force than its commanders in Buenos Aires (never very keen on Galtieri's war) were prepared to accept. Fortunately, too, the Argentine submarines stayed in port; while their land forces, though they outnumbered the British by 2–1, turned out to be unwilling conscripts from the warmer climate of northern Argentina, physically and psychologically less suited to the bitter Falklands winter than the Arctic-trained British professionals. Once the Marines and the Paras had begun their advance on Stanley – by way of a diversion to Goose Green – there was little doubt that they would get there; but the casualties could have been much greater had the Argentines put up more determined resistance. As it was, the last big blow to the British forces was the sinking of the troopship *Sir Galahad* at Fitzroy on 8 June, with the loss of fifty-one Welsh Guardsmen. The inadequately protected landing at Fitzroy was one perilous operation that went tragically wrong, giving a chilling glimpse of what might easily have been; but it did not delay the final push towards Stanley. Six days later the tin-roofed settlement was surrounded and the Argentine commander surrendered without need for a final onslaught.

During these climactic three weeks, when the fate of the task force, and of her Government, hung on events 8,000 miles away which were beyond her control, Mrs Thatcher lived on her nerves, barely sleeping, impatient for news, yet obliged to keep up as far as possible a normal round of duties and engagements. On the day of the San Carlos landing she was due to open a warehouse in Finchley: a date she had already cancelled once. 'Of course,' she told her daughter Carol, 'all my thoughts were in the South Atlantic. I was desperately worried . . . But if I hadn't gone to the function, people would have thought something was wrong – I had to carry on as normal.'[33] On the way to the constituency she was told that the operation had started badly: three helicopter pilots had been killed. She was photographed climbing into her car, her face awash with tears, but tactfully the picture was never printed. Back at the constituency office, she rested for an hour and a half before another engagement. 'Her exhaustion was almost complete.' While she was there, however, the news came through that the bridgehead had been established at San Carlos Bay:

> For the second time that day the Prime Minister froze . . . and she stayed motionless for a full thirty seconds. Then her whole body came alive again with a huge jerk, as she said: 'That's it. That's what I've been waiting for all day. Let's go!' The bustling practical Margaret Thatcher was back in action.[34]

Back in Downing Street later that evening she was transformed. 'These are nervous days,' she told the crowd which had by then gathered, 'but we have marvellous fighting forces: everyone is behind them. We are fighting a just cause, and we wish them Godspeed.'[35]

The following days were intensely difficult for her. She only visited operational HQ at Northwood twice, first during the South Georgia action on 23 April, when her supportiveness and determination made a deep impression, and then at the very end, when she and Nott went to monitor the final hours of the campaign. In the latter stages she was very hyped up and sometimes, in the words of one member of the War Cabinet, 'dangerously gung-ho': she had to be restrained from ordering an attack on the Argentine aircraft carrier *Veinticinco de Mayo* which at that stage would have been seen as a gratuitous provocation of world opinion, far worse than the *Belgrano*.[36] Her impatience was reinforced by renewed American and UN pressure for a ceasefire. Once the beachhead at San Carlos had been achieved, still more once Goose Green had been taken, the Americans urged that Britain had made her point: to go on would merely be to inflict humiliation on Argentina. But Mrs Thatcher had no problem with that. It would have been 'quite wrong', she wrote in her memoirs 'to snatch diplomatic defeat from the jaws of military victory'.[37] Besides, she could not leave her troops stranded in inhospitable terrain halfway to Stanley. So she was 'dismayed' and 'horrified' when Reagan (prompted by Jeane Kirkpatrick) telephoned her again on 31 May, begging her to follow Churchill's dictum of 'magnanimity in victory'. So far as she was concerned the victory was not yet won.

On 4 June Parsons had to use Britain's veto to block a Security Council resolution calling for a ceasefire (while the Americans performed a humiliating 'flip-flop' and ended up facing both ways at once). Simultaneously at the G7 summit at Versailles Reagan presented new proposals for a UN peace-keeping administration, with US involvement to prevent the Argentines using it to swamp the islands with new immigrants. By now both the Foreign Office and the Ministry of Defence were becoming alarmed at the implications of a military victory which would commit Britain to defending the islands for an indefinite future. On 6 June Henderson even found Mrs Thatcher herself marginally more ready to consider a solution short of the restoration of full colonial rule. 'I can't say that she liked it, but she listened.' Realising that there was a problem, however, she persuaded herself that the answer lay in the economic development of the islands. She toyed with the idea of a South Atlantic Federation of British dependencies, including Ascension, St Helena and South Georgia, which would attract Latin American investment, under US protection; but she still resented the need to show flexibility in order to secure American support. She insisted that she would be very reasonable – 'provided I get my way'.[38]

She finally got her victory on Monday 14 June. Just seventy-two days after the traumatic Saturday debate on 2 April she was able to tell a cheering House of Commons that white flags were flying over Port Stanley[39] – though the official Argentine surrender did not come until some hours later. She then returned to Downing Street where the crowd sang 'Rule, Britannia!'. This was the defining moment of her premiership. While careful to share the credit with the commanders who had planned the campaign and with 'our boys' who had executed it so heroically, there was no mistaking her determination to extract the maximum political dividend for herself and her Government. In the flush of victory, recriminations about the responsibility for letting the Argentine invasion happen in the first place were easily brushed aside. A commission of inquiry, chaired by the veteran mandarin Lord Franks, had to be set up, with a carefully balanced team of senior privy councillors and civil servants to look into the course of events leading up to the invasion. But it was inconceivable that its report – delivered the following January – would seriously criticise the victorious Government. From the humiliation of 2 April Mrs Thatcher had plucked a national and personal triumph; she had gambled dangerously but she had hit the political jackpot and no one could take her winnings from her now. 'A Labour Government,' she told Foot scornfully, 'would never have fired a shot.'[40] Over the weeks and months following the Argentine surrender she had no compunction about exploiting her victory for all it was worth.

Clearly she could not make a habit of exalting her own contribution – she attracted a good deal of criticism when she took the salute at a victory parade through the City of London, usurping, many thought, a function that was properly the Queen's – but over the summer she lost no opportunity to beat the patriotic drum. 'We have ceased to be a nation in retreat,' she claimed in a speech at an open-air rally on Cheltenham racecourse on 3 July. 'Britain found herself again in the South Atlantic and will not look back from the victory she has won.'[41]

Margaret Roberts had always been a flag-waving British patriot. From the very start of her career as a young Tory candidate in Dartford in 1949, her speeches were full of the ambition of restoring British 'greatness'. Thirty years later she entered Downing Street passionately committed to reversing the sense of national 'decline'. She had relished fighting Britain's corner against the rest of the EC at Dublin and Strasbourg; she hated lowering the flag on Rhodesia. But nothing gave her such an opportunity to wrap herself in the Union Jack as did the Falklands. The symbolism and language of military leadership gave her patriotism a new resonance. A Prime Minister in war – with a real enemy, troops committed, ships being sunk, lives lost – is a national leader in a way that he or she can never be in peace. Most other contemporary British politicians would have been uncomfortable in the role of war leader: Mrs Thatcher instinctively embraced it, enthusiastically identifying herself with 'our boys' and glorying unashamedly in the combat, the heroism and the sacrifice of war. Victory in war lent her an iconic status as a national emblem matched by none of her predecessors, with the single exception of Churchill.

It also transformed her political prospects. Despite the precedent of Churchill in 1945, it was now practically impossible that she could lose the next election, whenever she should choose to hold it. Only six months earlier she had been the most unpopular Prime Minister in polling memory, her Government divided and her party facing wipeout at the hands of a two-pronged opposition. By March there had been some recovery, but just a week before the invasion of the Falklands Roy Jenkins had won the Hillhead by-election to keep the SDP momentum rolling; the electorate was still divided equally between the Government, Labour and the Alliance. Both opposition parties had had a difficult war – Labour increasingly critical but constrained by Foot's initial support for the task force, the Alliance (despite David Owen's best efforts) looking weak and irrelevant. By July Mrs Thatcher's personal approval rating had doubled (to 52 per cent) and the Conservatives had left the other parties scrapping for a distant second place – which is how the position remained up to June 1983. Mrs Thatcher was not only virtually guaranteed a second term in Downing Street; after three years of battling her own colleagues, her authority within the Tory party was suddenly unassailable.

The Falklands war was a watershed in domestic politics, leading directly to the unprecedented domination that Mrs Thatcher established over the next eight years. As well as hugely boosting her authority and self-confidence, the experience of war leadership encouraged autocratic tendencies which had hitherto been contained. In particular the speed and convenience of working through a small War Cabinet led her increasingly to by-pass the full Cabinet in favour of decision-making through hand-picked *ad hoc* committees and her personal advisers. Meanwhile, the conviction that it was only her firmness which had brought victory encouraged her belief that a refusal to compromise was the only language foreigners understood.

The Falklands gave Mrs Thatcher a unique opportunity to become a truly national leader. Matthew Parris was one Tory MP who hoped that she might now 'emerge as a bigger person; she will acquire mercy; she will find grace'.[42] Unfortunately it had the opposite effect. Victory in the South Atlantic exacerbated her worst characteristics, not her best. After 1982 she used her augmented authority to pursue more self-righteously than before her particular vision of British society, and to trample on those groups, institutions and traditions which did not share it. Having routed the external enemy, she was soon looking for enemies within on whom she could visit the same treatment.

The war undoubtedly enhanced British prestige in the world, though possibly to a lesser extent than Mrs Thatcher wished to believe. It certainly confirmed the high professional reputation of Britain's armed forces: the Americans frankly contrasted the success of the Falklands operation with some of their own forces' bungled efforts in Lebanon and Iran, and British military advisers found themselves in demand around the world to train foreign armies. It also increased Mrs Thatcher's personal visibility on the international stage: her status as a global superstar, mobbed by crowds wherever she went, reflected credit, or at least heightened interest, back on Britain. But the world was as much amazed as it was impressed by the lengths Britain was prepared to go to recapture the Falklands. Mrs Thatcher invoked fine principles of defending democracy and standing up to dictators, investing the war with high global symbolism that went down well in Berlin, Hong Kong, Gibraltar and other threatened enclaves. But to many elsewhere the Falklands seemed a cause too petty to justify the expense of lives and treasure.

Of course it was disproportionate. The final casualty count was astonishingly low – 255 British servicemen killed, 777 wounded (and about one-tenth of those permanently disabled). This was actually fewer than were killed in the first five years of the Northern Ireland 'troubles'; but it was still a high human price, and it could easily have been much higher.* The material cost was six ships and twenty aircraft lost. The immediate financial cost has been reckoned anywhere between £350 million and £900 million, the longer-term expense of replacing lost vessels, ordnance and equipment at nearly £2 billion. Another £250 million was spent over the next three years on extending the runway at Port Stanley and improving the islands' defences, quite apart from the expense of keeping a garrison on the Falklands for the foreseeable future. Altogether the cost of the war and its immediate aftermath was around £3 billion.[43] It would have been cheaper to have given every islander £1 million to settle elsewhere. This was an ironic outcome of a crisis whose

---

* In fact it was much higher. It was revealed in 2002 that more Falklands veterans have taken their own lives since the end of the war than were killed during it.

origins lay in the MoD's plans to cut defence expenditure. Moreover, those cuts themselves had to be substantially reversed. The sale of *Invincible* to Australia was cancelled, and the navy's complement of frigates and destroyers was restored to fifty-five. If Sir Henry Leach had an ulterior motive in proposing sending the task force on 31 March he was resoundingly successful. By recovering the Falklands the navy saved itself. But from the global perspective of British strategic defence policy, the war was a disastrous diversion from sanity. Its outcome was to preserve in perpetuity, at vastly increased expense, the anomaly which successive British governments, including Mrs Thatcher's, had been trying to offload.

Having staked her political destiny on the recovery of the islands, Mrs Thatcher could not subsequently admit to any doubts that they were worth it.[44] She invested the homely names of Goose Green and Tumbledown with the glamour of Alamein and Agincourt; and in January 1983, accompanied by Denis and Bernard Ingham, she made the long uncomfortable flight by VC-10 to Ascension Island, then on by Hercules bomber to Port Stanley to receive the islanders' gratitude in person. She reverently walked – in most unsuitable shoes – over the hallowed ground where her boys had fought and died, while Denis memorably characterised the islands as 'miles and miles of bugger all' and longed for a snifter in the Upland Goose.[45] The return journey was even more uncomfortable, since their intended Hercules developed engine trouble. The replacement, hurriedly made ready for them, offered light or warmth, but not both. Mrs Thatcher chose light, huddled herself in as many blankets as could be found, and settled down to read the Franks Report into the causes of the war.

The Falklands was a war that should not have happened. Politically and diplomatically it arose from a sequence of miscalculations. Actuarially it was a nonsense. Yet once diplomatic blunders had created an unstoppable momentum for war, it cannot be denied that it was, in its way, magnificent – in part *because* the cause was so ludicrous.

Mrs Thatcher saw recapturing the Falklands as a matter of honour – her honour as well as the nation's honour – which could not be ducked without lasting national shame. Having determined to accept the challenge, the manner in which she and her forces carried it through was an astonishing feat of will, courage, skill and improvisation, a legitimate source of national pride. Generally speaking, Thatcherism was a utilitarian philosophy which subjected every aspect of national life to rigorous accountancy and undervalued what could not be costed. The Falklands war was the one great exception on which money was lavished unstintingly for the sake of an idea, an obligation, a conception of honour. Many would have preferred the coffers to have been opened for some other cause nearer home. But overall the public approved, believing that the war – like landing on the moon – was something which had to be done, without regard to cost, and took pride that it was done supremely well. It was unquestionably Mrs Thatcher's finest hour. She never achieved that moral grandeur again.

14

Falklands Effect

The emergence of Thatcherism

WITH the successful conclusion of the Falklands war, Mrs Thatcher's position was transformed. She could now look forward to almost certain re-election whenever she chose to go to the country. There was some speculation that she might cash in on the euphoria of victory by calling a quick 'khaki' election in the autumn. But that, she told George Gale in an interview for the *Daily Express*, would be 'basically wrong. The Falklands thing was a matter of national pride and I would not use it for party political purposes.'[1] This was humbug. In fact, she had no scruple about claiming the war as a specifically Conservative – indeed Thatcherite – achievement.

But she realised that to call a snap election would have looked cynically opportunist and might have backfired. Besides, it was unnecessary. Why should she cut short her first term just when she had finally secured her dominance? She could carry on for nearly two more years if she wished, to the spring of 1984. Her preference, she hinted was to go on to the autumn of 1983.[2] That gave her another full parliamentary year to reap the political harvest of her enhanced authority, and time to show some clear economic results from the pain of the last three years.

In the meantime something like normal politics resumed, and the Government could still be embarrassed by the unexpected. On 9 July there occurred an incident, trivial as it turned out, that was potentially almost as humiliating as the seizure of the Falklands. An intruder named Michael Fagan not only broke into Buckingham Palace, but found his way into the Queen's bedroom and sat on the end of her bed; fortunately he was unarmed and harmless, and she coolly engaged him in conversation until help arrived. (The Duke of Edinburgh, the public was fascinated to learn, slept in another room.) But the implications were alarming. It turned out that it was not the first time that Fagan had broken into the Palace. If security at the Palace was so poor, was it any better at Downing Street and Chequers? 'I was shocked and upset,' Mrs Thatcher told George Gale. 'Really I was very, very upset . . . Every woman in this country was upset because we all thought, oh lord, what would happen to me?'[3] Willie Whitelaw accepted responsibility as Home Secretary and initially felt he must resign. Having already lost Carrington, however, Mrs Thatcher could not face losing Whitelaw too, and persuaded him to change his mind. Whitelaw's popularity in the House protected him. Security at the Palace was tightened, and the bizarre episode passed off with no lasting political damage.

Yet the economic upturn was slow to materialise. Though Geoffrey Howe declared that the recession had officially ended in the third quarter of 1981, growth during 1982 was still only 0.5 per cent; industrial output was the lowest since 1965. Several times the Department of Employment massaged the basis of calculating the unemployment figure, but still it went on rising. Many analysts reckoned the true figure to be nearer four million than the three million the Government admitted. From within the Cabinet, too, Jim Prior continued to warn that the present level of unemployment was unsustainable and claimed that it could easily be relieved by 'some additional activity' which need not involve any more Government spending.[4] Howe and Mrs Thatcher rejected such siren voices as firmly as ever. 'When the rulers of old started to debase and clip the coinage,' she asserted, 'they were in difficulty. That's what reflation is and I'll have nothing of it.'[5]

On the other hand inflation – the Government's preferred measure of its success – continued to fall. It was down to 5 per cent by the end of 1982, enabling Howe to reduce interest rates steadily (to 9 per cent by November), which helped raise both living standards and the sense of wellbeing of those in work. The heavy shedding of manpower eventually produced higher productivity in those parts of the manufacturing economy that had survived, while industry was relieved by a steep fall in sterling – due largely to a fall in the oil price – which eventually forced Howe to raise interest rates again in December. While maintaining a tight spending framework overall, Howe also pursued an imaginative supply-side programme of deregulation and targeted incentives: more free ports, double the number of enterprise zones, loan guarantee schemes, grants to assist in the introduction of computers. For all these reasons, economic activity slowly picked up. Public spending, though still higher as a proportion of GDP than in 1979, was at last coming under control – despite the war, which was indeed paid for out of the contingency reserve, as Mrs Thatcher had promised – so that by the spring of 1983 Howe was in a position to make some modest but timely tax concessions in what was likely to be his election-year budget.

Then after three years of restraint the Chancellor and Prime Minister provoked general amazement in late 1982 by suddenly urging local authorities and other public bodies to spend more on capital investment. In fact, she was not telling local authorities to spend more, but rather to spend more of the money provided on capital projects and less on wages.

She was much more confident now in dismissing Labour allegations that she did not care about unemployment. 'I have come to the conclusion,' she retorted, 'that they do not want to get rid of unemployment. They wallow in it.'[6] In a changing economy, new jobs came from new industries and small businesses, not from declining industries. 'It is no good the Opposition yowling about it. It is a fact.'[7] The Government, she insisted, could not create jobs. 'One gains jobs by gaining customers. There is no other way.'[8]

By the time Mrs Thatcher went to the country in June 1983, the Government could plausibly claim, against all its critics, that its central economic strategy was working: inflation was being squeezed out of the economy and the way was now clear for a soundly based recovery which would soon bring real jobs. Sceptics countered that, on the contrary, Britain had suffered a more severe recession than the rest of Europe, while the Government's boasted recovery was shallow and patchy and concentrated in the south of England, leaving the manufacturing regions of Scotland, South Wales and the north of England permanently devastated. Economically this is undeniable; the impact of the Government's policies was cruelly unbalanced. The political fact, however, was that the Government had won the argument. Mrs Thatcher's toughness could be seen to be showing results. A level of unemployment hitherto held to be insupportable was discovered to be tolerable after all: there were no more riots. Meanwhile, as the political world adjusted to the probability of a second Thatcher term, a number of distinctively 'Thatcherite' policies were beginning to take shape.

First, Norman Tebbit carried the Government's second instalment of trade-union reform. With the reputation of a right-wing hard man, Tebbit had been appointed Employment Secretary in September 1981 specifically to do what Prior had successfully resisted. In fact he displayed a more subtle touch than his aggressive rhetoric suggested and produced another carefully judged package which was considerably less punitive than the Institute of Directors and right-wing backbenchers had been demanding.

The main thrust of his Employment Bill, introduced in January 1982, was to remove the unions' immunity from civil action arising out of unlawful trade disputes, while narrowing the definition of what constituted lawful action, thus rendering unions liable for damages (up to £250,000) for secondary and sympathetic strikes. Henceforth the law would only recognise disputes over pay, jobs and working conditions between groups of workers and their own employers. This was the crucial step which ended the privileged legal status granted the unions in 1906 – the anomaly on which the whole history of the abuse of union power since the 1960s had been founded.

Tebbit's Bill simultaneously tightened restrictions on the operation of closed shops; made it easier for employers to dismiss persistent troublemakers and offered Government funds to finance union ballots. But it still did not require ballots to be held before official strikes. It did not try to outlaw strikes in essential services. Nor did it touch the Tories' oldest grievance, the unions' political levy, which still required members to contribute to the Labour party unless they specifically opted out. Strike ballots and abolition of the political levy were foreshadowed in another Green Paper in January 1983, but their implementation was left to a third instalment of reform brought in by Tebbit's successor, Tom King, in 1984.

Once again this was shrewd strategy, which disarmed opposition by its carefully calculated moderation. As usual trade-union and Labour leaders furiously denounced the proposed legislation. But polls showed that public opinion overwhelmingly supported Tebbit's Bill; more important, the great majority of ordinary trade unionists supported it. By acting moderately but firmly to curb the abuses of the past fifteen years the Government was seen to be redeeming one of the clearest promises on which it had been elected.

The unions were additionally weakened by the level of unemployment, which severely cut their bargaining power. 1982 saw two long-running public-sector strikes – one on the railways, one by NHS workers – both of which ended in clear defeat for the unions without the Government's new legislation even being called upon. Mrs Thatcher vigorously condemned the strikers. 'If you want more unemployment and more job losses,' she told them bluntly, 'then keep on striking. Don't blame me.'[9] Tebbit's Bill was really a case of kicking the unions when they were already down. The industrial climate had been transformed since 1979. The unions' power to enforce unproductive overmanning and delay the introduction of new technology was already broken; management was recovering the power to manage. Some major battles still lay ahead, but by 1982 the dinosaur which had humbled Wilson, Heath and Callaghan was already mortally wounded.

The second distinctively Thatcherite policy which began to take clear shape in 1982 was large-scale privatisation. The breakthrough from a limited programme of asset disposals to the selling of whole industries came about quite suddenly as a result of the convergence of a number of factors. First the arrival of Patrick Jenkin at the Department of Industry and Nigel Lawson at the Department of Energy gave a new impetus to policies which Keith Joseph and David Howell had initiated but failed to carry through. Then the easing of the recession offered a more propitious economic climate. The likelihood of the Government winning a second term on the back of post-Falklands euphoria gave potential investors the confidence to buy shares in privatised companies without fear of a returning Labour Government immediately renationalising them. Perhaps most important, the newly established telephone company British Telecom urgently needed a massive injection of capital to finance the new digital technology. Mrs Thatcher took some persuading that privatisation was practical; but she eventually gave Jenkin the green light to go ahead.

She also needed some persuasion to privatise Britoil (the former British National Oil Corporation). This time her reservations were patriotic, reflecting a widely shared feeling that North Sea oil was a national asset which should remain under national control. Lawson's solution was to split the production side of the business from the trading side and sell only the former, retaining for the Government a 'golden share' to prevent the company falling into unsuitable (that is, foreign) hands. The first 51 per cent of Britoil shares were put on the market in November 1982. Despite an unexpected drop in the price of oil which left the underwriters with large losses, the sale raised £334 million for the Treasury, making it by far the biggest privatisation to date. The BT privatisation – much bigger again – was not ready to go before the 1983 election and had to be restarted in the next Parliament.

'We are only in our first term,' Mrs Thatcher told the party conference in October 1982. 'But already we have done more to roll back the frontiers of socialism than any previous Conservative Government. In the next Parliament we intend to do a lot more.'[10] In due course the 1983 manifesto earmarked BT, British Airways and 'substantial parts' of British Steel, British Shipbuilders and British

Leyland, plus the offshore interests of British Gas, as targets for the second term. As it turned out, building on the unexpected success of the BT sale, the Government went much further than this, privatising the whole of British Gas before moving on to target electricity and water. But already, she admitted in her memoirs, this was a programme 'far more extensive than we had thought would ever be possible when we came into office only four years before'.[11]

The form of popular capitalism she did enthusiastically embrace before 1983 was the sale of council houses. Michael Heseltine had enshrined the 'right to buy' – at a substantial discount – in his 1980 Housing Act. By October 1982, 370,000 families had already taken advantage of the legislation to buy their homes. While the Government was still feeling its way gingerly towards the privatisation of public utilities, she now knew that with the sale of council houses she was on to an electoral winner. It is probably too simple to suggest that those 370,000 families – it was 500,000 by the time of the election – were turned from Labour to Conservative voters overnight: many of them had already made the crucial switch in 1979. But more than anything else this one simple measure, promised in opposition and spectacularly carried out, both consolidated and came to symbolise Mrs Thatcher's capture of a large swathe of the traditionally Labour-voting working class.

The limits of radicalism

Council-house sales, trade-union reform and the beginnings of privatisation were major initiatives which changed the landscape of British politics. Yet beyond these three areas, some of Mrs Thatcher's keenest supporters were disappointed that her avowedly radical government did not have more to show for its first term.

The reason was partly that she simply did not have time to spare for social policy: at this stage the economy, the trade unions and the nationalised industries were her domestic priorities. In truth she was not really very interested in it: having served her ministerial apprenticeship in social security and education, she was happy to have escaped to wider horizons. But she was also very wary of the political danger in tackling the welfare state – particularly the National Health Service – which, for all its emerging inadequacies, was rooted in popular affection. 'She feared that the welfare state was Labour territory – that we weren't going to win on it.'[12] The result was that health, social security, education and public-sector housing were all squeezed to a greater or lesser degree by spending cuts, which gave practical effect – as it were by stealth – to the Prime Minister's instincts. But this was just tinkering, not the radical shake-up that Tory radicals had hoped to see.

The biggest question concerned the funding of the NHS. Almost since its inception in 1948, Conservative policy-makers had been looking at ways to switch funding at least partly from general taxation to an insurance basis. But insurance schemes had always been found to be less efficient and more impractical. Both Howe and Jenkin were still keen to explore the insurance option, however, and in July 1981 Jenkin set up a departmental working party to study alternative funding options. Mrs Thatcher was sympathetic. In her very first Commons speech as Prime Minister she had warned, with a clear echo of Milton Friedman, that 'there is no such thing as a free service in the Health Service'.[13] She never forgot that the cost of universal health care fell on the public purse and believed that self-reliant individuals should bear the cost of insuring themselves instead of relying on the state. She was keen, as a matter of principle as well as of economy, to encourage private health provision, which duly mushroomed after 1979 with an influx of American health care companies, a rush of private hospital building and more private beds in NHS hospitals. Kites flown by free-market think-tanks like the Adam Smith Institute and the Social Affairs Unit fuelled the impression – sedulously fostered by Labour – that the Tories were planning to privatise the NHS. But when it came to the point the Government drew back.

Social security was less of a sacred cow than health, largely because it was less used by Tory voters. There was no comparable embargo on radical reform; but here too policy proceeded by an accumulation of small cuts rather than a coherent programme. All short-term benefits – unemployment benefit, housing benefit, even child benefit were devalued more rapidly simply by not being uprated in line with inflation.

From her experience as a parliamentary secretary in the Ministry of Pensions twenty years before, Mrs Thatcher retained the conviction that the benefit system was a wasteful mechanism for recycling money from the hard-working to the lazy. Then at least it had been her job to face the reality of a lot of individual cases. Now she saw only the huge cost to the Treasury and a disincentive to enterprise and self-reliance. She believed that the prosperity of those in work would – in the American phrase – 'trickle down' to lift the living standards of all. She averted her eyes from the impoverishment of millions of families whose breadwinners were desperate to work if only the jobs had been there. Apart from throwing ever-larger sums at complicated youth-training schemes – money not for the most part well directed – the Government in its first term made no serious attempt to reform the benefit system.

Housing was the area where the Government most clearly favoured the better off at the expense of the poorer. The central plank of its housing policy was the sale of council houses. But while the best houses were sold on generous terms to those more prosperous tenants in secure jobs who could afford to buy them, rents for the rest – usually on the least desirable estates – were steeply increased. New council building almost completely ceased. Local authorities were debarred from using the revenues from council-house sales to renew their housing stock, leading in time to a housing shortage and the very visible phenomenon of home-lessness which emerged at the end of the decade. Housing was another service Mrs Thatcher did not really believe the state should be providing at all: her Government's purpose was to encourage and reward home-ownership. While cutting subsidy to council tenants, therefore, she was determined to protect and even extend mortgage-interest tax relief for home buyers – an anomalous middle-class subsidy which the Treasury had long wanted to phase out, but which she candidly defended as a well-deserved reward for 'our people'.[14]

As Education Secretary from 1979 to 1981, Mark Carlisle had an unenviable task, with the Treasury demanding heavy cuts in his budget and Mrs Thatcher bullying him to punish her old department. Less than a decade earlier she had been vilified for cutting free milk for primary schoolchildren, yet she finished up as a notably expansionist Education Secretary, having announced ambitious plans particularly for pre-school education, which sadly were aborted by the 1973 oil crisis. As Prime Minister, however, she showed no interest in reviving these plans, only the memory of the Milk Snatcher. Carlisle was compelled to enforce cuts in the provision of school meals and rural school transport – though the latter was partly reversed following a rebellion in the House of Lords. The axe fell hardest on the universities, which suffered a 13 per cent cut in funding over three years. This was the beginning of a decade of confusion, demoralisation and falling standards in higher education.

'We are the true peace movement'

The Government had given curiously little thought to the agenda for a second term. Given the enormous problems of trying to promote an enterprise economy against the background of a severe recession, it is understandable that the Government attempted so little major reform of social institutions before 1983. It is much harder to explain why, after the Falklands victory had transformed the political landscape and her own authority, Mrs Thatcher did not then grasp her opportunity with a radical programme for the next stretch of road that now extended before her. She evidently found it difficult to explain herself. In her memoirs she blamed Geoffrey Howe.

The truth is that a Government's energy stems from its head, and even Mrs Thatcher confessed to being a little tired by the end of the Falklands summer. Just before the recess she admitted that she intended to take a good holiday 'after this momentous year' – quickly adding, in case anyone should see this as a sign of weakness: 'I do not think I could take more than another ten years such as this has been.'[15] She actually went to Switzerland for ten days before going into hospital – briefly and, of course, privately – for an operation for varicose veins. After the high tension of the Falklands she was perhaps mentally unprepared for her sudden breakthrough to popularity and genuinely did not know what to do next. A year earlier she would not have dared talk of another ten years. There is a sense in the autumn of 1982 of Mrs Thatcher – still only fifty-seven years old – pausing for breath, resting on her oars for a moment, until she got used to the idea of going on and on.

With a dearth of new policies to unveil, Central Office was preparing to fight the coming election on the perennial appeal of Tory Governments seeking re-election: 'Life's Better under the Conservatives: Don't Let Labour Ruin it.' In 1983 the claim was rather that life was *getting* better under the Conservatives. It was admitted that the country had been through a tough three years, but the rewards were now becoming clear: inflation and interest rates were coming down, economic activity was picking up and unemployment – the Government's Achilles heel – would soon begin to fall as prosperity returned. The warning was the same, however: the return of a Labour Government would throw away all the hard-won gains.

A bland manifesto, giving no hostages to fortune, was all that was needed to win the election. The opposition parties – divided, poorly led and easily dismissed as respectively extreme (Labour) and woolly (the SDP-Liberal Alliance) – offered no serious challenge to Mrs Thatcher's inevitable return. Yet the failure to put forward a positive programme for its second term, besides being democratically dishonest, left the Government directionless after the election, prey to untoward events for which it tried to compensate, as the next contest approached, with hasty initiatives.

The trouble was that Labour offered too easy a target. Even after the defection of the SDP in 1981, the party was still riven by a bitter civil war. The hard left had seized control of the party's internal arrangements – the mechanism for electing the leader, the selection of candidates and the formation of policy. Yet senior social democrats like Denis Healey, Roy Hattersley and Gerald Kaufman remained in the Shadow Cabinet, visibly unhappy but helpless to arrest the leftward slide. In Michael Foot the party was stuck with an elderly leader, elected in a vain effort to preserve unity, whom the electorate found it impossible to imagine as Prime Minister: his approval rating – rarely over 20 per cent – was consistently the lowest since polling began. Moreover, as the election approached, Labour saddled itself with an entire platform of unpopular left-wing policies, any one of which might have rendered the party unelectable: wholesale nationalisation, massive public spending, the restoration of trade-union privileges, withdrawal from Europe and unilateral nuclear disarmament. If the Tories' manifesto was vague, Labour's was appallingly specific: Gerald Kaufman famously dubbed it 'the longest suicide note in history'.[16] Of all its suicidal policies the most crippling handicap was Foot's passionate commitment to unilateral nuclear disarmament.

Not for half a century had the major parties been so far apart on the issue of national defence. Ever since 1945 a broad consensus had obtained between the two front benches on the question of nuclear weapons. The left had kept up a more or less constant agitation for unilateral disarmament; but successive Labour leaders had maintained a firm line on the retention of the British independent deterrent. Now, with the election of a lifelong unilateralist to the leadership coinciding with a revival of support for the Campaign for Nuclear Disarmament, that consensus was ended. For the first time, nuclear weapons were set to be a major issue at the coming General Election. In the triumphant afterglow of her Falklands victory nothing could have suited Mrs Thatcher better.

Ever since becoming Tory leader in 1975, she had taken a strong line on the need to maintain and modernise NATO's nuclear defences against the Soviet nuclear threat. Her blunt warnings about Soviet expansionism had led the Russian press to christen her 'the Iron Lady', and she wore the intended insult with defiant pride. She had no interest in the polite bromides of 'peaceful coexistence' with Communism but believed that the West was engaged in a life-or-death struggle with the Soviet Empire – a struggle which she confidently expected the West to win, though she did not foresee the timescale. As early as May 1980, in a newspaper interview on the first anniversary of her election, she was looking forward to the fall of Communism. 'The major challenge to the Communist creed is coming now,' she told *The Times*:

> For years they were saying the march of communism and socialism is inevitable. Not now, not now. I would say that in the end the demise of the communist creed is inevitable, because it is not a creed for human beings with spirit who wish to live their own lives under the rule of law.[17]

In the Commons she promised to wage 'the ideological struggle . . . as hard as I can'.[18]

That meant imposing sanctions following the Soviet invasion of Afghanistan, and trying to persuade British athletes to boycott the Moscow Olympics. It meant supporting the struggle of the Polish Solidarity movement, which began in 1981, and keeping up the pressure over Soviet treatment of dissidents in breach of the Helsinki undertakings on human rights. It meant increasing Britain's contribution to NATO military spending by 3 per cent, as she had promised in opposition. Above all, it meant firmly rejecting the siren call of nuclear disarmament and matching the Russians' nuclear deployment missile for missile.

When the Conservatives came into office they were faced almost immediately with the need for a decision – which Labour had postponed – on replacing Britain's obsolescent nuclear deterrent, Polaris. As is the way with nuclear decisions in every government, this one was confined to a small *ad hoc* subcommittee composed of the Prime Minister, her deputy, the Foreign and Defence Secretaries and the Chancellor.[19] They lost no time in opting to buy the American submarine-launched Trident system, at a cost of £5 billion spread over ten years. The problem was that the expenditure could only be afforded by making cuts elsewhere. Mrs Thatcher, however, had no doubts. She believed passionately in nuclear weapons, both as a positively good thing in themselves, which had kept the peace in Europe for thirty years and would continue to do so as long as the balance of deterrence was preserved, but still more as an emblem of national power, prestige and independence. She never had any truck with the criticism that Britain's 'independent' deterrent was in practice wholly dependent on the Americans for spares and maintenance and would never in any conceivable military circumstances be used without American consent. The decision to buy Trident, she told the Commons in July 1980, 'leaves us master of our own destiny . . . We are resolved to defend our freedom.'[20]

But then the Americans changed the arithmetic by developing a new, more sophisticated version of Trident. In January 1982 the Government had to decide all over again whether to buy the upgraded D5 model in place of the original C4, at still greater expense. Mrs Thatcher was worried, but she was still determined that Britain must have the best and latest system, whatever it cost. This time she deployed the full Cabinet to outnumber the doubters. She also drew on her special relationship with President Reagan to persuade him to let Britain buy the D5 on exceptionally favourable terms, assuring the Commons – like a housewife in a soap-powder commercial – that 'the expenditure of this money secures a far greater degree of deterrence than expenditure of the same amount of money on ordinary conventional armaments'.[21]

Mrs Thatcher was also eager to accept the deployment of American cruise missiles at military bases in Britain as part of NATO's response to Soviet SS-20s targeted on the West. The deployment of cruise in several European countries had first been proposed by the West German Chancellor, Helmut Schmidt, as a way of locking the Americans into the defence of Europe at a time when it was feared they might otherwise walk away. Mrs Thatcher strongly supported it, not only to keep the Americans committed but also to demonstrate Europe's willingness to share the burden of its own defence. She was witheringly scornful when the Germans and other European governments began to weaken in the face of anti-nuclear protests; but at the same time she relished the opportunity to demonstrate once again that Britain was America's only reliable ally. When Britain agreed in September 1979 to station 144 cruise missiles at Greenham Common in Berkshire and RAF Molesworth in Cambridgeshire, the announcement caused little stir. But over the next three years, as the time for deployment approached, the mood changed. Increased tension between the superpowers, the spectre of a new nuclear arms race and the West's rejection of several plausible-sounding Soviet disarmament offers fuelled a Europe-wide revival of the fear of nuclear war, fanned by a widespread perception of Ronald Reagan as a sort of trigger-happy cowboy who might be tempted to use nuclear weapons against what he called (in March 1983) 'the evil empire'.[22] In Britain the Campaign for Nuclear Disarmament (CND), dormant since the early 1960s, suddenly sprang back to life, drawing large numbers to marches, rallies and demonstrations. Moreover, its cause was now backed by the official opposition.

Mrs Thatcher welcomed a fight on the issue, first because she thought defence more fundamental even than economics; second because she believed that unilateral disarmament was absolutely wrong in principle and would make nuclear war more likely, not less; and third because she was confident that the country agreed with her. Opinion polls reflected public anxiety about specific weapons systems. Yet when it came to the point the public over-whelmingly wanted to retain Britain's independent nuclear capacity. Keeping the bomb was at bottom, for the electorate as for Mrs Thatcher, a matter of national pride and identity. She was scornful of the woolly-minded wishful thinking of those who imagined that the USSR would respond in kind if the West tamely dismantled its weapons. 'Any policy of unilateral disarmament,' she told the Commons in June 1980, 'is a policy of unilateral surrender.'[23] The Warsaw Pact currently possessed a 3–1 superiority over NATO in nuclear weapons in Europe, she pointed out in July. 'Those who seek to have a nuclear-free Europe would do well to address their efforts in the first place to Soviet Russia.'[24] So long as the Soviets enjoyed superiority she scorned Brezhnev's offer of a moratorium. She was all for disarmament, but only on a basis of equality. In the meantime, she insisted in November 1982, 'We should have every bit as much strategic nuclear weaponry at our disposal as the Soviet Union, every bit as much intermediate nuclear weaponry at our disposal as the Soviet union.'[25]

Her enthusiasm for the latest hardware sounded alarmingly aggres-sive to those worried about the threat of nuclear escalation. The next time she spoke in the House about deploying cruise she was greeted with cries of 'Warmonger'.[26] Her response to this allega-tion was to insist repeatedly that nuclear weapons did not cause war but were actually the surest way to prevent it. She gave her fullest exposition of this argument at that year's party conference, when she devoted a long section of her televised speech to spelling out the ABC of deterrence:

I understand the feelings of the unilateralists. I understand the anxieties of parents with children growing up in the nuclear age. But the fundamental question for all of us is whether unilateral nuclear disarmament would make a war less likely. I have to tell you that it would not. It would make war more likely . . .

Because Russia and the West know that there can be no victory in nuclear war, for thirty-seven years we have kept the peace in Europe . . . That is why we need nuclear weapons, because having them makes peace more secure.[27]

It was at a joint press conference with Helmut Kohl at the end of the Chancellor's visit to London in February 1983 that she found the phrase that encapsulated her paradoxical faith. 'We really are a true peace movement ourselves,' she claimed, 'and we are the true disarmers, in that we stand for all-sided disarmament, but on a basis of balance.'[28] She always loved stealing Labour's slogans for herself. 'We are the true peace movement' became her favourite refrain throughout the General Election and beyond.[29]

Realising that defence, and the nuclear argument in particular, was going to be a key battleground in the coming contest, Mrs Thatcher took the opportunity of John Nott's intention to leave politics by removing him from the Ministry of Defence in January 1983 and replacing him with the much more combative figure of Michael Heseltine. Much as she distrusted Heseltine, she recognised that he had the populist flair to tackle CND head on. This was one of her most successful appointments; Heseltine responded exactly as she had hoped in the months leading up to the election, energetically countering the unilateralists in the television studios and on the radio. His most successful coup was to upstage CND's Easter demonstration, when they had planned to form a human chain around the Greenham Common airbase on Good Friday. Heseltine stole their thunder by visiting Germany the day before and having himself photographed looking over the Berlin Wall, thus dramatising the enemy whom NATO's nuclear weapons were intended to deter. Even with all its other doctrinal baggage, unilateralism was the biggest millstone round the Labour party's neck, and Heseltine made the most of it. The contrast with the recapture of the Falklands did not need spelling out.

Landslide: June 1983

If the result of the election was never in much doubt, its timing was uncertain up to the last moment. All Mrs Thatcher's habitual caution inclined her to carry on until the autumn. But she was under strong pressure from the party managers to go as soon as possible after the new electoral register came into force in February 1983: the redrawn constituency boundaries were expected to yield the Tories an extra thirty seats. The party chairman, Cecil Parkinson, and Central Office wanted to go early, and the temptation was great.

Nevertheless she sought every excuse for indecision. First she argued that she had promised President Reagan that she would attend the G7 summit at Williamsburg, Virginia, at the end of May: this would entail her being out of the country at a crucial stage of the campaign. She was persuaded that her absence could be turned to electoral advantage, with media coverage underlining her stature as an international stateswoman. Then she worried that the manifesto was not ready. Parkinson told her that it could be made ready in a couple of hours, at which she immediately started rewriting it herself. Still she wanted to sleep on the decision. But the next morning she went to the Palace as arranged. Polling day was set for Thursday 9 June.

The Tory campaign was frankly concentrated on Mrs Thatcher, highlighting her strength and resolution, clear convictions and strong leadership. The contrast with Foot was so obvious that it scarcely needed pointing out. Each day the Prime Minister herself chaired the morning press conference at Central Office, flanked by two or three colleagues; most of the Cabinet was paraded, but few featured more than once, and their role was clearly subordinate. Mrs Thatcher answered most of the questions. Besides herself only three ministers appeared in the party's television broadcasts.

The campaign closely followed the successful pattern of 1979. After the press conference each morning she set off by plane or helicopter for whistle-stop visits around the country, meeting up with her campaign coach to inspect shiny new factories or do walkabouts in shopping malls, carefully chosen to provide good pictures for the local media and the national TV news; she went mainly to Tory constituencies, where only the local members were told in advance that she was coming, to ensure that she met an enthusiastic reception and to minimise the risk of hostile demonstrations. She made only a handful of major speeches – and those were delivered to carefully vetted audiences of Tory supporters well supplied with Union Jacks. In addition, she gave two interviews to friendly newspapers, did two major radio interviews and five major TV interviews – two taking audience questions and three with heavyweight interviewers.

Each evening when she came back to Downing Street she would have a quick supper and then get on with preparing speeches for the following day. Mrs Thatcher would rewrite and correct them far into the night. Next morning she would arrive at Central Office at 8.15 for an hour's briefing before the 9.30 press conference. Gordon Reece attended these briefings and also helped rehearse her for her television appearances. But above all in this election she put herself in the hands of Cecil Parkinson, who had the knack of soothing tensions and keeping her calm when things went wrong.

She trusted him completely. 'If Cecil says not to do it,' she said after one mix-up on the bus when she had wanted to change plans, 'we won't do it.'[30] When it was all over she was generous in giving him the credit for victory.

Throughout the campaign she offered little that was new or positive, but concentrated on attacking Labour relentlessly on what she called 'the gut issues' – nationalisation, industrial relations and, above all, defence.[31] Characteristically she covered her own weakest flank – unemployment – by counter-attacking Labour's record in the 1970s. 'In the end Labour always runs away,' she jeered in her adoption speech at Finchley on 19 May:

> They are running away from the need to defend their country . . . They are fleeing from the long overdue reform of the trade unions . . . They are running out on Europe . . . Above all, Labour is running away from the true challenge of unemployment.

Promising to create millions of jobs, she insisted, was 'no more than an evasion of the real problem'. Real jobs could only be created by gradually building up a competitive economy with profitable industries that could hold their own in world markets. 'We Conservatives believe in working with the grain of human nature, in encouraging people by incentives, not in over-regulating them by too many controls.' 'A quick cure,' she repeated several times in another favourite formulation, 'is a quack cure.'[32]

The Tories' only other weak point was the widespread belief that the Government had a secret agenda to 'privatise' or somehow dismantle the National Health Service. Mrs Thatcher had already declared repeatedly that the NHS was 'safe with us'; but she had to go on repeating it until she finally rebutted it with the strongest disclaimer at her disposal: 'I have no more intention of dismantling the National Health Service,' she declared at Edinburgh, 'than I have of dismantling Britain's defences.'[33]

She had no doubt that she wanted the biggest majority possible. 'The Labour party manifesto is the most extreme ever,' she declared on a whistle-stop tour of Norfolk on 25 May, 'and it deserves a very big defeat.'[34] 'As a professional campaigner,' Carol Thatcher observed, 'she did not think there was such a thing as winning too well.' Mrs Thatcher warned repeatedly against complacency, believing that 'You can lose elections in the last few days by not going flat out to the winning post.'[35] 'We need to have every single vote on polling day.'[36]

Just as she dominated her colleagues, she also reduced television interviewers to pliant ciphers. Robin Day – the original tough interrogator – felt that he had let his viewers down by letting the Prime Minister walk all over him; but in all his long experience he had not been treated like this before. He was used to asking questions which the politicians would then make some attempt to answer: he was unprepared for Mrs Thatcher's new technique of ignoring the questions and simply delivering whatever message she wanted to get across.[37] 'In all her set-piece encounters,' Michael Cockerell wrote, 'the top interviewers scarcely succeeded in laying a glove on her. She said what she had come prepared to say and no more.'[38] By comparison both Foot and Jenkins were clumsy, longwinded and old-fashioned.

The only person who rattled her was an ordinary voter, a geography teacher named Diana Gould, who pressed her about the sinking of the *General Belgrano* on BBC TV's *Nationwide*, seizing on the discrepancy in her answers about whether or not the ship was sailing towards or away from the British task force, and refusing to be deflected. 'No professional would have challenged a Prime Minister so bluntly,' wrote Martin Harrison in the Nuffield study of the election, 'and precisely because she was answering an ordinary voter Mrs Thatcher had to bite back her evident anger.'[39] She came off the air talking furiously of abolishing the BBC. 'Only the BBC could ask a British Prime Minister why she took action to protect *our* ships against an enemy ship that was a danger to our boys', she railed, forgetting that it was a listener, not the presenter, who had asked the question.[40] Nevertheless she was entitled to resent armchair strategists who persisted in questioning the sinking of the *Belgrano* long after the event. 'They have the luxury of knowing that we came through all right,' she told Carol. 'I had the anxiety of protecting our people on *Hermes* and *Invincible* and the people on the vessels going down there.'[41]

Recriminations about the Falklands did Mrs Thatcher no harm, however, merely keeping the memory of her triumph before the electorate without the Tories having to boast about it. Labour knew the war was bad territory for them, and tried to keep off it. But two leading figures could not resist. First Denis Healey, in a speech in Birmingham, talked about Mrs Thatcher wrapping herself in the Union Jack and 'glorying in slaughter'; he was obliged to apologise the next day, explaining that he should have said 'glorying in conflict'. Then Neil Kinnock – Labour's education spokesman – responded still more crudely on television to a heckler who shouted that at least Mrs Thatcher had guts. 'And it's a pity that people had to leave theirs on Goose Green in order to prove it,' he retorted.

Kinnock was publicly unrepentant; but he too was obliged to write to the families of the war dead to apologise.[42] These wild charges only damaged Labour. There was no mileage in trying to denigrate Mrs Thatcher's achievement in the Falklands – particularly since the opposition was supposed to have supported the war. Such carping merely confirmed her charge that Labour never had the guts to carry anything through.

She started and finished her campaign, as usual, in Finchley. Mrs Thatcher always appeared at her most modest and humble among her own people, where she was still the model constituency Member they had elected in 1959. In all her years as Tory leader and Prime Minister she never missed a constituency function if she could help it. Except when she was out of the country she still held her regular surgery every Friday evening, usually preceded by meetings with businessmen or a visit to a local school or hospital, and followed by supper with her constituency officers and perhaps a branch meeting. Her insistence on keeping these appointments made for a running battle with Number Ten, which always had more pressing calls on her time. She was deeply possessive about Finchley and was furious when press reports suggested that she might seek a safer seat in Gloucestershire. Finchley had been her political base for more than twenty years and she liked everything there to be as it always had been.

As well as Labour and the Alliance, she faced for the first time a phalanx of fringe candidates – not only the imperishable 'Lord' David Sutch of the Official Monster Raving Loony Party, but a Greenham Common peace campaigner; anti-motorway, anti-licensing and anti-censorship campaigners; and a 'Belgrano Blood-hunger' candidate (who came bottom with just thirteen votes). All these diversions delayed the declaration of her result until 2.30 a.m., long after the Conservatives' national victory was confirmed. When the 326th Tory seat was formally declared, Alastair Burnet on ITN announced that 'Mrs Thatcher is back in Downing Street'. 'No, I'm not!' she shouted furiously at the screen, 'I'm still at Hendon Town Hall.'[43] Eventually she secured a slightly increased majority over Labour, with the Alliance third and the rest nowhere:

Mrs M. Thatcher (C)	19,616
L. Spigel (Lab)	10,302
M. Joachim (Lib/All)	7,763
(Eight others)	736
Majority	9,314

She left almost immediately for Conservative Central Office, where she thanked the party workers and was photographed waving from a first-floor window with the architect of victory, Cecil Parkinson. She had won, on the face of it, an enormous victory. The eventual Conservative majority was 144 over all other parties: they held 397 seats in the new House (compared with 335 in the old) against Labour's 205 and just 23 for the Alliance, 2 Scottish Nationalists, 2 Plaid Cymru, and 17 from Northern Ireland.

Nationally, however, the scale of her victory owed a great deal to the Alliance. Her hugely swollen majority actually rested on a lower aggregate vote, and a lower share of the vote, than she had won in 1979 – down from 43.9 to 42.4 per cent. Though it was rewarded with pitifully few seats, in terms of votes the Alliance ran Labour very hard for second place, winning 25.4 per cent to Labour's 27.6 per cent – less than 700,000 votes behind. The effect of the Alliance surge, which nearly doubled the Liberal vote of 1979, was not, as the Tories had feared, to let Labour in but, on the contrary, to deliver the Government a majority out of all proportion to its entitlement. Behind the triumphalism, therefore, June 1983 was by no means the massive endorsement of Thatcherism that the Tories claimed. It was 'manifestly less a victory for the Conservatives', the *Annual Register* concluded, 'than a catastrophe for the Labour Party'.[44] Perhaps the most significant statistic to emerge from analysis of the result was that less than 40 per cent of trade-union members voted Labour (31 per cent voted Conservative and 29 per cent Alliance).[45] What Mrs Thatcher had achieved since 1979 – with critical help from the Labour leadership itself, the SDP defectors, General Galtieri and the distorting electoral system – was to smash the old Labour party, leaving herself without the inconvenience of an effective opposition for as long as she remained in office.

Into the second term

With the second term secured and her personal authority unassailable, Mrs Thatcher now had an almost unprecedented political opportunity before her. Her opponents within the Tory party were conclusively routed. For the first time she was in a position to appoint her own Cabinet. Yet she made remarkably few changes. June 1983 largely confirmed the team that fought the election. There were, indeed, only three casualties. By far the most significant was Francis Pym. She had never wanted him as Foreign Secretary, but in April 1982 she had had little choice. Now she called him in the morning after the election and told him bluntly: 'Francis, I want a new Foreign Secretary.'[46] What she really wanted, as she grew more confident of her capacity to handle foreign policy herself, was a more amenable Foreign Secretary from her own wing of the party, preferably one without a traditional Foreign Office background. The man she had in mind was Cecil Parkinson, as his reward for masterminding the election. In the very moment of victory, however, at Central Office in the early hours of Friday morning, Parkinson confessed to her that he had been conducting a long-standing affair with his former secretary, who was expecting his child. She reluctantly concluded that he could not become Foreign Secretary with this incipient scandal hanging over him, but thought he would be less exposed in a less senior job. She sent him instead to Trade and Industry. With some misgiving she then gave the Foreign Office to Geoffrey Howe.

By the time she came to write her memoirs Lady Thatcher had persuaded herself that this was a mistake.[47] At the Treasury Howe's quiet determination had been invaluable both in riding the political storms and in stiffening her own resolve. At the Foreign Office, by contrast, his views – particularly towards Europe – increasingly diverged from hers, while his dogged diplomacy and air of patient reasonableness exasperated her as much as Pym's had done. She also became convinced that Howe was ambitious for her job. Yet in truth it was an excellent appointment. For the whole of Mrs Thatcher's second term, at summits and international negotiations, they made an effective combination on the global stage, each complementing the other's qualities, while Howe put up heroically with being treated as her punchbag.

The hot tip to become the new Chancellor was Patrick Jenkin. But Mrs Thatcher now had the self-confidence to choose the more flamboyant Nigel Lawson. If Howe had been the perfect helmsman for the first term, Lawson's slightly Regency style presented the right image of prosperity and expansion for the calmer waters of the second. This combination too worked well for the next four years, though Lawson was always more independent and self-confident than Howe had been.

Below these two key appointments, the rest of the Cabinet-making was largely a rearrangement of the pack. Willie Whitelaw left the Commons and the Home Office to become Lord President of the Council and Leader of the House of Lords. This was a position from which he could better exercise his non-departmental role as deputy Prime Minister; but it entailed the displacement of Lady

Young, thus ending the short-lived experiment of a second woman in the Thatcher Cabinet. There was never another.

Whitelaw's replacement at the Home Office was one of Mrs Thatcher's least successful appointments. Leon Brittan had done well as Chief Secretary to the Treasury and seemed to be a rising star. But he was at once too junior, too brainy and – it must be said – too Jewish to satisfy the Tory party's expectations of a Home Secretary. He was never convincing in the job and was shifted after two years.

This was the new team. It was a measure of the change already wrought since 1979 that the Cabinet could no longer be usefully classified into 'wets' and 'dries'. In the medium term the only likely threat to Mrs Thatcher's dominance came from the undisguised ambition of Michael Heseltine.

15

Popular Capitalism

High noon

A QUARTER of a century on, the second Thatcher Government
looks like the zenith of Thatcherism. This, after all, was the period
of economic recovery, when the economy – at least in the south of
England – finally emerged from the recession of the early 1980s into
the heady expansion of what came to be known as the 'Lawson
boom'; it was the heroic period of privatisation, with the successful
sell-off of whole utilities undreamed of in the first term; it was the
time of deregulation in the City of London – the so-called 'Big
Bang' – when quick fortunes were suddenly there to be made by
young men in red braces known to the press as 'yuppies'; a time of
tax cuts, easy credit and rapidly increased spending power for the
fortunate majority able to enjoy it, leading to a heady consumer
boom which helped float the Government back to office for a third
term amid excited talk of a British economic 'miracle'. It was the
moment when the hundred-year-old political argument between
capitalism and socialism seemed to have been decisively resolved in
favour of the former. The moral and practical superiority of the
market as an engine of wealth creation and the efficient delivery of
public services was incontestably established, its critics reduced to
impotent irrelevance, while the Conservative party, under its all-
conquering leader, the tireless personification of this liberation of
the nation's energy, seemed likely to retain power for as long as she
wanted. Her hegemony appeared complete; or, in the catchphrase
of the day, picked up from graffiti scrawled on a thousand walls,
'Maggie Rules OK'.

Yet it did not feel quite like that at the time. The years 1983–7
were seen by many of the Prime Minister's keenest supporters as

a period of drift and wasted opportunity when the Government, if not exactly blown off course, was distracted from pursuing its long-term objectives by a series of bruising political battles and an accumulation of accidents which so sapped its energy and authority that, contrary to the legend of unchallenged dominance, the Tories actually trailed the supposedly unelectable Labour party – and sometimes the Alliance too – in the opinion polls for more than half the period. Margaret Thatcher's hyperactive personality unquestionably dominated the political stage; but her popularity steadily dwindled so that in 1986 her poll rating was barely higher than in the darkest days of 1981. Though in the event she was comfortably re-elected the following year, her ascendancy was never so secure as the triumphalism of her instant myth-makers contrived to suggest.

The second term got off to a bad start with a series of minor embarrassments described by the press as 'banana skins'. Then most of the second year, 1984–5, was overshadowed by a critical confrontation with the Tories' old nemesis, the National Union of Mineworkers, which stirred deep passions on both sides and brought parts of the country close to civil war. The Government eventually prevailed, but it used up a lot of political energy and capital in doing so. At the same time it had picked a harder battle than it expected over the abolition of the Greater London Council, as well as several more tussles with Labour-controlled local authorities around the country over the level of their spending. It faced serious challenges to public order at the Greenham Common air base, where the first American cruise missiles arrived in November 1983; in parts of London, Birmingham and Liverpool, where another wave of riots erupted in September 1985; and in London's docklands, where through much of 1986 the police fought pitched battles with the printing unions who were attempting to defy the Australian magnate Rupert Murdoch's imposition of new technology in the newspaper industry. A series of security controversies further served to keep the Government on the defensive.

In October 1984 an IRA bomb planted at the Conservative Party Conference hotel in Brighton claimed five lives, seriously injured two members of the Cabinet and only narrowly failed to kill Mrs Thatcher herself. The Government was more seriously destabilised in January 1986 by a major political crisis arising from the future of the Westland helicopter company, which cost two senior ministers their jobs and for a time even threatened the Prime Minister. Between them these events necessitated several hasty reshuffles which disrupted the ministerial team. In addition Mrs

Thatcher's attention was increasingly diverted from the domestic front by an exceptionally demanding foreign-policy agenda: not only the European Community, but Hong Kong, South Africa, Anglo-Irish negotiations on the future of Northern Ireland, the fallout from American military adventures in Grenada, Lebanon and Libya, and the emergence of a promising new leader in the Soviet Union who held out the possibility of an end to the Cold War – all these helped to ensure that even Mrs Thatcher's phenomenal energies were very fully stretched. There was not much time to chart the way ahead.

As a result, she was never quite so dominant as she appeared. Immediately after the 1983 election Michael Foot announced that he was standing down as Labour leader. Though the party's laborious processes took three months to elect his successor, the result was never in much doubt. Neil Kinnock was young (forty-one), inexperienced (he had never held even junior office) and came from the left of the party: he was as emotionally committed as Foot to CND, and not much less hostile to Europe. Nevertheless he was fresh, idealistic and eloquent, if incurably verbose; he had grasped that Labour must change to make itself electable and quickly showed himself ready to jettison most of the left's unpopular ideological baggage. From the moment he took over, Labour's fortunes began to improve. There was, as it turned out, still a long way to go; but in the summer of 1984 the opposition registered its first lead in the polls since the invasion of the Falklands two years earlier.

At the same time Roy Jenkins was replaced as leader of the SDP by the much younger, more dashing and dynamic Dr David Owen. Owen's relationship with the Liberal leader David Steel was never easy; yet under the double-headed leadership of the two Davids the Alliance recovered its standing quickly too and from the end of 1984 maintained a regular presence between 25 and 33 per cent in the polls, winning a string of spectacular by-election victories as it had done in 1981–2. Mrs Thatcher's command of her party was never seriously challenged. Yet a powerful chorus of senior dissidents kept up a steady critique of the Government and its policies. Contrary to collective memory, the Thatcherite revolution did not carry all before it, even in 1983–7.

Banana skins

The first 'banana skins' began to afflict the Government as soon as the new Parliament met. On the very first day Mrs Thatcher was rebuffed over the choice of a new Speaker. She was sorry to see George Thomas retire, and made the mistake of allowing it to be known that she did not favour his deputy, Bernard Weatherill, to succeed him. She had hoped to use the job as a suitably dignified niche for Francis Pym or, when he declined, one of the other ex-ministers she had put out to grass. But the House of Commons is jealous of its independence and Tory and Labour backbenchers alike rallied to Weatherill. 'What seems to have clinched his election,' *The Times* commented, 'was the discovery by his fellow MPs that he did not have the Prime Minister's full approval.'[1]

There quickly followed two more parliamentary rebuffs. On 13 July the Government gave the new House an early opportunity to debate the reintroduction of capital punishment. With a large influx of new Tory Members, supporters of hanging, including the Prime Minister, hoped that this time – having failed in 1979 – they might be able to restore the death penalty, at least for terrorist murders and the killing of policemen. The new Home Secretary, Leon Brittan, reversed his previous opposition and spoke in favour of restoration. In the event capital punishment was still rejected by unexpectedly decisive majorities.

The second slap in the face was on the question of MPs' pay. The Government threw out a recommendation by the Top Salaries Review Body that would have given Members an increase of 31 per cent. 'We thought that Ministers could not possibly take increases of that magnitude,' Mrs Thatcher explained. 'And we trusted that Members of Parliament would take the same view.'[2] She was too sanguine. The Government's offer of just 4 per cent provoked fury on both sides of the House. In the event John Biffen was able to negotiate a compromise: increases of 5.5 per cent every year for the 1983 Parliament. This was further evidence that Mrs Thatcher's swollen majority would not always do her bidding, at least where their own interests were involved.

Just before the summer recess Lawson signalled his arrival at the Treasury by announcing a £500 million package of emergency spending cuts designed to reassure the City that there was to be no loosening of monetary policy. The cuts fell most heavily on defence and on the NHS, thus angering both the Tory right and the opposition simultaneously. The health cuts caused particular outrage, coming so soon after an election at which Mrs Thatcher had promised that the NHS was 'safe' with the Tories.

For some time Mrs Thatcher had been suffering from a torn retina in her right eye, which was affecting her vision. So, at the beginning of August, she underwent a laser operation at a private hospital in Windsor. This time she was obliged to stay in for three days – she was said to have done some work on the third day – and emerged wearing tinted glasses. She then went to Switzerland for a full two-week holiday to recover.

During September she visited first Holland and Germany, then the United States and Canada, returning just in time to face a new headache when *Private Eye* broke the story of Cecil Parkinson's adulterous affair. Mrs Thatcher tried hard to save him – she was remarkably relaxed about sexual matters – but in the end he was forced to resign. 'The only person who comes out of the affair with any credit is the Prime Minister,' Norman St John Stevas wrote in the *Sunday Express*. 'She has been compassionate, concerned, tolerant and Christian.'[3] By insisting that Parkinson should go back to his wife she was represented as fighting for the sanctity of marriage. In truth she too was fighting for her man. Parkinson was not just a personal favourite, but her chosen heir, whom she had been grooming for the eventual succession. Even after his resignation she remained keen to bring him back as soon as possible.

Parkinson's downfall necessitated the first unintended Cabinet reshuffle. Norman Tebbit moved to the DTI; Tom King took over the Department of Employment; and Nicholas Ridley finally made it to the Cabinet, taking King's place at Transport. In addition Mrs Thatcher had already taken the precaution, before the conference, of appointing a new party chairman: her surprising choice was the youthful but lightweight John Selwyn Gummer. Her reasoning was that she needed someone young – Gummer was forty-four – to combat Kinnock, Steel and Owen;[4] but Gummer was not a success and lasted only two years in the job. John Major, at the time an assistant whip, remembers being 'astonished' at Ridley's elevation: he had 'an original mind' but was 'wonderfully politically incorrect'.[5] Once arrived, Ridley was to remain one of the Prime Minister's most loyal disciples until one final indiscretion brought him down just before her own fall.

The worst embarrassment of all was the American invasion of Grenada – a Commonwealth country – to put down a Communist coup, with minimal reference to Britain. Both Geoffrey Howe, who in the Commons just the day before had confidently ruled out any prospect of American action, and Mrs Thatcher herself, whose vaunted special relationship with President Reagan was called into question, were publicly humiliated. 'There are always banana skins,' Mrs Thatcher had told the BBC's John Cole in May, 'but you don't have to tread on them.'[6] Since June she seemed unable to avoid them.

From bust to boom

Amid all the Government's minor embarrassments, however, the central political front was, as always, the economy: and here there were definite signs of recovery. An OECD (Organisation for Economic Cooperation and Development) report in December showed Britain enjoying the fastest growth in Europe. GDP, Mrs Thatcher told the Commons, was now back to its 1979 level – a somewhat limited success after four and a half years, but one which had been achieved, she pointed out, 'with 1.7 million fewer people in the workforce'.[7] In other words unemployment was up, but so was productivity. She insisted that unemployment would soon start to fall with the creation of new jobs.

In Nigel Lawson she now had a Chancellor who shared her own ability to project a bullish sense of optimism. Her relationship with Lawson was very different from that with Geoffrey Howe. Whereas she was frequently impatient with Howe's pedestrian manner, knowing that he was no more of an economist than she was, she respected Lawson's expertise to the extent that she was slightly in awe of him. This was a recipe for trouble in the long run, since their views increasingly diverged; but for the moment she was happy to indulge him

Lawson's first budget, in March 1984, delighted her. In their respective memoirs he recalled that the Prime Minister was 'ecstatic', while she characterised it as 'Nigel at his brilliant best'.[8] Though no further cut in the basic rate was possible just yet, the new Chancellor boldly signalled his ambitions as a tax reformer. First, he took Howe's switch from direct to indirect taxation a stage further by raising personal thresholds, taking 850,000 low earners out of income tax altogether, compensating by raising excise duties and extending VAT. More important, he cut corporation tax; abolished the 15 per cent surcharge on investment income; and completed Howe's phasing out of the National Insurance surcharge (the so-called 'tax on jobs'). One friendly commentator called this 'the most Thatcherite' budget so far.[9]

Clever tax changes, however, did nothing – at least in the short term – to meet the rising clamour for action to tackle unemployment. The Falklands Factor was now double-edged: if Mrs Thatcher could spend millions recapturing and now defending some barely inhabited islands in the South Atlantic, it was asked, why could she not apply some of the same resolution to conquering the great social evil on her doorstep? She now enjoyed a huge majority; the recession was officially over and the economy was supposed to be recovering; yet unemployment was still rising. She was running out of alibis. Just before the summer recess, Mrs Thatcher was forced to make an unusually defensive reply to Neil Kinnock's first no-confidence motion since becoming Labour leader.

'Creating new jobs is the main challenge of our time,' she acknowledged. But the Government was meeting it by tackling the 'fundamental causes' of unemployment, not just the symptoms. Thanks to the 'prudent financial policies' of Howe and Lawson, she insisted, 'the prize of lower inflation has been won, and we shall not put it in jeopardy now. Stable prices remain our eventual goal.' New jobs would come from new technology, but she accepted an obligation to mitigate the hardship of transition 'by generous redundancy payments, by retraining and by helping to create new businesses'.[10]

This was all very well, but it did not cut much ice against the relentlessly rising headline figure of 3.2 million unemployed. In August Mrs Thatcher bowed to pressure to be seen to be doing something by appointing David Young from the Manpower Services Commission (MSC) as an unpaid Minister without Portfolio to head a new 'Enterprise Unit' in the Cabinet Office – or, as Bernard Ingham encouraged the press to spin it, 'Minister for Jobs'. His appointment inevitably upset the Employment Secretary, Tom King, on whose territory he was set to trespass.[11] But Mrs Thatcher would hear not a word against her latest favourite. 'Others bring me problems,' she was reported as saying. 'David brings me solutions.'[12]

At the party conference at Brighton in October – this was the conference overshadowed by the IRA's bombing of the Grand Hotel – she devoted the longest section of her speech to unemployment. 'To suggest . . . that we do not care about it is as deeply wounding as it is utterly false.' Rejecting 'Keynesian' arguments for government stimulation of the economy, she asserted that Keynes' modern followers misrepresented what he actually believed. 'It was all set out in the 1944 White Paper on employment. I bought it then. I have it still . . . I re-read it frequently,' she claimed. 'On page one it states, "employment cannot be created by Act of Parliament or by Government action alone" . . . It was true then. It is true now.' The White Paper, she said, was full of 'basic truths' about the danger of inflation and the importance of enterprise.

She listed some projects for which the Government had – 'by careful budgeting' – found money: the M25 motorway, the electrification of British Rail ('if it can make it pay'), forty-nine new hospitals since 1979. 'Of course we look at various things like new power stations, and in a year after drought we look at things like more investment in the water supply industry.' But the overriding message was clear: there would be no massive spending programme to create jobs.[13] On the contrary, she specifically repeated during the autumn that the road to prosperity lay through tax cuts.

Accordingly the chorus of criticism swelled. Pym, Heath, Walker – the usual dissidents – were joined in December by Harold Macmillan, making his maiden speech in the House of Lords at the age of ninety, twenty years after leaving the Commons. The alarm of these grandees was magnified by the news that for the first time in modern history the UK was about to record a trading deficit on manufactured goods. This, combined with the strength of the dollar, caused a sharp fall in the value of sterling, leading in January 1985 to a full-scale crisis when the pound – from a value of $1.40 twelve months earlier – practically touched parity with the dollar. To show that the Government was not prepared to let sterling fall any further, Lawson raised interest rates by 2 per cent and then had to repeat the dose, to 14 per cent, when a second panic followed at the end of the month; while Mrs Thatcher privately persuaded President Reagan to lend American support and publicly went on television to 'talk up' the pound by insisting that its current valuation was too low (and the dollar too high). The medicine worked. By March the pound was back to $1.25, and Lawson was able to start bringing interest rates down again. But it had been a nasty few weeks.

So the pressure was unrelenting. At Mrs Thatcher's insistence, Lawson was obliged to flag his 1985 budget as 'a budget for jobs'. This was not at all his real priority. The previous autumn he had declared that unemployment was a social, not an economic problem, and cheerfully told an American journalist that 'economically and politically, Britain can get along with double-digit unemployment'.[14] His headline priority was sterling, and his real interest was further tax reform. He wanted to finance a further reduction in the basic rate by cutting middle-class tax perks – not only mortgage-interest tax relief but also relief on private pension payments. Lawson believed as a matter of principle in phasing out the accumulated clutter of sticks and carrots in pursuit of a 'neutral' tax system. But Mrs Thatcher would not hear of it. 'Our people won't stand for it,' she told him.[15] Second, Lawson wanted to extend VAT to newspapers and magazines and to children's clothes: the latter was an obvious vote loser, which the Prime Minister was firmly pledged against, while she insisted that it was no time to antagonise the press. All he could do – with patently little enthusiasm – was cut National Insurance contributions, and put another £400 million into the Youth Training Scheme and the Community Programme. After the plaudits for his first budget twelve months earlier, this lacklustre package pleased nobody.

That spring, for the first time since before the Falklands war, there was talk of a leadership challenge in the autumn. Francis Pym launched a new Tory dissident group, Centre Forward, asserting in a speech at Cambridge that 'responsible financial management does not itself constitute an economic strategy'.[16] In fact most of the grumblers were still afraid to put their heads above the parapet and the group entirely failed to establish an identity. But the evidence of discontent – focused perhaps more effectively in a new all-party pressure group, the Employment Institute – was sufficient to force Mrs Thatcher to promise, in a radio interview on 24 May, that the Government would take further action if unemployment did not fall within a year.

The traditional response to party jitters is a Cabinet reshuffle; so at the beginning of September Mrs Thatcher rearranged her pack to bring on some fresh faces – mainly from the Heathite wing of the party. 'I generally found', she wrote in her memoirs, 'that the Left seemed to be best at presentation'.[17] Better presentation was what the Government badly needed at this moment. First she moved David Young to the Department of Employment, with the rumbustious Kenneth Clarke to represent him in the Commons; then she replaced Patrick Jenkin with the smooth-tongued Kenneth Baker at Environment; and finally she moved Norman Tebbit from the DTI to replace Gummer as party chairman. In another populist touch she appointed the millionaire novelist Jeffrey Archer – a former Tory MP – to be deputy chairman to help re-enthuse the faithful in the constituencies. Mrs Thatcher never trusted Archer very far, but she thought he could do no serious harm, and might possibly raise morale, as a cheerleader.

Tebbit's replacement at the DTI was Leon Brittan, woundingly removed from the Home Office where he had never looked convincing. Douglas Hurd, a much safer pair of hands, stepped up from Belfast to be the new Home Secretary, while Tom King took over Northern Ireland. The old wets had been severely culled since 1979, and the Thatcherite true believers had begun to take their places in September 1981; but September 1985 marked a third stage in the evolution of the Thatcher Cabinet, with the advance of a new generation who – though happy to serve her – were not instinctive Thatcher supporters. As it happened, the Westland imbroglio forced yet another reshuffle only four months later, in January 1986. The effect of the rapidly changing personnel around her was to focus attention more than ever on Mrs Thatcher herself.

The autumn of 1985 brought no relief. In September and early October another wave of rioting broke out. The spark in every case was tension between black youths and the police. But despair arising from unemployment, not race, was clearly the underlying cause. Soon afterwards a House of Lords select committee published a report warning of the irreparable loss of industrial capacity since 1979 and challenging the Government's belief that expanding service industries would fill the gap. Services could not bridge the looming balance-of-payments deficit for the simple reason that they were not exportable. As the *Observer*'s William Keegan put it, 'A proliferation of part-time barmaids was not enough.'[18] Again at the party conference Mrs Thatcher insisted that there was 'no problem which occupies more of my thinking' than unemployment.[19] But still unemployment went on rising. In December the Church of England joined in the chorus of concern with a report on social breakdown and demoralisation in the inner cities, entitled *Faith in the City*. An unnamed Cabinet Minister's attempt to dismiss the report as 'Marxist' was ridiculed as ludicrously wide of the mark.

A significant divide now began to open between the Prime Minister and her Chancellor over monetary policy. In a speech in the City of London in October Lawson signalled his abandonment of formal monetarism. In its pure form, at the time of the Medium Term Financial Strategy, monetary targets – £M3 – had been the 'judge and jury'. Hit those, Lawson had then believed, and low inflation would inevitably follow. Now he had lost faith in £M3. Inflation had fallen since 1982 even though £M3 had far exceeded its target. Seeking a more reliable indicator, he had started targeting the exchange rate instead, believing that a stable pound would keep inflation under control.

It was the traumatic plunge and recovery of sterling at the beginning of 1985 which converted Lawson to the idea that the time had come to join the Exchange Rate Mechanism of the European Monetary System. Initially sceptical of international cooperation, he had become fascinated – Lady Thatcher would later say seduced – at meetings of the G7 finance ministers by the flattering delusion that a handful of wise men could manage the money markets. The first fruit of this international action was the Plaza Agreement – signed in the Plaza Hotel, New York – in September 1985, by which the Americans agreed to try to drive the dollar down by 10 per cent. As part of this process Lawson was ready to recommend to Mrs Thatcher that Britain should sign up to the ERM. He was supported by all his senior officials, by his predecessor Geoffrey Howe, now converted to the Foreign Office line, and by the Governor of the Bank. But Mrs Thatcher was resolutely opposed.

'I knew they were ganging up on me,' she later declared on television.[20] So on 13 November she convened a carefully chosen meeting of colleagues whom she thought she could count on to support her: Leon Brittan, Norman Tebbit, John Biffen and Willie Whitelaw. Contrary to her expectations, however, Brittan and Tebbit both supported Lawson, which persuaded Whitelaw to lend his weight, as usual, to what he thought was the consensus. Faced with the unanimity of her senior colleagues, Mrs Thatcher told them bluntly: 'I disagree. If you join the EMS you will have to do so without me.'[21] 'There was a deathly silence,' Lawson recalled, 'and then she left the room.'[22] Lawson wondered if he should resign; but Whitelaw and Tebbit assured him that if he persisted she would eventually come round, as she did on so many other issues to which she was initially opposed.[23] In fact this was one matter on which she remained immovable right up to October 1990.

Though she framed her objections as matters of timing and judgement, she was actually adamantly opposed on principle – or rather two principles, economic and patriotic. On the one hand she believed, as part of her free-market economic philosophy, that exchange rates could not be fixed and it was folly for governments to try to buck the markets. On the other hand, and somewhat contradictorily, she was instinctively opposed to sacrificing any shred of sovereignty over the value of the pound or the British Government's right – illusory as it might be in practice – to set its own interest rates to try to fix it. These two objections, fiercely maintained for the next five years against the growing determination of both Lawson and Howe to join the ERM by the back door if necessary, represented a ticking bomb at the heart of the Government. This fundamental disagreement between a determined Prime Minister and an equally stubborn Chancellor ultimately destroyed them both.

1986 was the year in which Lawson's economic management finally began to show results. In February Mrs Thatcher was driven to admit that unemployment would probably not begin to fall before the next election.[24] In fact David Young's training schemes at last began to take effect, and in October the headline figure turned down, for the first time since 1979. At the beginning of the year a sudden drop in the price of oil stymied Lawson's hopes of dramatic cuts in income tax in his budget; but he still contrived to take a penny off the standard rate (bringing it to twenty-nine pence). The sliding oil price proved unexpectedly beneficial: sterling fell against other European currencies, giving British exports over the year the benefit of an effective 16 per cent devaluation, without the political odium that accompanies a formal devaluation. Suddenly the economy entered a 'virtuous circle'.[25] Low inflation and low interest rates combined to promote 3 per cent growth. Faster growth meant falling unemployment and higher tax revenues. Higher revenues, further boosted by increased VAT on soaring consumer spending and the windfall proceeds of privatisation, enabled the Chancellor in his 1987 budget to achieve the elusive hat-trick of higher spending, reduced borrowing and further tax cuts, just in time for a summer election. No wonder that from the autumn of 1986 the polls began to move back in the Government's favour, or that by the spring the Tories were once again ahead.

The key to this dramatic turnaround was that most of the population – the twenty-five million in work – had more money to spend and were spending it, stimulating an explosion of small businesses and services: new shops, restaurants and wine bars, electrical consumer goods like videos and microwaves, conservatories and home improvements of every sort. Economic growth was visible, the City of London was booming and there was suddenly a heady whiff of optimism and opportunity in the air – just as the Tories had always promised would flow from deregulation and incentives.

Even as the Lawson boom took off, however, sceptical critics warned that it was not merely partial and unbalanced, but even on its own terms fragile and unsustainable. It was a boom founded on reckless consumer spending, stimulated by pay rises way above the rate of inflation, by easy credit and tax cuts paid for by oil and privatisation revenues, not based on long-term investment or increased domestic production. In fact it blatantly belied all Mrs Thatcher's homilies about good housekeeping. Both individual families and the nation as a whole were living beyond their means. While average incomes rose by 35 per cent between 1983 and 1987, personal indebtedness rose four times as fast in the same period: new bank lending trebled, and the number of mortgages doubled in 1986–7 alone. For the first time ever, the average British household was spending more than it earned. On the national scale, increased consumption was sucking in imports at twice their 1979 level, while manufacturing output was only just back to the 1979 figure. The deficit was covered only by the temporary bonus of North Sea oil, which was not being invested for the future. The domestic manufacturing capacity to supply the new demand had been destroyed in 1979–81 and was no longer there to be revived: industrial investment was actually 16 per cent less in 1986 than it had been in 1979. The illusion of an economic miracle since 1983 was a statistical sleight of hand achieved by measuring growth only from the trough of the economic cycle in 1981; measured from peak to peak, average growth over the cycle was still only 1.8 per cent – actually lower than in the previous Labour cycle of the late 1970s.[26] In 1987 Britain's GNP fell behind that of Italy – an event gleefully hailed by the Italians as *il surpasso*.

Lawson's boom, in short, contained the seeds of both renewed inflation and the next slump. Having abandoned the excessive restraints of monetarism, he had swung to the opposite extreme and unleashed a headlong pre-election spending spree similar to those of 1963 and 1973, except that he had now deprived himself of the traditional tools which previous Chancellors had used to check overheating: incomes policy, credit controls, exchange controls. Exuding a gambler's confidence, Lawson professed himself blithely unconcerned about the growing trade gap, still insisting that manufacturing no longer mattered.[27] His priority was, frankly, to win the election, then make any necessary adjustments afterwards.[28] Like the sorcerer's apprentice, he assumed that he could turn the tap off when he needed to.

Mrs Thatcher was instinctively more prudent: already in the autumn of 1986 she sensed that something was going wrong. Lawson dismissed her fears; but her intuition was right. 'Perhaps,' the former Labour minister Edmund Dell commented, 'if Lawson had paid more attention to her hunches and less to her reasoning, his economic management might have been better. But that would have been too much to expect from so cerebral a Chancellor.'[29] For her part, Mrs Thatcher failed to act decisively on her hunch. On the one hand she was still in thrall to her Chancellor's greater expertise. On the other she was grateful for the turn-up in the polls and was swept up in the general excitement surrounding what she called 'popular capitalism'.

The phrase is said to have been coined, ironically, by Michael Heseltine, shortly after he walked out of the Cabinet in January 1986. A year earlier Lawson had hailed the privatisation of British Telecom as marking 'the birth of people's capitalism'.[30] Mrs Thatcher first used the words on 26 February 1986, when she declared: 'We've got what I call popular capitalism.'[31] Thereafter she made the phrase her own. She adopted it as the defining slogan of her political project in a speech to the Conservative Central Council, meeting on 15 March. This was a critical speech in which Mrs Thatcher tried to put the trauma of the Westland crisis behind her and came out fighting for her political life. First she looked back, listing the principal achievements of her Government so far – taming the unions, curbing inflation and beginning to dismantle the public sector:

> Seven years ago, who would have dared forecast such a transformation of Britain? This didn't come about because of consensus. It happened because we said: This we believe, this we will do. It's called leadership.

By contrast, she concluded, socialist crusades to go back to the old ways were 'muted nowadays':

> Socialists cry 'Power to the people', and raise the clenched fist as they say it. We all know what they really mean – power over people, power to the State. To us Conservatives, popular capitalism means . . . power through ownership to the man and woman in the street, given confidently with an open hand.[32]

Property-owning democracy

'Popular capitalism' was Thatcherite shorthand for three separate revolutions in British economic life: wider home-ownership, wider share-ownership and an 'enterprise economy' characterised by more small businesses and more people becoming self-employed. The first revolution was well under way in Mrs Thatcher's first term, with half a million council houses already sold before the 1983 election. But the second and third took off only in the second term. The first was simple and irreversible, a major social change. The second turned out to be rather less significant than was pretended at the time, at least so far as individuals were concerned. The third was economically by far the most important: though stimulated by the Government's supply-side reforms and initially associated with the unsustainable euphoria of the Lawson boom, it represented the British reflection of universal trends – globalisation and computerisation – and an irresistible transformation of economic attitudes and behaviour, which long outlasted Mrs Thatcher and carried on vertiginously until it suddenly collapsed in the 'credit crunch' of 2008.

The sale of council houses was a specifically British social revolution which reflected the national obsession with home-ownership. From a mixture of prejudice and principle Mrs Thatcher believed that public-sector housing should really be abolished. She was convinced that council estates were breeding grounds of socialism, dependency, vandalism and crime. She had no interest in trying to improve them because she believed in principle that housing was not a commodity which the Government ought to provide, except for special categories like the elderly and disabled. In her memoirs she wrote unambiguously that the state should withdraw from the building and management of housing 'just as far and as fast as possible'.[33] She could not, when in office, act on this principle as decisively as she might have wished; but she certainly did everything she could to shrink the public sector and very little to help those compelled by circumstances to live in it.

Mrs Thatcher thought the sale of council houses an unalloyed good, both social and economic. She made a point of attending the handover of the millionth house to be sold. By the time she fell in 1990, the number sold was up to nearly 1.5 million, and the total proceeds had accrued £28 billion to the Treasury, which counted them – 'duplicitously', in Simon Jenkins' view[34] – against public spending. Spread over eleven years, this was the biggest privatisation of them all, bigger than British Telecom, British Gas and electricity put together. But the blessings were not so unmixed as she believed.

For one thing, some of those families who were persuaded to buy their houses, particularly towards the end of the decade, tempted by the easy mortgages on offer from banks falling over themselves to lend, soon found themselves, when inflation rose and the recession of the early 1990s bit, committed to payments they could not keep up. As prices fell back to more realistic levels, many found that their houses were worth less than their mortgages – the phenomenon of 'negative equity'. Many bright dreams of ownership ended in the nightmare of repossession five years later.

Second, it was naturally the best and most desirable houses that were sold – very few flats – and the more prosperous and upwardly mobile tenants who bought them, leaving the less salubrious high-rise estates to become sinks for the unemployed and problem families. The effect of Mrs Thatcher's sell-off was to leave the social mix narrower than before, with a much higher proportion of tenants dependent on benefit. Her belief that there were no good estates was therefore self-fulfilling.

Third, the non-replacement of the houses sold and the consequent decline in the stock of council housing, combined with the late 1980s explosion in house prices in the private sector, at a time when there were still nearly three million unemployed, left an absolute shortage of affordable housing and led by the end of the decade to the shocking appearance of a tribe of homeless people sleeping on the streets of London and other major cities. This was the most serious negative consequence of a popular policy to which Mrs Thatcher resolutely closed her eyes.

The family silver

The second 'crusade' of popular capitalism was privatisation. It had, of course, been under way, from cautious beginnings, since 1979. But it only really took off as a rolling process in Mrs Thatcher's second term, when it quite suddenly became the Government's 'big idea', the central pillar of Thatcherism, both the symbolic embodiment and the practical realisation of the reversal of socialism which she had been talking about since 1975. Now, starting with British Telecom, the Government moved on to the major state-owned corporations which had supplied the nation's essential services since 1945, services which only a few years earlier no one but a few free-market fanatics had imagined could be run by anyone but the state: the telephone system, gas and electricity, the national airline, the airports, even water supply. The expectation was successfully created that, as Nigel Lawson had asserted in 1981, 'No industry should remain under State ownership unless there is a positive and overwhelming case for doing so.'[35] A momentum was established which led on – after Mrs Thatcher's own fall – even to the two great behemoths of the public sector, coal mining and the railways. This was a huge and unexpected transformation of the economic landscape. Each successive privatisation was fought tooth and nail by both opposition parties, by the unions and most of those who worked in the affected industries, and opposed by the public as a whole, as measured by opinion polls. But each was accepted once it had happened, even by the Labour party, as an irreversible *fait accompli*. More than that, the privatisation process itself, to ministers' amazement, actually generated a wave of popular excitement, fanned by an enthusiastic press. The key was the sale of shares, at knockdown prices, directly to the public.

Suddenly, John Redwood, then head of the Downing Street Policy Unit, recalled, the issue was not 'will the public buy it?' but 'how can we do it technically?'[36] Lawson remembers a dinner with merchant bankers, all of whom – with one exception – 'roundly declared that the privatisation [of BT] was impossible: the capital market simply was not large enough to absorb it'.[37] The answer was to by-pass the bankers and sell the shares direct to the public by mail order, television and newspaper advertisements. Mrs Thatcher 'became excited by the possibilities' and gave Redwood the backing he needed to convince the Treasury and the City.[38]

The response exceeded all expectations: two million people applied for a prospectus, and when the first instalment went on sale in November 1984, the offer was four times oversubscribed. More than a million small investors applied for shares, including 95 per cent of BT employees, defying the advice of their union; most of these had never owned shares before, but the sale was weighted to favour those who applied for the smallest number. The price was kept deliberately low – 130 pence – for political reasons, since from the Government's point of view the sale simply had to succeed. The result was a bonanza for the lucky applicants; the price rose 90 per cent on the opening day, as many buyers sold on immediately. The second instalment in June 1985 was similarly oversubscribed. In the end the sale – of just 51 per cent of the company at this stage, in three instalments over eighteen months – raised nearly £4 billion. The company's profits jumped spectacularly and by the end of 1985 the share price – for those buyers who had retained them – stood at 192 pence.[39]

Immediately the success of the BT sale became clear, Mrs Thatcher was impatient to repeat it.[40] The obvious next candidate was British Gas. 'For sheer size, prodigality of advertising, and the opportunity to involve small punters and large investing institutions alike in the calculation of a quick profit', the *Annual Register* wrote, 'the launch of British Gas in the private sector made history.'[41] With the whole City now keen to get a share of the action, Rothschilds won a 'beauty contest' to handle the sale; four and a half million rushed to buy the shares. Once again they were deliberately undervalued and once again they were hugely oversubscribed: on the first day of trading the price leapt by 50 per cent. Labour furiously condemned the Government's cynical underpricing of a national asset in order to bribe the public with their own money: in his first front-bench job as a Treasury spokesman Tony Blair alleged that the sell-off would cost the taxpayer £20–30 per household.[42] But the Government had achieved its aim of making shareholding popular as never before.

The third high-profile privatisation of the second term – though in revenue terms much smaller than British Telecom and British Gas – was British Airways, which had been successfully brought into profit by one of Mrs Thatcher's favourite businessmen, Sir John King, and was sold off in February 1987. 'The World's Favourite Airline' was now a successful international leader which investors were keen to buy into; this time the shares were eleven times over subscribed, and the price jumped 82 per cent on the opening day. Just before the election another glamorous name, Rolls-Royce – controversially nationalised by the Heath Government in 1971 – was also returned to the private sector. The only hiccup in this stage of the programme came with Britoil, which was floated in 1985 just when the oil price was falling. Millions of shares were not taken up; but the loss was the underwriters', not the Government's, and the political embarrassment at least did something to counter the charge that the share price of the assets sold was always set too low.

With the success of privatisation Mrs Thatcher had stumbled on an ongoing narrative which gave a central theme to her Government, and she was keen to keep the momentum going. British Steel, drastically slimmed down and restored to profitability by Ian MacGregor, was already well down the road. The 1987 Tory manifesto earmarked electricity and water as the next targets. Both posed special problems: nuclear energy on the one hand, and the public-health implications of commercialised water on the other. Still she was determined to press ahead. At the same time, however, she had not abandoned her habitual caution. She was no ideologue, but a canny politician, and she foresaw only trouble in trying to privatise the railways. Nicholas Ridley, Transport Secretary from October 1983 to May 1986, accepted the Prime Minister's veto. But his successors were all keen to grab a share of the privatisation glory. There is no better example of Mrs Thatcher's shrewd political instinct than the fact that she persistently warned them off. She was happy to see British Rail forced to sell off its profitable assets – hotels, ferries, hovercraft and acres of undeveloped trackside property – which only made privatisation of the rest of the business harder; but she had the good sense not to try to sell the track or the trains.

For somewhat similar reasons she would not touch the Post Office, pleading the Queen's attachment to the Royal Mail as an excuse, or the remaining coal mines that were left after the trauma of the miners' strike. In fact, with her usual mixture of timing and luck, Margaret Thatcher triumphantly rode the first wave of privatisation, accomplishing all the easier sell-offs where public opinion, though initially sceptical, was fairly quickly persuaded of the benefits, while leaving the really hard cases to her successor.

A single phrase in a characteristically nostalgic speech by Harold Macmillan did more damage to the idea of privatisation than all the outraged anathemas of Neil Kinnock. Speaking to the Tory Reform Group in November 1985, the former Prime Minister was said to have likened privatisation to a once wealthy family fallen on hard times 'selling the family silver'.[43] Despite the remoteness from most voters' experience of the aristocratic world he conjured up, Macmillan's words touched a chord. In vain the Government's supporters retorted that the industries being sold off were not assets at all, but liabilities which the Treasury was well rid of. Six days after the original speech Macmillan himself explained in the House of Lords that he was not against the principle of transferring loss-making public utilities to more efficient private ownership.'I ventured to criticise the fact that these huge sums were used as if they were income.'[44] In other words, what he was warning against was not privatisation itself, but the way the proceeds were being spent on consumption, not investment. In this he was voicing a critique that was beginning to be widely shared.

Unquestionably privatisation yielded real benefits, to the consumer and to the Treasury. The level of service to the customer undoubtedly improved. Arguably this reflected the spread of a more commercial culture generally and the loss of power by the unions, rather than simply the change of ownership. The major efficiency gains in both British Steel and British Airways, for instance, occurred while they were still in the public sector. But the privatisers would argue that the crucial factor was the removal of the safety net hitherto provided by the bottomless public purse.

The result was that the Treasury, instead of endlessly subsidising losses, now actually drew revenue from the profits. As Mrs Thatcher boasted at the 1989 party conference: 'Five industries that together were losing over £2 million a week in the public sector [are] now making profits of over £100 million a week in the private sector.'[45] Beside this, the argument that the shares had been sold too cheaply paled into irrelevance. The real criticism of Lawson and Mrs Thatcher is that they blew this windfall on a short-term consumer boom, instead of investing it on long-overdue repairs to the crumbling national infrastructure.

The Government's other great boast – that privatisation had created a nation of small capitalists – also turned out to be something of an illusion. On paper the number of individuals who owned shares certainly rocketed, from around three million in 1980 to eleven million in 1990. But few owned very many; and this was anyway a smaller number than appeared to have been lured into the stock market in the heady days of 1984–6. Many of these new investors immediately cashed in their allocation for a quick profit; others proudly retained their original small purchase of BT or British Gas shares but bought no more. The number who went on to build up portfolios of shares in different companies was disappointingly small, so that the proportion of shares owned by private individuals actually fell.

Finally, disappointment with privatisation, particularly among those who had most supported it, focused on the failure to promote real competition in most of the newly privatised industries, and on the fact that prices were still not properly subject to the market but regulated by a succession of unaccountable bodies appointed by the Government and still in practice sensitive to political pressure. This was perhaps an inevitable function of the way privatisation happened – pragmatically, opportunistically and piecemeal. There was an aspiration, but never a clearly worked-out blueprint – any more than there had been for nationalisation forty years earlier. Nevertheless it turned out – at least in Mrs Thatcher's time – to be an outstanding political success: the problems only revealed themselves over the following decade. Moreover, the idea had universal application. In the global retreat from socialism of which Thatcherism was merely the British reflection, it was Britain which pioneered both the concept and the techniques of moving state-owned industries into the private sector. As early as 1986 Mrs Thatcher was boasting that privatisation was on the agenda in countries as various as Turkey, Malaysia, Japan, Mexico and Canada. At home Thatcherism had many strands and different connotations; but around the world the word was synonymous with privatisation.

An enterprise society?

Meanwhile, there were signs of real cultural change at all levels of the economy, from the City of London to every provincial high street, a tangible liberalisation of all those attitudes and practices which had held back the performance of the British economy for decades. In large part this was the deliberate result of the Government's 'supply-side' strategy of cutting regulation, cutting taxes, increasing incentives, curbing the unions and generally freeing up the labour market. But equally important was the fact that all this

coincided with an explosion of new technology, above all communications technology – the so-called 'third industrial revolution' –
which was rapidly making the old ways obsolete by promoting
small-scale consumer-driven service industries in place of the mass-
employment heavy industry of the past. In this respect Thatcherism
merely reflected and facilitated the march of global progress. Nevertheless the revolution in British life was palpable.

First, there was 'Big Bang' which transformed the City in October
1986, sweeping away centuries of tradition by admitting foreign
brokers and jobbers and switching to a global standard of regulation in place of the gentlemanly conventions – 'my word is my
bond' – on which the Square Mile had hitherto prided itself. This
was an overdue recognition of a technological imperative which
was pushed through by Nigel Lawson in alliance with Cecil
Parkinson during the latter's brief time at the DTI. As with the
abolition of exchange controls in 1979, of which 'Big Bang' was a
natural corollary, Mrs Thatcher was initially cautious, worried that
the Government would appear to be intervening to rescue its friends
in the City while manufacturing industry went to the wall. But the
political flak was short-lived and the outcome was a spectacular
success, allowing London to join fully in the emerging computerised global economy by enabling it – just in time – to compete
successfully with Tokyo, Frankfurt and New York.

The effect of 'Big Bang', combined with Lawson's tax cuts and
the bonanza of privatisation, which offered huge rewards not only
to the merchant banks which bore the risk but also to an army of
consultants, advertising agencies and public-relations companies
which rode the wave of lucrative new business, meant that quite
suddenly the City became glamorous. In the mid-1980s, as never
before, it was in finance and related activities, not in industry or
the professions, that big money was to be made. The new wealth
was manifest in the rise of huge new glass and steel towers. But
the phenomenon which caught the public imagination was the new
class of computerised whizz-kids – dubbed 'yuppies', an acronym
for young upwardly mobile professionals – who suddenly materialised to populate these palaces of mammon.

But it was not only in the City that money was being made.
Out in the real economy too, things were changing. Deregulation,
the easy availability of credit and the rapid proliferation of personal
computers created a climate in which small businesses flourished,
helping to create more than three million new jobs (mainly in the
service sector) between 1983 and 1990 to make up for those lost
in manufacturing at the beginning of the decade. More people

than ever before left their employers – often involuntarily but in many cases voluntarily – to strike out on their own in small desktop enterprises which identified a gap in the market and set out to fill it. By 1989 three million people – 11 per cent of the workforce – were self-employed. Enterprise flourished not only in the south of England but in the north and Scotland as well, irrespective of politics.

Not only yuppies had more to spend than ever before: everyone in work benefited. As income tax fell, average real wages rose by more than 20 per cent a year between 1983 and 1987. At the same time hire-purchase restrictions had been lifted in 1982, and financial deregulation led to an unprecedented credit boom as banks and building societies competed to offer ever easier loans; credit cards and hole-in-the-wall cash dispensers also took off in the middle of the decade, and shops stayed open longer too, so that opportunities to spend multiplied. Higher disposable incomes created demand for every sort of home improvement. Above all, big salaries and easy credit fuelled a boom in property. Average household indebtedness rose by 250 per cent between 1982 and 1989, and most of this borrowing went into mortgages. While it lasted everyone seemed a winner, and those who had bought their council houses at a discount did best of all. Former tenants who had bought their houses for £10,000 found a few years later that they were worth four times as much.

All this was exactly what Mrs Thatcher and her Chancellors had dreamed of. But at the same time a lot of people were left out. Unemployment went on rising inexorably until January 1986; and even when it began to fall the shadow did not suddenly go away. Not until 1989 did the headline figure drop below two million, and then it promptly started rising again, back to three million in 1993. The blight was heavily concentrated in the old manufacturing regions which were devastated by the loss of the mills, factories, mines and steelworks which had been their livelihood since the nineteenth century. The 1997 film *The Full Monty* – about a group of Sheffield steelworkers driven to stripping to survive – extracted comedy from one enterprising response to the desperation of long-term unemployment, but its defiant humour did not disguise the bitter sense of rejection felt by whole communities while the rest of the country prospered.

In addition to those officially registered as unemployed – and their families – there were many others trapped outside the virtuous circle of success: old people dependent on the shrinking state pension; single parents, mainly unmarried or abandoned mothers, struggling with low-paid part-time jobs to make ends meet; and a growing number of young, rootless dropouts, the victims of unemployment, homelessness, family breakdown, drugs or a self-reinforcing combination of them all: in other words all those dependent on state benefits, whose real value was steadily cut as the cost of living rose. While the average household saw its income rise by 36 per cent over the decade (and the top tenth by 62 per cent), that of the bottom tenth fell by 17 per cent. It was obvious to anyone who walked around any of Britain's city centres at night that in the midst of rising wealth, poverty was also increasing, creating a new and permanently excluded underclass.

Mrs Thatcher strenuously denied that poverty was growing alongside wealth, insisting that everyone benefited from the increasing prosperity. In one part of her mind she genuinely believed that her purpose was to spread the ownership of wealth more widely so as to create what she called in her memoirs 'a society of "haves", not a class of them', and persuaded herself that council-house sales and wider share ownership were having this effect.[46] But at the same time she also believed that inequality was not just inevitable but necessary, indeed positively beneficial, as a stimulus to enterprise, a reward for success and a penalty for failure or lack of effort. At heart she believed that no one remained poor for long except by their own fault: everyone could make a success if only they worked hard and showed a bit of gumption.

The truth was that she had very little understanding of people whose life experience was different from her own. She approved of those she called 'our people', the hard-working, home-owning, tax-paying middle class whom she regarded as the backbone of England and correspondingly disapproved of those so lazy, feckless or lacking in self-respect that they were content to live in subsidised housing or on benefits. But this strict moral framework founded on thrift and self-improvement also meant, paradoxically, that she was not comfortable with the culture of unapologetic greed that was popularly associated with Thatcherism in practice. In fact she was extraordinarily ambivalent about the consumerist philosophy which bore her name.

On the one hand she vigorously defended the urge to make and spend money as the essential motor of a thriving economy, and was irritated when sanctimonious church leaders condemned the Government for encouraging materialism. Yet she was personally puritanical about money. She did not really approve of the stock exchange, believing that wealth should be earned by making and selling real goods and services, not by gambling and speculation.

For the same reason she refused to sanction a national lottery so long as she was Prime Minister; and she disapproved of credit cards, even as she presided over an unprecedented credit explosion.

The foundation of her political faith was moralistic, derived from the thrifty precepts of her father and her Methodist upbringing. Yet she also believed that the pursuit of wealth was a force for good in the world. 'Only by creating wealth,' she argued, 'can you relieve poverty. It's what you do with your wealth that counts.'[47] She claimed that charitable giving – encouraged by tax relief – had doubled in the ten years since 1979. In this way she hoped that the shortfall in public funding of schools, hospitals, universities and libraries would be filled, as in America, by private benefactions. The trouble was that despite her wishful harking back to the Victorians, that culture of philanthropy did not exist on a sufficient scale in Britain. There were still not enough huge corporations and public-spirited millionaires to fill the gap. As a result over the last thirty years Britain has suffered from the worst of both worlds, with public services receiving neither European levels of public spending nor American levels of private finance. The Blair Government went further than Mrs Thatcher ever dared in trying to attract private money to build public projects; but the level of public resistance is still high, and the legacy is plain to see.

The central paradox of Thatcherism is that Mrs Thatcher presided over and celebrated a culture of rampant materialism – 'fun, greed and money' – fundamentally at odds with her own values which were essentially conservative, old-fashioned and puritanical. She believed in thrift, yet encouraged record indebtedness. She lauded the family as the essential basis of a stable society, yet created a cut-throat economy and a climate of social fragmentation which tended to break up families, and tax and benefit provisions which positively discriminated against marriage. She disapproved of sexual licence and the public display of offensive material, yet promoted an untrammelled commercialism which unleashed a tide of pornography, both in print and on film, unimaginable a few years earlier.

Above all, she believed passionately in the uniqueness of Britain among the nations. She still believed that Britain had a mission to 'teach the nations of the world how to live'.[48] Indeed, she came close to believing that the individual's duty was not to serve the general good by pursuing his own self-interest – the orthodox Adam Smith view – but rather to serve his country. 'It is not who you are, who your family is, or where you come from that matters,' she told the 1984 party conference. 'It is what you are and what you can do for your country that counts.'[49] Yet market forces respect no boundaries. While beating the drum for Britain, Mrs Thatcher presided over an unprecedented extension of internationalism – not only in the European Community, where she did try, in her last three years, to slow the momentum towards further integration, but rather in the explosion of American-led global capitalism, eliminating economic sovereignty and homogenising local identities, in Britain as across the world.

Mrs Thatcher rode this liberalising tide and averted her eyes from consequences which offended her deepest values. She enjoyed huge political success by releasing the power of the middle class. Her revolutionary discovery was that the middle class – and those who aspired to be middle class – formed the majority of the population. Labour had assumed that the working class, if properly mobilised, was the majority. All previous Tory administrations had likewise taken it for granted that no Government could hope to be re-elected with more than a million unemployed. Mrs Thatcher demonstrated that, on the contrary, Governments could ignore the unemployed and still win elections so long as the middle class felt prosperous. On this analysis she was not a true liberal at all, but a class warrior who waged and won the class war on behalf of her own kind by using free-market policies tempered with blatant bribes like mortgage-interest tax relief as methods of social reward, switching the emphasis of society from collective provision to individual gratification. While she denied that individualism was merely a cover for selfish hedonism, she was helpless to dictate how the new middle class should spend its money; still less could she control the amoral power of international capital.

The paradox of Thatcherism is piquantly embodied in the history of her own family. Think back to Alfred Roberts in his Grantham grocery, the small town shopkeeper, patriot and preacher, husbanding the ratepayers' pennies and raising his clever daughter to a life of Christian service, diligence and thrift. Then look forward to the future Sir Mark Thatcher, an international 'businessman' possessed of no visible abilities, qualifications or social conscience, pursued from Britain to Texas to South Africa by lawsuits, tax investigations and a persistently unsavoury reputation. Imagine what Alfred would have made of Mark. It is well known that Denis – a businessman of an older generation – took a dim view of his son's activities. Yet for his mother Mark could do no wrong. The world in which he acquired his mysterious fortune was the world she helped to bring to birth: the values he represents are the values she promoted. Torn between pious invocations of her sainted father and fierce protectiveness towards her playboy son, Mrs Thatcher is the link between two utterly opposed moral systems which reflect not only the ambivalence of her own personality but the story of Britain in the twentieth century: Alfred Roberts to Mark Thatcher in three generations.

16

Iron Lady I:
Special Relationships

Mrs Thatcher and the Foreign Office

BY the time she embarked on her second term in June 1983, Mrs Thatcher was far more confident in foreign affairs than she had been in 1979. Then she had been the new girl on the international block, admittedly inexperienced and up against established leaders at the head of all her major allies: Jimmy Carter in Washington, Helmut Schmidt in Bonn and Valéry Giscard d'Estaing in Paris. But already by October 1982 – when Schmidt was replaced by Helmut Kohl – she was boasting in her constituency that she was now the most senior Western leader.[1] (She did not count Pierre Trudeau, who had been Prime Minister of Canada on and off since 1968.) The longer she remained in office, the more she was able to exploit what she called in her memoirs the 'huge and cumulative advantage in simply being known both by politicians and by ordinary people around the world'.[2] She had scored a notable diplomatic success in Zimbabwe, partial victory on the European budget issue and above all a stunning military triumph in the Falklands. Before the Paras had even landed in San Carlos Bay she was proclaiming, in refutation of Dean Acheson's famous gibe that Britain had 'lost an empire and not yet found a role': 'I believe Britain *has* now found a role. It is in upholding international law and teaching the nations of the world how to live.'[3] Once the war was won there was no holding her belief that Britain was once again a model to the world.

From now on she travelled extensively and was royally received wherever she went; she milked her global celebrity to the full. But she always travelled with a purpose, to promote her views and British interests, not just to inform herself as she had done in opposition. Wherever she went she exploited the Falklands triumph as a symbol of Britain's rebirth under her leadership, her resolution in the cause of freedom, and proven military prowess. 'Better than any Prime Minister since Macmillan,' David Reynolds has written, 'she understood that prestige was a form of power.'[4] Every foreign leader who came to London, however insignificant, wanted to be photographed with Madame Thatcher to boost his prestige back home. She posed with them all in front of the fireplace in the entrance hall of Number Ten, and sent them away with a lecture about the free market or the need to combat Communism.[*]

Like all long-serving Prime Ministers, she increasingly wished to be her own Foreign Secretary. She quickly replaced Francis Pym with the more amenable Geoffrey Howe, then treated Howe as little more than her bag carrier, entrusted with the tiresome detail of diplomacy while she handled all the important conversations. She liked dealing directly with the heads of government but had no inhibitions about receiving their foreign ministers or lesser emissaries and thoroughly enjoyed subjecting them to the same sort of interrogation she gave her own ministers: few of them came up to scratch. As Charles Powell put it: 'She was ready to go toe-to-toe with any world leader from Gorbachev to Deng Xiaoping . . . She had the huge advantage of being unembarrassable.'[6] As a woman she could say things to foreign leaders – most of whom had little experience of female politicians – that no male Prime Minister could have got away with.[7]

Howe and Mrs Thatcher made an excellent partnership precisely because he was the perfect foil to her rampaging style. She positively prided herself on being undiplomatic; but for that very reason she needed him to smooth ruffled feathers and mend broken fences in her wake. In truth she resented the fact that the policies she followed were very often closer to Foreign Office advice than her rhetoric implied. Howe deserves as much of the credit for her foreign policy successes in the second term as he does for holding firm at the Treasury in the first.

---

[*] Raymond Seitz, American Ambassador in London in the mid-1980s, accompanied numerous Senators and Congressmen to see her. 'The visitor would start the conversation with something such as "Thank you for seeing me, Madam Prime Minister" . . . to which Mrs Thatcher would respond for about thirty minutes without drawing breath.' She would finish with 'one or two courtesy points about Ronnie' before the visitor emerged dazed into Downing Street repeating, 'What a woman! What a woman!'[5]

Mrs Thatcher's conviction that the Foreign Office – officially the Foreign and Commonwealth Office – was a limp institution dedicated to giving away Britain's vital interests had only been reinforced by her experience since 1979. After the Falklands war she appointed Sir Anthony Parsons, fresh from his brilliant performance at the UN, to be her private foreign-policy adviser in Number Ten. A large part of Parsons' job, as he described it, was to try to anticipate crises, so that she would not be 'caught short again as she had been over the Falklands'.[8] He stayed for only a year, but was replaced by Sir Percy Cradock, a China specialist who initially handled the Hong Kong negotiations but stayed on to become her general foreign-policy adviser right up to 1990.

Increasingly she travelled with no Foreign Office presence in her party at all, but was accompanied even on important trips only by her own private entourage. When she first visited President Reagan in 1981, for example, she took with her a whole phalanx of senior mandarins and several juniors. By the time she flew right round the world from Beijing and Hong Kong to bend the President's ear about his 'Star Wars' programme in December 1984 she was accompanied only by her two private secretaries, Robin Butler and Charles Powell, and her press secretary, Bernard Ingham. And towards the end it was usually just Powell and Ingham.

She continued to seek foreign-policy advice from independent academic experts outside the Foreign Office. Though to an extent these tended to tell her what she wanted to hear – or, more accurately, she chose advisers who would tell her what she wanted to hear – it is to her credit that she tried to go beyond the narrow circle of official advice. Nevertheless both her special advisers, Parsons and Cradock, were former FCO insiders; and the most influential of all from 1984 onwards – Charles Powell – was, ironically, a Foreign Office man *par excellence*.

A career diplomat in his early forties, Powell succeeded John Coles as Mrs Thatcher's foreign-affairs private secretary in June 1984 and immediately established an exceptional rapport with her. The basis of their relationship was his skill at drafting: he was brilliant at finding acceptable diplomatic language to express what she wanted to say without fudging it. Second, he needed as little sleep as she did: he was unflagging and ever-present, never went to bed but seemed to be always at her side. In addition, he had a knack of getting things done by informal personal diplomacy of his own: he would go direct to Washington or Paris, behind the back of the official Foreign Office, and fix what she wanted with a word in the right place. He came to be seen as the second most powerful figure in the Government, no longer confined exclusively to foreign affairs but the real deputy Prime Minister, practically her *alter ego*. 'It was sometimes difficult,' Cradock wrote, 'to establish where Mrs Thatcher ended and Charles Powell began.'[9]

After three or four years, by normal Whitehall practice it would have been time for Powell to move on, but Mrs Thatcher refused to let him go. This might not have mattered if he had been just an indispensable Jeeves. But, in fact, the longer he stayed the more his views began to influence Mrs Thatcher's. Whereas in the earlier years of her premiership Mrs Thatcher was surrounded by overwhelmingly pro-European advice, from about 1986 Powell's informed and articulate Euroscepticism increasingly encouraged her to follow her own anti-Community and anti-German prejudice – with serious consequences both for herself and for Britain.

For most of her premiership, however, she actually followed Foreign Office advice far more than she liked to pretend – on Zimbabwe, Hong Kong, Northern Ireland, Eastern Europe and even during her second term on the EC. Though she went to war for the Falklands, she liquidated most of the last vestiges of empire around the world; though famously hostile to Communism, she was persuaded that she could do business with a new generation of Soviet leaders; though an instinctive Unionist, she was likewise persuaded that the only chance of peace in Northern Ireland was with the involvement of Dublin; and against her instinct she took the decisive steps in committing Britain to an integrated Europe.

Judged by the objectives she set herself, she was 'hugely successful' in foreign affairs.[10] First, she played Ronald Reagan skilfully to revive and maximise the US 'special relationship'; then she spotted and encouraged Mikhail Gorbachev, and acted successfully as an intermediary between him and Reagan. She finally settled the EC budget row and went on to set the pace in promoting the introduction of a single European market. She achieved as good a settlement as could be hoped for in Hong Kong. She defied the world by pursuing her own route to ending apartheid in South Africa and arguably was vindicated by the result. And despite her strongly expressed views, she managed to maintain good relations with almost everyone, not only the leaders of both superpowers, but on both sides of the Jordan and the Limpopo too. In short, one recent history concludes, she 'utterly transformed Britain's standing and reputation in the world'.[11]

Ron and Margaret

The unshakeable cornerstone of Mrs Thatcher's foreign policy was the United States. She had no time for subtle formulations which saw Britain as the meeting point of overlapping circles of influence, maintaining a careful equidistance between America on the one hand and Europe on the other, with obligations to the Commonwealth somewhere in the background. She had no doubt whatever that Britain's primary role in the world was as Washington's number-one ally. No Prime Minister since Churchill had believed so unquestioningly in the mission of 'the English-speaking peoples' to lead and save the rest of the world. But she had no illusions about who was the senior partner, nor did she seek to deny the reality of British dependence on the United States. It was the Americans – with British help – who had liberated Europe from the Nazi tyranny in 1944; it was American nuclear protection which had defended Western Europe from Soviet aggression since 1945. 'Had it not been for the magnanimity of the United States, Europe would not be free today,' she reminded the Tory Party Conference in 1981 (and repeated on innumerable other occasions). 'We cannot defend ourselves, either in this island or in Europe, without a close, effective and warm-hearted alliance with the United States.'[12]

Moreover, she increasingly believed that it was not just America's military might that underwrote the survival of freedom in the West, but American capitalism, which was the pre-eminent model of that freedom. Nothing made her angrier than the condescension of the British political establishment which viewed America as crude, refreshingly vigorous but sadly naive. She envied the energy and optimism of American society – the unapologetic belief in capitalism and the refusal to look to the state for the solution to every social problem – and wanted Britain to become in every respect (from penal policy to the funding of the arts) more American. She was herself, as one US Ambassador in London shrewdly noted, a very American type of politician: patriotic, evangelical, unafraid of big abstract words, preaching a message of national and even personal salvation quite unlike the usual British (and European) style of ironic scepticism and fatalistic damage limitation.[13] Proud as she was of Britain's glorious past, at the end of the twentieth century a part of her would really rather have been American. Her entourage felt the almost physical charge she got whenever she visited America. 'When she stepped onto American soil she became a new woman,' Ronnie Millar noted. 'She loved America . . . and America loved her back. There is nothing like the chemistry of mutual admiration.'[14]

She was distressed and angered by the overt anti-Americanism of British liberals who professed to see little difference between the Americans and the Russians, or nuclear disarmers who painted the United States as a greater threat to peace than the Soviet Union. There was no group she more passionately despised than academics who abused their personal freedom by equating Tyranny and Freedom. Her world view was uncomplicatedly black and white. 'This party is pro-American,' she declared roundly at the 1984 Tory Party Conference.[15] Whatever differences she might have with the Americans on specific issues, she was determined to demonstrate on every occasion Britain's unqualified loyalty to the Atlantic alliance. If she could not be the leader of the free world herself, the next best thing was to be his first lieutenant.

Just as she was lucky in her enemies, Mrs Thatcher was extraordinarily fortunate to coincide for most of her eleven years in Downing Street with an American President who allowed her to play a bigger role within the Alliance than any other Prime Minister since the days of Roosevelt and Churchill. During her first year and a half in office she tried hard to cultivate a good relationship with Jimmy Carter. Deeply as she revered his office, however, she enjoyed no rapport with the well-meaning but in her view hopelessly woolly-minded Democrat. The election of Ronald Reagan in November 1980, by contrast, changed everything. It was not just that Reagan was an ideological soulmate, elected on the same sort of conservative backlash that had brought her to power in Britain. Ideological symmetry does not guarantee a good relationship: it can just as easily make for rivalry. Far more important than the similarity of their ideas was the difference in their political personalities.

Temperamentally Reagan was Mrs Thatcher's opposite, an easygoing, broad-brush politician who made no pretence of mastering the detailed complexities of policy, but was happy to let others – including on occasion Mrs Thatcher – lead and even bully him. The bond of their instinctively shared values was reinforced by sexual chemistry: he had an old-fashioned gallantry towards women, while she had a weakness for tall, charming men (particularly older men) with film-star looks. Out of his depth with most foreign leaders, Reagan knew where he was with Mrs Thatcher, if only because she spoke his language: he understood her, liked her, admired her and therefore trusted her. Unlike Helmut Schmidt, he did not feel threatened in his 'male pride' by a strong woman: as Americans often remarked, Margaret Thatcher held no terrors for a man who had been married for thirty years to Nancy Davis. For a politician, Reagan was unusually secure in his own skin. Unlike Mrs Thatcher he did not have to win every argument: he knew what he believed, but shrank from confrontation. Once when she was hectoring him down the telephone from London, he held the receiver away from his ear so that everyone in the room could hear her in full flow, beamed broadly and announced: 'Isn't she marvellous?'[16] Their contrasting styles served to disguise the disparity in power between Washington and London and for eight years made something approaching reality of the comforting myth of a 'special relationship' between Britain and the United States.

Mrs Thatcher exploited her opportunity with great skill – and uncharacteristic tact. Privately she was clear-sighted about the President's limitations. 'If I told you what Mrs Thatcher really thought about President Reagan it would damage Anglo-American relations,' Nicholas Henderson told Tony Benn some years later.[17] 'Not much grey matter, is there?' she once reflected.[18] But she would never hear a word of criticism from others. In Reagan she put up with a bumbling ignorance she would have tolerated in no one else, partly because he was the President and leader of the free world, but also because she realised that his amiable vagueness gave her a chance to influence American policy that no conventionally hands-on President would have allowed her – as was quickly demonstrated when Reagan was succeeded by George Bush.

The basis of their partnership was laid back in 1975, when Mrs Thatcher was a newly elected Leader of the Opposition and the ex-Governor of California was just beginning to be talked of as a Presidential candidate. They had immediately found themselves on the same wavelength, and in due course each was delighted by the other's election. Yet their relationship in office took a little time to develop. By no coincidence Mrs Thatcher was the first major foreign visitor to Washington after Reagan's inauguration. She stated her position unambiguously at the welcoming ceremony on the White House lawn: 'We in Britain stand with you . . . Your problems will be our problems, and when you look for friends we will be there.' Reagan responded in kind. 'In a dangerous world,' he asserted, there was 'one element that goes without question: Britain and America stand side by side.'[19]

But this was the conventional rhetoric of these occasions. At this stage the two leaders were still addressing each other formally on paper as 'Dear Mr President . . . Dear Madame Prime Minister'.[20] Their working partnership really began at the Ottawa G7 in July 1981. This was Reagan's first appearance on the global stage, while she was now relatively experienced: he was grateful for her support, both personal and political. She chaperoned and protected him, and made the case for American policy more effectively than he could, on the one hand for market solutions to the world recession against most of the other leaders who favoured more interventionist measures; and on the other in standing firm in support of the deployment of cruise missiles, from which the Europeans – faced with anti-nuclear demonstrations – were beginning to retreat. At the same time she warned Reagan privately that American criticism of European 'neutralism' risked provoking exactly the reaction it sought to prevent.[21]

Afterwards Reagan wrote to her for the first time as 'Dear Margaret', thanking her for her 'important role in our discussions. We might still be drafting the communiqué if it were not for you.' She in return addressed him for the first time as 'Dear Ron'.[22] Nine months later the Falklands crisis caused a temporary hiccup; but after some initial hesitation Reagan gave Britain the full support Mrs Thatcher felt entitled to expect. Arrangements had already been made for Reagan to visit London after the Versailles summit in June 1982. The trip had been planned at the nadir of Mrs Thatcher's domestic unpopularity to lend support to an embattled ally; in the event it took place a few days before the Argentine surrender, at the climax of her military triumph. As well as meeting the Prime Minister in Downing Street, the President went riding with the Queen in Windsor Great Park and addressed members of both Houses of Parliament in the Royal Gallery, where he overcame a sceptical audience by praising Britain's principled stand in the Falklands and borrowing freely from Churchill in asserting the moral superiority of the West. Freedom and democracy, he predicted, would 'leave Marxism-Leninism on the ash-heap of history'.* While the rest of his visit to Europe was disrupted by anti-nuclear demonstrations, the warmth of his reception in London moved the 'special relationship' visibly on to a new level.[23]

At subsequent summits Reagan treated Mrs Thatcher explicitly as his prime ally. He was particularly pleased that she found time to attend the Williamsburg summit in the middle of the June 1983 election. White House files show how his staff coordinated with hers to advance their joint agenda, and afterwards he thanked her for her help. 'Thanks to your contribution during Saturday's dinner

---

* This was the first time anyone in Britain had seen a teleprompter – Reagan's 'sincerity machine' – which enabled him to speak with unnatural fluency without looking down at his notes. Mrs Thatcher quickly adopted it for her own major speeches.

discussion of INF [Intermediate-range Nuclear Forces],' he told her, 'we were able to send to the Soviets a clear signal of allied determination and unity.'[24] And before the London meeting the following year he wrote to her that he planned to provide her with 'the same stalwart support' that she had given him at Williamsburg.[25] They made a powerful and well-rehearsed double act.

From now on Mrs Thatcher invited herself to Washington at the drop of a hat. As soon as she had secured her re-election in June 1983 she asked to come over in September 'to continue bilateral discussions with the President'.[26] 'She will speak plainly about British interests', the US Embassy in London warned, 'and will appreciate plain speaking from us'.[27] Henceforth this was the basis of the relationship, as Lady Thatcher explicitly acknowledged in her memoirs: 'I regarded the *quid pro quo* for my strong public support of the President as being the right to be direct with him and members of his Administration in private.'[28] 'She not only had her say,' Richard Perle remembered, 'but was frequently the dominant influence in decision-making.'[29]

If, as an outsider, she was able to have this degree of influence, it was because, compared with Whitehall, Washington is highly decentralised. American government is a continuous struggle between different agencies – the State Department, the Pentagon, the National Security Adviser, the CIA and others – all competing for the President's ear. Well briefed by the British Embassy, Mrs Thatcher knew the balance of views on every issue and where her intervention, judiciously applied, might be decisive. It was well known that Reagan did not like quarrelling with her, so those Presidential advisers on her side of a particular argument had every incentive to deploy her to clinch their case. George Shultz, who replaced Al Haig as Secretary of State in the summer of 1983, recalled that he always found her influence with Reagan 'very constructive', and was 'shameless' in calling on her aid when required.[30] Others, however, found her interventions maddening.

When she could not come to Washington in person, she would write or telephone. She regularly reported to Reagan her views on other leaders she had met on her travels, and pressed her ideas of the action he should take in the Middle East or other trouble spots. Sometimes their letters were purely personal, as when they remembered each other's birthdays, congratulated one another on being re-elected, or expressed horror and relief when the other narrowly escaped assassination. At least once, at the height of the miners' strike in 1984, Reagan simply sent his friend a note of encouragement. 'Dear Margaret,' he wrote:

In recent weeks I have thought often of you with considerable empathy as I follow the activities of the miners and dockworkers' unions. I know they present a difficult set of issues for your government. I just wanted you to know that my thoughts are with you as you address these important issues; I'm confident as ever that you and your government will come out of this well. Warm regards, Ron.[31]

Two years later, when Reagan in turn was in trouble over damaging revelations about his administration's involvement in the exchange of arms for the release of Iranian hostages, in defiance of its declared policy, Mrs Thatcher rushed publicly to his defence: 'I believe implicitly in the President's total integrity on that subject,' she told a press conference in Washington.[32] As the Iran–Contra scandal deepened the following year and America was seized by a mood of gloomy introspection, she visited Washington again – fresh from her own second re-election – and toured the television studios, vigorously denying that Reagan was politically weakened and defending his honour. 'I have dealt with the President for many, many years,' she told a CBS interviewer, 'and I have absolute trust in him.' Moreover, she insisted, 'America is a strong country, with a great President, a great people and a great future. Cheer up! Be more upbeat! . . . You should have as much faith in America as I have.'[33]

Such fulsome encomiums, repeated every time she went to Washington and lapped up by the American media, were regularly condemned by her opponents at home for showing an excessive degree of grovelling subordination. Yet the truth is that in her private dealings with Washington she never grovelled. On a whole range of issues, from the Falklands to nuclear disarmament, on which she had differences with the Americans, she fought her corner vigorously. As Richard Perle remembered: 'She never approached the conversations she had . . . with American officials and with the President from a position of supplication or inferiority. Quite the contrary.'[34]

Her first battle was over the consequences for British firms of American sanctions on the Soviet Union following the imposition of martial law in Poland in December 1981. She passionately supported the Polish Solidarity movement and was all in favour of concerted Western action to deter the Russians from crushing the flicker of freedom in Poland as they had done in Czechoslovakia and Hungary. But the Americans' chosen sanction was to halt the construction of an oil pipeline from Siberia to Western Europe, which they proposed to enforce by applying sanctions to European firms, including the British company John Brown Engineering, which had legitimate existing contracts to build the pipeline. This, Mrs Thatcher objected, would hurt the Europeans more than the Russians, while it was not matched by comparable American sacrifices: the Americans had actually ended an embargo on grain exports to Russia which was hitting American farmers in the Midwest. She also objected to the Americans trying to impose American laws on British firms operating outside the USA.

For once she was speaking for Europe against America. In truth she was fighting for British interests, but, with her usual ability to clothe national interest in a cloak of principle, she was also standing up for sovereignty and the rule of law against American extra-territorial arrogance. 'The question is whether one very powerful nation can prevent existing contracts being fulfilled,' she told the House of Commons on 1 July. 'I think it is wrong to do so.'[35] The British Government instructed John Brown not to comply with the US embargo.

Yet her main concern was still to prevent damage to the Alliance. 'The only fly in the ointment,' she told Weinberger in September, 'is the John Brown thing.' 'She fervently hoped,' he cabled Reagan, 'that what the US did would be so minimal that she could ignore it. She desperately needed some face-saving solution.' Characteristically she was worried about fuelling anti-Americanism. 'Mrs Thatcher said she had a serious problem with unemployment and bankruptcies, and she didn't want her closest friend, the United States, to be blamed by her people.'[36]

As so often, she knew that she had allies in Washington. In this instance her pressure helped the new Secretary of State, George Shultz, to get the pipeline ban lifted in return for a package of joint measures limiting Soviet imports and the export of technology to Russia. Telling her of his decision on 12 November, Reagan thanked her – and Pym and the British Ambassador in Washington, Sir Oliver Wright – for helping achieve this consensus.[37] This was the special relationship in action.

But the Polish pipeline question was just one of a number of 'chronic economic irritants' which Mrs Thatcher felt she had to raise with the Americans every time she visited Washington in the mid-1980s.[38] First there was the fallout of British Airways' price war with Freddie Laker's independent airline, Laker Airways, which succeeded in forcing the price-cutting upstart out of business in 1982. Much as she admired Laker as a model entrepreneur, Mrs Thatcher was worried that an American Justice Department investigation into BA's unscrupulous methods was holding up plans to privatise the national carrier. In March 1983 she appealed 'personally and urgently' to Reagan to suspend the investigation, once again threatening that it 'could have the most serious consequences for British airlines' and warning that if it was not stopped, 'our aviation relationship will be damaged and the harm could go wider'.[39] Advised by his staff that he could not interfere in the judicial process, Reagan replied regretfully that 'in this case I feel that I do not have the latitude to respond to your concerns'.[40] But seven months later he did stop the investigation – an 'almost unprecedented' intervention which left the Justice Department 'stunned'. In March 1985 Reagan intervened again to persuade BA's biggest creditors to settle out of court, thus clearing the way for privatisation to begin in 1986.

Another running sore was the attempt of some American states to tax multinational companies on the proportion of their profits deemed to have been earned in that state. British objections to this 'unitary taxation' – at a time when British companies were investing heavily in America – bedevilled several of Mrs Thatcher's meetings with Reagan and his colleagues, before this too was eventually settled to her satisfaction. In this case, however, the resolution probably owed more to American multinationals making the same complaint than it did to Mrs Thatcher's protests.

Above all, she worried about the impact on Europe of the Americans' huge budget deficit, caused by the Reagan administration's policy of tax cuts combined with increased defence spending. After five years the deficit was running at $220 billion a year and the US was the world's largest debtor nation – especially heavily indebted to Japan. This was Mrs Thatcher's one serious criticism of her ally's economic policy. When she had been unable to bring spending under control in 1981 she had felt bound to raise taxes and she could not understand Reagan's insouciance. At successive G7 summits she warned that the unchecked deficit would raise interest rates and 'choke off world recovery'.[41] In fact US interest rates fell in the second half of 1984 and the booming US economy led the world out of recession. But still Mrs Thatcher worried, though she was reluctant to criticise in public. She wrote to him that she remained 'very concerned by . . . the continuing surge of the dollar':

A firm programme for the reduction of the budget deficit is the most important safeguard against financial instability and I wish you every success with your Budget proposals to Congress.

Reagan tried, in his fashion; but in practice the conflicting priorities of the Republican White House and a Democrat-dominated Congress ensured that the deficit persisted for the rest of the decade.

An even more sensitive issue on which Mrs Thatcher's intransigence exasperated Washington was the future of the Falklands. The Americans had, with some misgivings, eventually backed what the *Washington Post* called her 'seemingly senseless, small but bloody war' in the South Atlantic.[42] But as soon as the fighting was over, Washington's priority was to resume normal relations with Argentina (and South America as a whole) as quickly as possible, and renew the search for a lasting peace settlement. Even in his message of congratulation on her victory, Reagan stated firmly that 'A just war requires a just peace. We look forward to consulting with you and to assisting in the building of such a peace.'[43] An invitation to her to visit Washington a few days later was couched explicitly as an opportunity to consider how to achieve this goal.[44]

But Mrs Thatcher was not interested in a just peace. So far as she was concerned, she had defeated the aggressor, at great risk and considerable sacrifice, and she was not now willing to negotiate away what her forces had won. As she defiantly put it: 'We have not sent British troops and treasure 8,000 miles to establish a UN trusteeship.'[45]

The first test of her flexibility came that autumn, when several Latin American countries sponsored a UN resolution calling for renewed negotiations to end what they called 'the colonial situation' in the Falklands. Mrs Thatcher immediately cabled Reagan asking that the US should oppose the resolution. But George Shultz and others in the administration – not least Jeane Kirkpatrick, still the American Ambassador at the UN – believed that the US should support it, since the whole purpose of the UN was to promote the peaceful resolution of disputes. Shultz initially feared that Reagan would take Mrs Thatcher's side. 'But I found that he too was getting a little fed up with her imperious attitude in the matter.'[46] The President ticked his agreement to Mrs Kirkpatrick backing the resolution, and wrote a delicate letter – in reply to what his staff called 'Mrs Thatcher's latest blast' – to explain why. Nevertheless the sting was that he was still going to support the UN resolution, which was duly carried by a large majority, with only a dozen Commonwealth countries joining Britain in opposing it.

Mrs Thatcher continued adamantly to reject any possibility of negotiations on the question of sovereignty. A year later, however, with a democratically elected government now installed in Buenos

Aires, the State Department took a further step towards normal-ising relations by 'certifying' Argentina as eligible for a resumption of American arms sales. This, Reagan assured Mrs Thatcher, merely ended the embargo imposed in 1982. 'Certification does not mean arms sales.'[47] The announcement was tactfully postponed for a day to spare her embarrassment in the House of Commons; Vice-President George Bush thanked her for her understanding response.[48] For the next three years Reagan deferred to her sensitivity, and no arms were sold; but by 1986 the pressure from the Pentagon was becoming irresistible. Once again Mrs Thatcher went straight to the top. 'You should expect a typical Thatcher barrage,' John Poindexter briefed Reagan before their meeting at Camp David following the Reagan–Gorbachev summit at Reykjavik. 'You will want to tell Mrs Thatcher that we cannot continually put off how best to nurture Argentina's democracy.'[49] But this time she was more subtle, waiting until almost the last minute before dropping a final item almost casually into the conversation, as Geoffrey Smith described. '"Oh, arms to Argentina," she said, for all the world like a housewife checking that she had not forgotten some last piece of shopping. "You won't, will you?"' To the horror of his officials, Reagan fell for it. '"No," he replied. "We won't." So in one short sentence he killed weeks of careful preparation within his administration.'[50]

The most serious public disagreement of their whole eight-year partnership came in October 1983, when the Americans sent troops to the tiny Caribbean island of Grenada to put down a coup by a gang of left-wing thugs against the elected – but already Marxist – government led by Maurice Bishop. The Americans were always concerned about any left-wing takeover on their Caribbean doorstep and, fearful of another Cuba, had already been doing their best to destabilise Bishop's regime ever since 1979. But Grenada was a member of the Commonwealth, whose head of state was the Queen. The Foreign Office was alarmed at events on the island, but believed there was nothing to be done, since Grenada was a sovereign country. Several neighbouring Caribbean states, however, concerned for their own security, did want something done, and appealed to Washington for help. The Americans responded by diverting ships to the island, ostensibly to evacuate several hundred American students, but in fact to mount a counter-coup. They did so without consulting or even informing Mrs Thatcher until it was too late to halt the action. As a result she was humiliated by the revelation that her vaunted relationship with Washington was rather less close than she pretended.

The story of her reaction to the news of the American invasion has been vividly told from both sides of the Atlantic. According to Carol's life of Denis, Reagan telephoned while her mother was attending a dinner – ironically at the US Embassy. As soon as she got back to Downing Street she phoned Reagan back and railed at him for several minutes: some versions say a quarter of an hour. 'She didn't half tick him off,' Denis told Carol. '"You have invaded the Queen's territory and you didn't even say a word to me," she said to him, very upset. I think that Reagan was a bit shocked. There was nothing gentle about her tone, and not much diplomacy either.'[51]

The diplomatic exchanges tell a slightly different story. Washington received the call for help from the Organisation of Eastern Caribbean States (OECS), led by the formidable Mrs Eugenia Charles, Prime Minister of Dominica, on Sunday 23 October. The same day a suicide attack in Beirut killed some 300 American soldiers serving in the multinational peacekeeping force in Lebanon. There was no logical connection, but there was no doubt in British minds that the American resolve to act quickly in Grenada was fuelled by the outrage in Beirut: it was easier to hit back in Grenada than in Lebanon. Reagan and his military advisers decided almost immediately to accede to the OECS request and began planning the operation in the greatest secrecy. At four o'clock on Monday afternoon, in reply to a question from Denis Healey about the possibility of American intervention in Grenada, Howe told the Commons in good faith that he knew of no such intention: American ships were in the area solely to take off US citizens if it should become necessary, just as Britain had HMS *Antrim* in the area for the same purpose. Pressed further by a Labour MP, he assured the House that 'we are keeping in the closest possible touch with the United States Government . . . I have no reason to think that American military intervention is likely.'[52]

Less than three hours later, however, at 6.47 p.m., while Mrs Thatcher was still in Downing Street hosting a reception, there came a cable from Reagan telling her that he was giving 'serious consideration' to the OECS request. He assured her that if an invasion did go ahead, the British Governor-General would be the key figure in appointing a provisional government as soon as the troops had landed. He also promised categorically: 'I will . . . undertake to inform you in advance should our forces take part in the proposed collective security force, or of whatever political or diplomatic efforts we plan to pursue. It is of some assurance to know I can count on your support and advice on this important issue.'[53]

Mrs Thatcher received this message before she went out to dinner but, in view of the promise of further consultation, did not think it required an immediate reply. Only three hours later, however, at ten o'clock, there came a second, much shorter cable, in which the President informed her curtly: 'I have decided to respond positively to this request.'

> Our forces will establish themselves in Grenada. The collective Caribbean security force will disembark on Grenada shortly there-after . . . We will inform you of further developments as they occur. Other allies will be apprised of our actions after they are begun.
>
> I expect that a new provisional government will be formed in Grenada shortly after the collective security force arrives. We hope that Her Majesty's government will join us by extending support to Grenada's new leaders.[54]

What these two cables clearly show is that the Americans were perfectly well aware of Britain's primary responsibility in Grenada, but had decided that Mrs Thatcher's support for unilateral US action could be taken for granted. As a robust Cold Warrior, they assumed, the Iron Lady would applaud the suppression of a Communist coup anywhere in the world. But if they thought she would be gratified to be informed a few hours before the other allies, they were badly mistaken. She was outraged, first that the Americans should think of invading the Queen's territory, which touched in her the same patriotic trigger as the Argentine invasion of the Falklands; worse still that they should do it without telling her. There is no doubt that she felt personally let down. But she did not get on the telephone immediately. First she held a midnight meeting with Howe and Michael Heseltine. They agreed a reply setting out Britain's objections to military action and urging the Americans to hold their hand. In addition, Mrs Thatcher worried that America intervening militarily in the Caribbean would be used by the Russians to legitimise their invasion of Afghanistan. She told her staff that she remembered seeing newspaper placards in 1956 reading 'Britain Invades Egypt' and knew instantly that it was wrong.[55]

Only after sending Britain's reasoned objection did she telephone Reagan, at about two o'clock in the morning, London time. Unfortunately no transcript of her call was made. But both Howe, in his memoirs, and Mrs Thatcher at the time, contradict the story that she gave the President an earful. All she did was to ask him to consider carefully the advice in her cabled message. So much for her giving Reagan 'a prime ticking off'.

A few hours later – just before 7.00 a.m. in London, just before 2.00 a.m. in Washington and only three hours before the troops landed – came Reagan's reply, diplomatic but uncompromising. He thanked Mrs Thatcher for her 'thoughtful message', claimed to have 'weighed very carefully' the issues she had raised, but insisted that while he appreciated the dangers inherent in a military operation, 'on balance, I see this as the lesser of two risks'. He stressed the danger of Soviet influence in Grenada, felt that he had no choice but to intervene, and repeated his hope that 'as we proceed, in co-operation with the OECS countries, we would have the active co-operation of Her Majesty's Government' and the support of the Governor-General in establishing an interim government.[56]

That afternoon Howe had to explain to the Commons why he had inadvertently misled the House the day before. He still claimed to have kept 'closely in touch' with the American Government over the weekend, and confirmed that he and Mrs Thatcher had opposed military intervention; but he could not deny that their advice had not been asked until it was too late and had been ignored when given. He could not endorse the American action, but neither could he condemn it, leaving himself open to the mockery of Denis Healey, who savaged the Government's 'impression of pitiable impotence'. Not for the first time, he charged, Mrs Thatcher had allowed 'President Reagan to walk all over her'.[57]

Next day – during an uncomfortable Commons debate – Reagan rang to apologise for the embarrassment he had caused her. This time the transcript shows Mrs Thatcher to have been uncharacteristically monosyllabic. But the action was under way now and she hoped it would be successful.

When her turn came to face questions in the Commons, Mrs Thatcher was obliged to put the best face possible on her humiliation. Needled by Labour glee at the breach of her special relationship, she made the best case she could for the American action, recalling that they had intervened to restore democracy in Dominica in exactly the same way in 1965.[58] Nevertheless, she was still seething. 'That man!', she railed. 'After all I've done for him, he didn't even consult me.'[59] On a late-night BBC World Service phone-in, she vented her fury on an American caller who accused her of failing to stand alongside the Americans in fighting Communism:

We in the Western countries, the Western democracies, use our force to defend our way of life. We do not use it to walk into other people's countries, independent sovereign territories . . . If you are pronouncing a new law that wherever Communism reigns against the will of the people . . . there the United States shall enter, we are going to have really terrible wars in the world.[60]

The Americans were bewildered by Mrs Thatcher's attitude. They did not understand her sensitivity about the Commonwealth and could not see that their action was any different from what she herself had done in the Falklands. Senior members of the administration were angry that Britain did not give them the same support they had given Britain in the South Atlantic. Reagan regretted the dispute, but was unrepentant because he thought she was 'just plain wrong'.[61] And in due course, as it became clear that the invasion – unlike some other American military interventions – had been wholly successful in its limited objectives, Mrs Thatcher herself came to feel that she had been wrong to oppose it. At any rate she quickly put the episode behind her and set herself to making sure that there was no lasting damage to her most important international relationship.

The tension passed. Nevertheless Mrs Thatcher's initial reaction to Grenada was a telling glimpse of her ultimate priority. Disposed as she was to defer to American leadership, her instinct was to repel any infringement of what she saw as British – or in this case Commonwealth – sovereignty. Had she been consulted she might well have agreed to a joint operation to restore democracy. She wanted to be America's partner, not its poodle. She was deeply hurt by Reagan's failure to consult her, but the lesson she learned was that next time the Americans needed her she must not let them down.

The test came in April 1986, when Washington was provoked by a spate of terrorist attacks on American tourists and servicemen in Europe, presumed to be the work of Libyan agents. Libya's eccentric President, Colonel Gaddafi, had been a particular *bête noire* of Reagan's from the moment he entered the White House, and by 1986 Reagan was itching to punish him. When a TWA plane was sabotaged over Greece on 2 April, and five servicemen were killed by a bomb in a Berlin nightclub three days later, the President determined to bomb Tripoli in retaliation. The US plan involved using F-111s based in Britain, partly for accuracy, but also deliberately to involve the European allies in the action. But Reagan's request put Mrs Thatcher on the spot at a time when her authority was weakened by the Westland crisis. France and Spain refused the Americans permission to overfly their territory; and Mrs Thatcher knew she would invite a political storm if she agreed to let the American mission fly from British bases.

Britain too had suffered from Libyan terrorism – notably the shooting of a London policewoman in 1984. MI5 had no doubt of Libya's responsibility for the latest attacks. But again Mrs Thatcher worried about the legality of the proposed action. Just three months earlier, speaking to American journalists in London, she had explicitly condemned retaliatory action against terrorism. 'I must warn you that I do not believe in retaliatory strikes that are against international law,' she declared. 'Once you start going across borders then I do not see an end to it . . . I uphold international law very firmly.'[62] Some time earlier she had refused to endorse an Israeli attack on the headquarters of the Palestine Liberation Organisation (PLO) in Tunis, asking Garret FitzGerald to imagine what the Americans would say if Britain 'bombed the Provos in Dundalk'.[63] She had also refused to follow a unilateral American embargo on Libyan oil.

But when Reagan asked her permission, late in the evening of 8 April, she felt that she had no choice but to agree. Particularly after Grenada, she could not afford to deny the Americans the payback to which they felt they were entitled after the Falklands. In her view – and theirs – this was what the Alliance was all about. 'The cost to Britain of not backing American action,' she wrote in her memoirs, 'was unthinkable.'[64] Her only escape was to try to convince the Americans that retaliation would be counterproductive. After hasty consultation she sent back a holding reply asking for more detail about intended targets, warning of the risk of civilian casualties and spelling out the danger that the United States would be seen to be in breach of international law unless the action could plausibly be justified under Article 51 of the UN Charter as 'self-defence'.

The next day she held more *ad hoc* meetings with relevant ministers, including the Attorney-General, Michael Havers. All were unhappy, but their doubts only hardened Mrs Thatcher's resolve, as Charles Powell recalled:

> The Foreign Office were whole-heartedly against it, believing it would lead to all our embassies in the Middle East being burned, all our interests there ruined. But she knew it was the right thing to do and she just said, 'This is what allies are for . . . If one wants help, they get help.' It just seemed so simple to her.[65]

After the event, when the television news showed pictures of the dead and injured in the streets of Tripoli, the opposition parties once again condemned her slavish subservience to American wishes, asserting that British complicity in the bombing would expose British travellers to retaliation. Opinion polls showed 70 per cent opposition to the American action – 'even worse than I had feared', Mrs Thatcher wrote in her memoirs.[66] But in public she was defiant. 'It was inconceivable to me,' she told the House of Commons, 'that we should refuse United States aircraft and personnel the opportunity to defend their people.'[67]

One opponent who backed her was the SDP leader David Owen. In his view Mrs Thatcher not only displayed courage and loyalty, but demonstrated 'one of the distinguishing features of great leadership – the ability to turn a blind eye to . . . legal niceties'. In the event, he believed, 'the bombing did deter Libya . . . even though it was, by any legal standard, retaliation not self-defence and therefore outside the terms of the UN Charter'.[68] In her memoirs Lady Thatcher too defended the bombing as having been justified by results. 'It turned out to be a more decisive blow against Libyan-sponsored terrorism than I could ever have imagined . . . The much-vaunted Libyan counter-attack did not . . . take place . . . There was a marked decline in Libyan-sponsored terrorism in succeeding years.'[69] There is a problem, here, however. The Thatcher–Owen defence is contradicted by the verdict of the Scottish court in the Netherlands which convicted a Libyan agent of the bombing of the US airliner over Lockerbie in 1989 which killed 289 people, the most serious terrorist outrage of the whole decade. Oddly, Mrs Thatcher fails to mention Lockerbie in her memoirs. This might be because it dents her justification of the American action in 1986. Alternatively it could be because she knew that the attribution of guilt to Libya – rather than Syria or the PLO – was false.*

But her principal reason at the time for backing the American raid was to show herself – by contrast with the feeble Europeans – a reliable ally; and in this she was triumphantly successful. Doubts raised in Washington by her reaction to Grenada were drowned in an outpouring of praise and gratitude. 'The fact that so few had stuck by America in her time of trial,' she wrote, 'strengthened the "special relationship".'[71] She got her payback later that summer when Congress – after years of Irish-American obstruction – approved a new extradition treaty, closing the loophole which had allowed IRA terrorists to evade extradition by claiming that their murders were 'political'. The Senate only ratified the new treaty

* In *Statecraft* (2002) she did assert that Libya was 'clearly behind' the Lockerbie bombing.[70]

after pressure from Reagan explicitly linking it to Britain's support for the US action in April. Here was one clear benefit from the special relationship.

Defusing the Cold War

But these were side shows. The central purpose of the Atlantic alliance was to combat the Soviet Union; and it was here that the eight years of the Reagan–Thatcher partnership saw the most dramatic movement. The sudden breach of the Berlin Wall in 1989, followed by the collapse of the Soviet Union itself a couple of years later, were totally unpredicted and, even as the events unfolded, unexpected. Yet both Reagan and Mrs Thatcher had been working for exactly that result; and with hindsight it can be seen that their dual-track strategy in the mid-1980s was staggeringly successful in bringing it about.

Though Mrs Thatcher had always been unrestrained in condemning the Soviet Union as a tyrannical force for evil in the world, she also believed – just because it was so repressive – that it must eventually collapse from lack of popular support and economic failure. She wanted to win the Cold War by helping it to do so: to encourage the Russian people and their subject populations in Eastern Europe to throw off the shackles by their own efforts and find freedom for themselves. She was very excited by the Solidarity movement in Poland, and disappointed when it seemed to peter out under the initial impact of General Jaruzelski's martial law. Beneath her hatred of Communism she even retained traces of a wartime schoolgirl's admiration for the heroic sacrifices of the Russian people in the struggle against Hitler. She never lost sight of the ordinary people behind the Iron Curtain.

At this time the Cold War appeared to be at its bleakest. NATO was in the process of stationing cruise missiles in Europe in response to Soviet deployment of SS-20s. Reagan – widely portrayed in Europe as a trigger-happy cowboy – had embarked on an expensive programme of modernising America's nuclear arsenal, and in March 1983 made his famous speech in Orlando, Florida, labelling the Soviet Union an 'evil empire . . . the focus of evil in the modern world'.[72] The Russians had a propaganda field day denouncing his warmongering provocation; but just six months later they furnished graphic evidence of what he meant by shooting down a South Korean airliner which strayed accidentally into Soviet air space, with the loss of 269 lives.

Yet it was at this very moment that Mrs Thatcher started making overtures to the Soviet Union. Leonid Brezhnev had died in November 1982 and she was keen to establish early contact with the new General-Secretary, the younger but still stone-faced Yuri Andropov. She began to look seriously for openings after June 1983.

On 8 September she held an all-day seminar at Chequers with academic experts on the Soviet Union to look at the possibilities. An urgent consideration was the recognition that defence spending could not go on rising indefinitely.[73] Britain (5.2 per cent) already spent a substantially higher proportion of GDP on defence than either France (4.2 per cent) or West Germany (3.4 per cent).[74] Reagan might reckon that the US could always outspend the Soviets, but Mrs Thatcher did not have the same resources. She needed a fresh approach. In Washington three weeks later, therefore, and in her party conference speech a fortnight after that, she surprised her hearers by sounding a new note of peaceful coexistence based on realism: 'We have to deal with the Soviet Union,' she asserted. 'We live on the same planet and we have to go on sharing it.'[75]

Her next step was to make her first trip as Prime Minister behind the Iron Curtain. In February 1984 she visited Hungary, selected as one part of the Soviet empire that was marginally freer than the rest, and had a long talk with the veteran leader, János Kádár, who welcomed her new concern for East–West cooperation and filled her in on the personalities to watch in the Kremlin. As usual, she passed on her impressions to the White House. 'I am becoming convinced,' she wrote to Reagan, 'that we are more likely to make progress on the detailed arms control negotiations if we can establish a broader basis of understanding between East and West . . . It will be a slow and gradual process, during which we must never lower our guard. However, I believe that the effort has to be made.'[76]

A few days after she returned from Hungary, Andropov died. Mrs Thatcher immediately decided to attend his funeral. There she met not only his successor, the elderly and ailing Konstantin Chernenko; but also Mikhail Gorbachev, who was clearly the coming man. 'I spotted him', she claims in her memoirs, 'because I was looking for someone like him.'[77] In fact the Canadians had already spotted him – Trudeau had told her about Gorbachev the previous September; and nearer home Peter Walker had also met him and drawn attention to him before she went to Moscow.[78] Even so, she did well to seize the initiative by inviting Gorbachev – at that time the youngest member of the Soviet politburo – to visit Britain. 'Our record at picking winners had not been good,' Percy Cradock reflected. But in Gorbachev's case 'we drew the right card'.[79]

Gorbachev came to Britain the following December. He was not yet Soviet leader, and Mrs Thatcher was accompanied by several of her colleagues; but over lunch at Chequers the two champions quickly dropped their agendas and simply argued, so freely that their interpreters struggled to keep up. Gorbachev was 'an unusual Russian', Mrs Thatcher told Reagan at Camp David the following week, 'in that he was much less constrained, more charming, open to discussion and debate, and did not stick to prepared notes'.[80]

'I found myself liking him', she wrote in her memoirs.[81] Even Denis – equally pleasantly surprised by Gorbachev's wife Raisa – was aware that 'something pretty special' was happening.[82] The fact was that Mrs Thatcher relished having an opponent who was prepared to argue with her. 'He was self-confident and though he larded his remarks with respectful references to Mr Chernenko . . . he did not seem in the least uneasy about entering into controversial areas of high politics.'[83] Gorbachev evidently enjoyed their exchange as much as she did, even though – on her home ground – he was necessarily on the defensive much of the time. Despite their fundamental differences, Gorbachev and Mrs Thatcher were temperamentally alike: each recognised the other as a domestic radical, battling the forces of inertia in their respective countries. Famously, therefore, when she spoke to the BBC next day, Mrs Thatcher declared that this was a man she could 'do business with'.[84]

They met again briefly at Chernenko's funeral in March 1985, soon after which Gorbachev finally stepped into the top job. But she still made a point of being wary and had no intention of lowering her guard. The reality, she warned in Washington that summer, was that 'the new brooms in the Soviet Union will not be used to sweep away Communism, only to make it more efficient – if that can be done'.[85] Two months later, as if to demonstrate to Moscow that the Cold War was not over, Britain expelled twenty-five Soviet diplomats exposed as spies by the defector Oleg Gordievsky. When Gorbachev retaliated in kind, Mrs Thatcher expelled six more Russians. Yet all the while Geoffrey Howe was following up her diplomatic initiative by quietly touring all the Warsaw Pact capitals during 1984–5.

With her impeccable track record of standing up to the Soviets, Mrs Thatcher's advice that Gorbachev was a different sort of Soviet leader undoubtedly impressed the Americans. James Baker – Reagan's chief of staff, later Treasury Secretary – testified that she had 'a profound influence' on US thinking about Russia.[86] Yet this almost certainly exaggerates her role. The truth is that the Americans were already reassessing their own approach, at least from the time Shultz

1. Alfred Roberts soon after his election as Councillor, 1927.
2. Margaret, aged four, and Muriel, aged eight, in 1929.
3. Alfred Roberts' shop fallen on hard times after his retirement.

4. Denis and Margaret on their wedding day, December 1951.

5. Mother of twins, August 1953.

6. With Carol and Mark soon after her election to Parliament in 1959.

7. After her party conference speech, October 1976, with (*from left to right*) Reginald Maudling, Keith Joseph, Willie Whitelaw and Peter Thorneycroft.

8. 'Labour Isn't Working', summer 1978.

9. 'Where there is discord, may we bring harmony.'

10,11. Mrs Thatcher with her two long-serving Chancellors of the Exchequer, Geoffrey Howe (*above*) and Nigel Lawson (*below*).

12. The Prime Minister, with Ian Gow, leaves 10 Downing Street to face the House of Commons following the Argentine invasion of the Falklands, 3 April 1982.

SPECIAL RELATIONSHIPS
13. Mrs Thatcher's farewell
visit to Washington near
the end of Ronald
Reagan's presidency,
November 1988.

14. With Mikhail
Gorbachev in Moscow,
March 1987.

15. Mrs Thatcher's farewell speech on leaving Downing Street, with Denis and Mark looking on, 28 November 1990.

16. Baroness Thatcher in the House of Lords before the State Opening of Parliament, June 2001.

became Secretary of State, and Reagan personally was as keen as she was to engage the Soviet leaders. From the moment he became President he sent a series of handwritten letters to his opposite numbers in Moscow, trying to strike a human response. From Brezhnev and Andropov he received only formal replies, but he did not give up.[87] When Mrs Thatcher described her talks with Gorbachev, he was 'simply amazed' how closely she had followed the same line that he had taken when meeting Foreign Minister Gromyko the previous September.[88] What can be said is that her clear-sighted public praise of Gorbachev helped the White House assure American public opinion that the President was not going soft when he too started to do business with the Soviet leader. On the other side she helped convince Gorbachev of Reagan's sincerity, and encouraged him to go ahead with the November 1985 Geneva summit, despite his suspicion of the American 'Star Wars' programme. Once Reagan and Gorbachev had started meeting directly, however, her mediating role was inevitably reduced.

Reagan's dedication to 'Star Wars' – the Strategic Defense Initiative (SDI) – was a delicate problem for Mrs Thatcher which she handled with considerable sensitivity and skill. The idea was a futuristic scheme, at the very limits of American space technology, to develop a defensive shield against incoming ballistic missiles, ultimately, it was hoped, making strategic nuclear weapons redundant. Reagan announced the project – with no prior warning to Britain or the rest of NATO – in March 1983. The allies were immediately alarmed. First of all they were sceptical of the technology and doubted that SDI would ever work with the 100 per cent certainty needed to replace the existing deterrent. Second, they feared that such an American initiative would breach the 1972 ABM Treaty and wreck the chances of further arms-control agreements by triggering a new arms race in space. Third, they feared that SDI would detach the USA from NATO: if the Americans once felt secure behind their own shield they would withdraw their nuclear protection from Europe; while if the Russians successfully followed suit, the British and French deterrents would be rendered obsolete.

Mrs Thatcher shared these fears; but she did not want to criticise the American initiative publicly because she knew Reagan was deeply committed to it. Unlike most of his advisers, who saw SDI as just another high-tech toy in the military arsenal, Reagan genuinely believed in the dream of abolishing nuclear weapons. In addition she was excited by the science, believing that, unlike 'the laid-back generalists from the Foreign Office' she, with her chemistry degree from forty years before, 'had a firm grasp of the scientific concepts involved'. She was keen to support the research programme, since 'science is unstoppable'.[89] But deployment was another matter. More than anyone she worried about destabilising the Alliance, giving the Russians an excuse to walk out of arms-control negotiations, and possible American withdrawal into isolationism. She had invested too much political capital – and money – in buying Trident to be willing to see it scrapped. Above all she regarded the idea that nuclear weapons could ever be abolished as dangerous fantasy.

During 1984 her worries grew and she determined to take the lead in representing Europe's concerns positively to the Americans. On 8 November she wrote to ask if she could call on Reagan at his 'Western White House' in California on her way home from signing the Hong Kong Agreement in Beijing just before Christmas. When Reagan replied that he would not be there until after Christmas, she invited herself to Washington instead. This was the most punishing schedule she ever imposed on herself (and on her staff). She left for China on the Monday evening following her Sunday talks with Gorbachev at Chequers. She signed the agreement in Beijing on the Wednesday, went on to Hong Kong to reassure the population there on Thursday, and then flew on across the Pacific and the US to Washington, from where she was helicoptered to meet the President at Camp David on Saturday morning, returning to London overnight. This involved flying right round the world – fifty-five hours of flying time – in five and a half days. Quite apart from the hours in the air, this must surely make her the only leader to have held substantial talks, on three continents, with Russian, American and Chinese leaders inside a single week.[40]

Yet she gave no sign of jet lag. First, as already described, she gave Reagan her favourable impression of Gorbachev; but she also passed on his defiant response to SDI. 'Tell your friend President Reagan,' Gorbachev had told her, 'not to go ahead with space weapons.' If he did, 'the Russians would either develop their own or, more probably, develop new offensive systems superior to SDI.' Reagan assured her that 'Star Wars was not his term and was clearly not what he had in mind'. If the research proved successful he had actually promised to share the technology. 'Our goal is to reduce and eventually eliminate nuclear weapons.' Mrs Thatcher repeated that she supported the American research programme; but when the President was joined by Shultz and his National Security Advisor 'Bud' Macfarlane she launched into her own worries about SDI.

She took seriously Gorbachev's threats to retaliate. 'We do not want our objective of increased security to result in increased Soviet nuclear weapons.' But her real fear was that SDI would undermine nuclear deterrence, which she passionately believed had kept the peace for forty years. Moreover, in response to Reagan's optimism that SDI would turn out to be feasible, she admitted that 'personally she had some doubts'. Macfarlane tried to convince her, but she remained sceptical. Finally, she asked 'if someone could come to London to give her a top-level US technical briefing'. Reagan 'nodded agreement and said it was time to break for lunch'.

Before, during and after lunch Mrs Thatcher banged on about British Airways and the Laker anti-trust case, followed by discussion of the US economy and the Middle East. All this gave time for Charles Powell to work up a statement which she now circulated, embodying four assurances that she wanted to be able to give to the press at the end of the meeting. 'We agreed on four points,' the statement declared:

(1) The US, and Western, aim was not to achieve superiority, but to maintain balance, taking account of Soviet developments;
(2) SDI-related deployment would, in view of treaty obligations, have to be a matter for negotiations;
(3) The overall aim is to enhance, not undercut deterrence;
(4) East–West negotiations should aim to achieve security with reduced levels of offensive systems on both sides.[91]

This was a brilliant diplomatic coup. Reagan's staff were not pleased at being bounced in this way; but the President happily accepted her four points, saying 'he hoped they would quell reports of disagreement between us'.[92] Thus, in exchange for publicly expressing her strong support for the research, she secured – and promptly went out and publicised – assurances that the Americans would not deploy SDI unilaterally and would not abandon deterrence. Of course she knew that Shultz and others in the American administration shared her doubts and welcomed her support: she could not have done it alone. But she knew exactly what she wanted and played her hand skilfully to obtain it. When Reagan sent a long cable to allied leaders setting out the American negotiating position for the resumed arms-control talks in Geneva a few weeks later it specifically included Mrs Thatcher's four points – though he also reiterated his personal dream of eventually eliminating nuclear weapons entirely.[93]

She got her 'comprehensive briefing' in London two weeks later from the director of SDI.[94] But she was not yet ready to relax. 'Margaret Thatcher . . . was on the rampage for a year or more about SDI', Macfarlane recalled. 'She wouldn't let us hear the end of it.' She flew over to Washington again in February, looking for another 'concentrated discussion of the substantive problems'.[95] Accorded the rare honour of addressing both Houses of Congress, she contrived a neat quotation from Churchill speaking to the same audience in 1952, in the very early days of nuclear weapons. 'Be careful above all things,' the old warrior had warned, 'not to let go of the atomic weapon until you are sure and more than sure that other means of preserving peace are in your hands.' Implicitly repudiating Reagan's vision of a world without nuclear weapons, she emphasised that the objective was 'not merely to prevent nuclear war, but to prevent conventional war as well' – and nuclear weapons were still the surest way of doing that.[96]

At her meeting with Reagan she raised a new worry, as she reminded him when she got home:

> As regards the Strategic Defense Initiative, I hope that I was able to explain to you my preoccupation with the need not to weaken our efforts to consolidate support in Britain for the deployment of cruise and for the modernisation of Trident by giving the impression that a future without nuclear weapons is near at hand. We must continue to make the case for deterrence based on nuclear weapons for several years to come.[97]

'Bud, you know, she's really missing the point,' Reagan told Macfarlane. 'And she's doing us a lot of damage with all this sniping about it.'[98] In fact, Mrs Thatcher was very careful not to snipe in public, but kept her criticism for the President's ear alone.

In July she was back in Washington, where she had persuaded the White House to set up a seminar on arms control attended by Reagan, Shultz, Weinberger and the whole American top brass. Over lunch she confronted the President directly with the implications of his enthusiasm for getting rid of nuclear weapons altogether. 'If you follow that logic to its implied conclusion,' she told him, 'you expose a dramatic conventional imbalance, do you not? And would we not have to restore that balance at considerable expense?' In response, Macfarlane recalled, Reagan 'looked her square in the eye and said, "Yes, that's exactly what I imagined"'.[99]

In truth, no one else in the administration believed in Reagan's naive vision of a nuclear-free future. Though Reagan would never admit it, the real point of SDI was that it was a massive bargaining chip, which raised the technological stakes higher than the struggling Soviet economy could match. Gorbachev recognised this, which was why he tried to rouse Western public opinion against it. Mrs Thatcher initially did not: she was more concerned that the Russians would meet the American challenge, leaving Europe exposed. But she assuaged her anxiety by concentrating on the lucrative crumbs she hoped British firms might pick up from the research programme. 'You know, there may be something in this after all,' she responded when Macfarlane dangled the prospect of contracts worth $300 million a year.[100] In fact Britain gained nothing like the commercial benefits she hoped for from SDI – no more than £24 million by 1987 rather than the £1 billion the MoD optimistically predicted in 1985. But by the time she came to write her memoirs she realised that her fears had been misplaced. SDI, though never successfully tested, let alone deployed, achieved its unstated purpose by convincing the Russians that they could no longer compete in the nuclear arms race, so bringing them to the negotiating table to agree deep cuts in nuclear weapons, even before the fall of the Berlin Wall. And she gave the credit to Reagan for having, in his artless way 'instinctively grasped the key to the whole question'. By initiating SDI he 'called the Soviets' bluff. They had lost the game and I have no doubt that they knew it.'[101]

But that revelation lay ahead. In October 1986 she was horrified when Reagan met Gorbachev at Reykjavik and offered off his own bat not only to cut strategic nuclear weapons by half in five years, but to eliminate them entirely in ten years. The moment passed: Gorbachev overplayed his hand by trying to get Reagan to scrap his beloved SDI as well. This Reagan would not do, since his dream of eliminating nuclear weapons was dependent on SDI being successful. But it was a bad moment for Mrs Thatcher when she heard how far Reagan had been willing to go.

What alarmed her was not just that she regarded talk of abolishing nuclear weapons as a utopian fantasy. More immediately, in blithely proposing to eliminate a whole class of weapons in a bilateral deal with the Russians, Reagan was completely ignoring Britain's Trident and the French independent deterrent. Implicitly Trident would have to be scrapped too: there was no way Britain could have continued to buy a weapon that the Americans themselves had abandoned. But the merest suggestion of scrapping Trident would play straight into the hands of the British peace movement which she had spent so much energy combating over the past five years. In 1983 maintaining the British deterrent had been her trump card against Michael Foot's unilateralist rabble. Now, with the next election looming and Labour posing a serious challenge, her best friend in the White House was casually threatening to tear it up. British press coverage of Reykjavik largely blamed Reagan for blocking a historic deal by refusing to give up 'Star Wars'. Mrs Thatcher was much more worried about what he had been willing to give up.

So she lost no time in getting back to Washington as soon as she could, inviting herself to Camp David for another flying visit on 15 November. The Americans were anxious to help her, recognising that she was 'in a pre-election phase', while Labour's unilateralism 'would deal a severe blow to NATO'.[102] 'Mrs Thatcher's overriding focus will be the British public's perception of her performance,' an aide noted. 'Our interest is in assuring that the results of the meeting support a staunch friend and ally of the US.' Nevertheless, White House staff were determined not to be bounced again, as they believed they had been in 1984, by Mrs Thatcher arriving with a document already up her sleeve. 'We have found,' Poindexter noted, 'even with friends like Mrs Thatcher – that joint statements, which are usually a compromise, do not serve our policy interests.'[103] This time they took care to have their own text prepared in advance.

US objectives, Shultz explained to Reagan, were first, to 'strengthen Alliance cohesion . . . by reconciling your commitment to eliminate offensive ballistic missiles within ten years with Mrs Thatcher's commitment to deploy UK Tridents within the same time frame'; second, 'to find a mutually acceptable formula [five or six words are here blacked out] that drastic nuclear reductions . . . are inadvisable as long as conventional and chemical imbalances exist in Europe'; and third, to secure British endorsement of US policies.[104]* It is clear that the Americans' real objective was the last. Just as she had done on SDI two years earlier, Mrs Thatcher secured the assurance she wanted that nuclear deterrence remained central to NATO policy and Trident would go ahead. This was spun to the British press as another triumph of Thatcherite diplomacy. The reality was rather different.

The Americans were happy to let her claim a triumph. But the truth is that this time the paper she came away waving was written in the White House. The assurances she secured were part of an 'agreed statement to the press' which explicitly endorsed Reagan's Reykjavik objectives and most of his specific proposals: a 50 per cent cut in strategic weapons over five years, deep cuts in intermediate nuclear forces – which Mrs Thatcher did not like at all – and

---

* The censored words are presumably something like 'to meet Mrs Thatcher's view'. But then why censor them? One can only guess that they are less complimentary than that – something like 'Mrs Thatcher's obsession'.

a ban on chemical weapons, plus continuing SDI research. Only the aspiration to phase out strategic weapons altogether in ten years was tactfully omitted.

Mrs Thatcher was still deeply worried about where American policy was heading. To her mind, even talking about abolishing nuclear weapons in the future dangerously undermined the West's defensive posture. It was only the balance of terror – 'mutually assured destruction' – which had kept the peace in Europe for forty years. Not only would it be foolish to abandon nuclear weapons: it was even more foolish to imagine it was possible to abandon them. 'You cannot act as if the nuclear weapon had not been invented,' she told the American interviewer Barbara Walters in January 1987. 'The knowledge of how to make these things exists.' New countries were acquiring that knowledge all the time. 'If you cannot be sure that no one has got them, then you have got to have a weapon of your own to deter other people.'[105] Her unapologetic enthusiasm invited the charge, both at home and in America, that she was a nuclear fanatic. On the contrary, she insisted, she was simply a realist. 'You cannot disinvent the nuclear weapon,' she told the *Daily Express* in April, 'any more than you can disinvent dynamite.'[106] She was right; but she did seem to make the argument with a disturbing relish.

Reagan's *démarche* at Reykjavik briefly shook her confidence in the American alliance. But her wobble did not last long. Having gained the reassurance she sought, at least for the moment, she redoubled her commitment to NATO. She was still alarmed by the speed with which the Americans were pressing on with INF cuts and then cuts in short-range battlefield weapons. She worried that the Russians were skilfully drawing the Americans into agreements which undermined the West's deterrent capability; while Reagan's willingness to do a private deal with Gorbachev still gave her nightmares. But she took comfort from the fact that, as she told a CBS interviewer in July 1987, 'they did not come to an agreement . . . It did not happen.' She was determined to see that it never happened; but she admits in her memoirs that the unshakeable importance of nuclear deterrence was 'the one issue on which I knew I could not take the Reagan Administration's soundness for granted'.[107]

At the same time, paradoxically, her other special relationship with Mikhail Gorbachev flourished, highlighted by a triumphal visit to Moscow in March 1987. This was a shameless piece of pre-election theatre designed to play well on television screens at home, projecting the Prime Minister as a world leader as welcome in the Kremlin as she was in the White House.

First, she had another seven hours of formal talks with Gorbachev, plus several social meetings. As before, their conversation ranged widely from the relative merits of Communism and capitalism to regional conflicts, arms control and the future of nuclear weapons. Once again Gorbachev gave as good as he got, rejecting Mrs Thatcher's criticism of Soviet subversion in Africa and Central America and meeting her lectures about human rights by pointing out the inequality of British society. But when she repeated her objection that eliminating strategic weapons would leave the Russians with conventional superiority in Europe, he admitted Moscow's opposite fear of being unable to match America's military spending. 'He was clearly extremely sensitive and worried about being humiliated by the West.'[108]

Just as important as her talks with Gorbachev, however, was the fact that she was also allowed to meet privately a number of prominent dissidents, most notably the nuclear physicist Andrei Sakharov and his wife Elena, who were now supporting Gorbachev's *perestroika*, and a number of Jewish refuseniks who exemplified its limits. She was permitted to attend a Russian Orthodox service at Zagorsk, forty-five miles outside Moscow, where she spoke to some of the worshippers and lit a candle symbolising freedom of conscience. Above all she was granted unprecedented access to the Soviet public. She was given fifty minutes unedited prime time on the main television channel, and she seized her chance brilliantly. Rather than talk straight to camera she insisted on being interviewed, so that she could be seen to *argue* with her three interviewers in the same way that she argued with Gorbachev. When they dutifully trotted out the party line and questioned how she could support nuclear weapons, she repeatedly interrupted them, contradicted them and tried to convince them from Russia's own experience of invasion and war. 'The Soviet Union suffered millions of losses in the Second World War,' she reminded them:

> The Soviet Union had a lot of conventional weapons. That did not stop Hitler attacking her. Conventional weapons have never been enough to stop wars. Since we have had the nuclear weapon, it is so horrific that no one dare risk going to war.

At the same time she told them bluntly that the Soviet Union had far more nuclear weapons than any other country; that it was the Soviet Union which had introduced intermediate-range weapons by deploying SS-20s, forcing the West to match them with Pershing and cruise; and the Soviet Union which had led the United States in developing anti-missile laser defences in the 1970s. The three stooges had no answer to this assault. The impact of her spontaneity was sensational. 'Her style, her appearance, her frankness about security matters made her appear like a creature from another planet,' wrote the *Guardian*'s Moscow correspondent, Martin Walker, '– and they found her terrific.'[109]

Finally, she undertook an unprecedented walkabout in a Moscow housing estate, meeting and talking to ordinary Russians who flocked to meet and touch her. 'Journalists with no liking for her at all came back from Moscow saying that they had never witnessed anything like it.'[110] The experience confirmed her faith that the peoples of the Soviet empire would eventually throw off their yoke. Her 1987 visit – for which Gorbachev also deserves credit – was almost certainly a factor in hastening the collapse of the Soviet system only three years later.

Undoubtedly Lady Thatcher played a part in the sudden ending of the Cold War in 1989–91. In retirement, she counted her championing of Gorbachev among her greatest achievements. But how much influence she really had is questionable. Events in the Soviet Union had a momentum of their own which even Gorbachev was unable to control. She certainly helped convince Gorbachev that the Soviet Union could never win the arms race, that Reagan would not give up 'Star Wars' but was nevertheless serious in wanting to engage in balanced arms reductions. Her relationship with Reagan and to a lesser extent with Gorbachev enabled her to punch – or at least appear to punch – above Britain's real weight in the world. For a heady time in the late 1980s she almost seemed to have recreated the wartime triumvirate of Roosevelt, Stalin and Churchill. But her role should not be exaggerated. Just as in 1945, only more so, Britain was always the junior partner. It was the Americans who called the shots; and the brief illusion of equality was swiftly exposed when Reagan was succeeded by George Bush.

Meanwhile, her love affair with America pulled Britain away from Europe.

17

Iron Lady II:
Europe and the World

Good European

DURING Mrs Thatcher's first term her relations with her European partners had been poisoned by the interminable wrangle over Britain's contribution to the Community budget. Later, her third term would be dominated by her increasingly bitter opposition to closer economic integration. Despite her strong bias towards the United States, however, her middle period (1983–7) was an interlude of improving relations with Europe. It was, as it turned out, only a temporary calm between two storms; but once the budget question had finally been resolved at Fontainebleau in June 1984, Britain actually took the lead for a time in Community affairs, with Mrs Thatcher the leading advocate of a rapid completion of the single European market.

Even in her most positive period, however, she set in hand no long-term thinking about the future of Europe or Britain's place in it. She simply dismissed as fantasy the idea that there could ever be a 'United States of Europe in the same way that there is a United States of America';[1] and assumed that her own idea of what the EC should be – a free-trade area and a forum for loose cooperation between sovereign nations – would naturally prevail.[2] As a result, from lack of imaginative empathy with other views and lack of her usual thorough homework, she failed to take seriously the fact that most other European governments had a quite different conception of how Europe should develop. They had given a good deal more thought to how to achieve their goal than she ever did to how she might prevent it.

Her relations with her Community partners were greatly improved in 1981 by the replacement of the haughty and supercilious Giscard d'Estaing as President of France by the veteran socialist François Mitterrand. Though on the face of it Mitterrand and Mrs Thatcher might have been thought to be chalk and cheese, they actually got on unexpectedly well. First, he was a very sexy man with the confidence to treat her as a woman – and she responded, as she often did to a sexual challenge. Far more explicitly than with Reagan, there was an erotic undercurrent in her relations with Mitterrand which predisposed her to like him. It was he who famously – and to the bewilderment of her British critics – described her as having 'the eyes of Caligula and the mouth of Marilyn Monroe'.[3] The former were undisputed, but it took a Frenchman to appreciate the latter.

Second, she quickly found that Mitterrand, though nominally a socialist, was a *patriotic* socialist – 'unlike ours', as she once tartly told Harold Evans.[4] Ten years older than Giscard (who was slightly younger than Mrs Thatcher), Mitterrand had fought in the Resistance and was still grateful for British support in the war. When he visited London in September 1981 the Foreign Office cleverly managed to find the pilot who had flown him to England in 1940. He was as firmly committed to maintaining the French independent *force de frappe* as she was to the British nuclear deterrent, and thus shared her alarm at SDI and Reagan's bilateral negotiations at Reykjavik.

Third, quite early in their relationship Mitterrand won her undying gratitude by his prompt and unequivocal support for Britain's cause in the Falklands. Mrs Thatcher never forgot this timely assistance. For the rest of the decade there persisted a strong mutual respect between Mrs Thatcher and Mitterrand which transcended their political differences.

By contrast, she never warmed to Helmut Kohl, who succeeded Helmut Schmidt as Chancellor of West Germany in 1982. She was as glad to see the back of Schmidt as she was of Giscard; but she thought Kohl boring, clumsy and provincial and persistently underestimated him. A huge man with a dominating physical presence and an enormous appetite, he perfectly embodied her resentment of Germany's post-war prosperity, which was never far below the surface. At first she patronised Kohl (as Schmidt and Giscard patronised her). But the longer he survived, as he grew in political stature and increasingly came to rival her as the dominant figure in Europe, the more her dislike grew. Kohl tried hard to woo her: but she would not be wooed.

She regarded every European summit as another battle in a protracted war to defend British interests against the greedy and scheming foreigners. More than this, she despised the whole ethos of compromise, deal-making and fudge, which was how the Community worked. 'She was quite simply too straight, too direct, too principled and altogether too serious for them', in Bernard Ingham's view.[5] But by disdaining to play by the Community's prevailing rules she reduced her own effectiveness and damaged British interests.

After five years of wrangling, she finally achieved a budget settlement which satisfied her in June 1984. Up until then she continued to block all other progress in the EC – on VAT payments and reform of the Common Agricultural Policy – until she got her way. The three-year deal secured by Peter Carrington in 1981 was about to expire. In the end she settled for less than she wanted – a 66 per cent rebate, not the 'well over 70 per cent' which had been her goal.[6] She also accepted an increase from 1 per cent to 1.4 per cent of each country's VAT returns that should be payable to the Community. The critical fact was that Mitterrand wanted a settlement under the French presidency. Mrs Thatcher knew that this was her best chance, and wisely took it. The other countries were just relieved that the 'Bloody British Question' was resolved at last.

With the budget dispute finally settled, it certainly appeared that Britain was now ready to play a more constructive role. The rest of the Community was also ready to open a new chapter, marked by the appointment of an energetic new President of the Commission – Jacques Delors, formerly Mitterrand's Finance Minister. With hindsight, Mrs Thatcher dismissed Delors as a typical French Socialist. But she was largely instrumental in his appointment, since she vetoed the first French candidate, Claude Cheysson. Delors had impressed the British as tough and practical: he had been responsible for scrapping most of the left-wing policies on which Mitterrand had been elected and implementing instead what Howe called 'our policies'.[7] Delors was indeed tough and practical, but he was also a European visionary, as she soon discovered.

Taking office in January 1985, Delors quickly fixed on the completion of the single market as the next big advance in the evolution of the Community. He looked first at other areas – common defence policy, progress towards a single currency, the reform of Community institutions – but he could not get sufficient agreement on any of these. So he settled for what he called '*les quatre libertés*' – free movement of goods, services, capital and people. This Mrs Thatcher was happy to go along with. It seemed consistent with her idea of the Community as essentially a free-trade area – a true common market – and an opportunity for advancing Thatcherite economic ideas of deregulation and free enterprise on a European scale. Carried away with her vision of Thatcherising the Community, she did not realise that Delors – and Mitterrand and Kohl and almost all the smaller countries – saw the single market as part of a wider process of European integration.

At first, however, all went swimmingly. She appointed Arthur Cockfield as one of Britain's two members of the new Commission. He wasted no time in publishing a detailed programme entitled *Completing the Internal Market*, listing 292 specific measures of deregulation to be achieved by 1992. Mrs Thatcher was delighted. This, she thought, was Britain at last leading the Community, as pro-Europeans had aspired to do ever since Macmillan first applied for membership, and extending to the overgoverned Continent the benefits of British free enterprise. But it was not so simple as that. Mrs Thatcher did not understand that creating a single market necessarily involved not just deregulation, but the harmonisation of regulations across the Community, which impinged on matters hitherto the prerogative of national governments. In her view Cockfield, in his missionary zeal for the project to which she had appointed him, betrayed her by straying too far into the forbidden area of integration. Like practically every British politician who has ever been appointed to Brussels, he 'went native' and adopted a quasi-federalist perspective. Though the rest of the Community regarded him as a conspicuous success, Mrs Thatcher declined to reappoint Cockfield for a second term.

In the meantime, however, in order to make progress on the single market, she realised that she would have to acquiesce in other developments which she subsequently came to regret. The so-called Single European Act – Delors' major initiative to carry the process of European integration forward – extended the application of weighted majority voting into new areas and increased the powers of both the Commission and the Parliament. Mrs Thatcher was afraid that the completion of the single market would be held up by other countries exercising their national vetoes, and positively bullied her partners to accept majority voting in this area.

She did what she could to block what she regarded as the most utopian proposals and drove forward agreement on the practical measures required to implement the single market, believing that the wider implications of the new treaty were no more than woolly aspirations which would come to nothing. In particular she believed that she had qualified the 'irrevocable' commitment to economic and monetary union (EMU) originally signed up to by Heath, Brandt and Pompidou in 1972, substituting instead a reference to economic and monetary 'co-operation'; and also that she had preserved the right of national veto in such sensitive areas as border controls, customs and drugs policy, and indeed any matter which any member country regarded as vital, under the so-called Luxembourg Compromise.

As a result of these assurances, the Single European Act was whipped through Parliament with scarcely a murmur of dissent. The Labour party was in the process of reversing its former opposition to all things European, while Tory Eurosceptics – as they were later called – believing that Mrs Thatcher shared their antipathy to any hint of federalism, trusted in her vigilance and accepted her assurances that they had nothing to worry about. In fact, whatever she and the Foreign Office believed, the Single European Act as interpreted in Brussels did very significantly extend the powers of both the Commission and the Strasbourg Parliament, and led on logically to the Treaty of Maastricht in 1992 and eventually to the single currency.

The fact is that Mrs Thatcher 'gave away' more sovereignty in 1985 than Heath in 1973 or Major in 1992. She subsequently claimed that she was deceived by the other leaders who broke assurances that they had given her. 'I trusted them,' she recalled bitterly in 1996. 'I believed in them. I believed this was good faith between nations co-operating together. So we got our fingers burned. Once you've got your fingers burned, you don't go and burn them again.'[8] But the idea that Mrs Thatcher, of all people, did not read the Act closely before signing it is incredible to anyone who knew her. David Williamson, Secretary-General of the Community from 1987, recalled her telling him specifically, 'I have read every word of the Single European Act.'[9] So why did she sign it? Bernard Ingham thought she knew what she was doing: 'I think she knew at the time that she was taking risks . . . She was taking a calculated risk with a very clear view in mind.'[10] In other words, she believed that the substantial bird in the hand was worth a flock of shadows in the bush. Delors confirms this interpretation, recalling that she hesitated and asked for an extra few minutes to think about it before she signed.[11]

As usual, she blames others, but has only herself to blame. Blinded by the strength of her own conviction, she did not understand the equal strength of the other leaders' will to maintain the momentum of economic, political and social integration. She believed that she had preserved Britain's essential independence by steadfastly refusing to join the ERM, and trusted in her ability to continue to do so. Having got what she wanted – the single market – she believed she could send back the rest of the menu.

Yet Mrs Thatcher did, ironically, sanction one powerfully symbolic act of European integration – the old dream of linking Britain physically to the Continent by building a Channel tunnel. This was a project she had strongly supported as a member of Ted Heath's Government in the early 1970s. When the incoming Labour Government scrapped it in 1974, she condemned their short-sighted penny-pinching, arguing – somewhat out of character – that the country could not live on bread and cheese alone but needed some 'visionary ideas' as well.[12] Now, as Prime Minister, she still liked the idea of a 'grand project', but insisted that it would have to be financed and built entirely by private enterprise. Initially it seemed that this condition would be enough to sink the project.

At her first meeting with Mitterrand in 1981 they both spoke warm words about wanting a tunnel in principle; but it did not become a serious possibility until the economy improved. Then a number of her favourite businessmen began to show an interest. The National Westminster Bank took the lead in persuading the DTI that a tunnel could be financed without a Government guarantee. On this basis, Mrs Thatcher's enthusiasm cautiously increased. Ideologically she was keen to give the private sector a chance to show what it could do, while she could see a political dividend from a big project which would create a lot of jobs.

Visiting Paris for a bilateral summit in December 1984, she and Mitterrand duly agreed to inject 'a new urgency' into studying the options. Both of them initially favoured a road, rather than a rail link: he wanted a bridge, she a drive-through tunnel. In practice, however, it became clear that a rail link was cheaper and more practical. Over the next year several bidders competed for the contract, but in the end it was the Channel Tunnel Group, headed by the former Ambassador to the US (and before that France), Nicholas Henderson, which gained the Prime Minister's ear and won the prize.

The decision was announced by the two leaders at Lille in northern France in January 1986. Mrs Thatcher made a humorous speech recalling previous attempts to build a tunnel, going back to Napoleon, and claimed that Churchill had supported a Channel bridge on condition that the last span was a drawbridge which could be raised in case of French attack. Times had now changed, she suggested.[13] As a rare gesture to Anglo-French fraternity she was persuaded to deliver the final part of her speech in French, which she learned phonetically with characteristic professionalism. This was the high point of Mrs Thatcher's enthusiasm for Europe.

Opened in 1994, the Channel tunnel does indeed stand today

as one of the few concrete legacies of Mrs Thatcher's rule. For travellers to the Continent it is an established success. But as a demonstration of what private enterprise could do it was an ambiguous success. It was indeed financed (on the British side) by private capital, as Mrs Thatcher insisted it should be; but only at a loss to the shareholders who were persuaded to invest in it. It did not make money. Then private enterprise was not willing to fund the projected high-speed rail link from London to Folkestone, a necessary part of the service which fell years behind schedule and had, after all, to be paid for by the taxpayer. The lesson, as of so much of the privatisation experience, is that big infrastructural projects of this sort cannot be built without public money.

Pragmatism in Hong Kong

Outside the major theatres of Europe and the Cold War, Britain still faced a troublesome legacy of post-imperial problems in other far-flung corners of the world. During her first term Mrs Thatcher had been confronted with two such hangovers of empire, in Africa and the South Atlantic, both of which she handled successfully, though in opposite ways. Now in her second term she faced a more intractable problem than either: the approaching expiry of Britain's hundred-year lease on Hong Kong, which was due to revert to China in 1997. Britain had immense commercial interests at stake as well as political responsibility for this anomalous enclave of Far Eastern capitalism, which was threatened with extinction in a decade's time unless the Chinese Communists could be persuaded to permit its survival after the handover.

Once again all Mrs Thatcher's instincts were aroused. First, Hong Kong was, like the Falklands, a British colony threatened with takeover by a neighbouring state. Although undeniably most of the territory was legally due to be returned to China, Hong Kong island itself was British sovereign territory which could in theory be retained, or at least used as a bargaining counter. Second, Hong Kong was a haven of freedom, prosperity and economic enterprise – though little democracy – besieged by Communism. Third, she did not like the Chinese. She accepted China as a fact of life and an ancient civilisation, culturally different and commanding respect on its own terms. But she had a 'visceral dislike' of the Chinese system and felt deeply that it should be possible to save Hong Kong from being swallowed by it. Coming straight after the Falklands, the problem of Hong Kong caused her 'a lot of mental difficulty'.[14]

Yet the facts of the two situations were entirely different. On the one hand, China's legal claim on 90 per cent of the territory was irrefutable – and Mrs Thatcher believed profoundly in the sanctity of law – while no one suggested that Hong Kong island was economically viable on its own. On the other, China possessed overwhelming military superiority, and anyway the island was indefensible: the Chinese could simply have cut off the water supply. Defiance was not an option.

So Britain had no choice but to negotiate – from a weak position – and try to secure the best possible result by diplomacy. Unwelcome as it was, Mrs Thatcher recognised the reality; but she still hoped, at the outset, to be able to bargain the sovereignty of Hong Kong island for continued British administration of the whole colony under nominal Chinese rule: in other words a form of the 'leaseback' idea originally proposed for the Falklands.

But when she met Deng Xiaoping in Beijing in September 1984 she found him unyielding. Believing that it was in China's interest to preserve the prosperity of Hong Kong, she held out the possibility of ceding sovereignty in return for continued British administration. But Deng knew that he held all the cards and called her bluff. Like Mrs Thatcher herself in regard to the Falklands, he regarded sovereignty as non-negotiable. If Britain made difficulties, he warned, China would simply reoccupy Hong Kong before 1997.

In March 1983 she was persuaded to send a letter to the Chinese Prime Minister Zhao Ziyang indicating a more positive approach. Specifically, she undertook that she would not merely consider but 'recommend' ceding sovereignty in return for certain assurances about Hong Kong's future. That cleared the way for Geoffrey Howe to open negotiations with Beijing on the basis of Deng's characteristically paradoxical formula 'one country, two systems', which offered the possibility of preserving the essentials of Hong Kong's capitalist way of life under Chinese rule. What this might mean in practice was impossible to know. The people of Hong Kong were suspicious that they were being sold down the river; but Howe still had no cards to play. In principle the Chinese recognised no distinction between sovereignty and administration, so he had nothing to bargain with. But he persisted, with quiet skill, and eventually secured an agreement in September 1984, guaranteeing Hong Kong's 'special status' within China for fifty years after 1997, plus agreement on passports, air travel and land ownership. Mrs Thatcher was persuaded to accept it as the best deal that could be achieved. At the end of the year she flew to China again to sign the agreement and reassure the people of Hong Kong in person. It was a realistic settlement and the best she could do.

South Africa and the Commonwealth

Though greatly diminished in importance compared with the Atlantic alliance and the European Community, the Commonwealth was still another set of relationships which Mrs Thatcher had to maintain, and a biennial forum of international diplomacy which gave her considerable trouble. At the beginning of her first term she earned considerable credit by the unexpectedly pragmatic way she resolved the Rhodesian problem, and by her willingness to recognise the new Zimbabwe. But that success only brought into greater salience the affront to the conscience of a multiracial organisation represented by the persistence of white minority rule in South Africa. Before long Mrs Thatcher had dissipated most of the credit she had won in Rhodesia by her determined refusal to support economic sanctions against the regime in Pretoria. As a result she was soon even more embattled within the Commonwealth than she was in Europe, portrayed by much of the rest of the world as a friend and protector of apartheid – whereas she saw herself as its most practical opponent.

There is no clearer example of Mrs Thatcher's refusal to acquiesce in a fashionable consensus than her stubborn resistance to sanctions against South Africa. She became the focus of all the frustration and hatred of the anti-apartheid movement not only in Britain but around the world. As with her perverse support for nuclear weapons, progressive opinion could not understand how anyone could be against such an obviously virtuous cause. Once again her insensitivity to others' passionately held beliefs, her certainty that she was right and her appearance of revelling in her isolation seemed wilfully provocative. Yet again there is a good case for maintaining that she was proved right by the eventual outcome, and her critics wrong.

Mrs Thatcher understood South Africa, like every other regional problem, as just another battleground in the global struggle between Western freedom and Soviet Communism. She regarded white South Africa, despite apartheid, as part of the West – Christian, capitalist, subject to the rule of law and in principle democratic – threatened by a Soviet-backed black liberation movement which aimed to destabilise the economy, destroy those liberal traditions and move South Africa into the Soviet camp. She opposed the principal black party, the African National Congress (ANC) – led by Oliver Tambo and a largely exiled leadership from outside South Africa while Nelson Mandela and other leaders served indefinite jail sentences – first as socialists, the tools of Communists if not actually Communists themselves; and second as terrorists, devoted to victory through 'armed struggle'. Making no allowance for the fact that so long as they were denied the vote the ANC had no legal outlet for political struggle, she was adamant that a precondition of any settlement in South Africa must be the cessation of violence.

She was certainly influenced by the scale of British business interests in South Africa. The UK was the biggest outside investor in South Africa, which was Britain's fourth-biggest trading partner. British industry – and particularly the defence industry – was heavily dependent on South African minerals. Sanctions, she constantly reminded the left, would damage not just British profits but British jobs. Moreover, around 800,000 white South Africans would be entitled to come to Britain if they were forced to flee South Africa, just as Portugal had been obliged to take an influx of ex-colonials from Angola and Mozambique. Other countries which jumped on the sanctions bandwagon did not have the same direct economic interest at stake.

Altogether she thought there was a lot of hypocrisy and easy moral outrage in the anti-apartheid movement. Her object – as she explained in an interview in the *Sowetan* in 1989 – was to end apartheid without destroying the South African economy in the process:

> We do not want to see a future South African Government which really does represent the majority of South Africans inheriting a wasteland . . . In far too many countries in Africa 'liberation' has been followed by economic disaster and has brought few practical benefits to ordinary people. This can and must be avoided in South Africa.

The way to avoid this outcome was not less trade, but more. 'What the country needs is opening up to the outside world. The last thing it needs is to close in on itself even more.'[15] The policy of demonising South Africa as if it was uniquely wicked, she believed, was not only unfair, but positively counterproductive. 'Insofar as sanctions did work,' she declared on a visit to Norway in 1986, 'they would work by bringing about starvation and unemployment and greater misery amongst the immense black population . . . I find it morally repugnant to sit here or anywhere else and say that we decide that should be brought about.'[16] Some of the most prominent South African opponents of apartheid agreed with her, which only strengthened Mrs Thatcher's suspicion that the ANC demanded sanctions precisely because its aim was to destroy South Africa's capitalist economy.

Convinced of the rightness of her analysis, Mrs Thatcher set herself to block the imposition of further Commonwealth and EC sanctions beyond those already in place, like the ban on sporting contacts, while working behind the scenes to try to influence the Pretoria Government from within. Casting herself as President Botha's candid friend – 'probably', as she claimed in her memoirs, 'the only helpful contact he had with western governments'[17] – she invited him to Chequers in June 1984, provoking inevitable demonstrations, and treated him (in Bernard Ingham's words) to some 'very plain speaking'. She urged him to release Mandela, to stop harassing black dissidents, stop bombing ANC camps in neighbouring states and grant Namibian independence. She kept up the pressure in a sustained correspondence over the next five years. But all this was in private: she refused publicly to join the clamour for the release of Mandela, so she earned no credit with the anti-apartheid movement. Botha was grateful for her friendship but ignored the candour. There was no significant movement in South Africa so long as he remained in power.

Mrs Thatcher's attitude to South Africa was much more principled and honourable than her critics recognised. At the same time she was less constructive than she could have been because she badly misjudged the internal opposition to apartheid. First, by insisting on classing the ANC as Communist terrorists, she completely failed to appreciate that Mandela and the rest of the ANC leadership were as deeply rooted in Western democratic values, liberal humanism, the Bible and Shakespeare as she herself was. Mandela was brought up as a Methodist on the very same hymns and prayers and poems as she was – though after his enforced leisure on Robben Island he had a rather deeper knowledge of English literature and history.

Then she compounded her reluctance to recognise the ANC by seeking a more 'moderate' and pro-Western alternative which she could promote instead. She pinned extravagant hopes on the Inkatha party led by the Zulu chief Mangosuthu Buthelezi. The more the world's attention focused on Mandela the more stubbornly she championed Buthelezi as 'the representative of the largest group of black South Africans'[18] and 'the head of the biggest nation in southern Africa'.[19] She praised him as a friend of free enterprise and 'a stalwart opponent of violent uprising' – unaware that Pretoria was secretly arming Inkatha to fight the ANC.[20] In taking sides in this way Mrs Thatcher was playing with fire.

It was in 1985 that she first set herself in direct opposition to the conscience of the world. That summer, as violent uprisings in townships all over South Africa brought the country close to civil war, President Botha declared a state of emergency. Alarmed, American and Swiss banks called in their debts and refused to make further loans, causing a devastating run on the rand. Under pressure from American public opinion, Reagan felt reluctantly obliged to tighten US sanctions before Congress passed a tougher package; and France and other European countries began to press for concerted EC action. In September Mrs Thatcher successfully vetoed the proposed EC sanctions; so when the Commonwealth heads of government assembled at Nassau in the Bahamas in October it was already clear that she was going to be isolated.

The only way she managed to delay further sanctions was by proposing to send a group of 'eminent persons' (EPG) to South Africa to assess the situation on the ground. President Botha let the EPG into the country in the spring of 1986, and allowed them to meet ANC leaders, including Mandela. They were impressed by Mandela and were close to negotiating a formula for his release when Botha wrecked their efforts by bombing ANC bases in Zambia, Zimbabwe and Botswana. They immediately abandoned their mission and soon afterwards submitted a gloomy report concluding that there was 'no genuine intention on the part of the South African government to dismantle apartheid' and advocating strengthened sanctions.

Privately Mrs Thatcher warned Botha that by falling back on a policy of 'total crackdown' he was making it hard for her to hold the line against sanctions. Behind the scenes she was urging him to do all the things the opponents of apartheid around the world wanted him to do: release Mandela, unban the ANC and start negotiating before it was too late. Having committed herself so vehemently against sanctions, she needed him to show some willingness to embrace reform voluntarily; but this he was refusing to do.

Publicly Mrs Thatcher revelled in her isolation. She had one important ally in the White House. 'As you,' President Reagan wrote to her, 'I remain opposed to punitive sanctions which will only polarise the situation there and do the most harm to blacks.' But Reagan too found himself under pressure to give ground:

You noted you may be forced to accept some modest steps within the European and Commonwealth contexts to signal your opposition to apartheid, and in all frankness we may be faced with the same situation if Congress, as expected, passes some sanctions Bill later this summer or fall.[21]

The Senate duly voted 84–16 to approve a comprehensive package of economic sanctions. The EC too went ahead with a further package, agreed in June. Mrs Thatcher now had no choice but to acquiesce. Yet at a special Commonwealth Conference held in London in August she was still defiant. For the first time in the history of the Commonwealth, the London conference overrode British dissent and agreed to implement measures.

In 1987 Mrs Thatcher took her most positive step with the appointment of a new ambassador to South Africa. Robin Renwick had taken a leading part in devising the Zimbabwe settlement, and subsequently wrote a book demonstrating that economic sanctions never worked. In July 1987 Mrs Thatcher sent him back to southern Africa to pursue what he called 'unconventional diplomacy' in Pretoria. Publicly he was still required to echo her exaggerated faith in Buthelezi. But at the same time he was implicitly authorised to build bridges to the ANC. Over the next three years, he wrote later, he received 'no instructions but full backing from her' for the important part he played in helping to negotiate the release of Mandela and eventually the peaceful transition to majority rule.[22]

The critical opening came in 1989 when President Botha suffered a stroke and was forced – unwillingly – to step down. His successor, F. W. de Klerk, was not at first sight a great improvement. But Renwick had already identified him as a genuine reformer who had learned the lesson of Rhodesia and wanted to talk to the responsible black leaders before it was too late; Mrs Thatcher seized on him as a South African Gorbachev and was hopeful that there would now be some movement in Pretoria.

When in February 1990 de Klerk announced the immediate release of all remaining political prisoners, including Mandela, and the unbanning of all political organisations, including not only the ANC but the South African Communist Party, she regarded it as the vindication of her lonely struggle. To the Commons the day after Mandela's release she insisted: 'I do not think sanctions have achieved anything.'[23] She immediately lifted those measures which Britain could rescind unilaterally and pressed European and Commonwealth leaders to follow suit. She was correspondingly disappointed that Mandela's first speech before the massed cameras of the world's press rehashed all 'the old ritual phrases' about socialism and nationalisation. She had hoped that he would now distance himself from the ANC; she should have realised that this was the last thing he was likely to do.[24]

They finally met in July when Mandela visited London and called on the Prime Minister in Number Ten. Tactfully, he recognised that Mrs Thatcher had opposed apartheid in her own way, and thanked her for her efforts to get him released. He also thanked her for her role in Zimbabwe and in improving East–West relations, but urged her again to maintain the pressure on de Klerk for a negotiated settlement. She in turn urged him to give up the armed struggle, talk to Buthelezi and abandon the ANC's commitment to nationalisation. When a reporter asked Mandela how he could talk to someone who had once denounced him as a terrorist, he replied that he was working with South Africans who had done much worse things than that. For her part, Mrs Thatcher found Mandela dignified and impressively unbitter, but still 'stuck in a kind of socialist time warp'; she still feared he might turn out a 'half-baked Marxist' like Mugabe.[25]

South Africa showed Mrs Thatcher at her best and worst. She was principled and courageous, but at the same time stubborn and self-righteous. She had a good case against sanctions but failed to win support for her view, preferring to lecture and thereby alienate potential allies rather than try to persuade them. Rather, she seemed to glory in her isolation, as if the fact of being isolated made her right. Her only powerful ally outside South Africa was President Reagan: but while he personally shared her Cold War perspective, South Africa was not an issue on which he wished to upset black America or pick a fight with Congress, so she got less help there than she might have hoped.

Was she right? The outcome might suggest so. But most of those who supported sanctions still believe that they were an essential part of the pressure that eventually compelled white South Africa to change. Undoubtedly she played a part in persuading de Klerk to move as far and as quickly as he did. The night before his historic speech in February 1990 he passed a message via Renwick to tell Mrs Thatcher that she would not be disappointed. But her role should not be exaggerated: there were bigger forces at play. As with Gorbachev in Russia, she was lucky that a leader came along at the right moment whom she could appear to influence.

The Middle East

By the 1980s Britain had no remaining direct responsibility in the Middle East, but it was still a part of the world in which Mrs Thatcher took a close interest. She regarded Israel – like South Africa – as essentially part of the West: the only true democracy in the region, with a prosperous and enterprising economy, ringed by hostile neighbours and threatened by Palestinian terrorism. Her instinct was to class the PLO with the IRA and the ANC as terrorist organisations which should be treated as international pariahs until they abjured the use of violence. At the same time, however, she knew that the State of Israel had itself been founded in terrorism. She could not forget that the current Israeli Prime Minister, Menachem Begin, had been the leader of the Irgun gang which bombed the King David Hotel in Jerusalem, killing ninety-one British soldiers, in 1946, and swore never to shake his hand – though eventually she did. She also recognised that Israel had seized Palestinian territory by force in 1967 and had occupied it ever since in defiance of the UN. She was sympathetic to the fate of the displaced Palestinians – she had visited a refugee camp in Syria when she was Leader of the Opposition in 1976 – and believed, as a friend of Israel, that the Israelis would only secure peace when they were prepared to give up some of the occupied territory to get it. Her hope – as in South Africa – was to encourage 'moderate' Palestinians to come forward with whom the Israelis could negotiate.

Whenever she visited the region, or received Middle Eastern leaders in London, she made a point of reporting to President Reagan her conversations and impressions. After visiting the Gulf in September 1981, for instance, she sent Reagan what his staff described as 'a rather somber assessment of views she picked up during her recent talks with a variety of senior Arab political figures'. Richard Allen told the President he should read the whole letter, but summarised its main points for him:

- A mood of disappointment and alienation now dominates moderate Arab thinking about the US. (Arabs hesitate to express the true strength of their feeling directly to us.)
- The view prevails that we are one-sidedly committed to Israel and ignore the Palestinians.[26]

This message, an aide noted, 'calls for a response'. But two more letters followed before the White House got round to drafting a reply in which the President thanked her for 'the candid insights that you have shared with me'.

> I understand the perceptions of the Arab leaders on the peace process alluded to in your letter. A comprehensive Middle East peace remains our objective, and I agree fully that one cannot be achieved unless it addresses the Palestinian problem.[27]

The next month Reagan assured her that Israeli withdrawal must be 'the fundamental basis of a settlement on the West Bank and Gaza';[28] and this was the premise of proposals which he set out in September 1982. But Mrs Thatcher never felt the Americans put enough pressure on Israel. The following year she was again giving Washington 'her read-out on meetings with King Hussein in London . . . She makes a powerful case that the President weigh in with the Arabs to demonstrate again that we are committed to the September 1 proposals.'[29] She was critical of Israel's bloody invasion of southern Lebanon in June 1982, but equally sceptical of the value of the multinational – predominantly American – UN peace-keeping force sent to Beirut, and restricted British participation to a token contribution of just one hundred troops. The killing of 300 American and French troops by a suicide bomber in October 1983 only confirmed her view that they were a sitting target: she urged Reagan not to retaliate but to withdraw the multinational force.[30] The next year he did so. In her memoirs she described the American intervention in Lebanon as a lesson in the folly of military action without a clearly attainable objective.[31]

By February 1984, following the massacre of refugees in southern Lebanon Mrs Thatcher's patience with Israel was wearing thin. 'Whenever there was a problem', she told Caspar Weinberger, 'it seemed that Israel annexed what it wanted. She urged that there should be a reappraisal of Israeli policy.'[32] An opportunity arose later that year when Yitzhak Shamir's hard-line Likud Government was replaced by a Labour–Likud coalition to be headed by Shimon Peres and Shamir in turn. At Camp David before Christmas she told the Americans that 'she personally knew the new Israeli Prime Minister very well and favourably. Prime Minister Peres wanted to be constructive, and if we are to get anywhere in the Middle East we should attempt to do it while he is Prime Minister.'[33]

In September 1985 she visited Egypt and Jordan to encourage President Mubarak and King Hussein to keep up the momentum for peace. 'I felt that President Mubarak and I understood one another', she wrote. She confessed to 'some sympathy' with his view that 'the Americans were not being sufficiently positive', and believed that King Hussein, too, had been taking 'a real risk' in trying to promote a peace initiative, but was being let down by the Americans.[34] Before leaving Jordan she and Denis made a point of visiting another refugee camp. The following spring she paid her first visit as Prime Minister to Israel, where she was again impressed by Peres, but dismayed by Shamir – another former terrorist – who rejected any question of giving up Jewish settlements on the West Bank in exchange for peace.

In 1986 Shamir took over as Prime Minister. Visiting Washington the next year Mrs Thatcher again vented her frustration with Israeli intransigence and chided the Americans for acquiescing in it.

> She regretted that there had been no major Western initiative since the Camp David accords; noted that President Reagan's 1982 speech had been superb but had been rejected by Begin; characterised Peres and Hussein as two positive figures who are doing everything possible to advance the peace process and deserve our support; and . . . asked rhetorically whether it was not timely to move forward by promoting an international conference.

Shultz replied that it was no good promoting a new initiative without Likud support: the American approach was 'to seek to find a way of getting Shamir and Likud on board'.

> Mrs Thatcher asked the Secretary whether he thought that Shamir ever intends to negotiate over the West Bank or Jerusalem or whether in fact it is Shamir's view that all of biblical Israel belongs to modern Israel. If the latter, Shamir is simply holding the entire world ransom and there will never be negotiations . . .
>
> Mrs Thatcher characterised this position by Shamir as hypocritical because it denies basic rights to the Arabs and removes Israel's credibility as the only Middle East democracy.[35]

Mrs Thatcher got nowhere on the Middle East, but she deserves credit for trying. Despite her instinctive admiration for Israel and substantial dependence on her own large Jewish vote in Finchley, she saw that there would be no serious pressure on Israel to negotiate so long as successive US administrations were terrified of offending the powerful American Jewish lobby. She told the Americans so, with her usual frankness, but this was one area in which they did not listen to her. Far from withdrawing from the occu-

pied territories, the Israelis carried on planting more Jewish settlements in the West Bank and Gaza. President Clinton made more
effort than any of his predecessors to broker a real compromise.
But nineteen years after Mrs Thatcher's fall, hope of an Arab-Israeli
settlement was as distant as ever. In her memoirs she reflected on
the paradox of modern Jews denying others the rights they were
so long and tragically denied themselves:

> I only wished that Israeli emphasis on the human rights of the
> Russian *refuseniks* was matched by proper appreciation of the
> plight of landless and stateless Palestinians.[36]

Aid and arms

Mrs Thatcher viewed the whole world through Cold War specta-
cles as a battleground for conflict with the Soviet Union, a struggle
for geopolitical advantage to be waged by all means – political,
cultural, economic and military. Whatever might be the particular
local circumstances of different countries, she saw Britain's role in
every corner of the globe as helping the Americans to combat those
they classed as Communists and support those regimes – however
undemocratic and repressive – approved by Washington as friends of
the West. As well as taking a high-profile role as a global evangelist
for the wealth-creating benefits of free enterprise, she had two practical means of exerting influence in the developing world: the provision of aid and the sale of military equipment. She was sceptical of
the former, and Britain's aid budget declined sharply during her
years in power. But she was a great enthusiast for the latter, and
Britain's share of the world arms trade grew spectacularly.

Her attitude to aid mirrored on a global scale her suspicion of
the welfare state at home. In defiance of the international liberal
consensus which inspired the 'North-South Commission' chaired
by Willy Brandt in the late 1970s, she believed that handouts from
rich countries to poor countries merely propped up corrupt regimes
and perpetuated dependency, instead of promoting free trade and
enterprise which would enable the underdeveloped to develop prosperous economies of their own. Far from trying to meet the target
agreed by all the industrialised countries (except the US and Switzerland) that they should raise their aid budgets to 0.7 per cent of
GNP, she allowed Britain's performance to decline from 0.52 per
cent in 1979 to 0.31 per cent in 1989. Moreover, most of the aid
that Britain did give was tied to British trade.

What she most resolutely opposed was coordinated international action. In October 1981 a global summit in Cancun, Mexico, chaired jointly by the Mexican President and Pierre Trudeau, raised exactly the sort of hopes she was determined to dash. Mrs Thatcher only attended – and persuaded Reagan to attend – because she thought it important that they should be there to argue the free-market case; specifically, she was anxious to block proposals to place the International Monetary Fund and the World Bank under direct UN control. She and Reagan deliberately set out to ensure that the conference imposed no new commitments, and by that standard she was happy to pronounce it 'very successful'.[37]

A particularly effective way of killing two birds with one stone was by linking aid to the sale of arms. By this means she could boost an important British industry while simultaneously supporting regional allies and helping to counter Soviet influence. The arms trade was a perfect marriage of her two primary concerns. Particularly after the Falklands, Mrs Thatcher took a close interest in the products of the defence industry. Acting as a saleswoman for British arms manufacturers also gave her a useful *entrée* to Third World kings and presidents: she had something to sell which they wanted, and she enjoyed dealing personally, leader to leader, trading in the very symbols and sinews of national power. Normally the Defence Secretary was the frontman in negotiating these sales; but Mrs Thatcher's role, as Michael Heseltine recalled, was 'not inconspicuous'. Her part in clinching sales to Saudi Arabia, the Gulf States and Malaysia was widely reported, and he found her always very supportive. 'I knew I had only to ask my office to contact No. 10 to wheel in the heavy guns if they could in any way help to achieve sales of British equipment.'

In 1985 Heseltine, with Mrs Thatcher's support, appointed Peter Levene, the managing director of his own arms-trading company, at an unprecedented salary to become head of defence procurement at the MoD. As a poacher-turned-gamekeeper, Levene earned his salary over the next six years by forcing down the prices the Government paid for military equipment. One way of cutting the manufacturers' costs was by helping them sell their products around the world. Partly as a result of his efforts Britain climbed during the 1980s from being the fifth- to the second-largest supplier of military equipment after the United States. But Mrs Thatcher herself set up many of the biggest and most contentious deals, including major contracts with King Hussein of Jordan, General Suharto of Indonesia and General Augusto Pinochet of Chile. She lubricated these deals by soft loans and vigorous use of the export credit system. The result was a less good deal for the taxpayer than at first appeared. Many of the arms supposedly purchased – by Jordan, Iraq and probably others – were never paid for at all. Even before the Gulf war intervened, Nicholas Ridley admitted that Iraq owed £1 billion and the true figure may have been nearer £2.3 billion.[38] In practice Mrs Thatcher was subsidising British companies with public money – something she refused to do in other areas of industry.

Her greatest coup was the huge Al-Yamamah contract with Saudi Arabia, negotiated in two parts in 1985 and 1987, said to be the biggest arms deal in history, worth something like £40 billion to British Aerospace and other British companies, and partly paid for in oil. Mrs Thatcher met Prince Bandar, a nephew of King Fahd and son of the Saudi Defence Minister, at least twice in 1985, once in Riyadh in April, the second time in Salzburg in August, when she was supposed to be on holiday. On the announcement of the first part of the deal – for forty-eight Tornado fighter/bombers, twenty-four Tornado air-defence aircraft, thirty Hawk advanced training aircraft and thirty basic training aircraft – Heseltine told the press that Mrs Thatcher's contribution 'cannot be overstated'.[39] She secured the second part at a stopover in Bermuda on her way to Australia in 1988. Given her usual readiness to boast of her achievements, however, it is curious that this went unmentioned in her memoirs.

The obvious reason was embarrassment over reports which soon emerged of huge commissions, running into millions of pounds, paid to middlemen – among them her own son. Mark's business interests had already attracted attention in 1984, when questions were raised about a large contract for the building of a university in Oman, which Mrs Thatcher had personally secured on her visit – with Mark in attendance – in 1981. The company principally concerned was Cementation Ltd, for which Mark was then acting as a 'consultant'. With no relevant qualifications or experience, his only possible value was his contacts, and specifically his name. 'We did pay him,' the company admitted, 'and we used him because he is the Prime Minister's son.'[40] In the Commons and on television Mrs Thatcher indignantly denied any impropriety: she had been 'batting for Britain' not for any individual company, and Mark's activities were his own affair.[41] In fact, since Cementation was the only British company bidding for the university contract, this defence was disingenuous. Mrs Thatcher must have known that her son stood to profit if Cementation won the contract, though that is not necessarily to say that she should therefore not have lobbied for them. The allegation that Mark was enriching himself on the back of his mother's patriotic salesmanship, however, did not go away. Much bigger sums were involved five years later in the Al-Yamamah contract, from which Mark was alleged to have pocketed £12–20 million for his role as a 'facilitator'. There is no doubt that he became inexplicably wealthy around this time, nor that he and his partner were active in the arms trade and in the Middle East.[42] The evidence is only circumstantial, however, since an investigation of the Al-Yamamah deal by the National Audit Office was never published.

A second criticism of Mrs Thatcher's enthusiasm for arms sales is that it distorted the allocation of the aid budget – a charge highlighted by the saga of the Pergau Dam project in Malaysia. Mrs Thatcher visited Malaysia in April 1985. On that occasion she 'got on rather well' with the Prime Minister, Dr Mahathir. Three years later she went back and negotiated – without reference to the Foreign Office – a deal whereby Britain financed the construction of an economically unviable and environmentally damaging hydroelectric power station in northern Malaysia in return for an agreement to buy British defence equipment worth £1.3 billion. Subsequently a pro-Third World pressure group took the Government to court, alleging that this was an improper diversion of 'aid' for commercial purposes, and in 1994 won their case when the High Court ruled the deal illegal. Douglas Hurd, then Foreign Secretary in John Major's Government, was obliged to refund the aid budget £65 million from Treasury reserves.

The Pergau affair threw a murky light on Mrs Thatcher's cavalier way with aid. In December 1994 Hurd was forced to reveal that three more aid projects – in Turkey, Indonesia and Botswana – had been found to breach the criteria of the 1980 Overseas Development and Co-operation Act. The money wasted on the Pergau project was more than Britain gave over the same period to Somalia, Ethiopia and Tanzania combined, while wealthy Oman alone received more British 'aid' than Ethiopia. Moreover, it emerged that nearly half the money expended under the Aid and Trade Provision (ATP) for projects in Third World countries went to finance contracts won by a handful of favoured companies all of which were major contributors to the Conservative party.[43] In short, British aid was recycled to the Prime Minister's friends and supporters at home and abroad.

The third charge against Mrs Thatcher's pursuit of arms sales is that much of it was carried on secretly, in contravention of the Government's declared policy. The most glaring instance was the supply of military equipment to Saddam Hussein's Iraq throughout the eight years of the Iran–Iraq war when Britain was supposed to be restricting the flow of arms to both sides. This turned into a major embarrassment in 1990 when Saddam invaded Kuwait and Britain and her allies found themselves at war with a country they had been busily arming just a few weeks earlier. But this is an occupational hazard of the arms trade: much the same had happened with Argentina in 1982. The real scandal was the secrecy – duplicity – with which the policy had been conducted for the previous ten years.

Officially the West was neutral in the bloody war of attrition which began in 1980 when Iraq launched its troops against Iran: up to 1985 Britain continued to train pilots and supply low-level equipment impartially to both sides. In practice, however, both Britain and the United States covertly supported Iraq. Saddam was a revolting tyrant, but he was a tyrant of a familiar sort whom they could get along with: Iran's fanatical Ayatollah Khomeini, on the other hand, seemed much more dangerous. With the trauma of the Teheran hostage crisis still fresh in American minds, Iran outranked even Gaddafi's Libya as Washington's 'public enemy number one'. As Mrs Thatcher told Caspar Weinberger in 1984, 'the West did not need another success by Moslem fundamentalists'.[44] Moreover, the war provided a tempting opportunity. So long as the Shah was on the Peacock Throne, Britain had been a major supplier of arms to Iran. But Khomeini's Islamic revolution had closed that market. British manufacturers were now keen to get into Iraq instead. Their American counterparts were hamstrung by Congress, which not only imposed an embargo on trade with both sides, but actually enforced it, so the Reagan administration was happy to see Britain secretly supply Baghdad. It was easier to deceive the House of Commons than it was to deceive Congress.

Officially Britain followed the American lead by banning the export of 'lethal' equipment to either side. But a meeting of the Cabinet's Overseas and Defence Committee (OD) on 29 January 1981, chaired by Mrs Thatcher, agreed to define the critical word 'as flexibly as possible'.[45] Before the end of the year the MoD's arms-trade subsidiary International Military Services (IMS) had won a contract to build an integrated weapons complex at Basra in southern Iraq; and this was just the beginning. Over the next four years 'something like ten times as much defence equipment [was] exported to Iraq than to Iran'.[46]

For a time in 1983–4, when an Iranian victory seemed likely, however, the Foreign Office worried that this 'tilt' to Iraq might be imprudent and began to hedge for a more balanced neutrality. In November 1984 Richard Luce proposed more detailed 'guidelines' to restrict the supply of arms to either side. By the time Howe disclosed them to Parliament in October 1985 they had already been in operation for nearly a year.

Except that they never really operated at all. Giving evidence at the Matrix Churchill trial in 1990, Alan Clark dismissed them with typical candour as 'tiresome and intrusive', mere 'Whitehall cosmetics'.[47] They were framed to be deliberately ambiguous. Only finished weapons were classed as 'lethal'. Every other sort of military equipment, from aircraft spares to laser range-finders, and above all lathes for manufacturing artillery shells, went through without difficulty. They were made by a number of firms, all of which enjoyed a close relationship with the MoD, with little effort to disguise either their purpose or their destination. One of those most heavily involved, Matrix Churchill in Coventry, was actually acquired in 1987 by a subsidiary of the Iraqi Government, presumably to get round the fact that Britain had just signed a pact banning the export of ballistic missile technology to the Third World. Matrix Churchill was then developing the Condor 2 missile with a range of 1,000 kilometres and capable of carrying nuclear warheads, in which Baghdad was known to be interested.[48] When questions were asked in Parliament they were batted away by junior ministers.

On 2 December 1986, when there was some question of changing the guidelines, Charles Powell wrote to the Foreign Office that Mrs Thatcher found them 'very useful' when answering questions in the House of Commons and had no wish to alter them.[49] Two days later she gave a perfect example of what he meant when she told the House that 'British policy on arms sales to Iran and Iraq is one of the strictest in Europe and is rigidly enforced, at substantial cost to British industry. That policy has been maintained scrupulously and consistently.'[50] Presumably this formula accorded with her reading of the guidelines. But the reality was very different from the impression given to Parliament.

Is it possible that she did not know what was really going on? There is no doubt that some individuals in all the relevant departments knew. But did Mrs Thatcher know? Quite apart from the fact that no Prime Minister so prided herself on knowing what was going on in every corner of Whitehall, the involvement of the intelligence service is the clearest indication that she was fully informed. After the scandal broke, the Scott Inquiry set up by John Major concentrated – so far as Mrs Thatcher was concerned – on whether she knew that the 1985 guidelines were secretly relaxed in 1988, when the Iran–Iraq war ended. But this was a very minor issue. More important is the overwhelming evidence that she knew

– she must have known – that the guidelines had been worthless ever since 1985.

For one thing she received a quarterly report listing arms sales, country by country, all round the world, and she had given explicit approval to a substantial (and unannounced) level of exports to Iraq. Of course the undercover trade might have been omitted from this list. But she also received intelligence reports, and we know that she read them avidly. More specifically, Scott quotes an intelligence digest dated 29 March 1988 – before the guidelines were changed – summarising the British machine-tool industry's involvement in Iraqi weapons manufacture and singling out Matrix Churchill as 'heavily involved'. This was initialled by Mrs Thatcher.[51]

Then there was the fact that large amounts of British equipment reached Iraq indirectly via other countries – notably Jordan. In her evidence to the Scott Inquiry, Mrs Thatcher claimed to have been deeply shocked by the discovery of this 'glaring loophole' (as Scott called it).[52] She attached great importance to Britain's relationship with Jordan and took pride in the three big arms deals she had made with King Hussein since 1979 – suspiciously large for such a tiny country. Other ministers followed her lead in claiming to have no idea that much of this equipment was destined for Iraq. But as usual there was one exception. Alan Clark told Scott that it was common gossip in the MoD that 'more than half the material purchased by Iraq was actually consigned to Jordan'. An instance came to light in 1983 when HM Customs intercepted a consignment of 200 sub-machine guns bound for Iraq via Jordan: three men were charged and fined, but their conviction was later set aside.[53] But Mrs Thatcher did not need customs to tell her that this was happening. In October 1985 the Joint Intelligence Committee circulated a confidential document entitled 'Use of Jordanian facilities for the transshipment of war material to Iraq'; and the Scott Inquiry was given details of twenty-five more intelligence reports on the same subject between 1986 and 1991.[54] Is it possible that the Prime Minister read none of them? She had certainly done so by July 1990 when she commissioned from the Cabinet Office a document known as the 'Iraqnote' tracing the history of defence exports to Iraq, which stated: 'Iraq systematically uses Jordan as a cover for her procurement activities almost certainly with the connivance of senior figures within the Jordanian administration.'[55] Her pretence that this came as a great shock to her the following month is demonstrably untrue.

The scandal of the arms trade to Iraq only began to unravel in the last months of Mrs Thatcher's premiership, and the Scott Inquiry concentrated largely on when she had known what after 1988. But the covert arming of Iraq had begun very much earlier, in 1981, and was well established during her second term, when British manufacturers were given every encouragement and assistance to export military equipment energetically to Iraq, both directly and (via Jordan) indirectly, in cynical contradiction of the Government's professed policy of scrupulous restriction. There is ample evidence that Mrs Thatcher both knew of and encouraged this policy: it would have been very remarkable if she had not. So why did she do it? She was not normally cynical, and she prided herself on her high ethical standards. The answer is twofold.

First, she genuinely believed that every country was entitled to purchase the means to defend itself, that a free trade in armaments promoted peace, not war, and that others would sell them if Britain did not. Second, however, her Manichean world view disposed her to the dangerous doctrine that 'my enemy's enemy is my friend'. If Iran was the enemy of the West, then it was in Britain's interest to help arm Iraq. In her own mind she knew that it was right, even though it might be difficult to defend the policy to Parliament. So she closed her mind to the impropriety of deceiving Parliament, and probably also deceived herself. But there can be no doubt that she both willed the end and winked at the means. The policy stemmed from the same robust world view that she applied to every area of her foreign policy, from the Falklands war to nuclear disarmament, from the bombing of Libya to the ending of apartheid. But in all those theatres she stood up boldly for what she believed. In the case of Iraq the execution of her policy required that Parliament was systematically misled over a period of eight or nine years. This was a major stain on her record.

18

Enemies Within

A need for enemies

ONE of Margaret Thatcher's defining characteristics as a politician was a need for enemies. To fuel the aggression that drove her career she had to find new antagonists all the time to be successively demonised, confronted and defeated. This is unusual: the normal instinct of politicians the world over is to seek agreement, defuse opposition and find consensus. The taste for confrontation is particularly alien to the British Tory party, whose traditional preference has always been to emphasise national unity around common values. By contrast Mrs Thatcher actively despised consensus: she needed always to fight and to win. She viewed the world as a battleground of opposed forces – good and evil, freedom and tyranny, 'us' against 'them'. The overriding global struggle between capitalism and Communism was reflected at the domestic British level by the opposition of Conservative and Labour, and more generally in a fundamental distinction between, on one side, 'our people' – honest, hard-working, law-abiding, mainly middle-class or aspiring middle-class taxpayers, consumers and home-owners – and, on the other, a ragtag army of shirkers, scroungers, socialists, trade unionists, 'wets', liberals, fellow-travelling intellectuals and peace campaigners. All these anti-social elements had to be taken on and beaten to make a world safe for Thatcherism.

The second term was the time to deal with her domestic opponents. For most of her first term she was on the back foot. But once the Falklands had helped her to survive the crises of her first three years, Mrs Thatcher returned to office with a clear intention to take the offensive. She had routed the Labour party at the polls. But socialism was a many-headed hydra, which still held important citadels of power beyond Westminster, and which must be reduced before the Thatcherite vision of Britain could be fully realised. Two, above all, threatened her authority. First, left-wing Labour councils still controlled local government in most of the country's major cities: most visibly, just over the river from Westminster, the leader of the Greater London Council, Ken Livingstone, was mounting a cheekily provocative challenge which she could not endure. She had already determined in the 1983 manifesto to deal with Livingstone by the simple expedient of abolishing the GLC (and with it the other metropolitan councils). That, however, would require legislation. Meanwhile, she faced a still more dangerous challenge from the Tories' old nemesis, the National Union of Mineworkers, now headed by the militant class warrior and would-be revolutionary Arthur Scargill, openly bent on destroying her government as he had previously destroyed Heath's. Having prudently backed off in 1981, Mrs Thatcher was now ready for this challenge too. But first she signalled a tough new attitude to trade unionism by picking a fight with the small but significant group of white-collar workers employed at the Government's top-secret satellite listening post, Government Communications Head-quarters, based at Cheltenham.

The problem of trade unionists at GCHQ had caught her attention during the 1981 Civil Service strike. The fact that striking tax collectors cost the Government £350 million in lost revenue merely irritated her; but the idea that intelligence personnel could endanger national security by industrial action enraged her, confirming her suspicion that trade unionism was fundamentally anti-patriotic. Codebreakers, she believed, should no more be unionised than members of the armed forces. She wanted to ban unions from GCHQ there and then, but at that time she was talked out of it. The Americans had been alarmed by the disruption of intelligence, however, and Mrs Thatcher placed the highest priority on Britain's intelligence relationship with the US. Particularly after the Falklands and Grenada crises she wanted to assure them that it would not be repeated. So in January 1984, with no prior consultation with the unions concerned, she persuaded Howe to announce an immediate ban on GCHQ employees belonging to unions.

The case was a reasonable one – MI5 and MI6 were not unionised, and it was something of an historical anomaly that GCHQ was different. But the abrupt way in which the Government proposed to end the anomaly seemed high-handed and unreasonable. The right to union membership, she told the Commons, was a 'privi-lege' which did not extend to security personnel.[1] To the unions this was tantamount to accusing their members of treason. The left claimed that the Government was removing a basic civil right and won a temporary victory when the High Court declared the ban illegal on the ground that the lack of consultation was 'contrary to natural justice'. This judgement was later overturned in the Court of Appeal, but the case of the handful of GCHQ workers who chose to be sacked rather than give up their membership remained a live grievance for the rest of the Thatcher years.

Scargill and the miners

The skirmish over GCHQ was no more than a curtain raiser to the real battle which overshadowed the whole of 1984: the Government's life-or-death showdown with the NUM. Mrs Thatcher had always known that she would have to face a miners' strike sooner or later. In February 1981, she accepted temporary humiliation by postponing a confrontation she was not yet ready to win. Since then, however, the Government had been quietly making its dispositions. An *ad hoc* committee, MISC 57, met 'in conditions of extreme secrecy for most of 1981' to devise ways to ensure that the Government would be able to sit out a long strike whenever it came. Over the next two years cash limits on the Central Electricity Generating Board (CEGB) were relaxed to allow the unobtrusive build-up of large stocks of coal in the power stations, which had been lacking in 1981. At the same time power stations were converted where possible to burn oil instead of coal, and fleets of road hauliers were recruited to move coal if the railwaymen should come out in support of the miners.[2] This, as Hugo Young pointed out, was a very rare example of strategic foresight on Mrs Thatcher's part.[3]

Then, in February 1983, Nigel Lawson signalled that the Government was ready by appointing Ian MacGregor from British Steel to become chairman of the National Coal Board. Fresh from turning round the steel industry, with the loss of almost half the workforce, MacGregor was plainly being sent to do the same for coal: his track record in the United States included the defeat of a two-year strike by the United Mineworkers. Finally, in her post-election reshuffle Mrs Thatcher persuaded Peter Walker to take on the Department of Energy with the explicit expectation that he would face a challenge from Scargill.

The economic case for shrinking the coal industry was incontestable. The rundown had been going on under governments of both parties since the 1960s. The moderate President of the NUM from 1971 to 1982, Joe Gormley, had broadly accepted it. But the industry was still overproducing coal that could not be sold. When MacGregor took over, the NCB was heading for a loss of £250 million in 1983–4. If the Government's policy towards nationalised industries was to mean anything this had to be stopped. But to achieve economic viability the NCB would have to close loss-making pits in traditional mining areas in Yorkshire, Scotland and South Wales and concentrate production in profitable modern pits. Coal mines, however, cannot be closed as easily as factories; whole communities with a proud and deeply rooted way of life depend on them. The new NUM leaders, Arthur Scargill and his saturnine Vice-President Mick McGahey, were not only militant left-wingers looking to break another Tory Government: they also came from Yorkshire and Scotland respectively. They took their stand on the view that the union could not allow the closure of any pit at all except on grounds of safety or geological exhaustion: they did not accept the concept of an uneconomic pit. This was the economics of the madhouse.

But Scargill was not making an economic case at all. Behind the Luddite insistence that miners' jobs must be guaranteed for life, his purpose was to mount a political challenge to the Government. He openly boasted of leading a socialist – more accurately a syndicalist – revolution to overthrow capitalism, asserting that after Mrs Thatcher's 1983 landslide, extra-parliamentary action was 'the only course open to the working class and the labour movement'.[4] He had first come to prominence by leading the mass picketing of the Saltley Gate coke works, which was perceived – rightly or wrongly – as having forced the Heath Government to cave in to the miners in 1972, and from the moment he was elected to succeed Gormley in December 1981 he was thirsting to repeat that revolutionary moment. Three times in 1982–3 he called on the NUM membership in national ballots to vote for strikes: three times, by majorities rising from 55 to 61 per cent, they voted him down. After the successful strikes of the 1970s too many miners – those whose jobs were not threatened – had too much to lose by going on strike: they had good pay, cars, mortgages and an increasingly middle-class way of life. They were no longer the down-trodden proletariat of Scargill's imagination. Moreover, the Coal Board, with Walker's encouragement, was offering generous redundancy terms to those who did lose their jobs when pits closed. By 1984 it was plain to Scargill that he would never get his strike if he relied on the membership voting for one – certainly not by the 55 per cent majority required by the NUM constitution. So when the NCB announced on 6 March 1984 that another twenty uneconomic pits would close over the next twelve months, with the loss of 20,000 jobs, he determined to engineer a national strike without the tiresome inconvenience of a national ballot.

He contrived it by encouraging a series of regional strikes, starting in the most directly affected and most militant areas, Yorkshire and Scotland, which would put moral pressure on the others to join in. As McGahey bluntly put it: 'We shall not be constitutionalised out of a strike ... Area by area will decide and there will be a domino effect.'[5] Pickets were dispatched to less militant areas to help them to the right decision. But only Yorkshire, Scotland and the small Kent coalfield – where there were no ballots – were solid in support of the strike. Most other areas which did ballot voted against striking: the crucial moderate coalfield, Nottinghamshire, recorded a majority of nearly four to one against and most pits in the county carried on working. In South Wales only ten out of twenty-eight pits supported the strike, but the local leaders called all their members out anyway. Thus Scargill's strategy split the union whose strength in the past had always been its unity. In fact, there were indications that, had he held a ballot in the early weeks of the strike, he might have won it – especially after he had pushed through a rule change requiring only a simple majority.[6] But by refusing to hold a ballot he not only set area against area but miner against miner within each area, pit and village. By mid-April, when the strategy was approved – by a majority of only 69–54 – by a special delegate conference, forty-three out of 174 pits were still working. To enforce and widen the strike Scargill revived on a much bigger scale his old weapon from 1972 – the mass picketing of working pits and also of ports and depots to prevent the movement of coal. Flying pickets were organised as a quasi-military operation, with men bused from all over the country to key sites: they were given strike pay only if they were prepared to picket. But this time the police were equally organised – the Government had made its preparations on this front too – and met them in equal numbers. Soon the television news every night led with what looked like pitched battles between medieval armies, one side armed with batons and riot shields, the other with bricks, spikes, darts, ball bearings and all manner of home-made weapons.

The public was appalled; but though there was widespread sympathy for the miners, faced with the loss of their livelihood, there was remarkably little public support for the strike, because of Scargill's methods. By waging the dispute with such blatant contempt for democracy – by defying the rules of his own union and openly challenging the elected Government – by strutting and ranting like a tinpot demagogue, refusing to condemn the violence of the pickets (which he blamed entirely on the police) and refusing to admit the possibility of closing any pits at all, Scargill alienated not only the public at large but also those who should have been his allies, the Labour party and the other unions. Neil Kinnock, less than a year into his leadership of the party, was cruelly exposed: emotionally disposed to support the miners but aware that it would be political suicide to do so, able neither to condemn the strike nor fully support it. He did criticise the failure to hold a ballot, condemned the violence – but also the police response – and did his best to express support for the miners without endorsing Scargill's more extreme objectives. But the more uncomfortably he wriggled, the more contemptuously Mrs Thatcher was able to pillory him as a weasely apologist for the enemies of democracy.

Likewise the rest of the union movement gave the miners verbal but little practical support. The steel unions above all were desperate to keep what was left of their industry working, and defied the NUM pickets designed to stop coal getting to the steel plants. But the electricians, the power workers and even the railwaymen also turned a deaf ear to Scargill's truculent demand for 'the total mobilisation of the trade union and labour movement'.[7] Passionately as Scargill appealed to working-class solidarity, he was asking others to risk their jobs when thousands of his own members were still working. By flouting the NUM's own rulebook Scargill had thrown away the public sympathy which was the miners' greatest asset.

So the Government held all the cards. And yet the year-long strike still represented a major crisis for Mrs Thatcher. The longer it dragged on the more it highlighted the division of the country which she seemed to embody. Its defeat was vital to her political survival, yet she could not afford to appear too directly involved and above all must not appear vindictive. It was no secret that she loathed the coal industry – the archetypal union-dominated, loss-making nationalised industry which, she wrote in her memoirs, 'had come to symbolise everything that was wrong with Britain'.[8] It was dirty, too; the future, she believed, lay with clean, modern nuclear energy. Yet she was bound to keep saying warm words about coal and what a bright future it could have once production was concentrated on the profitable pits, in order to counter Scargill's repeated allegation that the Government was intent on destroying it.

At the same time she had to pretend to treat the strike as an ordinary industrial dispute and leave the handling of negotiations with the NUM to the Coal Board. In the Commons Kinnock continually accused her of abdicating the Government's responsibility to bring the two sides together. But Government interference to impose a solution, she insisted, would be tantamount to surrender. 'The Government will leave the National Coal Board to deal with the matter as it thinks fit.'[9]

The Government's only role was to uphold the liberty of those miners – and others – who wanted to work. It was the job of the police to protect the freedom to work, and the job of the Government to support the police. The most serious confrontation took place at the Orgreave coke depot near Sheffield, just down the road from Scargill's headquarters, where 5,000 pickets gathered on 29 May to try to stop the movement of coal. They were beaten back by even greater numbers of mounted and heavily armoured police, but the battle was renewed daily for three weeks, with incidents of appalling violence on both sides: on the first day alone 104 police officers and twenty-eight pickets were injured, and by the end several hundred – including Scargill himself – had been arrested. The issue here was no longer the future of the coal industry but the maintenance of law and order, and on that subject Mrs Thatcher could not be neutral. 'What we have got,' she said on 30 May, 'is an attempt to substitute the rule of the mob for the rule of law, and it must not succeed . . . The rule of law must prevail over the rule of the mob.'[10] After three weeks it did. The battle of Orgreave was a decisive defeat for Scargill's storm troops.

The police operation, too, was centrally controlled. As soon as the strike began the Home Secretary, Leon Brittan, set up a National Reporting Centre in New Scotland Yard to coordinate intelligence between the forty-three independent police forces in England and Wales and ensure that adequate manpower and equipment was available to the chief constables wherever it was needed. The Home Office had learned a lot from the 1981 riots: as a result of that experience the police were far better equipped and trained to deal with mass violence than ever before. Coordination between local forces, it was alleged, was a sinister step in the direction of a national police force under the control of the Government, and ultimately a police state. But Brittan, strongly supported by Mrs Thatcher, insisted that the police had always had the power to prevent a breach of the peace wherever they anticipated one and were quite right to do so.[11] In due course the High Court agreed. Undoubtedly there were disturbing implications in the level of policing needed to contain the strike. But at least it was contained by the police. When MacGregor told Mrs Thatcher that in America they would have brought in the National Guard with tanks and armoured cars, she was quite shocked. 'Oh my goodness,' she exclaimed, 'we can't do that. That would be political suicide in this country.'[12] Most of the public recognised that centralised policing was needed to prevent centralised intimidation. If they did not like it they blamed Scargill more than the Government.

Thus Scargill's bully-boy tactics played into the Government's hands. No Prime Minister could have failed to denounce them, and Mrs Thatcher did not restrain her condemnation of his calculated assault on freedom, democracy and the rule of law. But once or twice she went too far with overtly military talk of 'victory' or 'surrender'. It was in an end-of-session speech to Conservative MPs on 19 July that she was reported to have described the striking miners as 'the enemy within'.[13]

Like most such phrases, this one was not original: the *Daily Express* had already applied it jointly to Scargill and Livingstone in a front-page headline the previous year.[14] But it sparked a furious reaction. Mrs Thatcher was forced to explain that she had meant only the militant minority, not the miners in general. But she never retracted the expression. In October she repeated and explained it in an interview with the *Sunday Mirror*: 'The "Enemy Within" are those people who turn to violence and intimidation to *compel* people to do what they can't *persuade* them to do.'[15]

Three weeks later the *Sunday Times* revealed that the NUM had sent a representative to Tripoli to seek money – successfully – from the Libyan President Colonel Gaddafi, who also made no secret of funding the IRA. Coming just a few weeks after Libyan agents had shot dead a young policewoman from the diplomatic sanctuary of their London embassy, this was Scargill's most spectacular blunder, condemned as strongly by Kinnock and the TUC as it was by Mrs Thatcher. But it allowed her to widen her attack still further. In a third speech, delivered at the Carlton Club in November, she equated the striking miners – and the hard left in general – with Libyan and Palestinian terrorists.

By such speeches Mrs Thatcher deliberately raised the stakes. By defining the coal strike as part of the global struggle against Communism and terrorism she nailed her authority to the outcome of a contest which the Government could not afford to lose and on which she repeatedly declared there could be no compromise. Contrary to her public denials, she took the closest interest in every aspect of the dispute. She not only chaired a large ministerial committee, MISC 101, consisting of nearly half the Cabinet, which met once a week throughout the strike, but more importantly she met both Peter Walker and Leon Brittan nearly every day to keep an eye on developments, and constantly had to be restrained from ringing chief constables with her views on detailed aspects of policing.[16]

In September the High Court ruled that the union had indeed breached its own constitution by calling a strike without a ballot. Scargill was fined £1,000 (which was paid by an anonymous donor) and the union £200,000. When it refused to pay, its assets were ordered to be sequestrated. It turned out that they had already been transferred abroad, out of reach of the court. But the judgement further deterred other unions from any thought of risking their own funds.

By far the most serious alarm of the whole dispute, however, arose from the possibility that the pit deputies' union NACODS, representing the men responsible for the maintenance and safety of the pits, might join the strike, which would have closed all the mines immediately and caused irreparable damage. Up until the summer enough deputies had kept working to keep the pits in good repair: local managers had turned a blind eye to those who stayed away. But in August the NCB suddenly announced that it would stop paying those who refused to cross NUM pickets. NACODS promptly voted by a majority of 82 per cent to strike from the end of October – principally over their own grievance but also in support of the miners' campaign against pit closures. Mrs Thatcher was furious at MacGregor's clumsiness. 'We were in danger of losing everything because of a silly mistake,' she recalled on television in 1993.[17] MacGregor was told in no uncertain terms that the deputies must be bought off; and after anxious talks under the auspices of the arbitration service ACAS, they were.

For the Government the key to victory lay with the 50,000 miners in Nottinghamshire and other 'moderate' coalfields who had continued working in the face of verbal and physical pressure to join the strike. To Mrs Thatcher they were heroes of democracy. '"Scabs" their former workmates call them,' she told the Tory Party Conference. 'Scabs? They are lions.'[18] There is no question that it took courage to defy the bullies. Her praise, however, did them no favours in their own communities, where being lauded by the Prime Minister made them look like the stooges of a hated Tory Government – as to an extent they were.

Eventually the strikers started to go back. By the end of October the realisation that they were going to get no significant support from other unions, and the evident fact that the CEGB had enough coal to sit out the winter, led all but the most militant to conclude that the cause was hopeless. The NCB bribed them with deferred bonuses – puffed in newspaper advertisements as 'the best package ever offered to any group of workers'[19] – and in the middle fortnight of November some 11,000 took the bait. By the end of the year 70,000 out of 180,000 miners were working (Scargill, of course, disputed the figure) and MacGregor announced that as soon as the number reached 51 per cent the strike would be over. Yet still it lasted for another two months, partly because a new TUC initiative raised hopes of a face-saving compromise. Again Mrs Thatcher was alarmed. She wanted nothing short of outright victory but was afraid that MacGregor was weakening. Now she intervened to insist that the NCB should require not just an assurance but a written guarantee that it alone could decide when pits must be closed, and went on television on 25 January 1985 to make her involvement perfectly clear.

She finally got her victory on 3 March – almost exactly a year after the strike had begun. With men now going back at the rate of 9,000 a week, a delegate conference voted to preserve what remained of the union's authority by ordering an orderly return to work the following Monday, even though nothing at all had been achieved. There was no agreement over pit closures; no pay rise until the overtime ban was lifted; and no promise of an amnesty for convicted pickets. Scargill still wanted to fight on, while simultaneously claiming a famous victory. But the majority of his members, and almost the whole of the rest of the country, could see that in a battle of two stubborn wills, Mrs Thatcher's had proved the stronger.

Yet it was not a popular victory. Mrs Thatcher expressed 'overwhelming relief' and tried not to crow.[20] Most of the public accepted that the NUM's position had been untenable. But there was no public celebration. Despite Scargill's tactics there was real sympathy for the miners and particularly for their wives, seen as long-suffering heroines of their communities' doomed struggle. Mrs Thatcher reaped no political credit for having defeated them. On the contrary, she was felt to have been as inflexible and divisive a class warrior as Scargill himself. Instead of getting a lift in the polls, as ministers expected, the Government soon found itself trailing in third place behind both Labour and the Alliance.

The economic costs of the dispute were high. In his 1985 budget Nigel Lawson reckoned the direct cost to the Government in public expenditure at £2.75 billion. The highest price, however, was paid by the coal industry itself. Scargill had always claimed that the Government's purpose was to destroy the industry. Over the next ten years the rate of pit closures accelerated, so that by 1994 there were only nineteen left in operation, employing just 25,000 miners. The bright future repeatedly promised by MacGregor and the Government throughout 1984 never materialised, mainly because the privatisation of electricity supply ended the protected market for overpriced coal. Thus Scargill could claim to have been vindicated. But in truth, until his determination to stage a political confrontation, the Thatcher Government had been no more ruthless than its Labour predecessors in trying to manage the inevitable rundown as generously as possible.

Nevertheless the strike left a lasting legacy of anger, bitterness and social division. At a time when unemployment was still rising ineluctably, it dramatised the human suffering in those parts of the country which felt themselves thrown on the scrap heap while London and the south of England boomed. Challenged politically by what she called 'Mr Scargill's insurrection', Mrs Thatcher did not seem to care, but concentrated all her attention on defeating the 'enemy within', who in turn became a focus of admiration for all other deprived and alienated groups who loathed her Government. In the long run the defeat of the NUM marked her decisive victory not just over the miners but over the unions and the left as a whole. When all is said it was a necessary victory; but it was a flawed and bitterly contested one, which highlighted the negative side of Thatcherism as vividly as the positive.

Livingstone and local government

Scargill's counterpart in local government was Ken Livingstone – the provocatively left-wing thirty-six-year-old leader of the Greater London Council. Livingstone was the figurehead for a number of local council leaders around the country determined to defy the Tory Government. But the Government's protracted showdown with Livingstone was in some respects the mirror image of its confrontation with Scargill. 'Red Ken', too, was defeated in the end. But whereas Scargill's blatant contempt for democracy dissipated public sympathy for the miners' cause, Livingstone by skilful public relations contrived to make corrupt and extravagant municipal socialism appear a great deal more popular than it really was and successfully cast Mrs Thatcher as the enemy of democracy for abolishing it. The GLC and six other metropolitan councils outside London were finally wound up in 1986, removing another focus of opposition to the Government's centralising hegemony. But the abolition of London-wide local government was another messy operation which left a sour taste in the mouth and an uneasy democratic void which was not filled for fifteen years. When London government was eventually restored by Tony Blair the voters promptly showed what they thought by twice electing Livingstone as Mayor. The fact that Lady Thatcher barely mentioned the abolition of the GLC in her memoirs suggests that she felt in retrospect not very proud of it herself.

Scrapping the metropolitan councils, however, was just one part of a wider assault on local government which ran all through Mrs Thatcher's three administrations, starting with Michael Heseltine's efforts to control local spending in her first term and ending with the fiasco of the poll tax in her third. The second term began with the new Environment Secretary introducing legislation to place a statutory ceiling on the amounts that local authorities could raise from the rates. This, though targeted at allegedly spendthrift Labour councils, seriously infringed what had hitherto been a hallowed Conservative principle, the autonomy of local government, and was vehemently opposed by a phalanx of senior party figures in both the Commons and the Lords. Whatever the case for each of these measures, the determination with which Mrs Thatcher pursued them suggests an extraordinary degree of hostility to local government.

Margaret Thatcher grew up in local government. She always claimed that she 'owed everything' to her father; and Alfred Roberts' whole life was local politics. Whatever was the case in her father's day, however, she believed by the 1970s that local government had become inefficient, extravagant and unrepresentative. As successive governments piled more and more functions and responsibilities on to them, she thought that local authorities had become both too big and intrinsically socialistic, providing all sorts of previously undreamed-of services and bleeding the ratepayers – not usually the same people as the recipients – to pay for them. Increasingly, as Prime Minister, she saw local authorities (of whatever colour) as obstacles blocking the implementation of Thatcherite policies of privatisation, deregulation and consumer choice. Hence the thrust of her Government's policies across the whole range of service provision was to take responsibility away from local authorities to give it instead to other agencies, private enterprise or central government. It has been calculated that more than fifty separate Acts of Parliament between 1979 and 1989 directly reduced the powers of local government; and the process continued after 1990.[21]

In this way, by an accumulation of *ad hoc* policies over ten years, Mrs Thatcher undermined the vitality and the very purpose of local government. The Government claimed that it was returning power to individuals and consumers, breaking the power of town-hall empires of self-serving local politicians and politicised council officers, particularly in housing and education. Undoubtedly there were abuses, particularly in London, and it was unquestionably true that Labour councils in deprived inner cities fostered an anti-business ethos and a culture of benefit dependency which actually perpetuated poverty. That said, however, the practical effect of her policies was to use the abuse of local government as an excuse to diminish it still further, concentrating power ever more centrally on Whitehall. This contradicted the historic Tory tradition of backing the local against the central power. With the rise of socialism in the twentieth century, fear of the overmighty state had become an even stronger article of Conservative faith. Tory councils in the 1960s and 1970s had seen themselves as bastions of liberty against the creeping interference of Whitehall. But the Tory Government of the 1980s, finding itself opposed by some high-profile socialist authorities in the cities, reversed this tradition. Behind her libertarian rhetoric, Mrs Thatcher's instinct to impose her views was authoritarian, interventionist and essentially centralising.

In diminishing the autonomy of local government she damaged many of the values which Conservatives – herself included – had always stood for: local pride, local responsibility, dispersed power, and a tradition of active local government. Mrs Thatcher often seemed to proceed on the assumption that there would never be another Labour Government. But it was not only shire Tories who were alarmed that their Government was destroying something precious: Tory radicals who were the strongest supporters of free-market economic policies were even more suspicious of the state gathering to itself ever greater power. If Mrs Thatcher thought she was serving democracy by weakening local government, she should have been reminded of Friedrich Hayek's warning in *The Road to Serfdom*: 'Nowhere has democracy worked well without a great measure of local self-government, providing a school of political training for the people at large as much as for their future leaders.'[22] Principle aside, this was a factor of direct practical relevance to the Conservative party, whose local organisation was largely based in local government. With so few significant powers left to local councils by the end of the 1980s, fewer able and public-spirited people came forward to serve on them, while activism at the grass roots of the party shrivelled. Thus, when the triumphs of her General Election victories had passed away she left her successors a much weakened – and ageing – power base.

Spies, moles and 'wimmin'

Behind the open political challenges of Scargill and Livingstone, Mrs Thatcher believed that her Government – and the country – also faced a persistent threat from a variegated coalition of left-wing dissidents, subversives and fellow-travellers, all more or less knowingly serving the interests of the Soviet Union, which must be countered by all means necessary in the cause of Freedom. Believing that she was engaged in a life-or-death struggle with the forces of evil both at home and abroad, she took very seriously anything which could be seen as a threat to national defence or the armed forces. Of Mrs Thatcher's recent predecessors, Harold Wilson was the one whose obsession with security most nearly matched her own; but he was worried much of the time that the security services were spying on him. Mrs Thatcher, by contrast, had no doubt that she and they were fighting the same global enemy, and she welcomed enthusiastically all the help MI5 and MI6 could give her. She read all the intelligence reports with close attention, and after the Falklands became the first Prime Minister to attend meetings of the Joint Intelligence Committee, now located in the Cabinet Office.

It cannot really be said that the women's 'peace camp' at Greenham Common posed a serious threat to national security. The 1983 election had delivered a resounding defeat to nuclear unilateralism, which was quite clearly a massive vote-loser for the Labour party. Nevertheless CND continued to march and campaign vigorously against nuclear weapons, while a few hundred heroically determined women kept up their stubborn vigil outside the US base in Oxfordshire where the first cruise missiles arrived at the end of the year, making occasional attempts to breach the perimeter before they were ejected. Their protest was ramshackle, eccentric, idealistic and very British, but essentially futile. In the Commons Mrs Thatcher worried that 'such protests tend to give the impression to the Soviet Union that this country has neither the capacity nor the resolve to defend itself or to keep defence expenditure at a sufficient level to deter'.[23] Fighting for Freedom with a capital F, she was not so keen to see that freedom exercised. But in fact nothing burnished her Iron Lady image more effectively than the contrast between herself, with her immaculate hair and powerful suits, and the woolly-hatted feminists and mystical tree-huggers of the peace camp. She gloried in the contrast, confident that on this issue at least Middle England identified overwhelmingly with her.

Yet the women of the peace camp and other CND supporters were subjected to continual surveillance and harassment by the police and MI5. Not only was the camp itself frequently raided and broken up, but activists' phones were tapped, their mail was opened and several suffered mysterious break-ins at their homes – leaving aside the unsolved murder of an elderly rose-grower of strong unilateralist convictions named Hilda Murrell. Nor was it only nuclear dissidents who were targeted. MI5 infiltrated NUM headquarters during the miners' strike and made unprecedented use of bugging and phone-tapping to track the deployment of pickets. In 1985 it emerged that MI5 had also been asked to vet senior figures in the BBC; in January 1987 the police actually raided the Glasgow offices of the BBC and confiscated material relating to a series of programmes the Government did not like. The centralisation of policing during the miners' strike; persistent allegations that the RUC and the security forces were operating a shoot-to-kill policy in Northern Ireland; the removal of union rights from workers at GCHQ; and a new readiness to use the Official Secrets Act to pursue civil servants who leaked embarrassing documents – all created a disturbing sense of an authoritarian government using unprecedentedly heavy-handed methods to suppress what it regarded as dangerous dissent.

The Government also appeared needlessly authoritarian by its efforts to block publication of the memoirs of a retired MI5 officer, Peter Wright. There is no question that the book, *Spycatcher*, was a serious breach of the confidentiality expected of secret-service personnel; the Government was thoroughly entitled to ban it, as it had done many less sensational books before. The problem was that Wright was now living in Australia and he published his book there, as well as in Ireland and America, whence its contents quickly became available in Britain; extracts even appeared in the British press. Trying to stop its publication now was a classic case of shutting the stable door after the horse had bolted. Nevertheless Mrs Thatcher was determined to pursue *Spycatcher* – 'irrespective of the outcome' – in order to assert the principle that former spies could not with impunity write about their experiences.[24] In vain. Both the Supreme Court of New South Wales and eventually the House of Lords ruled that it was too late to keep secret what everyone who was interested had already read. The Government's persistence long after the cause was lost merely made it appear stubborn and vindictive.

Faith in the City

Mrs Thatcher did not see enemies only in the shadows. She believed that the very pillars of the Establishment were against her. She considered that the whole professional class – the upper middle-class liberal intelligentsia and the distinguished generation of public servants which had dominated Whitehall since 1945 – was riddled with a sort of pale-pink socialism which was scarcely less corrosive than outright Trotskyism. Of course she made exceptions of individuals: but her instinctive preconception was that the whole traditional governing elite was made up predominantly of quislings and appeasers.

This liberal Establishment had several centres, only one of which – the Civil Service – was under her direct control. Over her decade in office she made a systematic effort, by a mixture of patronage and example, to mould the Whitehall village to her view of the world, and to a considerable extent succeeded. Four other centres of influence, however, remained more or less independent and overwhelmingly resistant to the Thatcherite gospel: the churches (particularly the Church of England); the universities; the broadcasters (particularly the BBC); and the arts community. Together these overlapping elites comprised what used to be called the political nation; nowadays sociologists classify them as 'opinion formers', while the tabloids call them the 'chattering classes'. All felt themselves under attack by a Conservative Government which was out of sympathy with all their values and assumptions. Seen from Downing Street, conversely, they were all faces of the same hydra-like enemy which Mrs Thatcher believed she had been called to office to defeat.

More publicly than any other recent Prime Minister before Tony Blair, Mrs Thatcher was a practising Christian. Alec Home, Harold Wilson and Ted Heath had all in their different styles professed to be believers; but Mrs Thatcher advertised the religious basis of her politics more than any of them. She not only attended the parish church near Chequers most Sundays when she was there, but she never shied from asserting what she believed should be the central place of Christianity in national life. It is impossible to know the exact nature of her personal faith, but she was steeped in the language and practice of Christianity from childhood and believed in it implicitly as a force for good.

She blamed the Church, however – all the churches – for their abdication of moral leadership in the face of permissiveness and for a general loss of moral values in society. Whereas the Church of England had once been known as 'the Conservative Party at prayer', and her father's brand of Methodism had been identified with self-reliance, individual responsibility and thrift, she thought the churches had become politically wet if not actually left wing, infected by a sort of soggy collectivism which looked to the state, instead of the individual, to solve all social ills. No one personified this sort of hand-wringing churchmanship better than the Archbishop of Canterbury, Robert Runcie, whom she appointed – in preference to the still more liberal Hugh Montefiore – soon after she became Prime Minister and who was therefore in office for almost her entire premiership. From the start Runcie did not shrink from criticising the harsh social consequences of her Government's economic policies; and he particularly outraged her by his sermon at the thanksgiving service at the conclusion of the Falklands war when he prayed even-handedly for those who had died on both sides.

She was constrained from responding in public, partly because Runcie was a good friend of Peter Carrington and Willie Whitelaw but also because – improbably in the light of his donnish manner – he had a distinguished war record, winning the Military Cross as a tank commander, and therefore could not easily be dismissed as a pacifist wimp.

However, she was hurt by the allegation that her social policies showed a lack of compassion, and worried by the widespread impression that Christians could no longer be Conservatives. She believed absolutely the contrary. Her politics and her religion were based alike on the primacy of individual choice and individual responsibility. 'The heart of the Christian message,' she told Laurens van der Post in a 1983 television interview with her favourite mystic, 'is that each person has the right to choose.'[25] She did not believe in collective morality or collective compassion, via taxation, but in individual charity – which depended on a degree of individual wealth. 'No one would remember the Good Samaritan if he'd only had good intentions,' she told Brian Walden in another interview. The important point was that 'he had money as well'.[26]

Unless provoked, she was generally careful not to bring religion into her political speeches.[27] She recognised that many sincere Christians were not Tories, and knew that it would cause an outcry if she suggested that they should be. But at the same time she was keen to demonstrate that good Christians could be – and in her view, should be – Conservatives; so she was not afraid to preach her own distinctive political theology whenever she was given the chance in an appropriate setting. In March 1981 she revisited the City church of St Lawrence Jewry, where she had preached once before when she was Leader of the Opposition, to expound her favourite parable of the talents: 'Creating wealth,' she told her lunchtime audience of bankers and stockbrokers, 'must be seen as a Christian obligation if we are to fulfil our role as stewards of the resources and talents the Creator has provided for us.'[28] And in 1988 she outraged the General

Assembly of the Church of Scotland with her gospel of unfettered individualism.

Though the Prime Minister's initiative in the appointment of bishops had been greatly curtailed by a new system introduced in 1976 whereby she was given only two names to choose from, Mrs Thatcher took her diminished responsibility very seriously and made a point of trying to appoint the more conservative of the options put up to her. 'They only give me two choices,' she once complained, 'both from the left.' Another time, when Woodrow Wyatt asked her why she had appointed so-and-so, she said, 'You should have seen the other one.'[29] In fact, she could ask for more names and at least once did so. Right at the end of her time she had the chance to replace Runcie at Canterbury. With no obvious front-runner, she made a bold choice by picking a complete outsider, the very non-Establishment, state school-educated evangelical George Carey – a moral and theological conservative who nevertheless supported the ordination of women – in preference to any of the Establishment candidates. 'In choosing him,' *The Times*'s religious correspondent Clifford Longley commented, 'Mrs Thatcher's known impatience with theological and moral woolliness . . . will have been a factor.'[30]

She found a much more effective champion of her religious views in the person of the Chief Rabbi, Immanuel Jakobovits, whose robust preaching of clear Old Testament values reminded her of her father. She frequently stated her admiration of the way the Jews in her constituency looked after their own community, without relying on the state. 'In the thirty-three years that I represented it', she wrote in her memoirs, 'I never had a Jew come in poverty and desperation to one of my constituency surgeries . . . I often wished that . . . Christians . . . would take closer note of the Jewish emphasis on self-help and acceptance of personal responsibility.'[31] The number of ministers of Jewish extraction in her Cabinets – Keith Joseph, Nigel Lawson, Leon Brittan, David Young, Malcolm Rifkind and later Michael Howard – and also among her private advisers, attracted some notice and even suggestions of favouritism; but it was largely accidental. She certainly liked clever, classless outsiders, which many of these people were; but the description also covered plenty of others not Jewish. There is no suggestion that she showed undue favour towards Jews, only that she was, as Nigel Lawson wrote, unusually free of 'the faintest trace of anti-Semitism'.[32] She was very far from being uncritically supportive of the State of Israel. But she did find it politically useful to hold up Jakobovits as a model by which implicitly to criticise Runcie. She knighted him – rather incongruously – in 1981; and wanted to send him to the

House of Lords to balance the Anglican bishops there, but with curious deference to protocol was not sure she could, until she finally took the plunge – to general applause – in 1988.

'Academic poison'

The Prime Minister might grumble about the bishops, but she could not do very much about them: and perhaps they did not greatly matter anyway. The case of the universities was different. If the nation's institutions of higher education were obstructing the realisation of the Government's vision, it was within the Government's power to bring them to heel. And that was precisely what she set out to do.

Mrs Thatcher's relations with the academic community were paradoxical. Though not herself an intellectual, she used intellectuals to advise her more systematically and effectively than any previous Prime Minister. She used the deliberately homely language of housewife economics to lead the most ideologically driven government of the century. And Thatcherism prevailed: she won the ideological argument and shifted the political agenda decisively in her direction for a generation. Ideas that had been derided when she and Keith Joseph first began to argue them in 1975 were taken for granted by a Labour Government twenty-five years later. Yet the intellectuals never forgave her. Of course, she had her academic supporters. But Thatcherite academics were always a minority – if, by the end of the decade, a highly visible and vocal one. The great majority of university teachers loathed her, and she equally despised them.

Her experience as Education Secretary in the early 1970s, visiting universities at the height of student radicalism and being shouted down by left-wing demonstrators who mindlessly denounced all Tory ministers as 'Fascists', confirmed both her dim view of the quality of education being taught and her contempt for the trendy professors and craven vice chancellors who permitted this sort of intolerance to go on. Remembering her own student days of hard work and plain living, she regarded modern students and most of their lecturers as idle parasites who lived off the taxpayer while abusing the hand that fed them. But she blamed the students less than their tutors. 'Revolutionary doctrines like communism,' she told Brian Walden in 1988, 'usually came from intellectuals and academics . . . Some academics and intellectuals . . . are putting out what I call poison. Some young people, who were thrilled to bits to get to university, had every decent value pounded out of them.'[33]

She resented the universities' claims to intellectual autonomy while expecting to be funded by the state, and complained of their anti-capitalist culture. Only two institutions were exempt from this blanket condemnation. The Open University, which she had saved from being strangled at birth in 1970, gave good value for the Government's money by turning out graduates more cheaply than conventional residential universities; she worried about left-wing bias in some of its correspondence material, but at least its students were highly motivated adults who did not waste their time on drink, sex and campus politics. Better still, the independent University College of Buckingham, founded in 1974, was a private university on the American model which got no funding from the Government at all.

Keith Joseph had tried to convert the universities to the beauty of the free market by his brave campaign around the campuses between 1975 and 1979, during which he was regularly abused, spat at and shouted down. Once in power Mrs Thatcher adopted more direct methods, first by simply cutting their budgets, later by taking them under direct political control, forcing them on the one hand to seek alternative sources of income and on the other to process more students with fewer staff and resources.

Curiously some of the heaviest cuts fell on science. Part of the problem was that the increasing emphasis on profitable development diverted money away from pure research. The result was that over the five years 1981–6 the proportion of national GDP devoted to research and development together fell from 0.72 per cent – which already compared poorly with other European countries – to 0.62 per cent.[34] Now Mrs Thatcher realised that if she was going to be her own Minister of Science she must be seen to do something. So she set up a Cabinet committee, with herself in the chair, to try to redirect resources to pure science. But the damage was done. The squeeze on the universities in general and science in particular had already driven many of the country's best scientists to move to the United States.

It was this more than anything else which provoked Oxford to the unprecedented snub of refusing the Prime Minister an honorary degree. All her recent Oxford-educated predecessors, from Attlee to Heath, had received this honour within a year of taking office. But the university had missed the moment in 1979 because it was already embroiled in controversy over an honorary degree to President Bhutto of Pakistan. It funked it again in 1983 and by the time the proposal came up for a third time in 1985 the opposition had grown formidable. Supporters of the award argued that the university would look petty in the eyes of the world if it denied the customary honour to a Prime Minister who – like her or loathe her – was not only the first woman but already one of the longest-serving holders of the office. Opponents, however – with scientists to the fore – argued that it would be monstrous to award such an honour to the head of a government which had inflicted 'deep and systematic damage to the whole public education system in Britain, from the provision for the youngest child up to the most advanced research programme'. By a majority of more than two to one – 738 to 319 – the dons voted to withhold the degree. The inevitable effect was to extinguish any lingering affection for her *alma mater*. 'I went to Oxford University,' she only half joked at the 1989 party conference, 'but I've never let it hold me back.'[35] A decade later, when she had finished her memoirs, she pointedly donated her papers to Cambridge.

'Trotskyists' in the BBC

All Prime Ministers become paranoid about the BBC. As problems mount and their popularity slides, they invariably accuse the media of turning against them, unfairly criticising the Government while giving the opposition a soft ride. Margaret Thatcher was no exception. It is in the nature of governments to resent criticism, particularly at the hands of a state-owned broadcaster. But Mrs Thatcher disliked the BBC on principle, long before she became Prime Minister, just because it was state-owned and publicly financed. She saw it as a nationalised industry, subsidised, anti-commercial and self-righteous: like the universities, she believed, it poisoned the national debate with woolly liberalism and moral permissiveness at the taxpayers' expense.

She was always particularly concerned about the reporting of terrorism. Her first public criticism of the BBC as Prime Minister was provoked by a contentious edition of *Panorama* in November 1979 which showed masked IRA men enforcing roadblocks in Northern Ireland: the allegation was that the programme makers had set up the incident in order to film it. She was still more outraged by the reporting – particularly the BBC's – of the Falklands war. She thought that in this crisis the Corporation was not just anti-Government and anti-Conservative, as usual, but anti-British, as exemplified by programmes examining in great detail alternative possible landing places on the islands and above all by the broadcasters' punctilious insistence on referring objectively to 'British forces' instead of 'our forces' as she expected.

The truth was that she did not really understand the idea of journalistic freedom. At a Chequers seminar with some of her favourite academics in January 1981, she worried about the penetration of the media by subversives. The historian Professor Michael Howard tried to assure her that the people she objected to were not Communists, just healthily opposition-minded sceptics exercising a hallowed British tradition of dissent; but she was not convinced.[36] She believed not only that in time of war the broadcasters should form part of the nation's war effort, but that in the context of terrorism and the Cold War the BBC had a duty to be on 'our' side. Instead she believed it gave 'covert support' to unilateralism and was 'ambivalent' in its coverage of the IRA.[37]

Mrs Thatcher had two means to discipline the BBC: first by exercising the Government's power to appoint the chairman and governors, who in turn appointed the Director-General; and second by keeping it on a tight financial rein. Over five years she was able to appoint three chairmen and nine new governors who gave the board 'a more hostile and opinionated composition'.[38] She also made no secret of her dislike of the licence fee – 'a compulsory levy on those who have television sets', whether they watched the BBC or not – but in March 1985 she was constrained to renew it for another five years, pegged for the first two years but rising in line with inflation after that, while making clear in the Commons that 'we do not rule out the possibility of changes' – specifically not excluding advertising – in the future.[39] The same month Leon Brittan set up a departmental committee which was expected to recommend funding the BBC by advertising. In the event the Peacock Committee came down in favour of the status quo, mainly because studies showed that there was not enough advertising to go round.[40] Mrs Thatcher was 'greatly disappointed'[41] and was obliged to back down; but she still hoped to reopen the matter in five years' time.

Friends in Fleet Street

The constantly simmering conflict between Mrs Thatcher and the BBC certainly contrasted with – and arguably balanced – the generally reliable support she enjoyed from most of the printed media. Of course there were exceptions. Among the broadsheets, the *Guardian* was the house magazine of the progressive establishment, read by all those Labour and Alliance-voting teachers, lecturers, social workers and local-government officers who most hated her: in her view the printed equivalent of the BBC, but without the BBC's obligation to at least appear impartial. Among the tabloids, the *Daily Mirror* remained solidly Labour, in opposition to its deadly rival the *Sun*. But the bulk of Fleet Street* from the relatively high-brow *Times* and *Telegraph* through the crucial mid-market *Mail* and *Express* – all with their Sunday sisters – to the soaraway Thatcherite *Sun* and the even more populist *Daily Star*, was firmly, if not always uncritically, in the Tory camp. Measured by total circulation, the press supported the Government in the 1987 election by a margin of roughly three to one.[42]

Mrs Thatcher was naturally very happy with this situation. She was not worried by the *Guardian*'s hostility, but rather welcomed its opposition as confirmation that she was doing all right. She expected her enemies to oppose her, just as she expected her allies to support her. But she took it for granted that anyone not for her was against her. When a new broadsheet, the *Independent*, was founded in 1986 she quickly classed it as an enemy. 'It is not independent at all,' she told Wyatt in 1989. 'It is dedicated to trying to destroy me.'[43] The corollary was that she took great care to keep her supporters loyal.

Unlike many Prime Ministers she did not actually read the papers very much. She received a daily digest from Bernard Ingham first thing every morning, which gave her the flavour and told her what he thought she ought to know. She was well aware of the importance of the press – particularly the *Sun* and the *Daily Mail* – in maintaining a swell of support for her personality and policies. She liked to have her attention drawn to helpful or supportive articles. But she did not often give interviews to favoured editors. If she did meet editors, it was not to learn what was on their mind but to tell them what was on hers.

On the other hand she was shameless in rewarding supportive editors with knighthoods and their proprietors with peerages. The great exception to this plethora of inky nobility was Rupert Murdoch, who could not be offered a peerage because he had become an American citizen and would probably not have accepted anyway. But Mrs Thatcher did everything else she could to show

---

* 'Fleet Street', of course, ceased to be located in Fleet Street during the 1980s, largely as a result of Rupert Murdoch's removal of News International to Wapping in 1985, which was followed by practically all the rest of the national press. But the name is still useful, and it was still correct at the start of the decade.

her appreciation of his support. In November 1979 she marked the tenth anniversary of News International's acquisition of the *Sun* with a glowing message of congratulation, making clear that she saw the paper as a loyal ally, or even partner. In return she did all she could to advance Murdoch's ever-expanding media interests.

First she helped him to snap up *The Times* and *Sunday Times* when Lord Thomson relinquished them in 1981. The rest of Fleet Street was dismayed and the Establishment horrified at seeing the former 'top people's paper', known around the world as 'The Times of London', sold to a brash Australian who already owned the *Sun*, the *New York Post* and a whole stable full of other titles in Australia and the US. Though Murdoch gave assurances of editorial independence, and elaborate safeguards were erected to try to ensure that he observed them, in practice they quickly turned out to be worthless.

Second, the Government was very helpful towards Murdoch's battle with the print unions when he moved his entire operation to Wapping in 1985. Like the miners' strike, this was another symbolic struggle between old-style trade unionism, defending jobs – and in the printers' case grotesque overmanning and the systematic blackmail of a peculiarly vulnerable industry – and management's right to manage. As in the coalfields, angry pickets tried to prevent Murdoch's new workforce getting to work, turning the streets around 'Fortress Wapping' into a nightly battleground. The Government was fully entitled to treat it as a law-and-order issue which had to be won; but at the same time it was an intensely political confrontation and another vital test of Thatcherism on the ground. According to Andrew Neil – editor of the *Sunday Times* from 1983 to 1994 – Murdoch obtained Mrs Thatcher's personal assurance before the dispute began that 'enough police would be available to allow us to go about our lawful business. She assured him that there would be . . . and she kept her word.'[44] As with the NUM, she wanted victory, not compromise.

The curiosity of Mrs Thatcher's gushing support for Murdoch is how she squared it with her dislike of pornography. Had she ever turned the pages of the *Sun*, she would have been appalled; but Ingham's daily digest spared her this embarrassment. Of course she knew about the topless Page Three girls; but she frankly closed her eyes to the rest of the paper's daily diet of sleazy sex in exchange for its robust support, rationalising it as the price of freedom.

In 1990 she once again showed Murdoch outrageous favouritism by allowing him to hijack satellite television in its infancy by buying out the competition, without reference to the Monopolies Commission. Her anxiety to keep Murdoch's newspapers on side, and her willingness to bend the regulations to buy their continuing support, was the grubbiest face of Thatcherism. Murdoch enjoyed a special place in the Prime Minister's circle of the elect – not a courtier but a powerful independent ally and family friend, rather like Ronald Reagan – who had direct access to her whenever he sought it. He was the only newspaper proprietor invited to the Downing Street lunch to mark her tenth anniversary in 1989, and was several times invited to spend Christmas with the family at Chequers. Yet she never once mentioned him in her memoirs.

The arts in the market place

Mrs Thatcher had an educated person's proper respect for the arts, but she had little feel for them. Like Christianity, the great books, paintings and music of the past provided a cultural heritage to be praised and raided for validation of the present. From her diligent childhood she retained a superficial familiarity with the major English classics; she could still quote from memory large chunks of poetry she had learned at school; and having both played the piano as a girl and sung in the Oxford Bach Choir at university she had a better than average knowledge of music. Within the fairly narrow limits of what she liked, she was by no means a philistine. As Prime Minister she occasionally went to the opera. She collected porcelain and (with advice from experts) Chinese scrolls. And if she did not have much time or taste for reading fiction – beyond the occasional Freddie Forsyth or John le Carré thriller, or Solzhenitsyn read as homework on the Soviet Union – she did read an astonishing amount of serious non-fiction (philosophy, theology, science and history) not directly related to the business of government.

Yet her taste in the arts was characteristically simple and relentlessly functional. She had no patience with complexity or ambiguity, no time for imagination. She thought art should be beautiful, positive and improving, not disturbing or subversive. She liked books which told her things she needed to know. She had a retentive memory and liked to be able to quote things that she had read long ago. But she could not talk about the arts. The paintings she really liked were the portraits of national heroes – Nelson, Wellington, Churchill – and great British scientists – Newton, Faraday – with which she filled the walls of Number Ten; and she always took visitors on a tour of the pictures, pointing the political moral of each one. Her idea of art was essentially didactic.

What she disapproved of was the view of the arts as yet another nationalised industry, a playground of spoiled children – gifted maybe, but self-indulgent – who expected to be supported by the taxpayer for the gratification of an elite who should be made to pay for their own pleasures. As a result, Government policy towards the arts was a matter of containing public spending, requiring value for the money allocated and demanding that arts organisations should become more self-supporting – in other words, more commercial. Her model for arts patronage was the United States: companies and galleries, she believed, should not look to the state for funding but to private enterprise. In fact, the level of public subsidy – already pretty static since 1973 – was not cut in absolute terms. The Arts Council's budget actually increased from £63 million in 1979–80 to £176 million in 1990–91, which on paper more than kept ahead of inflation. It did not feel like that on the ground, however, where costs rose faster than general inflation and most institutions felt their income constantly reduced. No doubt this made arts organisations leaner, more efficient and more anxious to get 'bums on seats'. But the need to attract sponsorship also dictated that artistic criteria were increasingly subordinated to commercial considerations, resulting in big, safe exhibitions, middle-brow plays with small casts and bankable TV stars, and frequent revivals of the most popular stalwarts of the operatic repertoire.

Towards the end of the decade, however, Mrs Thatcher did start to think that the country should do something memorable to mark the millennium. 'We are really going to be rather lucky if we live to that day', she told an audience of magazine editors in July 1988. 'We must celebrate it with something special'.

I am very well aware that if we are going to do something great . . . it will take about ten years to do it, but . . . I think we should not only build something special or do something special – we should be able to do something which affects every town, city and every village.

'I think', she concluded, 'that come the 1990s we will have to set up a group to really take this in hand'.[45] Whatever project was ultimately chosen she clearly expected the decision to be hers. We can be sure she would have commissioned something more enduring than New Labour's vapid dome.

19

Irish Dimension

The IRA: a real enemy

MRS Thatcher faced one real enemy within: Irish republican terrorism. When she came into office in 1979 the 'troubles' in Northern Ireland were already ten years old. Ever since Harold Wilson had sent in the army – originally to protect the Catholic minority from the Protestant backlash against their demand for civil rights – Britain had been caught up in a bloody security operation in Northern Ireland, attempting to keep peace between the communities while increasingly targeted as an occupying force by the Provisional IRA. Since then successive Secretaries of State had striven to devise new initiatives to resolve the conflict, while the 'provos' kept up a vicious guerrilla campaign against military and Unionist targets alike. From a peak in 1971–3, when 200 British soldiers and around 600 civilians died in three years, the toll had settled down to about a dozen soldiers, a similar number of police and forty or fifty civilians killed each year; but there were also regular bombings and murders on the British mainland, mostly in London, though the worst single incident was the bombing of a pub in Birmingham in 1976 which killed twenty-one people and injured a hundred more.

Over the next decade the terror continued, and several times it touched Mrs Thatcher herself very closely. At the outset of the election campaign which brought her to power, her mentor Airey Neave was blown up in his car in the precincts of the Palace of Westminster, apparently by the INLA, a splinter faction from the IRA. At the very end of her time in office another of her closest confidants, Ian Gow – another staunch Unionist – was murdered at his house in Sussex. Exactly midway between these two horrors the IRA's most audacious coup, the bombing of the Grand Hotel in Brighton in October 1984, came close to killing the Prime Minister herself and did kill or seriously injure several of her ministerial colleagues or their wives. At a purely human level, Margaret Thatcher had more reason than most to loathe the IRA.

Her instinctive political response was resolutely Unionist. Northern Ireland was British; the majority of its people professed their loyalty to the British Crown and flag: they were therefore entitled to the same unquestioning support as the people of the Falklands, Gibraltar or Hong Kong. Moreover, she always set her face against any cause – anywhere in the world, let alone in her own country – which sought to advance itself by violence. Insofar as she thought about it at all she saw the Northern Ireland situation primarily as a security matter.

She regularly repeated the promise that Northern Ireland was British and would remain British so long as the majority of its population wished it. Every autumn her party conference speech included an emotionally worded tribute to the courage and endurance of the people of Ulster. Yet in truth she had no deep concern for the province or its people. Ministers and officials who worked with her on Northern Ireland agree that she regarded it as a place apart whose customs and grievances she did not begin to understand.[1]

The more she saw of Unionist politicians over the years the less she liked them. Increasingly she saw Ulster as a drain on British resources and a diversion of her hard-pressed defence budget. What really moved her was the steady toll of young British lives – 'our boys' – lost in the province. From thirty-eight in 1979 the figure dwindled over the next decade to an average of nine a year. But there was no year in which at least two soldiers were not killed. She made a point of writing a personal letter to the family of each one. She also made several unannounced visits to the troops to demonstrate her support for them. She was strongly in favour of the policy of 'Ulsterisation' by which the army was withdrawn as far as possible to a reserve role and replaced on the streets with the Royal Ulster Constabulary (RUC). In fact she was as keen as any nationalist to get the troops out of Northern Ireland if only it had been possible. Yet the irreducible fact, as she acknowledged in a lecture dedicated to the memory of Airey Neave in 1980, was that 'No democratic country can voluntarily abandon its responsibilities in a part of its territories against the will of the majority of the population there.'[2] Like every other Prime Minister since Gladstone, Mrs Thatcher found herself with an insoluble problem. But the longer she lived with it, the more she too eventually moved towards making an effort to resolve it.

Her first Secretary of State, Humphrey Atkins, was a natural conciliator whose approach was to try to bring the two communities together. He immediately started talks about talks which, with no political impetus behind them, swiftly foundered.

Meanwhile, the republicans greeted the new government with an upsurge of violence. In August 1979 the IRA killed eighteen soldiers at Warrenpoint in County Down and blew up Lord Mountbatten – the Queen's cousin and Prince Charles' godfather – with two other members of his family on holiday in the Republic. Mrs Thatcher responded with typical defiance by flying immediately to visit the troops at Crossmaglen near the border in South Armagh: ignoring official advice she insisted on being photographed wearing a combat jacket and beret of the Ulster Defence Regiment. She also went on a courageous forty-five-minute walkabout in central Belfast. This visible demonstration of her support made a powerful impact in Northern Ireland. She went again on Christmas Eve, when a member of the Parachute Regiment kissed her under the mistletoe. Thereafter she made a similar morale-boosting visit nearly every year.

She found no rapport with the Irish Taoiseach, Jack Lynch, when he came to Downing Street in September. But at the end of 1979 Lynch handed over to the flamboyant Charles Haughey, a different style of leader altogether, with whom she initially got on surprisingly well. Despite his reputation as an unreconstructed nationalist – Haughey came to office determined to find a solution to what he provocatively termed the 'failure' of Northern Ireland. He bounced into Downing Street in May 1980 with a terrific charm offensive and came out claiming to have inaugurated an era of 'new and closer cooperation' between Dublin and London based on increasing security cooperation on both sides of the border and an apparent willingness on the Irish side to consider almost anything – short of joining the Commonwealth – to woo the north to throw in its lot with a united Ireland. He even hinted at ending Ireland's cherished neutrality by joining NATO.[3] Mrs Thatcher was tempted, but remained cautious.

In December 1980 they met again in Dublin, under the shadow of the first republican hunger strike. Mrs Thatcher took with her an unprecedentedly high-powered team, including Lord Carrington and Geoffrey Howe as well as Atkins. Again Haughey exerted all his charm to create a sense of momentum, and succeeded in slipping past her guard an optimistic *communiqué* which recognised that

Britain, Northern Ireland and the Republic were 'inextricably linked' and called for joint studies of 'possible new institutional structures' giving 'special consideration of the totality of relationships within these islands'. Though he later denied the words, the spin was that the two leaders had achieved 'an historic breakthrough'.[4] Mrs Thatcher was plainly embarrassed. On her return to London she gave two television interviews repeating that Northern Ireland was an integral part of the UK and stating firmly that 'there is no possibility of confederation'. She subsequently blamed the Foreign Office for stitching her up; but her discomfort was due to the fact that she had let herself be carried along by Haughey's blarney.

In fact Haughey's boldness outraged his own hardliners in Fianna Fail as much as it did the Unionists. He quickly retreated back into old-style nationalism, and his relationship with Mrs Thatcher never recovered. But Unionist alarm was not so easily assuaged. Opinion polls in Britain showed a swell of public support for being rid of Northern Ireland altogether. Mrs Thatcher's strenuous denials that Ulster had anything to fear from the 'new institutional structures' discussed at Dublin did not reassure them that Carrington and the Foreign Office were not in the process of talking her round as they had done successfully in relation to Rhodesia.

At the same time tension and violence in the province were stretched to breaking point by republican prisoners in the Maze prison going on hunger strike in pursuit of their demand for 'political' status. The first hunger strike began in October 1980 when seven men started a 'fast to death'. They were later joined by thirty more, but this action was called off in December. The real propaganda battle was joined at the beginning of March 1981 when Bobby Sands began a second fast, followed at staggered intervals over the spring and summer by several others.

Mrs Thatcher's attitude to the hunger strikes was uncompromising. Just as she would not submit to terrorism, she vowed that she would never give in to moral blackmail by convicted murderers. She repudiated absolutely the suggestion that the offences for which the IRA prisoners were imprisoned were 'political'. 'There can be no political justification for murder or any other crime,' she told the Commons on 20 November 1980.[5]

Conditions in the H-Blocks were actually far better than in prisons on the mainland, with single cells, regularly cleaned when the prisoners messed them, and excellent facilities for exercise and study. The Government had implemented all the recommendations of the European Commission on Human Rights, and Mrs Thatcher was entitled to claim that the Maze was now 'one of the most liberal and humane regimes anywhere'.[6] The new demands made by Sands and his colleagues in the second hunger strike would have given the prisoners almost complete internal control of the prison – something no government could have conceded. All this was widely recognised. Yet the hunger strikers won enormous public sympathy in the nationalist community, both north and south, and the prospect of a succession of young men starving themselves to death disturbed liberal consciences in Britain too.

The strike gained a fortuitous boost just after it started with the death of Frank McGuire, the independent republican MP for Fermanagh and South Tyrone. Sinn Fein immediately nominated Sands as an 'anti-H-Block' candidate. On 9 April 1981 he was elected by a majority of 1,400 votes over the former Unionist leader Harry West, a result which resounded powerfully in the United States and around the world. Four weeks later Sands died: 'murdered' – so the republicans charged – in a British 'death camp'.[7] In vain did Mrs Thatcher insist that Sands had died by his own volition and was himself – 'let us not mince our words' – a convicted murderer.[8] The 'true martyrs', she declared, were the victims, not the perpetrators of terrorism.[9] On 21 May two more strikers died. Courageously visiting Northern Ireland one week later, Mrs Thatcher was determined to stick the responsibility where it belonged.

'It is a tragedy,' she declared in a speech at Stormont Castle, 'that young men should be persuaded, coerced or ordered to starve themselves to death in a futile cause. Neither I nor any of my colleagues want to see a single person die of violence in Northern Ireland – policeman, soldier, civilian or prisoner on hunger strike . . . The PIRA [provisional IRA] take a different view. It would seem that dead hunger strikers, who have extinguished their own lives, are of more use to PIRA than living members. Such is their calculated cynicism. This Government is not prepared to legitimise their cause by word or by deed.'[10]

She was brave and she was right. The IRA's claim to be treated as political prisoners or prisoners of war was entirely spurious. Had they confined their attacks to military targets they might have claimed to be an 'army' conducting a dirty but defensible guerrilla war against an occupying power, but by cold-bloodedly targeting random civilians, as they regularly did, in defiance of the accepted norms of warfare as formulated in the Geneva Convention, they forfeited any right to be treated as soldiers. To this day Sinn Fein accuses the British Government of 'criminalising the Irish struggle'.[11] But it was they themselves who did that by espousing methods that were purely criminal. No government could have conceded the legitimacy of terrorism.

Nevertheless, her ruthlessness was breathtaking. Over that summer – this was the same summer when Brixton and Toxteth were torn by riots and her personal popularity touched its lowest level – seven more martyrs went, one by one, to their slow deaths inside the Maze, while outside another seventy-three civilians, RUC men and soldiers were killed in the accompanying violence, before the IRA finally bowed to pressure from the Church and some of the remaining strikers' families and called a halt at the beginning of October. In a sense Mrs Thatcher had won. She had stood firm in the face of all the allegations of heartlessness and inflexibility that could be thrown at her, and it was the IRA which eventually blinked. This was perhaps the first time the world realised what she was made of. Her resolution certainly impressed the Americans. When six months later General Galtieri tried to tell Alexander Haig's envoy that 'that woman wouldn't dare' try to retake the Falklands, General Vernon Walters told him: 'Mr President, "that woman" has let a number of hunger strikers of her own basic ethnic origin starve themselves to death without flickering an eyelash. I wouldn't count on that if I were you.'[12]

But in another sense the gunmen had won a huge propaganda victory. Not only did Jim Prior, newly appointed Secretary of State in September, immediately concede many of the strikers' demands as soon as they ended their action, but the undeniable courage of the strikers, the depth and selflessness of their devotion to their cause, however cruelly they had pursued it when at large, made a deep impression both in Ireland and around the world. Within Ireland, Bobby Sands' face displayed on posters made him as potent a recruiting sergeant for the IRA as Lord Kitchener for the British army seventy years before; while from America a fresh stream of dollars flowed into its coffers, giving it the funds to buy more sophisticated weaponry and sufficient Semtex to supply the bombers for the next ten years. For most of the world, knowing little of the details of the situation, the deaths of the hunger strikers brutally dramatised the impression that Britain was indeed a colonial power occupying Northern Ireland against the will of its oppressed population. The IRA's manipulation of the hunger strikes was as cynical as Mrs Thatcher said; but it was highly successful. It even had an effect on Mrs Thatcher herself.

In the short run Prior's latest scheme for restoring a power-sharing Executive was stillborn. Meanwhile, continuing shootings and bombings in Northern Ireland were dramatically supplemented by several more spectacular atrocities in London. In October 1981 a nail bomb at Chelsea Barracks killed two passers-by and horrifically injured another forty, mainly soldiers. The same month a bomb disposal expert lost his life defusing a device in Oxford Street. In July 1982 bombs in Hyde Park and Regent's Park killed eight military bandsmen – the softest of military targets – along with a number of their horses; and in December 1983 a bomb outside Harrods killed five Christmas shoppers and wounded another ninety-one. Each time Mrs Thatcher dropped whatever she was doing to hurry to the scene and visit the survivors in hospital, solemnly renewing her pledge to defeat the bombers.

But in fact she did not attempt to confront the IRA head on. Military intelligence told her that it could not be done. There were allegations that the army operated an unofficial 'shoot to kill' policy in Northern Ireland, eliminating rather than attempting to arrest suspected terrorists; and continued nationalist protests against heavy-handed interrogation and the use of plastic bullets against demonstrators. But the number of troops deployed actually fell slightly over the decade, from 13,000 in 1979 to 11,500 in 1990. Rather, as she faced up to the prospect of unending carnage, Mrs Thatcher began to look seriously at the possibility of promoting a political solution.

The Anglo-Irish Agreement

Several factors pushed her in this direction. First was the return of Garret FitzGerald as Taoiseach in December 1982, soon followed by her own re-election in June 1983. FitzGerald recognised that Ireland could only be united by consent. He had spoken in 1981 of a 'republican crusade' to reform those aspects of the Irish constitution which antagonised Protestants, and specifically of scrapping clauses 2 and 3 which laid territorial claim to the Six Counties.[13] But instead of grand gestures, he was anxious to proceed incrementally by rebuilding the confidence of northern nationalists and diminishing support for Sinn Fein and the IRA. Though she found him at times tiresomely verbose and academic, Mrs Thatcher 'trusted and liked and perhaps even admired Garret FitzGerald', in the words of one of her junior ministers in the Northern Ireland Office. 'She thought he was straight and that he wasn't trying to pull a fast one on her.'[14] Geoffrey Howe has spoken of 'an extraordinary chemistry' between the two leaders which he compares to her relationship with Mikhail Gorbachev.[15]

Second, despite her Unionist sympathies Mrs Thatcher did actually come to a partial appreciation of the nationalist case. When she was persuaded that the IRA and their Sinn Fein apologists were not Irish infiltrators but predominantly British citizens, an indigenous northern movement poorly supported in the Republic, and that the legitimate nationalist party, the SDLP, won a lot of impeccably democratic votes – 18 per cent in 1983, compared with 13 per cent for Sinn Fein – she became convinced that the law-abiding Catholic community had somehow to be reconciled to the British state. She could never accept the idea of dual allegiance – she resented the anomalous right of the Irish to vote in British elections, and thought that they should be treated logically as foreign – but she came to see that the legacy of history gave the Republic an interest in the equitable government of the north.[16] In other words she recognised that there was not just a security problem in Northern Ireland, which might be solved by stronger policing, but a real political problem which required a political solution.

Third, she was influenced – as on Rhodesia, Hong Kong and other comparable issues – by the Foreign Office. The Anglo-Irish Agreement which eventually emerged in 1985 was the fruit of painstaking spadework by the Foreign Office and the Irish foreign ministry with minimal involvement of the Northern Ireland Office and behind the backs of the Unionists.

Most important of all, she was significantly influenced by American pressure. The Irish lobby in Washington, led by the Speaker of the House of Representatives, Tip O'Neill, and Senators Edward Kennedy and Daniel Moynihan, was very powerful – second only to the Jewish lobby – and very partisan, continually issuing violent denunciations of British colonial oppression and the alleged denial of human rights in Northern Ireland. Ronald Reagan, with his own Irish background, was susceptible to this line; while Mrs Thatcher, faced with hostile demonstrators every time she visited America, was uncomfortably aware that Northern Ireland strained her special relationship with the US. At the time of the hunger strikes in 1981 the President refused to become involved in Britain's internal affairs, though the White House delicately warned London that it was in danger of 'losing the media campaign here in the United States'.[17] But following his sentimental visit to the land of his fathers in the summer of 1984 – at a time when Washington horsetrading additionally required him to buy O'Neill's acquiescence in American aid to the Nicaraguan Contras – Reagan became increasingly anxious to encourage his favourite ally to be more constructive.

For all these reasons, then, from the moment she was re-elected in June 1983, Mrs Thatcher began to look more favourably on the idea of recognising an 'Irish dimension' in tackling the Ulster problem. The catalyst was provided by the New Ireland Forum, established in May 1983 by the new leader of the SDLP, John Hume, with the encouragement of Garret FitzGerald, to bring together all the constitutional nationalist parties on both sides of the border to seek a peaceful way forward to undercut Sinn Fein and the IRA. Mrs Thatcher was slow to grasp the opportunity it offered. At the same time she and FitzGerald – meeting in the margin of the European summit at Stuttgart in June 1983 – agreed to revive the Anglo-Irish Council, under whose aegis officials of both countries were able to meet without fanfare sixteen times between November 1983 and March 1985. Then, in September 1984, when Prior left the Government (more or less at his own wish), she signalled a fresh start by appointing Douglas Hurd to the Northern Ireland Office, telling him she wanted 'someone of intellect and toughness' there.[18]

Four weeks later the process was derailed when the IRA exploded a massive bomb in the Grand Hotel in Brighton, where the Prime Minister and most of the Conservative hierarchy were staying during the party conference. She was very lucky to survive unscathed. The bomb ripped out the whole central section of the hotel and badly damaged her bathroom. When it went off, just before three in the morning, she had just been putting the finishing touches to her speech for the next day with Ronnie Millar and John Gummer. As they left, Robin Butler came in with a last letter for her to sign before she got ready for bed. But for that, she would have been in the bathroom at the critical moment and, though she might not have been killed, she would certainly have suffered serious injury from flying glass. Her sitting room, however, and the bedroom where Denis was asleep, were undamaged. Her first thought was that it was a car bomb outside; her next was to make sure that Denis was all right. 'It touched me,' Butler recalled, 'because it was one of those moments where there could be no play-acting.'[19] As Denis quickly pulled on some trousers over his pyjamas, she crossed the corridor to the room where the secretaries had been typing the speech. Only now did the scale of what had happened become clear.

Amazingly, the lights had stayed on. Millar, who had been thrown against a wall by the explosion as he walked away from her room, described the scene. 'There were no cries for help, no sound at all, just dust, clouds of dust, followed by the occasional crunch of falling masonry from somewhere above. Otherwise silence. It was eerie.' Pausing only to gather up the scattered pages of the precious speech which had burst from his briefcase, he hobbled back the way he had come and found Mrs Thatcher in the secretaries' room 'sitting on an upright chair, very still. The girls were standing on chairs peering out of a side window, bubbling with excitement . . . At length she murmured, "I think that was an assassination attempt, don't you?"'[20] Geoffrey and Elspeth Howe, the Gummers, David Wolfson and others who had been sleeping on the same corridor gathered in various states of undress, speculating about the possibility of a second device. They still did not know whether anyone had been hurt. It was a quarter of an hour before firemen arrived to escort them to safety down the main staircase and out through the kitchens, to be driven to Brighton police station. There they were gradually joined by other members of the Cabinet. Mrs Thatcher was still wearing the evening gown she had worn to the Conservative Agents' Ball a few hours earlier. Following a quick consultation with Willie Whitelaw, Leon Brittan and John Gummer, she insisted that the final day of the conference must go on as planned. She refused to return to Downing Street but – with her security men anxious to hustle her away – changed into a blue suit and gave a calmly determined interview on camera to the BBC's John Cole. 'Even under the most appalling personal strain,' he noted, 'Margaret Thatcher . . . was a supreme political professional.'[21] She was then driven to Lewes Police College, where she snatched a couple of hours' sleep.

She woke to see the television pictures of Norman Tebbit being pulled agonisingly out of the rubble and hear the news that five people had been killed and Margaret Tebbit badly injured. She was shocked but still determined that the conference should go ahead. At 9.30 a.m. precisely Mrs Thatcher walked into the conference centre to emotional applause to give her speech, shorn of the normal party point-scoring but prefaced by a defiant denunciation of the bombers. The bomb, she said, was not only 'an inhuman and undiscriminating attempt to massacre innocent, unsuspecting men and women'. It was also 'an attempt to cripple Her Majesty's democratically elected Government':

> That is the scale of the outrage in which we have all shared, and the fact that we are gathered here now, shocked but composed and determined, is a sign not only that this attack has failed but that all attempts to destroy democracy by terrorism will fail.[22]

Mrs Thatcher's coolness, in the immediate aftermath of the attack and in the hours after it, won universal admiration. Her defiance was another Churchillian moment in her premiership which seemed to encapsulate both her own steely character and the British public's stoical refusal to submit to terrorism. 'We suffered a tragedy not one of us could have thought would happen in our country,' she told her constituents in Finchley the following weekend. 'And we picked ourselves up and sorted ourselves out as all good British people do, and I thought, let us stand together, for we are British.'[23] Her popularity rating temporarily recovered to near-Falklands levels. In public she appeared unruffled by the attack. But the psychological damage may have been greater than she showed. Carol immediately flew back from Korea and found her mother at Chequers on the Sunday morning 'calm but . . . still shaken'. For ever afterwards she felt that Margaret Tebbit's fate – confined to a wheelchair for life – had been intended for her.[24] Though the lights had not gone out at Brighton, she always carried a torch in her handbag thereafter. The assassination of Indira Gandhi two weeks after Brighton underlined how vulnerable she was. Denis bought her a watch and wrote her a rare note: 'Every minute is precious.'[25]

Brighton had a political effect as well. 'Though it killed only a few unfortunate people,' Alistair McAlpine suggested some years later, 'it had a profound effect on the Tory party.'[26] The annual conference, hitherto remarkably open, was henceforth ringed by tight security. Many felt that not only Norman Tebbit, but Mrs Thatcher too, was never the same again. She seemed to lose some of her self-confidence and her political touch.

In the short run Mrs Thatcher's enthusiasm for talks with Dublin was understandably dented. The next month Garret FitzGerald came to Chequers to try to make progress on the lines explored by the New Ireland Forum, whose report had been published in May. This set out three possible solutions: a united Ireland, a federal or confederal Ireland, or some form of joint sovereignty. FitzGerald recognised that the first two were out of the question; but he hoped to win Mrs Thatcher's support for some version of the third option. If she would agree to give Dublin a role in the government of Northern Ireland – he was happy to call it 'joint authority' rather than joint sovereignty if that helped – he thought he could win a referendum in the south to scrap clauses 2 and 3 of the Irish constitution which laid claim to the whole island. Mrs Thatcher, however, doubted whether he could deliver this, except in return for an unacceptable degree of southern interference in the north. She was not prepared to pay a high price to be rid of clauses which she did not think should have been in the Irish constitution in the first place. She only wanted to commit the Irish to closer security cooperation across the border, ideally by means of a security zone on the Irish side where British troops would be allowed to operate. Alternatively she was prepared to consider redrawing the border and repatriating nationalists to the Republic.[27] FitzGerald was disappointed, but still unprepared for the devastating post-summit press conference in which Mrs Thatcher dismissed all three of the Forum's options out of hand. She started positively, but right at the end, when asked about the Forum's proposals, she slipped her leash:

> I have made it quite clear . . . that a unified Ireland was one solution that is *out.* A second solution was confederation of two states. *That is out.* A third solution was joint authority. *That is out.*[28]

It was not so much what she said but the withering tone in which she said it. Her uncompromising triple repetition 'out . . . out . . . out' was taken as a gratuitous slap in the face for FitzGerald and seemed to slam the door on all the hopes that had been raised by their relationship. The Irish press next day was seething with fury, and London–Dublin relations seemed to be back to square one. But in fact this diplomatic disaster turned out to be the low point from which the 1985 Agreement emerged. Mrs Thatcher herself realised that she had gone too far and recognised that she would have to give some ground to repair the damage. Above all, her provocative language persuaded Reagan that it was time to get involved. Not only was the White House bombarded with the usual wild communications from Irish pressure groups like the Ancient Order of Hibernians;[29] but, more constructively, O'Neill, Kennedy, Moynihan and forty-two other Senators and Congressmen wrote to him that 'Mrs Thatcher's peremptory dismissal of the reasonable alternatives put forth by the Forum' had dashed the most hopeful opportunity for peace since the Sunningdale accord of 1973.[30] They urged Reagan to press her to reconsider when she came to Camp David in December; and he did exactly as they asked.

The record confirms that Northern Ireland was discussed over lunch. Mrs Thatcher assured the President that, 'despite reports to the contrary, she and Garret FitzGerald were on good terms and we are working toward making progress on this difficult question'. He replied that 'making progress is important, and observed that there is great Congressional interest in the matter', specifically mentioning O'Neill's request that he appeal to her to be 'reasonable and forthcoming'.[31] To the Speaker himself Reagan wrote that he had 'made a special effort to bring your letter to her personal attention . . . I also personally emphasised the need for progress in resolving the complex situation in Northern Ireland and the desirability for flexibility on the part of all the involved parties.'[32]

An appeal from this quarter was not one that Mrs Thatcher could ignore. In the negotiations that followed her first concern was still security; but she realised that in order to get this she must concede what were called 'confidence-building measures' on the ground – mainly addressing practical grievances over policing, prisons and the court system – to reconcile the northern Catholic population to the British state. She still ruled out the sort of comprehensive constitutional settlement FitzGerald had originally wanted. Yet she was now prepared to accept some sort of 'Irish dimension' in exchange for assurances that Dublin accepted Ulster's right to remain British so long as the majority wished it, without formally amending the Irish constitution. It still took months of tortuous negotiation between officials, and a crucial meeting between Mrs Thatcher and FitzGerald in the margin of the Milan EC summit in May, to overcome her doubts; she was still worried that they were going too far, too fast. But eventually she bit the bullet and agreed to accord Dublin not just consultation on Northern Irish matters, but guaranteed institutional input in the form of a commission to be jointly chaired by the Secretary of State for Northern Ireland and an Irish minister, with a permanent secretariat housed outside Belfast. This was the core of the Anglo-Irish Agreement finally signed by the two leaders at Hillsborough Castle on 15 November 1985.

It was a measure of how tightly the negotiations had been conducted within a narrow circle of insiders that Mrs Thatcher was unprepared for the fury of the Unionist response. While Dublin had kept John Hume closely informed throughout, the Unionist leaders – James Molyneaux of the official Unionist party and Ian Paisley of the still more uncompromising Democratic Unionists – were deliberately excluded. They were excluded, obviously, because everyone knew there would be no agreement if they were included. But then no one should have been surprised that they objected. In fact they had inevitably picked up hints of what was in the wind and had made their position very clear to the Prime Minister personally.

She could not say she had not been warned. But she had closed her mind to the Unionist reaction in the interest of being seen to make an effort. She was shaken by the violence of the Unionist rejection of the Agreement and the storm of denunciation which they levelled at her, which was 'worse than anyone had predicted to me'.[33] But if these reactions were predictable she was most upset by the resignation of her former PPS, Ian Gow, from his junior job in the Treasury, to which she had only just appointed him. Gow was her Unionist conscience, as well as her most devoted supporter: if he could not bring himself to accept the Agreement, she feared that perhaps she had gone too far.

It was true that there was a fundamental inequity in the way the Agreement was negotiated behind the back of one of the two communities that would have to make it work. Always hypersensitive to any hint of a sell-out, the Unionists were bound to try to wreck it, as they had wrecked other promising initiatives in the past. But this time their bluff was called. Claiming that the Agreement could not be implemented against the democratic will of the majority community, all fifteen Unionist MPs resigned their seats and stood again in by-elections, held simultaneously on 26 January. They made their point, slightly spoiled by the loss of one seat to the SDLP. But in the House of Commons they gained the support of only thirty Conservative MPs: the Government won an overwhelming all-party majority of 473–47. The fact that FitzGerald faced a much closer vote in the Dail, where Haughey – following Sinn Fein – charged his rival with abandoning the goal of Irish unity, helped convince British opinion that Ulster was crying wolf as usual. Polls in both Britain and the Republic showed strong public support: most people felt that an agreement denounced by the diehards on both sides was probably on the right lines.

As time passed Mrs Thatcher came to regret the Anglo-Irish Agreement. She was bitterly disappointed that it failed to deliver the sort of cross-border cooperation against terrorism that she had hoped for. In 1987 Haughey returned to power in the Republic, and though he did not tear up the Agreement he remained truculent and unhelpful. Far from reducing violence, the Agreement provoked the paramilitaries on both sides to increased activity. Over the next two years the IRA stepped up attacks on British military personnel in Northern Ireland itself (where twenty-one soldiers were killed in 1988 and twelve in 1989), on the mainland (ten bandsmen were killed in an attack on the Royal Marines School of Music in September 1989) and on the Continent. In March 1988 the SAS thwarted a planned attack on bandsmen in Gibraltar by shooting dead three suspects before they could plant their bomb. Mrs Thatcher had no time whatever for critics who charged that the security services were operating an illegal 'shoot to kill' policy. She would not admit that the security forces themselves ever overstepped the limit, but promised once again that 'this Government will never surrender to the IRA. *Never.*'[34]

By 1993 Lady Thatcher had concluded that the whole philosophy behind the 1985 Agreement had been a mistake. She did not suggest what an alternative approach might be: the implication was tougher security, even a 'military' solution. But she had not attempted that in office, nor were her successors tempted by it. The same logic that impelled her, against her instincts, drove them too; and the 1985 Agreement gradually bore fruit. It can now be seen as the start of a process which eventually led to the Good Friday Agreement of 1998 and the power-sharing government of 2007. First, it served a warning to the Unionists that their bluff could be called: London's repeated guarantee that Northern Ireland would remain a part of the United Kingdom, so long as the majority of its people wanted, did not give them a veto on how Britain chose to implement its sovereignty. Second, it did help to reconcile the nationalists to British rule, shored up the position of the SDLP and, most significantly, began to convert Sinn Fein and the IRA itself to the idea that more might be achieved by negotiation than by endless violence. At the same time the machinery of cooperation established in 1985 provided mechanisms to defuse problems between the two governments; and the Agreement did – as was perhaps Mrs Thatcher's primary motivation – convince the United States that Britain was genuinely trying to resolve the problem, which led to better American understanding of the Unionist position and encouraged increased international, particularly American, investment in Northern Ireland.[35] All these beneficial developments flowed from the 1985 Agreement. It was understandable, as the murder of soldiers continued unabated, that Mrs Thatcher should have felt disappointed; understandable too, when Ian Gow was killed in the drive of his own house in 1990, that she should feel guilty that perhaps she had betrayed Ulster after all. But she was wrong to disparage the Agreement. She was brave and far-sighted to have concluded it, and it should stand among her diplomatic achievements alongside the Zimbabwe and Hong Kong settlements. If lasting peace finally comes to Northern Ireland, she will have played her part in the process.

20

Elective Dictatorship

'She who must be obeyed'

THE idea that the Prime Minister is merely the first among equals has long been a fiction. The power of the Prime Minister *vis-à-vis* his Cabinet colleagues has increased steadily for a number of reasons to do with the growth of the state, the increasing complexity of the government machine and the escalating demands of the media. Both Harold Wilson and Ted Heath in their day were criticised for being excessively 'presidential'. Unquestionably, however, the concentration of power in the person of the Prime Minister grew still more pronounced under Mrs Thatcher, as a result partly of her longevity in the job, partly of her personality.

During her first term she was to some extent constrained by her own relative inexperience, by the presence in the Cabinet of several heavyweight colleagues profoundly sceptical of her approach and by the dire economic situation. Even so, by placing her few reliable allies in the key departments, she broadly got her way most of the time and managed to remove or neutralise most of her critics. By the middle of her second term she had achieved a Cabinet much more nearly of her own choice. Though the old wet/dry dichotomy had been resolved, there were still three identifiable groups around the table. Despite the loss of Parkinson, she now had a solid core of true believers: Lawson, Howe and (till 1986) Keith Joseph, reinforced by Norman Tebbit, Leon Brittan, Nicholas Ridley, David Young and (from 1986) John Moore. In the middle there was the ballast of steady loyalists who took their cue from Willie Whitelaw: Tom King, Norman Fowler, Nicholas Edwards, George Younger, Michael Jopling and (from 1986) Paul Channon, to whom may be added the senior, sometimes cantankerous but generally supportive figure of Lord Hailsham. Then, coming into the Cabinet between 1984 and 1986 was a new generation of ambitious former Heathites who were happy, after a period of probation, to turn their coats: Douglas Hurd, John MacGregor, Kenneth Baker, Kenneth Clarke and Malcolm Rifkind.

Mrs Thatcher's most ardent allies and supporters worried that she was storing up trouble for the future by promoting too many of these fair-weather friends from the left of the party, rather than true believers from the right. But she scarcely seemed to worry any more about the left–right balance, because by 1983 she thought the economic argument had been won. She was uneasily aware that the ablest candidates tended to be of the left; but she appointed them as individuals to serve her, not as representatives of wings of the party.

In addition there were three unclassifiable individuals who belonged to no group: Peter Walker, the last survivor of the old wets; John Biffen, one of Mrs Thatcher's original 'true believers', now increasingly out of sympathy with her approach; and Michael Heseltine, an ambitious loner already identified as the likeliest challenger if ever the Prime Minister's authority should slip.

This was the personnel: but the Cabinet as a body had a much diminished sense of corporate identity. It met only once a week, on Thursday, compared with twice a week under previous administrations, and rarely enjoyed anything approaching general discussion. Moreover, Mrs Thatcher created fewer Cabinet committees than her predecessors. Sometimes she would set up an *ad hoc* committee of three or four ministers, often chaired by herself, to deal with a subject that had arisen; more often than not she would simply get the relevant minister to prepare a paper for herself alone; she would then interrogate him on it personally with two or three of her advisers from the Cabinet Office or the Policy Unit, thus acting as 'judge and jury in her own cause' without reference to the Cabinet.[1] This might almost be a definition of presidential government. None of these practices originated with Mrs Thatcher: but she took them further than any of her predecessors. Cabinet was reduced to an occasion for reporting decisions, not the mechanism for taking them.

Dealing with the Prime Minister one to one was a testing business, too. She was still always formidably well briefed from a variety of different sources – the official departmental brief, another from the Policy Unit and often a third in her handbag whose origin the unfortunate minister never quite knew, which she would produce triumphantly to catch him out; she could always find a weak point even when he thought he had everything covered. At her best she had not only read everything but had, in Charles Powell's words, 'a phenomenal recall of detail'. She did not just absorb information but actively digested what she read.[2]

She made it her business to give ministers a hard time. 'I think sometimes a Prime Minister should be intimidating,' she once declared. 'There's not much point in being a weak floppy thing in the chair, is there?'[3] Much of the time this approach was highly effective, so long as she was dealing with a strong character who could handle her firmly, argue his corner and bring her round to a sensible policy if necessary. On this view her destructive style was simply a way of testing policies – and the minister who would have to defend them – against every possible line of attack before she agreed to them. But the longer she stayed in the job, the more she tended to have formed her view in advance and the less prepared she was to listen to other arguments. After 1983 she became increasingly irrational and harder to deal with. Ministers would look forward to a vigorous discussion, one recalled, only to find themselves subjected to a one-sided tirade: they became afraid to mention this or that subject for fear of setting her off on some hobby horse.[4] Her briefing was now not always so well focused.

Mrs Thatcher prided herself on liking a good argument: but she argued to *win* – or, as she told Nigel Lawson bluntly during their difference about the exchange rate in 1988: 'I must prevail.'[5] She never learned to concede even a small point with good grace. There was another revealing episode when John Major first caught her attention at a whips' dinner at Number Ten in July 1985, at a time when the Government was trailing in third place in the polls. Major took the chance to tell her frankly about backbench worries: she became angry and attacked him in unfairly personal terms. The story is that she was impressed by the way he stood up to her and promoted him soon afterwards. Denis actually congratulated him and told him, 'She enjoyed that.' But Major did not enjoy it at all: he thought she had behaved unforgivably when he was only doing his job, part of which was to tell her unpalatable truths.[6] Viewed positively, this was an example of Mrs Thatcher working constructively, testing subordinates through tough argument with no quarter given but no grudges taken. Alternatively, it was an example of sheer bad manners which nearly provoked Major to resign: a bullying type of man management which was not productive but steadily alienated her best supporters.

If a Prime Minister needs to be a good butcher, Mrs Thatcher passed that test with flying colours. As well as those she got rid of for ideological reasons, several ministers who in her view failed to deliver were sacked. The turnover of ministers was extraordinarily high. Over the whole eleven years from 1979 to 1990 no fewer than thirty-six Cabinet Ministers departed. Eight resigned as a result of a policy failure, personal or political embarrassment or disagreement with the Prime Minister. Thirteen retired more or less voluntarily either through ill health, to 'spend more time with the family' or to go into business. But fifteen were involuntarily removed. Though Mrs Thatcher always claimed to hate sacking people, the casualty rate was designed to keep the survivors on their toes. By the time Howe resigned in October 1990 the Prime Minister herself was the only survivor from her first Cabinet.

The decline of Parliament

Mrs Thatcher was never a great parliamentarian. Though she revered the institution of Parliament she never liked the place or had any feel for its ambience or traditions. Her sex was a factor here, partly because as a young female Member she could never be one of the boys – she had a young family to get back to, and she would never have been one for sitting around in bars anyway – but also because she found it difficult to make herself heard without shouting, particularly when she became leader and a target for Labour heckling. But even after she had established her command of the House, she never wooed or flattered it: her manner was always to hector and assert, and when she was interrupted or in difficulties she would simply shout louder.

She knew she was not a good speaker, was nervous before she had to make a speech and consequently overprepared. Her speeches tended to be loaded with statistics and came alive only when she was interrupted and had something to respond to. As a result she spoke as rarely as possible in debates – far less frequently than her predecessors. More often she made statements (after every European summit, for instance) and then answered questions, which was what she was good at. The twice-weekly circus of Prime Minister's Questions suited her down to the ground. She had no respect for Neil Kinnock and took great delight in exposing his inadequacy in front of her baying supporters. But it did not add much to the dignity or usefulness of Parliament.

The abuse of Prime Minister's Questions had started with Harold Wilson, but it became more systematic under Mrs Thatcher. Bernard Weatherill, who succeeded George Thomas as Speaker in 1983, tried to put a stop to these abuses, but Mrs Thatcher would not hear of

it. She did not see Question Time as an opportunity for accountability to the House, but as her chance to project her message to
the nation – via radio, which had started broadcasting the proceedings in 1978. Weatherill wanted to restore the former practice
whereby questions of detail were deflected to the departmental
minister concerned, leaving the Prime Minister to answer for broad
strategy.[7] But Mrs Thatcher liked open questions precisely because
they enabled her to display her command of detail: the fact that
she might be asked about anything gave her the excuse she needed
to keep tabs on every department. She regarded Prime Minister's
Questions as 'the real test of your authority in the House' and
prepared for them with obsessive thoroughness: she prided herself
that 'no head of government anywhere in the world has to face
this sort of regular pressure and many go to great lengths to avoid
it'.[8] This shallow gladiatorial bunfight, she thought, was what Parliament was all about.

With the security of huge majorities after 1983 Mrs Thatcher
had no need, most of the time, to bother about the House of
Commons. She certainly did not bother about the opposition. She
saw no need to cut any deals with the Labour party, and was suspicious of Leaders of the House like Pym and Biffen who were too
accommodating to them. Whenever any difficulty arose, her bible
was Erskine May, the parliamentary rule book.[9] She was more sensitive to her own back benches. During her first term, when her
position in the Cabinet was precarious and she still remembered
who it was that had made her leader, she was careful to keep her
lines of communication open. On several contentious issues in the
second term she backed down in the face of party anxiety. But
inevitably, as all Prime Ministers do, she became increasingly remote
from her backbench troops.

To compensate for the lack of serious opposition in the
Commons, the House of Lords became increasingly assertive, to the
extent that the Government suffered regular defeats in the Upper
House – more than 200 between 1979 and 1987. Though the Tories
always had a large nominal majority in the Lords, there was a
substantial component of crossbenchers – in addition to Labour and
Alliance peers – who did not take a party whip but considered
issues on their merits. Mostly these defeats were reversed when the
legislation came back to the Commons, but on some major issues
the Lords' will prevailed. Mrs Thatcher was not pleased by this show
of independence by the peers, particularly since she had appointed
so many of them. She considered reducing their powers, but
concluded that it was not worth the effort.[10]

The House of Lords, despite its indefensible composition, was a useful counterweight to the Government's unchecked hegemony in the Commons; but it could not redress the increasing irrelevance of Parliament in the political process. The 'elective dictatorship' of which Lord Hailsham had warned in 1975 – when he objected to a Labour Government elected by 39 per cent of the votes cast (and only 29 per cent of the electorate) ruling as though it commanded a majority mandate – was a far more pressing reality in the mid-1980s when Mrs Thatcher used her huge parliamentary majorities to push through her revolution on the basis of no more than 43 per cent support (or 31 per cent of the whole electorate). The size of her majorities, Labour's impotence and her own functional view of Parliament as a legislative sausage factory meant that opposition to her policies found expression elsewhere: in local government, in parts of the press, occasionally on the streets, but above all on television and radio. Again, this shift of the political debate from Westminster to the airwaves had been under way for some time, but it was markedly accelerated in the Thatcher years, measured by the steep decline in serious press reporting of Parliament: insofar as debates were reported at all, it was in the form of satirical sketches. The journalists would say that the debates were no longer worth reporting, and they might be right; the process was self-fulfilling. But all that most of the public ever heard of Parliament was the crude knockabout of Prime Minister's Questions.

The obvious response to the usurpation of Parliament by television was to televise Parliament. But Mrs Thatcher strongly opposed letting cameras into the chamber, partly because she believed that they would damage the reputation of the House by showing in full colour the rowdiness which was already offending radio listeners, and change its character by encouraging publicity seekers to play to the gallery; but partly also because she thought it would do her personally no good. Gordon Reece and Bernard Ingham both tried to persuade her that she would only gain from being seen trouncing Kinnock at the dispatch box twice a week; but she was afraid she would come over as strident (as well as being seen wearing glasses to read her brief) and feared that the BBC would edit the exchanges to her disadvantage. When the issue came to a vote in late 1985 – at the height of her vendetta with the BBC – she did not speak publicly against it, but Tory MPs waited to see which way she was voting before following her into the 'No' lobby. The proposal was defeated by twelve votes. Two years later, in February 1988, she spoke and lobbied openly against the cameras: a majority of Tories still followed her line, but this time a six-month experiment was agreed by a majority of fifty-four.[11] The televising finally started in November 1989. Most observers thought the effect was, as Reece had anticipated, to underline the Prime Minister's dominance. But the cameras caught their first moment of real parliamentary drama when they were able to broadcast Geoffrey Howe's devastating resignation speech in November 1990. After that there was no going back – though still very little is ever shown on terrestrial channels apart from Question Time.

The power of patronage

For most of its life the Thatcher Government was not popular. Between General Elections it usually trailed in the polls – often in third place – and even its two landslide election victories were gained with well under half the votes cast. Yet except for a brief period in the spring of 1986, after the Westland crisis and the bombing of Libya, few commentators anticipated anything other than a third Tory victory in 1987 and probably a fourth after that. Labour under Neil Kinnock was slowly rowing back from the extremism of the early 1980s, becoming a better organised and credible opposition; yet such was Mrs Thatcher's dominance that it took an extraordinary leap of faith to imagine anyone else forming the next government. There was a despairing fatalism on the left, and a corresponding complacency on the right, that the political pendulum had been halted and the Tories would be in power for ever. The restraints traditionally imposed by the expectation of a periodic alternation of power between the main parties consequently exerted a diminishing force. As a result, from the mid-1980s, the Government began to give off an unmistakable odour of corruption arising from overconfidence, constitutional corner-cutting and mounting hubris.

First, Mrs Thatcher had no scruples about using the Prime Minister's power of patronage in a frankly partisan manner to reward her supporters. She revived the award of honours for political services – abandoned by Harold Wilson – and gave them in abundance: peerages to discarded ministers and an average of four or five knighthoods a year to long-serving MPs. She was even more blatant in honouring the proprietors and editors of loyal newspapers and other friendly journalists. And then there was a steady flow of honours to businessmen and industrialists in recognition of donations to Tory party funds, a well-documented correlation unequalled since the time of Lloyd George.

One of Mrs Thatcher's most provocative announcements on taking office was to declare her intention of reviving hereditary honours, which had been in abeyance since Macmillan's invention of life peerages in 1960. Having asserted the principle, however, she did nothing about it for four years, and then undercut the point by awarding them only to those – Willie Whitelaw and George Thomas – with no heir to inherit. She also wanted to give a hereditary title – the only sort he would accept – to Enoch Powell (who also had only daughters), but was dissuaded by Whitelaw. The following year Macmillan, at the age of ninety, belatedly accepted the earldom traditionally due to former Prime Ministers. But that was the extent of the revival until 1992 when John Major was persuaded, allegedly at Mrs Thatcher's personal request, to award a baronetcy to Denis. Though she herself took only a life peerage in 1992, this bizarre resurrection ensured that on Denis's death in June 2003 Mark inherited his title.

A second area where Mrs Thatcher was blatantly partisan was in making appointments to public bodies. From the chairmanship of nationalised industries to the dozens of obscure quangos, boards and advisory bodies of which British public life is made up, she took a close interest in getting into place men (and occasionally women) who were, in the phrase indelibly associated with her premiership, 'one of us' – that is, if not actually paid-up Conservatives, at least sympathetic to her purpose. She had equally little compunction about getting rid of people she found unhelpful, like the Governor of the Bank of England, following differences over monetary policy in 1980–81. His replacement was a former Tory leader of Kent County Council and chairman of the National Westminster Bank, with no central banking experience at all, but a sound monetarist.

Perhaps the Governor of the Bank needed to be a supporter of the Government's central policy. But Mrs Thatcher's interest in public appointments extended far beyond economic matters into the area of culture and the arts. Potential bishops and potential governors of the BBC were blackballed on frankly political grounds, and even nominations for trustees of national galleries were closely scrutinised and sometimes rejected on a hint from Downing Street. Right across the board Mrs Thatcher used the power of patronage systematically to assert her hegemony in every corner of national life.

A change of government in 1997 made very little difference. Tony Blair inherited the new conventions of Mrs Thatcher's patronage state and simply exploited them more ruthlessly than even she had dared, for the benefit of New Labour. Thus Thatcherite hubris in the 1980s met the nemesis it deserved in the late 1990s. But the civilised tradition of bipartisanship – hitherto one of the unsung decencies of British life – had been destroyed for ever.

Rival queens

One question that continued to fascinate the public about the phenomenon of a woman Prime Minister was how she got on with the Queen. The answer is that their relations were punctiliously correct, but there was little love lost on either side. As two women of very similar age – Mrs Thatcher was six months older – occupying parallel positions at the top of the social pyramid, one the head of government, the other head of state, they were bound to be in some sense rivals. Mrs Thatcher's attitude to the Queen was ambivalent. On the one hand she had an almost mystical reverence for the institution of the monarchy: she always made sure that Christmas dinner was finished in time for everyone to sit down solemnly to watch the Queen's broadcast. Yet at the same time she was trying to modernise the country and sweep away many of the values and practices which the monarchy perpetuated. She and Elizabeth had very little personally in common – though Denis and Prince Philip got on well. The Queen was said to dread her weekly audience with her Prime Minister because Mrs Thatcher was so stiff and formal. It was not, as some suggested, that Mrs Thatcher was too grand, rather that she displayed an exaggerated reverence. 'Nobody would curtsey lower,' one courtier confided;[12] and the Queen wondered 'Why does she always sit on the edge of her seat?'[13]

If the Queen dreaded Mrs Thatcher coming to the Palace, however, Mrs Thatcher loathed having to go once a year to Balmoral. She had no interest in horses, dogs or country sports and regarded the outdoor life – long walks and picnics in all weathers – which the Royal Family enjoyed on holiday, as 'purgatory'.[14] Though she frequently told interviewers that she loved nothing better than a country walk, she never had any suitable shoes and had to be forced into borrowed Hush Puppies or green wellingtons.[15] She could not wait to get away and on the last morning was up at six as usual, with her thank-you letter written, anxious to be off as soon as Denis was ready. The Queen was almost certainly equally glad to see her go.

More seriously, while Mrs Thatcher regarded having to attend the Queen as a waste of time – by contrast with every other engagement in her day, she would read the agenda only in the car on the way to the Palace – the Queen had real grounds for resenting Mrs Thatcher. First, she feared that the Government's policies were wilfully exacerbating social divisions: she worried about high unemployment and was alarmed by the 1981 riots and the violence of the miners' strike. Second, she was upset by Mrs Thatcher's ill-concealed dislike of her beloved Commonwealth: she was disturbed by the whole South African sanctions controversy which regularly pitted Britain against all the other members, with embarrassing calls for Britain to be expelled. At the Commonwealth heads of government conference every other year, from Lusaka in 1979 onwards, the Queen worked hard to make herself the focus of unity while Mrs Thatcher often seemed bent on splitting the organisation apart.

The Queen also worried about defence cuts affecting the survival of cherished regiments with which she or other members of her family had connections: while Mrs Thatcher was concerned solely with military capability, Her Majesty was more interested in cap badges and mascots. She worried about Mrs Thatcher's hostility to the Church of England, of which she was the Temporal Head, and about the effect of constant cost-cutting on other voluntary organisations of which she was patron. Sometimes Mrs Thatcher was obliged to defer to her. But she refused to allow the Queen to visit the European Parliament or – following her own triumphant visit – the Soviet Union. More than by any of these minor tussles, however, the Queen could not fail to be irritated by Mrs Thatcher's increasingly regal style.

The impression that Mrs Thatcher was developing monarchical pretensions first gained currency when she took the salute at the forces' victory parade through the City of London at the end of the Falklands war. Then the following January her visit to the islands was unmistakably a royal progress to accept the thanks and adoration of the population. Conor Cruise O'Brien wrote in the *Observer* that she was developing a parallel monarchy, becoming 'a new style elective executive monarch, as distinct from the recessive ceremonial one.'[16]

From now on the trend only increased. Her foreign tours were more and more like the Queen's, with all the trappings of crowds and walkabouts, little girls presenting bouquets, guards of honour and nineteen-gun salutes. As the Queen grew older and less glamorous – royal glamour being increasingly concentrated on the young Princess of Wales – Mrs Thatcher became more powerful and wreathed in myth, the very embodiment of Britannia. To the crowds who came out to see her, she far more than the Queen now embodied Britain.

She was also quicker off the mark than the Palace in visiting the scene of disasters. Whenever there was an accident or terrorist attack Mrs Thatcher always dropped everything to go at once – as her schedule allowed her to do: when the IRA bombed Harrods at Christmas 1983, for instance, she and Denis were attending a carol service at the Festival Hall, but immediately left at the interval. By contrast, Downing Street briefed, 'the Royal Family couldn't be relied on to go' at all, and certainly not for several days.[17]

Mrs Thatcher was embarrassed by reports of differences with the Palace and did her best to play them down. Strongly though she supported the monarchy, however, both with loyal words and with public money, the indirect effect of Thatcherism during the 1980s was not kind to the Royal Family. On the one hand, the management of the royal finances – like those of other national institutions – came under closer scrutiny as the old deference waned: palaces, yachts, trains and retainers once taken for granted now had to be justified on a value-for-money basis. On the other, the media – led by the increasingly uninhibited Murdoch press – threw off all restraint in prying into the private lives and marriages of the younger members of the family. The 1990s was a difficult decade for the House of Windsor.

As Prime Minister, Mrs Thatcher drew skilfully on a range of feminine roles – housewife, mother, nurse, headmistress – to project her message; but the longer she went on, the more she grew into the role of queen, which she could play so much better than the frumpy occupant of Buckingham Palace. The Falklands transformed the Iron Lady almost overnight into Boadicea, the warrior queen who had fought the Romans. Increasingly she came to identify with Elizabeth I – Gloriana – who had presided over England's first great period of mercantile expansion and national assertion, surrounded by her court of flatterers and buccaneers, all eager to do her bidding and dependent on her favour. She encouraged the comparison by her susceptibility to handsome protégés like Cecil Parkinson, flatterers like Woodrow Wyatt, favourite businessmen like Lord King; and even adopted the chilling phrase, when one of her ministers displeased her, 'Shall we withdraw our love?'[18] In her memoirs she echoed Elizabeth by writing that 'I did not believe I had to open windows into men's souls.'[19] And it was surely no accident that at the crisis of her premiership in November 1990 she appeared at the Lord Mayor's Banquet in the City wearing a defiantly regal, high-collared Elizabethan dress, looking like Judi Dench in *Shakespeare in Love*.

Above all she increasingly used the royal plural. In truth the widespread mockery she attracted for this habit is a bit unfair. In her early years she was criticised for the opposite habit of talking about the Government in the first person singular. 'Unemployment is the most difficult problem that I face,' she told Sue Lawley in 1981. 'I do feel deeply concerned when I have people who want jobs and can't get them. But I know that I can't conjure them out of thin air.'[20] She even talked possessively about 'my coal mines'[21] and 'my housing estates'.[22] This language inevitably provoked allegations of personal rule. Nevertheless, when she was later criticised for using the plural she protested that she did so because she was 'not an "I" person':

> I am not an 'I did this in my Government', 'I did that', 'I did the other' person. I have never been an 'I' person, so I talk about 'we' – the Government . . . It is not I who do things, it is we, the Government.[23]

Sometimes, when she wanted to stress collective responsibility, this was true. At other times, however, she distanced herself from the Government and used the first person singular to give the impression that its failings had nothing to do with her. In fact she veered wildly between singular and plural, sometimes in the same sentence, as in her assurance to Sue Lawley that she cared about unemployment: 'I wouldn't be human if we didn't.'[24] Her every waking thought was so taken up with the business of governing that she really made no distinction between herself as an individual and herself as leader of the Government, or more specifically the leader of the travelling circus which accompanied her.

Increasingly, however, she began to use the plural when she quite unambiguously meant herself alone. 'We are in the fortunate position in Britain,' she told an interviewer on her way to Moscow in 1987, 'of being, as it were, the senior person in power.'[25] 'When I first walked through that door,' she declared in January 1988, 'I little thought that we would become the longest serving Prime Minister of this century.'[26] And most famously, the following year, again on the steps of Downing Street: 'We have become a grandmother.'[27]

The cult of Maggie

By the middle of the decade Mrs Thatcher had become an institution, a seemingly permanent part of the national landscape, around whom there grew up a personality cult unlike anything seen in

Britain before. For a start she gave her name to an '-ism' as no previous Prime Minister had done: a relatively clear, if sometimes contradictory body of ideas, attitudes and values to which her personality gave unusual coherence. She exerted a hold on the national imagination that went far beyond politics. Old and young alike could not imagine life without her. When elderly patients were asked by psychiatrists to name the Prime Minister, it was said that for the first time in forty years they always got it right. Meanwhile, small boys were reported wistfully asking their fathers: 'Dad, can a man be Prime Minister?' To her admirers she was 'Maggie', to her opponents simply 'Thatcher' – but both held her responsible for everything, good or bad, that happened in what a flood of books inevitably called the Thatcher decade: half the population believed that she was single-handedly saving the country, the other half that she was single-handedly wrecking it.

Love her or hate her, she was inescapable, like a force of nature. Alternative nicknames proliferated, invented by Julian Critchley, Denis Healey and others: 'The Great She-Elephant', 'Attila the Hen', 'Catherine the Great of Finchley', 'the Maggietollah' (by analogy with Iran's Islamic revolutionary dictator, Ayatollah Khomeini), or just 'That Woman'. But all were too contrived and none replaced the simple 'Maggie' which in itself contained all the different personas she had adopted. There is a wider range of resonant role models available to a woman politician than to a man, and Mrs Thatcher played them all, from housewife and mother (even, to the troops in the Falklands, a pin-up), through a variety of female authority figures to domestic battleaxe. When her enemies tried to turn these images against her, they only enhanced her aura of power. The domestic battleaxe bullying feebler men fitted into a well-loved British comic tradition immortalised in music hall and seaside postcards; while the image of the cruel queen – Rider Haggard's chilling *She* ('She Who Must be Obeyed') or Kali ('the grim Indian goddess of destruction') – merely lent her a semi-mythical capacity to inspire fear that is not available to a male Prime Minister. Male tyrants are simply loathed, but a powerful woman attracts fascinated admiration from both sexes.

The media were equally fascinated by the feminine side of her personality: they were always on the lookout for tears or other signs of weakness which might reveal 'the woman within'. She famously wept twice on television, once when Mark was lost in the desert in 1981, and again in 1985 when telling Miriam Stoppard about her father's deposition from Grantham council. Yet to the despair of feminists, Britain's first female Prime Minister did nothing to feminise the male world of politics. She never had any truck with equal opportunities or political correctness. 'What has women's lib ever done for me?' she once demanded.[28] The virtue she admired above all others and claimed for herself was strength. 'If you want someone weak,' she once told Jimmy Young, 'you don't want me. There are plenty of others to choose from.'[29]

Yet at the same time she was very feminine, and derived much of her power from exploiting her femininity. 'I like being made a fuss of by a lot of chaps,' she once remarked.[30] Whether by calculation or instinct, she was skilful at wrong-footing men who did not know how to argue with a woman as bluntly as they would have with another man. They never knew whether she was going to mother them, flirt with them or hit them over the head – metaphorically – with her handbag. Her handbag (that most feminine appendage, carried by practically every woman from the Queen downwards) became an important component of her image. Other Prime Ministers have had their identifying props, like Churchill's cigar or Wilson's pipe, but Mrs Thatcher's handbag became much more than that. It was the physical symbol of her authority, like a royal mace or sceptre, which announced her presence. It was also a miraculous receptacle, like Mary Poppins' portmanteau, from which she could seemingly produce at will the killer quotation or statistic to win an argument. And above all it became an active verb, so that when she belaboured some offending minister she was said to 'handbag' him. Nothing more potently embodied a woman's dominance over a Cabinet of men.

She enjoyed denigrating men while asserting the superiority of women. Yet she found very few others of her own sex worthy of promotion either within government or the wider public service. Janet Young, the only other woman to sit briefly in her Cabinet, was sharply disparaged in her memoirs as not up to the job.[31] Lady Young in turn commented that Mrs Thatcher simply did not like women.[32] She claimed special virtue for women, but liked being the only one. Increasingly as she got older she did not encourage other women to follow the example of her own career, but told them that their special role was as home-makers and mothers, bringing up the family. She supported the right of women to be lawyers, doctors, engineers, scientists or politicians, she told the Conservative Women's Conference in 1988. How could she not? But, she went on, 'many women wish to devote themselves mainly to raising a family and running a home. And we should have that choice too.'[33]

She recognised that clothes were of huge importance to a woman politician, an asset if chosen with care, a liability if worn badly. 'She was convinced,' Nigel Lawson wrote, 'that her authority . . . would be diminished if she were not impeccably turned out at all times. She was probably right.'[34] From about 1985, however, as her power grew, so her style of dressing became more commanding. Charles Powell's wife Carla was credited with getting her into what was called 'power-dressing', following the styles set by the matriarchs of the American TV series *Dynasty* and *Dallas*: stronger, simpler cuts, darker colours and big shoulders. It was before her 1987 visit to Moscow that she discovered Aquascutum: thereafter she got most of her clothes from there, though she was still said to use a 'little lady' in Battersea who had been making clothes for her since the 1970s.[35]

By now she was extraordinarily dominant on television. An academic study of her technique showed that she intimidated even the most experienced interviewers by turning the tables and attacking them, refusing to be interrupted, while accusing them of interrupting her. She put them on the defensive by using their Christian names. 'She tends to personalise issues and take questions as accusations,' Donald McCormick commented. For instance, he once dared to suggest that she was inflexible. 'Inflexible?' she retorted. 'I am inflexible in defence of democracy, in defence of freedom, in defence of law and order and so should you be, so should the BBC be and so should everyone else be.'[36]

And yet she hated television. She rehearsed intensively for major interviews, and when she got to the studio she had to be handled very carefully. 'She needs settling like a horse, highly spirited', Gordon Reece told Woodrow Wyatt. 'She gets nervous if people surround and crowd her. She must be kept calm.'[37] As she once told Ronnie Millar, 'I'm not a performer, dear.'[38] Like everything else in her life, she only taught herself to dominate by willpower and hard work.

Above all she still needed very little sleep. Four hours a night was perhaps an exaggeration, but she could certainly go for several days on that little, and never slept for more than five or six. She sometimes caught up a bit at Chequers at weekends, but during the week she rarely went to bed before two o'clock, and was up again at six. She dominated the Government by sheer physical stamina.

Her health was generally robust, though she did suffer from colds and a number of minor ailments which never laid her low for long. She never put on weight, although she took no exercise; but she took a number of vitamin pills and was widely believed to have some form of hormone replacement therapy to keep her young. She had three minor operations while she was Prime Minister: one for varicose veins in 1982, the second for a detached retina in 1983; and the third to correct a contraction of the fingers of her right hand, Dupuytren's contracture (also known as 'coachman's grip'), in 1986. She had a painful tooth abscess during the June 1987 election, and generally her teeth gave her increasing trouble. She also – inevitably in her sixties – needed reading glasses, but did not like to be seen wearing them in public, so her briefs for Prime Minister's Questions and speech scripts had to be printed in large type. She would never admit to any hint of weakness. She was particularly annoyed, therefore, when she nearly fainted from the heat during a diplomatic reception at Buckingham Palace in November 1987, giving rise to speculation that she was finally cracking up and a spate of articles offering pseudo-medical advice that she should slow down.[39] She was sensitive to any suggestion that she was beginning to show her age, and tried to stop the party conference in 1989 serenading her sixty-fourth birthday by singing 'Happy Birthday to You'.

She had no real friends, because she had never left time in her life for friendship. In a sense Denis was her best friend. They were much closer in Downing Street than they had been in the earlier part of their marriage. He had friends, certainly, but they had few as a couple, because they had never operated as a couple. They never entertained privately in Downing Street; but they did very occasionally go out to dinner quietly with other trusted couples where she could briefly and genuinely relax.

Janet Young once wished Mrs Thatcher a happy Christmas and was appalled when she replied that she was having a houseful of colleagues and advisers to Chequers. Of course she had the family too (Mark and Carol if they were around, and at least once her sister Muriel and her husband) but they were always outnumbered by political friends. Christmas Day was rigidly structured around church in the morning, a traditional lunch which ended punctually in time for the Queen's broadcast at 3.00 p.m., then a short walk followed later by a cold buffet supper, often joined by other political guests who lived nearby. On Boxing Day there would be another lunch for favoured friends and allies – people like Rupert Murdoch, the American Ambassador, Lord King and Marmaduke Hussey. On these occasions Mrs Thatcher was the perfect hostess, not overtly political but tirelessly devoted to ensuring that everyone had everything they wanted. At the same time, though the atmosphere was carefully relaxed, these lunches like everything else in her life were unmistakably political gatherings – a symbolic summoning of key supporters at the turn of the year.

The sad truth is that Mrs Thatcher, behind the hugely successful front which enabled her to dominate her generation, was a driven, insecure and rather lonely woman who lived for her work and would be lost when her astonishing career ended, as one day it eventually must. In her early days her phenomenal energy, her single-mindedness, her inability to relax, to admit any weakness or trust anyone to do anything better than she could do it herself, were all strengths and part of the reason for her success; but the longer she went on, the more these strengths turned to weaknesses – a loss of perspective, growing self-righteousness, a tendency to believe her own myth, an inability to delegate or trust her colleagues at all, so that instead of leading a team and preparing for an eventual handover to a successor, the Government became ever more centred on herself. There were bound to be tears in the end, and there were.

21

Stumble and Recovery

Helicopters, leaks and lies

THE episode that threw the sharpest light on Mrs Thatcher's conduct of government was the crisis over the future of Westland helicopters which erupted at the beginning of 1986. More than any other incident in her whole premiership, Westland exposed to public gaze the reality of her relationship with her colleagues and the far greater trust she placed in unelected officials in her private office. The issue was relatively trivial in itself; but the questions raised went to the heart of constitutional government. As a result, the Westland affair came closer than anything else – before the combination of Europe and the poll tax arose in 1990 – to bringing her rule to an untimely end.

It arose from the refusal of one ambitious and independent-minded minister to be bullied. Michael Heseltine had always been the cuckoo in Mrs Thatcher's nest. Neither a monetarist nor a wet, he was an energetic and unapologetic corporatist very much in the manner of Ted Heath: his political hero was David Lloyd George. Mrs Thatcher was forced to recognise him as an effective minister, both at the Department of the Environment and later at Defence, where he deployed the case against unilateral nuclear disarmament with conviction and flair. But she distrusted both his interventionist instincts and his ambition, and doubted his grasp of detail. Likewise she resented his exploitation of the sort of photo-opportunity – looking over the Berlin Wall or wearing a flak jacket to visit Greenham Common – that she regarded as her own preserve. In the MoD he was dealing with matters in which she took a particularly close interest. It was inevitable that the two biggest egos in the Cabinet would clash on this territory.

Among other things they differed over nuclear policy, and specifically the British response to President Reagan's Strategic Defense Initiative. In her memoirs Lady Thatcher made no apology for keeping this question under 'tight personal control' since in her view 'neither the Foreign Office nor the Ministry of Defence took SDI sufficiently seriously'.[1] Though she had her own doubts about the programme, she was adamant that Britain must be seen to back it. Heseltine was much less enthusiastic and resented her taking this sort of major defence decision unilaterally without reference to himself as the responsible minister.

These tensions formed the background to the Westland affair. Lady Thatcher subsequently blamed the whole crisis on one man's overweening ambition and egotistical refusal to accept the discipline of collective responsibility.[2] Certainly Heseltine was riding for a fall. Unquestionably he got the relatively minor issue of the future of a small helicopter manufacturer out of perspective. He elevated the question of whether Westland should join up with the American firm Sikorsky or a somewhat shadowy consortium of European arms manufacturers (including British Aerospace and GEC) into a major issue of principle reflecting an American or European orientation in foreign policy, and by extension a trial of strength between himself and the Prime Minister. When she threw the Government's weight behind the American option – which was also the Westland board's preference – he blatantly flouted her authority by continuing to lobby energetically for the European alternative. First he induced the European national armaments directors to declare that in future they would buy only European-made helicopters. Then he planted correspondence in the press still pushing the European case after Leon Brittan, the new Trade and Industry Secretary, had announced the Government's support for Westland's decision in favour of Sikorsky.

This was outrageous behaviour by a Cabinet minister, defying the decision of his own government. Heseltine's justification was that he had been denied the opportunity to press the European option within the Government, so was forced to take the fight outside. In particular he accused the Prime Minister – after his resignation – of having unilaterally cancelled a meeting of the Cabinet's Economic Affairs Committee arranged for 13 December 1985 because, at a previous meeting four days earlier, he had won too much support. On the contrary, Mrs Thatcher insisted, there was no need for a second meeting since the majority view was quite clear at the first: the Government had made its decision and Heseltine alone refused to accept it.

Most testimony suggests that by this time she was right. Initially Heseltine had gained a good deal of support. Always a cat who walked by himself, however, Heseltine played his hand extremely badly. When it came to a stand-up fight with the Prime Minister, the relative merits of rival helicopter manufacturers were forgotten: his potential allies slipped back to the Prime Minister. Nevertheless he did have grounds for grievance. Mrs Thatcher was by no means as neutral as she pretended. Not only did she clearly favour the American option, but she was just as determined to defeat Heseltine as he was to defeat her. Colleagues like Willie Whitelaw believed as a matter of principle that a senior minister with a strongly held conviction in his own area of responsibility was entitled to take his case to Cabinet.[3] But Westland never went to Cabinet. The one time Heseltine tried to force it on to the agenda, on 12 December, he was peremptorily ruled out of order.

The trouble was that Mrs Thatcher was prepared neither to accommodate Heseltine by giving him the chance to put his case in full Cabinet, nor to confront him directly and force him to back down. By mid-December it was plain that he did not accept the Government's decision. With hindsight, she should have sacked him, or required his resignation, then. But he was too powerful: she did not dare. He would not have gone quietly, like the despised wets: on the back benches he would have become a much more dangerous rallying point for her critics than Pym. She chose instead to try to undermine him by the familiar method of press manipulation and inspired leaking deployed over the past six years against several less formidable colleagues. This time she – or someone on her behalf – carelessly laid a charge which blew up in her own face, and came closer than anything between the Falklands invasion and the poll tax to bringing her down.

The mistake was to leak a Law Officer's letter. There is a strict convention, jealously guarded by the Law Officers themselves, that legal advice is confidential. Yet Mrs Thatcher, who had once been a lawyer and was generally a stickler for correct procedure – however she might bend the spirit of it – and Brittan, a QC who should certainly have known his brother lawyers' sensitivity, chose to use a letter commissioned from the Solicitor-General, Sir Patrick Mayhew, without his permission, to discredit Heseltine. They had ample provocation. Over Christmas and the New Year Heseltine continued his efforts to keep the European option in play. On 3 January 1986 he gave *The Times* an exchange of letters with the merchant bankers acting for the European consortium in which he warned that Westland risked losing future European orders if it accepted the American rescue – explicitly contradicting assurances which Mrs Thatcher had given Sir John Cuckney a few days earlier. Mrs Thatcher understandably determined that this must be repudiated. Instead of doing so directly, however, she persuaded Mayhew to write to Heseltine querying the basis for his warning, and then arranged for a damaging simplification of his letter to be made public.

Mrs Thatcher subsequently admitted that it was she who initiated Mayhew's letter. 'I therefore, through my office, asked him to consider writing to the Defence Secretary to draw that opinion to his attention.'[4] In fact, she thought Mayhew's effort pretty feeble. He did no more than suggest, tentatively, that on the evidence he cited Heseltine might be overstating his case.[5] He asked for clarification – which Heseltine promptly provided (and Mayhew accepted).[6] But Mayhew's letter did contain the words 'material inaccuracies'; and it was these two words, torn out of context, which were leaked to the Press Association with a crude spin which was reflected in the next day's headlines. 'YOU LIAR' screamed the *Sun*; while *The Times* paraphrased the same message more sedately as 'Heseltine Told by Law Chief: Stick to the Facts'.[7] Mrs Thatcher afterwards maintained that, while she regretted the way it was done, 'it was vital to have accurate information in the public domain'.[8] 'It was a matter of duty that it should be known publicly that there were thought to be material inaccuracies' in Heseltine's letter.[9] But there was no contrary information in Mayhew's letter. The only possible purpose of leaking it was to discredit Heseltine and maybe provoke him to resign. The difference between this and earlier operations to discredit failing or dissenting ministers was that Mayhew – and his senior, the Attorney-General, Sir Michael Havers – were outraged by the use made of his letter and demanded an inquiry to discover the culprit.

The leaked letter by itself did not provoke Heseltine to resign. Of course when he dramatically walked out of the Cabinet two days later there was speculation that his action was premeditated, especially since he was able within a few hours to publish a 2,500-word statement detailing his complaints about Mrs Thatcher's style of government. But it was no secret at Westminster that he had been close to resignation for months; so it is not surprising that he should already have roughed out his grievances, to be polished up when the moment arose. His closest associates in the Cabinet were convinced that he did not mean to resign that day. The more interesting question is whether Mrs Thatcher deliberately forced his hand. She certainly laid down the law very firmly in Cabinet, insisting that the public wrangling between ministers must stop and that all future statements about Westland must be cleared though the Cabinet Office. But Heseltine accepted this without demur, until Nicholas Ridley intervened to spell out that this requirement should apply to the repetition of past statements as well. It was this that seemed to be gratuitously aimed at humiliating Heseltine. His response was to gather up his papers and leave the room. No one was sure whether he had resigned or merely gone to the bathroom. But Lady Thatcher wrote with undisguised satisfaction in her memoirs that while some of the Cabinet were 'stunned' by his *démarche*, 'I was not. Michael had made his decision and that was that. I already knew who I wanted to succeed him.'[10] The suspicion is that Ridley had been primed to push Heseltine over the brink.

Obviously Mrs Thatcher was not sorry to see her most dangerous colleague self-destruct. She adjourned the Cabinet for coffee, conferred briefly with Whitelaw and Wakeham, then called George Younger back and offered him the Ministry of Defence. Younger insisted that he had not been tipped off; but the MoD was the job he had always wanted and he accepted on the spot. Never was a resigning minister so quickly replaced.[11]

A few hours later Heseltine published his statement giving his side of the argument and alleging 'the complete breakdown of Cabinet government'.[12] Heseltine was not the first or the last of Mrs Thatcher's ministers to conclude that this was no way to run a government. But the argument over helicopters, and Heseltine's departure, were only the beginning of the Westland affair. Far more serious was the unravelling of the apparently trivial matter of the leak of Mayhew's letter, which called into question not the Prime Minister's strength but her honesty.

Sir Michael Havers took a serious view of the leaking of the Solicitor-General's advice to a colleague. The morning that Mayhew's letter was splashed all over the papers he went straight to Number Ten threatening to go to the police unless an inquiry was set up immediately to find the source. Mrs Thatcher had no choice but to agree. The difficulty was that she was being asked to investigate a process which she herself had set in motion and in which her own private office was, at the least, involved. If she did not know already how the letter had reached the Press Association, she had only to ask her own staff to be told in five minutes. So inviting Robert Armstrong to undertake a ten-day inquiry was a charade from the start. It could only be a cover-up, and it was.

After all the inquiries and the testimony of most of the protag-onists there remains only a narrow area of disagreement about what happened. It is admitted that Mrs Thatcher asked Mayhew to write a letter over the weekend. He took his time, but did so on the Monday morning, sending copies to the Treasury, the Foreign Office and the DTI. Mrs Thatcher made it clear to the DTI that she considered it 'urgent that it should become public knowledge before 4 p.m.', when Westland was due to hold a press conference to announce its decision.[13] Brittan's head of information at the DTI, Colette Bowe – a Civil Service high-flier only temporarily serving a spell as an information officer – was well aware that she was being asked to do something irregular. She tried to consult her Permanent Secretary, but unluckily he was out of the office and out of contact. So she contacted her superior in the Government Information Service, Bernard Ingham, hoping that he would handle the matter through the Number Ten press office. One way or another he declined. He wrote in his memoirs: 'I told Colette Bowe I had to keep the Prime Minister above that sort of thing.'[14] But Miss Bowe clearly understood that in leaking the letter she was acting on her minister's behalf, with Number Ten's knowledge, if not directly on instructions.*

In view of the subsequent controversy, it is important to note that Mrs Thatcher, in reporting to the Commons the result of Armstrong's inquiry, plainly acknowledged Number Ten's complicity in the leak. '*It was accepted that the DTI should disclose the fact* [that Mayhew considered Heseltine's letter inaccurate] *and that, in view of the urgency of the matter, the disclosure should be made by way of a telephone call to the Press Association.*' That admission unambiguously implicates her office, which is usually taken to mean Ingham and Charles Powell. She insisted that she herself was not consulted, but only because she did not need to be. She repeated, however, that 'had I been consulted, I should have said that a different method must be found of making the relevant facts known'.[15]

Under questioning she several times repeated that she wished the disclosure had been made by 'a more correct method' – even though there is no correct method of making public a Law Officer's advice. But in answer to a friendly question from Cranley Onslow she let slip an admission that she *had* given her approval. '*It was vital to have accurate information in the public domain . . . It was to get that accurate information to the public domain that I gave my consent.*'[16] Only the maverick Labour backbencher Tam Dalyell seems to have picked

---

* Colette Bowe is the one leading participant in the Westland drama who has not yet published her account of these events; but she has placed it in a bank for ultimate disclosure.

this up. When he quoted it back to her in the main Westland debate four days later she explained that she had meant her consent to an inquiry, not her consent to the leak. But the context makes it plain that this was not so. Later, before the select committee which investigated the affair, Robert Armstrong glossed her words as 'a slip of the tongue'.[17] But slips of the tongue not infrequently betray the truth. It is extraordinary that the persistent Dalyell let this critical admission go.

Instead she was allowed to continue to maintain that she had not known about the leak, or at least the method of it, until 'some hours later'.[18] She then went through the charade of setting Armstrong to inquire into the actions of her own office. For ten days, while Armstrong pretended to pursue his bogus inquiry, Mrs Thatcher pretended still to know nothing. Then, when he presented his report, concluding that the DTI had leaked the letter on Brittan's instruction, she made a pantomime of shocked amazement. 'Leon, why didn't you *tell* me?'[19] Michael Havers, promised his scapegoat, was impressed. 'Unless the PM is the most marvellous actress I've ever seen in my life she was as shocked as anybody that in fact it was on Leon Brittan's instructions.'[20]

It was the Prime Minister's veracity that was at stake in the House of Commons on 23 and 27 January. More strictly, it was her ability to avoid being caught in a demonstrable untruth, since most MPs of all parties found it impossible to believe that she had not checked up, either in advance or very soon afterwards, on how her closest aides had implemented her instructions.

Her statement was carefully framed to protect all parties: Brittan and his officials, the Prime Minister and her officials, all had 'acted in good faith'. The Attorney-General, in agreement with the Director of Public Prosecutions, had accordingly decided that no one should be prosecuted. Most significantly, Mrs Thatcher acknowledged that the DTI had not only 'the authority of its Secretary of State [but] cover from my office for proceeding'.[21] That word 'cover' was included at Brittan's insistence; yet it was not enough to save him. He was forced to resign next day – not because he took responsibility for the leak, but because he 'no longer commanded the full confidence of his colleagues'.[22]

The ugly truth was that Brittan had never been popular. He was too brainy, supercilious, soft – and Jewish. He had made a poor showing in the House, most glaringly when Heseltine tricked him into denying that he had received a letter from the Chief Executive of British Aerospace. He had to come back to the House a few hours later to admit that he had in fact received it. In the matter of Mayhew's letter he had been, at worst, naive. He was not a willing scapegoat. But the Tory party's famous 'men in grey suits' told him firmly that the backbenchers wanted his head. Like Lord Carrington after the Falklands invasion, someone had to be sacrificed to save the Prime Minister. Brittan's price was a fulsome exchange of letters in which she put on record that she had tried to persuade him to stay – thereby implicitly acknowledging that he had done no wrong – and all but promised to bring him back into the Cabinet very soon.

Brittan's sacrifice did not get her off the hook. Labour had set down an adjournment motion for Monday 27 January. There were still unanswered questions, above all about the role of Bernard Ingham and Charles Powell. If Mrs Thatcher had not personally authorised the leak, then one or both of them must have done so, in which case they had abused their position as civil servants. Likewise the Cabinet Secretary Robert Armstrong appeared to have lent himself to a sham inquiry designed not to discover the truth but to obscure it. The trivial matter of the leaked letter seemed to have exposed a culture of manipulation and deceit at the heart of the Government which the Prime Minister had still to clear up. Her speech, like her statement four days earlier, had to be carefully drafted to cover every angle. A form of words had to be agreed with Brittan to ensure his silence, and Heseltine might yet torpedo her. She and her staff, including Armstrong, spent the whole weekend – except for Saturday evening when she had to attend her annual dinner dance in Finchley – working on it, unusually in the Cabinet Room, the Cabinet table piled high with files. On Monday morning a group of senior ministers was allowed to vet the draft. Never again before November 1990 was Mrs Thatcher's dependence on colleagues so painfully exposed.

Simultaneously Ronnie Millar was summoned to lend his final polish to the text. He found Mrs Thatcher exceptionally tense and indecisive. It was then that she remarked that she might not be Prime Minister by six o'clock that evening.[23] Ingham maintains that this was a joke;[24] and she herself later claimed on television that it was 'just one of those things you say'.[25] But she unquestionably believed it at the time; and it could have come true, if Neil Kinnock had taken his opportunity.

But Kinnock blew it. He had two possible lines of attack. He might have taken the constitutional high ground and tried to mobilise the disquiet felt on both sides of the House at the blurring of the conventions of good government and the politicisation of the Civil Service. Or he might have conducted a forensic examination of the gaps, evasions and admissions in her previous testimony. Instead he plunged straight into a vague rhetorical denunciation of the Government's 'dishonesty, duplicity, conniving and manoeuvring' which instantly created a partisan atmosphere and united the Tories in the Prime Minister's defence. Within a minute he was punctured when the Speaker obliged him to withdraw the word 'dishonesty'.[26] 'For a few seconds', Alan Clark wrote, 'Kinnock had her cornered, and you could see fear in those blue eyes. But then he had an attack of wind, gave her time to recover.'[27]

The result of Kinnock's blustering was that she was able to get away with adding almost nothing to her previous story, beyond admitting that it was she who had initiated Mayhew's letter, that it was leaked without his permission and that it was Havers who had demanded an inquiry. These details apart, she held to her line that the leak arose from 'a genuine difference of understanding between officials as to exactly what was being sought and what was being given'. She apologised after a fashion, but repeated that she knew nothing about the disclosure 'until some hours after it had occurred'. She said nothing at all about Powell or Ingham. As she gained in confidence she turned the attack back on Kinnock for 'playing politics with people's jobs', and ended with a defiant promise to carry on with 'renewed strength to extend freedom and ownership . . . and to keep our country strong and secure'.[28] Clark thought it 'a brilliant performance, shameless and brave. We are out of the wood.'[29]

Mrs Thatcher managed to hide behind her officials, with the repeated insistence that she was not consulted, while at the same time denying that they had exceeded their powers. She blocked the committee of inquiry by refusing to allow Powell and Ingham to give evidence; instead Robert Armstrong appeared for the Civil Service as a whole and performed a masterly whitewash on the whole business. But by then it did not matter. The crisis passed the moment Neil Kinnock failed to put Mrs Thatcher on the spot on 27 January. No one recognised this more clearly than the man who had started it all, Michael Heseltine, who described Kinnock's speech as the worst parliamentary performance for a decade. 'It is the constitutional duty of the Opposition to exploit the Government's difficulties,' he reflected with a touch of frustration, 'but they cannot even make a decent job of that.' Realising that there was no more mileage to be got out of pursuing the Prime Minister, he congratulated her instead on her 'difficult and very brave' statement and pronounced himself satisfied with the words she had used. 'What the Prime Minister said today brings the politics of the matter to an end.' He would be supporting the Government in the lobby that evening.[30]

In that moment of prudent political calculation Heseltine set his course for the next five years. Resigning from the Government in January 1986 did his career no harm at all. He would have received no further promotion from Mrs Thatcher – certainly not the department he most coveted, the DTI. By walking out, instead of waiting to be sacked, he was able to carve out a distinctive position as a dissenting but loyal alternative Prime Minister, touring the Tory constituency associations as the challenger-in-waiting if and when she stumbled. When the moment came in November 1990 he wielded the knife yet failed to claim the crown. But by keeping clear of the wreckage of her final years he gained another seven years of office under John Major – five of them at the DTI – ending as a more than usually powerful deputy Prime Minister.

By contrast Leon Brittan's career in domestic politics was finished. The promises Mrs Thatcher made to buy his silence were not kept. Instead she sent him to Brussels as an EC Commissioner, over-looking – in her anxiety to be rid of him – his record as a convinced pro-European. Released from his debt of silence, Brittan lost no time in stating explicitly on television (in April 1989) what he had declined to spell out in 1986, that Powell and Ingham had expressly authorised the Westland leak.[31]

Mrs Thatcher herself was the biggest loser from the Westland imbroglio, for she lost what had hitherto been her most priceless asset, her reputation for integrity. The Westland cover-up concerned nothing more serious than a leaked letter: yet she left the inescapable impression that she had misled the House of Commons to save her own embarrassment and protect her entourage, letting a hapless colleague take the rap for a piece of skulduggery she had initiated. For one who prided herself on her honesty and preached a moral-istic politics based on a clear sense of right and wrong, it was a painful and humiliating shock, the lowest point of her career. She recovered, but never fully regained the moral high ground. Hence-forth she was just another slippery politician who would lie when cornered.

'That Bloody Woman'

The early months of 1986 were the lowest period of Mrs Thatcher's premiership. She had been unpopular in 1980–81, but then she was sustained by her own burning belief that what she was doing was right and by the support of a small band of like-minded believers. There was something epic, Churchillian, in her defiance of the odds. In 1986, by contrast, the revelations and evasions of Westland had left her morally damaged, her reputation for straight-talking integrity in tatters. Having lost two ministers and only narrowly survived herself, her authority was palpably weakened: she could not afford any more resignations, so was temporarily obliged to pay more deference to her colleagues than had become her habit since the Falklands war. Just as the attention of Westminster was beginning to turn towards the next election there were suggestions that she was becoming a liability, no longer an asset to the Government's chances of re-election, and increasing talk that after seven years she was running out of steam, had been in office long enough and would have to step down some time in the next Parliament. Commentators began to speculate that the succession would lie between Michael Heseltine and Norman Tebbit.

This was not Mrs Thatcher's intention at all. She was uneasily aware that her second term, despite economic recovery and the success of privatisation, had not been the unqualified triumph it should have been. Too much of the Government's energy had been diverted into defeating the miners and other distractions, at the expense of more positive objectives. In retrospect, she attributed the loss of momentum to the lack of detailed preparation before the 1983 election, for which she unfairly blamed Geoffrey Howe. But it was not in her nature to think of giving up. On the contrary, she was determined to demonstrate that both her energy and her radicalism were undiminished. With the economy apparently sorted out, unemployment falling at last and Lawson proclaiming an economic miracle, she was eager to turn to what had always been her real purpose, the remoralisation of British society. ('Economics is the method. The object is to change the soul.')[32] In her first two terms she had cut inflation by busting the taboo of full employment and begun a radical rebalancing of the mixed economy, but she had barely touched the third pillar of the post-war settlement, the welfare state. Belatedly, as many of her supporters believed, she now resolved to regain the political initiative by fighting the next election on this social agenda, with 'a set of policies . . . which my advisers, over my objections, wanted to call Social Thatcherism'.[33] In practice she was much less certain of exactly what these reforms should be than her missionary language implied; but she was absolutely determined to regain the sense of forward movement.

The problem was that if she was not exhausted, there was plenty of evidence that the public was growing tired of her. The Conservatives lagged consistently third in the polls behind both Labour and the Alliance, and in April her personal popularity rating fell to its lowest point – 28 per cent – since the inner-city riots of 1981. On 13 April Tebbit and his chief of staff Michael Dobbs (seconded from Saatchi & Saatchi) paid an uncomfortable visit to Chequers to present the Prime Minister with the results of polling carried out by Saatchis, which showed not only that the Government was seen to have 'lost its way' and 'run out of steam' but that she herself had ceased to be an asset on the doorsteps. She was given credit for having defeated General Galtieri, conquered inflation and tamed the unions, but now seemed to have run out of worthwhile enemies:

> With the lack of new battles to fight the Prime Minister's combative virtues were being received as vices: her determination was perceived as stubbornness, her single-mindedness as inflexibility and her strong will as an inability to listen.[34]

Collectively, Tebbit and Dobbs had to tell her, these attributes were becoming known as the 'TBW factor' – standing for 'That Bloody Woman'. Saatchis' recommended strategy for the next election involved the Prime Minister taking a lower profile. Of course she vehemently disagreed. She had no intention of being pushed into the background. She was already suspicious that Tebbit was pursuing his own agenda, and her suspicions can only have been confirmed when he went public a few weeks later with a singularly lukewarm endorsement of her leadership.

Rejecting Saatchis' polling, therefore, she commissioned alternative research from the American firm of Young and Rubicam which was already pitching to displace Saatchis and duly came up with more acceptable results. Their finding suggested not that Mrs Thatcher herself was the problem, but that too much of the Tories' appeal had been directed at the ambitious and successful ('succeeders' in advertising jargon), and not enough at ordinary people ('mainstreamers'). On this reading her strength of purpose was still an asset so long as she did not appear doctrinaire but committed to delivering real improvements in people's lives.[35] This was much more what she wanted to hear. She always believed that she had a special rapport with the long-suffering, hard-working, law-abiding middle class whom she regarded above all as 'her' people, and specifically wanted to do more for them now that she had got the economy right and sorted out the unions. That was to be her mission for the third term. From now on she received two parallel sets of polling advice, the official line from Saatchis via Tebbit and Central Office, and unofficial material from Young and Rubicam behind Tebbit's back, which she shared only with a small group of trusted ministers – Whitelaw, Wakeham, Lawson and Hurd – and her private office. This damaging duplication continued right through 1986 and into the election the following year.

She tried to counter the image of bossiness by presenting a more collective style of leadership. She accepted John Wakeham's advice that she should set up (and, most importantly, be seen to set up) a Strategy Group to take a grip on policy and presentation in the run-up to the election. In appearance this was a sort of inner cabinet of a sort she had never previously admitted since the 'Thursday breakfasts' attended by the inner core of monetarist economic ministers in 1979. Its members – immediately dubbed the 'A-Team', from a current television programme – were Willie Whitelaw, the holders of the three senior offices of state (Howe, Lawson and Hurd), Tebbit as party chairman and Wakeham as Chief Whip. In reality the A-Team was more for show than substance: it had less to do with sharing power than with shackling Tebbit, a means of retaining election planning in her own hands. Most of the groundwork for the reforms of the third term was done under her eye in the Downing Street Policy Unit rather than in the departments.

There was one very important exception. The policy initiative which turned out to be the most contentious after 1987 was agreed as far back as 1985, and originated not in the Policy Unit but in the Department of the Environment. After it blew up in her face, the poll tax was regularly cited as the epitome of Mrs Thatcher's domineering style, the result of her personal obsession with abolishing the rates, pushed through a tame Cabinet purely by her insistence. In fact, no reform of the Thatcher years was more exhaustively debated through all the proper committees. As usual, the Prime Minister was one of the last to be persuaded that it was practicable. Once convinced, she was unswerving in her refusal to abandon it and in her memoirs she still defended it as right in principle. But it was successive Secretaries of State for the Environment and Scotland (and their juniors) who made all the running at the beginning.

Of course Mrs Thatcher's desire to honour her 1974 commitment to abolish domestic rates was undiminished. She had always disliked the rates on principle as a tax on property which acted as a disincentive against making improvements; and she was keen to find a way to stop Labour councils piling heavy rate demands on

Tory householders in order to spend the money on their own voters who were largely exempt from payment. But since Michael Heseltine's abortive search for a workable alternative in 1979–83, her attention had been diverted into other ways of controlling local extravagance. It was Patrick Jenkin who unwisely revived the question by setting up yet another departmental inquiry in late 1984, delegating his juniors, Kenneth Baker and William Waldegrave, to find the holy grail. Waldegrave in turn consulted his old boss in Ted Heath's think-tank, Victor Rothschild. Mrs Thatcher later credited Rothschild with 'much of the radical thinking' which produced the community charge;[36] but many other bright sparks on the cerebral fringe of the Tory party, including the Adam Smith Institute, also had a hand in it.

The event which overcame her initial scepticism was the furious outcry against the revaluation of Scottish rates in February 1985, which threatened a steep hike in rateable values particularly in middle-class areas. Willie Whitelaw came back 'severely shaken' by the anger he encountered on a visit to the affluent Glasgow suburb of Bearsden in March.[37] Whitelaw and George Younger convinced the Prime Minister that something must be done urgently: their alarm coincided neatly with Waldegrave's review team coming up with an alternative which they believed would work. So she convened a conference at Chequers on 31 March at which Baker, Waldegrave and Rothschild gave a glossy presentation of their proposal, complete with colour slides and flip charts. Waldegrave ended his pitch with words allegedly suggested by Patrick Jenkin: 'And so, Prime Minister, you will have fulfilled your promise to abolish the rates.'[38] She was persuaded.

Five weeks later she paid her annual visit to the Scottish party conference and was able to tell the representatives that the Government had listened to their anger. 'We have reached the stage where no amount of patching up of the existing system can overcome its inherent unfairness,' she announced. The Government was now looking at a fundamental reform of local government finance. 'The burden should fall, not heavily on the few, but fairly on the many.'[39] The idea that everyone who used council services should pay equally towards the cost of them was, on paper, not a bad one. It was wrong in principle, and corrupting in practice, that only one-third of households paid full rates, yet everyone could vote for expenditure to which they did not contribute. 'My father always said that everyone ought to pay something,' she told Woodrow Wyatt, 'even if it is only sixpence.'[40] It was not envisaged that the charge would be more than £50–100 per head.

Nigel Lawson had missed the Chequers seminar but later submitted a paper warning the Cabinet committee which considered it that the proposed flat-rate charge would prove 'completely unworkable and politically catastrophic'.[41] He correctly predicted that it would be hard to collect, while Labour councils would simply hike up their spending and blame the Government for the new tax. He proposed instead a banded tax on capital values (very similar to that with which Heseltine eventually replaced the poll tax in 1991). Having voiced his dissent, however, Lawson subsequently lay low: he neither exerted his authority as Chancellor, nor attempted to combine with Heseltine and Walker (both former Environment Secretaries) to coordinate opposition to the charge. In his memoirs Lawson sought to distance himself from the disaster that followed. But no new tax can be introduced against the opposition of the Treasury. Having identified the flaws in the poll tax so accurately, Lawson bears substantial responsibility for having failed to stop it.

It was Kenneth Baker (having succeeded Jenkin the previous autumn) who published in January 1986 a Green Paper, *Paying for Local Government*, setting out the detail of what was officially called the community charge. His presentation to the Commons was given a mixed welcome by Tory MPs. Four months later Baker departed to Education, leaving Nicholas Ridley holding his baby. Nevertheless, at that year's Scottish conference Mrs Thatcher basked in the applause of the representatives for her promise of immediate legislation in Scotland, ahead of England and Wales.[42] Contrary to subsequent claims, the Government did not use Scotland cynically as a test bed for an unpopular policy, but introduced it there first because the existing grievance was most urgent there. The following year, opening her General Election campaign in Perth as usual, Mrs Thatcher boasted that the Scottish legislation had passed its final stage the previous week. 'They said we couldn't do it. They said we wouldn't do it. We did it.'[43] She had no doubt that the change would be popular, at least with her own party.

At the same time other ministers were encouraged to develop a whole range of new policies on housing, health and education. The 1986 Conservative Party Conference was a brilliant public-relations exercise, choreographed by Saatchi & Saatchi under the slogan 'The Next Moves Forward' and designed to convey the message that the Government was not a one-woman band but a young and vigorous team full of energy and new, practical ideas for improving public services. Each day a succession of ministers trooped to the platform to set out their wares. On Tuesday Norman Lamont offered further privatisation, including water supply, the British Airports Authority and the return of Rolls-Royce to the private sector. On Wednesday Norman Fowler unveiled an ambitious hospital building programme, while Douglas Hurd announced longer sentences and new powers to seize criminals' assets. Thursday brought Nigel Lawson holding out the prospect of zero inflation and income tax coming down to twenty-five pence. The coverage was everything Tebbit and Central Office could have hoped for, climaxing when Mrs Thatcher grabbed the spotlight back to herself on Friday morning.

The Government's poll ratings picked up immediately, so that by December the Tories were back in a clear lead for the first time for nearly two years: 41 per cent against 32 per cent for Labour and 22 per cent for the Liberal/SDP Alliance, which had come badly unstuck over defence. Whereas in the early summer there had been growing belief in the likelihood of a Labour victory, by the end of the year the betting had swung overwhelmingly back towards the Tories. Over the spring that lead was maintained and even extended. Though she had no need to go to the country again before 1988, Mrs Thatcher had much less hesitation than in 1983 about seizing this advantage while the going was good. Having won twice previously in May and June she had become convinced that the early summer was a lucky time for her, and she was keen to get the ordeal over as soon as possible so that she could get back to work.

Then, on 17 March, Nigel Lawson introduced the perfect pre-election budget in which he was able to cut the standard rate of income tax by another two pence while simultaneously finding money for increased spending on health and other services, without even raising duties on petrol, drink or cigarettes. Two weeks later the Tories' resurgence was crowned by Mrs Thatcher's triumphant visit to Moscow. She was indignant when reporters dared to suggest that her visit was designed with an eye on the upcoming election. 'Enlarge your view,' she told them scornfully. 'I'm here for Britain.'[44] The impact was doubled by the contrast with Kinnock's disastrous trip to Washington a few days earlier when he and Denis Healey were received by President Reagan with a barely disguised snub. They were accorded just a quarter of an hour of the President's time, and the White House put out an uncompromising statement to the effect that Labour's non-nuclear defence policy would be damaging to NATO. With the Tories making modest gains in the local elections on 7 May the omens could scarcely have been better, and it was no surprise that, having slept on it, Mrs Thatcher announced next day that the election would be on 11 June.

Hat-trick: June 1987

Yet June 1987 was by no means such a walkover as June 1983 had been. Despite the polls there was a nervousness in the Tory camp that perhaps the Government had been in office too long, that Mrs Thatcher's style of leadership had become a liability and that the oldest cry in democratic politics – 'Time for a Change' – might exert a potent effect. By contrast with the shambles of 1983, Labour mounted a very slick and professional campaign while there was always the possibility of a late surge by the Alliance. In fact, the outcome almost exactly mirrored the polls at the beginning and victory was almost certainly in the bag all along. But it was, as Lady Thatcher wrote with some understatement in her memoirs, 'not . . . a happy campaign'.[45]

It was vitiated by intense rivalry between Norman Tebbit, the party chairman, and David Young whom she had appointed unofficially to second-guess him. This tension boiled over on 4 June – 'Wobbly Thursday' – when a rogue poll almost persuaded some in both camps that the party might actually lose. Mrs Thatcher herself made a number of slips – notably in suggesting that she hoped to go 'on and on' – and was irritable throughout, suffering from a painful tooth and missing the soothing presence of Cecil Parkinson who had masterminded her previous re-election so smoothly in 1983.

Thus, at the very height of her electoral success, in securing her unprecedented third election victory, Mrs Thatcher did not dare to seek and certainly did not secure any sort of mandate for 'Social Thatcherism'. She won easily again, essentially because the voters did not trust Labour on the economy or defence, while the Alliance remained popular enough to split the opposition but too divided to make its dreamed-of breakthrough. 'Mr Kinnock had in his favour', *The Times* commented, 'eight years of the most vilified Prime Minister of modern times; three million unemployed and a country apparently enraged by the condition of its health service. Yet he could not win.'[46] By keeping the Government on the defensive on health, employment and the state of the inner cities, Labour was widely judged to have 'won' the campaign. Yet Kinnock managed to recover only about half of the three million votes Foot had lost in 1983, and that ground was almost all regained from the Alliance. This gave Mrs Thatcher 376 seats (a loss of twenty-three), Labour 229 (up just twenty) and the Alliance a mere twenty-two, with the Scottish and Welsh Nationalists at three each, trimming the Government's overall majority from the swollen 144 it had won in 1983 to a still more than comfortable 102. In raw parliamentary terms it was another landslide.*

In the hour of victory it seemed that Mrs Thatcher could be Prime Minister for life if she wanted. Speaking to the crowds in Downing Street on Friday morning she was openly delighted with her achievement. 'I think the real thing now is we have done it three times . . . With a universal franchise the third time is terrific, is it not?'[47] Pressed again about how long she intended to go on, she made no bones about her intention to complete the third term, dismissed the idea of grooming a successor ('Good heavens, no') and did not demur when Robin Day suggested that she might still be Prime Minister in the year 2000, when she would be only seventy-five. 'You never know,' she replied, 'I might be here, I might be twanging a harp. Let us just see how things go.'[48] She had no doubt that she had won a huge personal mandate.

Denis was more realistic. Watching with Carol from an upstairs window as Margaret acknowledged the cheering crowd below, he 'turned to get himself a refill and said, "In a year she'll be so unpopular you won't believe it".'[49] In fact, it took a bit longer than that. But it was prescient all the same.

---

* Mrs Thatcher's personal result in Finchley was very little changed from 1983:

Mrs M. Thatcher (C)	21,603
J. Davies (Lab)	12,690
D. Howarth (Lib/All)	5,580
(Two others)	190
Majority	8,913

22

No Such Thing as Society

'Society – that's no one'

IN June 1987 Thatcherism moved into a new phase. Having sorted out the economy, as she believed, Mrs Thatcher now wanted to take on British society and specifically the culture of dependency which had grown out of forty years of socialised welfare. But this ambition quickly brought the contradictions of her philosophy into sharp focus. With the exception of curbing the unions, which had required legislation, and privatisation (which only involved undoing what had been done in the past), most of what she had achieved so far had been achieved by *not* doing things – *not* intervening as previous governments had done to settle strikes or to save jobs. So far she, Howe and Lawson, with their advisers, had been following a clear programme which had worked more or less as intended. The hands-off, free-market approach had undoubtedly had a stimulating effect on those parts of the economy that survived its rigours. Now she proposed to tackle something much more difficult and amorphous, where there were not the same clear doctrinal guidelines. According to the pure milk of free-market economics, the state should not be in the business of providing education, housing or medical care at all. But in practice abolishing public provision was not an option: too many voters were indeed dependent on it. She could trim a little at the margins; but fundamentally she could only try to improve the delivery and quality of services. And she could only do this by inter-vening directly to reform the way they were run. Partly from this inexorable logic, therefore, partly from her own restlessly interfering temperament, she was driven into an activist, centralising frenzy at odds with the professed philosophy of rolling back the state. This was to cause all sorts of trouble in the next three years.

Usually Mrs Thatcher denied any conflict, insisting that all her reforms were simply aimed at giving power back to schools, parents, tenants and patients. But an article she wrote for the *Sunday Express* a week after the election reveals a rare awareness of this contradiction. (No doubt it was largely written for her; but nothing was ever published in Mrs Thatcher's name without her correcting every word.) Conscious of the criticism that her government since 1979 had served only the interests of the better-off, she set four goals for 'a Government which seeks to serve *all* the people *all* the time'. The first three were quite conventional: to ensure liberty and security, to preserve the value of the currency and (more vaguely) to ensure 'fairness' for all. But the fourth recognised the tension between the philosophy of minimum government and her instinct to tell people what to do:

> Fourth, in full recognition of human frailty, and together with all the other great institutions, it must seek to set standards by which people lead their lives. A society which knows what is expected of it has a sure base for progress.

Immediately she entered all sorts of disclaimers:

> We do not seek to lead people's lives for them, nor to boss them around, nor to regulate them into apathy . . . A government for *all* the people must have the humility to recognise its limitations and the strength to resist the temptation to meddle in the citizens' lives.[1]

Nevertheless the ambition had been declared in the first sentence: the Government 'must seek to set standards by which people live their lives'. That is unmistakably the voice of nanny.

It was during an interview for the magazine *Woman's Own* that autumn that Mrs Thatcher delivered the statement which seemed to define her philosophy more perfectly than anything else she ever said. Arguing that people should not look to 'society' to solve their problems, she asserted:

> There is no such thing as society. There are individual men and women, and there are families. And no Government can do anything except through people, and people must look to themselves. It's our duty to look after ourselves and then to look after our neighbour.[2]

As is usually the case with famous sayings, she had made the same point several times before, for instance in a 1985 television interview. She said it again in 1988: 'Don't blame society – that's no one', going on to explain that the streets would not be dirty if only people did not drop litter.[3] So her words were not a misquotation or taken out of context. But this time they created enormous outrage.

In her memoirs Lady Thatcher protested that she had been deliberately misunderstood. All she had meant was that society was not an abstraction, 'but a living structure of individuals, families, neighbours and voluntary associations . . . Society for me is not an excuse, but an obligation.'[4] In a purely literal sense it is obviously true that society is made up of individuals, grouped into families and other associations. But because it is composed of small platoons does not mean that society, as an aggregate of those components, does not exist. On the contrary, society has a collective existence on at least two levels. First there is the emotional sense of a national community, a concept traditionally important to Conservatives of all stripes, whether One Nation paternalists or gung-ho imperialists. Mrs Thatcher more than most professed a semi-mystical view of Britain as a family united by common values, an ideal to which she frequently appealed when it suited her. But more concrete than that, modern society has also a statutory existence as a network of legal and financial arrangements built up to discharge collective responsibilities beyond the capacity of the immediate neighbourhood. It was a perfectly legitimate Conservative position to argue that society in this sense had taken on too many responsibilities, which should be reduced. It was not meaningful for the head of a government charged with administering those responsibilities to maintain that it did not exist.

Her statement that there was 'no such thing as society' gave offence mainly because it seemed to legitimise selfishness and reduced public provision for the poor to the bounty of the rich. It denied that sense of social solidarity which Conservatives as much as socialists had in their different ways always tried to inculcate, replacing it with an atomised society bound together only by contractual obligations. But it also had implications for other public amenities beyond the social services: transport, art and leisure facilities, sewers and prisons. The doctrine that citizens should be allowed to keep as much as possible of their own money to spend on personal consumption, while essential public facilities like roads and railways, museums and libraries, swimming pools and playing fields were financed wherever possible by private enterprise – or private benefaction – rather than by the state, as in most other European countries, derived from the same belief that Adam Smith's multiplicity of individual decisions would somehow work their magic and the market would provide. But by the end of the decade – still more by the end of the century – it was becoming apparent that this was not the case. There was necessary collective investment in public facilities which only the state could provide. There was such a thing as society after all.

The consequence of the Prime Minister's denial of society at the very moment when she was promising, at the party conference, to devote her third term to 'social affairs' was that she found herself embarked on a hotchpotch of incoherent reforms, in some respects more ambitious than originally intended and generally ill-thought out. It was not only that reform of the National Health Service forced itself on to the agenda, in addition to the plans already announced in the manifesto for education, housing and the poll tax. The Government soon became embroiled in a swathe of other legislation involving broadcasting, football supporters, firearms, the legal profession, official secrets, pubs, homosexuality, child support and war criminals. Mrs Thatcher's promise to 'resist the temptation to meddle in the citizens' lives' was soon forgotten. The drive to reform every corner of British society was taken up by a new generation of ambitious younger ministers – many of them originally Heathites, now keen to make up for lost time by jumping on the Thatcher bandwagon, believing they could get away with anything, with no cautionary elders like Whitelaw and Hailsham left in the Cabinet to restrain them. Meanwhile, the economic miracle which was supposed to make all things possible was turning sour.

Thus Mrs Thatcher's third term was a saga of boastful talk and loudly proclaimed radicalism, but also a lot of misdirected energy due to a fundamental contradiction at the heart of the Government's purpose and a crippling lack of trust and sympathy between an increasingly irrational Prime Minister and her closest colleagues, which eventually resulted in her brutal deposition.

The new Cabinet

The old division of the Cabinet into 'wets' and 'dries' had long since been superseded. Of the original wets, only Whitelaw and Walker now survived. From 1981, with the accession of Lawson, Tebbit, Parkinson and Ridley to senior positions, Mrs Thatcher had begun to forge a Cabinet much more in her own mould than the one she had been obliged to form in 1979. By 1987, however, with the departure of Tebbit, Brittan and Biffen, the balance was tilting against her again. The critical mass of the new Cabinet was made up of up-and-coming pragmatists from the centre-left of the party – Hurd, Baker, Clarke, MacGregor, Fowler, King, Rifkind and Major – who had come into politics under Heath. They had absorbed the lessons Keith Joseph and Mrs Thatcher had taught, but they were by no means natural Thatcherites. Of course the Cabinet as a body counted for very little in the determination of policy. Most of its members would continue to support her so long as she was riding high. But its changing composition should have been another warning that it would not automatically back her when the going got rough.

In addition, after only seven months she lost Willie Whitelaw, who was taken ill at a carol service in December and resigned in January 1988. Many see this as a critical turning point. It was during a late-night speechwriting session with her wordsmiths at Blackpool that Mrs Thatcher famously remarked that 'Every Prime Minister should have a Willie'. When she realised what she had said she swore them all to secrecy; but the story inevitably got out.[5] The unconscious *double entendre* drew a lot of ribaldry, but her point was absolutely true: every Prime Minister does need a Willie, though few are lucky enough to have one. Whitelaw was not only rigidly loyal himself, but he had the authority to impose loyalty on others. For eight and a half years his reassuring and defusing presence was hugely important to the survival and success of Mrs Thatcher's governments. His departure left the Government without its sheet anchor in the increasingly heavy seas of the next three years.

'What's to stop us?'

The Government made a much more purposeful start to its third term than it had done to its second. Following her usual very brief holiday in Cornwall – interrupted on 19 August by a horrific incident in the quiet Wiltshire town of Hungerford when a single gunman ran amok, killing sixteen people – she used the latter part of the recess to demonstrate that she did care about the forgotten parts of Britain which she had seemed wilfully to ignore in the election. She visited several run-down inner cities – Glasgow, Cleveland and Wolverhampton – touring carefully selected scenes of urban decay to preach her message that enterprise, not Government subsidy, would create the jobs to bring regeneration. A photo-call in Cleveland resulted in a famous picture of the Prime Minister, with her handbag, marching determinedly into a wasteland which had once been a steelworks. When a journalist asked where the money would come from to revive such areas, she demanded that *he* tell *her*.[6] She saw the solution less in terms of money than in the anticipated impact of the three Bills already announced – Ridley's new forms of tenancy, Baker's education reforms and the community charge, all designed to weaken the grip of Labour councils which she saw as the cause, not a reflection, of urban deprivation. 'Where one finds poverty in the inner cities,' she had declared back in 1979, 'there one finds that Socialist government has operated for many years.'[7]

So far as physical regeneration was concerned her model was the redevelopment of London's docklands, which she praised during the election as 'a classic example of Toryism at work. Take the dereliction, improve it, make progress, do it by putting in a little bit of taxpayer's money to prime the pump and along comes industry.'[8] There was actually nothing specifically Tory about it – the proposal for a Docklands Development Corporation had first been put forward by the Labour MP Bob Mellish in the 1960s – but it fitted well with Mrs Thatcher's desire to bypass obstructive councils. The idea was to create a body which could override the local authorities, cut through the jungle of local planning regulations, buy up and redevelop derelict land and offer incentives to attract business to the area. The London Docklands Development Corporation was eventually established in 1981 by Michael Heseltine, with a similar body for Merseyside (planned before that summer's riots). Their success encouraged Ridley to announce another four Urban Development Corporations in 1986. Now Mrs Thatcher resolved to set up four more and more than double the amount of money put into them. In December Ken Clarke – rather than Ridley – was put in charge of the inner-city programme, initially with a budget of £2 billion. By the time Mrs Thatcher herself chaired a multi-departmental press conference in March 1988 to launch a White Paper, *Action for Cities*, that figure had been raised to £3 billion.

The programme, with a multiplicity of subordinate schemes – Enterprise Zones, Business in the Community, City Action Teams, Derelict Land Grants – achieved considerable success over the next decade, at least in physically redeveloping derelict areas. Much of the benefit, however, particularly in London, accrued to 'yuppies' and other middle-class incomers, rather than to the original inhabitants who could not afford the new housing and found themselves either displaced or servicing the new population.

The 1987 party conference at Blackpool was an unabashed victory rally not spoiled as the 1983 equivalent had been by revelations about Cecil Parkinson. 'That makes three wins in a row,' Mrs Thatcher told the adoring faithful. 'Just like Lord Liverpool. And he was Prime Minister for fifteen years. It's rather encouraging.' Dismissing calls for a period of 'consolidation', she insisted that the third victory was just 'a staging post on a much longer journey', and tempted fate by demanding 'What's to stop us?' [9]

One week later the mood was abruptly punctured by the collapse of the New York stock market. When the markets reopened on Monday morning, London duly followed New York and Tokyo down the tube: 23 per cent was wiped off share values in one day. 'Black Monday' delivered a devastating blow to Mrs Thatcher's view of Britain's restored 'greatness'. Though in principle she believed in the global market, she was shocked by the reminder of the British economy's vulnerability to a crash on Wall Street, and the helplessness of her government to act independently.

The most embarrassing effect in the short run was the wreck of the privatisation of British Petroleum, whose shares went on sale at the worst possible moment. After a string of successes over the spring and summer with British Airways, the British Airports Authority and Rolls-Royce, the Government was suddenly left with millions of shares on its hands in what *The Times* called 'the biggest flotation flop in history'.[10] Lawson refused to 'pull' the sale, but the Treasury was obliged to underwrite the issue itself at just seventy pence a share – instead of 120 pence – giving rise to gleeful Labour jeers of renationalisation. In fact, the losers were neither the Government nor the public, but the bankers. The episode proved to be only a blip in the sequence of successful privatisations. The second instalment of BP shares the following summer netted the taxpayer the biggest yield yet.

Far more serious in the long run were the measures Lawson took to try to mitigate the impact of the stock-market crash on the British economy. Amid widespread – but as it turned out erroneous – fears of an American-led recession, he cut interest rates by half of one per cent on 20 October, then by another half per cent on 4 November, to boost demand. Both he and Mrs Thatcher claim to have been unmoved by the general panic over a perfectly normal 'correction' of overvalued stocks.[11] Nevertheless, with the economy in fact already beginning to overheat, cutting interest rates at all turned out to be the wrong medicine at the wrong time.

Social Thatcherism: education, housing and health

In November all the key planks of the Government's programme were unveiled, starting with Baker's Education Bill, known as the Great Education Reform Bill, or 'Gerbil' for short. It was really five Bills in one, each one of which – setting up a National Curriculum, giving schools the right to opt out of local-authority control, establishing City Technology Colleges, reforming the universities, and (as an afterthought) abolishing the Inner London Education Authority – could have been a substantial measure on its own. But the perils of introducing major legislation with inadequate prior consultation were illustrated as Baker and his colleagues, battered by conflicting pressures from various parts of the educational establishment on the one hand and the Prime Minister on the other, were forced to improvise policy as they went along. By the time the Bill finally concluded its passage through Parliament in July 1988 it had swollen from 137 clauses to 238 and taken up 370 hours of parliamentary time – a post-war record.

By comparison with Baker's monster, Ridley's Housing Bill was modest and attracted relatively little controversy. Here too council tenants were empowered to opt out of local-authority control. Housing Action Trusts (HATs) were supposed to improve rundown estates by converting them to private ownership. At the same time new forms of rented tenure ('assured' and 'shorthold' tenancies) were designed to bring more private rented property on to the market. In fact, little of this came to pass. Despite large sums of public money on offer as an inducement, tenants proved unwilling to exchange the public-sector landlord they knew for the uncertainty of the private sector: as a result, no HATs at all were set up before November 1990 and only four by 1996, while the amount of private renting increased only marginally.

The real story of housing in the late 1980s was a shocking increase in the number of people without homes at all, who resorted to sleeping on the streets, under flyovers and in shop doorways in London and other big cities. This sudden phenomenon of visible homelessness was due to a combination of reasons, at least three of them the direct result of Government policy: the reduction in the public housing stock due to the non-replacement of the million former council houses sold to their tenants; higher rents in both council and private rented housing; and the withdrawal of benefits from several categories of claimant, specifically the young and single unemployed. In addition, an increasing rate of family break-up was creating more demand for homes, while more young people, for a variety of reasons, good and bad, were leaving home. The situation was further exacerbated towards the end of the decade by the number of homes repossessed when their proud purchasers – who had been encouraged to buy their houses in the heyday of council-house sales a few years earlier – were unable to keep up the mortgage payments when interest rates soared after 1988. All these factors together made homelessness a disturbingly visible – and for the Government politically embarrassing – problem by 1990.

Mrs Thatcher was extraordinarily unsympathetic towards the homeless. In the Commons she regularly listed all the measures the Government was taking to provide alternatives: hostels, bed-and-breakfast accommodation and the like. But she revealed her true feelings in her memoirs. 'Unfortunately there was a persistent tendency in polite circles to consider all the "roofless" as victims of middle class society', she wrote, 'rather than middle class society as victim of the "roofless".'[12] From her cosy suburban perspective she regarded the young homeless on the streets as social misfits who should go back to their families – ignoring the fact that many had not got families, had been thrown out, abused by their families, or simply (in approved Thatcherite manner) had left homes in areas of high unemployment and moved to London or other big cities looking for work. She lumped them all together as suffering from 'behavioural problems'.

Nor was poverty merely a matter of income. The 1987 edition of *Social Trends*, published by the Central Statistical Office, reported not only a widening gap between rich and poor but specifically a widening health gap, with the poor showing much greater liability to illness and shorter life expectancy, while a number of poverty-related illnesses like rickets and even consumption, previously eradicated, were making a comeback.[13] The Government's Chief Medical Officer, Sir Donald Acheson, blamed the effect of poor diet and poor housing.[14] Back in 1980 a report on inequalities in health commissioned by the Labour Government from Professor Sir Douglas Black had sounded the same warning: the DHSS, on Mrs Thatcher's instructions, had buried it. Seven years later, after repeated cuts in benefits, the position was very much worse.

Meanwhile, very much against Mrs Thatcher's will, the Government was drawn into major reform of the National Health Service. It was already clear during the election that the state of the NHS was at the top of the public's concerns. However strenuously the Prime Minister insisted that the NHS was not merely 'safe' in her hands but was being funded with unprecedented generosity, the public saw only underfunding, deteriorating services and mounting crisis. That autumn the situation deteriorated further, with seemingly daily stories of staff shortages, long waiting lists, bed closures, postponed operations and deaths – all attributed to a deliberate policy of 'Tory cuts'. At first Mrs Thatcher kept on reeling off her statistics, claiming that real spending on the NHS had risen by 30 per cent since 1979. But increasingly, as the *Annual Register* commented, 'this tactic began to seem arid and repetitious'.[15] Her figures were also misleading: health spending had indeed increased between 1979 and 1983 – reaching 6.7 per cent of GNP that year – but it had fallen over the past four years, while the British Medical Association (BMA) reckoned that the NHS needed to grow by 2 per cent a year just to keep up with the demands of an ageing population and new medical developments. International comparisons showed that Britain's *per capita* spending on health was now the lowest in northern Europe. In December the combined Royal Colleges published a report entitled *Crisis in the NHS*; the *British Medical Journal* declared the service to be 'in terminal decline'; while in the Commons Neil Kinnock told Mrs Thatcher that she was 'making a fool of herself' by continuing to deny what every shade of expert opinion was telling her.[16] In the end she had to be seen to respond.

In the short term there was nothing for it but to inject more money. But more money alone could not be the whole answer – and it was certainly not one that Mrs Thatcher or her Chancellor were prepared to contemplate. Opinion polls indicated public willingness to pay higher taxes to fund the health service, and some – though by no means all – Tory MPs were urging Lawson to put higher NHS spending before further tax cuts in his next budget. But this was contrary to everything Mrs Thatcher believed in. In her heart she was perfectly clear what she would have liked to do: she would have liked to move away from tax-funded health care altogether. But in practice she knew that privatisation on any significant scale was out of the question. Public opinion demanded that the NHS must remain essentially taxation-based and free to patients at the point of service. That being so, and the tax base being finite, the only alternative was to look at ways of improving delivery of the service.

The policy which Ken Clarke finally unveiled in January 1989 had two main features. On the one hand, hospitals were given the power to choose to become self-governing 'NHS Trusts' within the health service, funded by the taxpayer but in control of their own budgets, independent of the Regional Health Authority. On the other, doctors were encouraged to become 'GP fundholders', managing their own budgets to buy the most appropriate services for their patients: instead of sending them automatically to the local hospital, they should be able to shop around to find the best – or best-value – provider. Money would thus follow the patient, and the most efficient hospitals (those that actually knew what operations cost, for a start) would secure the biggest funding.

Most hospitals did opt to become trusts – fifty-seven came into operation in April 1991 and almost all had followed suit by 1994. The spread of GP fundholding, by contrast, was slow, patchy and unpopular. The more idealistic doctors objected to being asked to run their practices as businesses, while it was widely alleged that preference was given to the patients of fundholders over non-fundholders, creating a two-tier system with more resources going to wealthier practices than to the poorer. In fact, the system gradually settled down and was working quite well when it was abolished by Labour after 1997 and replaced by a not so very different system of Primary Care Groups.

The NHS reforms, ironically, were one of Mrs Thatcher's most successful achievements, securing, in Simon Jenkins' words, 'a real change in the management of the NHS without undermining its principle'.[17] Treatment was still delivered free to all patients at the point of service and was overwhelmingly funded out of general taxation. By the mid-1990s the NHS was treating more patients, more efficiently than in the 1980s, and the creaking old service was enabled to stagger on for another decade.

The final verdict on Social Thatcherism is a mixed one. Nicholas Timmins, the 'biographer' of the welfare state, concludes that despite her instincts Mrs Thatcher actually strengthened the welfare state – at least the NHS, education and those parts of the social services used by the middle class, making them more efficient in order to keep her key constituency happy. She might have wished that 'her' voters did not look to the state for their health and education – and mortgage tax relief – but the fact was that they did: opinion surveys consistently showed that the public remained as firmly wedded to the basic principles of the welfare state as ever.[18] As a result services were trimmed at the edges by charging for things like dentals checks and eye tests which had previously been free, and greatly increasing the cost of prescriptions, but the central pillars remained untouched. The main exceptions were those services principally relied on by the poor: public sector housing and the basic state pension, whose value was allowed to wither away, and other forms of income support. Poverty visibly increased as a substantial 'underclass' was cut off from the rising prosperity of the majority.

But in the big picture the scale of social provision was undiminished over the Thatcher years: it still took around 25 per cent of GDP at the end as it had at the beginning. 'The welfare state remained remarkably un-rolled back thirteen years after Margaret Thatcher took power . . . The stark change . . . was the growth in economic inequality.'[19]

The poll tax

Meanwhile, the poll tax, launched as the 'flagship' of the Government's programme for the third term, was facing an increasingly difficult passage through Parliament and was building into a major political disaster. Back in 1985 Mrs Thatcher had been slow to be convinced that it was practicable. Once sold on it, however, she set her face against the swelling chorus of opposition and determined to stake her own position and the electoral prospects of the Tory party on forcing it through. She elevated support of it into a test of loyalty to herself, with ultimately fatal results. In particular she insisted – almost alone – on calling it the 'community charge'. Already within weeks of the election the first whispers of revolt were stirring within the party. Sir George Young emerged as a leading dissenter on grounds of equity, pointing out that his personal liability would fall from £2,000 to around £300 a year while others, much poorer, would pay more. In the Commons Mrs Thatcher agreed that some people would gain under the new system, but insisted that the losers would be those unlucky or foolish enough to live in high-spending boroughs. It was up to the electors in those authorities to vote for lower spending. Moreover, she claimed, the principle that every local resident should pay the same community charge, regardless of income, was *not* regressive, since the charge still covered only 25 per cent of local-authority expenditure (less in Scotland): the rest was met by central government out of general taxation, so higher-level taxpayers would still pay more.[20]

At this stage, however, she still envisaged phasing the charge in over several years. But then for the second time on this issue the Government let itself be bounced by the unrepresentative enthusiasm of the party faithful. Ridley and Mrs Thatcher were impressed by speaker after speaker at the Blackpool conference in October 1987 calling for the hated rates to be scrapped without delay. 'We shall have to look at this again, Nick,' she whispered to him on the platform.[21] A few weeks later Ridley announced that 'dual running' would be abandoned and the community charge introduced all at once in April 1990. In her memoirs Lady Thatcher confessed that this 'may have been a mistake'.[22]

In fact, the poll tax was not really a flat-rate charge: it did allow means-testing at the bottom of the scale. The Government was never given credit for the fact that around seven million poorer people – later increased to nine million, or one in four of the total number of charge payers – were eligible for rebates of up to 80 per cent of their liability; while those on Income Support had even the remaining 20 per cent taken into account in calculating their benefit. So the very poorest were not greatly affected, though households on low wages certainly were. But these substantial rebates compromised the initial simplicity of the idea, while increasing the burden on those who were liable for the full whack, who still numbered twenty-five million compared with just nineteen million who paid rates. 'What you vote for, you pay for,' Mrs Thatcher told her restless backbenchers the following year.[23] 'The community charge is a way of asking people to pay for what they vote for, and when they do they will vote against Labour authorities.'[24] The problem was how they were to pay the bill in the meantime.

The Bill finally received the Royal Assent in July 1988. The average charge was then expected to be about £200 per head. A year later that estimate had risen to £278; by January 1990 it was £340, with many councils anticipating even higher levels. In her memoirs Lady Thatcher blamed 'the perversity, incompetence and often straightforward malice of many local councils' for seizing the chance to push up spending and let the Government take the blame. But this was precisely what Lawson and Heseltine had predicted they would do. Lawson argues that they should have capped spending first; and in retrospect she agreed.[25]

Instead, opposition continued to build right across the political spectrum. In April 1989 the charge came into force in Scotland, a year ahead of England and Wales, amid widespread refusal to pay, orchestrated by the Scottish National Party and supported by some left-wing Labour MPs. The Labour leadership, while opposing the tax, was careful to avoid the illegality of being seen to advocate non-payment. But by September between 15 and 20 per cent of those registered had not paid; while a significant number simply did not register. This Scottish resistance fuelled alarm among Tory MPs in England, prompting a series of ever more desperate efforts to cushion the impact by offering transitional relief over the first few years – in effect a return to dual running.

In July 1989, realising that Ridley was a public-relations liability in this area, Mrs Thatcher replaced him with the much more voter-friendly Chris Patten, who warned her that the flagship was threatening to sink the whole fleet but nevertheless took on the job of trying to save a policy he did not believe in. At first she was 'quite adamant that she was not going to have the Treasury dish out all this money' to ease the transition.[26] But in October Patten did squeeze substantial additional funding out of Lawson to head off the latest revolt. In theory, Patten now claimed, no one should be more than £3 a week worse off. But that calculation was based on an average bill of £278, which was already out of date. When Labour members pointed out that even Mrs Thatcher's own Barnet council was preparing to set a charge well above the Government's guideline, she was reduced to retorting that the charge in neighbouring Labour boroughs was even higher.[27]

In February 1990 Tory councillors in Oxfordshire and Yorkshire resigned from the party rather than be responsible for introducing the tax. In March there were disturbances in Manchester, Bristol, Birmingham, Hackney, Lambeth, Swindon and even true-blue Maidenhead. The Government's popularity, which had held up well for two years, went into free fall. The climax came with a huge demonstration in Trafalgar Square which turned into the worst riot seen in the capital for decades. Cars were burned, shops looted and some 450 people injured – mainly police.

Mrs Thatcher was horrified by such 'wickedness'. By focusing on the violent minority, however, she missed the point: though the far left as usual hijacked a peaceful demonstration to their own pseudo-revolutionary ends, the poll-tax disturbances up and down the country were predominantly a middle-class revolt. 'I was deeply worried', she wrote. 'What hurt me was that the very people who had always looked to me for protection from exploitation by the socialist state were those who were suffering most.'[28] Alan Clark nailed the essential flaw in his diary for 25 March:

> As usual the burden will fall on the thrifty, the prudent, the responsible, those of 'fixed address' who patiently support society and the follies of the chattering class.[29]

In other words the charge missed those it was intended to hit and punished those it was designed to protect: in Chris Patten's words, it was 'targeted like an Exocet missile' on the middle class in marginal constituencies.[30] It was not surprising that Tory MPs began to fear for their seats.

The community charge was finally introduced in England and

Wales on 1 April 1990 at an average of £363 per head. Some councils were soon reporting levels of non-payment as high as 50 per cent. Mrs Thatcher set up a Cabinet committee, chaired by herself, to consider further measures of relief, but she still refused to consider any serious retreat from the basic principle. The only alternative was to keep on dishing out money from the Treasury to try to reduce the impact in the second year, which was likely to be election year. In July Patten secured from John Major – the new Chancellor, following Lawson's resignation the previous October – a further £3.2 billion to extend transitional relief to another four million people (making eleven million in all). This was a grotesque inversion of Thatcherite economics. By now the charge had become a fiasco from which the only escape seemed to be through ditching the Prime Minister herself.

Nothing did more than the poll tax to precipitate Mrs Thatcher's downfall. It seemed to epitomise the least attractive aspects of her political personality – a hard-faced inegalitarianism combined with a pig-headed authoritarianism – and at the same time demonstrated a fatal loss of political judgement. The last was the most surprising. Despite her cultivated image of bold radicalism and unbending resolution, she had actually shown herself, in office and before that in opposition, a very shrewd and cautious politician who had always taken care not to get too far ahead of public opinion. The poll tax was the one issue on which her normally sensitive political antennae really let her down. It was the most spectacular failure of Mrs Thatcher's premiership and it cost her her job.

Permanent revolution

As if it had not already got enough on its plate with the reform of education, the health service and local taxation, the third Thatcher Government was also hyperactive on practically every other front of domestic politics. As is the way with Governments when things start to go wrong, however, practically all of these restless interventions ran into difficulties of one sort or another.

Privatisation had been the unexpected triumph of the second term. But the attempt to maintain momentum after 1987 led the Government into more problematic territory. British Steel, sold back to the private sector in December 1988, was the last relatively straightforward operation. At least Mrs Thatcher had the political sense not to rush into privatising the railways: she left that poisoned chalice to her successor. But she was committed to privatising water and electricity, both of which raised sensitivities which had not applied to telephones or gas.

Water was a particularly emotive issue – rather as she had found milk to be when she was Education Secretary. The public had a strong instinctive feeling that water, unlike gas and electricity, was a precious natural resource, a God-given necessity of life like air itself, which should not be owned or even distributed for profit but held by the Government in trust for everyone. Most of this was irrational: water supply was a customer service like any other, and one crying out for new investment to replace antiquated pipework, sewage treatment plants and the like: it made sense to seek this from the private sector. It was not widely realised that a quarter of the industry was privately owned already; or that, as Mrs Thatcher never tired of pointing out, water was privately run in many other countries: 'Even Socialist France knows that privatised water is a better deal than nationalised water.'[31] Nevertheless, there persisted a deeply held belief that private companies were not to be trusted with public health. There were also concerns about continued access to rivers and reservoirs for leisure use: millions of anglers feared being barred from private property.

The solution was not simply to sell off the nine existing Water Authorities, but to separate the commercial business of supplying water from the environmental responsibility for monitoring purity and pollution. Public opinion remained resolutely hostile, and in March 1989 Mrs Thatcher admitted that 'the subject of privatisation of water has not . . . been handled well or accurately'.[32] One of the first acts of Chris Patten, on taking over as Environment Secretary in July, was to write off the industry's debts to the tune of £4.4 billion and promise another £1.1 billion of public money – described as a 'green dowry' – to tempt investors to risk their money. With this inducement the sale went ahead successfully in December 1989, with a second instalment the following July. Over the next ten years, when steeply increased charges failed to prevent hosepipe bans in summer and flooding in winter, the water companies were regularly criticised for putting profits before investment. But the fact was that much higher investment went into the water industry after privatisation than before; while fears about public health largely melted away.

Electricity posed different problems. The minister responsible in this case was the rehabilitated Cecil Parkinson, who was keen to demonstrate that his Thatcherite credentials were unimpaired. But Mrs Thatcher herself was torn between the desire of Nigel Lawson, on the one hand, to break up the industry (as Peter Walker had failed to do with gas) and the equal determination of Lord Marshall, the chairman of the Central Electricity Generating Board and one of her favourite businessmen, to keep it together. Parkinson devised a compromise involving just two new companies, PowerGen and National Power, the larger of which (the latter) would keep control of nuclear power. The problem was that, when subjected for the first time to proper commercial analysis, the cost of nuclear power turned out to be prohibitive: the private sector would not take it on without open-ended guarantees which the Government could not give. First Parkinson had to remove the cost of decommissioning the nine oldest power stations from the package; then John Wakeham, who succeeded him in July 1989, was forced to exclude nuclear power from the scheme altogether and postpone the planned flotation of the twelve new distribution boards from the spring to the autumn of 1990. This was a huge embarrassment, particularly in view of Mrs Thatcher's personal commitment to nuclear power. The sale of the two new generating companies, twelve regional distribution companies and the National Grid eventually went ahead in 1991. The nuclear industry was finally privatised in 1996.

If privatisation was one Thatcherite policy which was running into rougher water the longer it went on, the reverse was true of trade-union legislation. Norman Fowler, in 1998, followed by Mrs Thatcher's sixth and last Employment Secretary, Michael Howard, in 1990, tied up some loose ends. Fowler's Act reinforced the requirement to hold strike ballots, strengthened the rights of individual members against their union and banned the misuse of union funds; Howard's finally outlawed the closed shop and ended the unions' legal immunity from civil damages. The fact that these Bills were passed with scarcely a murmur of protest was a measure of how thoroughly the unions had been cowed since 1979.

Another important area of national life which Mrs Thatcher was determined to sort out was broadcasting. Thwarted in her attempt to commercialise the BBC, she still wanted to break up the cosy BBC/ITV duopoly. As Home Secretary, Douglas Hurd weakly allowed himself to be bullied into auctioning off the existing ITV franchises to the highest bidder – with results which even Mrs Thatcher regretted. Meanwhile, she did everything she could to help Rupert Murdoch dominate the new medium of satellite television. Just as John Biffen had allowed Murdoch to buy *The Times* and *Sunday Times* without reference to the Monopolies Commission back in 1981, so now Hurd's successor, David Waddington, bent the Government's own rules governing satellite broadcasting to allow Sky TV to swallow its only rival, BSB. Whereas other newspaper proprietors were allowed to own no more than 20 per cent of terrestrial television channels, Murdoch's News International was permitted to own nearly 50 per cent of BSkyB by the device – which Waddington admitted was technically illegal – of classifying it as 'non-domestic'.[33] Mrs Thatcher 'loves the whole idea' of Sky, Wyatt recorded, 'because it whittles down the influence of the BBC. It makes the area of choice more open and it is more difficult for people of left-wing persuasion to mount steady drip-drip campaigns against her.'[34] Also in the name of 'choice' existing restrictions were relaxed to allow television companies to buy exclusive rights to major sports events – the plums with which Murdoch tried to woo audiences to his satellite channels.

Other botched reforms between 1987 and 1990 – all of which bore the stamp of the Prime Minister's personal initiative – included a misguided scheme to require football supporters to carry identity cards; an attempted shake-up of the legal profession, largely abandoned in the face of professional resistance; the ill-considered Child Support Agency, intended to force absent fathers to meet their obligations; and an impractical attempt to pursue elderly war criminals. All these, on top of the poll-tax fiasco, contributed to a mounting impression of a government which had lost its way. Hitherto Mrs Thatcher had been seen as hard-faced but competent. Now after ten years in office she suddenly appeared as alarmingly incompetent – especially since the economic achievement on which her authority depended was suddenly going wrong.

Inflation again

If the Thatcher Government had one overriding objective in May 1979 it was the conquest of inflation. Conquer inflation, the Prime Minister and her economic advisers believed, by means of sound monetary policy, and everything else would follow. By June 1983 they were able to boast that inflation was conquered – if not in quite the way they had projected – and over the next four years steady growth and rising living standards for the majority duly followed. Unemployment was falling at last, public spending was under control, the balance of payments was in surplus, interest rates were at their lowest for years. By June 1987 Lawson was hailed as the 'miracle' Chancellor who had found the holy grail which had eluded all his post-war predecessors. But the control of inflation always remained, as he had once rashly described it, 'judge and jury'.[35] Not content with getting it down to 3 per cent by 1987, he announced that his next ambition was to bring it down to zero.[36]

Yet within a year the miracle started to go badly wrong. Hubris met its poetic nemesis. A combination of overconfidence, poor forecasting and consequent policy errors fuelled a credit boom which sucked in massive quantities of imports, leading to a runaway trade deficit and an upturn in inflation. Far from the zero Lawson had targeted, by the end of 1989 the figure was pushing 10 per cent, practically back to where it had been in 1979. After ten years of Mrs Thatcher, in other words, inflation was actually higher than it ever was under Harold Macmillan – the supposed father of inflation – while unemployment, though down, was still around two million and likely to rise again as a new recession threatened. This was where the Conservatives had come in. More than the poll tax or divisions over Europe, this central failure of economic management called into question the success of the whole Thatcherite project since 1979. As the huge bonus of North Sea oil began to run out, all the old problems seemed to be returning. As unemployment fell from its 1986 peak, the trade unions were beginning to recover their confidence. Pay was growing faster than productivity which – though much improved – still lagged behind most comparable economies. Manufacturing had never recovered from the previous recession; investment had been low and the national infrastructure was visibly crumbling. Moreover, of particular concern to Mrs Thatcher, the combination of renewed inflation and high interest rates hit particularly hard the new middle class of self-employed small businesspeople, entrepreneurs and new home-owners, whose aspirations she had specifically set out to advance and protect. 'Good housekeeping' suddenly seemed a sour joke.

Several factors contributed to this mortifying reversal. Always more cautious than her expansive Chancellor, Mrs Thatcher was already worried that the boom was getting out of hand in the autumn of 1986: Lawson was confident that he could rein it back after the election if necessary. But 'Big Bang' and the deregulation of the City had removed from his armoury many of the controls which previous Chancellors had been able to use to cool an overheating economy. Moreover, in the autumn of 1987 Treasury forecasts underestimated how rapidly the economy was already growing. Lawson raised interest rates a point, to 10 per cent, in August. But when the stock market crashed in October, his concern – shared by almost all the City pundits – was to prevent a downturn such as had followed the Wall Street crash of 1929, leading to a world recession. To forestall this threat he cut interest rates again, in three steps between October and December, down to 8.5 per cent. In his defence, Lawson points out that the pundits and the opposition parties were all urging him to do more. Cutting interest rates, however, turned out to be the wrong medicine at the wrong time. The economy was already growing faster than the Treasury realised, and the cuts gave it an additional stimulus which was not needed. Mrs Thatcher was in America at the time of the crash, where the Federal Reserve took the opposite course and tightened credit. Nevertheless she approved Lawson's strategy, as she wrote in her memoirs, 'to make assurance double sure'.[37]

Then Lawson's first budget of the new Parliament threw further fuel on the fire. Undeterred by warnings that it might be the wrong moment, he was determined to crown his reputation as a great reforming Chancellor with another spectacular tax-cutting package. With revenues buoyant, he was able to balance the books with a surplus for 1988–9 and plan for zero public borrowing in 1989–90, while leaving himself £4.2 billion to give away. Not only was he able to trim the standard rate of income tax by another two pence to twenty-five pence in the pound, while announcing his ambition to cut it eventually to twenty pence; but he simultaneously slashed the top rate – which Howe had cut to 60 per cent back in 1979 – down to 40 per cent, one of the lowest rates in the world. All intermediate tax bands were abolished. At the same time Capital Gains Tax was reformed and simplified, and married women were at last assessed separately from their husbands – an equalisation which Mrs Thatcher strenuously opposed.

This was Lawson's apogee. The opposition parties – and some Tories – denounced the budget for blatantly favouring the rich, at the very moment when social-security reforms were withdrawing many benefits from the poor. 'It's tax cuts galore but not if you're poor' was the *Daily Mirror*'s headline. Executives earning £70,000 a year gained an extra £150 a week, while families struggling on that much a week had their income cut.[38] Mrs Thatcher privately had her doubts: she would have settled for a top rate of 50 per cent, and she thought announcing a 20 per cent target an unnecessary hostage to fortune.[39] But most Tory MPs were ecstatic, and she could not fail to join in the general enthusiasm. 'Nigel's budget,' she told the Conservative Central Council four days later, was 'a humdinger' which wrote 'the obituary for the doctrine of high taxation ... It was the epitaph for Socialism.'[40]

But 1988 was a classic instance of the maxim that the morning-after verdict on budgets is usually wrong. Lawson's tax cuts, whether or not they were equitable, were fatally mistimed. They were followed the next day by yet another cut in interest rates. But over the next few months, as consumers rushed to spend their gains, the deficit soared and inflation turned up, the Chancellor was forced into an embarrassing reversal: he was obliged to raise interest rates again repeatedly but without effect, so that by September the base rate was back to 12 per cent, and a year later reached 15 per cent, thus clawing back from home-owners all the benefit given away in March.

But this was not the ground of Mrs Thatcher's quarrel with Lawson. His real error, for which she could not forgive him, was not the budget but his monetary policy. The rot set in, she believed, when Lawson lost faith in the Medium Term Financial Strategy, which he himself had devised, stopped targeting £M3 or any other measure of money supply because of the difficulty of measuring it, and started to pay more attention to the sterling exchange rate as a more reliable indicator, until during 1986 he had begun to target a particular rate – between 2.80 and 3.00 Deutschmarks – not as a rough guide, but as a fixed goal. In her memoirs she explained that this was a fundamental error of economic principle. 'It is . . . quite impossible to control both the exchange rate *and* monetary policy . . . You can either target the money supply or the exchange rate, but not both.'[41]

The value of a currency, to a monetarist, is no different from that of any other commodity: it must be allowed to find its level in a free market. All attempts to peg it are futile. By targeting a particular value Lawson unaccountably forgot all the hard-learned lessons of the past decade and went back to the bad old days of Harold Wilson trying to defend the fixed parity of sterling in 1964–7. By using monetary policy to target a desired exchange rate, he was obliged first to *cut* interest rates when he should have raised them, fuelling inflation, and then when the pound began to fall to *raise* them when the economy (and home-owners) were crying out for them to fall. On this analysis Lawson's policy – which Mrs Thatcher claimed to have known nothing about in its initial stages – was simply wrong.

But in reality it was not so simple. Her own attitude at the time was not as clear as she later pretended. On the contrary she was, in Lawson's word, 'schizoid' about sterling. Though in theory a good monetarist who was happy to see its value determined by the market, in practice she saw the national currency – 'our pound' – as a symbol of national pride and national strength. She liked to see it going up, as an expression of the world's confidence in Britain, and hated to see it fall.

In fact, between a low exchange rate on the one hand and low interest rates on the other she was ambivalent. She could see the benefit of the low pound between 1983 and 1987, which helped Britain recover from the 1980–81 recession. She liked the lower interest rates which that involuntary devaluation made possible and did not want to tie sterling into the Exchange Rate Mechanism of the European Monetary System for fear of having to raise interest rates to protect a fixed parity. She was not initially against the ERM on principle – she had criticised the Callaghan Government for failing to join in 1978 – but increasingly became so from a contradictory mixture of patriotism and free-market economics. She both feared having to defend an unrealistic parity and resented the loss of national independence in being tied, officially or unofficially, to the Deutschmark. Where chauvinism and economics pulled her different ways, the former generally prevailed; but both chauvinism and economics led her to distrust Lawson's hankering to manage the markets by international agreement. 'Something always goes wrong,' she complained, 'when Nigel goes abroad.'[42]

But she was – on her own admission – isolated. Most of the Cabinet would have happily gone along with the judgement of the Chancellor and the Foreign Secretary, supported by the overwhelming consensus of Fleet Street and the City, in favour of joining the ERM as soon as possible. She had imposed a personal veto in 1985, and maintained it until 1990; but she could not stop Lawson working to achieve the same result by informal means. Part of her problem was that currency management was the jealously guarded preserve of the Treasury and the Bank; but that had never worried previous Prime Ministers with more amenable Chancellors. Her real difficulty was that Lawson was intellectually and politically too strong for her. After five years in the job – and two more as Financial Secretary before that – he had, as she acknowledged, 'complete intellectual mastery of his brief' and complete confidence in his own ability.[43] Mrs Thatcher was not often at a disadvantage, but she lacked the technical expertise to argue successfully with Lawson, even when all her instincts told her he was wrong. She could not bully him, as she did most of her other ministers. Moreover, his reputation gave him an unusual independence. He was widely believed to have no further political ambition but to be only waiting for his moment to step down for a lucrative job in the City. So long as the party and the press believed that he could do no wrong she could not afford to lose him, let alone sack him. She had no choice but to go along publicly with his policy while doing her best to undermine it from within – rather as she had done with Heseltine, and ultimately with the same result.

For another year, therefore, the Government was hobbled by this damaging rift at its heart. Nicholas Ridley – now almost Mrs Thatcher's last uncritical ally in the Cabinet – describes the 'deep and mutual hostility' that now existed between the Prime Minister and the Chancellor and their 'considerable feat of acting' in broadly concealing it from the rest of their colleagues.[44] Publicly she continued to endorse him in lavish terms – 'I fully, gladly, joyfully, unequivocally, generously support the Chancellor,' she declared in June 1989 – though the extravagance of her language only confirmed that the Lady did protest too much.[45]

In terms of immediate policy, in fact, they were no longer so far apart during 1989 as they had been the previous year. Bitterly as she blamed Lawson's misguided exchange-rate policy for having let inflation take hold again, she had no doubt that, since it had taken hold, bringing it back under control must be the Government's paramount priority. Since she continued to rule out joining the ERM so long as inflation was high, she had no alternative to Lawson's only other anti-inflationary instrument, the use of interest rates. There are hints that she might have preferred to raise taxes instead, repeating the formula of Howe's 1981 budget, which she increasingly looked back on as her Finest Hour. But Lawson had no intention of reversing what he regarded as the crowning achievement of his Chancellorship. His reliance on interest rates was widely condemned, most memorably by Ted Heath, who compared him to 'a one-club golfer'. Criticism from Heath, however, was usually enough to convince Mrs Thatcher that she was on the right track. She was clear that inflation, misguidedly unleashed, must be wrestled down again whatever the pain involved. 'I don't want Nigel to go,' she told Wyatt. 'He has got to finish what he started first.'[46]

In retrospect she realised that she should either have let him go or sacked him. It was clearly an intolerable position to have the two dominant personalities of the Government locked in fundamental disagreement, neither trusting the other, each determined to prevail. Mrs Thatcher's partisans maintain that she, as Prime Minister, held the ultimate authority: Lawson was arrogant and overweening to set his will against hers and she would have had every right to sack him. Lawson, on the contrary, insisted that in managing the exchange rate in preparation for entering the ERM he was following the Government's declared policy: it was Mrs Thatcher who was covertly undermining it. If she wanted to change the policy she should have done so openly, by agreement with the Cabinet or at least – as in 1980–81 – with an inner group of economic ministers. Instead she continued to pay lip service to joining the ERM 'when the time is ripe' and winked at his policy which, he insists, she was perfectly aware of.

Like the dispute with Heseltine over Westland, the issue in the end was not the rights or wrongs of policy but the way the Prime Minister ran her Government. In her central dispute with Lawson, Mrs Thatcher may well have been right: her instincts were sometimes sounder than his intellectual chutzpah. He unquestionably let the economy run out of control in 1987–8. Faced with a strong minister whom she could not dominate, however, she once again worked to undermine him instead of confronting him. In 1986 Heseltine kicked over the traces and walked out. Lawson stuck to his post, probably longer than he should have done; but in the end she made his position untenable by openly preferring the advice of her private adviser. By this time she was doing much the same in foreign policy, listening to Charles Powell rather than Geoffrey Howe and the Foreign Office. Fundamentally the problem was that she did not trust her colleagues. Heseltine, Tebbit, Lawson, Howe – she saw them all in turn as challenges to her authority; and she could not tolerate rivals. It was this inability to lead a team which ultimately brought her down. Lawson unquestionably made mistakes and overplayed his hand. But the responsibility for resolving the dispute within the Government was hers: instead she let it fester. It was no way to run a Government and it eventually destroyed her.

23

A Diet of Brussels

The declaration of Bruges

MARGARET Thatcher's aggressive style of politics was founded on the identification of enemies. Her success was measured by the trophies stuffed and mounted on her walls: Ted Heath in 1975; the 'wets' and General Galtieri in her first term; Arthur Scargill and Ken Livingstone in her second. For the third term she lit on a new antagonist worthy of her mettle: the President of the European Commission, Jacques Delors.

In most respects Delors was perfectly cast for the role: he was both a foreigner and a socialist, so that by fighting him she united in one crusade her two great causes, British patriotism and the defeat of socialism – a combination with maximum populist appeal to her supporters. But Delors turned out to be a more difficult opponent than Scargill or Galtieri, partly because she had been instrumental in appointing him in the first place, preferring him to his French rival Claude Cheysson in 1985; still more because she had taken a leading role in driving forward the first tranche of his reform of the Community, the Single European Act, in 1986; but above all because in anathematising Delors she was taking on a powerful section of her own party and the wider political establishment which was committed to Britain's role in Europe. Hitherto the Tory grandees, though sceptical of her policies and wary of her moral fervour, had been willing to let her fight their battles for them: they had no convincing alternative to her economic policies, but were agreeably amazed when they proved successful without provoking revolution. Now that she was directly challenging a central tenet of their faith, however, they stirred themselves to more active resistance which ultimately brought her down.

In her memoirs Lady Thatcher claimed that the European Community changed fundamentally in the later 1980s, and that Delors was 'a new kind of European Commission President' with grander ambitions than his predecessors – determined, now that the single market was agreed if not yet fully functioning, to press on to the next objectives enshrined in the founding treaties: economic and monetary union (EMU) and the harmonisation of social policy and labour law. The Treaty of Rome had set the nebulous objective of 'ever-closer union', building into European institutions the belief that there must always be movement – sometimes rapid, sometimes stalled, now in one area, now in another, but always in the direction of closer integration. Mrs Thatcher tried to portray Jacques Delors as a power-hungry bureaucrat determined to expand his empire. 'The French socialist,' she reflected grimly, 'is an extremely formidable animal.'[1] Certainly Delors was ambitious to maintain momentum: he had no intention of letting the single market settle down before seeking fresh areas of advance. But he could have done nothing without the active encouragement of the leaders of the major countries of the Community. Mrs Thatcher blamed the unelected bureaucrat Delors for exceeding his powers; but Delors was only pursuing a course set by François Mitterrand and Helmut Kohl and supported by all the other elected leaders.

She made a point of treating Delors as a mere official. By 1988, however, she believed that Delors had 'slipped his leash as a *fonctionnaire* and become a fully fledged political spokesman for federalism'. This might be acceptable to foreigners, she believed, with their shallower democratic tradition and well-founded distrust of their domestic politicians. 'If I were an Italian I might prefer rule from Brussels too. But the mood in Britain was different.'[2]

She had to believe that Delors was behaving improperly in order to argue that he was taking the Community into new areas of integration which Britain had not signed up for when it joined the Common Market. But the goal of economic and monetary union had been set in 1972 and it had been explicitly reaffirmed in the Single European Act which she had signed in 1986. Mrs Thatcher insisted that it did not necessarily entail a single currency or a single central bank, institutions which would involve an unacceptable pooling of national sovereignty. Her difficulty was that this was exactly what all the other members did think it meant. Her need to demonise Delors derived partly from her knowledge that she had been slow to grasp what she now perceived as a mortal threat to Britain's interest: on the contrary she had actually welcomed and promoted the Act from which the mandate to press on to economic union was derived. She now insisted that she had been tricked. She could not see, because she did not want to see, that movement towards economic and monetary union was, as John Major wrote in his memoirs, 'the logical extension of the changes she had set in train'.[3]

In resisting what she conceived as a mortal threat to Britain's historic identity – symbolised by the sanctity of sterling – Mrs Thatcher found the great cause of her last years in office, and of her retirement. Here was an external enemy, more threatening by far than a distant South American dictator, whose defeat required the Iron Lady once again to don the armour of Churchillian defiance. In opposing the insidious spectre of rule by Belgian bureaucrats and German bankers, while insisting that Britain's true interest lay with the United States – 'the new Europe across the Atlantic'[4] – she believed that she was indeed emulating her hero, not only the defiant British bulldog of 1940 but the half-American chronicler of 'the English-speaking peoples'. But her identification with 'Winston' was self-deluding: Churchill was not the simple cartoon patriot that she imagined. Not only did he issue a number of resounding (if vague) statements in support of European unity between 1945 and 1951, but in private letters, even before the end of the war, he had frequently voiced an emotional identity with Europe which was quite alien to Mrs Thatcher's overriding deference to the United States.

Europe was her greatest blind spot. She knew and reluctantly accepted that Britain was irreversibly a member of the Community: but in her heart she wished it was not so. She had no respect for European politicians of any stripe. She veered between denouncing federalist ambitions as a mortal threat to Britain's sovereignty and dismissing them as fantasy that would never happen. As a result she never engaged seriously with what Britain's role in the evolving Community should be. On other subjects, from Russia to global warming, she set out to inform herself, listened to advice and devised a coherent diplomatic strategy which she then adhered to. On the subject of Europe, however – the central problem of British foreign policy – there were, as her policy adviser Percy Cradock wrote, 'no large strategic discussions; no seminars'.[5] She knew what she thought, and she knew what the rest of the Community ought to think, too, if they knew what was good for them. Consequently she was always two steps behind events, unable to lead or even to participate fully, but only to react angrily to what others proposed.

Of course she had a case. She was entitled to point out – as she did repeatedly – that Britain was 'way ahead' of other countries in implementing the provisions necessary to allow a single market – let alone a single currency – to function properly: the abolition of exchange controls (which Britain had ended in 1979), free capital movements and the dismantling of a host of protectionist barriers. She was constantly complaining that the French were still blocking the import of Nissan cars manufactured in Britain, or imposing unfair duties on Scotch whisky;[6] and she believed they should honour what was already agreed before they went on to grander schemes. She believed in small practical steps, an incremental approach, rather than grand schemes. This she thought was the British way, and therefore by definition the better way. But the truculent manner in which she told them so only irritated her partners and alienated potential allies. The merits of her argument for a Europe of independent nations were smothered by the self-righteousness of her performance.

Moreover, she saw divisions over Europe as a threat to her authority at home. With only two reliable allies in the Cabinet – Ridley and Parkinson – and flanked by a Chancellor and Foreign Secretary who both, for different reasons, wanted to join the ERM as soon as possible, she became obsessed with the idea that Lawson and Howe were 'in cahoots' against her and must be kept from ganging up on her if her will was to prevail. In fact Howe and Lawson had scarcely any contact with each other. Their attitudes to the ERM were entirely distinct. Since going to the Foreign Office, Howe had become a convert to the full EMU package, including the single currency, and wanted to join the ERM as soon as possible in order to maintain Britain's standing as a leading member of the Community. Lawson, by contrast, was as strongly opposed to the single currency as Mrs Thatcher herself. He wanted to join the ERM primarily as a monetary discipline; but he also thought that being inside the ERM would give Britain greater leverage to *prevent* a single currency than it could exercise outside it. This difference in objectives should have allowed Mrs Thatcher to play them off against each other while maintaining her own authority: instead she dealt with each of them separately, while demonstrating no confidence in either, which eventually, just before the Madrid summit in June 1989, did drive them to make common cause.

At Hanover in June 1988 Mrs Thatcher set out to block the establishment of a European Central Bank; but as so often she was outmanoeuvred. Chancellor Kohl persuaded her to agree to a committee mainly composed of central bankers – including her own appointee, the Governor of the Bank of England – to study the question; then they slipped in Delors to chair it. Still she convinced herself that the creation of a central bank was not within the committee's terms of reference. Lawson was amazed at her naivety. 'Prime Minister,' he claims to have told her, 'there is no way that a committee with those terms of reference can possibly do anything else than recommend the setting up of a European Central Bank.'[7] Charles Powell confirms that the committee, once set up, 'put on an unexpected turn of speed' and within nine months came up with the three-stage timetable for EMU which was to be the next great bone of contention between Mrs Thatcher and the rest of the Community.[8] If she had been seriously engaged with the issue, she should have fought it from within. On the contrary, either she still thought it would never happen or she believed that she could veto it later.

Another example of her deafness to what she did not want to hear was her choice of Leon Brittan to replace Arthur Cockfield as Britain's senior commissioner in Brussels. She refused to reappoint Cockfield because she thought he had 'gone native', and persuaded herself that Brittan, because he had been dry on economic policy at the Treasury and tough on policing as Home Secretary, would naturally be sound on Europe as well. She should have known that he was solidly pro-European and had long supported joining the ERM. But she was so anxious to push him out of domestic politics into a suitably prestigious job, to get out of her promise to bring him back into the Cabinet, that she overlooked his record – and then felt betrayed when he too 'went native'.[9]

The turning point in Mrs Thatcher's public attitude to the Community was her speech to the College of Europe in Bruges in September 1988. She had been booked to speak there, ironically, by the Foreign Office, which hoped it would provide a suitable occasion for a 'positive' speech on Europe. By the time she came to deliver it, however, two more developments had determined her to use it as an opportunity to slap down Jacques Delors. First, in a speech to the European Parliament in July, Delors had deliberately trailed his coat by suggesting that 'an embryo European government' should be established within six years and that in ten years '80 per cent of laws affecting the economy and social policy would be passed at a European and not a national level'.[10]

Then Delors compounded his offence by bringing his federalist pretensions into the British political arena. Again it was the Foreign Office which thought it might be helpful to have him address the TUC at Bournemouth. Delors gave what he regarded as a fairly standard speech, expounding the vision of harmonised laws on hours of work, working conditions and collective bargaining which the following year became the European Social Charter. But he succeeded in converting the traditionally anti-European British trade unionists almost overnight to the realisation that Europe could offer a way of regaining some of the ground they had lost during ten years of Thatcherism – which of course was exactly what Mrs Thatcher objected to. If the Foreign Office had hoped to soften Labour hostility to the Community, they succeeded, as Lawson put it, 'beyond their wildest dreams'.[11] But for twenty years Labour's hostility had been a major factor in keeping Mrs Thatcher positive towards Europe: the moment Labour began to reverse itself, she immediately felt free to do the same.

In fact Mrs Thatcher's Bruges speech as eventually delivered contained a good deal that was positive, including the assertion that 'Our destiny is in Europe, as part of the Community.' But Britain, she insisted, had its own view of that future. 'Europe is not the creation of the Treaty of Rome . . . The European Community is one manifestation of that European identity, but it is not the only one.' She went on to set out five 'guiding principles', of which the most important was the first: the best way to build a successful Community was not through closer integration but through 'willing and active co-operation between independent sovereign states'. Of course, she conceded, Europe should 'try to speak with a single voice' and 'work more closely on the things we can do better together than alone'. But then came the two killer sentences:

> But working closely together does not require power to be centralised in Brussels or decisions to be taken by an appointed bureaucracy . . . We have not successfully rolled back the frontiers of the State in Britain, only to see them re-imposed at a European level with a European superstate exercising a new dominance from Brussels.

This was the key passage. She went on to set four more guiding principles: that solutions should be practical, not utopian; that Europe should be committed to enterprise and open markets; that it should not be protectionist; and that it should maintain its commitment to NATO.[12] But most of the controversy the speech aroused centred on her first point.

It was not so much the content, but the highly charged language which ruffled feathers. It seems commonplace today, but in 1988 no one had spoken of a European 'superstate' before. Talk of a 'European conglomerate' with bureaucrats exercising 'dominance from

Brussels' was – in the words of Michael Butler, until 1986 Britain's permanent representative in Brussels – 'very dangerous stuff indeed'.[13] Mrs Thatcher's dichotomy between a free-trade area (good) and a superstate (bad) was false, in Butler's view, since the Community had already developed far beyond the one, and no one wanted the other. By signing the Single European Act Mrs Thatcher herself had already agreed to everything that was now on the table.[14]

It was not in fact what she said at Bruges but the way the speech was 'spun' by Bernard Ingham which ensured that it haunted the Tory party for years to come. 'In fact,' Lawson admitted, 'it said a number of things that needed to be said, in a perfectly reasonable manner . . . But the newspaper reports, which reflected the gloss Bernard Ingham had given when briefing the press . . . were very different in tone and truer to her own feelings: intensely chauvinistic and . . . hostile to the Community.'[15]

Mrs Thatcher herself was delighted with the effect of the speech, and repeated its central message in even less diplomatic language at the Tory Party Conference a few weeks later. She was convinced that she had struck a popular chord, she told *The Times*, because federalism was 'against the grain of our people'.[16] To keep her up to the mark a number of prominent Eurosceptics formed a pressure group to campaign against ceding any further powers to the Community. The Bruges Group was mainly composed of leading Thatcherite academics – the sort of people who had provided much of the intellectual excitement of early Thatcherism but now merely purveyed an increasingly strident nationalism.

The problem with the Bruges speech was that it did not represent a policy. It was, rather, as Nye Bevan described unilateral nuclear disarmament in 1957, 'an emotional spasm'.[17] Its impact on the development of the Community was minimal; while its effect on the Conservative party over the next decade was almost wholly disastrous. In the short term, it split the party, releasing in the grass roots a vein of suppressed hostility to the Community which had been building up for years and now burst out unchecked with the leader's undisguised approval, while at the same time infuriating most of the Cabinet and the party hierarchy whose lifelong commitment to Britain's role in Europe as pursued by Macmillan and Heath was undiminished. The Prime Minister's abrupt reversal of the party's established attitude to Europe led inexorably to Geoffrey Howe's resignation from the Government just over two years later and to the parliamentary party's withdrawal of support which forced her own downfall in November 1990.

The 'ambush' before Madrid

Delors unveiled his programme in April 1989, in two parts: one his three-stage timetable for economic and monetary union, the other the so-called 'Social Charter'. Mrs Thatcher immediately rejected both documents out of hand. The first, she told the Commons, 'is aimed at a federal Europe, a common currency and a common economic policy which would take economic policies, including fiscal policy, out of the hands of the House, and that is completely unacceptable'.[18] The second was 'more like a Socialist charter of unnecessary controls and regulations which would . . . make industry uncompetitive and . . . increase unemployment and mean that we could not compete with the rest of the world for the trade that we so sorely need'.[19] Outright opposition to both initiatives formed the basis of her platform for the elections to the European Parliament on 15 June.

Since the introduction of direct elections in 1979 the Tories had always won these five-yearly polls quite easily. They were, after all, the pro-European party. June 1989, however, found the Conservatives not only beset by rising inflation and the poll tax, but in disarray over Europe too. Mrs Thatcher authorised a manifesto, and a campaign, at odds with the views of most of her candidates, who were almost by definition Europhiles. The tone was set by a disastrously negative poster, displayed on hoardings all round the country, showing a pile of vegetables with the slogan: 'Stay at home on 15 June and you'll live on a diet of Brussels.'[20] In campaign speeches and television interviews she cast herself as Battling Maggie fighting off the foreign foe.

The result was the Tories' first defeat in a national election under Mrs Thatcher's leadership. On a significantly increased poll, up from 32 to 37 per cent, the party gained only 33 per cent of the vote – its lowest-ever share – and lost thirteen seats to Labour, precisely reversing the 1984 result so that Labour now held forty-two to the Tories' thirty-five. Of course the outcome owed less to enthusiasm for a federal Europe than to the Government's growing unpopularity for other reasons nearer home. Nevertheless the result delivered a sharp warning to Tory MPs that Neil Kinnock's Labour party had finally become electable again, while the Prime Minister was becoming a liability whom they might need to jettison before the next election if they wanted to save their seats.

The next week the simmering tension between Mrs Thatcher and her senior colleagues came to a head in the run-up to the European Council in Madrid, when she persisted in trying to exclude her Chancellor and Foreign Secretary from any consultation about the decisions that might be taken at the summit. In public she continued to insist that there was no disagreement between them about the ERM. That might have been strictly true insofar as neither Howe nor Lawson thought it practical to join immediately; but they were both convinced that it would strengthen Britain's hand in forthcoming negotiations about EMU if she would come off the fence at Madrid and give a commitment to join within a set timescale. She was more determined than ever to do no such thing. She prepared for the summit by convening a conference of her private advisers with no elected colleagues present at all.

On Wednesday 14 June Howe and Lawson sent her a joint minute setting out their advice that she should give a 'non-legally binding' undertaking at Madrid to join the ERM by the end of 1992, and asked her for a meeting.[21] She was furious – she describes their request in her memoirs as an attempt to 'ambush' her – but grudgingly agreed to see them the following Tuesday, 20 June, when she bluntly rejected their arguments and refused to tie her hands. A few hours later she sent Howe a paper adding further conditions before Britain could contemplate joining, including the final completion of the single market, which might take years. Their response was to ask for another meeting. She was angrier than ever, tried to talk to the two of them separately by telephone but eventually agreed to see them together at Chequers early on Sunday morning, just before she left for Madrid. There is not much disagreement between the three of them about what happened at this 'nasty little meeting', as she called it. In her view they tried to 'blackmail' her by threatening to resign if she would not agree to state her 'firm intention' to join the ERM not later than a specified date. 'They said that if I did this I would stop the whole Delors process from going on to Stages 2 and 3. And if I did not agree to their terms and their formulation they would both resign.'[22] 'The atmosphere was unbelievably tense,' Lawson confirms:

> Margaret was immovable. Geoffrey said that if she had no time whatever for his advice . . . he would have no alternative but to resign. I then chipped in, briefly, to say, 'You know, Prime Minister, that if Geoffrey goes I must go too.' There was an icy silence, and the meeting came to an abrupt end, with nothing resolved.[23]

'I knew that Geoffrey had put Nigel up to this,' Lady Thatcher wrote. 'They had clearly worked out precisely what they were going to say.'[24] Lawson does not deny it, but insists that this was 'the only instance in eight years as Cabinet colleagues when we combined to promote a particular course of action'.[25] All they were doing, in the first instance, was asking – as Chancellor and Foreign Secretary – to be consulted. Yet she bitterly resented what she called 'this way of proceeding – by joint minutes, pressure and cabals'.[26] It is difficult to argue with Percy Cradock's verdict that the fact that 'a ministerial request for consultation could be construed as a conspiracy . . . illustrated an alarming breakdown of communication and trust within government'.[27]

Prime Minister and Foreign Secretary flew together to Madrid, but Mrs Thatcher did not speak to her colleague on the plane and when they got to the British Embassy she closeted herself all evening with Powell and Ingham, while Howe enjoyed a relaxed supper downstairs with the Ambassador and his staff. When she spoke in the Council the next morning, 'her Foreign Secretary still had not the least idea what she intended to say'.[28]

In fact she was unwontedly conciliatory and constructive. It was widely suggested that following her rebuff in the European elections she came to Madrid with 'diminished clout' and conducted herself less stridently as a result – though she of course denied it.[29] She insisted afterwards that she had defied Howe and Lawson's 'blackmail' by still refusing to set a date for joining the ERM. But in reality she did move most of the way to meet them, by advancing from the vague formula that Britain would join 'when the time is right' to a much more specific set of conditions – not, as she had threatened on 20 June, the final completion of the single market, but merely further progress towards completion, plus British inflation falling to the European average, progress by other countries towards the abolition of exchange controls, and further liberalisation of financial services. These new tests were much more flexible and open to interpretation than her stance hitherto, as was demonstrated just over a year later when John Major was able to persuade her that sufficient progress had been made to declare that the conditions had been met.

On the wider issues at Madrid, EMU and the Social Charter, Mrs Thatcher congratulated herself that she had stood firm. She claimed to have prevented President Mitterrand fixing a timetable for the second and third stages of the Delors Report before the first stage had been completed.

The faithful Wyatt thought that she had done 'brilliantly'.[30] But she had not really achieved anything at all, as the following year showed. Whether, as Lawson and Howe believed, she would have gained herself more leverage at future meetings by agreeing to set a clear timetable to join the ERM cannot be proved. The fact is that Britain was now isolated, however she conducted herself. She did not significantly hold up progress towards EMU by being marginally more constructive; but neither would she have achieved any more by being intransigent. It was too late.

Her fury was reserved for Howe and Lawson, who had backed her into a corner and demonstrated that they had the power to bring her down. At the time she pretended that she had called their bluff. In fact there was no need for resignations since the threat had achieved most of what they wanted. Years later she admitted: 'They overpowered me.'[31] She knew she could not have survived either or both of them resigning. But she vowed, 'I would never, never allow this to happen again.'[32] Four weeks later she employed the Prime Minister's ultimate power to break the Howe–Lawson axis. She resolved to punish Howe – and warn Lawson – by removing him from the Foreign Office. But it was a messy operation.

She was due for a reshuffle anyway – she normally held one before the summer holidays – but this was exceptionally sweeping. Only eight out of twenty-one Cabinet ministers stayed where they were. Two she removed, and two more left voluntarily. The other nine were switched around. Into the Cabinet for the first time came Peter Brooke, Chris Patten, John Gummer and Norman Lamont. Of these only the last could be called a Thatcherite. The overall effect of the changes, Lady Thatcher noted in her memoirs, was that the balance of the Cabinet 'slipped slightly further to the left'. But 'none of this mattered', she assured herself, 'as long as crises which threatened my authority could be avoided'.[33]

But all this minor juggling was overshadowed by the removal of Geoffrey Howe from the job he had held for the past six years. Howe had no warning of what was coming. It was a brutal way to treat one of her most loyal colleagues, her shadow Chancellor in opposition and the architect of the 1981 budget, who in his quiet way had borne the heat of the early economic reforms. The debt she owed Howe's dogged persistence for her survival and success was incalculable; yet Mrs Thatcher had come to despise but simultaneously fear him, believing that he was positioning himself to replace her.

Having decided to remove Howe from the Foreign Office she offered him the choice of becoming Leader of the House or Home Secretary. He accepted the former, but held out for the consolation title of deputy Prime Minister to salve his pride. With hindsight she thought she should have sacked him altogether, rather than leave him bruised but still in a position from which he could wound her fatally the following year. Howe, too, quickly realised that he would have done better to make a clean break. By becoming deputy Prime Minister he hoped to inherit the sort of position within the Government that Willie Whitelaw had occupied before his illness. If Mrs Thatcher had not by this time lost all sense of Cabinet management she would have invited him to fill that crucial vacancy: Howe would have made a very good Willie, had she been prepared to trust him. But 'because Geoffrey bargained for the job,' she sneered, 'it never conferred the status which he hoped'.[34] Bernard Ingham made a point of telling the press that there was no such job as deputy Prime Minister anyway.

And that was not the end of it. If she was determined to remove Howe, Douglas Hurd was by far the best-qualified replacement. After Peter Carrington, Francis Pym and Howe, however, Mrs Thatcher did not want another pro-European toff at the Foreign Office; and at this point she was still strong enough to appoint whomever she wished. She wanted a Foreign Secretary with no 'form', who would uncomplainingly do her bidding. So she appointed John Major.

She had already identified Major as a possible long-term successor. As Chief Secretary at the Treasury since 1987 he had impressed her with his quiet mastery of detail and calm judgement. Always on the lookout for competent right-wingers, she had persuaded herself that he was more of a Thatcherite than he really was. 'He is another one of us,' she assured a sceptical Nicholas Ridley.[35] In fact, though dry on economic issues, Major was by no means a Thatcherite on social policy; he was also unenthusiastic about the poll tax. Even if she had been right, however, thrusting him into the Foreign Office at the age of forty-five, with no relevant experience or aptitude, was bad for him and also bad for her: he could not help looking like her poodle.

Altogether the 1989 reshuffle was a political shambles which antagonised practically all her colleagues, dismayed her party and delighted only the opposition. Loyal supporters like Ian Gow foresaw trouble ahead;[36] while even Wyatt worried that 'she has made a bitter enemy of Geoffrey Howe'.[37] For her part Mrs Thatcher quickly recognised that by leaving Howe in office she had got the worst of all worlds. Meanwhile the rest of the Cabinet felt that if she could treat Howe like that, none of them was safe.

From now on Mrs Thatcher took a positive delight in flaunting her hostility to all things European. When France hosted a G7 summit in Paris that summer to coincide with the bicentenary of the French Revolution she took the chance to deliver a patronising lecture on the superiority of the British tradition of human rights going back to Magna Carta. Then at Strasbourg in December she unilaterally vetoed the adoption of the Social Charter. She was happy to accept common rules in some areas, like health and safety and freedom of movement, but she rejected the harmonisation of working hours, compulsory schemes of worker participation and the like. More importantly, however, she was unable to block the next stage of progress towards EMU. It needed only a majority of member countries to call an Intergovernmental Conference (IGC) to set a definite timetable. But she still insisted that it would require unanimity for the conference to decide anything, and so long as she was there this was out of the question.

'I do not think we are out of step,' she declared at her post-summit press conference. 'I think steadily others are coming in step with us.'[38] Alternatively she persuaded herself that it was actually good to be isolated, that in being isolated she was actually leading Europe. 'Sometimes you have to be isolated to give a lead.'[39] But this was self-delusion. She had a legitimate alternative vision of Europe. But right or wrong she was the worst possible advocate for her vision. Her ceaselessly confrontational style became – in the view of her long-suffering colleagues who had to try to pick up the pieces after her barnstorming performances – 'counterproductive'.[40] 'It wears out a bit,' Douglas Hurd recalled. 'I think that quite a lot of her colleagues began to regard it as theatre.'[41]

The truth is that Mrs Thatcher's European policy was no policy at all. It reflected, but also greatly exacerbated, instinctive British suspicion of the Continent. It pointed up real difficulties – of sovereignty, of democratic accountability, of economic divergence – in the way of 'ever-closer union' of the Community. There was a case for proceeding one step at a time, just as there was – and still is – a case for preferring a community of independent nations to a superstate. But by continually saying 'no' Britain only lost influence on a process from which it was in the end unable to stand aside, thus repeating the dismal game of catch-up which it had been playing at every stage of Europe's development since 1950. Europe was the greatest challenge facing Mrs Thatcher's premiership. It was also the greatest failure of her premiership. And it was a failure directly attributable to her own confrontational, xenophobic and narrow-minded personality.

24

Tomorrow the World

The export of Thatcherism

BY the mid-1980s Thatcherism had become an international phenomenon. Partly just because she was a woman, which meant that in all the photographs of international gatherings she stood out, in blue or red or green, from the grey-suited men around her (and was always placed chivalrously in the middle); partly on account of the strident clarity of her personality, her tireless travelling and her evangelical compulsion to trumpet her beliefs wherever she went; partly as a result of Britain's unlikely victory in the Falklands war; partly in recognition of her close relationship with Ronald Reagan and her intermediary role between the Americans and Mikhail Gorbachev – for all these reasons Margaret Thatcher had become by about 1985 one of the best-known leaders on the planet, a superstar on the world stage, an object of curiosity and admiration wherever she went and far more popular around the world than she ever was at home.

Above all she was the most articulate and charismatic champion of a wave of economic liberalisation which was sweeping the world, turning back the dominant collectivism of the past half-century. She did not, of course, originate it. The anti-socialist and anti-corporatist counter-revolution was a global phenomenon observable literally from China to Peru. It originated, if anywhere, in Chicago, where both Friedrich Hayek and Milton Friedman had been at different times professors. The turning of the intellectual tide was reflected before Mrs Thatcher even became Tory leader by both of them being awarded the Nobel prize for economics – Hayek in 1974, Friedman in 1976. It was in Chile that their heretical ideas were first determinedly put into practice when General

Augusto Pinochet, having overthrown (with American help) the democratically elected Marxist government of Salvador Allende in 1973, brought in the so-called 'Chicago boys' to instigate an extreme experiment in free-market reform enforced by the methods of a police state. The politics were detestable, but the economics set a model for the rest of South America and beyond.

In the early days of her leadership Mrs Thatcher knew that she was riding, or hoped to ride, a global wave. 'Across the Western world the tide is turning', she declared in March 1979, just before the General Election which brought her in to power, 'and soon the same thing will happen here.'[1] The idea that she was the pathfinder only seized her some years later. 'In 1981,' she recalled, 'a finance minister came to see me. "We're all very interested in what you're doing," he said, "because if you succeed, others will follow." That had never occurred to me.'[2] By 1986, however, she had begun to glory in the claim that Britain had led the world.

Incontestably the British example – particularly privatisation – played a part. But equally obviously the counter-revolution had its own momentum, in both East and West, as one social democratic country after another ran into the same sort of problems that Britain had encountered in the 1970s and responded in more or less the same way. Over the next decade the same necessity imposed itself right across Europe. In the fifteen years from 1985 over $100 billion worth of state assets were sold off, including such flagship national companies as Renault, Volkswagen, Lufthansa, Elf and the Italian oil company ENI, adding up to 'the greatest sale in the history of the world'.[3]

Above all the free-market contagion spread to the citadels of Communism itself – to China as early as 1981 (where the experiment of economic liberalisation remained under strict political control) and then to the Soviet Union in the form of Mikhail Gorbachev's *perestroika* programme, whose inherent contradictions rapidly precipitated the collapse of the whole Communist system. Mrs Thatcher was entitled to celebrate the triumph of ideas which she had not only followed but proselytised with missionary fervour. But the very fact that the phenomenon has been virtually universal – so that, as Mrs Thatcher herself noted, not just conservative but even nominally socialist governments were equally forced to conform to the global *Zeitgeist* – is the proof that it had its own irresistible momentum, irrespective of her contribution, significant though that was.

The collapse of Communism and the 'problem' of Germany

Nevertheless the sudden and quite unexpected collapse of Communism in the autumn of 1989 was a triumphant vindication of all that Mrs Thatcher had stood for and striven to bring about since 1975. Whether you call it Thatcherism or some other name, the fall of the Berlin Wall, the liberation of the Soviet empire and the disintegration within two years of the Soviet Union itself represented the ultimate victory for her philosophy and her – and Ronald Reagan's – military strategy. The overriding context of all her politics for forty years had been the Cold War; and now suddenly the West had won it.

In her memoirs she gave the principal credit to Reagan 'whose policies of military and economic competition with the Soviet Union forced the Soviet leaders . . . to abandon their ambitions of hegemony and to embark on the process of reform which in the end brought the entire Communist system crashing down'. But since the actual collapse had occurred after Reagan's time she felt obliged to extend the credit to his successor, George Bush, who 'managed the dangerous and volatile transformation with great diplomatic skill'; and even, through gritted teeth, to some of the other European allies, 'who resisted both Soviet pressure and Soviet blandishments to maintain a strong western defence – in particular Helmut Schmidt, Helmut Kohl, François Mitterrand and . . . but modesty forbids'.[4] This was false modesty, however. As the President's staunchest ally she had no doubt who deserved most credit, after Reagan himself, for the success of their joint strategy. In retirement she had no doubt that this was her greatest achievement.

Nevertheless the implosion of Communism did not bring her unmixed joy. On the contrary, her last year in office was one of her most difficult on the international front. For the immediate consequence of the opening of the Berlin Wall was an irresistible momentum to reunite the two parts of Germany, a prospect which exacerbated her fear and loathing of the former enemy. At the same time she was having to come to terms with a new administration in Washington in which she had much less confidence than she had in Ronald Reagan. At her moment of ideological victory, therefore, she found herself more isolated on the world stage than ever before.

She was relieved when Vice-President George Bush trounced the Democrat Michael Dukakis in November 1988 to ensure continuity of Republican rule. But she would never have the same rapport with Bush that she had with Reagan. She was now the senior partner, but Bush, unsurprisingly, had no wish to be patronised. Guided by a new team of advisers – James Baker as Secretary of State, Dick Cheney as Secretary of Defense, Brent Scowcroft as National Security Adviser – he determined to make his own alliances. In particular, even before the fall of the Berlin Wall, Bush had identified Helmut Kohl as the European leader with whom he should forge a special relationship. With Mrs Thatcher it was necessary for him to show that he was his own man.

Bush's relations with his European allies are fully documented in *A World Transformed*, his remarkably candid joint memoir written with Brent Scowcroft, which reprints a lot of documents, transcripts of telephone conversations and diary accounts of the intense diplomacy accompanying the end of the Cold War – far more than has yet received security clearance at the Bush Library in Texas.* From this there emerges a vivid picture of the tensions between the leading players and the extent of Mrs Thatcher's isolation as Bush and Kohl, with much less objection than she hoped for from Mitterrand and Gorbachev, rushed to consummate the reunion of the two Germanies far faster than she thought wise or desirable.

Even before the heady events of November, however, from the very beginning of Bush's presidency she was afraid that Washington was going soft on nuclear disarmament. Gorbachev was trying to split NATO by offering cuts to prevent the alliance modernising its short-range nuclear forces (SNF). Kohl, under domestic pressure from the Social Democrats and Greens, wanted to delay modernisation and reduce the number of missiles immediately. By contrast, Scowcroft wrote, 'Thatcher was unyielding on any changes that might weaken NATO defences.'[5] She wanted the Americans to let her handle Kohl, which they were unwilling to do – partly because 'Margaret . . . was even more unyielding than we, and far more emotional about the dangers of compromise', but also because Bush was not willing to play second fiddle to her.

She was very annoyed when Kohl's Foreign Minister, Hans-Dietrich Genscher, tried to 'bounce' the alliance into SNF cuts by announcing them in the Bundestag before they had been agreed. She gave Bush her views in a telephone conversation which he described as 'vintage Thatcher': 'We must be firm with Germany

---

* Much of the material relating to Bush's dealings with Chancellor Kohl has been declassified, however, confirming the accuracy of what appears in *A World Transformed*. Only a few disparaging remarks by Kohl about Mrs Thatcher are omitted.

. . . There could be no question, no question, she repeated, of negotiations on SNF.'[6]

But the Americans did change their position on SNF negotiations. Mrs Thatcher, Scowcroft recalled, was 'not happy . . . particularly since we had not consulted with her beforehand':

> The truth of the matter was that we knew what Thatcher's reac-
> tion would be . . . We believed we had to make this gesture to
> the Germans . . . and, had we consulted the British, it would have
> been very awkward to proceed over their strong objections.[7]

Before the May 1989 NATO summit in Brussels she was still
'unhappy and apprehensive' about the American proposal for immediate cuts in conventional forces, linked to SNF negotiations; but
at the end of the day she knew the limits of her influence. She told
the envoys who came to brief her in London, 'If the President
wants it, of course we will do it.'[8] Yet even as they sat down to
dinner in Brussels she buttonholed Bush. 'We must not give in on
this,' she told him. 'You're not going to give in, are you?' In the
end James Baker and the Foreign Ministers – still Howe for Britain
– found a form of words she could accept. 'Our strategy of using
our conventional forces proposal to encourage a deal over the nuclear
forces problem worked,' Bush wrote. The next morning, to his relief,
'Margaret waxed enthusiastic. I suspect she did not want to be sepa-
rated from the United States.'[9] But while the Americans congratulated themselves on 'a resounding success', the press had no doubt
that Mrs Thatcher had suffered a humiliating defeat.[10]

The next day Bush went on to Germany and delivered a speech
at Mainz in which he referred to West Germany and the United
States as 'partners in leadership'. Mrs Thatcher took this as a snub
to her special relationship with Washington. 'In truth she need not
have worried,' Scowcroft wrote. 'The expression had no exclusionary
intent and was meant only for flourish and encouragement.'[11] Nevertheless it was widely interpreted as reflecting a real and important
shift in transatlantic relationships. Bush tried to make up by describing
Britain as America's 'anchor to windward'. 'This was kindly meant,
but not exactly reassuring,' Percy Cradock commented. 'The anchor
to windward is a lonely position and not the one we had imagined we occupied.'[12]

At least one special relationship did persist, however, between
Scowcroft and Charles Powell, whom Scowcroft regarded as 'my
opposite in the British Government'. Secure lines were installed so
that the National Security Adviser could speak directly to his coun-

terparts in London, Paris and Bonn. 'All either one of us had to do was to push a button and lift the receiver to have the phone ring on the other's desk . . . We soon learned how to explore in a comfortable, offhand manner the limits of the flexibility we felt our principals would have on various issues.' Scowcroft felt that by this time Powell was 'the only serious influence on Thatcher's views on foreign policy'.[13]

Mrs Thatcher naturally watched the dominoes come down across Eastern Europe with unrestrained delight, as first Poland and Hungary moved towards democracy without provoking Soviet intervention; then the Hungarians allowed refugees from East Germany to cross into Austria; and finally the East German authorities themselves opened the Berlin Wall on 9 November and the population emerged like the prisoners in *Fidelio* to tear it down with pickaxes, crowbars and their bare hands and dance exultantly on the ruins. Bulgaria, Czechoslovakia and Romania followed before the end of the year as the so-called 'velvet revolution' brought the dissident playwright Václav Havel to power in Prague, while President Ceauşescu and his monstrous wife were summarily executed in Bucharest on Christmas Day. Bliss was it in that dawn to be alive. But Mrs Thatcher, mindful of the excesses of the French Revolution 200 years before, was already wary of things getting out of hand. Back in 1982 she had predicted that the Wall would fall one day:

> The day comes when the anger and frustration of the people is so great that force cannot contain it. Then the edifice cracks: the mortar crumbles . . . One day, liberty will dawn on the other side of the wall.

But she admitted she had not expected it so soon. When it happened, she told reporters in Downing Street that she had watched the television pictures with the same enthusiasm as everyone else and celebrated 'a great day for liberty'. But even at that moment she was quick to stamp on questions about German reunification. 'I think you are going much too fast, much too fast,' she warned. 'You have to take these things step by step and handle them very wisely.'[14] But she quickly found that the impetus of events was too strong for her.

She had three admissible reasons for resisting the prospect of a united Germany. First, she was afraid that its sheer economic strength would upset the balance of the European Community. Second, she was afraid that a neutral or demilitarised Germany would leave a gaping hole in NATO's defences against a still-nuclear Soviet Union. Third, she feared that the loss of East Germany (and the disintegration of the Warsaw Pact generally) might destroy Gorbachev and thus jeopardise the biggest prize of all, democracy in the USSR. All these were rational arguments for caution. But they were underpinned in Mrs Thatcher's mind by another, inadmissible reason – her virulent and unappeased loathing of the wartime enemy.

There is no easy explanation of why Margaret Thatcher found it so much harder than others of her generation to forget the war. Certainly it dominated her adolescence from the age of fourteen to twenty – her last four years at school, her first two at university – but she was not alone in that. Grantham suffered fairly heavy German bombing – probably heavier than anywhere outside London except for Coventry and Plymouth; also from 1941 Lincolnshire was full of US airbases and US airmen, which sharpened her awareness of the Americans' role in saving Europe from itself. She had heard first-hand testimony of the nature of the Nazi regime from the young Jewish refugee whom her parents briefly had to stay before the war; later she had a large Jewish community in her Finchley constituency. But all this pales in comparison with the experience of her male contemporaries who actually fought in France, Belgium, North Africa and Italy, let alone those who liberated the concentration camps, almost all of whom – certainly the future politicians among them – seem to have come back determined to rebuild the continent, ready to forget the war and move on. She had suffered no personal loss of family or close friends to explain her enduring bitterness. Yet forty years later she was still consumed by an 'atavistic fear of Germany and [a] suspicion of the German people *qua* people'.[15]

As soon as the Wall came down in November 1989 she knew that Kohl would lose no time in pressing for reunification of the two Germanies; but she believed that the four wartime allies, if they were resolute, could still prevent it, or at least delay it for ten or fifteen years. Unification was not a matter for the Germans alone, she insisted, but affected NATO, the EC, the Russians and the whole balance of power in Europe. She even tried to argue that the Helsinki Agreement precluded any alteration of borders. In Paris she hoped to form an Anglo-French axis to contain Germany, but found Mitterrand unhelpful. A week later she flew to Camp David to share her fears with the President directly. 'She particularly worried that talk of reunification or changing borders would only frighten the Soviets,' Bush recorded:

'The overriding objective is to get democracy throughout Eastern Europe,' she told me. 'We have won the battle of ideas after tough times as we kept NATO strong' . . . She added that such change could take place only in an environment of stability.[16]

'The atmosphere,' Mrs Thatcher acknowledged, 'did not improve as a result of our discussions.'[17] In fact, Brent Scowcroft felt 'some lingering sympathy for Thatcher's position', believing that she 'had her eyes on some very important priorities'.[18] But from the moment Kohl had telephoned him to describe the 'festival atmosphere [like] an enormous fair' as the Wall came down, the President was firmly on Kohl's side.[19] 'We don't fear the ghosts of the past,' he assured the Chancellor. 'Margaret does.'[20] For his part Kohl was exasperated by Mrs Thatcher's obstruction. 'I think it is a great mistake on Maggie's part to think this is a time for caution,' he complained.[21] Her ideas were 'simply pre-Churchill. She thinks the post-war era has not come to an end. She thinks history is not just. Germany is so rich and Great Britain is struggling. They won a war but lost an empire, and their economy. She does the wrong thing. She should try to bind the Germans into the EC.'

Kohl still professed to see reunification as a long process over several years, with West Germany meanwhile remaining in NATO and the GDR in the Warsaw Pact – as Mrs Thatcher wanted.[22] Bush suspected that Kohl really hoped for unification much sooner than this, but did not want to prejudice it by seeming to press too fast. Nevertheless he was happy to give Kohl 'a green light. I don't think I ever cautioned him about going too fast.' In his relaxed view 'self-determination was the key, and no one could object to it'.[23]

Brent Scowcroft still shared Mrs Thatcher's worry about Gorbachev's response. 'It was still possible that the Soviets would conclude that a united Germany was intolerable and oppose it, by force if necessary. Or they would successfully impose conditions on it taking place which would render it unacceptable to us.'[24] The difference was that while the Americans, determined that the new Germany should be a member of NATO, were working to overcome Soviet opposition, Mrs Thatcher was trying to deploy Gorbachev's objections as a brake. From their private conversations she believed that Mitterrand also shared her alarm and hoped that he would join with her to slow the process down; but whatever he may have said in private, Mitterrand was realistic. He had no intention of opposing the cherished project of his friend Helmut Kohl, but still put the preservation of the Franco-German axis before her idea of a Franco-British one. 'He made the wrong decision for France,' she asserted in her memoirs.[25]

The diplomatic method eventually agreed was the 'Two-plus-Four' process, whereby the two Germanies negotiated the domestic details of unification in an international context approved by the United States, the Soviet Union, Britain and France. This met Mrs Thatcher's wish to involve the Russians, despite American fear that it would give them a chance to be obstructive. But Bush gambled that Gorbachev could be won over, and he was right.

Mrs Thatcher's other concern was that premature euphoria about the end of the Cold War would lead to reductions in defence spending. When she met Bush at Camp David – just before he was due to meet Gorbachev in Malta for the latest round of arms-limitation talks – she was adamant that he should give nothing away. 'We had a good visit,' Bush wrote, 'but she did not want to see any defense cuts at all of any kind.' Once again, however, she recognised the limits of her influence. 'In the end . . . Margaret sent me a nice telegram pledging her full support in very comforting words.'[26]

At the NATO summit in Brussels in December she was very unhappy about American proposals for cutting conventional forces in Europe, fearing that the Russians would simply pull their forces back beyond the Urals, from where they could easily sweep west again at a moment's notice. Despite Kohl's repeated assurances that neutralisation was out of the question, he was under strong domestic pressure to reduce the number of allied troops and NATO missiles on German soil; she was afraid that Gorbachev might exploit this weakness to make neutralisation his condition for accepting unification. In the end, however, Scowcroft noted, 'it became apparent that, while not happy, she would acquiesce in what we wished to do'.[27]

By February 1990 she accepted that she was losing the battle, but was still anxious to save Gorbachev's face. 'I fear that Gorbachev will feel isolated if all the reunification process goes the West's way,' she told Bush by telephone. 'He's lost the Warsaw Pact to democratic governments.' Then Bush's account went on:

> Margaret's fears of a united Germany, however, came ringing through. She darkly perceived that Germany would be 'the Japan of Europe, but worse than Japan. Japan is an offshore power with enormous trade surpluses. Germany is in the heart of a continent of countries most of which she has attacked and occupied. Germany has colossal wealth and trade surpluses. So we must

include a bigger country, the Soviet Union [or] you, in the political area.'

'It was not enough to anchor Germany in the EC,' she believed.
'That might become Germany's new empire: the future empires
will be economic empires.'[28] On this occasion Scowcroft found her
arguments becoming more sophisticated and her tone 'much
improved', but still found her fears 'worrying'.[29] He was 'dismayed'
that her anxiety not to upset Gorbachev led her to back a 'demilitarised East Germany', outside NATO, instead of a united Germany
in NATO as the Americans wanted. Meeting Bush in Bermuda in
April, she still argued that 'we should allow Soviet troops to remain
for a transitional period – it would help Gorbachev with his military'. 'I don't agree,' Bush replied, 'I want the Soviets to go home.'[30]

In fact she had already accepted the inevitable at the end of
March when Kohl came to Britain. Heaping insincere encomiums
on the Chancellor, Mrs Thatcher formally gave her blessing to the
new Germany, so long as it was in NATO and retained 'sizeable'
British, French and American forces, including short-range nuclear
weapons, on its soil.

Her acceptance was made easier by the results of the first free
elections held in the old GDR. One of her arguments for delay
had been that the East had lived under authoritarian rule for so
long – first under the Nazis, then under Communism – that it
could not be expected to adapt quickly to democracy. In fact the
voters confounded her by voting heavily for Kohl's CDU, giving a
clear endorsement both to his policy of rapid unification and to
broadly free-market economic policies (the former Communists
won only 16 per cent) and allaying her fears of neutralism. Visiting
Moscow in June, Mrs Thatcher played her part in helping to secure
Gorbachev's acquiescence that the reunited Germany could join
NATO – in return for badly needed Western credits to shore up
the Soviet economy. In July Gorbachev survived a last-ditch challenge from his own hardliners; and Kohl flew to Moscow to receive
the Soviet blessing in person. The new Germany came into being
on 3 October 1990, less than eleven months after the opening of
the Wall.

Even with Germany locked into NATO she still worried that
facile talk of a 'peace dividend' from the ending of the Cold War
would lead to a short-sighted lowering of the West's nuclear guard.
Washington was pressing for an early NATO summit, eventually
held in London in July, to bring forward cuts in both nuclear and
conventional forces in Europe. To her dismay Mrs Thatcher found

herself once again 'at odds with the Americans'. As Bush relates, she still objected to weakening nuclear deterrence by diluting the doctrine of flexible response:

> She argued that we were abandoning the fundamentals of solid military strategy for the sake of 'eye-catching propositions' . . . She saw the move to declare nuclear weapons 'weapons of last resort' as undermining our short-range forces and as slipping us to a position of 'no first use of nuclear weapons', leaving our conventional forces vulnerable . . . She demanded an entirely new draft.[31]

Once again, however, Mrs Thatcher had to swallow her objections and accept 'a compromise text close to the original draft'. Flexible response was modified and the Alliance declared that it was 'moving away' from forward defence. At her insistence the words 'weapons of last resort' were stiffened with an assertion that there were 'no circumstances in which nuclear retaliation in response to military action might be discounted'. Mrs Thatcher was still not happy with 'this unwieldy compromise'.[32] But she had no veto in NATO as she had in Europe, so she had to accept it. 'It was a landmark shift,' Bush wrote. 'It offered the Soviets firm evidence of the West's genuine desire to change NATO. Our offer was on the table.'[33]

The final act of the Cold War was also, suitably enough, the final act of Mrs Thatcher's premiership. In November 1990, as the votes were being cast in London which forced her resignation, she was in Paris attending a meeting of the Conference on Security and Cooperation in Europe (CSCE), at which she committed Britain to substantial cuts in the stationing of conventional forces in Germany. In reality it was a largely ceremonial occasion, with congratulatory speeches celebrating the victory of freedom over tyranny and resolution over coexistence. But it was the triumph of everything Mrs Thatcher had been fighting for all her political life.

The environment and global warming

A major new issue appeared on the political agenda in the late 1980s – and Margaret Thatcher, with all her other domestic and international concerns, deserves much of the credit for putting it there. Since the 1970s 'the environment' had been the fashionable term for a ragbag of relatively minor problems to do with planning and land use. Around 1988, however, environmental concerns suddenly acquired a new dimension with the discovery of global warming, caused – probably – by the build-up in the earth's atmosphere of so-called 'greenhouse gases': carbon dioxide, methane and chlorofluorocarbons. From parochial questions of road building and waste disposal which were normally beneath a Prime Minister's notice, the environment assumed, almost overnight, the status of an international challenge which transcended even the Cold War.

In the early years of her premiership Mrs Thatcher had not taken environmental concerns very seriously. As a combative Tory politician she saw environmental campaigners, particularly Greenpeace, as just another branch of CND, a mix of sincere but naive sentimentalists. She insisted that socialism, inherently inefficient and unaccountable, was the great polluter, whereas free enterprise was both more efficient and better able to spend resources on environmental protection. Indeed, she suggested in 1988, cleaning up pollution was 'almost a function of prosperity, because it is the East European block, their chemical factories, that have been pouring stuff into the Rhine'.[34]

She also believed that coal and other fossil fuels beloved of the left were intrinsically dirty, whereas nuclear energy was clean and safe. Those who campaigned against nuclear power on environmental grounds were simply wrong, like those who imagined they were promoting peace by opposing nuclear weapons. She saw it as her business to cut through this sort of emotive nonsense to deal with the facts. Proud of her credentials as a scientist in a world of arts-educated generalists, she believed that she understood the scientific arguments. She believed that scientific problems would be solved by the further development of science, not by regulation.

One project she had always backed, even before the Falklands gave her a special interest in the region – was the British Antarctic Survey (BAS). It therefore gave her great patriotic satisfaction that it was the scientists of the BAS who in 1985 discovered a large hole in the earth's ozone layer, nearly as large as the United States and growing. International efforts had already been under way for some time to limit the emission of halogen gases, principally chlorofluorocarbons (CFCs) used in refrigerators and aerosol sprays: a UN-sponsored conference in Montreal in 1987 set a target of halving the use of CFCs in ten years. But the fact that the hole in the ozone layer was a British discovery undoubtedly helped persuade Mrs Thatcher to throw her weight into efforts to remedy it. She was also greatly influenced by Britain's Ambassador to the United Nations from 1987 to 1990, Sir Crispin Tickell, a career diplomat who happened to be a serious amateur meteorologist. It was Tickell who brought the urgency of the problem to Mrs Thatcher's attention and persuaded her to make it the subject of a major speech, which he then helped her to write.

A decade later her speech to the Royal Society in September 1988 was remembered as 'a true epiphany, the blinding discovery of a conviction politician, which overnight turned the environment from being a minority to a mainstream concern in Britain'.[35] At the time it made rather less impact. Most of it was a standard affirmation of the Government's commitment to science; only towards the end did she turn to the three recently observed phenomena of greenhouse gases, the hole in the ozone layer, and acid rain. She stressed the need for more research, as well as immediate steps to cut emissions, and emphasised how much money the Government was already spending on cleaning Britain's rivers.[36]

In March 1989 Mrs Thatcher chaired a three-day conference in London on Saving the Ozone Layer, attended by 123 nations, which strengthened the Montreal protocol by setting a new target of ending CFC emissions entirely by the end of the century: she spoke at both the beginning and the end. Within Whitehall and the EC she chased progress vigorously on the tightening of anti-pollution regulations, backing the DoE against the Treasury and other departments which raised the sort of objections on grounds of cost that she herself used to make a few years earlier.[37] In August she told President Bush of 'her intention to overhaul Britain's environmental legislation' – clearly trying to encourage him to do the same;[38] and in November she made a major speech to the UN General Assembly in which she announced the establishment of a new climate research centre in Britain and called for 'a vast international co-operative effort' to save the global environment.[39]

All this was before the final report of the Intergovernmental Panel on Climate Change was published in June 1990. This – the unanimous conclusion of 300 international scientists – warned that if no action were taken to curb the emission of greenhouse gases, average global temperatures would rise by anything between 1.4 and 2.8 per cent by 2030, causing sea levels to rise with disastrous consequences for low-lying areas such as Bangladesh, Holland and East Anglia. (Mrs Thatcher was particularly fond of pointing out that one Commonwealth country, the Maldive Islands, with a population of 177,000, would disappear entirely.)[40] This was the first authoritative international confirmation that global warming was really happening, though the evidence was already visible in severe drought leading to famine in Sudan, Ethiopia and much of central

Africa. But Mrs Thatcher, encouraged by Crispin Tickell, had already anticipated its recommendations. Opening the promised new research centre – the Hadley Centre for Climate Prediction and Research – near Bracknell in Berkshire in May 1990, she committed Britain to stabilising carbon dioxide emissions by 2005, which actually meant a 30 per cent cut over fifteen years, back to the 1990 figure. 'This,' she told George Bush pointedly, 'is a demanding target.'[41]

But the Americans dragged their feet. At the London conference the previous year they had combined with the Soviet Union and Japan to reject an earlier target date for the elimination of CFCs. Now Bush told a conference in Washington that more research was needed before action on carbon dioxide would be justified. Mrs Thatcher pressed him to take the matter seriously.

Her words fell on deaf ears. At the second World Climate Conference in Geneva in November, 137 countries agreed that global warming was a reality and pledged themselves to take action. But while the EC, Japan and Australia advocated freezing CO_2 emissions at 1990 levels by the year 2000, the Americans, this time supported by the USSR and Saudi Arabia, opposed the setting of firm targets. In her speech at the conference – one of her last appearances on the world stage before her fall – Mrs Thatcher tactfully made no direct criticism of American or Russian reluctance. But for once she had to admit that Europe was showing the way. 'I hope that Europe's example will help the task of securing worldwide agreement.'[42]

In Tickell's view the 1992 Earth Summit in Rio de Janeiro, at which 170 countries including the Americans finally agreed to cut CO_2 emissions by 2000, would never have happened without her effort. Five years later the 1997 Kyoto Agreement set a new target of cutting emissions back to the 1990 level by 2010 – only for the US, now led by Bush's resolutely isolationist and oil-oriented son, to refuse to ratify it.

But by then Lady Thatcher had changed her mind. As part of her increasingly slavish subservience to American leadership in the late 1990s, she concluded in her last book, *Statecraft*, that 'President Bush was quite right to reject the Kyoto protocol'. Half-baked scaremongering about climate change, she now believed, had been seized on by the left to furnish 'a marvellous excuse for worldwide supra-national socialism'. The environmental movement was just the latest manifestation of fashionable anti-capitalism, containing 'an ugly streak of anti-Americanism'.[43] This U-turn, made for frankly political reasons, marks a sad retreat from her brave pioneering in the late 1980s, when she had in her own way been a good friend of the earth.

Arms and the Gulf

Meanwhile, in her last months in office, the scandal of the covert arming of Iraq began to break. When the Iran–Iraq war finally ended in stalemate in July 1988, Alan Clark (then still in the DTI) and the latest Minister for Defence Procurement in the MoD, Lord Trefgarne, immediately began lobbying the Foreign Office to lift the 1985 guidelines restricting arms sales to both combatants. Geoffrey Howe was sympathetic and in August minuted Mrs Thatcher, spelling out the commercial benefits of 'a phased approach to borderline cases'. Charles Powell replied that she was 'in general content with the strategy', but it would need careful watching: 'The PM will wish to be kept very closely in touch at every stage and consulted on all relevant decisions.'[44] One of the questions that Lord Justice Scott's subsequent inquiry had to answer was whether this instruction was obeyed. Having studied the exchanges between Clark, Trefgarne and the new Foreign Office minister William Waldegrave, Scott concluded that after December 1988 the relevant correspondence was not copied to the Prime Minister; she was therefore unaware of the subtle semantic revision which allowed the three ministers henceforth to interpret the guidelines more generously.[45] In truth, however, whether or not she knew of the new wording, she cannot have failed to notice that exports to Iraq increased rapidly as soon as the war ended. In October she specifically approved new export credits worth £340 million.[46]

The following month Saddam Hussein turned his violence against his own population and started murdering and gassing the Iraqi Kurds. Yet the flow of British machine tools to his munitions factories continued unabated. The only effect on British policy was to make those in the know more anxious to keep it secret: ministers, including Mrs Thatcher, continued to hide behind Howe's 1985 guidelines, insisting to Parliament that nothing had changed. On the ground the British sales effort could scarcely have been more blatant. In April 1989 no fewer than seventeen major British companies attended the Baghdad arms fair. At last some alarm bells began to ring in Downing Street. In May Mrs Thatcher was sufficiently disturbed by the intelligence she was receiving to set up a Cabinet Office working group on Iraqi procurement (WGIP). But what was it that had disturbed her? According to Scott – based on the evidence she gave to his inquiry in December 1993 – she 'had become concerned about the extent of the Iraqi network for the procurement of materials and equipment for proliferation purposes, as well as of conventional defence-related goods and equipment, from the UK'.[47] In other words she only became concerned when she thought the Iraqis were obtaining nuclear materials, not just conventional equipment, which she had been happy to supply for years.*

Within the Ministry of Defence at least one officer was becoming alarmed at 'the scale on which the Iraqis are building up an arms manufacturing capability'. In June Lt-Col. Richard Glazebrook circulated a paper drawing attention to 'the way in which UK Ltd is helping Iraq often unwittingly to set up a major indigenous arms industry'.[49] He managed to block the export of an infra-red surveillance system but still the build-up went on: he failed to stop a consignment of helicopter spares and a Marconi communications system which would enhance the Iraqi forces' effectiveness in the field. In July his Secretary of State, George Younger, put up to the Cabinet's OD committee a proposal to grant export licences for a £3 billion sale by BAe of 'the "know-how", equipment and components necessary to enable Iraq to assemble 63 Hawk aircraft'. This, according to Scott, was the first admission to senior ministers, including Mrs Thatcher, that the interpretation of the 1985 guidelines had been changed.[50] In their evidence Clark, Trefgarne and Waldegrave argued that the order fell within the revised guidelines, since the Hawk, though capable of being adapted for chemical weapons, was not strictly designed to be lethal. Sharp as ever, Mrs Thatcher wrote in the margin 'Doubtful'; but she failed to pick up the crucial word 'revised'.[51]

A note by the deputy Cabinet Secretary, Leonard Appleyard, set out the humanitarian case against this latest sale and warned of a hostile press if it was approved. Mrs Thatcher underlined several passages, indicating that she shared these concerns. Charles Powell had initially favoured the sale, since 'the pot of gold is enticingly large'; and Percy Cradock agreed. But after reading Appleyard's note Powell changed his mind. 'Iraq is run by a despicable and violent government which has gloried in the use of CW [chemical weapons] and a substantial defence sale to them would be seen as highly cynical and opportunistic.' Mrs Thatcher told the Scott Inquiry that she agreed – on moral grounds:

---

* The Americans were not even worried about helping Saddam acquire a nuclear capacity. In April 1989 Iraqi scientists attended an advanced thermo-nuclear seminar in Portland, Oregon.[48]

'Even though this is a big order,' she said, 'you cannot let [that] influence your judgement against your deep instinct and knowledge that it would be wrong to sell this kind of aircraft, that could be used for ground attack, to a regime that had in fact used chemical weapons on the Kurds.'[52]

On this occasion the committee refused an export licence.

Yet even now – despite her fine words – the Prime Minister was no more willing than her junior colleagues to stop supplying Iraq with the ability to build sophisticated weapons. Right up to the end of July she was seeking to ease rather than tighten restrictions. A meeting chaired by Douglas Hurd on 26 July confirmed the embargo on 'lethal' material but recommended relaxing controls on the export of lathes for the manufacture of weapons – and Powell minuted that 'the Prime Minister found the Foreign Secretary's presentation convincing'.[53] In the event the new policy was never implemented: it was wrecked by Saddam's invasion of Kuwait a few days later and hastily buried. But by approving it Mrs Thatcher retrospectively endorsed the earlier shift of practice on which the whole Scott Inquiry centred. The fact is that right up to the last moment she had been eager to arm Britain's new enemy.

'No time to go wobbly'

Mrs Thatcher had just arrived in the United States on Thursday 2 August 1990 to attend the fortieth anniversary conference of the Aspen Institute in Colorado when the news came in that Saddam Hussein had invaded Kuwait. She immediately took a clear view that the Iraqi action – like Argentina's in 1982 – must be reversed, by force if necessary. Little as she liked telephone diplomacy, she lost no time in making a series of calls: to European heads of government, starting with François Mitterrand, whose prompt support over the Falklands she had never forgotten; to Commonwealth leaders; friendly Arab leaders; and the current members of the Security Council. Most promised support for some form of collective action. The exception, to her disappointment, was King Hussein of Jordan who – as she later told President Bush – was 'not helpful. He told me the Kuwaitis had it coming.'[54]

Bush had, of course, been making many of the same calls himself, so by the time he joined Mrs Thatcher in Aspen the next morning they had already assembled the nucleus of an international coalition against Iraq. They talked for two hours, discussing economic sanctions but not at this stage military options, then went outside to speak to the press. 'Prime Minister Thatcher and I are looking at it on exactly the same wavelength,' Bush told them. But Mrs Thatcher sounded much the more forceful of the two. While Bush hoped for a peaceful settlement and called for the Iraqis to withdraw in accordance with UN Resolution 660 (carried 14–0 by the Security Council overnight), it was she – as he later recognised – who 'put her finger on the most important point by insisting that Iraq's aggression was a test of the international community's willingness to give the Resolution teeth': 'What has happened,' she added, 'is a total violation of international law. You cannot have a situation where one country marches in and takes over another country which is a member of the United Nations.'[55]

But, of course, it was not quite as altruistic as that. Though neither leader acknowledged it, their real concern was that – having annexed the Kuwaiti oilfields – Saddam might, if not prevented, go on to seize the even more important Saudi reserves. 'They won't stop here,' Mrs Thatcher told Bush. 'Losing Saudi oil is a blow we couldn't take. We cannot give in to dictators.'[56]

It is still disputed whether or not Mrs Thatcher's presence in Aspen at the critical moment helped determine Bush's response to the Iraqi invasion. The Americans insist that the President needed no stiffening; and Bernard Ingham (who was there) agrees. 'George Bush had a backbone before he arrived in Aspen and did not acquire it from Mrs Thatcher . . . Her familiar distinctive contribution [was] a clear and simply expressed analysis of the situation.'[57] Doubt arose from the fact that in his first public response the President had stated that he was 'not contemplating' military action. This choice of words, Scowcroft admitted, was 'not felicitous', but he insists that it was not meant to rule out the use of force, merely to keep all options open.[58] Nevertheless the belief took hold in Britain that Bush was a bit of a wimp who was impelled to strong action only by Mrs Thatcher's robust example – an impression which she was happy to perpetuate. Actually it was not until some weeks later that she told Bush that this was 'no time to go wobbly'. There was certainly a difference of emphasis between them: Bush was more concerned than Mrs Thatcher to assemble the widest possible coalition of Western and Muslim nations, and to take no military action without the specific authority of the United Nations, while she wanted to invoke Article 51 of the Charter to justify action in self-defence without further ado. But there is no doubt of Bush's personal resolve.

On her way home she stopped off in Washington to see the President again. While she was with him Defense Secretary Dick

Cheney called with the news that King Fahd had agreed to allow American forces to be stationed on Saudi soil: this was the key decision which made it possible to mount a military operation to expel Iraq from Kuwait. The same day the Security Council voted 13–0 to impose sanctions on Iraq. Mrs Thatcher immediately argued that this gave all the authority needed to impose a blockade to enforce them. But Bush shied away from the word 'blockade' which in international law constituted an act of war. He preferred the more diplomatic 'quarantine', which was the term President Kennedy had used to bar Soviet ships from Cuba in 1962.

The Gulf crisis came at an opportune moment for Mrs Thatcher, both internationally and domestically. So far as her relations with Bush were concerned, she was delighted to have the chance to demonstrate once again that Britain was still America's best friend in a crisis, while scoffing at the Europeans' feebleness. Whether or not her presence in Aspen significantly influenced Bush's reaction, their identity of view instantly recreated the sort of Anglo-American special relationship she had enjoyed with Reagan.

A major international crisis also seemed just the thing to rebuild her position at home. The possibility of military action to repel another aggressive dictator could only revive memories of the Falk-lands. As in 1982 Mrs Thatcher relished the chance to show that she was not afraid of war. Woodrow Wyatt found her on 10 August 'very bullish about the possibility of squashing Iraq'.[59] Eight days later there occurred the incident that put a new phrase into the vocabulary of politics. The question was what to do about two Iraqi oil tankers which were trying to beat the allied blockade. 'We had lengthy discussions with the British about it,' Scowcroft recalled, 'and of course Margaret Thatcher said go after the ships.' But this risked upsetting the Soviets, who still retained some influence with Iraq, so James Baker persuaded Bush to hold off for three days. 'Margaret went along with this delay only reluctantly', Bush wrote:

> I called her at about three in the morning her time – although I wasn't looking forward to it . . . We knew how strongly she wanted to stop those ships. She insisted that if we let one go by it would set a precedent. I told her I had decided to delay and why. It was here, not earlier, as many have suggested, that she said, 'Well, all right, George, but this is no time to go wobbly.'[60]

'George always loved that', Barbara Bush wrote, 'and wobbly he did not go.'[61] Thereafter, Scowcroft recalls, 'we used the phrase almost daily'.[62]

Meanwhile, Mrs Thatcher devoted her diplomatic efforts to berating anyone else she thought insufficiently robust – notably King Hussein who came to Downing Street in early September seeking support for a deal to save Saddam's face. 'He walked into a firestorm,' Charles Powell recalled. 'I was not discourteous,' she insisted later. 'I was firm – very firm indeed.'[63] Above all she was contemptuous of those – most prominently Ted Heath – who muddied the waters by flying to Baghdad to try to negotiate the release of a number of British hostages whom Saddam was holding as pawns in a cruel game of diplomatic poker. In the Commons she was curtly dismissive of Heath's freelance efforts: she was bound to welcome the return of thirty-three whom he had managed to bring out, but pointed out that there were still another 1,400 British nationals in the country.[64] She resolutely refused to negotiate with such barbarism.

In fact her bellicosity, in a situation where British territory was not at stake, probably did her less good than she expected. The polls registered no significant recovery of her popularity over the next three months and the fact that British troops were committed did not save her when her leadership was on the line. Nevertheless, she enjoyed having a 'real' crisis on her hands again. But this time – remembering the trouble she had had with the Foreign Office in 1982 – she was determined to keep control firmly in her own hands. Once again she formed a small war cabinet – but it was not a properly constituted Cabinet committee, just an *ad hoc* ministerial group.

Her first military commitment, as early as 7 August, was to send two squadrons of Tornados and one of Jaguars to Saudi Arabia, Bahrain and Oman, and a destroyer and three minesweepers to join the destroyer and two frigates already in the Gulf. She initially hoped to limit Britain's ground contribution to an infantry or parachute battalion. But the Americans were pressing for tanks, so in September the Chief of the General Staff persuaded her to send the 7th Armoured Brigade (the 'Desert Rats') from Germany, plus two armoured regiments and an infantry regiment, led by Sir Peter de la Billière but ultimately under the command of US General Norman Schwarzkopf. (The French, by contrast, retained operational independence.)[65] The army chiefs hoped that war in the Gulf would win them the same sort of reprieve that the Falklands had secured the Royal Navy.

Mrs Thatcher personally insisted on Peter de la Billière, who had impressed her as the SAS commander in charge of the Iranian Embassy siege back in 1980. He was what she called 'a fighting general' who even spoke passable Arabic. He was on the point of retirement, but she let it be known that if he was not appointed she would make him her adviser in Downing Street.[66] The MoD gave way and sent him to the Gulf, where he fully justified her faith in him.

Almost as if she sensed that her own time might be short, she was impatient to act quickly, without waiting to see if sanctions might do the job without recourse to war and without seeking further authority from the UN. When Parliament was recalled on 6 September dissenting voices in all parties called for caution and delay. She argued on the contrary that ruling out early military action only played into Saddam's hands. 'I told them we already *have* the authority and don't need to go back to the UN,' she reported to Bush. She worried that trying but failing to get a UN resolution, due to a Russian or Chinese veto, would be worse than not trying at all, and saw no need to take the risk. Bush and Baker, however, judged it essential to secure another UN resolution; and by patient diplomacy they eventually succeeded. Resolution 678, authorising the use of force unless Iraq withdrew from Kuwait by 15 January 1991, was carried on 29 November by twelve votes to two (Cuba and Yemen voting against, China abstaining). But by that time Britain had a new Prime Minister.

Colin Powell, then chairman of the American Chiefs of Staff, wanted to give sanctions longer to work. General Schwarzkopf did not think he yet had enough troops. But Bush shared Mrs Thatcher's fear that hanging about in the desert for months would put too much strain on the coalition. In Paris on 19 November she argued that Saddam's use of hostages alone was reason enough to use force and promised 'another brigade and some minesweepers'.[67] She still worried that giving the military everything they wanted would mean further delay. But at her very last Cabinet three days later, after she had tearfully announced her resignation, she was better than her word and pushed through the commitment of another armoured brigade and an artillery brigade, all from the British Army of the Rhine, making a total British contribution of 45,000 personnel.

Her removal from office just as these preparations were gathering pace left her feeling cheated of another war. 'One of my few abiding regrets,' she maintained in her memoirs, 'is that I was not there to see the issue through.'[68] Her fall, according to Peter de la Billière, 'caused consternation' among the troops in the Gulf and dismayed the allies, particularly the Saudis, who could not understand how a democracy could replace a leader without an election.[69] In fact

'Desert Storm' was so overwhelmingly an American operation that her absence made little difference.

As time passed, however, Lady Thatcher persuaded herself that she would not have acquiesced in the American decision to halt the pursuit of Saddam's fleeing forces and leave the dictator still in power. Yet the truth is, as Field-Marshal Sir Michael Carver wrote in 1992, that 'the decision to call a halt was a rare example of voluntarily ceasing hostilities at the right moment'.[70] Having achieved the limited objective of getting Iraq out of Kuwait, the coalition had no authority to go on to topple Saddam, while the Americans very wisely had no wish to get sucked into a long-term occupation of Iraq. 'When she was in office,' Percy Cradock recalled, 'there was no serious talk of that kind, for good reasons.'[71] In retirement Lady Thatcher forgot that when in office she was punctilious about respecting international law. From the start of the crisis she was always careful to limit the coalition's objective to reversing the occupation of Kuwait: she repeatedly denied any intention of removing Saddam which, she said on 19 November, was 'a matter for the people of Iraq'.[72] Though she believed strongly in the proper application of military force, she was also passionately legalistic.

25

On and On

Ten more years?

O N 3 May 1989 Margaret Thatcher chalked up ten years as Prime Minister. Sixteen months earlier, on 3 January 1988, she had already become the longest-serving Prime Minister of the twentieth century. Nevertheless she was reluctant to draw too much attention to the anniversary, partly from superstition, partly for fear that people would say ten years was enough.

Several of her senior colleagues, even as they applauded her achievement, felt she should have chosen this moment to announce that she would step down soon, when she could still have gone in triumph. Peter Carrington actually invited her to his house in Oxfordshire to urge her to retire 'rather sooner than had been in my mind'.[1] According to Carol, Denis had made up his mind as early as June 1987 that she should not fight another election as leader. He told her so around December 1988 and briefly thought he had convinced her. But at this stage Willie Whitelaw told her it would split the party. Denis knew she did not really want to give up and accepted defeat gracefully.[2] But from now on he made no secret of his longing to name the day. He did not force the issue: it was her decision, but he had seen enough of politics to suspect that she would be hurt in the end if she stayed too long.

Having worked so hard all her life Mrs Thatcher dreaded retirement. She loved the job and felt no loss of ability to do it. She believed she had much more still to do. Moreover, she could not think of going until she was sure that she could hand over to a worthy successor who would protect her legacy and carry on her work with the same zeal that she had brought to it; and like most dominant leaders she saw no one who fitted the bill. She was determined to deny any candidate of her own political generation – that is Howe, Heseltine, Lawson or Tebbit – but did not believe that anyone in the next generation was yet ready. Her real problem was that none of the leading contenders from the next two political generations were true Thatcherites.

If she had wanted to groom a Thatcherite successor in the short term, the obvious candidate was Norman Tebbit. But Tebbit's caustic style represented the unacceptable face of Thatcherism. 'I couldn't get him elected as leader of the Tory party even if I wanted to – nor would the country elect him if he was,' she once told Rupert Murdoch.[3] In any case – apart from the question of his injuries in the Brighton bomb – Tebbit had already fallen from favour before the 1987 election. The one presentable right-winger whom she had tried to bring on was John Moore, briefly puffed by the media as her chosen heir; but he had muffed his big chance at the Department of Health and disappeared from view in 1989. All this explains her identification, quite early on, of John Major.

Elected in 1979 with little ideological baggage, Major was not obviously either wet or dry but made his mark first as a whip, then as an able, industrious, self-effacing junior minister at Social Security until appointed Chief Secretary to the Treasury in 1987. Quietly ambitious, he allowed the Prime Minister to think he was more of a Thatcherite than he really was: in fact, having known poverty as a boy and unemployment as a young man, he had a strong sympathy for the underdogs in society. In May 1989 Major was the only current minister invited to her anniversary lunch at Chequers. Woodrow Wyatt had not met him before but was impressed. 'I am glad you like him,' Mrs Thatcher told Wyatt later, 'because I think he's splendid.'[4]

Given that she had no intention of stepping down in the foreseeable future, it was difficult to strike the right note in public. As she had already learned in 1987, talk of going 'on and on' was counterproductive. She must not sound as if she intended to stay for ever. In her determination to give the media no opportunity to treat her as a lame duck, however, she sometimes spoke incautiously of going on to a fourth or even a fifth term.[5]

If the party conference loved the idea of 'ten more years', most of her parliamentary colleagues were much less enthusiastic. In politics, any long-serving leader represents a block on the prospects of others. After ten years a very high proportion of Tory MPs not in the Government had either had their chance or knew that it was never going to come; while those in office were uncomfortably aware that the only way she could freshen the Government, since she had no intention of retiring herself, was to keep shuffling the faces around her. One way and another, her support base at Westminster was growing dangerously thin.

Even as Mrs Thatcher insisted on her determination and fitness to carry on, therefore, there was a growing sense that her time was inexorably running out. She had come through dreadful by-elections and dire opinion polls before, in 1981 and again in 1986, and recorded landslide victories less than two years later. She saw no reason why she could not do it again. But this time round two things had changed. First, whereas in those previous pits of unpopularity her personal approval rating had always kept ahead of the Government's, now her own figure fell commensurately. By the spring of 1990 it had settled at a lower level – around 25 per cent – than she had ever touched previously. At the same time Labour had begun to look – as John Biffen put it – 'distinctly electable'.[6] By late 1989 Labour was pushing towards 50 per cent in the polls and in February 1990 (for the first time since a brief moment in 1986) was the party thought most likely to win the next election.[7]

She was worried by the polls, but she half believed that everything would come right, as it always had before, as soon as the economy was back under control. She was most hurt by the personal polls. 'They say I am arrogant,' she complained to Wyatt. 'I am the least arrogant person there is.'[8] The trouble was, as an unnamed media adviser shrewdly put it in 1990, that she was the victim of her own success:

> In 1979, 1983, 1987, they needed Mrs Thatcher to slay dragons . . . Now in 1990 many of the dragons are perceived to be slain, i.e. trade unions, communism, socialism, unemployment . . . The new dragons are perceived to be of the Government's own making . . . The result of this is that people no longer know what they need Mrs Thatcher for.[9]

'The Chancellor's position was unassailable'

When Mrs Thatcher determined, after the Madrid summit, that she must break what she saw as the Lawson–Howe axis, she made the wrong choice by demoting Geoffrey Howe. Her real problem was with Nigel Lawson. There is a good case that she should have sacked Lawson the year before, when it became clear that they were pursuing irreconcilable financial policies. The trouble was that she admired and was slightly afraid of Lawson, despite her loss of trust in him, whereas she increasingly despised Howe; so Howe was the easy scapegoat, while she went on protesting her 'full and unequivocal and generous backing' for Lawson.[10] But the fundamental difference between the Chancellor and the Prime Minister remained, and within three more months it came to a head.

The catalyst was the return of Alan Walters as Mrs Thatcher's personal economic adviser. Lawson had warned her when she first mooted it that this was a bad idea. His difficulty was not simply that Walters reinforced her refusal to join the ERM. He had been living with that difference of opinion since 1986 and could have gone on living with it. His more serious problem was that Walters made no secret of his view that the Chancellor's determination to hold the value of sterling above three Deutschmarks was misguided and unsustainable. Thus what Lawson calls the 'countdown to resignation' was triggered at the beginning of October by the Bundesbank's decision to raise German interest rates, forcing Britain to follow suit with yet another increase at the worst possible political moment, just before the Tory Party Conference. Despite Walters' warning that high interest rates were already threatening to drive Britain into recession, Mrs Thatcher reluctantly agreed to go to 15 per cent, provoking further howls of protest. But the next day, despite the interest-rate hike, sterling fell below DM3.

The *Daily Mail*, representing the hard-pressed mortgage payers of Middle England, ran a front-page splash denouncing 'This Bankrupt Chancellor', and Fleet Street seethed with rumours of his imminent resignation.[11] Yet two days later Lawson still managed to win a standing ovation at Blackpool for a fighting speech defending high interest rates in the short term as the only way to beat inflation; and the next day Mrs Thatcher backed him with only an imperceptible difference of emphasis. Then she flew off for ten days to the Commonwealth Conference in Kuala Lumpur.

In her absence the *Financial Times* stirred the pot by printing extracts from an article by Walters congratulating himself that 'so far Mrs Thatcher has concurred' with his advice to keep out of the 'half-baked' ERM.[12] It had actually been written for an American magazine the previous year, some months before Walters returned to England. Mrs Thatcher maintained that this made it unobjectionable. Since it was still due to be published in America, and since Walters himself had given it to the *Financial Times*, Lawson was entitled to feel differently. It was not so much the fact of his difference with the Prime Minister which mattered. 'It was her persistent public exposure of that difference, of which Walters was the most obvious outward and visible symbol.'[13] He felt that his position was becoming untenable.

The two protagonists later published their own accounts of the series of meetings – four in all – that took place before his decision was announced. Thursday 26 October was an exceptionally fraught day for Mrs Thatcher. She had only got back from Malaysia at four o'clock on Wednesday morning, after an eighteen-hour flight, and was obviously 'absolutely exhausted'. In the circumstances Lawson felt it would be unfair to tackle her at their regular bilateral meeting that afternoon, but warned her that they needed to talk about the Walters problem. 'She replied that she saw no problem' – but she agreed to see him first thing on Thursday morning, with no secretaries present.

She listened quietly while Lawson told her that either Walters or he would have to go: he did not want to resign but unless she agreed that Walters should leave by the end of the year, he would have no choice. She begged him to reconsider and arranged to see him again at two o'clock. Later that morning he attended Cabinet as normal, betraying no hint of what was in his mind. But at two o'clock he was back, bringing with him his letter of resignation.

After Prime Minister's Questions Mrs Thatcher called John Major to her room at the Commons and told him, 'I have a problem.' When Lawson met her for the last time at around five o'clock, he says that she asked his advice about his successor; she says that she told him she had already chosen Major. Either way, they parted in what Lawson called 'an atmosphere of suppressed emotion'.[14] When she called Major in again he found her close to tears and felt the need to hold her hand for a moment.[15]

Mrs Thatcher wasted no time in carrying out a swift, limited and unusually well-received reshuffle, announced that same evening, which rectified some of the mistakes of July. Major was clearly much better suited to the Treasury than to the Foreign Office, and it was the job he had always wanted.[16] Yet he was initially reluctant to move again when he was just getting used to the Foreign Office. 'I told him that we all had to accept second best occasionally. That applied to me just as much as to him.'[17] Equally Douglas Hurd was still the obvious choice for the Foreign Office, as he had been in July. When she rang at about six to make the offer she was clearly 'still in shock' at Lawson's resignation – Hurd himself was 'flabbergasted' – and did not disguise her doubts. 'You won't let those Europeans get on top of you, will you, Douglas?'[18] The one move she was really happy with was the choice of David Waddington to go to the Home Office. This was the first time in four attempts, that she had managed to send a right-winger there.[19]

She was able to put a positive gloss on the whole reshuffle by emphasising that all three principal appointments – Major, Hurd and Waddington – had achieved their lifetime's dream. 'We are very sad to be without Nigel, but we have an excellent Chancellor of the Exchequer, an excellent Foreign Secretary, an excellent Home Secretary for each of whom it was their ambition.'[20] The press for the most part agreed. The ironic fallout of Lawson's resignation, however, was that Walters resigned too. He was in America when the news broke but immediately realised that his position would be impossible and, despite Mrs Thatcher's efforts to dissuade him, insisted on stepping down as well. Thus by sacrificing Lawson to try to keep Walters, Mrs Thatcher ended by losing both of them. Lawson reflected wryly that, 'however painful it was to me personally, I had performed a signal service to my successor and to the Government in general'.[21]

Despite the swift reshuffle, which arguably improved the Government, Lawson's resignation, following so soon after Howe's demotion, damaged Mrs Thatcher by throwing a fresh spotlight on her inability to retain her closest colleagues. The damage was compounded when Mrs Thatcher appeared on Brian Walden's Sunday morning interview programme on 29 October. Instead of telling the truth – that there had developed between herself and her Chancellor a difference of view which regrettably made it impossible for him to carry on – she gushingly repeated her claim that she had 'fully backed and supported' him. 'To me the Chancellor's position was *unassailable*,' she insisted; but she floundered when Walden asked the killer question:

Do you deny that Nigel would have stayed if you had sacked Professor Alan Walters?

I don't know. I don't know.

You never even thought to ask him that?

I . . . that is not . . . I don't know.[22]

The second instalment of this two-part trial by television the following Sunday gave Lawson the opportunity flatly to contradict her. He told Walden that he had made perfectly clear to the Prime Minister in their three conversations on the Thursday why he was resigning – 'quite clearly and categorically' because she refused to part with Walters.[23]

No one who watched these two programmes could have had any doubt which witness was telling the truth. Not for the first time, but more publicly than over Westland three years earlier, Mrs

Thatcher's reputation for straight speaking had taken a severe knock. It was no longer a question about which of them was right about the economics of the ERM and the exchange rate. Most economists would now say Lawson was wrong. But if she really did not understand why Lawson had resigned she was too insensitive to continue long in office. If she did understand, but chose to keep Walters anyway, that only confirmed that she valued her advisers more than her elected colleagues. Either way she was increasingly living in a world of her own.

The start of a new parliamentary session gave the Prime Minister's critics in her own party a chance to test their level of support. The rules under which Mrs Thatcher had successfully challenged Ted Heath in 1975 allowed for a leadership contest to be held every year. Alec Douglas-Home had never imagined that this provision would be used against an incumbent Prime Minister; but in November 1989, for the first time, an unlikely champion came forward in the person of Sir Anthony Meyer, a sixty-nine-year-old baronet whose political passion was a united Europe. Meyer was not a serious challenger; yet he attracted a significant degree of support. Only thirty-three Tory MPs voted for him, but another twenty-seven abstained. A margin of 314–33 was a convincing endorsement, but it was also a warning shot. The real significance lay not in the figures but in the fact that the contest had taken place at all. If Mrs Thatcher did not make a visible effort to address her backbenchers' mounting worries, she was likely to face a more serious challenge next year.

The Major–Hurd axis

Lawson's departure opened a new phase in the Thatcher Government. Though routinely portrayed by the media as a dictator, the Prime Minister was in fact profoundly weakened from November 1989. In place of Howe and Lawson, the twin pillars of her middle period, Mrs Thatcher now had a new pair of senior colleagues who, if they combined as their predecessors had done before Madrid, had her in an armlock. Neither John Major nor Douglas Hurd was 'one of us'; but she absolutely could not afford to lose another Chancellor or sack another Foreign Secretary. Though less senior and less assertive personalities than Lawson and Howe, Major and Hurd were thus, if they chose, in a position to dictate to the Prime Minister. And in the gentlest possible way they did.

Unlike their predecessors, Major and Hurd met regularly for

breakfast to coordinate their approach.[24] 'We both believed the Prime Minister needed to be coaxed, and not browbeaten,' Major recalled;[25] and his Permanent Secretary observed how skilfully he did it. 'Major went out of his way to be sensitive to what the PM wanted to do, and the fact that he was sensitive meant they got on pretty well. It also meant he got his way on most issues.'[26] For his part Hurd followed Howe's tactic of not attempting to argue with Mrs Thatcher but simply waiting till she had finished before going on patiently with what he had been saying.[27]

She still had doubts about Hurd's capacity to stand up to the wily Europeans. 'The trouble is Douglas is a gentleman and they're not,' she once expostulated.[28] But Major, she believed, was 'perfect'.[29] Several times over the next few months she told Wyatt that Major was her chosen successor. 'Yes, he is the one I have in mind.'[30] 'That has always been my intention, as you know.'[31] As a result she indulged him like a favourite son, averting her mind from the fact that he too lost no time in signalling his wish to join the ERM – the subject was never even mentioned when she appointed him – while he in turn suppressed his doubts about the poll tax.

Meanwhile, he had a difficult economic inheritance. The economy was slowing down. Unemployment, which had been falling steadily since 1986, turned up again over the winter; while inflation carried on rising, from 7.7 per cent in November to 9.4 per cent in April and 10.9 per cent in October 1990 – 'a figure', Lady Thatcher wrote, 'I had never believed would be reached again while I was Prime Minister.'[32] With interest rates at 15 per cent and the revolt against the poll tax in full swing, the Government's poll rating fell to just 28 per cent and Mrs Thatcher's personal approval rating to 23 per cent, two points lower than her previous nadir in 1981.

On these figures the Government faced complete wipe-out in the English local election results in May. In fact the Tories did less badly than expected; but with Labour winning 40 per cent to the Tories' 32 per cent, the Liberal Democrats' 18 per cent and the Greens' 8 per cent, the Tories' performance was still among their worst ever and they lost control of another twelve councils.

In the middle of July Mrs Thatcher suffered another blow when Nicholas Ridley was forced to resign following some unguarded comments about the Germans which were widely assumed to echo her views. Ridley was almost her last unqualified supporter in the Cabinet; losing him made her more than ever the prisoner of Major, Hurd and Howe.

Then, on 30 July, Ian Gow was murdered by the IRA. Though he had not been part of her private office since 1983, he and his wife Jane were still among her closest friends, one of the few couples with whom she and Denis would sometimes dine informally. 'Margaret is quite shattered,' Wyatt wrote. 'She spoke with more emotion than I have heard for a long time and for considerable length . . . She missed him and misses him.'[33] She immediately went down to Sussex to comfort his widow and read the lesson at his funeral on 10 August, still very upset.[34] But she forced herself to keep on with her normal programme, telling her staff to cancel no engagements but to give her plenty of work to keep her busy.[35] Work was always her best therapy, and on this occasion she had no time to grieve. On 1 August she flew off to Colorado, and a few hours later Saddam Hussein invaded Kuwait.

All the time Major, with Hurd in the background, was working at trying to bring the Prime Minister round to joining the ERM. Since Madrid, she had been publicly committed to joining as soon as the conditions she had laid down there were fulfilled: free movement of capital between all the major countries in the system; completion (or near-completion) of the internal market; and British inflation coming down to somewhere near the European average. Since France and Italy were due to free capital movements on 1 July and the single market was already virtually complete, the critical condition was inflation – which was still rising.

Major started trying to talk her round at the end of March. 'I felt from the outset that she could be persuaded to enter if the decision to do so did not humiliate her', he wrote. The next stage of EMU was due to be discussed at the intergovernmental conference in Rome in December 1990. 'Our exclusion from the EMU was making us bystanders in this debate. The Prime Minister did not like this argument, not least because it was true. Yet it did register with her' – though Major still felt she shied away from the topic.[36]

But in the end she did give way. On 14 June she conceded the principle but still insisted on delaying till the autumn. On 4 July she started to consider possible dates. By 4 September she was ready to agree on one condition: she wanted a simultaneous cut in interest rates. 'No cut, no entry,' she told Major. 'We had no choice but to defer to her.' At the last moment she had a fresh attack of doubt and had to be reconvinced.[37] But finally she gave the go-ahead on 4 October. 'Do it,' she now agreed. 'Do it tomorrow.'[38]

She made the announcement herself on the pavement outside Number Ten, with Major beside her but saying nothing: it was important that it should be seen as her decision. Accordingly she emphasised the interest-rate cut – back to 14 per cent – as much as ERM entry, asserting that 'the fact that our policies are working and are seen to be working have [*sic*] made both these decisions possible'. She admitted that inflation was not yet coming down, but argued that since other countries' inflation was rising faster, 'we are coming nearer to the European average', so the Madrid conditions 'have now been fulfilled'. She affirmed that ERM entry 'will underpin our anti-inflationary stance . . .We have done it because the policy is right.'[39]

The immediate reaction was euphoric, and share prices soared. In his memoirs Major took understandable pleasure in recalling the enthusiasm of some of the papers which were most critical, with the benefit of hindsight, when Britain was forced out of the mechanism less than two years later. 'Both politically and economically,' the *Financial Times* wrote, 'entry is shrewdly timed.'[40] But other commentators, even at the time, were not so sure.

The real argument that has raged ever since is whether sterling joined at the wrong rate: DM2.95, with a 6 per cent margin. But Major insists, 'Any suggestion that we could have entered at a significantly lower rate is utterly unrealistic.'[41] In fact, Mrs Thatcher decided that there should be no negotiation with Britain's partners at all. Having bitten the bullet, she insisted on joining at the existing parity, partly because she always liked a strong pound and partly because she did not want entry to be accompanied by devaluation. Major was obliged to present his fellow Finance Ministers with a *fait accompli*. This failure of consultation was not responsible for fixing the parity too high, but it threw away much of the goodwill that sterling's entry should otherwise have generated.[42]

Afterwards Lady Thatcher made a virtue of the fact that she had never wanted to join at all. She had been pushed into it by the cumulative pressure of Lawson and Howe before Madrid, then of Major and Hurd, to the point where she could no longer resist. When sterling was forced out of the mechanism again in September 1992 she felt that she had been vindicated. Major denies that he pushed her into it unwillingly. She agreed 'because she was a political realist and knew that . . . there was no alternative'.[43] But essentially it was true. The fact was that by October 1990 she was no longer in control of economic or European policy.

The irony of the ERM saga is that, after years of opposition, Mrs Thatcher finally agreed to join at an unsustainable rate at the worst possible moment. If she was thus proved right from one point of view, she was equally wrong from another. She was not only formally responsible, as Prime Minister, for the ultimate decision to go in; she was also, by imposing her personal veto from as far back as 1985, directly responsible for the fact that Britain did not join five years earlier, in more settled conditions, at a rate which sterling would have been able to sustain and at a time when membership would have helped contain inflation. Lawson's attempt to shadow the Deutschmark as a substitute for membership certainly contributed to – though it did not wholly cause – the resurgence of inflation after 1987. But it might have been a different story if she had listened to Lawson in 1985.

The decision finally to join the ERM led on to a euphoric party conference in Bournemouth. 'It's full steam ahead for the fourth term', she announced confidently, and her troops responded ecstatically – as Ronnie Millar ironically recalled:

> On the platform, surrounded by her applauding and apparently adoring Cabinet, the star ackowledges the rapturous acclaim of her public, both arms held aloft as they have been every year since 1975 . . . 'TEN MORE YEARS!' roar the faithful five thousand, stamping their feet in time with the words . . . 'TEN MORE YEARS!! TEN MORE YEARS!!' they cry fortissimo. The floor trembles. The rafters shake. It is as though by the sheer force of their utterance and its constant repetition they feel they can compel the future. Even by the Leader's standards it is a salute to end all salutes. As it turns out to be . . . [44]

Just over a month later she resigned.

26

The Defenestration of Downing Street

The sheep that turned

MRS Thatcher's downfall was a drama which unfolded with shocking suddenness. For political journalists those three weeks in November 1990 were a once-in-a-lifetime story of rumour and intrigue, calculation and backstabbing, all conducted in the bars and tearooms, clubs and private houses of the Westminster village. For the general public – angry, exultant or simply bewildered by the speed of events – it was a Shakespearean soap opera played out nightly in their living rooms. Though all the elements of a climactic bust-up had been coming together over a long period, with persistent talk of another leadership challenge, speculation about Michael Heseltine's intentions and questions about how long she could go on, few at Westminster or in the media really believed that she could be toppled as swiftly or abruptly as she was. The conventional wisdom of political scientists held that a Prime Minister in good health and in possession of a secure majority was invulnerable between elections. She might be given a warning shot but she could not be defeated. When suddenly she was gone, Tory MPs were amazed at what they had done. One recent textbook calls it 'the most ruthless act of political ingratitude in the history of modern Britain'.[1] Nicholas Ridley wrote of 'mediaeval savagery',[2] others of treachery, betrayal, assassination, defenestration, even ritual sacrifice. Matthew Parris wrote in anthropological terms of the Tory 'tribe' having to kill and eat its mother figure.[3] For the next decade the party was riven by the consequences of its act of regicide, and well into the new century the trauma shows little sign of healing. Yet like most great events, the drama of November 1990 was a sequence of accidents with only in retrospect an underlying inevitability. John

Biffen came up with the best metaphor for what happened. 'You know those maps on the Paris Metro that light up when you press a button to go from A to B?' he told Alan Watkins. 'Well, it was like that. Someone pressed a button and all the connections lit up.'[4]

Of all her colleagues Geoffrey Howe was perhaps the least likely political assassin. Yet there was poetic justice in the fact that it was he who pressed the button. Several of those closest to the Prime Minister had feared that the contemptuous way she treated Howe might in the end rebound on her. Though nominally deputy Prime Minister he was so comprehensively frozen out of policy towards Europe that he only learned that Britain was finally joining the ERM when the Queen asked him what he thought of the news. Mrs Thatcher believed that Howe was still deeply ambitious and scheming to replace her. 'You know what he's like and what he's up to now,' she complained to Wyatt in February.[5] Yet at the same time she did not really believe he would ever strike at her: she did not think he had the guts. When Howe finally cracked, George Walden wrote, it was 'like seeing a battered wife finally turning on a violent husband'.[6]

What caused him to crack was her intemperate reaction to the European Council held in Rome the last weekend in October 1990. In truth even Howe admitted that she had some ground to be upset. The next stage of EMU was due to be discussed at the inter-governmental conference fixed – over her objections – for December. But then the Italians called an extra Council in October and used it to try to pre-empt the wider discussions at the IGC by setting a timetable for the second and third stages of the Delors plan imme-diately. Contrary to prior assurances, Kohl and Mitterrand went along with this, and Mrs Thatcher found herself at Rome suddenly confronted by the other eleven ready to commit themselves to start stage 2 in 1994 and complete the single currency in 2000. Hurd was as shocked as Mrs Thatcher by the Italian ambush; once again Britain was cast as the lone obstructive voice. She objected that it was absurd to set a timetable before it was even agreed what form stages 2 and 3 should take. But her objections were heard 'in stony silence'.[7]

Back in Britain she reported to the House of Commons on Tuesday 30 October. At Prime Minister's Questions Kinnock seized on the more positive tone Howe had taken with with Brian Walden and tried to get her to endorse her deputy: this she pointedly declined to do, merely asserting that Howe was 'too big a man to need a little man like the right hon. Gentleman to stand up for him'. What Howe had actually said was that Britain's alternative proposal for a common currency – the so-called 'hard ecu' – might in time grow into a single currency. This was no more than Major had also said, and was in fact the Government's policy. In her written statement Mrs Thatcher duly toed this line – the first time, Howe believed, that she had done so:

> The hard ecu would be a parallel currency, not a single currency. If, as time went by, peoples and Governments chose to use it widely, it could evolve towards a single currency. But our national currency would remain unless a decision to abolish it were freely taken by future generations of Parliament and people. A single currency is not the policy of this Government.

So far, so moderate. But then Kinnock riled her with the usual charge that her performance in Rome had damaged Britain's interest and she was away.

> The President of the Commission, M. Delors, said at a press conference the other day that he wanted the European Parliament to be the democratic body of the Community, he wanted the Commission to be the Executive and he wanted the Council of Ministers to be the Senate. No. No. No.[8]

Once again it was her tone – defiant, intransigent and glorying in her intransigence – more than her actual words which horrified her colleagues. 'It was already clear,' David Owen wrote, 'that she was on an emotional high and the adrenalin was pumping round her system as she handbagged every federalist proposal'.[9] In particular – answering a question from a Labour Eurosceptic – she departed from her carefully phrased backing of the hard ecu:

> The hard ecu . . . could be used if people chose to do so. In my view, it would not become widely used throughout the Community . . . I am pretty sure that most people in this country would prefer to continue to use sterling.[10]

'I nearly fell off the bench,' Major wrote. 'With this single sentence she wrecked months of work and preparation. Europe had been suspicious that the hard ecu was simply a tactic to head off a single currency, and now the Prime Minister, in a matter of a few words, convinced them it was.' He had no doubt about the likely effect of her 'unscripted outburst'. 'I heard our colleagues cheer, but knew there was trouble ahead.'[11] From the SDP bench below the gangway, Owen kept his eye on Geoffrey Howe. 'He looked miserable and unhappy, truly, I thought, a dead sheep. How wrong I proved to be.'[12]

If Howe needed any further prompting the next day's press – led by the *Sun* with the gleeful headline 'Up Yours, Delors' – pushed him over the edge.[13] He had already drafted his resignation letter before he attended Cabinet on Thursday morning. With now characteristic insensitivity Mrs Thatcher lectured him in front of his colleagues over the fact that two or three Bills to be included in the Queen's Speech were not quite ready. Some of them felt later that this was the final provocation.[14] But Howe denies it. 'Far from being the last straw, this final tantrum was the first confirmation that I had taken the right decision.'[15]

His resignation letter – running to over 1,000 words – repeated his concern that Britain should remain on the 'inside track' in Europe. He insisted that he was '*not* a Euro-idealist or federalist'. He did not want a single currency *imposed* any more than she did, but 'more than one form of EMU is possible. The important thing is not to rule in or out any one particular solution absolutely.' 'In all honesty,' he concluded, 'I now find myself unable to share your view of the right approach to this question.'[16]

Mrs Thatcher regarded this as typically feeble stuff and tried to brush off Howe's complaints, as she had done Lawson's, as differences of style only, not of policy. 'I do not believe these are nearly as great as you suggest,' she replied.[17] They parted with mutual relief and a formal handshake – the first time, Howe thought, they had ever shaken hands in fifteen years – leaving the Prime Minister to carry out her fourth reshuffle of the year.

For nearly two weeks, Mrs Thatcher seemed to have ridden out this latest crisis, helped by Bernard Ingham's bullish briefings. 'She will survive it,' *The Times* asserted confidently.[18] Parliament was not sitting – her report on the Rome summit had been the fag end of the previous session – so Howe had no early opportunity to make a resignation statement. Michael Heseltine congratulated him on his 'courageous decision' but told him it did not materially affect his own position. Just to post a reminder that he was still in the wings, however, Heseltine reworked an article intended for the *Sunday Times* and published it as an open letter to his Henley constituents before leaving on a visit to the Middle East. This was a mistake which allowed Ingham to charge him with cowardice.

But why should Ingham have wished to provoke Heseltine? The answer would seem to be that Mrs Thatcher wanted to flush him into the open. The same rules that had allowed Meyer to challenge her the year before were still in place, and not a day passed without another Tory MP calling for a contest to 'lance the boil'.[19] That being so, she resolved to get it over quickly. On Tuesday 6 November she arranged to bring forward the date of any contest by two weeks, with the closing date for nominations on Thursday 15 November and the first round of voting the following Tuesday. What was extraordinary was not the haste but the fact that she was due to be out of the country on 20 November attending the CSCE conference in Paris. She knew this, but thought either that it did not matter, since she did not intend to canvass personally, or that it would be of positive benefit to her by reminding Tory MPs of her standing as an international stateswoman. The idea that she did not expect a serious contest when she changed the date does not stand up. On the contrary, she expected Heseltine to stand but thought the best way of beating him was to beat him quickly. 'It'll be a fortnight's agony,' she told Ronnie Millar. 'Oh well. Never mind.'[20] It was a fateful miscalculation.

Normal political business resumed on 7 November, with the opening of the new session of Parliament. Despite a concerted effort by Labour MPs to throw her off her stride, Mrs Thatcher opened the debate on the Queen's Speech in characteristically combative style, outlining new Bills ranging from longer sentences for criminals, through the setting up of the Child Support Agency, to privately financed roads and privatised ports. She wiped the floor as usual with Kinnock and played down the differences with Howe, squaring her own scepticism about the hard ecu with the possibility that it nevertheless *could* evolve into a single currency with the clever formula that 'We have no bureaucratic timetable: ours is a market approach, based on what people and governments choose to do.' When John Reid asked why in that case Howe had resigned, she replied – with a dangerous echo of the Lawson resignation – that only Howe could answer that.[21] Howe let it be known that he would make a statement the following Tuesday. Meanwhile, Major, in his autumn economic statement, was forced to admit that the economy was now officially in recession; and the next day the Conservatives were hammered in two more by-elections.

Howe made his statement on Tuesday afternoon, shortly after Prime Minister's Questions, to a packed House which nevertheless had no expectation that it was about to witness one of the parliamentary occasions of the century. Its impact was greatly enhanced by being one of the first major occasions to be televised. Howe never raised his voice above its habitual courteous monotone. But almost from his first words he gripped the House with a hitherto unsuspected passion. He started lightly by dismissing the idea that he had resigned purely over differences of style. He recalled the privilege of serving as Chancellor for four years, paying tribute to Mrs Thatcher's essential contribution to their economic achievements, but also suggesting that 'they possibly derived some little benefit from the presence of a Chancellor who was not exactly a wet himself'.

The core of his speech then spelt out their real differences over Europe. First, he recalled that he and Lawson had wanted to join the ERM since at least 1985 and revealed for the first time – with Lawson sitting beside him nodding his assent – that they had both threatened to resign if she did not make a definite commitment to join at the time of Madrid. He gently corrected Mrs Thatcher's increasingly public placing of all the blame for the renewal of inflation on Lawson by insisting that it could have been avoided if Britain had joined the ERM much earlier. Next, he mocked her 'nightmare image' of a Europe 'teeming with ill-intentioned people scheming, in her words, to "extinguish democracy" and "dissolve our national identities"', preferring to quote against it both Macmillan's 1962 warning against retreating into 'a ghetto of sentimentality about our past' and Churchill's vision of a 'larger sovereignty' which alone, he had declared in 1950, could protect Europe's diverse national traditions. Again he warned against getting left out of the forging of new institutions. Of course Britain could opt out of the single currency, but she could not prevent the others going ahead.

Personally, Howe concluded, he had tried to reconcile the differences from within the Government, but he now realised that 'the task has become futile: trying to stretch the meaning of words beyond what was credible, and trying to pretend that there was a common policy when every step forward risked being subverted by some casual comment or impulsive answer'. The conflict between the 'instinct of loyalty' to the Prime Minister, which was 'still very real', and 'loyalty towards what I perceive to be the true interests of the nation' had become intolerable. 'That is why I have resigned.' In the very last sentence came the killer punch. 'The time has come for others to consider their own response to the tragic conflict of loyalties with which I have myself wrestled for perhaps too long.'[22]

Lawson called it 'the most devastating speech I, or I suspect anyone else in the House that afternoon, had heard uttered in the

House of Commons . . . It was all the more powerful because it was Geoffrey, that most moderate, long-suffering and patient of men, that was uttering it.'[23] 'It was the measured way in which Howe gave the speech which made it so deadly,' Paddy Ashdown wrote in his diary. 'The result is that she appears terminally damaged'.[24]

Howe denied that his final sentence was a prearranged invitation to Heseltine to end his hesitation.[25] But it is hard to see what else it could have meant. Heseltine too denied collusion; yet his lieutenant Michael Mates was already canvassing possible allies, before Howe spoke, on whether it would be helpful for him to mention Heseltine by name.[26] In such a highly charged situation, a hint was more than enough. In fact Heseltine's mind was already made up; but Howe's speech gave him a more favourable wind than he would have had the previous week. An hour after Howe sat down, Cecil Parkinson made a last attempt to dissuade him. 'Cecil, she is finished,' Heseltine told him. 'After Geoffrey's speech, she is finished.'[27] The next day he announced his candidacy.

Tarzan's moment

He gave three reasons – a shrewd amalgam of real policy differences with an appeal to the survival instinct of Tory backbenchers. First, he agreed with Howe that Mrs Thatcher held 'views on Europe behind which she has not been able to maintain a united Cabinet. This damages the proper pursuit of British self-interest in Europe.' Second, and perhaps most important, polls showed that he was the alternative leader best placed to rebuild Tory support and win the next election. Third, he promised an immediate review of the poll tax. At this stage he did not promise to abolish it: the undertaking merely to look at it again was designed to attract both those who still believed in the principle and those who thought the only possible result of a review would be to scrap it entirely.[28] But he was careful not to repudiate Mrs Thatcher's record entirely. On the contrary he claimed with some justice to have been 'at the leading edge of Thatcherism' for the past ten years. His resignation from the Cabinet in 1986 had seemed to be a storm in a teacup at the time – but his criticism of her handling of Cabinet had subsequently been corroborated by Lawson and Howe. Finally, he was a charismatic politician of undoubted Prime Ministerial calibre who had scrupulously refrained from open disloyalty over the past four years, while assiduously cultivating the constituencies and anxious

MPs. Thus he was in every way a serious candidate and difficult for her to disparage.

In common with most political commentators, Mrs Thatcher did not really think it conceivable that a Prime Minister in possession of a good majority could be thrown out between elections by her own party. Though she had always known that she had enemies who would be glad to see the back of her, she took it for granted that her senior colleagues and her appointees in the party organisation would rally round to ensure that the challenge was seen off as it had been in 1989. In the event those she charged with running her campaign made a very poor fist of the job.

With hindsight she recognised that her insistence on going to Paris, which took her out of the country for the last two days of the campaign and the day of the ballot, was a mistake. It was not as if the CSCE was actually an important event. There was one symbolic treaty to be signed, cutting the levels of conventional forces; but it was more in the nature of an international celebration of the ending of the Cold War. President Bush, President Gorbachev, Chancellor Kohl and President Mitterrand were all going to be there, so Mrs Thatcher naturally wanted to be there too, to take her share of the credit. In truth it set the seal most appropriately on her premiership: but that was not her intention. By going to Paris she sent a signal that she was more interested in strutting the world stage than in meeting the worries of her troops at Westminster. She thought it was more important for her to be seen doing her job than grubbing for votes; for the same reason she spent the Friday before the poll in Northern Ireland. But this was not the message the party wanted to hear. 'The plaudits are abroad,' Kenneth Baker warned her, 'but the votes are back home.'[29] Heseltine by contrast, as Alan Clark noted, was working the Members' Lobby and the tea rooms every day.

Fundamentally, the very fact that the Prime Minister's supporters, with or without her presence, could not put together a decent campaign showed that she had lost the support of the central core of the parliamentary party. The necessary level of enthusiasm simply was not there. Those MPs who were neither passionately for her nor passionately against were listening to their constituencies. When George Walden consulted his local party in Buckingham, the show of hands was for loyalty. But in private three-quarters of those who said they supported her told him it was time for her to go, and he suspects this was typical.[30] Ironically Mrs Thatcher herself had articulated the clinching argument. Replying to Kinnock and Ashdown at Prime Minister's Questions the previous autumn, she had asserted that 'the country's best long-term interests consist of keeping those who are in opposition there in perpetuity'.[31] It was precisely to ensure this that a large minority of Tory MPs thought that Mrs Thatcher should be replaced. Moreover, they were right: with a new Prime Minister, Labour was kept in opposition – if not in perpetuity, at least for another seven years.

With even Tory newspapers increasingly doubtful whether she could – or should – survive, there was an unmistakable whiff of defeat in the air even before the vote. Douglas Hurd added to it by failing to deny categorically that he might stand himself. 'Against her, no,' he told an interviewer, thus betraying that he recognised at least the possibility of a second ballot.[32] Willie Whitelaw issued a statement of support but told Wyatt that the whole thing was 'absolutely ghastly'. He believed that Mrs Thatcher should win, but he was afraid she would not win by enough. If it came to a second ballot he might have to advise her to stand down.'Whatever happens, we can't have her humbled. But then she is wise enough to know that.'[33] John Major, nursing an infected wisdom tooth away from the snake pit of Westminster, thought that she would probably scrape through; but Jeffrey Archer, who came on Monday to tell him the gossip, told him that her chances were 'bleak'. Major's phone kept ringing with colleagues wanting him to be ready to stand if she did not win well enough.[34]

In Paris on Monday morning Mrs Thatcher had breakfast with George Bush at the American Embassy, followed by a joint press conference, mainly about the Gulf. She attended the first plenary session of the conference and emerged to give another press conference at the British Embassy, hailing the signing of what she called 'the biggest international disarmament agreement since the end of the last World War' and brushing off questions about the leadership.[35] After lunch with the other leaders at the Elysée Palace – at which her old adversary Helmut Kohl was particularly supportive – she made her own speech at the conference, confessing that she had initially been sceptical about the Helsinki process, but admitting that with the arrival of Gorbachev in the Kremlin it had worked in the end and hoping that the CSCE would provide a forum for continuing progress on establishing human rights in the old Soviet empire.[36] On Tuesday, while Tory MPs were voting in the House of Commons, she had talks with Gorbachev, Mitterrand and the President of Turkey and lunch with her favourite European leader, the Dutch Prime Minister Ruud Lubbers. The conference finished for the day around 4.30 p.m., and she returned to the British Embassy to await the result.

Back in London a meeting rather oddly composed of her campaign team plus party officials had drawn up alternative forms of words for her to use whatever the figures. Obviously if she won handsomely, or lost absolutely, there was no problem: discussion centred on what she should say if – as seemed increasingly likely – she led, but without the necessary margin to win on the first ballot. According to the rules she had to gain not only a simple majority (187) but a margin of 15 per cent of all those entitled to vote – that is fifty-six votes. In the event of her falling short, Norman Tebbit wanted her to make a clear commitment to fight on. Baker thought she should say she must consult her colleagues. It was John Wakeham who proposed the compromise formula that she should declare her 'intention' to contest a second ballot. Mrs Thatcher accepted this advice, so that when the result came through she had her response ready.

Waiting in Peter Morrison's room at the embassy – Morrison (her current PPS) had flown over to be with her for the result – she sat at the dressing table with her back to the company, displaying 'an inordinate calm'.[37] Charles Powell sat on the bed. Morrison, Bernard Ingham, Cynthia Crawford (her dresser), the deputy Chief Whip and the British Ambassador in Paris were also present. Around 6.20 p.m. Tim Renton (the Chief Whip) rang from London. Morrison answered, wrote down the figures and gave them to Mrs Thatcher. 'Not, I am afraid, as good as we had hoped.' (Powell, typically, had his own line and had got the news half a minute earlier: behind Mrs Thatcher's back he gave a thumbs down.) She had only 204 votes to Heseltine's 152, with sixteen void or spoiled ballots: four votes short of the margin needed. She received the news calmly and after checking with Hurd that he and Major would still support her, immediately marched downstairs and out into the courtyard to give her predetermined response to the waiting press. Dramatically interrupting John Sergeant's report for the BBC's *Six O'Clock News*, she seized his microphone and announced, live to the cameras:

I am naturally very pleased that I got more than half of the Parliamentary party and disappointed that it's not *quite* enough to win on the first ballot, so I confirm that it is my intention to let my name go forward for the second ballot.[38]

Despite her reflex defiance, both Powell and Ingham believe that those around her, and probably Mrs Thatcher herself, knew in their hearts that she was finished.[39] So, certainly, did Denis. The first thing she did on coming back into the embassy was to ring him. 'Denis was fabulous,' Carol remembered. '"Congratulations, Sweetie-Pie, you've won; it's just the rules," he said, as tears trickled down his face. He was crying for her, not for himself.' But when he put down the phone he turned to the friend who was with him and said: 'We've had it. We're out.'[40]

'Treachery with a smile on its face'

Mrs Thatcher returned to London next morning having had no sleep, still determined to fight on. She had, after all, comfortably defeated her challenger and fallen only four votes short of outright victory. Woodrow Wyatt toyed with the notion that she could ask the Queen to grant her a General Election.[41] She herself still believed she could win the second ballot 'if the campaign were to go into high gear and every potential supporter pressed to fight for my cause'.[42] She knew now that this had not been the case so far. But most observers shared the view bluntly expressed in his memoirs by Michael Heseltine. 'To anyone with the faintest knowledge of how Westminster politics work, her position was manifestly untenable. It says much for Mrs Thatcher's capacity for self-delusion that at first she stubbornly refused to recognise the fact.'[43]

The BBC's political editor John Cole felt the mood as soon as he got to the House of Commons on Wednesday morning. 'Conservative MPs began stopping me in the corridors and in the Members' Lobby to tell me that if she persisted in her declared intention to enter the second ballot, they would switch their votes to Michael Heseltine.' The Heseltine camp was now confident of winning if she stayed in the contest.[44] But by the same token, urgent discussions had already been going on all over London to prevent that eventuality. The younger members of the Cabinet had no wish to see Mrs Thatcher deposed to put Heseltine in her place. Whenever she went, they wanted her to be replaced by one of themselves. If it really looked as if she could not beat Heseltine, it followed that she should be persuaded to withdraw in favour of another candidate who could. The supposedly crucial meeting took place on Tuesday evening at the home of Tristan Garel-Jones. Those present included four Cabinet Ministers from the left of the party – Chris Patten, William Waldegrave, Malcolm Rifkind and Tony Newton – plus Norman Lamont from the right and two or three ministers from outside the Cabinet, including Alan Clark.

It was not really much of a conspiracy. 'The really sickening thing,' Clark wrote, 'was the urgent and unanimous abandonment of the Lady. Except for William's little opening tribute, she was never mentioned again.'[45] But with thirty to forty of her supporters on the first ballot said to have deserted, the conclusion that she was finished was pretty obvious. The consensus of the group at this stage was to back Hurd. The importance of the meeting was not that it decided anything, but simply that it showed the way several of the younger ministers were thinking. Ken Clarke, John Wakeham and John Gummer had reached the same conclusion without being present; and others were holding countless similar conversations by telephone.

Before Mrs Thatcher returned to London three more formal consultations had taken place. All told the same story of crumbling support. The question was who would tell Mrs Thatcher. Denis was the first to try when she returned to Downing Street at lunchtime. 'Don't go on, love,' he begged her. But she felt – 'in my bones' – that she owed it to her supporters not to give up so long as there was still a chance.[46] Wakeham warned that she would face the argument that she should step down voluntarily to avoid humiliation, but professed that this was not his own view. All the other emissaries ducked it. These were the famous 'men in suits' who were supposed to tell her when it was time to go. But over a working lunch at Number Ten 'the greybeards', as Hurd called them, 'failed to deliver the message'.[47] 'The message of the meeting, even from those urging me to fight on, was implicitly demoralising,' Lady Thatcher wrote in retrospect.[48] But for the moment she formed the impression that she should still fight on.

She still had a statement to make in the Commons on the Paris summit. As she left Downing Street she called out to reporters: 'I fight on. I fight to win', managing, as she later wrote, to sound more confident than by now she felt.[49] In the House she gave another characteristically brave performance, hailing 'the end of the Cold War in Europe and the triumph of freedom, democracy and the rule of law', spiritedly rebutting opposition taunts and thanking the one Tory loyalist who hoped that she would 'continue to bat for Britain with all the vigour, determination and energy at her command'. Only once, uncharacteristically, did she forget the second half of a question and have to be reminded what it was.[50] Then Tebbit took her round the tea room in a belated effort to shore up her support. 'I had never experienced such an atmosphere before,' she wrote in her memoirs. 'Repeatedly I heard: "Michael has asked me two or three times for my vote already. This is the first time we have seen you."'[51]

Around five o'clock she saw the Queen and assured her that she still intended to contest the second ballot. What finally convinced her that her cause was hopeless was a series of individual interviews with the members of the Cabinet between six and eight that evening. This procedure has been widely regarded as another misjudgement. The summons to see her individually meant that they all congregated along the ministerial corridor to concert what they were going to say before they went in. This explains why, when they saw her, so many of them said the same thing. Mrs Thatcher sat tense and upright at the end of one sofa next to the fireplace, the ministers on the opposite sofa. 'Almost to a man,' she wrote bitterly, 'they used the same formula. This was that they themselves would back me, of course, but that regretfully they did not believe I could win . . . I felt I could almost join in the chorus.'[52]

There were some variations. Clarke, Patten and Rifkind were the only three to tell her frankly that they would not support her if she stood again. Clarke – 'in the brutalist style he has cultivated' – warned her that Heseltine would become Prime Minister unless she made way for either Hurd or Major. She was 'visibly stunned' by this estimate.[53] Only Baker and Cecil Parkinson told her that she could still win. The rest, with varying degrees of embarrassment (some with tears in their eyes) advised her to give up.

The one interview she describes as light relief was that with Alan Clark, who also – though not a member of the Cabinet – somehow managed to get in to see her. He too told her she would lose, but encouraged her to go down fighting gloriously to the end. Earlier he had written in his diary that 'the immediate priority is to find a way, tactfully and skilfully, to talk her out of standing a second time'. Presumably this was his way of doing so. After a pause while she contemplated this Wagnerian scenario she said: 'It'd be so terrible if Michael won. He would undo everything I have fought for.'[54] So maybe Clark, while convincing her that he was still on her side, had more effect than the faint hearts whom she accused of betraying her.

By the end of this dismal procession Mrs Thatcher had accepted that the game was up. 'I had lost the Cabinet's support. I could not even muster a credible campaign team. It was the end.'[55] 'She was pale, subdued and shaking her head, saying "I am not a quitter, I am not a quitter",' Baker recalled. 'But the tone was one of resignation, not defiance.'[56] She was upset not so much by her poor vote in the ballot, which could be attributed to electoral nerves, nor by the frank opposition of those who had never supported her, but by what she saw as the treachery of those from whom she felt entitled to expect loyalty. 'What grieved me,' she wrote, 'was the desertion of those I had always considered friends and allies and the weasel words whereby they had transmuted their betrayal into frank advice and concern for my fate.'[57] It was treachery, she charged later on television. 'Treachery with a smile on its face.'[58]

The best answer to this allegation comes from Kenneth Clarke. 'There was no treachery,' he told one of his biographers. The Cabinet gave her 'wholly sensible advice' that, having failed to win by a sufficient margin on the first ballot, she would not win the second and should now withdraw. 'That was nothing to do with the Cabinet. It was the parliamentary party where she'd suffered the defeat.'[59] The fact was that not just her long-time enemies but many of her strongest supporters thought it was time for her to go, in order to protect her legacy. On this analysis it was not merely the party but Thatcherism itself which needed a new leader if it was to survive. It was cruel, but Margaret Thatcher had never been one to let personal feelings stand in the way of what she thought was right. Though she talked of loyalty, she had never shown much mercy herself to colleagues who threatened or disappointed her. As Prime Ministers go, she was a good butcher: that was part of her strength. But she could not complain when she was butchered in turn. She had only gained the leadership in the first place by boldly challenging Ted Heath when all his other colleagues were restrained by loyalty. She had lived by the sword and was always likely to perish by the sword. Really she would have wanted it no other way. As she said, she was not a quitter. What perhaps galled her most in retrospect about the Cabinet's advice was that it forced her to quit voluntarily when temperamentally she would rather have gone down to defeat, as Clark suggested. But her first priority was to defend her legacy, and she was reluctantly persuaded that self-immolation was the only way to do it.

At 11.15 p.m. she rang Tim Bell and told him: 'I've decided to go. Can you come and see me?' He went, collecting Gordon Reece on the way, and 'blubbed hopelessly' in the car on the way.[60] Her two 'laughing boys', as she had called them in happier times, sat up with her till two o'clock helping to write her resignation statement, while Andrew Turnbull, her private secretary rang the Governor of the Bank and others to give them advance warning of her decision.

As she always did before a big decision, she slept on it – briefly – before committing herself. At 7.30 she asked Turnbull to arrange another audience with the Queen. Then at 9.00 she chaired her final Cabinet. It was an intensely awkward occasion. She began by reading out her prepared statement, which was a model of dignified euphemism:

> Having consulted widely among colleagues, I have concluded that the unity of the party and the prospects of victory in a General Election would be better served if I stood down to enable Cabinet colleagues to enter the ballot for the leadership. I should like to thank all those in Cabinet and outside who have given me such dedicated support.[61]

Twice she almost broke down, but she rejected Parkinson's suggestion that the Lord Chancellor should read it for her. After embarrassed tributes from several ministers, she then expanded on her statement by emphasising the importance of the Cabinet now uniting to defeat Heseltine and protect her legacy. Insisting that she could handle business but not sympathy, she recovered her composure to conduct the rest of the meeting in her usual brisk manner. After a short coffee break she reported on her latest talks with Bush and Gorbachev in Paris, and it was agreed to send another armoured brigade to the Gulf.

The announcement of Mrs Thatcher's withdrawal from the contest was made at 9.25 a.m. (during the Cabinet's coffee break), though of course she remained Prime Minister until the party had elected her successor. The news, though not unexpected at Westminster, evoked extraordinary scenes of jubilation and disbelief among the public: she had been there so long that her departure was hard to comprehend.

Last rites

Even in defeat Mrs Thatcher still had a last bravura performance up her sleeve. Another leader might have chosen to let someone else answer Labour's 'no confidence' motion. On the contrary, she saw it as a last opportunity to vindicate her record. Even as her position crumbled the previous evening, she had not stopped working on her speech for the next day: never had her dedication been more impressive or her power of concentration more extraordinary. She was up before dawn to carry on crafting it. 'Each sentence,' she wrote in her memoirs, 'was my testimony at the Bar of History.'[62]

After Prime Minister's Questions – where she was given a fairly gentle ride – and a typically ungenerous speech by Kinnock, when a word of sympathy might have disarmed her, she started her speech by reminding the House of Nicholas Henderson's gloomy 1979 dispatch describing Britain's economic failure and loss of influence in the world since 1945. 'Conservative government has changed all that,' she boasted. 'Once again, Britain stands tall in the councils of Europe and of the world, and our policies have brought unparalleled prosperity to our citizens at home.' Once the interventions started she really got into her stride; and by the time she came on to defending her record in Europe she was ready to demolish Kinnock one last time. He did not know whether he was in favour of the single currency or not, she jeered, because 'he does not even know what it means'. When the Labour left-winger Denis Skinner suggested that she should become Governor of the European Bank she seized on the notion with delight. '*What a good idea! I had not thought of that . . . Now where were we? I am enjoying this.*'

From this moment, she had the House in the palm of her hand. A Eurosceptic Tory called out, 'Cancel it. You can wipe the floor with these people.' She went on to expound her vision of 'a free and open Britain in a free and open Europe . . . in tune with the deepest instincts of the British people', took credit for winning the Cold War, and ended with the Gulf, comparing it with the Falklands. Her last words were the apotheosis of the Iron Lady:

> There is something else which one feels. That is a sense of this country's destiny: the centuries of history and experience which ensure that, when principles have to be defended, when good has to be upheld and when evil has to be overcome, Britain will take up arms. It is because we on this side have never flinched from difficult decisions that this House and this country can have confidence in this Government today.[63]

It was an astonishing performance, a parliamentary occasion to equal – or, rather, trump – Howe's speech, which had precipitated the whole landslide just nine days earlier, never to be forgotten by anyone who was present in the House or watched on television. The Tory benches cheered wildly, wondering if they had made a dreadful mistake.

At the end of the debate Baker had a drink with her in her room. 'She was still resilient and looked as if she had freshly stepped off the boat after a great tour.'[64] She was still angry about what her own party had done to her. 'They've done what the Labour party didn't manage to do in three elections,' she told Carol. But for the moment she was still on a high. 'Carol, I think my place in history is assured.'[65]

Nominations for the second ballot had already closed. To maximise the anti-Heseltine vote, and avoid the appearance of a Cabinet stitch-up, it was decided that both Hurd and Major should stand, thus giving Tory MPs what many had been demanding: a wider choice. Hurd, the older and much more experienced man, was the safe pair of hands. Major was thirteen years younger and an unknown quantity. He had risen with astonishing speed and seemed to owe his career entirely to Mrs Thatcher's patronage. But the fact that he was her protégé made it natural for those who felt guilty at ditching her to make amends by supporting him, though anyone who knew him at all well knew he was not a Thatcherite. 'Many will vote for him thinking he is on the right wing,' Willie Whitelaw correctly predicted. 'They'll be disappointed and soon find out that he isn't.'[66] Mrs Thatcher already had doubts herself, and initially declared that she would not endorse any candidate; but this was quickly forgotten, and over the weekend she did more canvassing for Major – mainly by telephone – than she had ever done for herself. She told them – and tried to believe it herself – that the best way of preserving her legacy was to support Major. Though she recognised that Hurd had been loyal, she had never really trusted him; more than Heseltine in some ways, he represented everything in the party that she had striven to reject, as she explained to Wyatt:

John Major is someone who has fought his way up from the bottom and is far more in tune with the skilled and ambitious and worthwhile working classes than Douglas Hurd is.[67]

The short campaign was exceptionally gentlemanly, and, once the momentum had swung behind Major, the result was never in doubt. Heseltine had always known that his chance would have gone the moment Mrs Thatcher withdrew, and so it proved. The result of the voting on 27 November gave Major 185 votes to Heseltine's 131 and Hurd's 56. Though strictly speaking Major was still two votes short of an absolute majority, both Heseltine and Hurd immediately withdrew, leaving Major the clear winner – with, as Mrs Thatcher reflected wryly, nineteen votes fewer than she had won seven days earlier. Nevertheless it was the result she had campaigned for, so as soon as Hurd and Heseltine had made their statements she burst through the connecting door to Number Eleven to congratulate her successor. 'It's everything I've dreamt

of for such a long time,' she gushed. 'The future is assured.'[68] She
wanted to go outside with Major while he spoke to the media,
but was persuaded that she must let him have his moment of
glory alone. She was photographed peeping sadly from an upstairs
window while Major made his statement and answered questions.
This was the moment when the reality of her loss of office must
have hit her.

She had spent the previous few days packing up and holding
farewell parties for her staff and supporters. It was for just this eventuality that she and Denis had bought a house in Dulwich in 1986,
so at least she had somewhere to go; and the housewife in her was
good at the business of packing and clearing up. So long as she was
busy she had no time to grieve.

Margaret and Denis went to Chequers for the last time for the
weekend, attended church on Sunday morning and were heart-
broken to leave the country home they had made good use of
for the past eleven years. On Monday she paid a short visit to
thank the workers at Central Office. She had been 'very, very
thrilled', she said, that President Bush had telephoned after her
resignation was announced. They had discussed the Gulf and it
was in that context – in relation to Bush, not Major – that she
had declared: 'He won't falter, and I won't falter. It's just that I
won't be pulling the levers there. But I shall be a very good back
seat driver.'[69]

On Tuesday, while Tory MPs were still voting on her successor,
she made her last appearance answering Prime Minister's Questions. Again it was an occasion more for tributes than for recrim-
ination. She told a Tory member that his was the 7,498th question
she had answered in 698 sessions at the dispatch box. By the time
she answered her last question a few minutes later the final tally
was 7,501.[70]

Finally, on Wednesday morning, she left the stage, only with difficulty holding back the tears as she made her final statement:

> Ladies and Gentlemen. We're leaving Downing Street for the last
> time after eleven and a half wonderful years and we're very happy
> that we leave the United Kingdom in a very, very much better
> state than when we came eleven and a half years ago.

It had been 'a tremendous privilege', they had been 'wonderfully
happy years' and she was 'immensely grateful' to all her staff and
the people who had sent her flowers and letters:

Now it's time for a new chapter to open and I wish John Major all the luck in the world. He'll be splendidly served, and he has the makings of a great Prime Minister, which I'm sure he'll be in a very short time.

Thank you very much. Goodbye.[71]

When the car arrived in Dulwich, a journalist asked her what she would do now. 'Work. That is all we have ever known.'[72] Her trouble would be finding enough to do.

27

Afterlife

Unemployed workaholic

BRITISH democracy is peculiarly cruel to its defeated leaders. The familiar spectacle of the removal vans in Downing Street the morning after a General Election is an undignified one. Mrs Thatcher had witnessed at first hand Ted Heath's abrupt and unanticipated ejection from office in February 1974. It was very largely the example of his predicament, with no alternative home to retreat to, so that he was forced to squat for several months in a small flat lent him by a Tory MP, that had prompted her to buy an unsuitable house in Dulwich as some sort of insurance policy against a similar fate. Her dismissal was actually less abrupt than most: she had almost a week between her decision to resign and the moment of departure – six days to pack up and say her farewells. Yet her defeat was also more brutal, since it was inflicted not by the electorate but by her own MPs. In June 1983 and June 1987 she had been packed and psychologically prepared: in November 1990 she was not.

Mrs Thatcher was a compulsive workaholic, still full of energy, with no interests outside politics. The loss of office deprived her almost overnight of her main reason for living. She had always dreaded the prospect of retirement. 'I think my definition of Hell is having a lot of time and not having any idea of what to do with it,' she told *She* magazine in 1987.[1] 'Happiness is not doing nothing,' she reiterated to *Woman's Own*. 'Happiness in an adult consists of having a very full day, being absolutely exhausted at the end of it but knowing that you have had a very full day.'[2] When she talked of having a full day she meant a full day's *work*; and what she meant by work was politics. She could no more walk away from politics than she could stop breathing.

'There will always be work for me to do and I shall just have to find it,' she had said in 1989.[3] But she was quite unsuited for any of the big international jobs – NATO, the World Bank, even the United Nations – with which her name was sometimes linked: she was never cut out to be a diplomat. John Major would have liked nothing better than to keep her fully occupied, preferably out of the country: but as he wrote in his memoirs, there was 'no credible job to offer her'.[4]

It only made it worse that Major was her protégé whom she had promoted rapidly over the heads of his contemporaries and finally endorsed as her successor. While colleagues and commentators saw the importance of Major quickly proving himself his own man, free of nanny's apron strings, Mrs Thatcher continued to treat him as her unfledged deputy whose job it was to carry on the work which she had regrettably been prevented from finishing herself. Just as she had wanted to join him on the pavement outside Number Ten for his first press conference, so she had to be dissuaded from sitting immediately behind him at his first Prime Minister's Questions.[5] She thought she was still entitled to be informed and consulted, and the fact that Major's first big challenge was the Gulf war, which was in origin *her* war, helped cement that expectation: Charles Powell – who stayed with Major until the conclusion of the war in March 1991 – continued to give her weekly briefings far fuller than those given by convention to the Leaders of the Opposition. Yet still she felt cut off from the information flow which had been her lifeblood for eleven years, and as a result she became frustrated and increasingly critical.

As she voiced her criticism more and more publicly she was accused of behaving as badly towards Major as Heath had done towards her. Yet Heath was widely seen as an embittered failure pursuing a lonely sulk, whereas she still had a huge following in the party, the country and indeed the world which made her criticism far more damaging and imposed on her a greater responsibility to deploy her influence discreetly and judiciously. This she manifestly failed – or refused – to do. The result was that for the Tories' remaining seven years in office she made Major's position *vis-à-vis* his own backbenchers almost impossible. By helping to exacerbate divisions in the party she contributed substantially to its heavy defeat in 1992, after which she continued to undermine the efforts first of William Hague and then – until her health began to fail – of Iain Duncan Smith to reunite the party around a new agenda. The wounds inflicted on the Tory party by her traumatic overthrow will never heal until her still-unquiet ghost is exorcised.

Back-seat driver

Woodrow Wyatt rang Mrs Thatcher in Dulwich the day after she and Denis arrived there and found her 'coming down to earth with a bump'.[6] She had no one to type letters for her or to acknowledge the thousands of letters of sympathy and bouquets of flowers she was receiving from members of the public. She did not even know how to operate the telephone or the washing machine. The one reassuring element of continuity was the police protection which still guarded her at all times; so finding herself unable to dial a number, she sought help from the Special Branch officers established in the garage. She still had a room in the House of Commons and John Whittingdale as her political secretary, but her first practical need was for a proper office. Alistair McAlpine came to the rescue by lending her a house in Great College Street, and she soon recruited a staff of eight. This arrangement served for the first few months, until the newly established Thatcher Foundation acquired an appropriate headquarters in Chesham Place.

Meanwhile, she quickly realised that Dulwich was not a sensible place for her to live. The only attraction of the house – for Denis – was that it overlooked Dulwich and Sydenham Golf Club. But it was hopelessly impractical for an ex-Prime Minister who intended to remain fully involved in public life, and whose schedule required her to be able to get home quickly to change between engagements. She needed to remain symbolically as well as literally in the thick of things. After just three weeks of commuting from Dulwich, therefore, she and Denis were lent a luxurious ground floor and basement duplex apartment in Eaton Square, Belgravia, owned by Henry Ford's widow, while they looked for something more permanent. They eventually bought a ten-year lease – later extended to a life interest – on a five-storey, five-bedroom house nearby in Chester Square, just off Victoria, which was made ready for them to move into in the summer of 1991.

There were some consolations to salve her sense of rejection in the first few weeks. She received a warm – perhaps guilt-fuelled – reception in the Commons when she attended Major's first appearance at Prime Minister's Questions; and everywhere she appeared she was met with sympathy, tributes to her historic stature and admiration for her dignified bearing in adversity. On 9 December it was announced that the Queen had awarded her the Order of Merit – the highest honour in the sovereign's gift, limited to just twenty-four individuals: Mrs Thatcher filled the vacancy left by the death of Laurence Olivier. More controversially, Denis was created a baronet. A few days earlier she and Denis had paid a well-publicised call on Ron and Nancy Reagan, who were passing through London, and took tea with them at Claridge's, reliving past glories.

She was still resilient, determined to look forward and keep herself busy. 'I have got to do a positive job, and do positive things,' she told Wyatt. 'I intend to go on having influence.'[7] She knew she had to step back from daily domestic politics, but in the very first days she set herself three tasks. First, she intended to travel widely and lecture, particularly in America, partly to keep on spreading her gospel, but also to make money. She soon signed on with the Washington Speakers' Bureau for a reported fee of $50,000 a lecture – second only to Reagan – and she commanded similar fees in Japan and all over the Far East. She made a clear rule, however, that she would accept no payment for speeches in Britain, or for speaking in Russia, China, Hong Kong or South Africa – anywhere, in fact, where she was speaking *politically* as opposed to just exploiting her name. She was determined not to compromise her independence where she felt she could still have influence.

Within two years she was placed 134th in the *Sunday Times* list of the country's richest people, with personal wealth estimated at £9.5 million.[8] Much the biggest part of this income, however, derived from her second task – the writing of her memoirs. These clearly had huge commercial potential. In June Mrs Thatcher signed up with an American agent, Marvin Josephson, who swiftly accepted an offer of £3.5 million from HarperCollins – part of Rupert Murdoch's empire – for two volumes to be published in 1993 and 1995.

It was a substantial deal. But the timetable was demanding, requiring her to write the first volume, covering her entire premiership, in not much more than eighteen months. It was announced that she would write every word herself; but no one seriously believed this. She had never claimed to be a writer. Her method of composing speeches had always been to edit, criticise and exhaustively rewrite the drafts of others; and it was the same with her memoirs. Like her valedictory speech to the House of Commons on the day she resigned, but on a vastly bigger scale, Mrs Thatcher took the project immensely seriously, treating every word as her vindication before the bar of history. She did not intend to pull her punches – and nor did she. But directing the writing of the book gave her something serious and all-consuming to do with her time; and completing it on schedule was a formidable achievement.

Her third project was to set up some sort of institution to preserve her legacy and propagate her ideas around the world, but this fell foul of British charity law. In July 1991 the Charity Commission refused to grant the Thatcher Foundation charitable status since it was not politically neutral: this seriously affected its ability to raise funds, since companies could not claim tax relief. By 1993 no more than £5 million had been raised. The Foundation was nevertheless established with its headquarters in Chesham Place (near Hyde Park Corner), which provided a suitably imposing office where Mrs Thatcher could receive foreign visitors: several remarked that its fine staircase and chandeliers, mementoes of the Falklands and a large globe were curiously reminiscent of Downing Street – though far grander.

Branches were also opened in Washington and Warsaw, with the object of spreading free-market ideas and Western business practice in the new democracies of Central and Eastern Europe. The specific initiatives announced, however, were small beer. The Foundation evolved instead into an educational trust. In 1998 it gave £2 million to endow a new chair of enterprise studies at Cambridge. The previous year Lady Thatcher had donated her papers to Churchill College, together with funds to catalogue them and build a new wing of the Archives Centre to house them. The Foundation also paid for the distribution to libraries all round the world of a CD-ROM of her complete public statements produced (at its own expense) by Oxford University Press, and it funds a Margaret Thatcher website. All this has helped to make the record of her life available to historians; but it was not the crusading vehicle for global Thatcherism that was originally envisaged.

In the short term the main thing she could do was to travel extensively, which both got her out of Major's hair and enabled her to enjoy the adulation of her admirers around the world. As a global superstar she was far more recognisable than her unknown successor, and she met with rapturous receptions wherever she went. During 1991 she made five visits to the United States – in February to attend Ronald Reagan's eightieth-birthday celebrations in California and inspect the still unfinished Reagan Library in Simi Valley, north of Los Angeles; in March to receive the congressional Medal of Freedom from President Bush at a lavish ceremony in the White House, followed by her first paid lectures in Republican strongholds like Dallas, Texas and Orange County, California; in June to give two major speeches about world affairs in New York and Chicago; in September and again in November for further lecture tours. America was more than ever her spiritual home, and during and after the Gulf war she still had some standing in Washington, even if more often than not she had to be content with seeing

Vice-President Dan Quayle – usually for breakfast – rather than the President. But she also went in May to South Africa for what was essentially the state visit she had never managed to make as Prime Minister, where she was fêted by President de Klerk but boycotted by the ANC; and then to Russia where she met both Gorbachev and Boris Yeltsin and was mobbed in the streets of Moscow and Leningrad. In September she aroused extraordinary enthusiasm in Japan and was given the red-carpet treatment in China (overshadowing a visit by Major a few days later). In October she was hailed as a heroine by crowds in Poland; and in November she was welcomed as the liberator of Kuwait, whence she returned 'reverberating with vitality'.[9]

Wherever she travelled she felt no inhibitions about plunging into local politics. In South Africa she urged Mandela and Chief Buthelezi to talk and it was even suggested that she might act as a mediator to bring them together.[10] In Russia she gave strong backing to her now embattled friend Gorbachev, urging students at Moscow University to keep faith with *perestroika*; at the same time, however, she firmly supported the right of the Baltic republics to independence (which was not then the view of the British Government).[11] Three months later, when Gorbachev was briefly deposed by a hardline Communist coup, and Western capitals held back to see the outcome before committing themselves, Mrs Thatcher took the lead in urging the Soviet people to take to the streets in protest. She openly supported the defiance of Boris Yeltsin, holed up in the Russian parliament building, and even managed to hold a twenty-five-minute telephone conversation with him to express her encouragement.[12] Likewise, arriving in Warsaw, where the post-Communist government had been making deep cuts in subsidies and public services, she was 'not at all shy about wading into the Polish election campaign, praising the embattled finance minister and dismissing left-wing parties'.[13] The whole world was now her constituency: or, as she herself put it with her habitual royal plural, 'We operate now on a global scale.'[14]

But she could not confine herself entirely to the world stage. The issues she felt most strongly about inevitably impacted on domestic politics. Any criticism she made of the Government's stance towards Iraq, the disintegration of Yugoslavia or – above all – Europe was inescapably a comment on her successor's lack of judgement, experience or resolution. At least she could have no complaint about the conduct of the war to liberate Kuwait. In her first intervention in the Commons on 28 February she simply congratulated Major on the war's successful conclusion and accepted his tribute to her staunchness the previous August. She did not yet criticise the coalition's failure to overthrow Saddam, though she did point out that the problem of Iraq was not resolved and warned darkly that 'the victories of peace will take longer than the battles of war'.[15] Within a few weeks, however, she was demanding that the Government should send troops to protect the Kurdish population fleeing from Saddam's forces in northern Iraq. In fact Major was already working on a plan to create 'safe havens' for the Kurds, for which he was able to secure French, German and eventually American backing; so on this occasion he was able to neutralise her intervention. It would not always be so easy.

In the autumn of 1991 Mrs Thatcher took an early, clear and courageous view on the break-up of Yugoslavia, which put her bitterly at odds with the Government over the following years as the complex inter-ethnic conflict escalated. As the Serbs sought to maintain by force their domination of the former federation, she boldly championed the right of the constituent republics – first Croatia and Slovenia, later Bosnia-Hercegovina – to break away. She saw the issue partly as one of nationalist self-determination, with echoes of her resistance to the federal pretensions of Brussels; but also as the latest front in the continuing battle of democracy against Communism.

Major and Hurd, however, were determined to avoid either Britain or NATO getting sucked into a Balkan civil war and asserted a policy of non-intervention, with an embargo on the supply of arms to all sides, to which they stubbornly adhered in the face of mounting evidence of Serb atrocities. For the next few years Mrs Thatcher's militant anti-Communism was unusually allied with the humanitarian conscience of the world in demanding action against the Serbs, beating in vain against the cautious pragmatism of the British Government, which took the lead in blocking direct NATO, EU or UN intervention.

But the issue on which Mrs Thatcher set herself most uncompromisingly against her successor was, inevitably, Europe. From the time of her Bruges speech her attitude towards the Community had been hardening, but so long as she was in office her growing antipathy was restrained by the need to negotiate the best deal for Britain that she could achieve. From the moment she left office that restraint was off. Now she was free to follow her instinct, to criticise the deals which Major and Hurd secured, and she did so without inhibition or consideration of the pressures that would have weighed with her if she had still been in government. On the contrary, she felt no compunction about putting herself at the head of the hitherto quite small section of the Tory party which was bitterly opposed to any further European integration, thereby helping to tip the party's centre of gravity over the next seven years from a broadly pro-European to a strongly Eurosceptic, even Europhobic, stance. By leading the opposition on this issue she not only thwarted Major's vague ambition to put Britain 'at the heart of Europe', but also undermined his authority more generally, fuelling a civil war in the party which not only destroyed his government in the short term, but wrecked the credibility of the Tories as a governing party for years to come. This was her revenge for November 1990.

So long as she remained in the Commons it was plain that Mrs Thatcher would dominate the House whenever she chose to speak. It therefore came as a huge relief to Major when she announced that she would stand down at the next election. She had been in two minds whether to stay in the Commons or go to the Lords. Though no great parliamentarian, she was clear that she must retain a platform in one or other House. Some of her supporters urged her to stay in the Commons, mainly to keep the Government up to the mark, but also to keep open the possibility of a comeback in the event of some future crisis. At the end of March she was still wavering. Finally she decided that she would be freer to speak her mind if she made it clear that she had ruled out the possibility of a comeback.

For all her disillusion with Major, she did want the Tories to win the coming election. On 12 December outward cordiality was restored when the Majors and most of the Cabinet attended the Thatchers' fortieth wedding-anniversary celebration at Claridge's. During the early months of 1992 she concentrated on her memoirs, paying just two visits to the United States where she managed to say nothing controversial.

Major called the election for 9 April. In appreciation of her restraint and doubtless in the hope that she would keep it up till polling day, he sent Mrs Thatcher a bunch of twenty-four pink roses. She was unimpressed. 'A bunch of flowers won't make up for a £28 billion deficit, Woodrow,' she complained.[16] But for the moment she bit her lip, so much so that Andrew Turnbull (now serving Major) told Wyatt on 17 March that 'her behaviour has been absolutely first-class . . . We couldn't have asked for more. She's been wonderful.'[17]

She played a fairly discreet part in the campaign, appearing just once with Major at a rally for Tory candidates where she raised morale with a strong endorsement of his leadership, and doing walkabouts in selected marginal seats. In his memoirs Major alleged that 'allies of my predecessor' did their best to undermine his campaign;[18] but Mrs Thatcher herself was in America for the last week, returning only on the evening of polling day in time to attend a round of election-night parties. She watched the results with Wyatt in a small room at the top of Alistair McAlpine's house in a mood of mellow magnanimity. She emerged to tell the press: 'It is a great night. It is the end of Socialism.'[19] The next day she hailed Major's 'famous victory' and urged him now to press 'full steam ahead'.[20]

Yet within days she published a devastating interview in the American magazine *Newsweek* which expressed her real feelings. Under the headline 'Do Not Undo My Work' she poured scorn on her successor's ability to fill her shoes:

> I don't accept the idea that all of a sudden Major is his own man. He has been Prime Minister for 17 months and he inherited all these great achievements of the past eleven and a half years which have fundamentally changed Britain.

Major, she insisted, was entitled to chart his own course only within the limits that she had set out.[21] This was a breathtakingly arrogant put-down of the elected Prime Minister on the morrow of his 'famous victory'. But she was unrepentant. 'I only said I would keep quiet during the election,' she told Wyatt.[22] She was determined not to be silenced.

There had been some speculation about what type of peerage she would take. Prime Ministers are traditionally entitled to an earldom, so there was a possibility that she might become a countess. Having resurrected hereditary titles for others, it would have been consistent to take one herself. Rather quaintly, however, she felt that she and Denis lacked the means to support a hereditary title.[23] Mark already had Denis's baronetcy to look forward to; so in the end she concluded: 'I thought it was enough to be a life peer.'[24] On 6 June she was gazetted as Baroness Thatcher of Kesteven in the County of Lincolnshire. Cynics noted that she had never cared for Grantham; Kesteven sounded so much more distinguished.

She took her seat in the Upper House on 30 June – 'like a lioness entering into what she must realise is something of a cage'[25] – just in time to speak in a debate on the Maastricht Treaty on 3 July. 'Your maiden speech is supposed to be non-controversial,' Wyatt reminded her. 'But I shall only be following precedent,' she protested. 'Macmillan in his maiden speech attacked me.'[26] In fact, she made a fairly gracious and even witty speech, written for her by Charles Powell, dissenting from the Government's support for Maastricht but expressing confidence in Major's ability to use Britain's forth-coming chairmanship of the Council of Ministers to influence the development of the Community in the right direction.

Her restraint was short-lived. She was working on her memoirs in Switzerland in August when the Vice-President of Bosnia came to beg her to make a fresh appeal on behalf of his country. She responded with a flurry of articles and TV interviews on both sides of the Atlantic, calling for military action to halt the continuing Serb assault on Gorazde and Sarajevo, end the brutal policy of 'ethnic cleansing' and save the Bosnian state. What was happening in Bosnia, she declared, was 'reminiscent of the worst excesses of the Nazis'.[27] Despairing of the 'paralysis' of the EU, she called on the Americans to take a lead. NATO, she wrote in the *New York Times*, was 'the most practical instrument to hand'. The Balkans were not 'out of area', but part of Europe.[28] In reply to those who argued that Western intervention would only exacerbate the conflict, she insisted that she was not calling for a full-scale military inva-sion, just the bombing of Serbian supply routes and the lifting of the arms embargo which prevented the Bosnians buying the means to defend themselves.[29] But her call fell on deaf ears. With a few exceptions, most MPs of both parties, most of the Establishment, elder statesmen like Ted Heath and most commentators backed the Foreign Office line that Britain had no interest in getting drawn into the conflict: many, frankly, took the view that the best outcome to be hoped for was a quick Serb victory. The most that Major and Hurd would do was to contribute British troops to a UN force protecting convoys of humanitarian aid; but this only strengthened the argument against military intervention, since these troops would have become vulnerable to retaliation if NATO had bombed the Serbs. Douglas Hurd still believes that active Western intervention would only have increased the bloodshed and made a bad situation worse.[30]

Nevertheless, Lady Thatcher kept up her demand, with mounting contempt for the Government's inertia, for the next three years, until eventually the Americans stepped in with enough force to bring the Serbs to the negotiating table. In December 1992 she warned of a 'holocaust' in Bosnia and insisted: 'We could have stopped this. We could still do so.' By treating the conflict as a purely internal matter, the West had 'actually given comfort to the aggres-sor'.[31] In April 1993, following the first massacre at Srebrenica – the second, even worse one, was in July 1995 – she rejected Hurd's plea that lifting the arms embargo would merely create 'a level killing field', as 'a terrible and disgraceful phrase'. Bosnia was 'already a killing field the like of which I thought we would never see in Europe again'. The horrors being perpetrated were 'not worthy of Europe, not worthy of the West and not worthy of the United States . . . It is in Europe's sphere of influence. It should be in Europe's sphere of conscience . . . We are little more than accomplices to a massacre.'[32] Privately she was said to have told Hurd: 'Douglas, Douglas, you would make Neville Chamberlain look like a warmonger.'[33]

In retrospect she was probably right. One can respect the reluctance of Major, Hurd and initially Bill Clinton (who succeeded George Bush as US President in 1993) to escalate the war by taking sides. Their instinct all along was to try to secure a ceasefire and a negotiated settlement via a succession of intermediaries: they could not believe that the Serbs could be so ruthless and unreasonable. But the fact was that the deployment of American force was in the end the only thing that brought the Serbs to conclude the Dayton Agreement in 1995. As so often, Lady Thatcher's bleak view of human nature and the necessity of military strength to defeat aggressors was more realistic than the pragmatism of those who thought themselves the 'realists'. The slaughter could have been stopped earlier if Europe had found the will to act firmly in its own back yard. It was ironic that she who so opposed Europe's ambition to develop a single foreign policy should have been the one calling for it to act unitedly in Bosnia. Sadly, events justified her scepticism and vindicated her view that no trouble anywhere in the world would ever be tackled without American leadership.

It was relatively easy for the Government to dismiss the former Prime Minister's lectures about Bosnia. She caused them more serious difficulty nearer home in the autumn of 1992 when the Maastricht Treaty finally came before Parliament. The Government suffered the worst possible curtain raiser to this debate on 16 September – 'Black Wednesday' – when Norman Lamont was humiliatingly forced to abandon Britain's membership of the ERM. After all the wrangles with Lawson and Howe about joining, culminating in Mrs Thatcher's reluctant acquiescence in October 1990, sterling crashed out of the system after just two years, at the cost of some £15 billion of the country's gold reserves and dealing a blow to the Government's reputation for financial competence from which it never recovered. Securing Mrs Thatcher's agreement to Britain's belated entry had been Major's personal triumph as Chancellor: now premature exit wrecked his premiership. Lady Thatcher – in Washington at the time – could not help but be delighted. 'If you try to buck the market, the market will buck you.'[34] She could not gloat too openly in public, but nothing would stop her trumpeting her vindication in private. Lamont told Wyatt that she was 'ringing all her friends saying, "Isn't it marvellous, I told you so etc."'[35] She warned against any thought of rejoining the ERM, but urged the Government to capitalise on its escape by cutting interest rates to beat the recession.

Back at Westminster on 4 November the Government faced two crucial Commons divisions on a so-called 'paving' vote, called by Major to reassure his European partners before the committee stage of the Maastricht Bill. With an overall Tory majority of just twenty-one, and two or three dozen Europhobes threatening to vote against the Government, Major's survival was on the line. The whips pulled out all the stops; but Lady Thatcher summoned wavering back-benchers to her room to tell them firmly what she expected of them. At the last moment Major personally cajoled leading Eurosceptics into the Government lobby with a promise that the Government would not finally ratify the treaty until after a second Danish referendum. By such means the Government won the first division by six votes, the second by three. Thus Major survived by the skin of his teeth. But he could not forget that at this crisis of his premiership his predecessor had done her best to destroy him.

For most of the first half of 1993 Lady Thatcher concentrated on her memoirs, while the Maastricht Bill ground through the Commons, suffering just two minor defeats in committee. But when it went up to the Lords in June she re-emerged to lead the attack in the Upper House, denying that the treaty followed naturally from the Single European Act which she had signed – 'I could never have signed this treaty' – and demanding a referendum before it was ratified.[36] With Willie Whitelaw, Geoffrey Howe and John Wakeham speaking for the Government, the treaty was overwhelmingly approved. But the schism that its passage caused in the Tory party has never fully healed.

The Mummy's curse

There was just one issue on which Lady Thatcher steadily supported the Government. Between 1992 and 1997 she probably devoted more time to Hong Kong than to any other subject. Maastricht and Bosnia made the headlines, but Hong Kong was the issue on which she felt she still had a responsibility and could exert an influence. The Chinese leadership still treated her with enormous respect and she handled them – particularly the charmless Prime Minister Li Peng – with a skilful mixture of outspokenness and tact. There was a particularly sharp diplomatic crisis in March 1995 when the Chinese were making difficulties about a number of thorny issues concerning the handover: among other things, they had got it into their heads that the British were planning to remove Hong Kong's entire gold reserves with them when they left. Lady Thatcher flew out, with the approval of Major, and broke the logjam by announcing sweetly but decisively in the hearing of journalists at the red-carpet ceremony at the airport exactly what she had come to get straight. No more was heard about the gold reserves or any of the other stumbling blocks.[37] In public and in private she boldly proclaimed her confidence that economic development in China would inevitably bring political freedom in its wake; and she protested firmly about Beijing's treatment of dissidents. In 1994 she announced that she had already booked rooms in Hong Kong so as to be present in person for the handover; and indeed when the day came, on 1 July 1997, she was there – with Tony Blair and Prince Charles – to witness the interminable ceremony in pouring rain. So far, she acknowledged in 2002, the Chinese had 'generally honoured their commitments'.[38]

Lady Thatcher did a good deal of unofficial lobbying on behalf of British firms bidding for contracts around the world. She intervened, for example, to stop Kuwait backing down on an agreement to buy armoured cars from GKN, by ringing the Crown Prince and telling him firmly that he should stick to his word; another time she flew secretly from Hong Kong to Azerbaijan to help BP secure a major oil contract under the noses of the French and American ambassadors.[39] As Prime Minister she had always believed in 'batting for Britain' – particularly in the arms trade – by face-to-face diplomacy with her opposite numbers, and after leaving office she did not cease to exert her personal influence wherever it could still be effective. Though it could never compensate for the loss of real power, this more than anything else did make her feel that she was still serving her country.

The first volume of her memoirs, *The Downing Street Years*, was published in October 1993. Although the real scores she had to settle were with those of her former colleagues who had ganged up on her, let her down or ultimately betrayed her, the media were sure to focus on what she had to say about her successor. Rumours abounded even before the *Daily Mirror* leaked her dismissive view that Major, as Chancellor in 1990, had 'swallowed . . . the slogans of the European lobby' and 'intellectually . . . was drifting with the tide'.[40] This was the start of an intensive blitz of book promotion accompanied by a four-part BBC television series.

Both the book and the series showed that the Iron Lady had lost none of her passionate intensity. The book has its longueurs, but it is still by far the most comprehensive and readable of modern prime ministerial memoirs: partisan, of course, but generally a clear and vivid account of her side of the arguments. Of course it aggrandises her role, exaggerates the degree to which she knew where she was going from the beginning, slides over her moments of doubt and hesitation and diminishes the contribution of most of her colleagues, aides and advisers. It is a shockingly ungenerous book. Nevertheless, it sold well. Lady Thatcher spent two weeks signing copies in bookshops all around Britain, then flew off in November to do the same in America and Japan. The paperback edition appeared in Britain in March 1995 and did even better. Meanwhile, her contract with HarperCollins obliged her to lose no time in getting on with the second volume covering her early years.

This, though autobiographically more interesting, had less commercial potential. Lady Thatcher was therefore persuaded to supplement the 450-odd pages describing her childhood and rise to power with another 150 pages giving her view of current events in the four and a half years since her fall. If *The Downing Street Years* had been unhelpful to her successor, *The Path to Power*, which appeared in May 1995 accompanied by another media circus, was much worse. This time she avoided personal criticism, but made it clear that she thought the Major Government had squandered her legacy and pursued the wrong policies in almost every area. At public meetings to promote the book she was still more outspoken. But by now she was simply ranting. Prejudice had finally taken over from politics, unmediated by the memory of responsibility. She was suddenly an opinionated and easily provoked old lady: press a button and she would respond with a tirade until she ran out of steam and had to be prompted with another question, which set her off again. Unfortunately for Major, she still made headlines and her words, as she set off on another whistle-stop signing tour around the country, gave encouragement to those in the party who were working for a change of leader.

Major accepted the challenge and got his response in first. On 22 June he startled the political world by resigning – as Tory leader, not as Prime Minister – and inviting his critics to 'put up or shut up': either put up a candidate to defeat him or else stop sniping. The obvious candidate, long seen as Lady Thatcher's favourite – though she had never publicly endorsed him – was Michael Portillo. But Portillo decided, after some contrary signals, not to stand, and the much less charismatic John Redwood came forward instead. In this crisis of his premiership one might have expected Lady Thatcher, who had been so affronted by the constitutional impropriety of a serving Prime Minister being driven from office by a party revolt, to have rallied to her successor's support, whatever her reservations about him. In fact she remained studiedly neutral. She was promoting her book in America at the time of the ballot on 4 July, but issued a curt statement saying merely that Major and Redwood were 'both good Conservatives'.[41] This was very pointedly not an endorsement. She did bring herself to congratulate Major, however, when he won just enough votes to secure his position – 218 to Redwood's 89 – and told Wyatt that she would henceforth support Major 'because the alternative is even worse'. Tony Blair might be a new sort of Labour leader, she conceded but his party was as socialist as ever – though now pursuing its goal through European federalism – so it was vital for the Tories to win again.

She saw a hopeful model for a Tory recovery in the Republicans' sweeping gains in the 1994 mid-term congressional elections in America, under the born-again leadership of Newt Gingrich. 'After an unhappy period when the momentum stalled,' she declared in Washington, the Republicans 'have now decided to regard the 1980s as a springboard, not an embarrassment. And the political dividend has been huge. I hope that British Conservatives will raise their sights and learn lessons from America.'[42] By the same token she saw the Democratic President Bill Clinton as 'nothing but a draft dodger and a coward',[43] as well as hopelessly woolly. 'He's a great communicator,' she acknowledged. 'The trouble is he has absolutely nothing to communicate.'[44]

She was on more solid ground when she kept to the world stage. In March 1996 she made one of her most prescient speeches when invited to speak at Fulton, Missouri, where, fifty years earlier, Churchill had coined his great image of an 'iron curtain' descending across Europe. With the help of her speechwriter, the now indispensable Robin Harris, she rose to the occasion with a Churchillian survey of the world after the end of the Cold War, highlighting the rise of 'rogue states' – was she the first to use the phrase? – 'like Syria, Iraq and Gaddafi's Libya' and the danger from 'the proliferation of weapons of mass destruction'. The world, she warned, 'remains a very dangerous place . . . menaced by more unstable and complex threats than a decade ago'. But she feared that with the risk of imminent nuclear annihilation apparently removed, 'we in the West have lapsed into alarming complacency about the risks that remain'. Her preference was explicitly for pre-emptive military action to remove the threat – a policy that would have to wait for the presidency of the younger George Bush, acting under the provocation of the attack on the World Trade Center in September 2001. In the meantime she merely urged the West to press on with the development of 'effective ballistic missile defence which would protect us and our armed forces, reduce or even nullify the rogue state's arsenal and enable us to retaliate'. She called for a reinvigoration of NATO both by extending its membership to include Poland, Hungary and the Czech Republic and by allowing it to operate 'out of area' to defend the West's security. But as always she saw all progress and safety in terms of American leadership, with Britain as America's first ally. 'It is the West – above all perhaps the English-speaking peoples of the West . . . which we all know offers the best hope of global peace and prosperity. In order to uphold these things, the Atlantic political relationship must be constantly nurtured and renewed.'[45]

With the 1997 General Election only months away and a Labour victory seemingly almost certain, she did not want to be seen to rock the boat. For some time she had been telling friends that the country had 'nothing to fear' from Tony Blair, a patriot who, she said, 'will not let Britain down'.[46]* But now an unnamed 'ally' told *The Times*: 'She will not be blamed, or allow the blame to be heaped on her friends, for losing the Tories the election . . . Whatever misgivings she may have, she fears a Blair Government even more.'[47]

Once again she was determined not to be sidelined when the election came. No sooner had Major announced the date than she was on the pavement outside Chesham Place giving an impromptu press conference, as she had so often done in Downing Street, to try to quash reports that she was secretly supporting Blair. 'The phrase "New Labour" is cunningly designed to conceal a lot of old socialism', she warned. 'Don't be taken in . . . Stay with us and with John Major until we cross the finishing line.'[48] She appeared with Major twice during the campaign, and made a number of barnstorming forays on her own to selected constituencies without rocking the boat too vigorously.

Eighteen years of Conservative Government ended on 1 May 1997 in an even bigger Labour landslide than the polls had predicted.

---

*If her definition of 'not letting Britain down' was backing America in every eventuality, Blair did her proud in 2003 by aligning Britain unswervingly behind George W. Bush's invasion of Iraq, in defiance of most of his party, public opinion and the United Nations. She herself at the height of her relationship with Ronald Reagan was never obedient to American leadership.

Labour won 419 seats and the Liberal Democrats – benefiting from widespread tactical voting – 46, reducing the Tories to a rump of 165 (their worst result since 1906) and giving Blair a majority of 179, which dwarfed even Mrs Thatcher's two big wins in 1983 and 1987. Lady Thatcher viewed this debacle with mixed feelings. On the one hand, she was a lifelong party warrior and believed enough of her dire warnings about resurgent socialism to deplore the state to which her old party had been reduced. On the other hand, she could not disguise a certain satisfaction in contemplating the shipwreck which she believed her successors had brought upon themselves by discarding her in 1990. She did not consider the alternative view that she had left Major a poisoned legacy – an economy running into recession, declining public services and a party already deeply split over Europe – and had done everything in her power over the past seven years to undermine his authority and widen the rift. Many commentators saw 1997 as the electorate's delayed verdict on Thatcherism. All but the most committed partisans thought a change of government overdue and healthy.

At a deeper level, however, 1997 can be seen as Mrs Thatcher's greatest victory, which set the seal on her transformation of British politics. She had set out, on becoming leader in 1975, to abolish socialism and twenty years later she had succeeded beyond her wildest dreams. By her repeated electoral success, by her neutering of the trade unions, by the privatisation of most of the public sector and the introduction of market forces into almost every area of national life, she – and her successor – had not only reversed the tide of increasing collectivism which had flowed from 1945 to 1979, but had rewritten the whole agenda of politics, forcing the Labour party gradually and reluctantly to accept practically the entire Thatcherite programme – at least the means, if not in its heart the ends – in order to make itself electable. Blair was a perfectly post-Thatcherite politician: an ambitious pragmatist with a smile of dazzling sincerity, but no convictions beyond a desire to rid Labour of its outdated ideological baggage. The rebranding of the party as 'New Labour' was the final acknowledgement of Mrs Thatcher's victory. 'We are all Thatcherites now,' Peter Mandelson acknowledged.[49] She had not only banished socialism, in any serious meaning of the word, from political debate, but she had effectively abolished the old Labour party. 'New' Labour was as dedicated as the Tories to wealth creation and market forces, even if it hoped – as Major, too, had done – to pursue them with more humanity than Mrs Thatcher had often shown. Back in the polarised 1970s the dream of most pundits had been that Britain should become more like

America, with two capitalist parties differing in style and tone but agreed on essentials, like the Republicans and Democrats. The rise of New Labour had now brought this to pass. But instead of an alternation of parties, the consequence was almost fatal to the Tory party.

Three weeks after the election, just before attending his first European summit, Blair outraged old Labour stalwarts by inviting Lady Thatcher to Downing Street. 'She has a mind well worth picking,' his spokesman explained, 'and he wants to see her again.'[50] She was happy to give him the benefit of her advice. Blair, with his huge majority, his personal self-confidence and vaguely messianic leanings, was – as William Rees-Mogg wrote in *The Times* – her 'natural successor' in a way that poor, insecure John Major had never been. Major's seven-year tenure in Number Ten quickly shrivelled to a mere fractious coda to the Thatcher years. Meanwhile the shattered Tory party had to elect a new leader. Lady Thatcher initially indicated that she would not back any candidate but when the thirty-six-year-old William Hague emerged as the fresh white hope, she came off the fence to lobby for him. Hague had first come to prominence as a precocious schoolboy at the 1977 party conference, speaking from the podium under the benign maternal gaze of the leader, then had won a by-election in 1988. He was Mrs Thatcher's political child if ever there was one; and she now appeared with him for an excruciating photo-call outside the House of Commons, at which she wagged her finger and lectured the camera as if it were a backward child:

> I am supporting William Hague. Now, have you got the name? William Hague. For principled government, following the same kind of government which I led, vote for William Hague on Thursday. Have you got the message?[51]

Hague was duly elected, but over the next four years failed dismally to dent Blair's popularity or restore the public's faith in the Tories. Apart from the odd embarrassing eruption, Lady Thatcher finally began to fade from public view.

Shortly before Blair went to the country again in May 2001, Lady Thatcher – now seventy-five – descended on the party's spring conference in Plymouth and made one of her characteristically cloth-eared jokes. On her way to the hall, she said, she had passed a cinema showing a film entitled *The Mummy Returns*. She did not seem to realise that this was a horror film – nothing to do with a cuddly mother figure. By applying it to herself she unwittingly evoked all the headlines and cartoons that had been portraying her for years as a ghost, a vampire, the undead or Frankenstein's monster still haunting the Tory party.[52] During the campaign Labour once again exploited her unpopularity with a poster combining Hague's face with her hair, and her every appearance in the campaign served only to remind the voters why they did not want the Tories back. Labour was returned with its huge majority virtually undented, and once again the Tories were looking for a new leader.

Rejecting the far better qualified Ken Clarke, whose pro-European views now made him unacceptable, the party next elected the totally inexperienced Iain Duncan Smith, whose only qualifications were that he had been a leading rebel against Maastricht in 1993–4 and was now Lady Thatcher's anointed favourite. The *Week* summed up the press consensus with a cover cartoon of her embracing the new leader under the headline 'The Kiss of Death?'[53] Three months later a BBC documentary entitled *The Curse of the Mummy* revived her Plymouth joke to lay on her much of the blame for the party's dire state.[54] Her refusal to go quietly into the political night had left the former Prime Minister now virtually friendless.

Silenced

Not only did she have few friends, but her family provided little consolation for her old age. 'We have become a grandmother,' she had proudly announced in 1989, when Mark's first child was born. Four years later Diane Thatcher gave birth to a second. But Margaret saw her grandchildren only rarely – and not much more of her children. In 1994 Mark and Diane moved from Texas to South Africa, but seldom came to Britain. Carol spent most of her time in Switzerland in an on-off relationship with a ski instructor, but has never married. Neither of the twins, who turned fifty in 2003, exemplified the ideal of a close-knot family which their mother always strove to project.

Mark's business dealings have continued to attract controversy. His American affairs came under investigation by the Texas courts in 1995. He was sued by his business partner for alleged conspiracy involving 'mail fraud, wire fraud, tax fraud, bankruptcy fraud, money laundering, usury, common law fraud, deceptive trade practices, perjury, theft and assault'.[55] Eventually he settled out of court for $500,000 but he still faced another $4 million case being brought against his Grantham Company (which traded in aviation fuel) by the Ameristar Fuel Corporation, as well as charges of tax evasion. After a family summit his mother was reported to have cleared his debts to the tune of £700,000[56]: yet he somehow still continued to live like a millionaire. Later that year he moved, with Diane and the children, to Cape Town; but his shady reputation followed him and he continued to attract the attention of both the police and the South African tax authorities.[57] In 2005 he was charged with involvement in an attempted coup to overthrow the President of Equatorial Guinea. He pleaded guilty and was lucky to escape with a suspended sentence and a fine of three million rand (£265,000) – again paid by his mother. Soon afterwards Diane divorced him and returned to America. Banned from entering the United States and several other territories, Mark settled appropriately among the expatriate criminal fraternity in southern Spain.

In 1996, Carol published an affectionate biography of Denis, which drew a devastating picture of Margaret's remoteness as a mother. She was even more explicit in some of the interviews that accompanied publication. 'As a child I was frightened of her,' Carol revealed. Mark had always been their mother's favourite. 'I always felt I came second of the two. Unloved is not the right word, but I never felt I made the grade.' Though as an adult she had plainly grown fond of her father, she described her parents' marriage as a union of two ambitious and primarily work-directed people, rather than a happy family unit. 'Their priorities were not to each other or to us.'[58] 'It was very much drilled into me that the best thing I could ever do for my mother was not to make any demands on her.'[59] In a curiously artless way Carol thus comprehensively torpedoed her mother's pretence that family had always been the most important thing in her life.

For seventy years Mrs Thatcher's health had been extraordinarily good. She had suffered from colds, from one or two specific conditions like varicose veins and Dupuytren's contracture which had required minor operations, and increasingly from problems with her teeth. But considering the demands she had made on her constitution for the past forty years, it had held up astonishingly well. In so-called retirement she still got up early and kept herself busy all day, still exhausted her staff by her relentless schedule on foreign trips. Yet eventually the Iron Lady did begin to show signs of metal fatigue. While speaking in Chile in 1994 she suddenly lost consciousness and slumped forward onto the lectern. She quickly recovered, and apologised profusely to her hosts for her uncharacteristic moment of weakness; but this was probably her first very minor stroke.[60]

The most visible sign of frailty over the next few years was a loss of short-term memory. She began to repeat herself and seemed not to take in what was said to her. So long as she had a script, she remained a true professional who could still turn in a faultless perform-ance. But off-script she could be a liability, either too predictable – simply repeating lines she had used a thousand times before, some-times just a minute earlier – or else alarmingly unpredictable. Denis or whoever was minding her at the time had to be skilled at nudging the needle on at the right moment. It was in Madeira, where she and Denis had gone to celebrate their golden wedding anniversary at the end of 2001, that she suffered a second minor stroke. Some-time early in 2002 she had a third, as a result of which it was announced on 22 March that she would do no more public speaking. But not before she had exploded one last bombshell with the serialisation of her latest book.

Statecraft: Strategies for a Changing World was neither a third volume of memoirs, though it had autobiographical elements, nor – as its title might suggest – an instruction manual in the art of govern-ment. Rather, it was a survey of the international scene at the start of the new millennium, comprising Lady Thatcher's view of how things had been allowed to slide since 1990 and what should now be done to put them right. Every few pages her prescription was summarised in four or five bullet points printed in bold type. The book was dedicated to Ronald Reagan 'to whom the world owes so much': its central message was contempt for the woolly inter-nationalism of the 'new world order' and the importance of Amer-ican global leadership. She seemed almost to welcome the terrorist attack on the World Trade Center on 11 September 2001 as a vindi-cation of her previous warnings, and positively looked forward to the Americans hitting back decisively and unilaterally:

> So far . . . I am heartened by the fact that President Bush seems to have concluded that this is an American operation and that America alone will decide how it is to be conducted . . . That means taking out the terrorists and their protectors, and not just in Afghanistan but elsewhere too.[61]*

Did she recall that she had once been a strong upholder of inter-national law who had criticised unilateral American action in

---

* On the specific question of Iraq she wrote, 'There will be no peace and security in the region until Saddam is toppled.' She was hesitant about attacking him unless he could be shown to have been involved in the atroc-ities of 11 September. 'But if he was, he must be made to pay the price.'[62]

Grenada, warned Reagan against retaliation against Libya and opposed carrying the Gulf war all the way to Baghdad without UN authority? Or that she had long argued that nuclear weapons helped preserve the peace and practically defined a country's sovereignty? Now, faced with the prospect of nuclear weapons falling into the wrong hands, she wrote that she 'certainly would not rule out pre-emptive strikes to destroy a rogue state's capabilities'[63] – while at the same time she dismissed 'pointless protests about India's or Pakistan's nuclear capabilities'.[64] Now it all depended on whether it was America's friends or enemies who had the weapons.

Other chapters dealt with Europe's feeble response to the disintegration of Yugoslavia; her high hopes of China, Hong Kong, India and Asia generally; rather more cautious optimism about Russia; and a somewhat muted restatement of her belief that Israel must eventually be persuaded to trade 'land for peace' to secure a just settlement in the Middle East. Most controversial, however, was her latest and definitive blast against the European Union, in which she finally laid bare the gut conviction which had underlain her attitude to the Continent all her life. 'During my lifetime', she declared, 'most of the problems the world has faced have come, in one fashion or another, from mainland Europe, and the solutions from outside it.'[65] Of course she was thinking primarily, as always, of the Second World War. But it applied also to the Cold War: Communism was the problem, America the solution.

The European Community, she had concluded, was 'fundamentally unreformable'. It was 'an empire in the making . . . the ultimate bureaucracy', founded on 'humbug'; inherently protectionist, intrinsically corrupt, essentially undemocratic and dedicated to the destruction of nation-states. 'It is in fact a classic utopian project, a monument to the vanity of intellectuals, a programme whose inevitable destiny is failure.'[66] That being so, she called for a fundamental renegotiation of Britain's membership and, if that failed – as it was bound to do – for Britain to be ready to withdraw and join the North American Free Trade Area instead, turning its back on the whole disastrous folly into which Ted Heath had led the country in 1973.

This sensational *démarche* was serialised in *The Times*, starting on 18 March. This time the consensus was clear, right across the political spectrum, that she had finally lost touch with reality. Several of her most loyal supporters, including leading Eurosceptics like Michael Howard, were quick to distance themselves. A poll of constituency party chairmen found 71 per cent rejecting Lady Thatcher's view. 'I love her to death,' the chairman of North East Hampshire Conservatives told *The Times*, 'but she's gone too far. We do not tolerate extremists and she has gone into the extremist bracket.' 'She has a special place in Conservative Party history,' echoed another. 'What she did for this country was something we should be proud of. But times have moved on . . . She should gracefully take a step back and let those in charge get on with it.'[67]

The very next day she caught the press off guard by doing exactly that. Having dominated the media all week with her views, she announced on Friday that she had been advised by her doctors to cancel all her scheduled speaking engagements and accept no more. 'SILENCED' ran the headlines from the *Daily Mail* to the *Sun*. The weekend papers were filled with retrospectives of her career, picture spreads, memorable sayings and virtual obituaries which proclaimed that this was the end of the story. Some commentators doubted if she would really be able to contain herself, since 'the sound of silence and Lady Thatcher are not natural allies'.[68] No one pointed out that she had only forsworn public speaking, and that she had sparked the latest uproar without uttering a word. Nevertheless, there was universal agreement that it was the end of an era.

Her three strokes, rather than memory loss, were given as the reason, though clearly the two were connected. She did in fact continue to make public appearances. In October 2002 she attended the opening of the new Archives Centre, built to house her papers at Churchill College, Cambridge, to which the Thatcher Foundation had contributed £5 million. And she continued to issue brief statements on current events – praising Blair's 'bold and effective' leadership in the war on Iraq, for instance, but at the same time accusing New Labour of 'reverting to Old Labour with its irresponsible policies of tax and spend'.[69] She could not quite give up the habit of a lifetime. But essentially she had now finally retired.

In 2003 Denis died, which added further to her confusion. For more than half a century he had been her rock and without him she was lost. It was now generally known that she was suffering – like Ronald Reagan – from Alzheimer's disease, and she slipped progressively from public view, cared for by a loyal bodyguard of old friends and devoted staff. In 2008 Carol published another book in which she spelled out – rather unnecessarily in many eyes – the extent of her mother's dementia. Even in her twilight state, however, her capacity to arouse controversy remained undimmed. On becoming Prime Minister in July 2007, Gordon Brown followed Tony Blair's example ten years earlier by inviting Lady Thatcher to tea in Downing Street. She was said to be pleased to be asked back to her old domain and posed happily for pictures on the doorstep; but both Labour and Tory supporters were outraged by Brown trying to exploit her reputation for his own political ends. Paradoxically, even as Brown embraced her, David Cameron was still trying to distance the Tories from her legacy. ('There *is* such a thing as society', he insisted. 'It's just not the same thing as the state.')[70] When her statue was erected in the lobby of the House of Commons in 2002 a protester decapitated it with an iron bar; then in 2008 it leaked out that plans were in hand to give her a state funeral – an honour last accorded to Churchill in 1965. It was as if she was no longer a living person but had already passed into history, a semi-mythical icon whose mantle was simultaneously claimed and rejected by both parties.

The debate will be joined in earnest when she finally joins the pantheon of departed leaders. Margaret Thatcher was not merely the first woman and the longest-serving Prime Minister of modern times, but the most admired, most hated, most idolised and most vilified public figure of the second half of the twentieth century. To some she was the saviour of her country who 'put the Great back into Great Britain' after decades of decline;[71] the dauntless warrior who curbed the unions, routed the wets, reconquered the Falklands, rolled back the state and created a vigorous enterprise economy which twenty years later was still outperforming the more regulated economies of the Continent. To others, she was a narrow ideologue whose hard-faced policies legitimised greed, deliberately increased inequality by favouring the middle class at the expense of an excluded underclass, starved the public services, wrecked the universities, prostituted public broadcasting and destroyed the nation's sense of solidarity and civic pride. There is no reconciling these views: yet both are true.

A third view would argue that she achieved much less than she and her admirers claim: that for all her boasts on one side, and the howls of 'Tory cuts' on the other, she actually failed to curb public spending significantly, failed to prune or privatise the welfare state, failed to change most of the British people's fundamental attitudes, but rather extended Whitehall's detailed control of many areas of national life, shrank freedom where she claimed to be enhancing it, downgraded Parliament and pioneered a style of presidential government which was developed still further by Tony Blair. Nor did she raise Britain's influence in the world. On the contrary, by binding the country more firmly than ever to the United States and refusing to engage constructively with Britain's opportunity in Europe, she repeated the historic error which kept Britain outside the European Union in its formative phase, perpetuating its ambivalent semi-isolation. This may prove in the long run her most damaging legacy.

There remains the question of how far Margaret Thatcher, as an individual, inspired and drove the policies that bore her name, or to what extent she simply rode a global wave of anti-collectivism and technological revolution which would have changed British society in most of the same ways, whoever had been in power. What she undeniably did was to articulate the new materialistic individualism with a clarity and moral fervour which appeared to win the argument by sheer force of personality, even when the reality was less radical than the rhetoric. She was not a creative or consistent thinker. There were huge contradictions between her belief in free markets and liberal economics, on the one hand, and her flagrant partiality to her own class and her increasingly strident English nationalism on the other. But that was not the point. She was a brilliantly combative, opportunist politician who, by a mixture of hard work, stamina, self-belief and uncanny instinct, bullied an awestruck country into doing things her way for more than a decade. Above all she was a tremendous performer, who raised genuine passions on both sides of the political divide which have been sadly absent in the bland, spin-doctored days since her departure. She may have achieved less than she claimed, but she still accomplished much that was necessary and overdue. Today the whole culture of incomes policies, subsidies and social contracts – and the double-digit inflation that made them seem inescapable – seems so remote that it is easy to forget how much courage was required in 1979–81 to set about dismantling it. The courage was not hers alone; but she was the leader. Ultimately the balance sheet will demand a judgement as to whether the benefits of that economic and cultural revolution outweighed the social cost.

Up till 2008 it was widely accepted that Thatcherism had not only restored the British economy but – hand in hand with Reaganism in the United States – set the template for the development of the world economy for the foreseeable future. Free market capitalism had triumphed all round the world, socialism was a discredited memory, and ever-growing prosperity was assumed to be infinitely assured on a tide of financial ingenuity and deregulated credit. While a few wise voices warned that the boom was founded on a confidence trick, the Labour governments of Blair and Brown bought into this dangerous optimism, partly because they too were carried away by it, but partly also because they could not be seen to stand against it. 'New Labour' regained power in 1997 precisely by accepting the Thatcher revolution, and its continued dominance over the next decade depended on leaving the Tories no political space to their right. The 2008 'credit crunch' – directly caused by the irresponsible lending of deregulated banks and other financial institutions in Britain and the United States – shattered this optimism and plunged the whole world into the worst recession since the 1930s. On the one hand this devastating collapse was specifically the failure of the Reagan/Thatcher model of 'light-touch' regulation which encouraged the pursuit of short-term profits at the expense of long-term security. On the other, the measures adopted on both sides of the Atlantic to salvage the situation – by the outgoing Republican administration in Washington as much as by Brown's Labour government in Britain, as well as by all the economies of the European Union and most of the rest of the world – resurrected almost overnight – with astonishingly little hesitation or opposition – all those discredited 'socialist' solutions which were thought to have been forsworn for ever: 'rescuing' the banks with large sums of taxpayers' money (stopping barely short of outright nationalisation) and pumping further large injections of borrowed money into the economy to try to maintain demand. Crude Keynesianism – which Thatcherism was supposed to have buried for ever – was suddenly resurgent, to the great glee of all those old socialists who had never in their hearts abandoned their hankering for state control. Now it was untrammelled capitalism which seemed to have imploded, with banks and building societies running to the state to be saved from the consequences of their own folly.

Seeking scapegoats, some in the media blamed Mrs Thatcher personally. Her defenders pointed out that she had always preached thrift, held that high remuneration should be the reward of hard work, not speculation, never owned a credit card and disapproved of the 'casino culture' of the City. One could even see the credit crunch as a spectacular vindication of her repeated warnings that 'you cannot buck the market'. Nevertheless it was undeniable that her government, by detonating the 'Big Bang' of 1986, had unleashed, perhaps unwittingly, all the consequences that flowed from deregulation of the financial sector, including the rocketing of house prices and a huge rise in household indebtedness as under-capitalised banks lent money they did not have to overmortgaged customers who could not repay it. She was, whether she liked it or not, the patron saint of the 'loadsamoney' culture, and when it collapsed it was inevitable, in the highly personalised world of modern politics, that she would be blamed, and her reputation as the saviour of British capitalism badly tarnished. Of course it was not just her government which inflated the bubble. One of Gordon Brown's first acts on taking over the Treasury was to ease still further the framework of financial regulation; Peter Mandelson famously declared that New Labour was 'intensely relaxed about people getting filthy rich';[72] and for ten years Tony Blair's overriding priority was to do everything necessary to retain the support of the City. But they were all operating within the climate created by eighteen years of Thatcherism. It was a measure of how fundamentally she had transformed the political landscape that even a Chancellor with such deep 'old Labour' roots as Brown – who had made his reputation excoriating Thatcherism in the 1980s – felt obliged in office to press on with her revolution, carrying it to lengths of imprudence at which her innate caution would have baulked. Her influence lived on long after 1990; that was her great achievement. But when the world she had bequeathed crashed, her reputation necessarily suffered with it.

No doubt the world economy will recover, as the counter-cyclical measures taken by all the major national economies – with Barack Obama's new Democrat administration in Washington in the lead – sooner or later take effect. 'Socialism' in the form that Mrs Thatcher banished it will not return. But there is bound to be a serious correction which will last for many years. The substantial stake which all Western governments have taken in their financial institutions will take time to unpick. Having had their fingers badly burned, the ideologues of the unregulated market will not be so arrogant – or so triumphalist again for a long time. Thus as the perspective on Margaret Thatcher's career lengthens it becomes clearer than ever that history moves in cycles. The solutions of today become the problems of tomorrow. Margaret Thatcher played a bold part in wrenching Britain – and by her example much of the world – out of the failed path of economic planning and stifling state control. Over a period of nearly thirty years Thatcherism released a huge amount of economic energy, created a great deal of new wealth and delivered many social benefits – as well as some enduring costs. That it eventually had to be corrected in its turn will not detract in the long run from her historic importance. For better and worse, the grocer's daughter from Grantham imprinted her personality, and her name, indelibly upon her era. She will always remain one of the transformative figures who shaped the twentieth century.

Notes and References

1. Dutiful Daughter

1. Private information.
2. *Grantham Journal*, 6 February 1981.
3. Ibid., January 1917.
4. Ibid., 8 February 1936.
5. Ibid., 9 October 1937.
6. Patricia Murray, *Margaret Thatcher* (W. H. Allen, 1980), p. 13.
7. Ibid., p. 21.
8. Russell Lewis, *Margaret Thatcher* (Routledge & Kegan Paul, 1975), p. 10.
9. Margaret Thatcher, *The Path to Power* (HarperCollins, 1995), p. 28.
10. Ibid., p. 19.
11. Ibid., p. 6.
12. George Gardiner, *Margaret Thatcher: From Childhood to Leadership* (William Kimber, 1975), p. 20.
13. *Sunday Telegraph*, 14 February 1982.
14. *The Times*, 5 May 1979.
15. Murray, p. 50.
16. BBC TV, *In the Limelight*, 11 August 1980.
17. Nicholas Wapshott and George Brock, *Thatcher* (Macdonald, 1983), p. 26.
18. Interview with Brian Walden, *Weekend World*, 28 January 1981.
19. Private information.
20. Lewis, p. 11.
21. Thatcher, p. 36.
22. Murray, p. 37.
23. Gardiner, p. 37.
24. Thatcher, p. 39.
25. Interview, Mrs Jean Darmon (née Southerst).
26. Wapshott and Brock, p. 46.

27. *Grantham Journal*, June 1945.
28. *Sleaford Gazette*, 29 June 1945.
29. Thatcher, p. 46.
30. Ibid., p. 38.
31. House of Commons, 23 October 1984.

2. Young Conservative

1. Wapshott and Brock, p. 51.
2. Conservative party archive (CCO 1/8/397).
3. Ibid.
4. E. J. Tranter to J. P. L. Thomas, 14 January 1949 (CCO 1/7/397).
5. Ibid., 2 March 1949.
6. Thatcher, p. 67.
7. *Erith Observer*, 10 February 1950.
8. Wapshott and Brock, p. 54.
9. Thatcher, p. 66.
10. Ibid.
11. Carol Thatcher, *Below the Parapet: The Biography of Denis Thatcher* (Harper-Collins, 1996), p. 63.
12. Thatcher, p. 67.
13. Penny Junor, *Margaret Thatcher: Wife, Mother, Politician* (Sidgwick & Jackson, 1983), p.33.
14. Carol Thatcher, p. 64.
15. Miriam Stoppard interview, *Woman to Woman*, Yorkshire TV, 19 November 1985.
16. Carol Thatcher, p. 69.
17. Murray, p. 48.
18. Election press conference, Glasgow airport, 26 April 1979.
19. Thatcher, p. 103.
20. Carol Thatcher, p. 72.
21. Ibid., p. 89.
22. Ibid., p. 88.
23. Interview, Lord Jenkin.
24. Miriam Stoppard interview, 19 November 1985.
25. Conservative party archive (CCO 1/12/375).
26. *Finchley Press*, 18 July 1958.
27. *Evening Standard*, 15 July 1958.
28. Conservative party archive (CCO 1/12/375).
29. *Finchley Press*, 13 February 1959.
30. Ibid., 25 September 1959.

3. **First Steps**

1. Peter Rawlinson, *A Price Too High* (Weidenfeld & Nicolson, 1989), pp. 246–7.
2. Henry Brooke in House of Commons, 5 February 1960 [Vol. 616, col. 1436].
3. *The Times*, 29 January 1960.
4. House of Commons, 5 February 1960 [Vol. 616, cols 1350–58].
5. Ibid., col.1358.
6. *The Times*, 14 April 1960.
7. House of Commons, 13 May 1960 [Vol. 623, col. 836].
8. *Finchley Press*, 18 August 1961.
9. Gardiner, p. 68.
10. TV interview with Laurens van der Post, 29 March 1983.
11. Thatcher, p. 123.
12. Ibid.
13. Interview, Lord Holderness.
14. Lewis, p. 32.
15. Interview, Lord Holderness.
16. *Finchley Press*, 9 October 1964.
17. Carol Thatcher, pp. 91–4.

4. **Opposition**

1. Thatcher, p. 133.
2. Ibid., p.134.
3. Election address, Finchley 1966 (Conservative party archive).
4. James Prior, *A Balance of Power* (Hamish Hamilton, 1986), p. 42.
5. Thatcher, p. 139.
6. *Daily Telegraph*, 13 October 1966.
7. *Sun,* 13 October 1966.
8. Thatcher, pp. 153–4.
9. Thatcher, p. 144.
10. *Sunday Telegraph*, 15 October 1967.
11. *The Times*, 13 September 1968.
12. *Guardian*, 11 October 1968.
13. Thatcher, pp. 146–7.
14. *The Times*, 13 September 1968.
15. Margaret Thatcher, *What's Wrong with Politics?* (CPC, 1968).
16. House of Commons, 29 November 1968 [Vol. 774, cols 946–56].
17. Thatcher, pp. 154–6.
18. *Finchley Press*, 17 October 1969.

19. Thatcher, p. 150.
20. *Financial Times*, 22 October 1969.
21. *Observer*, 26 October 1969.
22. *Finchley Press*, 25 March 1966.
23. Sir Edward Boyle to Alderman Fred Hutty, 29 September 1969 (Conservative party archive, CCO 505/3/9).
24. Thatcher, p. 159.
25. *The Times*, 7 November 1969.
26. House of Commons, 12 February 1970 [Vol. 795, col. 1535].
27. Thatcher, p. 161.
28. Michael Cockerell, *Live from Number 10: The Inside Story of Prime Ministers and Television* (Faber, 1988), p. 213.
29. Thatcher, pp. 162–3.
30. Carol Thatcher, p. 97.
31. *Finchley Press*, 26 June 1970.

5. Education Secretary

1. Thatcher, p. 166.
2. Interview, Sir Toby Weaver.
3. *Spectator*, 22 July 1972.
4. Thatcher, p. 38.
5. Nicholas Timmins, *The Five Giants: A Biography of the Welfare State* (HarperCollins, 1995), pp. 373–4.
6. Peter Hennessy, *Whitehall* (Secker & Warburg, 1989), p. 626.
7. Interview, John Hudson.
8. Conservative Party Conference, 7 October 1970.
9. Interview, Sheila Browne.
10. House of Commons, 5 November 1971 [Vol. 825, cols 510–27].
11. *The Times*, 26 June 1971.
12. Conservative Party Conference, 14 October 1971.
13. Confidential source interviewed by David Butler, June 1970.
14. House of Commons, 14 June 1971 [Vol. 819, cols 42–56].
15. *Sun*, 9 July 1971.
16. Ibid., 25 November 1971.
17. *Daily Mail*, 31 January 1972.
18. *The Times*, 18 January 1972.
19. *Education: A Framework for Expansion* [Cmnd 5774] (HMSO, 1972); House of Commons, 19 February 1973 [Vol. 851, cols 41–57].
20. Thatcher, pp. 190–91.
21. House of Commons, 28 January 1974 [Vol. 868, cols 39–49].
22. *The Times*, 17 May 1972.

23. *Finchley Press*, 16 February 1973.
24. Conservative Party Conference, 12 October 1972.
25. *Finchley Press*, 1 February 1974.
26. Ibid., 19 October 1973.
27. John Ramsden, *The Winds of Change: Macmillan to Heath, 1957–1975* (Longman, 1996), p. 359.

6. The Peasants' Revolt

1. Phillip Whitehead, *The Writing on the Wall: Britain in the Seventies* (Channel 4/Michael Joseph, 1985), p. 330.
2. Keith Joseph, *Reversing the Trend* (Barry Rose, 1975), p. 4.
3. Conservative party archive (LCC 74/9].
4. Interview, Sheila Browne.
5. Thatcher, p. 249.
6. David Butler and Dennis Kavanagh, *The British General Election of October 1974* (Macmillan, 1975), p. 122.
7. *Evening News*, 11 October 1974.
8. Thatcher, p. 266.
9. Whitehead, p. 327.
10. Thatcher, p. 267.
11. Ibid.
12. BBC Radio 4, *Any Questions?* 30 January 1970.
13. *The Times*, 25 November 1974.
14. *Daily Mirror*, 3 February 1975.
15. *Daily Express*, 3 February 1975.
16. *Daily Mail*, 5 February 1975.
17. Patrick Cosgrave, *Margaret Thatcher: A Tory and her Party* (Hutchinson, 1978), p. 72.
18. *Daily Telegraph*, 6 February 1975.
19. *Daily Mail*, 1 February 1975.
20. Cockerell, p. 219.
21. *Sun*, 12 February 1975.
22. Ramsden, p. 456.

7. Leader of the Opposition

1. Ramsden, p. 456.
2. Margaret Thatcher interviewed by David Butler and Dennis Kavanagh, 9 August 1978.
3. Thatcher, p. 334.

4. *The Times*, 9 April 1975.
5. House of Commons, 8 April 1975 [Vol. 889, cols 1021–33].
6. *The Times*, 7 June 1975.
7. Margaret Thatcher to Lord Home, 23 June 1975, in D. R. Thorpe, *Alec Douglas-Home* (Sinclair-Stevenson, 1996), pp. 450–51.
8. Margaret Thatcher to Lord Home, July 1975, loc. cit.
9. Lord Home to Margaret Thatcher, 13 August 1975, loc. cit.
10. Speech to Chelsea Conservative Association, 26 July 1975.
11. Cosgrave, p. 190.
12. Speech to the National Press Club, Washington, DC, 19 September 1975.
13. *The Times*, 18 September 1995.
14. Henry Miller, *Daily Telegraph*, 25 September 1975; Fred Emery, *The Times*, 26 September 1975.
15. Thatcher, pp. 305–6.
16. Ronald Millar, *A View from the Wings* (Weidenfeld & Nicolson, 1989), pp. 225–7.
17. Ibid., p. 275.
18. Speech to Conservative Party Conference, Blackpool, 10 October 1975.
19. Cosgrave, p. 195.
20. House of Commons, 16 October 1975 [Vol. 897, col. 1587].
21. Ibid., 6 November 1975 [Vol. 899, cols 605–6].
22. Speech at Kensington Town Hall, 19 January 1976; *Collected Speeches*, pp. 39–47.
23. Thatcher, p. 362.
24. Geoffrey Smith, *Reagan and Thatcher* (Bodley Head, 1990), p. 1.
25. Ibid., p. 2.
26. Cosgrave, p. 212.
27. Barbara Castle, *Fighting All The Way* (Macmillan, 1993), p. 513.
28. House of Commons, 7 March 1978 [Vol. 945, cols 1221–2].
29. Ibid., 9 May 1978 [Vol. 949, cols 971–2].
30. Ibid., 1 November 1978 [Vol. 957, cols 21–35].
31. Thatcher, p. 320.
32. *The Jimmy Young Programme*, BBC Radio 2, 31 January 1978.

8. Thatcherism under Wraps

1. Richard Cockett, *Thinking the Unthinkable: Think-Tanks and the Economic Counter-Revolution, 1931–83* (HarperCollins, 1994), p. 174.
2. Speech to the Junior Carlton Club, 4 May 1976.
3. David Butler and Dennis Kavanagh, *The British General Election of 1979* (Macmillan, 1980), p. 65.
4. Cosgrave, pp. 167–8.

5. Margaret Thatcher interviewed by Butler and Kavanagh, 9 August 1978.

6. Iain Macleod Memorial Lecture, Caxton Hall, London, 4.77 July 19 (*Collected Speeches*, pp. 58–69).

7. House of Commons, 25 July 1978 [Vol. 954, col. 1405].

8. Speech to CDU Conference, Hanover, 25 May 1976.

9. Nigel Lawson, *The View From Number 11: Memoirs of a Tory Radical* (Bantam, 1992), Corgi edition, p. 199.

10. House of Commons, 21 March 1978 [Vol. 946, cols 1326–8].

11. *The Conservative Manifesto, 1979.*

12. Speech to Conservative Party Conference, 8 October 1976.

13. Ibid.

14. House of Commons, 20 January 1976 [Vol. 903, cols 1129–30].

15. Ibid., 24 January 1978 [Vol. 942, cols 1174–5].

16. Ibid.

17. Ibid., 3 March 1977 [Vol. 927, cols 606–7].

18. ITN, 4 October 1976.

19. Party Political Broadcast, 4 May 1977.

20. John Cole, *As It Seemed To Me* (Weidenfeld & Niccolson, 1995), p. 189.

21. Granada TV, *World in Action*, 27 January 1978.

22. House of Commons, 31 January 1978 [Vol. 943, cols 241–5].

23. Ibid., 25 July 1978 [Vol. 954, col.1392].

24. Patrick Cosgrave, *The Lives of Enoch Powell* (Bodley Head, 1989), p. 444.

25. Enoch Powell interviewed for Brook Associates, *The Seventies.*

26. *Observer*, 25 February 1979.

27. Cole, p. 188.

28. *The Economist*, 31 March 1979.

9. Into Downing Street

1. Butler and Kavanagh, p. 151.

2. House of Commons, 6 December 1978 [Vol. 959, cols 1424–5].

3. Ibid., 1 December 1976 [Vol. 921, cols 920–21].

4. Ibid., 10 July 1978 [Vol. 953, cols 1027–8].

5. *Sun*, 11 January 1979.

6. BBC TV, 14 February 1979.

7. James Callaghan, *Time and Chance* (Collins, 1987), p. 561; Kenneth O. Morgan, *Callaghan* (Oxford 1997), p. 682.

8. Thatcher, p. 432.

9. House of Commons, 28 March 1979 [Vol. 965, cols 461–70].

10. Ibid., 28 March 1979 [Vol. 965, cols 470–79].

11. Kenneth Baker, *The Turbulent Years: My Life in Politics* (Faber, 1993) pp. 511–12.

12. Cecil Parkinson, *Right at the Centre* (Weidenfeld & Nicolson, 1992), pp. 26–7.
13. Cole, p. 188.
14. *Spectator*, 28 April 1979.
15. *Sunday Telegraph*, 22 April 1979; BBC Radio News, 21 April 1979.
16. *Daily Mail*, 19 April 1979.
17. Private information.
18. Butler and Kavanagh, p. 172.
19. *Observer*, 22 April 1979.
20. Millar, pp. 259–60.
21. Murray, p. 198.
22. *Daily Mail*, 30 April 1979.
23. Conservative party election broadcast, 30 April 1979.
24. Millar, pp. 263–4.
25. Election press conference, 2 May 1979.
26. *Daily Express*, 30 April 1979.
27. *Daily Mail, Daily Express, Sun*, 3 May 1979.
28. Interview, Lord McAlpine.
29. Butler and Kavanagh, pp. 197–9, 343, 393–5.
30. Millar, p. 266.
31. Remarks on the steps of Downing Street, 4 May 1979.

10. The Blessed Margaret

1. *Guardian*, 5 May 1979.
2. Ibid.
3. Margaret Thatcher interviewed in *Thatcher: The Downing Street Years* (BBC, 1993).
4. BBC interview with Michael Cockerell, 27 April 1979.
5. Margaret Thatcher, *The Downing Street Years*, p. 10.
6. Interview, Sir Kenneth Stowe.
7. *The Times*, 5 May 1980.
8. *Sunday Times*, 3 May 1981.
9. *Observer*, 25 January 1979.
10. Penny Junor, *Margaret Thatcher*, p. 231.
11. Edward Heath, *The Course of My Life*, p. 574.
12. *Guardian*, 7 May 1979.
13. e.g. *The Economist*, 12 May 1979.
14. Thatcher, p. 28.
15. Millar, p. 319.
16. House of Commons, 9 February 1970 [Vol. 795, col. 1019].
17. Prior, p. 66.

18. Interview, Sir Kenneth Berrill.
19. Sir John Hoskyns, interviewed for *The Thatcher Factor*.
20. Interview, Sir Charles Powell.
21. Nigel Lawson, *The View From Number 11*, p. 128.
22. Alan Clark, *Diaries*, p. 215 (14 June 1988).
23. Interview, Sir Charles Powell; Woodrow Wyatt, *Confessions of an Optimist* (Collins, 1985), pp. 345–6.
24. Lord Carrington, interviewed for *Thatcher: The Downing Street Years* (BBC, 1993).
25. Sir John Hoskyns, interviewed for *The Thatcher Factor*.
26. Murray, p. 170.
27. Peter Hennessy, *Cabinet* (Blackwell, 1986), pp. 97–8.
28. Interview, Lord Jenkin of Roding.
29. Murray, p. 200.
30. George Walden, *Lucky George: Memoirs of an Anti-Politician* (Allen Lane, 1999), p. 191; interview, Dr John Ashworth.
31. Walden, p. 191.
32. Peter Hennessy, Gresham Lecture, 20 February 1996.
33. Parkinson, p. 220.
34. Interviews, Sir John Nott, Sir Peter Middleton.
35. John Hoskyns, *Just in Time: Inside the Thatcher Revolution* (Aurum, 2000), p. 164.
36. Interview, Sir Kenneth Stowe.
37. Hoskyns, p. 108.
38. Interview, Lord Hunt of Tanworth.
39. Margaret Thatcher interviewed on *Aspel and Company*, LWT, 19 July 1984.
40. Diana Farr, *Five at 10: Prime Ministers Consorts since 1957* (André Deutsch, 1985), p. 200.
41. Junor, p. 264; Millar, p. 338.
42. Bernard Ingham, *Kill the Messenger* (HarperCollins, 1994), p. 293.
43. Millar, p. 327; John Junor, *Listening for a Midnight Tram*, (Chapman, 1990) p. 264.
44. Alan Clark, *Diaries* (Weidenfeld & Nicolson, 1993), p. 319 (30 July 1990).
45. Millar, p. 317.
46. Sir Peter Emery in Iain Dale (ed.), *As I Said to Denis: The Margaret Thatcher Book of Quotations* (Robson Books, 1997), p. 70.
47. Hoskyns, p. 230.
48. Millar, p. 330.
49. Ingham, p. 248.
50. Conservative Party Conference, 15 October 1980.
51. Hennessy, *Whitehall*, p. 598.
52. Ibid., p. 598.

53. Interviews, Sir Frank Cooper, David Tanner.
54. Thatcher, p. 303.
55. Hennessy, p. 585.

11. Signals of Intent

1. House of Commons, 15 May 1979 [Vol. 967, cols 73–87].
2. Ibid., 22 May 1979 [Vol. 967, cols 867–72].
3. Thatcher, p. 50.
4. Howe, p. 130.
5. Lawson, p. 35.
6. Thatcher, pp. 42–3.
7. Howe, p. 142.
8. House of Commons, 24 July 1979 [Vol. 971, cols 345–6].
9. *Daily Mirror*, 13 June 1979.
10. Murray, p. 225.
11. House of Commons, 13 November 1979 [Vol. 973, col. 1498].
12. Ian Gilmour, *Dancing with Dogma*, p. 25n; Peter Walker, *Staying Power*, p. 161.
13. e.g. House of Commons, 19 July 1979, 26 July 1979, 19 February 1980.
14. Thatcher, p. 26.
15. House of Commons, 19 November 1975 [Vol. 901, cols 19–28].
16. Clark, p. 219; interview, Sir Douglas Wass.
17. Murray, p. 219.
18. Hoskyns, p. 114.
19. Lord Carrington, interviewed for *The Thatcher Factor*, BBC TV, 1993.
20. Ibid.
21. Walden, p. 207.
22. Lord Carrington, interviewed for *The Thatcher Factor*.
23. Jimmy Carter, *Keeping Faith* (Collins, 1982), p. 113.
24. Nicholas Henderson, *Mandarin: The Diary of an Ambassador* (Weidenfeld & Nicolson, 1994), p. 269 (24 May 1979).
25. Thatcher, p. 68.
26. Speech on the White House lawn, Washington, DC, 17 December 1979.
27. Henderson, p. 316; Sir Frank Cooper, interviewed for *The Thatcher Factor*.
28. Speech to the American Foreign Policy Association, New York, 18 December 1979.
29. Thatcher, p. 88.
30. Summary of President Carter's telephone conversation with Mrs Thatcher, 28 December 1979 [Carter papers: vertical file – Afghanistan].
31. House of Commons, 26 June 1979 [Vol. 969, col. 289].
32. Gilmour, p. 289.

33. Alan Sked and Chris Cook, *Post-War Britain: A Political History, 1945–1992* (Penguin, 1993), p. 376.

34. Speech at dinner for Chancellor Schmidt, 10 May 1979.

35. House of Commons, 20 March 1980 [Vol. 981, col. 636].

36. e.g. Ibid., 13 March 1979 [Vol. 964, cols 455–6].

37. Roy Jenkins, *European Diary, 1977–81* (Collins, 1989), p. 466.

38. Thatcher, p. 64.

39. Walden, p. 194.

40. Jenkins, p. 479.

41. Ludovic Kennedy, *On My Way to the Club* (Collins, 1989), p. 354.

42. Lord Carrington, interviewed for *The Thatcher Factor*.

43. Winston Churchill Memorial Lecture, Luxembourg, 18 October 1979.

44. House of Commons, 25 October 1979, 20 November 1979 [Vol. 972, cols 619–20; Vol. 974, col. 208].

45. Jenkins, *European Diary*, p. 529.

46. Roy Jenkins, *A Life at the Centre* (Macmillan, 1991), p. 498.

47. Jenkins, *European Diary*, p. 529.

48. Henderson, p. 338 (9 May 1980).

49. Jenkins, *European Diary*, pp. 530–31.

50. Ibid., p. 450.

51. House of Commons, 11 March 1980 [Vol. 980, col. 1149].

52. Conservative Party Conference, 12 October 1979.

53. House of Commons, 12 June 1979 [Vol. 968, col. 229].

54. Ibid., 13 November 1979 [Vol. 973, cols 1149–50].

55. Jenkins, *European Diary*, p. 511.

56. BBC interview, *Campaign '79*, 24 April 1979.

57. *Thatcher: The Downing Street Years*, BBC TV, 1993.

58. Jenkins, *European Diary*, pp. 545–7.

59. Ibid., pp. 592–3.

60. Claude Cheysson, interviewed on *The Last Europeans* (Channel 4, 1995).

61. Jenkins, *European Diary*, p. 547.

62. Thatcher, p. 86.

63. Gilmour, pp. 292–4.

64. Thatcher, p. 86.

65. Gilmour, pp. 292–5.

66. Lawson, p. 111.

67. Jenkins, *Life at the Centre*, p. 500.

68. House of Commons, 15 May 1979 [Vol. 967, cols 73–87].

69. Thatcher, p. 73.

70. Sir Anthony Parsons, interviewed on 22 March 1996 for the British Diplomatic Oral History Project, Churchill College, Cambridge.

71. Gilmour, pp. 281–2.

72. Lord Carrington, interviewed for *The Thatcher Factor*.

73. Carrington, p. 295; Patrick Cosgrave, *Thatcher: The First Term* (Bodley Head, 1985), p. 81.

74. Ben Pimlott, *The Queen* (HarperCollins, 1996), pp. 467–8.

75. Interview, Sir Robin Renwick.

76. Lord Carrington, *Reflect on Things Past* (Collins, 1988), p. 286.

77. David Anderson, 'Mugabe is Right about Land', *Independent*, 4 May 2000.

78. *Guardian*, 30 August 1979.

79. *The Times*, 14 November 1979.

80. Conservative Party Conference, 12 October 1979.

81. *The Times*, 14 November 1979.

12. Heading for the Rocks

1. *The Times*, 12 November 1980.

2. Martin Holmes, *The First Thatcher Government, 1979–1983* (Wheatsheaf, 1985), p. 155.

3. House of Commons, 5 July 1979 [Vol. 969, col. 1553].

4. William Keegan, *Mrs Thatcher's Economic Experiment*, p. 148.

5. Ian Gilmour, *Dancing with Dogma*, p. 24.

6. House of Commons, 26 June 1979 [Vol. 969, col. 296].

7. Margaret Thatcher, *The Downing Street Years*, p. 97.

8. Lawson, p. 67; Geoffrey Howe, *Conflict of Loyalty* (Macmillan, 1994), p. 155.

9. Howe, p. 163.

10. Ibid.; Lawson, p. 71; interview, Sir Peter Middleton.

11. Thatcher, p. 97.

12. House of Commons, 27 July 1981 [Vol. 9, col. 828].

13. Howe, p. 162.

14. House of Commons, 9 March 1982 [Vol. 19, col. 719].

15. Jock Bruce-Gardyne, *Mrs Thatcher's First Administration: The Prophets Confounded* (Macmillan, 1984), p. 93.

16. *The Times*, 20 September 1980.

17. John Ranelagh, *Thatcher's People: An Insider's Account of the Politics, the Power and the Personalities* (HarperCollins, 1991), p. 227.

18. Whitehead, p. 380.

19. Hoskyns, p. 267.

20. Denis Healey, *The Time of My Life* (Michael Joseph, 1989), pp. 491–2.

21. Peter Clarke, *A Question of Leadership: Gladstone to Thatcher* (Hamish Hamilton, 1991), pp. 302–4.

22. *Guardian*, 26 March 1980.

23. Thatcher, p. 53.

24. House of Commons, 23 October 1979 [Vol. 972, col. 192].

25. Ibid., 30 October 1980 [Vol. 991, col. 692].

26. House of Commons, 12 June 1979 [Vol. 968, col. 230].

27. Ibid., 5 February 1981 [Vol. 998, cols 415–23].

28. IRN interview, 28 November 1980.

29. Lawson, p. 100.

30. House of Commons, 29 July 1980 [Vol. 989, cols 1301–14].

31. Conservative Party Conference, 15 October 1980.

32. John Hoskyns, interviewed for *The Thatcher Factor*; Ranelagh, p. 236.

33. House of Commons, 26 June 1979 [Vol. 969, col. 285].

34. Phillip Whitehead, *The Writing on the Wall*, p. 371.

35. House of Commons, 19 July 1979 [Vol. 970, col. 1989].

36. *Guardian*, 23 August 1979.

37. House of Commons, 15 May 1980 [Vol. 984, col. 1748].

38. LWT, *Weekend World*, 6 January 1980; House of Commons, 22 January 1980 [Vol. 977, col. 197].

39. Cockerell, p. 260.

40. House of Commons, 3 July 1980 [Vol. 987, col. 1759].

41. House of Commons, 15 May 1979 [Vol. 967, cols 73–87].

42. Ibid., 12 June 1979 [Vol. 968, col. 229].

43. Ibid., 19 June 1979 [Vol. 968, col. 1114].

44. Ibid., 4 November 1981 [Vol. 12, col. 23].

45. Ibid., 28 February 1980, 5 February 1981 [Vol. 998, col. 481]; 18 June 1981 [Vol. 6, col. 1175]; 30 July 1981 [Vol. 9, col. 980]; 4 February 1982 [Vol. 17, col. 539].

46. Ibid., 5 November 1981 [Vol. 12, cols 440–41].

47. Prior, p. 125.

48. Thatcher, pp. 114–15.

49. Morison Halcrow, *Keith Joseph: A Single Mind* (Macmillan, 1989), p. 149.

50. LWT, *Weekend World*, 1 February 1982.

51. House of Commons, 12 February 1982 [Vol. 998, col. 979].

52. Ibid. 10 February 1982 [Vol. 998, col. 737].

53. Thatcher, p. 141.

54. Lawson, p. 107; Howe, p. 221.

55. Thatcher, p. 132.

56. Philip Stephens, *Politics and the Pound: The Tories, the Economy and Europe* (Macmillan, 1996), p. 21.

57. *The Times*, 30 March 1981.

58. Gilmour, p. 35.

59. *The Times*, 13 July 1981.

60. *Daily Telegraph*, 11 March 1981; *The Times*, 11 March 1981.

61. Ranelagh, p. 235.

62. Conservative Central Council, Cardiff, 28 March 1981.

63. Thatcher, p. 574.
64. Hugo Young, *One of Us: A Biography of Margaret Thatcher* (Macmillan, 1989, 1991), p. 239.
65. Whitehead, p. 387.
66. House of Commons, 14 July 1981 [Vol. 8, cols 973–6].
67. Ibid., 16 July 1981 [Vol. 8, col. 1383].
68. Hoskyns, p. 301.
69. Nicholas Henderson, *Mandarin*, pp. 404–6.
70. Howe, p. 169.
71. Howe, p. 223.
72. *The Times*, 15 September 1981.
73. Prior, p. 173.
74. Conservative Party Conference, 14 October 1981.
75. Conservative Party Conference, 16 October 1981.
76. House of Commons, 28 October 1981 [Vol. 10, cols 881–7].
77. IRN interview, 31 December 1981.

13. Salvation in the South Atlantic

1. Speech in Finchley, 22 October 1982.
2. House of Commons, 2 April 1982 [Vol. 21, cols 633–8].
3. Peter Hennessy, *The Prime Minister: The Office and its Holders since 1945* (Allen Lane, 2000), p.104.
4. Sarah Curtis (ed.), *The Journals of Woodrow Wyatt*, Vol. 2 (Macmillan, 1999), p. 245, citing Norman Tebbit (22 February 1990).
5. Hennessy, p. 414.
6. Peter de la Billiere, *Looking for Trouble* (HarperCollins, 1994).
7. Speech at Conservative Party Conference, Brighton, 11 October 1978; BBC TV *Panorama*, 26 April 1982; House of Commons, 4 May 1982, 11 May 1982, 13 May 1982, 20 May 1982, 15 June 1982 etc.
8. Max Hastings and Simon Jenkins, *The Battle for the Falklands* (Michael Joseph, 1983), p. 271.
9. *Sunday Times*, 7 June 1987.
10. Patrick Cosgrave, reported in *The Times*, 26 May 1995.
11. ITN interview, 5 April 1982.
12. Ronald Millar, *From the Wings*, p. 298.
13. Interview with Miriam Stoppard, *Woman to Woman*, Yorkshire TV, 19 November 1985.
14. Nigel West, *The Secret War for the Falklands* (Warner Books, 1997), p. 230.
15. Hastings and Jenkins, p.167; Geoffrey Smith, *Reagan and Thatcher*, p. 86.
16. Caspar Weinberger, *Fighting for Peace: Seven Critical Years at the Pentagon* (Michael Joseph, 1990), p. 149.

17. Thatcher, p. 205.
18. Ibid., p. 219.
19. House of Commons, 29 April 1982 [Vol. 22, col. 981].
20. Ibid., 6 May 1982 [Vol. 23, col. 282].
21. Lord Lewin, interviewed for *The Thatcher Factor*.
22. Admiral 'Sandy' Woodward, *One Hundred Days: The Memoirs of the Falklands Battle Group Commander* (HarperCollins, 1992), pp. 148–63.
23. House of Commons, 4 May 1982 [Vol. 23, col. 16].
24. Thatcher, p. 215.
25. e.g. Paul Hirst, *After Thatcher*, p. 106.
26. Hastings and Jenkins, p. 196.
27. Interview, Lord Crickhowell; see also Lawson, pp. 126–7; and Hennessy, p. 420.
28. Interview, Sir John Nott.
29. House of Commons, 13 May 1982 [Vol. 23, col. 942].
30. Smith, p. 93.
31. House of Commons, 20 May 1982 [Vol. 24, cols 477–83].
32. Interview, Sir Frank Cooper.
33. Carol Thatcher, p. 197.
34. Andrew Thomson, *Margaret Thatcher: The Woman Within* (Allen Lane, 1989), pp. 174–8.
35. *The Times*, 22 May 1982.
36. Private information.
37. Thatcher, p. 230.
38. Henderson, pp. 468–70.
39. House of Commons, 14 June 1982 [Vol. 25, col. 700].
40. Ibid., 22 June 1982 [Vol. 26, cols 430–32].
41. *The Times*, 5 July 1982.
42. Matthew Parris, *Chance Witness: An Outsider's Life in Politics* (Viking, 2002), p. 294.
43. Sked and Cook, p. 418.
44. e.g. House of Commons, 23 November 1982, 18 January 1983 [Vol. 32, col. 705; Vol. 35, col. 178]
45. Carol Thatcher, p. 201.

14. Falklands Effect

1. *Daily Express*, 23 July 1982.
2. BBC Radio News, 22 July 1982.
3. *Daily Express*, 23 July 1982.
4. *The Times*, 16 August 1982.
5. *Daily Express*, 23 July 1982.

6. House of Commons, 3 November 1982 [Vol. 31, col. 18].
7. Ibid., 10 March 1983 [Vol. 38, col. 949].
8. Ibid., 12 May 1983 [Vol. 42, col. 917].
9. Speech in Finchley, 22 October 1982.
10. Conservative Party Conference, 8 October 1982.
11. Thatcher, p. 284.
12. Nicholas Timmins, *The Five Giants*, p. 372.
13. House of Commons, 15 May 1979 [Vol. 967, col. 81].
14. Ibid., 24 March 1983 [Vol. 39, col. 1013].
15. Ibid., 27 July 1982 [Vol. 228, col. 1226].
16. Kaufman is usually credited with the remark, but David Butler and Dennis Kavanagh, *The British General Election of 1983* (Macmillan, 1984) p. 62, attributes it to Shore.
17. *The Times*, 5 May 1980.
18. House of Commons, 5 June 1980 [Vol. 985, col. 1671].
19. Peter Hennessy, *Cabinet,* pp. 154–5.
20. Ibid., 24 July 1980 [Vol. 989, col. 761].
21. Ibid., 21 January 1982 [Vol. 16, col. 412].
22. Geoffrey Smith, *Reagan and Thatcher*, p. 113.
23. House of Commons, 26 June 1980 [Vol. 987, col. 742].
24. Ibid., 15 July 1980 [Vol. 988, col. 1229].
25. Ibid., 25 November 1982 [Vol. 32, col. 1010].
26. Ibid., 14 December 1982 [Vol. 34, col. 121].
27. Conservative Party Conference, 10 October 1982.
28. Press conference with Chancellor Kohl, London, 4 February 1983.
29. House of Commons, 28 April 1983 [Vol. 41, col. 994].
30. Carol Thatcher, *Diary,* pp. 34–5.
31. Ibid., p. 57.
32. e.g. speech at Fleetwood, 7 June 1983.
33. Speech at George Watson's College, Edinburgh, 31 May 1983.
34. Remarks electioneering in Norfolk, 25 May 1983; Carol Thatcher, *Diary*, p. 52.
35. Carol Thatcher, *Diary*, p. 104.
36. Ibid., p. 53.
37. Robin Day, *Grand Inquisitor* (Weidenfeld & Nicolson, 1989), p. 232.
38. Cockerell, p. 282.
39. Butler and Kavanagh, p. 167.
40. Cockerell, p. 283.
41. Carol Thatcher, *Diary*, p. 100.
42. Butler and Kavanagh, pp. 112–13.
43. Thomson, p. 80.
44. Butler and Kavanagh, p. 160.
45. Ibid., p. 296.

46. Francis Pym, *The Politics of Consent* (Hamish Hamilton, 1984), p. ix.
47. Thatcher, p. 309.

15. Popular Capitalism

1. *The Times*, 16 June 1983.
2. IRN interview, 28 July 1983.
3. *Sunday Express*, 16 October 1983, cited in Sara Keays, *A Question of Judgment* (Quintessential Press, 1985), p. 219.
4. Alan Clark, *Diaries*, pp. 37–8 (1 September 1983).
5. John Major, *The Autobiography* (HarperCollins, 1999), p. 108.
6. Interview with John Cole, BBC, 27 May 1983.
7. House of Commons, 31 January 1984 [Vol. 53, col.138].
8. Thatcher, p. 673.
9. Sked and Cook, p. 474.
10. House of Commons, 31 July 1984 [Vol. 65, col. 248].
11. Clark, p. 109 (24 April 1985).
12. e.g. *Observer*, 1 July 1990, cited in Tyler, p. 53n., though Tyler thinks she never actually said it.
13. Conservative Party Conference, Brighton, 12 October 1984.
14. William Keegan, *Mr Lawson's Gamble* (Hodder & Stoughton, 1989), p. 140.
15. Ibid., p. 158.
16. *The Times*, 15 May 1985.
17. Thatcher, p. 418.
18. William Keegan, *Mrs Thatcher's Economic Experiment* (Penguin, 1984), p. 139.
19. Speech at Conservative Party Conference, 11 October 1985.
20. Lady Thatcher, interviewed on *Thatcher: The Downing Street Years*.
21. Lawson, p. 499.
22. Nigel Lawson, interviewed on *Thatcher: The Downing Street Years*.
23. Lawson, p. 500.
24. Interview on *The Jimmy Young Programme*, BBC Radio 2, 26 February 1986.
25. Sked and Cook, p. 476.
26. Keegan, pp. 182–3; Christopher Johnson, *The Economy under Mrs Thatcher, 1979–1990* (Penguin, 1991), pp. 11–14.
27. Keegan, pp. 136–40.
28. Wyatt, Vol. 1, p. 242 (9 December 1986).
29. Edmund Dell, *The Chancellors: A History of the Chancellors of the Exchequer, 1945–1990* (HarperCollins, 1996), p. 532.
30. Lawson, p. 224.

31. Interview on *The Jimmy Young Programme*, BBC Radio 2, 26 February 1986.
32. Speech to the Conservative Central Council, Felixstowe, 15 March 1986.
33. Thatcher, p. 600.
34. Simon Jenkins, *Accountable to None: The Tory Nationalisation of Britain* (Hamish Hamilton, 1995), p. 179.
35. Lawson, p. 211.
36. John Redwood in Iain Dale (ed.), *Memories of Maggie*, p. 102.
37. Lawson, p. 222.
38. John Redwood, loc. cit.
39. *Annual Register*, 1985, p. 28; *Annual Register*, 1984, p. 21.
40. George Grimstone, a Treasury official, interviewed on *The Great Sell-Off*, BBC TV, 26 January 1997.
41. *Annual Register*, 1986, p. 22.
42. Ibid.
43. *The Times*, 9 November 1985.
44. Ibid., 15 November 1985.
45. Speech at the Conservative Party Conference, 13 October 1989.
46. Thatcher, p. 482.
47. Conservative Party Conference, 13 October 1989.
48. Speech to mid-Bedfordshire Conservatives, 30 April 1982.
49. Conservative Party Conference, 12 October 1984.

16. Iron Lady I: Special relationships

1. Speech in Finchley, 22 October 1982.
2. Thatcher, p. 487.
3. Speech to mid-Bedfordshire Conservatives, 30 April 1982.
4. David Reynolds, *Britannia Overruled: British Policy and World Power in the Twentieth Century* (Longman, 1991), p. 256.
5. Raymond Seitz, *Over Here* (Weidenfeld & Nicolson, 1998), p. 278.
6. Charles Powell in Dale, pp. 39–40.
7. Charles Powell, interviewed on *The Last Europeans*.
8. Sir Anthony Parsons, interviewed for the British Diplomatic Oral History Project, Churchill College, Cambridge.
9. Sir Percy Cradock, *In Pursuit of British Interests: Reflections on Foreign Policy under Margaret Thatcher and John Major* (John Murray, 1997), p. 14.
10. Sked and Cook, p. 504.
11. Ibid.
12. Speech to the Conservative Party Conference, 16 October 1981.
13. Interview, Raymond Seitz.
14. Millar, p. 335.

15. Speech to the Conservative Party Conference, 12 October 1984.
16. Smith, p. 26.
17. Tony Benn, *Free at Last: Diaries 1991–2001* (Hutchinson, 2002), p. 211 [4 November 1993].
18. Chris Ogden, *Maggie* (Simon & Schuster, New York, 1990), p. 236.
19. Speeches at the White House, Washington, DC, 26 February 1981.
20. Reagan papers, Box 35, 8100164–8102258.
21. Robin Renwick, *Fighting with Allies: America and Britain in Peace and War* (Macmillan, 1996), p. 50.
22. Ronald Reagan to Margaret Thatcher, 4 August 1981 (Reagan papers, Box 35, 8100164–8102258).
23. *Newsweek*, 21 June 1982.
24. Reagan to Mrs Thatcher, 17 June 1983 (Head of State file, Box 34, 152/04/4).
25. Reagan to Mrs Thatcher, 30 May 1984 (CO 167, 237000–245999)
26. John Poindexter memo, 29 July 1983 (CO 167, 160000–169999)
27. US Embassy briefing, September 1983 (European and Soviet Affairs Directorate, NSC, Box 90902).
28. Thatcher, p. 469.
29. Richard Perle, interviewed for *The Thatcher Factor*.
30. George Shultz, interviewed on *Thatcher: The Downing Street Years*.
31. Reagan to Mrs Thatcher, 18 July 1984 (Box 35, 88404781–8407224).
32. Press conference in Washington, DC, 15 November 1986.
33. *Face the Nation*, CBS, 17 July 1987.
34. Richard Perle, interviewed for *The Thatcher Factor*.
35. House of Commons, 1 July 1982 [Vol. 26, col. 1044].
36. Minute of meeting between Mrs Thatcher and Caspar Weinberger, 8 September 1982 (NSC, Box 91330).
37. Reagan to Mrs Thatcher, 12 November 1982 (Head of State file, Box 34, 152/04/4).
38. Robert Macfarlane/George Shultz memo, 22 December 1984 (NSC, Box 90902).
39. Mrs Thatcher to Reagan, 29 March 1983 (Box 35, 8301952–8303361).
40. Reagan to Mrs Thatcher, 6 April 1983 (loc. cit.).
41. Briefing paper, June 1984 (CO 1167, 270790–289999).
42. *Washington Post*, 17 June 1983.
43. Reagan to Mrs Thatcher, 18 June 1982 (NSC, Box 90902).
44. Reagan to Mrs Thatcher, 24 June 1982 (Head of State file, Box 34, 152/04/4).
45. William Clark memo to Reagan, 22 June 1982 (NSC, Box 91327).
46. George Shultz, *Turmoil and Triumph: My Years as Secretary of State* (Scribner's, New York, 1993), p. 1152.
47. Reagan to Mrs Thatcher, 7 December 1983 (Box 35, 8307330–83308843).

48. George Bush to Mrs Thatcher, 8 December 1983 (CO 167, 207000–215999).

49. John Poindexter memo to Reagan, 15 November 1986 (CO 167, 440030).

50. Smith, p. 224.

51. Carol Thatcher, p. 210.

52. House of Commons, 24 October 1983 [Vol. 47, cols 227–30].

53. Reagan to Mrs Thatcher, 24 October 1983 (Executive Secretariat, NSC, Box 91331).

54. Reagan to Mrs Thatcher, loc. cit.

55. Interview, Sir John Coles.

56. Reagan to Mrs Thatcher, 25 October 1983 (Executive Secretariat, NSC, Box 91330).

57. House of Commons, 25 October 1983 [Vol. 47, cols 143–6].

58. House of Commons, 27 October 1983 [Vol. 47, col. 422].

59. Brian Crozier, *Free Agent: The Unseen War, 1941–1991* (HarperCollins, 1993), p. 264.

60. BBC World Service, 30 October 1983.

61. Renwick, p. 244.

62. *New York Times*, 11 January 1986.

63. *Irish Times*, 20 May 2000.

64. Thatcher, p. 445.

65. Renwick, pp. 250–51.

66. Thatcher, p. 447.

67. House of Commons, 15 April 1986 [Vol. 95, col. 726].

68. David Owen, *Time to Declare* (Michael Joseph, 1991), pp. 641–2.

69. Thatcher, p. 449.

70. Margaret Thatcher, *Statecraft: Strategies for a Changing World* (HarperCollins, 2002), p. 232.

71. Thatcher, *The Downing Street Years*, p. 449.

72. Reagan speech in Orlando, Florida, 8 March 1983.

73. Baker, p. 262.

74. Reynolds, p. 277.

75. Speech in Washington, DC, 29 September 1983.

76. Thatcher, p. 457.

77. Ibid., p. 452.

78. Peter Walker, *Staying Power* (Bloomsbury, 1991), p. 193.

79. Cradock, p. 144.

80. Memorandum of conversation at Camp David, 22 December 1984 (NSC, Box 90902).

81. Thatcher, p. 461.

82. Carol Thatcher, p. 222.

83. Thatcher, p. 461.

84. BBC TV interview, 17 December 1984.
85. Speech in Washington, DC, 25 July 1985.
86. James Baker, interviewed on *Thatcher: The Downing Street Years.*
87. Letters displayed in the Reagan Library.
88. Memorandum of conversation at Camp David, 22 December 1984 (NSC, Box 90902).
89. Thatcher, pp. 463, 466.
90. Robin Butler in Dale, pp. 108–9.
91. Memorandum of conversation at Camp David, 22 December 1984 (NSC, Box 90902).
92. Ibid.
93. Reagan to NATO leaders, January 1985 (Box 35, 8590010–8590047).
94. Lt. Gen. James Abrahamson to Mrs Thatcher, 3 January 1985 (Box 35, 8500392–8500484).
95. Macfarlane, p. 284.
96. Speech to the US Congress, Washington, DC, 20 February 1985.
97. Mrs Thatcher to Reagan, 22 February 1985 (Box 35, 8590152–8590923).
98. Macfarlane, pp. 305–7.
99. Smith, p.177.
100. Macfarlane, p. 306.
101. Thatcher, pp. 467, 471.
102. John Poindexter memo to Reagan, 15 November 1986 (NSC, Box 90902).
103. Ibid.
104. George Shultz memo to Reagan, November 1986 (loc. cit.).
105. Interview for ABC, 21 January 1987.
106. *Daily Express*, 22 April 1987.
107. *Face the Nation*, CBS, I July 1987.
108. Thatcher, p. 482.
109. Cockerell, p. 318.
110. Rodney Tyler, *Campaign! The Selling of the Prime Minister* (Grafton Books, 1987).

17. Iron Lady II : Europe and the World

1. Speech to Franco-British Council, Avignon, 30 November 1984.
2. Thatcher, p. 536.
3. Young, p. 383.
4. Harold Evans, *Good Times, Bad Times* (Weidenfeld & Nicolson, 1983), p. 284.
5. Ingham, p. 265.
6. Thatcher, p. 543.

7. Sir Geoffrey Howe, interviewed on *The Last Europeans*, Channel 4, 1995.

8. Margaret Thatcher, interviewed on *The Poisoned Chalice*, BBC 1996.

9. David Williamson, interviewed on *The Last Europeans*.

10. Bernard Ingham, interviewed on *The Poisoned Chalice*.

11. Jacques Delors, interviewed on *The Poisoned Chalice*.

12. House of Commons, 30 April 1974 [Vol. 872, col. 967].

13. Speech at Lille, 20 January 1986.

14. Interview, Sir John Coles.

15. *Sowetan*, 2 October 1989.

16. Press conference in Oslo, 12 September 1986.

17. Thatcher, p. 515.

18. BBC, 27 June 1986.

19. Interview on Channel 10, Sydney, 4 August 1988.

20. Anthony Sampson, *Nelson Mandela* (HarperCollins, 1999), pp. 321, 356.

21. Reagan to Mrs Thatcher, 23 June 1986 (Box 35, 8690401-8690687).

22. Robin Renwick, *Unconventional Diplomacy in Southern Africa* (Macmillan, 1997), p. 152.

23. House of Commons, 13 February 1990 [Vol. 167, col. 140].

24. Sampson, p. 409.

25. Thatcher, p. 533; Sampson, p. 418.

26. Richard Allen memo to Reagan (Box 35, 8106458).

27. Reagan to Mrs Thatcher, November 1981 (loc. cit.).

28. Reagan to Mrs Thatcher, 1 December 1981 (loc. cit.).

29. Mrs Thatcher to Reagan, 22 March 1983 (Box 35, 8301952-8300964).

30. Mrs Thatcher to Reagan, 5 November 1983 (Box 35, 8391259-8391521).

31. Thatcher, p. 334.

32. Note of meeting between Mrs Thatcher and Caspar Weinberger, 29 February 1984 (Executive Secretariat NSC, Box 90902).

33. Memorandum of a conversation at Camp David, 22 January 1984 (NSC, Box 90902).

34. Thatcher, p. 509.

35. Memorandum of meeting between Mrs Thatcher and George Shultz, 17 January 1987.

36. Thatcher, p. 510.

37. Press conference at Cancun, Mexico, 23 October 1981.

38. Gerald James, *In the Public Interest* (Little, Brown, 1995), p. 67.

39. *The Times*, 27 September 1985.

40. *Observer*, 12 January 1986.

41. House of Commons, 17 January 1984, 24 January 1984 [Vol. 52, cols 159, 766]; *Weekend World*, 15 January 1984; *Panorama*, 9 April 1984.

42. Paul Halloran and Mark Hollingsworth, *Thatcher's Gold: The Life and Times of Mark Thatcher* (Simon & Schuster, 1995), pp. 178-86.

43. Andrew Marr, *Ruling Britannia* (Michael Joseph, 1995).

44. Note of meeting between Mrs Thatcher and Caspar Weinberger, 29 February 1984 (Executive Secretariat NSC, Box 90902).
45. *Not the Scott Report* (Private Eye, 1994), p. 13.
46. Ibid., p. 14.
47. Alan Friedman, *Spider's Web: Bush, Saddam, Thatcher and the Decade of Deceit* (Faber, 1993), p. 251.
48. *The Times*, 9 November 1989.
49. *The Scott Report* (HMSO, 1994), G12, 30.
50. House of Commons, 4 December 1986 [Vol. 106, col. 1078].
51. *Scott Report*, G12, 30.
52. Ibid., D2, 328–30.
53. *Not the Scott Report*, p. 9.
54. Ibid., p. 24.
55. Ibid.

18. Enemies Within

1. House of Commons, 26 January 1984 [Vol. 52, col. 1047].
2. Hennessy, *Cabinet*, pp. 32–3.
3. Young, p. 367.
4. Speech at NUM conference, 4 July 1983.
5. *Annual Register 1984*, p. 8.
6. Michael Crick, *Scargill and the Miners* (Penguin, 1985), p. 108.
7. *The Times,* 28 March 1984.
8. Thatcher, p. 340.
9. House of Commons, 13 March 1984 [Vol. 56, col. 279].
10. Speech to farmers at Banbury, Oxfordshire, 30 May 1984.
11. House of Commons, 15 March 1984; [Vol. 56, cols 512–13] *Panorama*, 9 April 1984 .
12. Sir Ian MacGregor on BBC TV, *The Downing Street Years*, 1993.
13. *Yorkshire Post*, 20 July 1984.
14. Wendy Webster, *Not a Man to Match Her: The Marketing of the Prime Minister* (Women's Press, 1990), p. 159.
15. *Sunday Mirror*, 3 October 1984.
16. Interview, Sir Michael Partridge.
17. BBC TV, *Thatcher: The Downing Street Years*, 1993.
18. Speech at Conservative Party Conference, 12 October 1984.
19. *Daily Express*, 31 December 1984.
20. *The Times*, 4 March 1985.
21. Simon Jenkins, p. 156; Marr, p. 104.
22. Pym, p. 19.
23. House of Commons, 16 December 1982 [Vol. 34, col. 476].

24. Wyatt, Vol. 1 p. 229, (24 November 1986).
25. *The Woman at No. 10*, ITV, 29 March 1983.
26. *Weekend World*, 6 January 1980.
27. Millar, p. 284.
28. Address at St Lawrence Jewry, 4 March 1981.
29. Wyatt, p. 496 (7 February 1988).
30. *The Times*, 26 July 1990.
31. Thatcher, pp. 509–10.
32. Lawson, p. 256.
33. *Sunday Times*, 8 May 1988.
34. Tom Wilkie in Dennis Kavanagh and Anthony Seldon (eds), *The Thatcher Effect: A Decade of Change* (Oxford, 1989), pp. 316–29.
35. Speech to Conservative Party Conference, 13 October 1989.
36. George Urban, *Diplomacy and Disillusion at the Court of Margaret Thatcher: An Insider's View* (Tauris, 1996), p. 23.
37. Thatcher, p. 267.
38. Michael Leapman, *The Last Days of the Beeb* (Allen & Unwin, 1986), p. 32.
39. House of Commons, 14 March 1985 [Vol. 75, col. 429].
40. Alastair Hetherington in Kavanagh and Seldon, p. 298.
41. Wyatt, p. 160 (29 June 1986).
42. David Butler and Gareth Butler, *British Political Facts*, p. 499.
43. Wyatt, p. 158 (15 November 1989).
44. Andrew Neil, *Full Disclosure* (Macmillan, 1986), p. 137.
45. Speech to the British Society of Magazine Editors, 29 July 1988.

19. Irish Dimension

1. Interviews, Tom King, Sir Frank Cooper.
2. Airey Neave Memorial Lecture, 2 March 1980.
3. Bruce Arnold, *Haughey: His Life and Unlucky Deeds* (HarperCollins, 1993), pp. 167–8.
4. Ibid, pp. 173–4.
5. House of Commons, 20 November 1980 [Vol. 994, col. 27].
6. House of Commons, 14 May 1981 [Vol. 4, col. 881].
7. Sinn Fein poster commemorating the twentieth anniversary of the hunger strikes, 2001.
8. House of Commons, 14 May 1981 [Vol. 4, col. 881].
9. Speech to Conservative Women's Conference, London, 20 May 1981.
10. Speech at Stormont, 28 May 1981.
11. Sinn Fein poster, 2001.
12. Renwick, *Fighting with Allies*, p. 230.

13. Garret FitzGerald, *All in a Life* (Macmillan, 1991), p. 378.
14. Chris Patten, interviewed for *The Thatcher Factor*.
15. Institute of Contemporary British History witness seminar, 26 April 1995.
16. Lord Gowrie, Chris Patten, interviewed for *The Thatcher Factor*.
17. Dennis C. Blair to Richard V. Allen, National Security Council memorandum, 10 June 1981 (Reagan Library).
18. Mark Stuart, *Douglas Hurd: The Public Servant* (Mainstream, 1998), p. 135.
19. Carol Thatcher, p. 219.
20. Millar, p. 301.
21. Cole, p. 278.
22. Speech to Conservative Party Conference, 12 October 1984.
23. Speech at Finchley, 20 October 1984.
24. Tyler, p. 245; George Gardiner in Dale, p. 46.
25. Wyatt, p. 415 (5 October 1987).
26. Alistair McAlpine in BBC TV, *Thatcher: The Downing Street Years* (1993)
27. FitzGerald, p. 517; Stuart, p. 140.
28. Press conference at 12 Downing Street, 19 November 1984.
29. Reagan papers, e.g. CO 167, 216000-226999.
30. Tip O'Neill, Edward Kennedy and others to Reagan, 20 December 1984 (NSC, Box 90902).
31. Record of meeting at Camp David, 22 December 1984 (NSC, Box 90902).
32. Reagan to O'Neill, 9 January 1985, in *Boston Globe*, 30 June 2002.
33. Thatcher, p. 403.
34. Speech to Conservative Party Conference, 14 October 1988.
35. Institute of Contemporary British History witness seminar, 26 April 1995.

20. Elective Dictatorship

1. Hennessy, *Whitehall*, p. 314.
2. Charles Powell, interviewed on *Thatcher: The Downing Street Years*.
3. Interviewed on *Thatcher: The Downing Street Years*.
4. Interview, Lord Crickhowell.
5. Lawson, p. 918.
6. Penny Junor, *John Major: from Brixton to Downing Street* (Penguin, 1996), pp. 117–19.
7. Lord Weatherill at ICBH witness seminar, 25 February 2002.
8. Thatcher, p. 41.
9. Interview, Lord Wakeham.
10. Ridley, p. 33.
11. Cockerell, pp. 300–302, 336–7.

12. Sarah Bradford, *Elizabeth: A Biography of her Majesty the Queen* (Heinemann, 1996), p. 381.
13. Pimlott, p. 460.
14. Lord Hunt in Pimlott, p. 461.
15. Bradford, p. 380.
16. *Observer*, 5 June 1983.
17. Bradford, p. 389.
18. Reference lost.
19. Thatcher, p. 755.
20. *Nationwide*, BBC TV, 14 June 1981.
21. *Sunday Times*, 5 August 1988.
22. Speech to WRVS, 19 January 1981.
23. *The Times*, 22 November 1989.
24. *Nationwide*, BBC TV, 14 June 1981.
25. BBC Radio interview, 23 March 1987.
26. Remarks in Downing Street, 3 January 1988.
27. Ibid., 3 March 1989.
28. Cosgrave, p. 14.
29. Interviewed on *The Jimmy Young Programme*, BBC Radio 2, 26 February 1986.
30. Thomson, p. 50.
31. Thatcher, p. 307.
32. Interview, Lady Young.
33. Speech to Conservative Women's Conference, 25 May 1988.
34. Lawson, p. 127.
35. Tyler, p. 191.
36. Interviewed on *Newsnight*, BBC TV, 30 July 1985.
37. Wyatt, p. 359 (4 June 1987).
38. Millar, p. 275.
39. *The Times*, 27 November 1987.

21. Stumble and Recovery

1. Thatcher, p. 463.
2. Ibid., p. 433.
3. Lord Whitelaw, John Biffen, interviewed for *The Thatcher Factor*.
4. House of Commons, 27 January 1986 [Vol. 90, col. 652].
5. The full text of Mayhew's letter is printed in Tam Dalyell, *Misrule: How Mrs Thatcher Misled Parliament from the Sinking of the Belgrano to the Wright Affair* (Hamish Hamilton, 1987), pp. 137–8.
6. House of Commons, 27 January 1986 [Vol. 90, col. 660].
7. *Sun*, 7 January 1986; *The Times*, 7 January 1986.

8. House of Commons, 23 January 1986 [Vol. 90, col. 455].
9. Ibid. [Vol. 90, col. 449–50].
10. Thatcher, p. 432.
11. Interview, Lord Younger.
12. *The Times*, 10 January 1986.
13. House of Commons, 23 January 1986 [Vol. 90, col. 450].
14. Ingham, p. 335.
15. House of Commons, 23 January 1986 [Vol. 90, col. 450].
16. Ibid. [Vol. 90, col. 455].
17. Young, p. 443.
18. House of Commons, 27 January 1986 [Vol. 90, col. 657].
19. Peter Jenkins, *Mrs Thatcher's Revolution: The Ending of the Socialist Era* (Jonathan Cape, 1987), p. 199.
20. Lord Havers, interviewed for *The Thatcher Factor*.
21. House of Commons, 23 January 1986 [Vol. 90, col. 450].
22. *The Times*, 25 January 1986.
23. Millar, p. 310.
24. Ingham, p. 337.
25. *TV-am*, 7 June 1987.
26. House of Commons, 27 January 1986 [Vol. 90, cols 646–51].
27. Clark, p. 135 (27 January 1986).
28. House of Commons, 27 January 1986 [Vol. 90, cols 651–8].
29. Clark, p.135 (27 January 1986).
30. House of Commons, 27 January 1986 [Vol. 90, cols 661–2].
31. Leon Brittan, interviewed for *The Thatcher Factor*.
32. *Sunday Times*, 3 March 1981.
33. Thatcher, p. 147.
34. Cockerell, p. 307.
35. David Butler and Dennis Kavanagh, *The British General Election of 1987*, pp. 32–4.
36. Thatcher, p. 647.
37. David Butler, Andrew Adonis and Tony Travers, *Failure in British Government: The Politics of the Poll Tax* (Oxford, 1994), p. 64.
38. Ibid.; Baker, p. 122.
39. Speech to the Scottish Conservative conference, Perth, 10 May 1985.
40. Wyatt, p. 467 (20 December 1987).
41. Lawson, pp. 573–4.
42. Speech to the Scottish Conservative conference, Perth, 10 June 1986.
43. Speech to the Scottish Conservative conference, Perth, 15 May 1987.
44. John Simpson, *Strange Places, Questionable People* (Macmillan, 1998), p. 246.
45. Thatcher, p. 573.
46. *The Times*, 13 June 1987.

47. Remarks in Downing Street, 12 June 1987.
48. Interview for BBC TV, 12 June 1987.
49. Carol Thatcher, p. 246.

22. No Such Thing as Society

1. *Sunday Express*, 21 June 1987.
2. *Woman's Own*, 31 October 1987.
3. Interview on *The Jimmy Young Programme*, BBC Radio 2, 27 July 1988.
4. Thatcher, p. 626.
5. Millar, p. 319.
6. Cockerell, p. 332.
7. House of Commons, 15 May 1979 [Vol. 967, cols 73–87].
8. Remarks visiting London docklands, 21 May 1987.
9. Speech to Conservative Party Conference, 9 October 1987.
10. *Annual Register 1987*, p. 31.
11. Lawson, p. 747; Thatcher, p. 700.
12. Thatcher, pp. 603–4.
13. *Social Trends*, 1987.
14. *Annual Register 1987*, p. 25.
15. Ibid., p. 9.
16. House of Commons, 15 December 1987 [Vol. 124, col. 918].
17. Simon Jenkins, p. 77.
18. Eric Jacobs and Robert Worcester, *We British: Britain under the Moriscope* (Weidenfeld & Nicolson, 1990).
19. Timmins, p. 508.
20. BBC TV, 24 July 1987.
21. Nicholas Ridley, *'My Style of Government': The Thatcher Years* (Hutchinson, 1991), p. 125.
22. Thatcher, *Downing Street Years*, p. 654.
23. Speech to 1922 Committee, 20 July 1989.
24. House of Commons, 20 July 1989 [Vol. 157, cols 516–17].
25. Thatcher, p. 654.
26. Wyatt, Vol. 2, p. 158 (17 September 1989).
27. House of Commons, 20 March 1990 [Vol. 169, col. 1008].
28. Thatcher, p. 658.
29. Clark, p. 287 (25 March 1990).
30. Chris Patten on BBC Radio 4, *Desert Island Discs*, 3 November 1996.
31. House of Commons, 28 November 1989 [Vol. 162, col. 576].
32. Speech to Conservative Local Government conference, 8 March 1989.
33. William Shawcross, *Murdoch* (Chatto & Windus, 1992), p. 511.

34. Wyatt, Vol. 2, p. 31 (12 February 1989).
35. Speech at the Mansion House, 17 October 1985.
36. *The Times*, 31 March 1987.
37. Thatcher, p. 701.
38. Timmins, p. 450.
39. Lawson, pp. 815, 824.
40. Speech to Conservative Central Council, Buxton, 19 March 1988.
41. Thatcher, pp. 689–90.
42. Keegan, *Mr Lawson's Gamble*, p. 188.
43. Thatcher, p. 703.
44. Ridley, p. 211.
45. Press conference, 14 June 1989.
46. Wyatt, Vol. 2, p. 99 (4 June 1989).

23. A Diet of Brussels

1. Thatcher, p. 558.
2. Ibid., p. 742.
3. Major, p. 345.
4. Thatcher, p. 744.
5. Cradock, p. 124.
6. e.g. *Daily Mail*, 17 May 1988.
7. Lawson, p. 903.
8. Charles Powell, interviewed on *The Poisoned Chalice*.
9. Interview, Sir Leon Brittan.
10. Hugo Young, *This Blessed Plot: Britain and Europe from Churchill to Blair* (Macmillan, 1998), p. 548.
11. Lawson, p. 907.
12. Speech to the College of Europe, Bruges, 20 September 1988.
13. Sir Michael Butler, interviewed on *The Poisoned Chalice*.
14. Sir Michael Butler, interviewed for DOHP, Churchill College, Cambridge.
15. Lawson, p. 907.
16. *The Times*, 25 October 1988.
17. John Campbell, *Nye Bevan and the Mirage of British Socialism* (Weidenfeld & Nicolson, 1986), p. 337.
18. House of Commons, 27 April 1989 [Vol. 151, col. 1089].
19. Ibid., 18 May 1989 [Vol. 153, col. 470].
20. Speech to Conservative Women's conference, 24 May 1989.
21. Howe, p. 578.
22. Thatcher, pp. 712–13.
23. Lawson, p. 933.

24. Thatcher, pp. 711–12.
25. Lawson, p. 932.
26. Thatcher, p. 711.
27. Cradock, p. 132.
28. Howe, p. 582.
29. Interview for ITN, 27 June 1989.
30. Wyatt, Vol. 2, p. 117 (26 June 1989).
31. Wyatt, reference missing.
32. Thatcher, p. 712.
33. Ibid., p. 758.
34. Ibid., p. 757.
35. Ridley, p. 40.
36. Ranelagh, p. 285.
37. Wyatt, Vol. 2, p. 139 (26 July 1989).
38. Press conference, Dublin, 26 June 1990.
39. Interview for BBC Radio, 14 June 1989.
40. Lawson, p. 898.
41. Douglas Hurd, interviewed on *The Poisoned Chalice*.

24. Tomorrow the World

1. House of Commons, 28 March 1979 [Vol. 965, col. 470].
2. Daniel Yergan and Joseph Stanislaw, *The Commanding Heights; The Battle Between Government and the Marketplace that is Remaking the Modern World* (Touchstone, New York, 1998), p. 124.
3. Ibid., p. 13.
4. Thatcher, p. 813.
5. George Bush and Brent Scowcroft, *A World Transformed* (Alfred A. Knopf, New York, 1998), p. 60.
6. Ibid., pp. 68–9.
7. Ibid., p. 72.
8. Bush and Scowcroft, p. 80.
9. ibid, pp. 82–3.
10. Ibid., p. 83; *The Times*, 30 March 1990.
11. Bush and Scowcroft, p. 84.
12. Cradock, p. 184.
13. Bush and Scowcroft, p. 84.
14. Press conference in Downing Street, 10 November 1989.
15. Urban, p. 99.
16. Bush and Scowcroft, p. 192.
17. Thatcher, p. 794.
18. Bush and Scowcroft, p. 193.

19. Transcript of telephone conversation, 9 November 1989 (Bush papers, OA/1D CFO 1731).
20. Bush and Scowcroft, p. 253.
21. Ibid., p. 195.
22. Transcript of telephone conversation, 3 December 1989 (Bush papers, OA/1D CFO 1729).
23. Bush and Scowcroft, pp. 198–9.
24. Ibid., p. 213.
25. Thatcher, p. 798.
26. Bush and Scowcroft, p. 159.
27. Ibid., p. 214.
28. Ibid., pp. 248–9.
29. Ibid., p. 249.
30. Ibid., p. 265.
31. Ibid., p. 294.
32. Thatcher, p. 811.
33. Bush and Scowcroft, p. 295.
34. *Financial Times*, 11 December 1989.
35. *Independent*, 25 October 2000.
36. Speech to the Royal Society, 27 September 1988.
37. The Earl of Caithness in Dale, p. 37.
38. Bush papers, 140654.
39. Speech to UN General Assembly, New York, 8 November 1989.
40. Speech to the Royal Society, 27 September 1988; interview in *She*, February 1989.
41. Margaret Thatcher to George Bush, 7 June 1990 (Bush papers, John Sonunu files CA/1D CF 00151).
42. Speech at World Climate Conference, Geneva, 6 November 1990.
43. Thatcher, *Statecraft*, pp. 449–57.
44. *Scott Report*, D3 11–15.
45. Ibid., D3 102.
46. Ibid., D3 11–15.
47. Ibid., C2 73.
48. James, p. 285.
49. *Not the Scott Report*, p. 22.
50. *Scott Report*, D3 105–6.
51. Ibid., D4 11–23.
52. Ibid., D 16.
53. Ibid., D3 164–5.
54. Bush and Scowcroft, p. 320.
55. Press conference at Aspen, Colorado, 2 August 1990.
56. Bush and Scowcroft, p. 320.
57. Ingham, p. 262.

58. Bush and Scowcroft, p. 315.
59. Wyatt, Vol. 2, p. 342 (10 August 1990).
60. Bush and Scowcroft, p. 352.
61. Barbara Bush, *A Memoir* (Scribners's, New York, 1995), p. 353.
62. Lawrence Freedman and Efraim Karsh, *The Gulf Conflict, 1990–91* (Faber, 1993), p. 177.
63. BBC, 7 January 1996.
64. House of Commons, 28 October 1990 [Vol. 178, col. 498].
65. Sir Michael Carver, *Tightrope Walking: British Defence Policy since 1945* (Hutchinson, 1992), p. 163.
66. Thatcher, *Downing Street Years*, p. 826.
67. Bush and Scowcroft, p. 407.
68. Thatcher, p. 828.
69. De la Billiere, pp. 401–2.
70. Carver, p. 163.
71. Cradock, p. 179.
72. Press conference in Paris, 19 November 1990.

25. On and On

1. Lady Thatcher, interviewed on *Thatcher: The Downing Street Years*.
2. Carol Thatcher, pp. 253–4.
3. Neil, p. 236.
4. Wyatt, Vol. 2, pp. 82–6 (7 May 1989).
5. Interview for IRN, 24 November 1989.
6. *Annual Register 1989*, p. 21.
7. Butler and Butler, pp. 256–7.
8. Wyatt, Vol. 2, p. 169 (9 October 1989).
9. Ranelagh, p. 306.
10. House of Commons, 13 June 1989 [Vol. 154, col. 702].
11. *Daily Mail*, 9 October 1989.
12. *Financial Times*, 18 October 1989.
13. Lawson, p. 959.
14. Thatcher, pp. 715–18; Lawson, pp. 960–64.
15. Major, p. 134.
16. Ibid., p. 133.
17. Thatcher, p. 717.
18. Stuart, p. 234.
19. Baker, p. 309.
20. *Daily Express*, 28 October 1989.
21. Lawson, p. 967.
22. Interviewed on *The Walden Interview*, 29 October 1989; reprinted in

David Cox (ed.), *The Walden Interviews* (Boxtree, 1900), pp. 30–52.

23. Nigel Lawson, interviewed on *The Walden Interview*, 5 November 1989, loc.cit., pp. 53–75.
24. Stuart, p. 236.
25. Major, p. 155.
26. Antony Seldon, *Major: A Political Life* (Weidenfeld & Nicolson, 1997), p. 112.
27. Cole, p. 349.
28. Private conversation, William Waldegrave, 10 December 1997.
29. Wyatt, Vol. 2, p. 189 (3 November 1989).
30. Ibid., p. 260 (21 March 1990).
31. Ibid., p. 288 (6 May 1990).
32. Thatcher, p. 719.
33. Wyatt, Vol. 2, pp. 339–40 (31 July 1990).
34. Ibid., p. 343.
35. David Waddington, in Dale, p. 217.
36. Major, p. 156.
37. Seldon, p. 104.
38. Major, p. 161.
39. Press conference in Downing Street, 5 October 1990.
40. *Financial Times*, 6 October 1990.
41. Major, p. 163.
42. Charles Powell on BBC TV, 16 September 1997.
43. Major, pp. 339–40.
44. Miller, p. 344.

26. The Defenestration of Downing Street

1. Sked and Cook, p. 551.
2. Ridley, p. 251.
3. *The Times*, 28 November 1990.
4. Alan Watkins, *A Conservative Coup: The Fall of Margaret Thatcher* (Duckworth, 1992), p. 213.
5. Wyatt, Vol. 2, p. 246 (25 February 1990).
6. Walden, pp. 301–2.
7. Thatcher, p. 767.
8. House of Commons, 30 October 1990 [Vol. 178, cols 869–92].
9. Owen, *Time to Declare* (Michael Joseph, 1991), p. 777.
10. House of Commons, 30 October 1990 [Vol. 178, cols 869–92].
11. *The Times*, 31 October 1990.
12. Owen, p. 777.
13. *Sun*, 31 October 1990.

14. Ranelagh, p. 285; Parkinson, pp. 118–19.
15. Howe, p. 647.
16. Howe to Mrs Thatcher, *The Times*, 2 November 1990.
17. Mrs Thatcher to Howe, *The Times*, 2 November 1990.
18. *The Times*, 2 November 1990.
19. Ibid., 3 November 1990.
20. Millar, p. 348.
21. House of Commons, 7 November 1990 [Vol. 180, col. 32].
22. Ibid., 13 November 1990 [Vol. 180, cols 461–5]; Howe, pp. 697–703.
23. Lawson, p. 1000.
24. Paddy Ashdown, *The Ashdown Diaries*, Vol. 1 (Allen Lane, 2000), p. 96.
25. *Independent*, 22 November 2000.
26. Walker, p. 233.
27. Parkinson, p. 25.
28. Michael Heseltine, *Life in the Jungle* (Hodder & Stoughton, 2000), pp. 362–3.
29. Baker, p. 363.
30. Walden, p. 302.
31. House of Commons, 12 December 1989 [Vol. 163, col. 849].
32. Stuart, p. 251.
33. Wyatt, Vol. 2, pp. 388–9 (15 November 1990).
34. Major, p. 184.
35. Press conference in Paris, 19 November 1990.
36. Speech at CSCE conference in Paris, 19 November 1990.
37. Ingham, p. 395.
38. Statement to reporters, Paris, 20 November 1990.
39. Charles Powell, interviewed on LWT, 17 September 2000; Ingham, p. 395.
40. Carol Thatcher, p. 264.
41. Wyatt, Vol. 2, p. 395 (20 November 1990).
42. Thatcher, p. 845.
43. Heseltine, p. 368.
44. Cole, p. 376.
45. Clark, pp. 359–61.
46. Thatcher, pp. 846–7.
47. Watkins, p.17.
48. Thatcher, p. 849.
49. Ibid.
50. House of Commons, 21 November 1990 [Vol. 181, cols 291–310].
51. Thatcher, p. 850.
52. Ibid., p. 851.
53. Watkins, p. 18.
54. Clark, pp. 364–5 (21 November 1990).
55. Thatcher, p. 855.

56. Baker, p. 407.
57. Thatcher, p. 855.
58. Interviewed on *Thatcher: The Downing Street Years*.
59. Malcolm Balen, *Kenneth Clarke* (Fourth Estate, 1994), p. 208.
60. Penny Junor, *John Major*, p. 197.
61. Resignation statement, 22 November 1990.
62. Thatcher, p. 859.
63. House of Commons, 22 November 1990 [Vol. 181, cols 445–53].
64. Baker, p. 414.
65. Carol Thatcher, p. 269.
66. Baker, p. 396.
67. Wyatt, Vol. 2, pp. 401–2 (23 November 1990).
68. Junor, p. 205.
69. Remarks at Conservative Central Office, 26 November 1990.
70. House of Commons, 27 November 1990 [Vol. 181, cols 737–42].
71. Statement on leaving Downing Street, 28 November 1990.
72. Carol Thatcher, p. 274.

27. Afterlife

1. *She*, 11 March 1987.
2. *Woman's Own*, 23 September 1987.
3. *TV-am*, 4 May 1989.
4. Major, p. 207.
5. Wyatt, Vol. 2, p. 411 (29 November 1990).
6. Ibid.
7. Ibid., p. 414 (2 December 1990).
8. *The Times*, 29 September 1992.
9. Wyatt, Vol. 2, p. 613 (29 November 1991).
10. *The Times*, 16 May 1991.
11. Ibid., 28 May 1991.
12. Ibid., 20, 21 August 1991.
13. Ibid., 2 October 1991.
14. Ibid.
15. House of Commons, 28 February 1991 [Vol. 186, col. 1120].
16. Wyatt, Vol. 2, p. 675 (15 March 1992).
17. Ibid., p. 677 (17 March 1992).
18. Major, p. 299.
19. Wyatt, Vol. 2, pp. 690–91 (9 April 1992).
20. *The Times*, 11 April 1992.
21. *Newsweek*, 17 April 1992; *The Times*, 21 April 1992.
22. Wyatt, Vol. 3, p. 12 (22 April 1992).

23. Wyatt, Vol. 2, p. 405 (26 November 1990).

24. Wyatt, Vol. 3, p. 22 (6 May 1992).

25. Ibid., p. 64 (30 June 1992).

26. Ibid., p. 64 (28 June 1992).

27. *The Times*, 6 August 1992.

28. *New York Times*, 6 August 1992.

29. *The Times*, 14 August 1992.

30. Douglas Hurd, *The Search for Peace* (Little, Brown, 1997), pp. 126, 141.

31. *Independent/The European*, 17 December 1992.

32. *The Times*, 14 April 1993.

33. Brendan Simms, *Unfinest Hour: Britain and the Destruction of Bosnia* (Allen Lane, 2001), p. 50.

34. *The Times*, 21 September 1992.

35. Wyatt, Vol. 3, p. 100 (18 September 1992).

36. House of Lords, 7 June 1993 [Vol. 546, cols 560–66].

37. Interview, Julian Seymour; Thatcher, *Statecraft*, pp. 191–2.

38. Thatcher, p. 193.

39. Interview, Julian Seymour.

40. Thatcher, *Downing Street Years,* pp. 719, 721.

41. Seldon, p. 579.

42. *The Times*, 14 July 1995.

43. Wyatt, Vol. 3, p. 581 (29 November 1995).

44. Dale, p. x.

45. Speech in Fulton, Missouri, 9 March 1996.

46. Paul Johnson in the *Sunday Telegraph*, 16 March 1997.

47. *The Times*, 23 November 1996.

48. Ibid., 18 March 1997.

49. *The Week*, 22 June 2002.

50. *The Times*, 26 May 1997.

51. *Independent*, 19 June 1997; Brenda Maddox, *Maggie: The First Lady* (Hodder & Stoughton, 2003), p. 225.

52. *Independent*, 23 May 2001.

53. *The Week*, 25 August 2001.

54. BBC 2, 3 November 2001.

55. *The Times*, 7 February 1995.

56. *Sunday Times*, 8 December 1996.

57. *Independent*, 12 August 1998.

58. *The Times*, 1 April 1996.

59. *Independent*, 4 April 1996.

60. Maddox, p. 225.

61. Thatcher, *Statecraft*, pp. 37–8.

62. Ibid., p. 228.

63. Ibid., p. 54.

64. Ibid., p. 206.
65. Ibid., p. 320.
66. Ibid., p. 321.
67. *The Times*, 22 March 2002.
68. *Independent on Sunday*, 24 March 2002.
69. *Independent*, 1 May 2003.
70. *Sun*, 23 March 2002.
71. *The Times*, 14 May 2008.
72. Andrew Rawnsley, *Servants of the People* (Penguin 2001), p. 213.

Sources and Bibliography

Primary sources

Margaret Thatcher, *Complete Public Statements, 1945–1990* on CD-Rom (Oxford University Press, 1999)
Parliamentary Debates, House of Commons, 1959–1992,
—, *House of Lords,* 1992-2001
George Bush presidential papers (George Bush Library, College Station, Texas)
Jimmy Carter presidential papers (Carter Library, Atlanta, Georgia)
Ronald Reagan presidential papers (Reagan Library, Simi Valley, California)
Conservative Party Archive (Bodleian Library, Oxford)
Conservative Party election manifestos, 1979, 1983, 1987, 1992 (Conservative Central Office)
Conservative Party Conference reports (Conservative Central Office)
David Butler/ Dennis Kavanagh interviews (Nuffield College, Oxford)
Interviews conducted for the British Diplomatic Oral History Programme (Archives Centre, Churchill College, Cambridge)
Interviews conducted for Brook Productions' TV series *The Seventies* and *The Thatcher Factor* (London School of Economics)
Annual Register
Dartford Chronicle
Economist
Erith Observer
Finchley Press
Grantham Guardian
Grantham Journal
Independent
Kentish Independent
The Times
KGGS Magazine, 1938–44

Palmer's Almanack (Grantham)

The Franks Report: Falkland Islands Review (Pimlico, 1992)

Indictment of Margaret Thatcher, Secretary of State for Education 1970–73, in *Defence of the Education Act,* 1944 (PSW Publications, Leicester. 1973)

Not the Scott Report (Private Eye, 1994)

The Right Approach (Conservative Central Office 1976)

The Right Approach to the Economy (Conservative Central Office 1977)

The Scott Report (HMSO, 1994)

Broadcast sources

The Woman at Number Ten (BBC 1983)

Woman to Woman (Yorkshire TV, 1985)

The English Woman's Wardrobe (De Wolfe Productions, 1986)

Thatcher: The Downing Street Years (BBC, 1993)

The Last Europeans (Channel 4, 1995)

The Poisoned Chalice (BBC, 1996)

Consequences (BBC Radio 4, 1996)

The Great Sell-Off (BBC, 1997)

Endgame in Ireland (BBC, 2001)

The Curse of the Mummy (BBC, 2001)

Maggie: The First Lady (Brook Lapping, 2003)

Secondary Sources

Leo Abse, *Margaret, Daughter of Beatrice: A Politician's Psycho-Biography of Margaret Thatcher* (Jonathan Cape, 1989)

Martin Adeney and John Lloyd: *The Miners' Strike, 1984–85: Loss Without Limit* (Routledge, 1986)

Jim Allen: *The Grantham Connection* (Grantham Book Centre 1986)

Kingsley Amis, *Memoirs* (Hutchinson, 1991)

Bruce Anderson, *John Major: The Making of the Prime Minister* (Fourth Estate, 1991)

Oliver Anderson: *Rotten Borough* (Ivor Nicholson & Watson, 1937; reissued, Fourth Estate, 1989)

Noel Annan, *Our Age: Portrait of a Generation* (Weidenfeld & Nicolson, 1990)

Bruce Arnold, *Margaret Thatcher: A Study in Power* (Hamish Hamilton, 1984)

—, *Haughey: His Life and Unlucky Deeds* (HarperCollins, 1993)

Paul Arthur and Keith Jeffery, *Northern Ireland since* 1968 (Blackwell, 1988)

Paddy Ashdown, *The Ashdown Diaries,* Vol.1, 1988-1997 (Allen Lane, 2000)

Jacques Attali, *Verbatim* (Fayard, Paris, 1995)

Kenneth Baker, *The Turbulent Years: My Life in Politics* (Faber, 1993)

Malcolm Balen, *Kenneth Clarke* (Fourth Estate, 1994)

Stuart Ball and Antony Seldon eds.: *The Heath Government, 1970–74* (Longman, 1996)

Anthony Barber, *Taking the Tide* (Michael Russell, 1996)

Anthony Barnett, *Iron Britannia: Why Parliament Waged its Falklands War* (Allison & Busby, 1982)

Nina Bawden, *In My Own Time* (Virago, 1994)

Andy Beckett, *Pinochet in Piccadilly: Britain and Chile's Hidden History* (Faber, 2002)

Robert Behrens: *The Conservative Party from Heath to Thatcher* (Saxon House, 1980)

Tony Benn: *Against the Tide: Diaries, 1973–76* (Hutchinson, 1989)

—, *Conflicts of Interest: Diaries, 1977–80* (Hutchinson, 1990)

—, *The End of an Era: Diaries, 1980–90* (Hutchinson, 1992)

—, *Free at Last: Diaries, 1991–2001* (Hutchinson, 2002)

Claire Berlinski: *'There Is No Alternative': Why Margaret Thatcher Matters* (Basic Books, 2008)

Paul Bew, Henry Patterson and Paul Teague, *Between War and Peace: The Political Future of Northern Ireland* (Laurence and Wishart, 1997)

Patrick Bishop and Eamonn Mallie, *The Provisional IRA* (Heinemann, 1987)

Tessa Blackstone and William Plowden, *Inside the Think Tank: Advising the Cabinet, 1971–1983* (Heinemann, 1988)

David Blair, *The History of the Oxford University Conservative Association* (OUCA, 1995)

Robert Blake, *The Conservative Party from Peel to Thatcher* (Faber, 1985)

Robert Blake and John Patten, ed.: *The Conservative Opportunity* (Macmillan, 1976)

John Boyd-Carpenter, *Way of Life* (Sidgwick & Jackson, 1980)

Andrew Boyle, *The Climate of Treason: Five Who Spied for Russia* (Hutchinson, 1979)

Rhodes Boyson, *Speaking my Mind* (Peter Owen, 1995)

Sarah Bradford, *Elizabeth: A Biography of Her Majesty the Queen* (Heinemann, 1996)

Gyles Brandreth, *Breaking the Code: The Westminster Diaries, May 1990–May 1997* (Weidenfeld & Nicolson, 1999)

Jock Bruce-Gardyne, *Mrs Thatcher's First Administration: The Prophets Confounded* (Macmillan, 1984)

—, *Ministers and Mandarins: Inside the Whitehall Village* (Sidgwick & Jackson, 1986)

Lisa Budreau: *An Analysis of the Anglo-American Alliance During the Second World War in Grantham* (Grantham Museum, 1993)

Barbara Bush, *A Memoir* (Scribners, New York, 1994)

George Bush and Brent Scowcroft, *A World Transformed* (Alfred A. Knopf, New York, 1998)

David Butler, *The British General Election of* 1951 (Macmillan, 1952)

David Butler and Richard Rose, *The British General Election of* 1959 (Macmillan, 1960)

David Butler and Anthony King, *The British General Election of* 1964 (Macmillan, 1965)

—, *The British General Election of* 1966 (Macmillan, 1967)

David Butler and Michael Pinto-Duchinsky, *The British General Election of* 1970 (Macmillan, 1971)

David Butler and Dennis Kavanagh, *The British General Election of February* 1974 (Macmillan, 1974)

—, *The British General Election of October 1974* (Macmillan, 1975)

—, *The British General Election of 1979* (Macmillan, 1980)

—, *The British General Election of 1983* (Macmillan, 1984)

—, *The British General Election of 1987* (Macmillan, 1988)

David Butler and Uwe Kitzinger, *The 1975 Referendum* (Macmillan, 1976)

David Butler, Andrew Adonis and Tony Travers, *Failure in British Government: The Politics of the Poll Tax* (Oxford, 1994)

Davis Butler and Gareth Butler, *British Political Facts, 1900-1994* (Macmillan, 1994)

Michael Butler, *Europe: More than a Continent* (Heinemann, 1986)

R.A.Butler, *The Art of the Possible* (Hamish Hamilton, 1971)

James Callaghan, *Time and Chance* (Collins, 1987)

Beatrix Campbell, *The Iron Ladies: Why do Women Vote Tory* (Virago, 1987)

John Campbell, *Edward Heath* (Jonathan Cape, 1993)

Humphrey Carpenter, *Robert Runcie: The Reluctant Archbishop* (Hodder & Stoughton, 1996)

Lord Carrington, *Reflect on Things Past* (Collins, 1988)

Jimmy Carter, *Keeping Faith* (Collins, 1982)

John Carvel, *Turn Again, Livingstone* (Profile Books, 1999)

Michael Carver, *Tightrope Walking: British Defence Policy since 1945* (Hutchinson, 1992)

Barbara Castle, *The Castle Diaries, 1964–70* (Weidenfeld & Nicolson, 1984)

—, *The Castle Diaries, 1974–76* (Weidenfeld & Nicolson, 1980)

—, *Fighting All The Way* (Macmillan, 1993)

Michael Charlton, *The Last Colony in Africa: Diplomacy and the Independence of Rhodesia* (Blackwell, 1990)

Alan Clark, *Diaries* (Weidenfeld & Nicolson, 1993)

—, *Diaries: Into Politics* (Weidenfeld & Nicolson, 2000)

—, *The Tories: Conservatives and the Nation State, 1922–1997* (Weidenfeld & Nicolson, 1998)

Peter Clarke, *A Question of Leadership: Gladstone to Thatcher* (Hamish Hamilton, 1991)

—, *Hope and Glory: Britain 1900–1990* (Allen Lane, 1996)

Michael Cockerell, *Live from Number 10: The Inside Story of Prime Ministers and Television* (Faber, 1988)

Michael Cockerell, Peter Hennessy and David Walker, *Sources Close to the Prime Minister: Inside the Hidden World of the News Manipulators* (Macmillan, 1984)

Richard Cockett, *Thinking the Unthinkable: Think-Tanks and the Economic Counter-Revolution, 1931–1983* (HarperCollins, 1994)

Richard Cockett, ed.: *My Dear Max: The Letters of Brendan Bracken to Lord-Beaverbrook, 1925–1958* (Historians' Press, 1990)

John Cole, *The Thatcher Years: A Decade of Revolution in British Politics* (BBC, 1987)

—, *As It Seemed to Me* (Weidenfeld & Nicolson, 1995)

Terry Coleman, *Movers and Shakers* (Bantam, 1987)

—, *Thatcher's Britain: A Journey through the Promised Lands* (Bantam, 1987)

John Coles, *Making Foreign Policy: A Certain Idea of Britain* (John Murray, 2000)

Patrick Cormack ed.: *Right Turn: Eight men Who Changed Their Mind* (Leo Cooper, 1978)

Patrick Cosgrave: *Margaret Thatcher: A Tory and her Party* (Hutchinson, 1978)

—, *Thatcher: The First Term* (Bodley Head, 1985)

—, *Carrington: A Life and a Policy* (Dent, 1985)

—, *The Lives of Enoch Powell* (Bodley Head, 1989)

Philip Cowley and Matthew Bailey: "Peasants' Uprising or Religious War?: Re-examining the 1975 Conservative Leadership Contest" in *British Journal of Political Science*, September 1999.

Maurice Cowling ed.: *Conservative Essays* (Cassell, 1978)

Brian Cox, *The Great Betrayal* (Chapman, 1992)

David Cox ed., *The Walden Interviews* (Boxtree, 1990)

Percy Cradock, *Experiences in China* (John Murray, 1994)

—, *In Pursuit of British Interests: Reflections on Foreign Policy under Margaret Thatcher and John Major* (John Murray, 1997)

Michael Crick, *Scargill and the Miners* (Penguin, 1985)

—, *Michael Heseltine* (Hamish Hamilton, 1997)

Julian Critchley, *Westminster Blues* (Hamish Hamilton, 1985)

—, *The Palace of Varieties: An Insider's View of Westminster* (John Murray, 1989)

—, *Heseltine: The Unauthorised Biography* (Andre Deutsch, 1987)

—, *Some of Us: People Who Did Well Under Thatcher* (John Murray, 1992)

Richard Crossman, *The Diaries of a Cabinet Minister* (Hamish Hamilton & Jonathan Cape, 1975, 1976, 1977)

Brian Crozier, *Free Agent: The Unseen War, 1941–1991* (HarperCollins, 1993)

Edwina Currie, *Life Lines: Politics and Health* (Sidgwick & Jackson, 1989)

—, *The Edwina Currie Diaries, 1987–1992* (Little, Brown, 2002)

Iain Dale, ed., *As I Said to Denis: The Margaret Thatcher Book of Quotations* (Robson Books, 1997)

—, *Memories of Maggie* (Politicos, 2000)

Ann Dally, *A Doctor's Story* (Macmillan, 1990)

Macdonald Daly and Alexander George, *Margaret Thatcher in her own Words* (Penguin, 1987)

Tam Dalyell, *Misrule: How Mrs Thatcher Misled Parliament from the Sinking of the Belgrano to the Wright Affair* (Hamish Hamilton, 1987)

A.J. Davies, *We, the Nation: The Conservative Party and the Pursuit of Power* (Little, Brown, 1995)

Rupert E. Davies: *Methodism* (Penguin, 1963)

Robin Day, *Grand Inquisitor* (Weidenfeld & Nicolson, 1989)

Peter de la Billière, *Looking for Trouble* (HarperCollins, 1994)

Michael De-la-Noy, *The Honours System: Who Gets What and Why* (Virgin, 1992)

Edmund Dell, *The Chancellors: A History of the Chancellors of the Exchequer, 1945–1990* (HarperCollins, 1996)

Andrew Denham and Mark Garnett, *Keith Joseph* (Acumen, 2001)

David Dimbleby and David Reynolds, *An Ocean Apart* (BBC/Hodder, 1988)

Jonathan Dimbleby, *The Prince of Wales* (Little, Brown, 1994)

—, *The Last Governor: Chris Patten and the Handover of Hong Kong* (Little, Brown, 1997)

Michael Dockrill, *British Defence since 1945* (Blackwell, 1988)

Bernard Donoughue, *Prime Minister: The Conduct of Policy Under Harold Wilson and James Callaghan* (Jonathan Cape, 1987)

Edward du Cann, *Two Lives: The Political and Business Careers of Edward du Cann* (Images, Upton-upon-Severn, 1995)

Michael Edwardes, *Back from the Brink* (Collins, 1983)

Harold Evans, *Good Times, Bad Times* (Weidenfeld & Nicolson, 1983)

Marcia Falkender, *Downing Street in Perspective* (Weidenfeld & Nicolson, 1983)

Ivan Fallon, *The Brothers: The Rise and Rise of Saatchi and Saatchi* (Hutchinson, 1988)

Diana Farr, *Five at 10: Prime Ministers' Consorts since 1957* (Andre Deutsch, 1985)

Nigel Fisher, *Iain Macleod* (Andre Deutsch, 1973)

—, *The Tory Leaders: Their Struggle for Power* (Hamish Hamilton, 1977)

Garret Fitzgerald, *All in a Life* (Macmillan, 1991)

Norman Fowler, *Ministers Decide* (Chapman, 1991)

Antonia Fraser, *The Warrior Queens: Boadicea's Chariot* (Weidenfeld & Nicolson, 1988)

Lawrence Freedman and Virginia Gamba-Stonehouse, *Signals of War: The Falklands Conflict of 1982* (Faber, 1990)

Lawrence Freedman and Efraim Karsh, *The Gulf Conflict, 1990–91* (Faber, 1993)

Alan Friedman, *Spider's Web: Bush, Saddam, Thatcher and the Decade of Deceit* (Faber, 1993)

Andrew Gamble, *The Conservative Nation* (Routledge & Kegan Paul 1974)

—, *The Free Economy and the Strong State: The Politics of Thatcherism* (Macmillan, 1988)

George Gardiner: *Margaret Thatcher: From Childhood to Leadership* (William Kimber, 1975)

—, *A Bastard's Tale* (Aurum, 1999)

Mark Garnett, *From Anger to Apathy: The British Experience since 1975* (Jonathan Cape, 2007)

Mark Garnett and Ian Aitken, *Splendid! Splendid! The Authorised Biography of Willie Whitelaw* (Jonathan Cape, 2002)

David Gergan, *Eyewitness to Power: The Essence of Leadership: Nixon to Clinton* (Simon & Schuster, New York, 2000)

Frank Giles: *Sundry Times* (John Murray, 1986)

Ian Gilmour: *Inside Right: A Study of Conservatism* (Hutchinson, 1977)

—, *Britain Can Work* (Martin Robertson, 1983)

—, *Dancing with Dogma: Britain under Thatcherism* (Simon & Schuster, 1992)

Ian Gilmour and Mark Garnett, *Whatever Happened to the Tories? The Conservative Party since 1945* (Fourth Estate, 1998)

Philip Goodhart, *The 1922: The Story of the Conservative Backbenchers' Parliamentary Committee* (Macmillan, 1973)

Mikhail Gorbachev, *Memoirs* (Doubleday, 1996)

Joe Gormley, *Battered Cherub* (Hamish Hamilton, 1982)

Alexander Haig, *Caveat: Realism, Reagan and Foreign Policy* (Weidenfeld & Nicolson, 1984)

Lord Hailsham, *The Dilemma of Democracy* (Collins, 1978)

—, *A Sparrow's Flight* (Collins, 1990)

Morison Halcrow, *Keith Joseph: A Single Mind* (Macmillan, 1989)

Paul Halloran and Mark Hollingsworth, *Thatcher's Gold: The Life and Times of Mark Thatcher* (Simon & Schuster, 1995)

Chris Ham, *The Politics of NHS Reform: Metaphor or Reality?* (King's Fund, 2000)

Kenneth Harris, *Thatcher* (Weidenfeld & Nicolson, 1988)

Robert Harris, *Gotcha! The Media, the Government and the Falklands Crisis* (Faber, 1983)

—, *The Making of Neil Kinnock* (Faber, 1984)

—, *A Good and Faithful Servant: The Unauthorised Biography of Bernard Ingham* (Faber, 1990)

Ralph Harris and Brendon Sewill, *British Economic Policy, 1970–74: Two Views* (Institute of Economic Affairs, 1975)

Brian Harrison, 'Mrs Thatcher and the Intellectuals' in *Twentieth Century British History*, 1994.

Max Hastings and Simon Jenkins, *The Battle for the Falklands* (Michael Joseph, 1983)

Bob Hawke, *The Hawke Memoirs,* (Heinemann, 1994)

Denis Healey, *The Time of my Life* (Michael Joseph, 1989)

Edward Heath, *The Course of My Life* (Hodder & Stoughton, 1998)

Simon Heffer, *Like the Roman: The Life of Enoch Powell* (Weidenfeld & Nicolson, 1998)

Nicholas Henderson, *Channels and Tunnels* (Weidenfeld & Nicolson, 1987)
Mandarin: The Diary of an Ambassador (Weidenfeld & Nicolson, 1994)

Peter Hennessy, *Cabinet* (Blackwell, 1986)

—, *Whitehall* (Secker & Warburg, 1989)

—, *The Prime Minister: The Office and its Holders since 1945* (Allen Lane, 2000)

Peter Hennessy and Anthony Seldon eds., *Ruling Performance: British Governments from Attlee to Thatcher* (Blackwell, 1985)

Michael Heseltine, *Where There's a Will* (Hutchinson, 1987) *Life in the Jungle* (Hodder & Stoughton, 2000)

Judy Hillman and Peter Clarke, *Geoffrey Howe: A Quiet Revolutionary* (Weidenfeld & Nicolson, 1988)

Paul Hirst, *After Thatcher* (Collins, 1989)

Simon Hoggart and David Leigh, *Michael Foot: A Portrait* (Hodder & Stoughton, 1981)

Mark Hollingsworth, *The Ultimate Spin-Doctor: The Life and Fast Times of Tim Bell* (Hodder & Stoughton, 1997)

Martin Holmes, *Political Pressure and Economic Policy: British Government, 1970–74* (Butterworth, 1982)

—, *The First Thatcher Government, 1979–1983* (Wheatsheaf, 1985)

Michael Honeybone, *The Book of Grantham* (Barracuda Books, Buckingham, 1980)

Alistair Horne, *Macmillan, 1957–1986* (Macmillan, 1989)

—, (ed)., *Telling Lives* (Macmillan, 2000)

John Hoskyns, *Just in Time: Inside the Thatcher Revolution* (Aurum, 2000)

Geoffrey Howe, *Conflict of Loyalty* (Macmillan, 1994)

Rex Hunt, *My Falkland Days* (David & Charles, 1992)

Douglas Hurd, *The Search for Peace* (Little, Brown, 1997)

Marmaduke Hussey, *Chance Governs All* (Macmillan, 2001)

Bernard Ingham, *Kill the Messenger* (HarperCollins, 1994)

Eric Jacobs and Robert Worcester, *We British: Britain under the Moriscope* (Weidenfeld & Nicolson, 1990)

Gerald James, *In the Public Interest* (Little, Brown, 1995)

Kevin Jefferys, *Finest and Darkest Hours: The Decisive Events in British Politics from Churchill to Blair* (Atlantic Books, 2002)

Peter Jenkins, *Mrs Thatcher's Revolution: The Ending of the Socialist Era* (Jonathan Cape, 1987)

Roy Jenkins, *European Diary, 1977–1981* (Collins, 1989) *A Life at the Centre* (Macmillan, 1991)

Simon Jenkins, *Accountable to None: The Tory Privatisation of Britain* (Hamish Hamilton, 1995)

—, *Thatcher & Sons: A Revolution in Three Acts* (Allen Lane, 2006)

Christopher Johnson, *The Economy under Mrs Thatcher, 1979–1990* (Penguin, 1991)

J.D.F. Jones, *Storyteller: The Many Lives of Laurens van der Post* (John Murray, 2001)

Keith Joseph: *Reversing the Trend: A Critical Reappraisal of Conservative Economic and Social Policies* (Barry Rose, 1975)

—, *Monetarism Is Not Enough* (Conservative Political Centre, 1976)

—, *Stranded on the Middle Ground* (Conservative Political Centre, 1976)

—, "Escaping the Chrysalis of Statism": Keith Joseph interviewed by Anthony Seldon in *Contemporary Record*, Vol.1, no.1, Spring 1987.

John Junor, *Listening for a Midnight Tram* (Chapman, 1990)

Penny Junor, *Margaret Thatcher: Wife, Mother, Politician* (Sidgwick & Jackson, 1983)

—, *John Major: From Brixton to Downing Street* (Penguin, 1996)

Dennis Kavanagh, *Thatcherism and British Politics: The End of Consensus?* (Oxford, 1987, 1990)

Dennis Kavanagh and Anthony Seldon, *The Thatcher Effect: A Decade of Change* (Oxford, 1989)

—, *The Major Effect* (Macmillan, 1994)

Sara Keays, *A Question of Judgement* (Quintessential Press, 1985)

William Keegan, *Mrs Thatcher's Economic Experiment* (Penguin, 1984, 1985)

—, *Mr Lawson's Gamble* (Hodder & Stoughton, 1989)

Richard N. Kelly, *Conservative Party Conferences: The Hidden System* (Manchester University Press, 1989)

Arnold Kemp, *The Hollow Drum: Scotland since the War* (Mainstream, 1993)

Ludovic Kennedy, *On my Way to the Club* (Collins, 1989)

Robert Kilroy-Silk, *Hard Labour: The Political Diary of Robert Kilroy-Silk* (Chatto & Windus, 1986)

Anthony King, *The British Prime Minister* (Macmillan, 1985)

Cecil King, *The Cecil King Diary, 1970–74* (Jonathan Cape, 1975)

Malcolm Knapp, *Grantham, The War Years 1939–45* (Lincolnshire Books, 1995)

—, *Grantham* (Sutton Publishing, Stroud, 1996)

Norman Lamont, *In Office* (Little, Brown, 1999)

Zig Layton-Henry ed., *Conservative Party Politics* (Macmillan, 1980)

Nigel Lawson, *The View from No. 11: Memoirs of a Tory Radical* (Bantam, 1992)

Michael Leapman, *Barefaced Cheek: The Apotheosis of Rupert Murdoch* (Hodder & Stoughton, 1983)

—, *The Last Days of the Beeb* (Allen & Unwin, 1986)

J.J. Lee, *Ireland,1912–85* (Cambridge, 1989)

Oliver Letwin, *Privatising the World* (Cassell, 1988)

Shirley Robin Letwin, *The Antomy of Thatcherism* (Fontana, 1992)

Geoffrey Lewis, *Lord Hailsham* (Jonathan Cape, 1997)

Russell Lewis, *Margaret Thatcher* (Routledge & Kegan Paul, 1975)

Magnus Linklater and David Leigh, *Not with Honour* (Sphere, 1986)

Alistair McAlpine, *Once a Jolly Bagman* (Weidenfeld & Nicolson, 1997)

Robert Macfarlane, *Special Trust* (Cadell & Davies, New York, 1994)

Ian MacGregor, *The Enemies Within: The Story of the Miners' Strike, 1984-85* (Collins, 1986)

Andy McSmith, *Kenneth Clarke: A Political Biography* (Verso, 1994)

Brenda Maddox, *Maggie: The First Lady* (Hoffer & Stoughton, 2003)

Lady Olga Maitland, *Margaret Thatcher: The First Ten Years* (Sidgwick & Jackson, 1989)

John Major, *The Autobiography* (HarperCollins, 1999)

Nelson Mandela, *Long Walk to Freedom* (Little, Brown, 1994)

Jean Mann, *Woman in Parliament* (Odhams, 1962)

David Marquand, *The Unprincipled Society: New Demands and Old Politics* (Jonathan Cape, 1987)

—, *Britain Since 1918: The Strange Career of British Democracy* (Weidenfeld & Nicolson, 2008)

Andrew Marr, *Ruling Britannia* (Michael Joseph, 1995)

Arthur Marwick, *British Society since 1945* (Penguin, 1990)

Reginald Maudling, *Memoirs* (Sidgwick & Jackson, 1978)

Anthony Meyer, *Stand up and be Counted* (Heinemann, 1990)

Keith Middlemas, *Power, Competition and the State*, Vol.3, *The End of the Post-War Era: Britains since 1974* (Macmillan, 1991)

Ronald Millar, *A View from the Wings* (Weidenfeld & Nicolson, 1993)

Alasdair Milne, *D-G: The Memoirs of a British Broadcaster* (Hodder & Stoughton, 1988)

Kenneth Minogue and Michael Biddiss eds., *Thatcherism: Personality and Politics* (Macmillan, 1987)

Ernle Money, *Margaret Thatcher, First Lady of the House* (Leslie Frewin, 1975)

Charles Moore and Simon Heffer, *A Tory Seer: The Selected Journalism of T.E. Utley* (Hamish Hamilton, 1989)

Kenneth O. Morgan, *The People's Peace: British History, 1945-1989* (Oxford, 1990)

—, *Callaghan: A Life* (Oxford, 1997)

Oliver Morrissey, Brian Smith and Edward Horesh, *British Aid and International Trade: Aid Policy Making, 1979–89* (Oxford, 1992)

Patricia Murray, *Margaret Thatcher* (W.H. Allen, 1980)

Andrew Neil, *Full Disclosure* (Macmillan, 1986)

H. G. Nicholas, *The British General Election of 1950* (Macmillan, 1950)

Philip Norton, *Conservative Dissidents: Dissent within the Parliamentary Conservative Party, 1970–74* (Temple Smith, 1978)

—, *Dissension in the House of Commons, 1974–1979* (Oxford, 1980)

John Nott, *Here Today and Gone Tomorrow* (Politico's, 2002)

Robin Oakley, *Inside Track* (Bantam, 2001)

Chris Ogden, *Maggie* (Simon & Schuster, New York, 1990)

Amy C. Old, *The History of Kesteven and Grantham Girls' School, 1910–1987* (Privately printed).

Arwel Ellis Owen, *The Anglo-Irish Agreement: The First Three Years* (University of Wales, Cardiff, 1994)

David Owen, *Face the Future* (Jonathan Cape, 1981)

—, *Time to Declare* (Michael Joseph, 1991)

Cecil Parkinson, *Right at the Centre* (Weidenfeld & Nicolson, 1992)

Matthew Parris, *Chance Witness: An Outsider's Life in Politics* (Viking, 2002)

Chris Patten, *East and West* (Macmillan, 1998)

Jeremy Paxman, *Friends in High Places: Who Runs Britain?* (Michael Joseph, 1990)

Edward Pearce, *Election Rides* (Faber, 1992)

—, *Denis Healey: A Life in our Times* (Little, Brown, 2002)

John Peyton, *Without Benefit of Laundry* (Bloomsbury, 1997)

Melanie Phillips, *The Divided House* (Sidgwick & Jackson, 1980)

Ben Pimlott, *Harold Wilson* (HarperCollins, 1992)

—, *The Queen* (HarperCollins, 1996)

Chapman Pincher, *Their Trade is Treachery* (Sidgwick & Jackson, 1981)

Clive Ponting, *Whitehall: Tragedy and Farce* (Hamish Hamilton, 1986)

James Prior, *A Balance of Power* (Hamish Hamilton, 1986)

Peter Pugh and Carl Flint, *Thatcher for Beginners* (Icon Books, 1997)

Stanislao Pugliese, ed., *The Political Legacy of Margaret Thatcher* (Politico's, 2003)

Francis Pym, *The Politics of Consent* (Hamish Hamilton, 1984)

Jonathan Raban, *God, Man and Mrs Thatcher* (Chatto & Windus, 1989)

Timothy Raison, *Tories and the Welfare State: A History of Conservative Social Policy since the Second World War* (Macmillan, 1990)

John Ramsden, *The Making of Conservative Party Policy: The Conservative Research Department since 1929* (Longman, 1980)

—, *The Winds of Change: Macmillan to Heath, 1957-1975* (Longman, 1996)

—, *An Appetite for Power: A History of the Conservative Party since 1830* (Harper-Collins, 1998)

John Ranelagh, *Thatcher's People: An Insider's Account of the Politics, the Power and the Personalities* (HarperCollins, 1991)

Peter Rawlinson, *A Price Too High* (Weidenfeld & Nicolson, 1989)

Ronald Reagan, *An American Life* (Arrow, 1991)

John Rentoul, *The Rich get Richer: The Growth of Inequality in Britain in the 1890s* (Unwin, 1987)

Robin Renwick, *Fighting with Allies: America and Britain in Peace and War* (Macmillan, 1996)

—, *Unconventional Diplomacy in Southern Africa* (Macmillan, 1997)

David Reynolds, *Britannia Overruled: British Policy and World Power in the Twentieth Century* (Longman, 1991)

Peter Riddell, *The Thatcher Decade* (Blackwell, 1989)

Nicholas Ridley, *'My Style of Government': The Thatcher Years* (Hutchinson, 1991)

Kenneth Rose, *Elusive Rothschild: The Life of Victor, Third Baron* (Weidenfeld & Nicolson, 2003)

Andrew Roth, *Heath and the Heathmen* (Routledge & Kegan Paul, 1972)

Paul Routledge, *Scargill: The Unauthorised Biography* (HarperCollins, 1993)

Anthony Sampson, *The Changing Anatomy of Britain* (Hodder & Stoughton, 1982)

—, *The Essential Anatomy of Britain: Democracy in Crisis* (Hodder & Stoughton, 1992)

—, *Nelson Mandela* (HarperCollins, 1999)

John Sergeant, *Maggie: Her Fatal Legacy* (Macmillan, 2005)

Raymond Seitz, *Over Here* (Weidenfeld & Nicolson, 1998)

Anthony Seldon, *Major: A Political Life* (Weidenfeld & Nicolson, 1997)

Anthony Seldon and Stuart Ball, *The Conservative Century: The Conservative Party since 1900* (Oxford, 1994)

William Shawcross, *Murdoch* (Chatto & Windus, 1992)

Robert Shepherd, *The Power Brokers: The Tory Party and its Leaders* (Hutchinson, 1991)

—, *Enoch Powell* (Hutchinson, 1996)

Norman Shrapnel, *The Performers: Politics as Theatre* (Constable 1978)

—, *The Seventies* (Constable, 1980)

George P. Shultz, *Turmoil and Triumph: My Years as Secretary of State* (Scribners, New York, 1993)

Brendan Simms, *Unfinest Hour: Britain and the Destruction of Bosnia* (Allen Lane, 2001)

Brian Simon, *Bending the Rules: The Baker 'Reform' of Education* (Laurence and Wishart, 1988)

John Simpson, *Strange Places, Questionable People* (Macmillan, 1998)

Alan Sked and Chris Cook, *Post-war Britain: A Political History, 1945–1992* (Penguin, 1993)

Robert Skidelsky ed., *Thatcherism* (Chatto & Windus, 1988)

Geoffrey Smith, *Reagan and Thatcher* (Bodley Head, 1990)

Ronald A. Smith, *The Premier Years of Margaret Thatcher* (Kevin Francis, 1991)

Jon Sopel, *Tony Blair: The Moderniser*

David Steel, *Against Goliath: David Steel's Story* (Weidenfeld & Nicolson, 1989)

Tom Stacey and Roland St. Oswald, *Here Come the Tories* (Tom Stacey, 1970)

Philip Stephens, *Politics and the Pound: The Tories, the Economy and Europe* (Macmillan, 1996)

Hugh Stephenson, *Mrs Thatcher's First Year* (Jill Norman, 1980)

Norman St John Stevas, *The Two Cities* (Faber, 1984)

Roy Strong, *Diaries, 1967–1987* (Weidenfeld & Nicolson, 1997)

Mark Stuart, *Douglas Hurd: The Public Servant* (Mainstream, 1998)

Robert Taylor: *The Trade Union Question in British Politics: Government and Unions since 1945* (Blackwell, 1993)

Norman Tebbit, *Upwardly Mobile* (Weidenfeld & Nicolson, 1988)

—, *Unfinished Business* (Weidenfeld & Nicolson, 1991)

Carol Thatcher, *Diary of an Election: With Margaret Thatcher on the Campaign Trail* (Sidgwick & Jackson, 1983)

—, *Below the Parapet: The Biography of Denis Thatcher* (HarperCollins, 1996)

—, *A Swim-On Part in the Goldfish Bowl: A Memoir* (Headline, 2008)

Margaret Thatcher, *What's Wrong With Politics?* (Conservative Political Centre, 1968)

—, *Let Our Children Grow Tall: Selected Speeches, 1975-77* (Centre for Policy Studies, 1977)

—, *In Defence of Freedom: Speeches on Britain's Relations with the World, 1976–1986* (Prometheus Books, 1987)

—, *The Downing Street Years* (HarperCollins, 1993)

—, *The Path to Power* (HarperCollins, 1995)

—, *The Collected Speeches*, edited by Robin Harris (Harper Collins, 1997)

—, *Statecraft: Strategies for a Changing World* (HarperCollins, 2002)

George Thomas, *Mr Speaker* (Century, 1986)

Andrew Thomson, *Margaret Thatcher: The Woman Within* (Allen Lane, 1989)

D.R. Thorpe, *Alec Douglas-Home* (Sinclair-Stevenson, 1996)

Kenneth R. Timmerman, *The Death Lobby* (Fourth Estate, 1992)

Nicholas Timmins, *The Five Giants: A Biography of the Welfare State* (HarperCollins, 1995)

Ian Trethowan, *Split Screen* (Hamish Hamilton, 1984)

Christopher Tugendhat, *Making Sense of Europe* (Viking, 1986)

Rodney Tyler, *Campaign! The Selling of the Prime Minister* (Grafton Books, 1987)

George Urban, *Diplomacy and Disillusion at the Court of Margaret Thatcher: An Insider's View* (Tauris, 1996)

Cento Veljanovski, *Selling the State: Privatisation in Britain* (Weidenfeld & Nicolson, 1987)

Anthony Verrier, *The Road to Zimbabwe* (Jonathan Cape, 1986)

George Walden, *Lucky George: Memoirs of an Anti-Politician* (Allen Lane, 1999)

Peter Walker, *Staying Power* (Bloomsbury, 1991)

Alan Walters, *Britain's Economic Renaissance: Mrs Thatcher's Reforms* (Oxford, 1986

—, *Sterling in Danger: The Economic Consequences of Pegged Exchange Rates* (Fontana/IEA, 1990)

Dennis Walters, *Not Always With the Pack* (Constable, 1989)

Nicholas Wapshott and George Brock, *Thatcher* (Macdonald, 1983)

Marina Warner, *Monuments and Maidens: The Allegory of the Female Form* (Weidenfeld & Nicolson, 1985)

Alan Watkins, *Brief Lives* (Hamish Hamilton, 1982)

—, *A Conservative Coup: The Fall of Margaret Thatcher* (Duckworth, 1991, 1992)

Charles Webster, *The National Health Service: A Political History* (Oxford, 1998)

Wendy Webster, *Not a Man to Match Her: The Marketing of the Prime Minister* (Women's Press, 1990)

Caspar Weinberger, *Fighting for Peace: Seven Critical Years at the Pentagon* (Michael Joseph, 1990)

Nigel West, *The Secret War for the Falklands* (Warner Books, 1997)

Martin Westlake, *Kinnock: The Biography* (Little, Brown, 2001)

Geoffrey Wheatcroft, *The Strange Death of Tory England* (Allen Lane, 2005)

Phillip Whitehead, *The Writing on the Wall: Britain in the Seventies* (Michael Joseph/Channel 4, 1985)

William Whitelaw, *The Whitelaw Memoirs* (Aurum Press, 1989)

Sandy Woodward, *One Hundred Days: The Memoirs of the Falklands Battle Group Commander* (HarperCollins, 1992)

Peregrine Worsthorne, *Tricks of Memory* (Weidenfeld & Nicolson, 1993)

Peter Wright, *Spycatcher: The Candid Autobiography of a Senior Intelligence Officer* (Viking, 1987)

Woodrow Wyatt, *Confessions of an Optimist* (Collins, 1985)

—, *The Journals of Woodrow Wyatt*, 3 Vols, (Macmillan, 1998, 1999, 2000)

Daniel Yergan and Joseph Stanislaw, *The Commanding Heights: The Battle Between Government and the Marketplace that is Remaking the Modern World* (Touchstone, New York, 1998)

Peter York, *Peter York's Eighties* (BBC, 1996)

Hugo Young, *One of Us: A Biography of Margaret Thatcher* (Macmillan, 1989, 1991)

—, *This Blessed Plot: Britain and Europe from Churchill to Blair* (Macmillan, 1998)

Hugo Young and Anne Sloman, *The Thatcher Phenomenon* (BBC, 1986)

Lord Young, *The Enterprise Years: A Businessman in the Cabinet* (Headline, 1990)

Index

NB. The use of titles in this index is not consistent. Most individuals are
referred to by the name or title under which they are first mentioned,
but some by that under which they are best known.